Media Controversy:

Breakthroughs in Research and Practice

Information Resources Management Association
USA

Volume I

IGI Global
DISSEMINATOR OF KNOWLEDGE

Published in the United States of America by
    IGI Global
    Information Science Reference (an imprint of IGI Global)
    701 E. Chocolate Avenue
    Hershey PA, USA 17033
    Tel: 717-533-8845
    Fax: 717-533-8661
    E-mail: cust@igi-global.com
    Web site: http://www.igi-global.com

Library of Congress Cataloging-in-Publication Data

Names: Information Resources Management Association, editor.
Title: Media controversy : breakthroughs in research and practice /
  Information Resources Management Association, editor.
Description: Hershey PA : Information Science Reference, [2020] | Includes
  bibliographical references.
Identifiers: LCCN 2019014111| ISBN 9781522598695 (hardcover) | ISBN
  9781522598701 (ebook)
Subjects: LCSH: Mass media--Social aspects. | Mass media--Political aspects.
Classification: LCC P95.54 .M39 2020 | DDC 302.23--dc23 LC record available at https://lccn.loc.gov/2019014111

British Cataloguing in Publication Data
A Cataloguing in Publication record for this book is available from the British Library.

The views expressed in this book are those of the authors, but not necessarily of the publisher.

For electronic access to this publication, please contact: eresources@igi-global.com.

List of Contributors

Table of Contents

Section 4
Media Representation and Bias

Section 5
Media Transparency and Press Freedom

Section 6
Role of Media in Politics

Section 7
Role of Media in Public Health

Section 8
Role of Media in War and Conflicts

Preface

The media, entrusted with providing clear and accurate information to its consumers, readers, and audience, plays an increasingly important role in modern society. Journalists, in particular, are educated to remain unbiased and to present all uncovered information to readers to allow those consumers to form their own opinions on the published events. While this is the basis for the media, it is increasingly common for media outlets and individuals within the media to include personal bias and opinions in their pieces and even use their roles as watchdogs and gatekeepers to sway public opinion on specific issues such as public health, warfare, and economic policies. Although this may be unintentional on the part of the journalist, the media has the power to play important roles in the global society and is responsible for uncovering all of the information and checking facts and sources before publishing a story.

Different laws around the world impact the level of transparency, clarity, and censorship that appear in published coverage with free media policies in some countries and government-run media approaches in others. Additionally, the subject matter that is reported can greatly impact the way a story is handled. Issues such as racial tension, warfare, and ethnic conflicts are often handled with more care though they are often the most difficult for the media to cover. Media coverage of these may be manipulated by extremists to cause a serious distortion of public perception. Because of this, outlets are vigilant to not report sensitive issues in inflammatory manners although outlets are often criticized as sensationalizing such events to increase readership, "clicks" on online articles, and increase profits.

The need and desire to increase profits, the emergence of social media sharing, and freedom of the press greatly impact which stories are published and which aren't, driving public opinion on those given areas. Social media and the amount of clicks a story receives from audiences sway the types of stories that continue to get posted. Social media shares and the easily publishable online articles through blogs or less credible sources compromises the integrity of news stories as readers can easily share an enticing article without doing any research into the facts behind the post and could subsequently perpetuate false information. As shown in the forthcoming chapters of this reference source, numerous factors attribute to the articles and media presented to consumers including information on the impact of the media in elections, after natural disasters, and violent conflicts while also presenting research on the importance of transparency and credibility in the media.

The changing landscape surrounding the diverse applications of different scientific areas can make it very challenging to stay on the forefront of innovative research trends. That is why IGI Global is pleased to offer this two-volume comprehensive reference that will empower journalists, news writers, columnists, broadcasters, newscasters, media professionals, media outlets, professors, students, researchers, practitioners, and academicians with a stronger understanding of media controversies.

This compilation is designed to act as a single reference source on conceptual, methodological, and technical aspects, and will provide insight into emerging topics including but not limited to social media news, ethical coverage of war conflicts, political communication, and the importance of gatekeeping in the media. The chapters within this publication are sure to provide readers the tools necessary for further research and discovery in their respective industries and/or fields.

Media Controversy: Breakthroughs in Research and Practice is organized into eight sections that provide comprehensive coverage of important topics. The sections are:

1. Media Advocacy
2. Media and Social Platforms
3. Media Credibility
4. Media Representation and Bias
5. Media Transparency and Press Freedom
6. Role of Media in Politics
7. Role of Media in Public Health
8. Role of Media in War and Conflicts

The following paragraphs provide a summary of what to expect from this invaluable reference source:

Section 1, "Media Advocacy," opens this extensive reference source by highlighting the latest trends in social change, hashtag activism, and advocacy among various media outlets. In the first chapter of this section, "Mediating Social Media's Ambivalences in the Context of Informational Capitalism," Prof. Marco Briziarelli and Prof. Eric Karikari from the University of New Mexico, USA explore the socially reproductive and transformative functions of social media in media dialectics from a political economic perspective. In the second chapter, "Trans-National Advocacy and the Hashtag Black Lives Matter: Globalisation and Reception in the UK and France," Prof. Danella May Campbell and Prof. Marie Chollier from Manchester Metropolitan University, UK offer insights into racial debates and equality advocacy in the 21st century through social media hashtags, and the authors focus on the long-lasting impact of #BlackLivesMatter in particular. In the following chapter, "Rethinking Media Engagement Strategies for Social Change in Africa: Context, Approaches, and Implications for Development Communication," the author, Prof. Adebayo Fayoyin from UNFPA, South Africa, investigates the imperatives for and the diverse approaches by development organizations in mobilizing the media for social change in Africa and call for a second look at existing media engagement approaches in achieving social change. Within a significant chapter of this section, "With a Little Help From My Friends: The Irish Radio Industry's Strategic Appropriation of Facebook for Commercial Growth," Prof. Daithi McMahon of the University of Limerick, Ireland studies strategic social media management as a way to enhance radio station audiences and revenues citing Facebook opportunities as a key factor in maximizing profits. In the following chapter, "The Personalized and Personal "Mass" Media – From 'We-Broadcast' to 'We-Chat': Reflection on the Case of Bi Fujian Incident," the author, Prof. Yu Zhang from New York Institute of Technology, USA, discusses the role two of China's major social media channels—Weibo and WeChat—played following the Bi Fijuan incident that turned the event into a national debate, created citizen journalists, and called for social justice in the country. In one of the concluding chapters, "Radical Political Communication and Social Media: The Case of the Mexican #YoSoy132," Prof. Lázaro M. Bacallao-Pino from the National Autonomous University of Mexico, Mexico analyzes the main uses of social media as part of mobilizations and the interrelationships between online communication and offline collective action while using a university student mobilization campaign during Mexico's 2012 electoral campaign—#YoSoy132—as a key case study. In the final chapter of this section, "The Resistance of Memories and the Story of Resistance: July 15 Coup Attempt and Social Movement in Turkey," the author, Prof. Fadime Dilber from Karamanoğlu Mehmet Bey University, Turkey, focuses on the story structure of struggle exhibited against the July 15, 2016 coup attempt in Turkey in the transmedia. Unlike previous coup attempts in Turkish history, the media moved with the people out in the streets as an anti-coup, and the author surmises that when the attitude of the national media is supported by citizens and mass media, new media, and those struggling against the coup gained strength and helped to make the coup attempt unsuccessful.

Section 2, "Media and Social Platforms," includes chapters on emerging innovations in social networks as journalistic tools. In the first chapter, "We the New Media: The Disruption of Social Media in Interpersonal and Collective Communication," Prof. Miguel del Fresno of the Universidad Nacional de Educación a Distancia (UNED), Spain presents a new model to describe and explain the emerging social media communication ecosystem that has put an end to the mediating exclusivity of professional media and maximizes collective interpersonal communication on one and the same social continuum. In the following chapter, "Social Media as Public Political Instrument," the author, Prof. Ikbal Maulana from the Indonesian Institute of Sciences, Indonesia, argues social media is an effective tool that gives a political voice to individuals who are otherwise silent on societal, public, and political issues while also explaining the ways in which conventional media hinders the public in expressing opinions. In the final chapter of this section, "The Politics of Immersive Storytelling: Virtual Reality and the Logics of Digital Ecosystems," Prof. Christian Stiegler from Brunel University London, UK applies and extends the concept of social media logic to assess the politics of immersive storytelling on digital platforms such as Facebook and Instagram.

Section 3, "Media Credibility," presents coverage highlighting media responsibility and tools to determine credible news sources. In the first chapter of this section, "Modeling Rumors in Twitter: An Overview," the authors, Prof. Rhythm Walia and Prof. M.P.S. Bhatia, both from Netaji Subhash Institute of Technology, India, focus on rumor analysis in the age of social media as more of the population receive and share news stories via social media platforms. In the next chapter, "Contribution of Mindfulness to Individuals' Tendency to Believe and Share Social Media Content," Prof. Peerayuth Charoensukmongkol from the National Institute of Development Administration, Thailand explores the effect of mindfulness on individuals' tendencies to believe social media content and share it without realizing the potential consequences through a survey of 300 full-time workers and college students in Bangkok, Thailand. In the concluding chapter of this section, "Arabic Rumours Identification by Measuring the Credibility of Arabic Tweet Content," Prof. Ahmad Yahya M. Floos from King Saud University, Saudi Arabia investigates Arabic rumor patterns on Twitter and explains the impact features the social media platform can have in spreading false information.

Section 4, "Media Representation and Bias," discusses ethical issues in media coverage and the possible introduction of bias by reporters in news stories, as well as showcases how media can help to represent minorities and women. In the first chapter, "Exploring the Complexities Associated to Victimization: Addressing Media Sensationalism and Race," Prof. Erica Hutton from Hutton Criminal Profiling and Associates, USA addresses the complexities in reports of victimization in the media in direct correlation to how racial disparities sensationalize certain incidents of crime. In the second chapter of this section, "Racial Spectacle and Campus Climate: Media Representations and Asian International Student

Perceptions at U.S. Colleges," the authors, Prof. Kenneth Robert Roth of California State University, USA and Prof. Zachary S. Ritter of the University of Redlands, USA, present the implications media representations may have on cross-cultural interactions by identifying the ways in which U.S. colleges are addressing campus climate issues. In the following chapter, "Portrayal of Women in Nollywood Films and the Role of Women in National Development," the authors, Prof. Suleimanu Usaini, Prof. Ngozi M. Chilaka, and Prof. Nelson Okorie from Covenant University, Nigeria, investigate how women are portrayed in Nollywood films and the interpretation of their representations among audiences. The authors argue that positive portrayal of women in film furthers national development and female portrayal can only be fully achieved through an increase in female screenwriters and directors. In a noteworthy chapter, "The Digital Politics of Pain: Exploring Female Voices in Afghanistan," Prof. Mary Louisa Cappelli from Globalmother.org, USA explores the power of the Afghan Women's Writing Project in empowering women to bear witness and share their stories. The group, the author states, operates as a social media campaign employing Western rhetoric to combat efforts that undermine protections against women and principles of free market democracy. In the concluding chapter of this section, "Islamophobic Discourse and Interethnic Conflict: The Influence of News Media Coverage of the ISIS Beheadings on Identity Processes and Intergroup Attitudes," Prof. Bobbi J. Van Gilder and Prof. Zach B. Massey from the University of Oklahoma, USA examine the Islamophobic discourse that is perpetuated by the news media coverage of the ISIS beheadings to explain the potential influence of news media on viewers' dissociative behaviors and the justifications made by social actors for such behaviors.

Section 5, "Media Transparency and Press Freedom," presents emerging research on journalistic limits and freedom of the press in modern news coverage. In the first chapter of this section, "The Uses of Science Statistics in the News Media and on Daily Life," Prof. Renata Faria Brandao from the University of Sheffield, UK investigates how journalists use scientific statistics as a means to communicate current scientific research as well as how the public decodes this information. In the second chapter, "Naming Crime Suspects in the News: 'Seek Truth and Report It' vs. 'Minimizing Harm,'" the author, Prof. Robin Blom from Ball State University, USA, examines the positive and negative aspects of news outlets exposing all information regarding a crime suspect as well as other outlets withholding this information. In the following chapter, "Mediatized Witnessing and the Ethical Imperative of Capture," Prof. Sasha A.Q. Scott of Queen Mary University of London, UK argues the need to rescue witnessing as a concept from its conflation with the watching and passive consumption of events. Within a noteworthy chapter in this section, "Online Free Expression and Its Gatekeepers," the author, Prof. Joanna Kulesza from the University of Lodz, Poland, covers the pressing issues of online free expression at the time of global telecommunication services and social media. She discusses each of the three composite rights of free expression (the right to hold, impart, and receive information and ideas) and identify the actual limitations originated by national laws. In the next chapter, "Information Control, Transparency, and Social Media: Implications for Corruption," Prof. Chandan Kumar Jha from Le Moyne College, USA discusses the implications that government control over information can have for the effects of social media on corruption. In one of the concluding chapters of this section, "Free Speech, Press Freedom, and Democracy in Ghana: A Conceptual and Historical Overview," the authors, Prof. Murtada Busair Ahmad, Prof. Chudey Pride, and Prof. Anthony Komlatse Corsy from Kwara State University, Nigeria, examine free speech, press freedom, and media ownership in Ghana with a focus on the roles of the colonialists, anti-colonial activists, post-independence democratic government, and business conglomerates. The authors also discuss specific factors that affect free speech and press activities within the framework of diverse political and legal settings that operate in Ghana. In the final chapter, "Press Freedom and Socio-Economic Issues in the Nigerian and Ugandan Democratic Landscape," Prof. Okorie Nelson from Covenant University, Nigeria compares the constitutional basis of press freedom in Uganda and Nigeria.

Section 6, "Role of Media in Politics," discusses the impact media coverage, or lack of coverage, can play in modern politics such as covering the positive or negative aspects of candidates or policies to sway popular opinion. In the first chapter of this section, "Neo-Populist Scandal and Social Media: The Finnish Olli Immonen Affair," the authors, Prof. Juha Herkman and Prof. Janne Matikainen from the University of Helsinki, Finland, analyze the impact social media has on politics by highlighting a scandal that occurred in Finland in 2015, when an MP of the populist right-wing Finns Party, Olli Immonen, published a Facebook update in which he used the same kind of militant-nationalist rhetoric against multiculturalism that Norwegian mass-murderer Anders Behring Breivik had used years earlier. In the following chapter, "Interacting With Whom?: Swedish Parliamentarians on Twitter During the 2014 Elections," the authors, Prof. Jakob Svensson of Uppsala University, Sweden and Prof. Anders Olof Larsson of Westerdals Oslo School of Arts, Communication, and Technology, Norway, explore Swedish Parliamentarians' Twitter practices during the 2014 general elections and investigate party uses such as only retweeting within a party's network and only @messaging towards political opponents. In the third chapter of this section, "Understanding the Role of Media in South Asia," Prof. Sukanya Natarajan from Jawaharlal Nehru University, India aims to understand the dynamics behind the rise of social media, print media, audio visual media, and film in these countries and describes the cultural and social continuum the media has to employ in shaping public opinion within the South Asian region. In a noteworthy chapter of this section, "Social Media and the Public Sphere in China: A Case Study of Political Discussion on Weibo After the Wenzhou High-Speed Rail Derailment Accident," Prof. Zhou Shan and Prof. Lu Tang from the University of Alabama, USA examine the political discussion and interrogation on Sina Weibo, China's leading microblog site, concerning the Wenzhou high-speed train derailment accident in July of 2011 through a critical discourse analysis. The authors use this event to investigate whether or not a microblog can function as a promising form of public sphere. In the following chapter, "Media Mediate Sentiments: Exploratory Analysis of Tweets Posted Before, During, and After the Great East Japan Earthquake," the authors, Prof. Naohiro Matsumura from Osaka University, Japan; Prof. Asako Miura from Kwansei Gakuin University, Japan; Prof. Masashi Komori from Osaka Electro-Communication University, Japan; and Prof. Kai Hiraishi from Keio University, Japan, analyze 89,351,242 tweets posted between December 11, 2010 to April 16, 2012 following the Great East Japan Earthquake to reveal the usage of various terms appearing in tweets concurrently with the terms expressing emotion. In another significant chapter in this section, "The Role of Mass Media in Women's Participation in 2013 Kenya General Election," Prof. Thomas Ibrahim Okinda of Moi University, Kenya assesses the role and performance of the Kenyan media in women's participation in 2013 Kenya general election with particular emphasis on radio, television and newspapers concluding that, while Kenya generally has a diverse and informative free media, it largely limited coverage and produced negatively biased coverage of the female candidates. In the next related chapter, "Kenya's Difficult Political Transitions Ethnicity and the Role of Media," Prof. Wilson Ugangu from the Multimedia University of Kenya, Kenya argues there is a close relationship between the country's political transitions, ethnicity, and the role of the media citing transitionary events of the 1960s, 1982, the 1990s, and 2007 as case periods that affected media. In a concluding chapter, "Media Coverage of the 2009 Afghan Presidential Election," Prof. Christopher Strelluf from Northwest Missouri State University, USA investigates how, despite tremendous obstacles that journalists faced in Afghanistan during the 2009 presidential election, the news sources leveled a range of critiques against incumbent president Hamid Karzai, the Afghan government, and foreign governments. Within another concluding chapter of this section, "ISIS Discourse in Radical Islamic Online News Media in Indonesia: Supporter or Opponent," the authors, Prof. Fajar Erikha from Universitas Indonesia, Indonesia; Prof. Idhamsyah Eka Putra from Persada Indonesia University, Indonesia; and Prof. Sarlito Wirawan Sarwono from Universitas Indonesia, Indonesia & Persada Indonesia University, Indonesia, aim to understand how discourses about Islamic State in Iraq and Syria (ISIS) are supported and/or rejected by radical Islamic groups through data collected from Islamic news sources, Voa-Islam, and Arrahmah. In the following chapter, "The Press and the Emergent Political Class in Nigeria: Media, Elections, and Democracy," Prof. Ibitayo Samuel Popoola from the University of Lagos, Nigeria investigates how the political class in colonial and post-colonial Nigeria established, maintained, improved, and controls the machinery of the state through the press concluding that the political class emerged because they were read, advertised, or packaged by the press. In the significant chapter, "Ethical and Legal Challenges of Election Reporting in Nigeria: A Study of Four General Elections, 1999-2011," Prof. Tayo Popoola from the UNESCO Centre of Excellence in Journalism and Media Training, Nigeria explores why the mass media, which are globally regarded as the playing field of politics and the road upon which presidential campaign travels every four years, could suddenly develop contours leading to serious disputes, crisis, violence, and bloodletting in Nigeria, especially between 1999 and 2011. In the final chapter of this section, "Communicating Democracy Through Participatory Radio in Nigeria: The Question of Political Economy," the authors, Prof. Murtada Busair Ahmad and Prof. Kamaldin Abdulsalam Babatunde of Kwara State University, Nigeria, argue a case for sustainability of community radio in a developing society with a focus on both sides of the equation (production and distribution) after finding that community media enables people from different socio-cultural backgrounds within a community, to share information and exchange ideas in a positive and productive manner.

Section 7, "Role of Media in Public Health," explores the ways in which modern media can impact public health both positively by promoting emerging research and negatively by spreading false information. In the first chapter of this section, "Social Media and Infectious Disease Perceptions in a Multicultural Society," Prof. Maria Elena Villar and Prof. Elizabeth Marsh of Florida International University, USA examine the influence and effect of social media on health communication during the Zika outbreak in Miami and the Ebola outbreak. In the following chapter, "Media Campaign on Exclusive Breastfeeding: Awareness, Perception, and Acceptability Among Mothers in Anambra State, Nigeria," Prof. Nkiru Comfort Ezeh from Nnamdi Azikwe University, Nigeria investigates the relationship between the media campaign for exclusive breastfeeding and mothers' decision to comply based on Symbolic Interactionism, Diffusion of Innovation, Social Responsibility, and Gate-Keeping Theories through a survey conducted among 400 mothers in Anambra, Nigeria. In the final chapter of this section, "Awareness and Education on Viral Infections in Nigeria Using Edutainment," the authors, Prof. Suleiman Usaini, Prof. Tolulope Kayode-Adedeji, Prof. Olufunke Omole, and Prof. Tunji Oyedepo from Covenant University, Nigeria, examine why edutainment—a fusion of education into entertainment programs—should be used and how it can be used to educate media audience in Nigeria on some viral infections that pose serious health risks and how they can live healthy lives.

Section 8, "Role of Media in War and Conflicts," tackles sensitive responsibilities of journalists when covering war-torn nations, violent conflicts, and other war issues. In the first chapter of this section, "The Benefits and Challenges of New Media for Intercultural Conflict," the authors, Prof. Amy Janan Johnson, Prof. Sun Kyong Lee, Prof. Ioana A. Cionea, and Prof. Zachary B. Massey from the University of Oklahoma, USA, examine current research on intercultural interactions over new media with a particular emphasis on those studies involving conflict. In the second chapter, "Art, Values, and Conflict Waged in Satirical Cartoons: The 10-Year Rhetorical Crisis," Prof. Z. Hall, an Independent Scholar from USA, investigates whether or not satire is an effective rhetorical device for resolving disagreements involving conflicting sacrosanct values, and if and how it ameliorates or contributes to conflict in increasingly multi-religious, multiethnic, and multicultural societies. In a significant chapter of this section, "Postracial Justice and the Trope of the 'Race Riot,'" Prof. Jennifer Heusel from Coker College, USA aims to understand the trope of "race riot" as a rhetorical strategy in news media that disciplines race-conscious protest, and the author compares coverage of the 1906 Atlanta riots with the 2014 unrest in Ferguson, Missouri. In a concluding chapter, "Using Media to Resolve Media Engendered Ethnic Conflicts in Multiracial Societies: The Case of Somalis of Kenyan Origin," the author, Prof. Agnes Lucy Lando of Daystar University, Kenya, exposes the ethnic conflicts Somalis of Kenyan origin endure and argues that the ethnic plights of Somalis of Kenyan origin are often created by media. In the final chapter of this section and reference source, "Boko Haram Insurgency in Cameroon: Role of Mass Media in Conflict Management," Prof. Afu Isaiah Kunock of the University of Yaounde I, Cameroon discusses the role of the media in managing the deadly attacks by the Islamic insurgent group Boko Haram in Cameroon through the critical analysis of documents as well as interviews and observations from the theoretical perspective of framing.

Although the primary organization of the contents in this work is based on its eight sections, offering a progression of coverage of the important concepts, methodologies, technologies, applications, social issues, and emerging trends, the reader can also identify specific contents by utilizing the extensive indexing system listed at the end.

Section 1
Media Advocacy

Chapter 1
Mediating Social Media's Ambivalences in the Context of Informational Capitalism

Marco Briziarelli
University of New Mexico, USA

Eric Karikari
University of New Mexico, USA

ABSTRACT

This essay explores the dialectics of media, by considering the socially reproductive and transformative function of social media from a political economic perspective. The authors claim that while media have consistently generated aspirations and fear of social change, their powerful capability of shaping societies depend on the historically specific social relations in which media operate. They engage such an argument by examining how the productive relations that support user generated content practices such as the ones of Facebook users affect social media in their capability to reproduce and transform existing social contexts. In the end, the authors maintain that the most prominent mediation of social media consists of the ambivalent nature of current capitalist mode of production: a contest in which exploitative/emancipatory as well as reproductive/transformative aspects are articulated by liberal ideology.

INTRODUCTION

In this essay we explore the deep level of ambiguities that characterize the relationship between social media and capitalism, the social, political economic context in which in several regions of world they operate. We provide this reflection in a particular moment of history in which media have become at the same time the main "language" in order to decipher contemporary economics as well as the material terrain in which those economic activities develop. Yet, while social media seem to have been more and more integrated within the logic of capitalism, and capitalism, has increasingly assumed the morphology of an informational dispositive, their relationship is not straightforward but defined by a series of deep rooted tensions.

DOI: 10.4018/978-1-5225-9869-5.ch001

We claim in fact that those tensions illustrate a long lasting relationship between our societies and the way we understood the normative role of media technologies. For instance, Mosco (2005) claims that every new wave of media technology seems to bring with it contradictory declarations of ultimate ends, a mixture of messianic and apocalyptic predictions of future, a *telos* that simultaneously implies modernity and anti-modernity. The radio for instance could connect distant communities, thus enhancing a common understanding of the world, but could also generate phenomena of mass hysteria. In the specific case of social media platforms, they are simultaneously perceived to be rescuing the public sphere (Habermas, 1991), promoting new sociability (Boyd, 2010) while concurrently, deteriorating more genuine forms of communication such as interpersonal and dialogic ones, and facilitating further levels of commodification of previously un-colonized spheres of social life (Terranova, 2004).

In relation to such a debate, this paper provides a framework that tries to synthetize both utopian and dystopian, socially reproductive and reformative aspects of media by focusing on the ways in which the user generated content activity of Facebook users mediate the structural and cultural contradictions of operating in the high-tech environment such as the tension between the liberal ideology of agency and the necessities to monetize their activity. Thus, drawing on Fuchs and Sevignani's (2013) distinction between the exploitative "labor" and the emancipatory "work," the paper suggests looking at Facebook practices as representative of such a synthesis. This is a political economic perspective that focuses on how social media activities are capable of emancipating and coercing their users and how those ambivalences are mediated by liberal ideology. As a result, the contradictions between viewing technology as emancipating or coercive tend to be normatively framed as politically engaged practices, which could simultaneously be considered as the unpaid labor of producing content for Facebook.

The main theoretical contribution of the paper consists in providing a political economic critical inquiry of the capability of social media to "mediate" multiple messages, to concurrently generate social transformation and social reproduction (Bloch, 1986). In order to advance our argument, we structure this paper in three main sections: the first one concerning the link between media and utopian/dystopian societal dispositions in which we show how consistent those aspirations and fears of social change triggered by media are; the second one expounding a perspective that understands those tensions within media as an ideological process that links two aspects of user generated content, i.e. working and laboring; and the third one that uses the case of Facebook to exemplify our framework, the synthesis between the working/utopic/transformative and the laboring/dystopic/reproductive features of social media.

UTOPIA AND DYSTOPIA IN SOCIAL MEDIATION AND SOCIAL FORMATIONS

The process of social formation— i.e. how a given society comes to organize itself through time— and the process of social mediation— i.e. different elements/subjects come to interact, communicate and exchange of information among each other, are indissolubly united. That is because both processes are based on the production and reproduction of social relations. In fact, media could not exist without a preexisting social field and a sense of sociability. At the same time, a social community could not be constructed without an adequate means of communication and social coordination.

In our view this explains why there seems to be a consistent ambivalent feelings associated with mediated communication that regard media as alternatively determining a feared or a welcome social change. Furthermore, it also explains why, as we will argue later on, while media technology can significantly change throw-out time, its conceptual role of mediation may remain fairly unvaried. More specifically, we see media as channeling technological utopia and dystopia. By technological utopia we refer to the specific modern ideology assuming that progress of science and technology will eventually fulfill an ideal society in which human scarcity, sufferance and mortality will be overcome (Gendron, 1977). Its *alter*, technological dystopia, describes how technology has also been consistently associated with catastrophic changes; images of technology mediating so much to actually contaminate our human-ness as well as compromising genuine social intercourse (Gendron, 1977). As a consequence, almost consistently media have been celebrated to overcome physical and temporal distance among human be-ings (e.g. the book, the telegraph, the radio, the email), and at the same time distancing otherwise close social relations (Jacobs, 1992). According to Peters (1999) fascination and fear for media went hand in hand with the first groundbreaking physics discoveries about magnetism and gravitational forces. In fact in both cases, people fantasized about the power of "*actio in distans*," the God-like idea of controlling an object without touching it, but also the utopic theory of labor in which production does not require physical force.

For Peters, the stupefying experience of receiving a message from wireless devices, or transposing bodily existences of a person into images were interpreted as the power of human intentions overcoming natural barriers but also as the bizarre and horrific way to create a fake double of a living person, i.e. a "doppelgänger," ghostly appearances and monstrosities. In more recent times, the cultural circumstances in which media operate have significantly changed but are also still consistent with the ideology of a technological driven history. In fact, according to Gendron (1977) post-industrial capitalism— the mode of economic development that has shifted its main goals from industrial production to consumption— serves as a base for utopian perspectives by bringing about a technological revolution, which supposedly will bring growth, progress and the elimination of any societal issues. Examined from the teleology of progress, in the end, post-industrial technological utopianism is not distant from earlier utopias of Owen (1995), Fourier (1971), and De Saint-Simon (1964). Those authors believed in the so called "utopian socialism" the project of realizing human being's happiness not in the state of nature as in Rousseau's *bonne savage* (2014) but in the state of culture, in other words in a society enlightened by rational (and therefore just) principles and technology.

However, as already mentioned, mediation, as a metaphor belonging to a conceptualization of modernity understood in its contradictory nature (Horkheimer & Adorno, 1973), has also consistently produced fear, anxiety and dystopic images, which materialized in different forms, as the literary and scholarly tradition of mass society theory confirms: mediation as the loss of contact with nature (Peters, 1999); mediation as alienating new model of society and rational apparatus that imprisons people in Kafka bureaucratic labyrinths (Marx, 1867);, mediation as a simulation of reality (Baudrillard, 1988), or mass mediation as a way of producing stereotypes (Lang and Lang, 2009). In other examples, Singer (1973) analyzed how mass media, contrary to the popular notion that its main function is to "homogenize the psyches of [men]" (p. 140), performs a disruptive function by offering minority groups transformative possibilities through protests; Rosten (1947) interrogated the role of movies as propaganda and observed that there is a higher sensitivity to movies because of their wider reach and thus the nature of their mass influence.

To summarize, mediated communication embodies the dialectics of modernity, with its promise of human emancipation and its constant danger to degenerate into humanity's imprisonment. Both represent dichotomous aspects of a general acknowledgment about the power of media to shape our society. In the next section, we will show how the aspirations and anxieties expressed via mediation have perpetrated in the so-called web 2.0 applications and social media as well.

Mediation of Old and New Ambivalences

Our distinction between the social role of media— i.e. mediation— and their historical development as media technologies allows us to reflect on the ambivalent sentiments that seem to have continuously accompanied (mediated) communication (Mosco, 1996), to the point that it is possible to draw a parallelism between the preoccupation of Classic Greek philosophy for diverse mode of communication and modern social media, understood here as Internet-based applications that allow the creation and exchange of user-generated content through web 2.0 technology (Kaplan & Haenlein, 2010).

Plato, in his seminal work *Phaedrus* (Peters, 1999), resumes very effectively the anxieties that mediated communication carried with its message. He narrates about the rhetorical confrontation between Socrates' apologies of dialogism against Phaedrus' support of written communication. The former, being face-to-face, direct and personal aims at the communion (*ergo* communication) of the communicating souls involved in the dialogue. The second one, reified into written word, puts distance between the author and his/her audience, between the original communicative goal and how the message is received. The first one is *ad personam* and fills the distance between two people/minds, the second one is wasteful because it disseminates messages indiscriminately.

Both modes of communication are considered to be fundamental in the social and political organization of a given community. According to Socrates, whereas the immediacy of dialogue creates bond, love and social relations, the mediation of written word can potentially create social lacunas, misunderstandings and it is lavish because it disseminates words that are not necessarily heard, received or understood (Peters, 1999). Phaedrus instead sees in mediation, the power of "mass" communication in mobilizing society as a whole, in broadcasting knowledge, therefore the power of affecting an entire community. Phaedrus is a supporter of what, in the early twentieth century, mass communication scholars would have called as propaganda.

Dissemination versus dialogue remains a fairly up-to-date category when it comes to examining inherent tensions of social media. For instance, in many ways, the same ambivalence about mediation is reproduced by the controversial notion of virality. A virus metaphorically embodies the idea of the dissemination of a disease that exploits the potential of modern means of communication as a vehicle of infection. At the same time, in a networked culture, a phenomenon can spread or gain popularity by digital vernacularity, by collective conversation, which for Hardt and Negri (2000) has a revolutionary potential. Thus, viruses embody the fear of contagion and the aspiration of social amelioration via interpersonal communication.

In similar ways, Jenkins, Green and Ford (2013), explore the phenomenon of "virality" as both the beneficial objective of business marketing to exploit close affective social relations (such as among friends and family), and at the same time as an impoverishing metaphor of audiences' agency. On the one hand, the term viral has been used to describe so many different practices such as buzz marketing, guerrilla marketing video mash-ups and remixes posted to YouTube that trigger dialogue and discussions, which all rely on the amplifying potential of robust communication among people, what Arvidsson and Colleoni (2012) define as "affective relations" (p.135). On the other, the idea of virality builds on the concept of quick replication of an original message, which implies a fairly passive conceptualization of the audience/consumer because it assumes an almost automatic and unaware process of communication predominantly propelled by marketing kind of interests.

Virality is only one of many examples that confirm how the critical question of mediation continues to emerge in current media applications as in the case of web 2.0 media and its specific application in social media. In fact, those utopic/dystopic-loaded narratives appear as constitutive of the paradigm shift represented by the transition from web 1.0 to Web 2.0, the second generation in the development of the World Wide Web and successive development of social media (Barbrook & Cameron, 1996). The passage to Web 2.0 implied the evolution from the production of software that created bounded environments in which users where constrained in utilizing the products into flexible platforms in which previously considered passive audiences now have the agency to participate in the provision of content and the construction of the web environment.

The philosophy behind web 2.0 reproduces the social Enlightenment utopia of creating a general intellect, a collective effort to produce human intellectual wealth though collaboration. Certainly, the Web 2.0 changeover did not happen in a vacuum but reflects the general economic shift of post-industrialism and its tendency to shift from an economy selling products to one providing services (Lazzarato, 1996). Both the post-industrial political economic model and the new participatory perspective materialized via web 2.0 based applications have created a milieu allowing the creation, re-creation and exchange of user generated content: i.e. social media.

Mosco (2004) reminded us that myths offer a means by which meaning is made and in many ways, technology is a powerful instrument of mass mediation. He, however, also noted the schizophrenic nature of mass mediation – particularly, communication technology - by exploring its utopic renderings on one hand and its dystopic manifestations on another; in one instance, the mythologizing effects of mass mediation provides a template of perfection and a moral framework, in another instance, mass mediation spatializes and commodifies.

Social media offer a highly interactive experience in which both individuals and communities produce cultural content as well as new practices. They have been integrated into practices that go well beyond the social sharing of the first weblogs of early 2000s, such as building reputation and bringing in career opportunities and monetary income, as discussed in Tang, Gu, and Whinston (2012). In scholarly literature there have been some debates about their definition (Boyd & Ellison, 2007; Selwyn, 2007), however there is also a significant consensus in using the term to refer to web-based multimedia production and distribution tools incorporating text (blogs, wikis, Twitter), audio (podcasting, Skype), photo (Flickr) and video (video casting, YouTube) capabilities.

The ongoing debate about how to best theorize social media is also propelled by the very utopic/dystopic ambivalences we have just discussed. *De facto*, whereas most scholarship agrees on the significant novelty brought by social media as well as the need to develop adequate theoretical tools to study them, a lively debate exists about their larger social and cultural implications. For instance, Reading (2014), through the lens of political economy interrogated the "socioeconomic and technical infrastructures that enable the capture, circulation and storage of data that then become the raw material of global memory" (p. 748). Again, in the field of media studies much of the interest in social media could be explained in relation to their alleged capability of radically redefining the meaning of mass communication: the rediscovery of sociability; the blurring of boundaries between the moment of production and moment of consumption, the moment of dissemination and the moment of reception of the message (Napoli, 2010). Ems (2014) similarly did a study of Twitter as a space where the intertwining of social and technological features provide a complex but useful means of political protest. She argued that social media like Twitter provide a new stage where old power struggles are manifested.

Such a debate reproduces the utopic /dystopic ambivalence, which, in media theory discourse, corresponds to the re-proposing of the classical question here paraphrased: 'whether social media do things with people or "people do things with (social) media' (Blumer & Katz, 1974). In other words, involving questions about where the meaning of a given text comes from or whether the audience can be considered passively or actively involved in the process of communication. For instance, Casemajor, Couture, Delfin, Goerzen, and Delfanti (2015) explored the value of non-participation in digital media and argued that non-participation – both active and passive forms of it – offers a unique avenue for political action.

According to such a narrative, while Internet applications until early 2000 were broadcasting information by the similar logic of traditional media (e.g. radio, TV), i.e. functioning by the logic of one-to-many, the evolution propelled by Web 2.0 information technology allegedly allowed a democratization and liberalization of information and communication technologies, that led to a many to many logic (Boyd, 2010). For instance, Starke Meyerring (2008) describes the democratic potential of social media to enable, challenge, reproduce or question established practices and social hierarchies rooted in print material, while offering alternative writing practices to those established around print.

As a result, social media such as Facebook are considered to have acquired a greater transparency and permitted cooperative formation of knowledge (Shirky, 2008), which would lead to an empowering experience of social media: "people build their own networks of mass self-communication, thus empowering themselves" (Castells, 2009, p.421). Furthermore, online social networks contribute to the personal development of people by facilitating self-expression (Boyd, 2010).

However, interest in social media could be linked to the dystopian concerns about this technology as well. As mentioned before, media mirrors the betrayal of modernity towards the dream of human emancipation. Accordingly, social media can be seen as limiting freedom and augmenting surveillance through monitoring of personal media practices to the point that Willcocks (2006) compared information society to "control society" (p. 4). Other dystopian views of social media include the intrusion into private communication and into classrooms (Dalsgaard & Paulsen, 2008); the potential for identity theft and lurking (Siciliano, 2013); and the way social media facilitates academic dishonesty during tests and examinations (Seitz, Orsini & Gringle, 2011).

Moreover, several scholars have scrutinized new media practices from the point of view of power, labor and value creation (e.g. Arvidsson & Colleoni, 2012; Dyer-Witheford, 1999; Ems, 2014: Fuchs, 2010, 2012; Hesmondhalg, 2010; Margonelli 1999; Napoli, 2008; Petersen 2008; Sawhney & Suri, 2014: Scholz, 2008; Wall & El Zaheed, 2011;Willmott, 2010; Zwick et al., 2009). Such a perspective rejects neoliberal "methodological individualism" (Popper, 1971) supposedly characterizing most positive depiction of social media. Most of this critical literature links social media to "digital labor," a productive activity of creating value (especially financial value) in digital environments.

According to Scholz (2012) digital labor has become one of the key concepts in order to both understand the political economic environment of new media and the reason why there is so much discussion around it. One of the most critical positions in such a debate states that the internet has been incorporated in a dominant corporate model of capital accumulation, which is grounded on the exploitation of unpaid labor of so-called "prod-users," i.e. the activity of creating content by users while involved in activities such as blogging, and social networking (Terranova, 2004; Cohen, 2008; Fuchs, 2010).

Toffler (1980), more than three decades ago, by the notion of "pro-sumer" (p.*i*) provided an influential standpoint through which understanding the user-driven, cooperative processes of content generation, which are currently associated with Web 2.0 and more in particular social media. However, the prosumer is not actually the producer of content but rather a more active, well-informed consumer, capable of orienting him/herself in the universe of consumer culture. Such an expert knowledge on consumer products would allow the pro-sumer to have better insights about production.

Only later on, when the so-called pro-sumer acquired inexpensive digital production tools, high internet connection, powerful computers, from the sophisticated consumer identified by Toefler, has he/she become the generator of content by producing blog material, joining social media such as Twitter and Facebook, producing audio visual material, a "prod-user" (Bruns, 2008). The "prod-user" seems to capture more closely those recent changes in the media landscapes. Prod-users are agents that come into this new collaborative space provided by web 2.0 as users but then become producers, thus occupying a liminal position between production and consumption. The kind of production prod-users engage with is not centralized or coordinated but extemporaneous, ongoing, open-ended process. For Bruns (2008), the concept of prod-usage is intended as "a means of connecting such development in the cultural social commercial, intellectual, economic social realms" (p.5). He points out how prod-usage is characterized by open collaborative participation, fluid hierarchic structure of production, unfinished artifacts and common property and individual rewards.

According to the critical political economists of media previously mentioned, it is in such porous boundaries of producing/consuming that the active user of social media, freely generate content for media corporations' interests. Therefore, in contrast to the positive depiction of social media previously exposed, linking those media practices to a process of liberalization and democratization of media, the political economic perspective tends to highlight the level of exploitation of audience labor.

Byung-Chul Han (2015) makes sense of such an ambiguity through the notion of a transparent society. He notices how transparency in the context of new media has become a normative trope dominating public discourse that calls for increased translucence of the political process and the freedom of information. While the author considers transparency as a condition of possibility of a true democracy, its positive (as opposed to negative) dialectics also created a major exposition to collective control and exploitation in current capitalist societies. Accordingly, media-powered transparency, becomes a false ideal, which leads to an insatiable appetite for performance, disclosure, and uncovering, a process that for Byung-Chul Han operates with the same logic of pornography: as an immediate display without meaning. Thus, dialectically enough, both the current dream and nightmare of mediation consists of its turning into immediacy.

To sum up, web 2.0 and social media seem to reproduce the same ambivalences about media, which can be synthetized into the opposition between utopia and dystopia but also the opposition between human emancipation and human subjugation via media technology. In this sense, a fundamental aspect of this paper's argument is that those ambivalences, and their apparent consistent reproduction in current media settings, should not be considered as linked to any inherent ideology of media but rather associated with the social relations in which those media emerge, operate and re-produce. Therefore, as we explain in the next section, in such a contest of material production, ideology does not produce those contradictions but actually mediates between them, thus defusing their potential frictions.

MATERIALLY PRODUCING THE WORLD THROUGH MEDIATION

Livingstone (2008), in a seminal address at the 2008 International Communication Association conference eloquently expressed this concern:

It seems that we have moved from a social analysis in which the mass media comprise one among many influential but independent institutions whose relations with the media can be usefully analyzed, to a social analysis in which everything is mediated, the consequence being that all influential institutions in society have themselves been transformed, reconstituted, by contemporary processes of mediation (p.2).

While mediation, in many ways, represents a quasi-ontological account of the complexity of social life as a whole, for Harvard (2008), it falls short in describing media as a historic force. A way in which current scholarship has tried to understand the prominent role of media as a historic driver is through the concept of mediatization, which constitutes a concept that tries to make sense of the long term structural and cultural effects of media (Couldry & Hepp).

Mediatization represents a meta-process, a force, together along with globalization, individualization and, especially, commercialization that have shaped modernity: 'By mediatization we mean the historical developments that took and take place as a result of change in (communication) media and the consequences of those changes.' (Krotz, 2008, p. 23). The force driving this meta-process is clarified by Harvard (2008) who claimed that media have gradually replaced former socializing institutions such as "family, school and church […] as providers of information and moral orientation" (p.13). However, while the mediatization literature provides an important historical account of media, the lens tends to be so wide that it overlooks the materially (re)productive function of media, thus preferring a broad notion of media effects over the perspective of media understood as a means of material production.

Accordingly, in this section, we provide a political economic account that incorporates the utopic/dystopic media perspectives as ideological reflections of an inherent contradiction of the post-industrial capitalism between emancipatory/transformative and exploitative/reproductive dimensions. In order to accomplish that, we first discuss the need to re-conceptualize ideology as a material force that allows the function of media as a means of production. Then, we discuss how one fundamental task of ideology in these particular productive relations is to weld together the tension between work and labor.

Ideology entered the dominant discourse of the media studies field possibly thanks to the intervention of Critical Theory and Cultural Studies and their interest in non-orthodox Marxist perspectives. Ideology represented the main access to a culturally materialist narrative of power (and counter power) in which media appeared as the main protagonists (e.g. Althusser, 1971; Atkinson, 2005; Horkheimer & Adorno, 1974; Debord, 1967; Freedman, 2015; Gramsci, 1971; Hall, 1982). However, as Peck (2006), Artz, Maceck and Cloud, (2006), Reading, (2014) and Aune (2004) claimed, most of media research seems to still operate within the idealist assumption that ideas produce social reality instead of social reality producing ideas. Furthermore, in many instances, the interest of media scholars in ideology is more focused on the communication process that channels ideology rather than ideology itself. As a result, ideology is almost never linked to labor and material production but reduced to a "result" within the still powerful tradition of mass communication effects.

Conversely, what intrigues us about social media is that the practical productive activity of the audience leads to problematize or at least sophisticate the idea of the audience as the alleged recipient of the ideological process. The audience should be regarded as simultaneously the predicate and the predicated of ideology. Such a perspective leads to the conceptualization of ideology not as "media effects" merely operating upon people but also actively operated by them, which echoes the Marxian notion of "productive consumption" (Nixon, 2012, p.443). This consists of the audience producing consciousness but also articulating ideas by consuming commodified culture.

Atkinson (2005), for instance, foregrounded issues of power and ideology in his assessment of global justice activism. He used an analysis of alternative media audiences to show that such avenues aid the resistance efforts of activists but do not provide a means of absolute inversion of power and ideological structures. In this sense, audiences of alternative media are simultaneously acting on and being acted upon. In another example, Stein (2013) expanded the concept of participation by looking at how, and to what extent, social media platforms like Facebook, YouTube and Wikipedia enable and disable audience engagement in the production of media content.

Marx and Engels in *German Ideology* (2001) maintain that the production of consciousness and the production of ideology are tightly linked to concrete human activity: "the production of ideas, concepts and consciousness is first of all directly interwoven with the material intercourse of man, the language of real life. Conceiving, thinking, the spiritual intercourse of men, appear here as the direct efflux of men's material behavior [...] Consciousness does not determine life: life determines consciousness" (pp. 35-36).

However, the audience's consciousness and his/her adoption of specific worldviews do not passively reflect so-called real life but interacts with it and therefore cannot simply be reduced to an instrumentalized epiphenomenon of productive logics. Following Bloch's (1986) consideration of the complexity of the ideological phenomenon, we would argue that the ideology of the prod-users is not simply false consciousness—in other words deception—in the same way as consciousness is not simply false ideology because, aside its concealing of exploitation, it comprises a genuine desire of the community for a better society. As Kellner and O'Hara explain (1976), Bloch considers ideology as an ambiguous two-sided phenomenon as it encompasses distortion, mystifications, techniques of manipulation and domination, but it also incorporates a utopian residue. Thus, the cognitive error of ideology and the cognitive accuracy of consciousness (as opposed to false consciousness) maybe distinct but are also highly intertwined, as we show in a moment when talking about the distinction between-work and labor.-

Such a process of production of ideology and consciousness generating through the prod-users' activity does not take place in a vacuum, but is immerged in a pre-existing ensemble of ideas and practices. In other words, it interacts also with previous existing worldviews that contribute to give meaning to both media and their usages. We see in social media practices, both the resurgence of a liberal public sphere ideology that tries to colonize all social experiences (Negt & Kluge, 1993) and the assertion of a technological utopianism that equates hi-tech progress with social progress and that consistently manifests with the introduction of (relatively) new means of communication (Mosco, 2005).

So how, more concretely, does this interaction between practical consciousness and practical activity function? In the next section we clarify how ideology mediates between two distinct but interconnected aspects of social media's productive practices (and capitalism in general): working and laboring.

The Distinction between Work and Labor

We believe that one of ideology's agencies in the social media environment consists in its capability to combine the objective element of producing media content and the subjective element of consciousness, thus combining the necessity of production of value with the subjective motivations that lead users to do that for free or to enjoy doing it. In this sense, Fuchs and Sevignani (2013) spelled the dialectical aspects of producing. With their investigation on how Marx conceives human practical activity, they suggested the need to distinguish between labor and work. They differentiated the two concepts as follows:

Labor is a necessarily alienated form of work, in which humans do not control and own the means and results of production. Work in contrast is a much more general concept common to all societies. It is a process in which humans in social relations make use of technologies in order to transform nature, culture and society in such a way that goods and services are created that satisfy human needs (p. 240).

Fuchs and Sevignani base their distinction on Marx's (1867) statement that "Labor which creates use-values and is qualitatively determined is called 'work' as opposed to 'labor'; labor which creates value and is only measured quantitatively is called 'labor', as opposed to 'work'" (p.138). The two moments oppose each other when it comes to human emancipation because the realm of freedom only begins where labors ends. Through work human intentions become bound to the product and in such a product people see and recognize themselves. Conversely, labor causes multiple kinds of alienation to the workers, thus disrupting the moment of genuine creative activity intrinsic in the experience of "working."

The two authors point out how productive work seems to be an inherent characteristic of human beings, which then turns into labor due to the development of capitalist social organization. However, work is not simply the general anthropological conceptualization of human productive activity. In relation to how, historically, labor developed in capitalist societies, work remains a more positive *alter*. In fact, Marx (1867) believes that work gives people the chance for human expression and signification, thus a chance to make of the product into signified matter. Instead waged labor appears as alienated work, the denial of the latter. Thus, one can find a dialectic unity of alienation and emancipation, which seems to be inherent in how human practical activity historically developed in capitalist societies.

Such a dual character of producing activities is also embodied in commodities, which present a series of binary oppositions along the axis of work/labor. Commodities comprise the distinct and concrete use-value of work and the abstract de-personalized exchange value of labor; the anthropological necessity of work and the artificial/historical surplus value of labor; the creative side of work and the automatism of labor. Thus a given commodity crystallizes the basic contradiction between freedom and exploitation, but also their fusion in the object itself.

Despite their contradiction, the two productive aspects coexist in capitalism and the survival of capital in fact depends on the interaction of those two aspects. This seemed true at the time Marx wrote and seems an even more fundamental characteristic in the postindustrial context, in which manual labor is increasingly giving up to intellectual labor. Especially in the contest of knowledge working, the valorization of labor heavily depends on the imaginative creative activity of people (Lazzarato, 1996).

In the concrete social relations that surround social media, working and laboring are in fact synthesized: on the one hand, the social media user is unpaid, alienated from his/her own product and from the work process and becomes a commodity sold to the advertising industry; on the other hand, the user is a worker who enjoys constructing his/her own identity by generating the social environment around and is also propelled by a sense of social and political engagement. Thus, the social media user is alienated by his/her unpaid laboring but feels emancipated by his/her working in building sociability.

Along the same line, Lund (2014) explored the distinction between work and labor trying to understand an economy that constantly welds together production and entertainment, by pointing out the parallel conceptual distance between 'work' and 'labor, and 'play' and 'game,' as well as parallel affinities between 'work'/ 'play and 'labour'/'game.' He distinguished between the open-endedness of playing and the confined challenge of games, the informal character of the former and formal strategic approach of the latter. While gaming is organized, play is capricious in its behavior and does not follow rules in an explicit and uniform way. Correspondingly, play and work are creative and their objectives—such as entertainment, expressive meanings—are qualitatively measurable. Contrariwise, game and labour operate in a formal and abstract framework that establishes quantitative relations— such as scoring or exchange value—among the people involved in the activity.

In the context of digital media, Lund's four categories of working, laboring, playing and gaming intersect each other and define a province in which production and consumption, free expression and exploitation meet. For instance, Barbrook and Cameron (1996) provide a study of how high-tech networking technologies have created a vision of the world in which all four dimensions are synthesized in the so called California ideology, a mix of high tech hypsterism and conservatory principles.

Jenkins, Ford and Green (2013) provided another important account that seems to acknowledge some of those aspects. In their reading, media landscape is characterized by multi-dimensional system, in which different broadcast logics, economies, media and cultural practices converge. Their interpretation of social media describes a reality in which for instance a top-down hierarchy of the broadcast era now coexists with the integrated system of participatory channels, thus suggesting that the same media operating in different social contests may function with different logics.

In fact, their concept of audience labor synthesizes activity and passivity. That is because they acknowledge the fundamental objective of monetizing such labor but also stressing how audience labor generates multiple values: "by contrast, engagement-based models see the audience as a collective of active agents whose labor may generate alternative forms of market value" (p. 117). Some of those values are monetizable, some others actually constitute subversive acts such as parody, mockery of capitalist values.

Dean (2009) would probably find the meaningful participation described by Jenkins, Ford and Green (2013) as an ideological fantasy used to sell products and services rather than a description of contemporary political and economic realities. In our view, both the fantasy and reality-are comprised in the ideological phenomenon: as meaningful participation coexists with the instrumental side just described, which are fused together in the audience's productive activities.

To sum up, so far we have shown how the utopic /dystopic ideologies of media may depend not on the very nature of media but rather on the nature of the social relations in which they operate. Historically, in the West, that implies acknowledging the overwhelming presence of capitalist relations and, in our view, it is the internal capitalist contradiction between work and labor that create utopia/dystopia, emancipatory/exploitative and transformative/reproductive ambivalences of social media as well as the ideology that mediates between them. In the next and last part of this chapter, we take Facebook as a powerful exemplification of how concretely digital social media reproduces such ambivalences and how those are articulated by liberal ideology.

UNDERSTANDING FACEBOOK: PRACTICES OF PRODUCTION AND TRANSFORMATION

Since its first formulations, liberalism has consistently been capable of fusing together a political and an economic project (Marx, 1867). For instance, in his manifesto of 1644 *Aeropagitica's* demand for a "free open encounter" (p.50) of ideas and trade implied that the liberalization of the market and the public sphere were tightly connected (Rosenblatt, 2011). In fact, the link between the two aspects is so profound that both in the public and academic discourse the market frequently becomes metaphor for democracy and democracy becomes a metaphor for the market.

In this sense, if it is true that communication technology has very often-embodied such a link in powerful ways, this is also the case of Facebook. Facebook, currently the world's most popular social network service, which has reached 1.55 billion active monthly users by the third quarter of 2015 (Statistica, 2014), is a perfect example, as its rhetoric intermeshes together political and economic arguments. Following the framework just discussed, in this last section of the paper, we examine how the working and laboring aspect of Facebook help us explain how this particular media application is simultaneously advancing social reproduction and social transformation.

The two dimensions can only be analytically distinguished for exposition purposes though, as in, reality appears to be consistently overlapping. In this sense, despite the important historical changes that brought capitalism to its current informational forms, I think that Marx's observation about the contradiction of the capitalist system caught in between revolution and reproduction of its logic are still very pertinent. In *Grundisse*, Marx (1973), on one hand, affirms that consistent extraction of surplus value from labor requires a consistent reproduction of exploitation, and on the other hand, that capitalism to do that must also 'revolutionize' its forms:

There appears here the universalizing tendency of capital, which distinguishes it from all previous stages of production and thus becomes the presupposition of a new mode of production, which is founded not on the development of the forces of production for the purpose of reproducing or at most expanding a given condition, but where the free, unobstructed, progressive and universal development of the forces of production is itself the presupposition of society and hence of its reproduction; where advance beyond the point of departure is the only presupposition (Marx, 1973, p.540).

Capitalism constantly changes everything so everything can remain the same. In other words, it constantly modifies the ways it shapes its labor relations in order to keep producing profit. This is in line with its schizophrenic logic which enables capital to universalize and stratify at the same time. According to Deleuze and Guattari (1987) capitalism is schizophrenic because it is interested in profit and thus must subvert/deterritorialize all territorial groupings – like religious, ethnic/familial, national groupings. At the same time, it relies on the continuous mythification of social groupings in order to continue functioning smoothly and to re-enforce social ordering needs. Such a tension can be consistently found in Facebook. Let us first examine some examples of how Facebook and the labor it exploits contribute to reproduce existing social relations.

Socially Reproducing Through Facebook

First of all, from a general point of view, Facebook outsources and crowdsources the labor of media production through the producer-consumer, a practice of cost reducing that, not accidentally, coincided with rising layoffs in media industries (Deuze, 2007). As Huws notices (2003) the exploitative aspect of unpaid labor in social media comes from a general tendency of capital to offload labor costs onto consumers just like in the case of self-service gasoline stations, ATM, grocery check out, which "burden the consumers of unpaid labor" (p. 69). Such a system of exploitation of prod-users has in the case of Facebook exhibited itself rather explicitly as in the case of the program *Facebook Diaries* (Cohen, 2008), which asks Facebook users to send stories and therefore "participate" in a contest that rewards the best stories by broadcasting them on TV.

More concretely, in order to start examining the reproductive function of this social network, Smythe's (1981) political economy and his concern of withdrawing attention to the place of communications in the wider system of social reproduction of capital" (Jhally & Livant 1986, p.129) offers a valuable point of view. According to such a perspective, Facebook represents a means of production, which transforms audience labor of lending attention and providing information/content to media program as commodities to be sold to the advertising industry. Smythe's analysis concerned media such as TV and radio. Consequently, the question at this point is how the context of an online social network such as Facebook— characterized by high levels of participation, by user-generated content, and by the ability to create varied channels of communication— can allow the application of audience labor just mentioned.

In this sense, Scholz (2010) argued that Facebook produces value through the audience by first of all providing invaluable information for advertisers. According to Fuchs (2012) the primary source of Facebook's value is communication and sociability, which derive from Facebook's extraordinary facility to have access to information, to store it, to process it, to analyze it, and finally to deliver it to its customers. The informational content consists of a variety of data: specific demographics of Facebook users; personal information regarding their tastes, habits, status; information about the kind communicative channels users utilize to socialize; performative information about the specific themes used for impression management, and associational information about the specific ways users socialize. In doing that, Facebook provides very detailed profiles of individuals, localized and networked communities, therefore offering important clues on consumers habits and consumer affective relations (Scholz, 2010).

Second, Facebook valorizes audience labor in having the audience provide unpaid services and volunteer work. Scholz (2010) indicates that many Facebook users deliver, willingly, their time and energy for Facebook usage. He provides the example of a translation application, where users translate Facebook into different languages totally for free. Thus, the more content and the more users join, the more profit can be made by advertisements. Hence the users are exploited as they "produce digital content for free in non-wage labor relationship" (Fuchs, 2011, p.299). Third, Facebook monetizes audience's labor by providing data and content for the site, making it more appealing for users who can enjoy looking at photos, videos, comments and links. In other words, the audience provides value to the social network by providing content that is used to attract and invite new users to join the network. Thus, the more content the higher the profit from audience's labor, and the more the content higher the chance to employ more labor by opening more accounts.

In the already discussed context of informational capitalism, the fact of Facebook being capable of monetizing unpaid knowledge work has an incredible reproductive power by replicating a logic of both labor and extraction of value from labor that, as already mentioned, tends to move an increasingly larger part of the economy. This is the kind of informational economy based on affective relations (Arvidsson & Colleoni, 2012), also described by terms such as "Thank you economy," "Social Economy," or the "Gift economy" (Vaynerchuck, 2011).

Another way in which Facebook reproduces existing social relations is by alienating its workers/ users, estranging them from a possible awareness of their actual position within Facebook 's process of valorization. According to Fuchs and Sevignani (2013), users are alienated from themselves because they are coerced to use Facebook by way of peer pressure and a lack of viable alternatives; users are alienated from "the instruments of labor" (p.257) because they do not own the communication platform itself and because their "brains, hands, mouths, ears and speech, the Internet and platforms"(p.258) are instrumentalized "for advertising" (p. 258); moreover, users are alienated from the "objects of labor" (p.259) on Facebook—which the authors identify as shared representations of experiences "through a legally binding agreement" (p. 259); and finally users are alienated from the product of labor due to the peculiar divide between use-value and exchange-value of symbolic produce online: the "use-values that Facebook users create are at the same time commodities that Facebook offers for sale on a market"(p.259).

Fuchs and Sevignani (2013) also talked about an inverse kind of fetishism which describes how users deny the reifying aspects in their relationship with Facebook by stressing the social gratifications they obtain from using the service. In the world of digital labor, the fetish character of the commodity takes on an inverted form. We can speak of an inverse fetish character of the social media commodity. The commodity character of Facebook data is hidden behind the social use-value of Facebook, i.e. the social relations and functions enabled by platform use. The inverse fetish of Facebook is typically expressed in statements like "Facebook does not exploit me because I benefit from it by connecting to other users" (p. 261).

Valtysson (2012) also noticed that Facebook reproduces the existing mode of production by enhancing the colonization process of exchange logic (commodities, instrumentalism) to more and more private spheres, thus opening more ground to the process of commodification and the subsumption by capital. For the author, services like instant personalization and user's timeline represent a continuation of the process of receiving/sharing information about its users to and from other websites. This information is used for commercial purposes, which makes it an act of colonization, as users are turned into consumers. Similarly, Netchitailova (2012), talking about privacy, claims that Facebook reproduces the same contradictory and discriminatory understanding of private property that capitalism conveys: socialization of production and privatization of the gains from that. On the one hand, privacy is celebrated as a universal value that protects private property; on the other hand, corporate interests of businesses like Facebook surveys and lures audiences' private lives in order to extract profit out of them. Such a contradiction manifests in the inconsistency between Facebook's rhetoric of discretionary privacy settings, and its systematic collecting of data from users.

Finally, Facebook has acquired another important role in replicating the existing social relations by becoming a fundamental factor in the reproduction of social and cultural capital (Fuchs, 2012; Briziarelli, 2013). In fact, users build and preserve relations not only for sociability purposes but also for the objective of performing networking kind of socialization. According to Bourdieu's notion of social, cultural and symbolic capital (1986), users spend time on Facebook (and other social media) to generate that kind of capital of affective relations that may facilitate their continuous effort to manage an impression but also useful for a business activity or for credentials. For instance, Yazan (2015) studied the means by which Facebook was utilized in a top-down language policing move to convince people "that they need Ottoman Turkish to secure their ties and reconnect with their ancestors' cultural heritage" (p. 335).

Through the discussion above, it is evident how Facebook reifies existing social relations and shows that in many ways, Facebook, as an alternative media form, does not operate under entirely different logics from those applied by mainstream media (Rauch, 2015). In Rauch's work, for instance, alternative media like Facebook and mainstream media lie on different portions of a converging spectrum.

To sum up, Facebook operates as a powerful re-producer of the necessary social relations (i.e. audience's unpaid labor, link to the advertising industry), and more broadly, the necessary ideological and cultural logic of capitalism. However, as previously mentioned, ideology does not simply serve instrumental goals but also link those to more utopic aspirations. Thus, in the next section, we examine how by reproducing main ideological components such as consumer choice, individual freedom, and the liberal idea of civic engagement, Facebook also offers a transformative potential. We show how liberal ideology is the mediating bridge that can manage to keep two apparently opposed poles united: exploitative labor and (potentially) emancipatory work.

Socially Transforming Through Facebook

Kushner in a *Rolling Stone* article applauded Facebook in terms of citizen-and consumer choice (2006): "the long epoch of top-down culture … is fading faster than anyone predicted. The more vibrant world is bottom up, powered by the people" (p.1). As Cohen notices (2008), innovations information and communication technology tend to be accompanied by the teleological narratives of progress and human perfectibility.

Indeed, Facebook reflects the liberal normative social projects to emancipate people through the market, through Smith's public use of instrumental and individualist reason, through Kantian publicity (i.e. the public use of reason), and through technology and communication ideological representations. Those are all facets of the liberal discourse/ideology of modernity (Passerin & Benhabib, 1997). They are at the same time ideological fictions but also relevant existing promises that have historically mobilized people for some time now and they still operate through the utopia of media as technological promises of human comprehension and social pacification. Facebook indeed combines both the already mentioned exploitative and utopic aspects of media

As Kessler (2007) notices, Mark Zuckerberg, the founder of Facebook, consistently utilizes the rhetoric of novelty, social change and promise of social amelioration through media technology, which, in its clear instrumentality, also resonates with genuine existing democratic sentiments. In the Facebook manifesto (2007), the founder describes the social mission of the platform as follows: Facebook aspires to build the services that give people the power to share and help them once again transform many of our core institutions and industries … We believe building tools to help people share can bring a more honest and transparent dialogue around government that could lead to more direct empowerment of people, more accountability for officials and better solutions to some of the biggest problems of our time. By giving people the power to share, we are starting to see people make their voices heard on a different scale from what has historically been possible. These voices will increase in number and volume. They cannot be ignored. Over time, we expect governments will become more responsive to issues and concerns rose directly by all their people rather than through intermediaries controlled by a select few (p.1).

Zuckerberg's rhetorical arguments make leverage on the technological utopianism which recovers liberal ideology through the reassertion of the public sphere and Kantian publicity, which is represented in the text by both the use of reason in public and the idea of political power under public scrutiny. Such a rhetoric is also conveyed by a more general narrative of social media, which are often described in the public discourse as Web 2.0, social media, participatory mediacitizen journalism, user generated content, user driven innovation, or social software. Such a civic consciousness ultimately re-articulates in terms of ethical work and ethical citizenship the (neo-) liberal ideological fiction of a civic society not ruled by the state as external apparatus but by the market as an internal, ethical, self-sufficient and self-balancing system.

However, the civic engagement that Facebook proposes reflects the kind of confusing all-encompassing civic engagement that Berger (2011) problematized as being even potentially counter-productive for the development of a truly democratic system. In this sense, when it comes to digital media, Ekman and Amnå (2012) point out the need to distinguish different degree of political activisms. They distinguish between political participation (including formal political behavior as well as protest or extra-parliamentary) and less direct or latent forms of participation, conceptualized here as civic engagement. Still, regardless of its actual effectiveness, the perception of a usage of Facebook for some degree of political activism reveals an important source of normativism towards alternative or improved forms of sociability (Valtysson, 2012).

Such a normative thrust is not simply present in the rhetoric of its founder but also in the daily practices of Facebook users. In fact, aside from the significant aspect of management impression according to which users utilize this platform to construct, negotiate and reproduce a given identity, many users understand the function of sharing links and content as a way to establish a platform for discussion of matter of public interests, to sensitize specific issues. Furthermore, as the study conducted by DeRosa (2013) confirmed, people use web 2.0 platform in order to construct a new understanding of citizenship, a digital citizenship that re-interprets democratic deliberation as e-democracy. As Dean (2009) observed, social media are less of places enhancing critical debate than platforms devoted to corporate profit. However, as we tried to demonstrate, they also work as platforms providing an ideological rationalization and moralization of free labor because they produce the impression of subjective visibility and social and political agency.

Thus, as Bloch (1986) recognized, although often mirroring "how the ruling class wishes the wishes of the weak to be" (p. 13), the ideologies in Facebook can also provide a 'transition' stage and display a drive towards a better life, and real possibilities to transform societies. In Facebook, Bloch (2004,) would probably find two different ideological utopian aspects First, via Facebook users embrace what Bloch defined as "wish-fulfillment" (p. 40) aspects which consist in the elimination of the roots of human un-happiness such as social solipsism, alienation, physical, social and cultural distance that otherwise would separate society's members. The second aspect, instead of eliminating constructs the utopia by contributing to re-agreements of organization, civic order and political arrangements.

The apparent openness of Facebook to whatever content or community organization would appear as promise of the reality not yet realized. The anticipatory consciousness of Facebook users perceives the unrealized emancipatory potential in Facebook. Indeed, as already mentioned, Facebook is not a public sphere for critical thought. Nevertheless, in that ideological surplus value of the bourgeois notion of citizenship with its individual rights, civil liberties, and actively engaged autonomy, users express something more than mere legitimation and apologetics for bourgeois institutions and practices.

Thus, what Facebook points out is an ambiguous reality. On the one hand, Facebook can and should be considered as a phenomenon that further rationalizes, colonizes and commodifies more spheres of our lives. On the other, the fact that our private sphere becomes a commodity that is sold in a particular market makes that market a liberal arena in which, aside goods, ideas can, wishfully enough, move freely. As a result, the unpaid and exploited labor of generating content also gives the impression of a more constructive and positive working.

Another aspect that reveals the potentially transformative feature of Facebook is its capability for connectivity, which facilitated the mobilization of people in specific circumstances. In other words, the very bases of Facebook political economy, what we described as "affective relations," allow exploitation and radical insurgency. In fact, Facebook is considered to have played an increasingly central role in facilitating and organizing social movements and political upheavals from the Anti-Globalization movement to the Arab Spring. Pollock (2011) reported how two underground Tunisian hackers known as Foetus and Waterman, and their organization, Takriz, played a remarkable role in the Arab Spring by taking advantage of social media such as Facebook, in order to send messages to document police repressions and to mobilize people.

Finally, if Facebook is considered as a source of alienation, it should also be evaluated for its de-alienating effects. Trying to explain the coexistence of exploitative and normative features, Fisher (2012) pointed out Facebook's promise of de-alienation: if alienation is about the lose authorship of the product of labor, social media such as Facebook grant users much more control over the production of process of communication, thus the self-expression, identity building aspects that frequently celebrated are for Fisher de-alienating mechanisms. According to Fisher, the paradox of Facebook consists of the fact that the more socially reproductive the higher the potential for de-alienation.

In Fisher (2012) there is an analysis of media "as a dynamic site of struggle between audience (labour) and media providers (capital), a struggle that revolves on time" (p. 172). This is made evident in the positioning of social media sites like Facebook a platform for de-alienation which simultaneously exhorting exploitative avenues of production. As is made explicit in Fisher's work – and as we have mentioned in this one – the distinction between the social reproductive function and the social transformative function of Facebook are never clear-cut but explicating the ambivalences, we are also able to identify the power of audiences.

To conclude, Facebook reproduces the ambivalences of a productive activity that in the Twenty First century capitalism involves a complex reality in which extraction of labor value and a degree of self-realization are all combined in a complicated picture held together by a liberal ideology. Recalling Byung-Chul Han's (2015) argument previously mentioned, Facebook exemplifies the dialectic of transparency. On the one hand, it asserts the progressive, quasi enlightenment, idea of casting light over power by mobilizing civil society resources against it. On the other, the operationalization of sociability also provides a breach for the commodification of social relations that instead of liberating exploits people.

CONCLUSION: THE (SOCIAL) MEDIATION IS THE MESSAGE

A recent study of the University of Pittsburgh (Lewis, 2016) claims how heavy users of social media such as Facebook are three times more likely to develop depression. It describes how people engaging in a lot of social media use frequently feel they are not living up to the idealized portraits of life that other people tend to present in their profiles. In doing so, the study seems to confirm some of the claims advanced by this essay. First of all, it shows how utopia and dystopia, the transformative and conservative potentials are tangled together in social media practices of impression management.

Second, in relation to the historical materialist conceptual apparatus provided by this essay, the study also suggests that the overly optimistic (self-)representations conveyed by social media users such as Facebook's find in the actual social relations in which the users live, a strong limit. Thus, as we have argued in this paper, Facebook's capability of producing social change is both enabled and constrained by the social relations in which it operates, thus, at a higher level, which are heavily shaped by political and economic interest but also by the persistence in the cultural and social life of powerful utopic/dystopic narratives.

This is a conclusion that celebrates human agency because, after all, social relations are only and exclusively produced by people working, playing, consuming producing, chatting and discussing. At the same time, it is a statement that problematizes individual and immediate kind of agency because those social relations, throughout time and because of specific interests annexed to them, become crystallized in institutions such as the market, the law, the state, and in worldviews, such as liberal ideology or democracy. Quite evidently, those social relations are not easily changeable in the same way in which a single user can re-appropriate and re-signify a given media text and a Facebook enthusiast can update his/her status.

Another important conclusion for this paper and its objective to examine both transformative and re-productive aspects, is that we tried to advance the understanding of one distinctive characteristic defining social media: the "relationship between willing participation and commercial exploitation" (Andrejevic, 2011, p. 83). From such a perspective, the utopia /dystopia associated with media become dimensions subsumed by capitalism as work and labor (and play and game) aspects: whereas applications such as Facebook appear to provide agency for pro-sumers, they also provide a powerful access for capitalist interests to exploit social media's sociability.

Therefore, we claimed that the utopian aspect of work and the dystopian aspect of labor can coexist thanks to the mediation of ideology. That is understood as a conception of the world as well as a consciousness that both develops thanks to the productive activity of Facebook users as well as echoes existing ideologies such as the liberal conceptualization of the market and the liberal democratic political process. In this sense, from a broader perspective, this paper has explored the richness of the concept of mediation, which in this case, presents various and distinct facets deserved to be explored more thoroughly in their complex interaction: mediation as communication, as technology, as ideology, as an embodied metaphor for social anxieties and social aspiration. Thus, as theorists such as McLuhan (1964) have observed, what is actually transmitted (or mediated) in a communication process consistently exceeds the mere message; it is a synthetic social commentary that speaks about a society as a whole.

REFERENCES

Althusser, L. (1970). *Lenin and philosophy and other essays*. London, NY: Monthly.

Andrejevic, M. (2008). Watching television without pity. *Television & New Media*, 9(1), 24–46. doi:10.1177/1527476407307241

Andrejevic, M. (2011). Social network exploitation. In a networked self: Identity, community, and culture on Social. In L. Artz, S. Maceck, & D. Cloud. (Eds.), Communication and Marxism. The Point is to Change it. New York: Peter Lang.

Arvidsson, A., & Colleoni, E. (2012). Value in informational capitalism and on the internet, *The Information Society. International Journal (Toronto, Ont.)*, 28(3), 135–150.

Atkinson, J. (2005). Conceptualizing global justice audiences of alternative media: The need for power and ideology in per formance paradigms of audience research. *Communication Review*, 8(2), 137–157. doi:10.1080/10714420590947700

Aune, J. (2004). *Rhetoric and Marxism*. Boulder: Westview Press.

Barbrook, R. & Cameron, A. (1995, August). The Californian Ideology.

Baudrillard, J. (1988). *Jean Baudrillard, Selected Writings*. Stanford: Stanford University Press.

Berger, B. (2011). *Attention deficit democracy: The paradox of civic engagement*. Princeton, New Jersey: Princeton University Press. doi:10.1515/9781400840311

Bloch, E. (1986). *The principle of hope*. Cambridge, Mass.: The MIT Press.

Blumer, J. G., & Katz, E. (1974). *The uses of mass communication*. Newbury Park, CA: Sage.

Bourdieu, P. (1986). The (three) forms of capital. In J. G. Richardson (Ed.), *Handbook of theory and research in the sociology of education*. New York: Greenwood Press.

Boyd, D. (2010). Social network sites as networked publics: Affordances, dynamics, and implications. In N. Papacharissi (Ed.), *Networked Self: Identity, Community, and Culture on Social Network Sites*. New York: Routledge.

Briziarelli, M. (2014). The dialectics of voluntariat 2.0: Producing neoliberal subjectivity through Facebook. *Sociologia del Lavoro*, *134*(133), 133–144. doi:10.3280/SL2014-133009

Bruns, A. (2008). *Blogs, Wikipedia, Second life, and Beyond: From production to produsage*. New York: Peter Lang.

Byung-Chul Han. (2015). *Transparency Society*. Stanford: Stanford University Press.

Casemajor, N., Couture, S., Delfin, M., Goerzen, M., & Delfanti, A. (2015). Non-participation in digital media: Toward a framework of mediated political action. *Media Culture & Society*, *37*(6), 850–866. doi:10.1177/0163443715584098

Castells, M. (2009). *Communication power*. Oxford: Oxford University Press.

Cohen, N. (2008). The valorization of surveillance: Towards a political economy of Facebook. *Democratic Communiqué*, *22*(1), 5–22.

Couldry, N., & Hepp, A. (2013). Conceptualizing Mediatization: Contexts, Traditions, Arguments. *Communication Theory*, *23*(3), 191–202. doi:10.1111/comt.12019

Daalsgard, C., & Paulsen, M. (2009). Transparency in cooperative online education. *International Review of Research in Open and Distance Learning*, *10*, 3.

Dean, J. (2009). *Democracy and other neoliberal fantasies: Communicative capitalism and left politics*. Durham: Duke University Press. doi:10.1215/9780822390923

Dean, J. (2010). *Blog Theory: Feedback and Capture in the Circuits of Drive*. Cambridge: Polity.

Deleuze, G., & Guattari, F. (1987). *A thousand plateaus: Capitalism and schizophrenia*. Minneapolis, MN: University of Minnesota Press.

Deuze, M. (2007). Toward an ethics of the sociable web: A conversation between Trebor Scholz and Mark Deuze. Retrieved from http://mailman.thing.net/pipermail/idc/2007-July/002652.html

Dyer-Witheford, N. (1999). *Cyber-Marx. Cycles and circuits of struggle in high-technology capitalism*. Urbana: University of Illinois Press.

Wall, M., & El Zahed, S. (2011). "I'll be waiting for you guys": A YouTube call to action in the Egyptian revolution. *International Journal of Communication*, *5(2011)*, 1333–1343.

Ekman, J., & Amna, E. (2012). Political participation and civic engagement: Towards a new typology. *Human Affairs*, *22*(3), 283–300. doi:10.247813374-012-0024-1

Ellison, N. B. (2007, October). Social Network Sites: Definition, History, and Scholarship. *Journal of Computer-Mediated Communication*, *13*(1), 210–230. doi:10.1111/j.1083-6101.2007.00393.x

Ellison, N.B. (2007). Social network sites: Definition, history and scholarship.

Ems, L. (2014). Twitter's place in the tussle: how old power struggles play out on a new stage. *Media, Culture & Society*, 36(5), 720–731.

Fisher, E. (2012). How less alienation creates more exploitation? Audience labor on social network sites. *Triple C,* 10(2), 171-183.

Fourier, C. (1971). *Design for Utopia: Selected Writings. Studies in the Libertarian and Utopian Tradition*. New York: Schocken.

Freedman, D. (2015). Paradigms of media power. *Communication, Culture & Critique*, 8(2), 273–289. doi:10.1111/cccr.12081

Fuchs, C. (2009). Information and communication technologies and society. A contribution to the critique of the political economy of the internet. *European Journal of Communication*, 24(1), 69–87. doi:10.1177/0267323108098947

Fuchs, C. (2010). Labor in informational capitalism and on the Internet, *The Information Society. International Journal (Toronto, Ont.)*, 26(3), 179–196.

Fuchs, C. (2012). With or without Marx? With or without Capitalism? A rejoinder to Adam Arvidsson and Eleanor Colleoni. *Triple C, 10(2)*, 1–12.

Fuchs, C., & Sevignani, S. (2013). What is digital labor? What is digital work? What's their difference? And why do these questions matter for understanding social media? *TripleC, 11*(2), 237–293.

Gendron, B. (1977). *Technology and the human condition*. New York: St. Martin's Press.

Gramsci, A. (1971). *Selections from the Prison Notebooks*. New York: International Publishers.

Habermas, J. (1991). *The structural transformation of the public sphere: An inquiry into category of bourgeois society*. Cambridge, MA: MIT Press.

Hardt, M., & Negri, A. (2000). *Empire*. Cambridge, MA: Harvard.

Hesmondhalg, D. (2010). User-generated content, free labor and the cultural industries. *Ephemera, 10*(3/4), 267–284.

Hjarvard, S. (2008). The Mediatization of Religion: A Theory of the Media as Agents of Religious Change. In Northern Lights 2008. doi:10.1386/nl.6.1.9_1

Horkheimer, M., & Adorno, T. (1974). *The Dialectics of enlightenment*. London: Verso.

Huws, U. (2003). *The making of a cybertariat: Virtual work in a real world*. New York: Monthly Review Press.

Jacobs, N. (1992). *Mass media in modern society*. New Brunswick, New Jersey: Transaction Publishers.

Jenkins, H., Ford, S., & Green, J. (2013). *Spreadable media: Creating value and meaning in networked culture*. New York: NYU Press.

Jhally, S., & Livant, B. (1986). Watching as working: The valorization of audience consciousness. *Journal of Communication, 36*(3), 124–143. doi:10.1111/j.1460-2466.1986.tb01442.x

Kaplan, A., & Haenlein, M. (2010). Users of the world, unite! The challenges and opportunities of social media. *Business Horizons, 53*(1), 61. doi:10.1016/j.bushor.2009.09.003

Kellner, D., & O'Hara, H. (1976). Utopia and marxism in Ernst Bloch. *New German Critique, NGC, 9*(9), 11–34. doi:10.2307/487686

Krotz, F. (2008). *Media Connectivity: Concepts, Conditions, and Consequences* (A. Hepp, F. Krotz, & S. Moores, Eds.). New York: Hampton Press.

Lang, K., & Lang, G. E. (2009). Mass Society, Mass Culture, and Mass Communication: The Meanings of Mass. *International Journal of Communication, 3*, 20.

Lazzarato, M. (1996). *Immaterial labor. In radical thought in Italy: A potential politics.* Minneapolis: University of Minnesota Press.

Lewis, K. (2016). Heavy Social Media Users Trapped in endless Cycles of Depression. *Independent. com.* Retrieved from http://www.independent.co.uk/life-style/health-and-families/health-news/social-media-depression-facebook-twitter-health-young-study-a6948401.html

Livingstone, S. (2009). On the mediation of everything. ICA Presidential address 2008. *Journal of Communication, 59*(1), 1–18. doi:10.1111/j.1460-2466.2008.01401.x

Lopez, L. K. (2014). Blogging while angry: The sustainability of emotional labor in the Asian American blogosphere. *Media Culture & Society, 36*(4), 421–436. doi:10.1177/0163443714523808

Lund, A. (2014). Playing, Gaming, Working and laboring: Framing the concepts and relations. *Triple-C, 12*(2), 735–801.

Margonelli, L. (1999). Inside AOL's cyber–sweatshop. *Wired*, 7(10).

Marx, K. (1867). *Capital: A critique of political economy* (Vol. 1). (P. C. Ben Fowkes, Trans.). London.

Marx, K. (1973). *Grundisse*. London, UK: Pelican.

Marx, K., & Engels, F. (2001). *The German ideology Part One. New York: International PublisherMcLuhan, M. (1964). Understanding media: The extensions of man.* Cambrdige, MA: MIT Pres.

Mosco, V. (2005). *The digital sublime - myth, power, and cyberspace.* Cambridge, MA: The MIT Press.

Napoli, P. (2010). Revisiting "mass communication" and the "work" of the audience in the new media environment. *Media Culture & Society, 32*(3), 505–516. doi:10.1177/0163443710361658

Negt, O., & Kluge, A. (1993). *Bourgeois and proletarian public sphere.* University of Minnesota Press.

Netchitailova, E. (2012). Facebook as a surveillance tool: From the perspective of the user. *TripleC, 10*(2), 683–691.

Nixon, B. (2011). Dialectical method and the critical political economy of culture. *TripleC, 10*(2), 439–456.

Number of monthly active Facebook users worldwide from 3rd quarter 2008 to 2nd quarter 2014 (2014) *Statistica*. Retrieved from http://www.statista.com/statistics/264810/number-of-monthly-active-facebook-users-worldwide/

Owen, R. (1995). *A new view of society and other writings*. New York: Penguin.

Passerin, M., & Benhabib, S. (1997). (Eds.), Habermas and the unfinished project of modernity: Critical essays on the philosophical discourse of modernity. Cambridge, MA, MIT Press.

Peck, J. (2006). Why shouldn't be bored with the political economy versus cultural studies Debate. *Cultural Critique*, *64*(1), 92–125. doi:10.1353/cul.2006.0029

Peters, J. (1999). *Speaking into the air: A history of the idea of communication*. IL: University of Chicago Press. doi:10.7208/chicago/9780226922638.001.0001

Petersen, S. (2008). Looser generated content. From participation to exploitation. *First Monday*, *13*(3). doi:10.5210/fm.v13i3.2141

Pollock, J. (2011, Aug. 23). Street book: How Egyptian and Tunisian youth hacked the Arab Spring. *MIT Technology Review*. Retrieved from http://technologyreview.com

Popper, K. (1971). *The open society and its enemies* (Vol. 2). Princeton: Princeton University Press.

Rauch, J. (2015). Exploring the Alternative–Mainstream Dialectic: What "Alternative Media" Means to a Hybrid Audience. *Communication, Culture & Critique*, *8*(1), 124–143. doi:10.1111/cccr.12068

Reading, A. (2014). Seeing red: A political economy of digital memory. *Media Culture & Society*, *36*(6), 748–760. doi:10.1177/0163443714532980

Rosenblatt, J. P. (2011). *Milton's selected poetry and prose: authoritative texts, biblical sources, criticism*. New York: W.W. Norton & Co.

Rosten, L. C. (1947). Movies and Propaganda. *The Annals of the American Academy of Political and Social Science*, *254*(1), 116–124. doi:10.1177/000271624725400119

Rousseau, J. J. (2014). *A discourse upon the origin and the foundation of the inequality among men*. New York: CreateSpace Independent Publishing Platform.

Saint Simon, H. (1964). *Social organization, the science of man and other writings*. New York: Harper & Row.

Sawhney, H., & Suri, V. R. (2014). From hierarchy to open configurations: Decentralization and user-generated content. *Media Culture & Society*, *36*(2), 234–245. doi:10.1177/0163443714526551

Scholz, T. (2008). What the MySpace generation should know about working for free. *Collectivate.net*. Retrieved from http://collectivate.net/journalisms/2007/4/3/what-the-myspace-generation-should-know-about-working-for-free.html

Scholz, T. (2010). Facebook as playground and factory. In D. E. Wittkower (Ed.), *Facebook and philosophy* (pp. 241–252). Chicago: Open Court.

Seitz, C., Orsini, M., & Gringle, M. (2011). YouTube: An international platform for sharing methods of cheating. *International Journal for Educational Integrity*, 7, 57–67.

Selwyn, N. (2007). Web 2.0 applications as alternative environments for informal learning—a critical review. *Paper presented for OECD-KERIS expert meeting—session 6—alternative learning environments in practice: using ICT to change impact and outcomes*. London: Institute of Education, University of London.

Shirky, C. (2008). *Here comes everybody: The power of organizing without organizations*. New York: Penguin Press.

Siciliano, R. (2013, March 30). The Social media identity theft of a school director via Twitter. *Huffington post*. Retrieved from http://huffimgtonpost.com

Singer, B. D. (1973). Mass society, mass media and the transformation of minority identity. *The British Journal of Sociology*, 24(2), 140–150. doi:10.2307/588374

Smythe, D. (1981). *Dependency road: Communication, capitalism, consciousness and Canada*. Norwood: Ablex.

Starke-Meyerring, D. (2008). Genre, knowledge, and digital code in web-based communities: An integrated theoretical framework for shaping digital discursive spaces. *International Journal of Web-Based Communities*, 4(4), 398–417. doi:10.1504/IJWBC.2008.019547

Stein, L. (2013). Policy and Participation on Social Media: The Cases of YouTube, Facebook, and Wikipedia Communication. *Cultural Critique*, 6(3), 353–371. doi:10.1111/cccr.12026

Tang, Q., & Whinston, B. (2012). Content contribution for revenue sharing and reputation in social media: A dynamic structural model. *Journal of Management Information Systems*, 29(2), 41–75. doi:10.2753/MIS0742-1222290203

Terranova, T. (2000). Free labor. Producing culture for the digital economy. *Social Text*, 18(2), 33–57. doi:10.1215/01642472-18-2_63-33

Terranova, T. (2004). *Network culture: Politics for the information age*. London: Pluto Press.

Toffler, A. (1980). *The third wave: The classic study of tomorrow*. New York, NY: Bantam.

Valtysson, B. (2012). Facebook as a Digital Public Sphere: Processes of Colonization and Emancipation. *Triple C, 10*(1), 77–91.

Vaynerchuck, G. (2011). *The thank you Economy*. New York: HarperBusiness.

Wilmott, H. (2010). Creating value beyond the point of production: Branding, financialization and market capitalization. *Organization*, 17(5), 517–542. doi:10.1177/1350508410374194

Yazan, B. (2015). Adhering to the language roots: Ottoman Turkish campaigns on Facebook. *Language Policy*, 14(4), 335–355. doi:10.100710993-015-9355-1

Zuckerberg, M. (2007). *Keynote speech delivered at the f8 conference at the San Francisco Design Centre*. Retrieved from http://developers.facebook.com/videos.php

Zwick, D., Bonsu, S., & Darmody, A. (2009). Putting consumers to work. "Co-creation" and new marketing govern-mentality. *Journal of Consumer Culture*, *8*(2), 163–196. doi:10.1177/1469540508090089

KEY TERMS AND DEFINITIONS

Audience Labor: a particular political economic perspective that considers audience as a key productive factor in media business.

Ideology: a particular worldview (such as liberal ideology) that acts as a mediating and reproductive force of a given set of social relations.

Labor: it is a historic specific kind of work resulting from a highly developed social organization of production, therefore specific social relations. It is coercive and exploitative.

Mediation: both a concrete and conceptual way to talk about mediated communication.

Political Economy of Media: the study of the social relations, particularly the power relations, which mutually constitute the production, distribution, and consumption of resources, including communication resources.

Pros-User: the user that operating in web 2.0 environment blurs the boundaries between production and consumption of media material.

Social Media: web-based multimedia production and distribution tools incorporating text audio, photo, and video, capabilities, which are characterized by enabling users to create and share content or to participate in social networking.

Social Transformation: a process that tends to significantly change a given set of social relations

Social Reproduction: a process that tends to significantly reproduce a given set of social relations.

Technological Utopia: the specific modern ideology assuming that progress of science and technology will eventually fulfill an ideal society in which human scarcity, sufferance and mortality will be overcome.

Transparency: a metaphor to describe a society that in which un-dialectical thinking, hyper-connectivity, hyper-sociability has prevailed with gloomy consequences.

Work: a basic anthropological necessity, which leads human beings to act upon nature and to "produce" material products for their own survival. It is also a practical and creative activity that allows people to express themselves through objects.

This research was previously published in International Journal of Civic Engagement and Social Change (IJCESC), 3(1); edited by Susheel Chhabra; pages 1-22, copyright year 2016 by IGI Publishing (an imprint of IGI Global).

Chapter 2
Trans–National Advocacy and the Hashtag Black Lives Matter:
Globalisation and Reception in the UK and France

Danella May Campbell
Manchester Metropolitan University, UK

Marie Chollier
Manchester Metropolitan University, UK

ABSTRACT

This chapter offers an insight into racial debates and equality advocacy in the 21st century and explores the emergence, the becoming and long-lasting effect of #BlackLivesMatter. The hashtag story is a traditional viral web content. Nevertheless, technologies allowed these initially local concerns, to become a world-wide plea. The first section summarises the past and current struggle for civil rights and equality in the USA. The second one focuses on the European reception of the hashtag in two structurally different countries. The last section discusses both outcomes and consequences in terms of social policies and international advocacy. A journalistic and critical analysis of the movement is here provided, with long term effects and reception case studies.

INTRODUCTION

For the majority of African-Americans, the reality is unemployment, barriers to education and health services and insufficient housing in poor urban areas highly militarized by the police. American statistics show that Black men are 31% more likely to be pulled over by the police than white men and 15 to 34-year-old black men are nine times more likely to be killed than any other person. American police killed around 1,100 black people in 2015 compared to three killed by police in the UK; it has one of the highest murder rates in the developed world and three million privately owned firearms (Murdoch, 2016). The ongoing war against police brutality in the United States persists for African-Americans.

DOI: 10.4018/978-1-5225-9869-5.ch002

From Malcolm X's marking of the 'movement' in the sixties as a nightmare… to King's dream attributed as a dream deferred, the killing of Michael Brown undoubtedly triggered the re-affirmation of the struggle for Blacks in America. The story of #blacklivesmatter is a lens through which both American and international racial inequalities can be analysed. This chapter offers an insight into racial debate and equality advocacy in the 21st century, based on journalistic and academic works.

The first section briefly summarises the past and current struggle for civil rights and equality in the USA documenting the birth and journey of BLM within the current social and political settings of America and identifying the political triggers contributing to a black uprising. It acts as a documentation of the timeline and adaptation of BLM, from hashtag, to movement, transcending to its recognition as a global network and describes how new technologies and social media offer new channels for advocacy, leading to potential new agencies.

The second one focuses on the European reception of the hashtag in two structurally different countries, the UK and France, exploring the transferability of an online movement born in the USA to other national contexts. The last section discusses both outcomes and consequences in terms of social policy, international advocacy and potential impact on people's lives interrogating the internationalisation of BLM as a global movement and its proficiency to advocate for the poorest of Black people in an ever-increasing globalised world.

BIRTH AND RISE OF THE #BLACKLIVESMATTER (#BLM): AMERICAN HISTORY

From Slavery to Civil Rights: A Brief History of Black Rights Movements

American history is complex. The structure of society and the legality are organised according to several levels leading to diverse impact and consequences. Several dates and historical periods are important to recall regarding the topic of this chapter.

Reconstruction Amendments

The first date is the abolition of slavery in 1865. The reformation following the civil war, led to Reconstruction Amendments and a will from President Lincoln to guarantee rights and equality to all citizens. The 13th amendment of the constitution - examined on January 31 and ratified on December 6 – declares "…neither slavery nor involuntary servitude, except as a punishment for crime whereof the party shall have been duly convicted, shall exist within the United States, or any place subject to their jurisdiction…" (Constitution of the United States of America, 1865/2016). The reformation following the civil war, led to Reconstruction Amendments and a will from President Lincoln to guarantee rights and equality to all citizens. Nevertheless, slavery even though abolished, found new social expressions (Daniel, 1979). One of the forms of slavery perpetuated in Southern states was through peonage (even if legally abolished) and sharecropping (Daniel. 1973; Nieman, 1994). Indeed, labour organisation and southern agriculture maintained a form of lifetime exploitation and implicit transmissibility to descendants.

From "Separate but Equal" to Structural Equality

In 1896, the law case Plessy v Ferguson confirmed the up to then latent doctrine of "separate but equal" (Groves, 1951). In 1890, Louisiana State passed the Separate Car Act (Rountree, 2004) that required separate railway cars and accommodations for Black and White people. Homer Plessy, an octoroon free man (reportedly of seven-eighths European descent and one-eighth African descent), bought a first-class train ticket but was refused the 'white' wagon. Homer Plessy appealed to the law for equal treatment. However, the Supreme Court followed the jurisprudence stating that separation was not anti-constitutional. Further to Plessy v Ferguson, national Black civil rights movements encompassed local communities and aimed at forming a national alliance. The national movement became organised and structured after World War 1 (for comprehensive details, see Maslow and Robinson, 1953), through the creation of different organisations, such as the Universal Negro Improvement Association[1]. From 1896, the doctrine (Roche, 1951) seemed officially promoted, considering the separation of public space between White and Black people (defined by one ancestor) as not entailing the 13th Amendment. The legal turn came in 1954 when the Supreme Court stated that separate public schools were unconstitutional (Brown v. Board of Education of Topeka).

Subsequently, a de-segregation process operated. However, mentalities and interpersonal relationships cannot be guided by legal decisions. The next decade saw the rise of two seminal works on prejudice (Allport, 1954) and stigma (Goffmann, 1963). Indeed, these works studied empirically, racial and religious prejudice and stigma in post 1954 America. These seminal works investigated, firstly, the social perpetuation of diverse types of prejudice against visible minorities, namely Black (up to then discriminated against) and Jewish people, secondly, how some members of these communities were ostracised. Further to this, racial and social preference studies started in the USA after the end of racial segregation in schools (Brand et al, 1974). Many of them focused on children's groups re-creating segregation (i.e. not playing together) and trying to formalise interventions or a good-enough environment to promote equality. Current studies focus on the conceptual acquisition of the notion of race/ethnicity (Cockerham, 2011) and racial favouritism (Rutland et al, 2015; Aboud, 2003). Almost Decades later, both the persistence of this field of study and the events leading to the rise of the #BLM indicate the structural shift from an unequal to a theoretically equal system is not enough to implement and achieve social change and equality.

Technologies and Advocacy: From Black Activism to Black Digital Activism

The history of Black Rights and Black Rights campaigning in the USA is not unequivocal and should be historically and geographically contextualised, as it determines both means and aims. The organisation and the modes of campaigning used to rely on in-person, sometimes hidden meetings, spreading by word of mouth and relying on printed materials when not prohibited (Cashmore and McLaughlin, 1991; Painter, 2006). Therefrom, the main impact of new technologies relates to the dematerialisation of both organisational aspects and campaigning materials and therefore to the rapidity of diffusion and potential snowball effect (Franklin, 2014).

New technologies and social media represent a new possible means for social interactions, personal and collective expression (Moore & Selchow, 2012). Virtual or online communities are dematerialised communities that can gather around specific common features; in the context of this chapter, around a common cause and purpose. This is named digital or online activism (Breindl, 2010); hashtag activism

(Stache, 2015), sometimes spelled hashtactivism (Ibahrine, 2017), as one of its subtypes. The codes and rules of writing and using the hashtag have been studied from a linguistic perspective, underlining the condensing mechanism aiming to produce a strong effect (Caleffi, 2015). More than a new linguistic practice condensing words, the hashtag and related social practices (e.g. posting, sharing) are a new way to aggregate both language and people when aiming at visibility and awareness. If the hashtag has a linguistic structure, each hashtag has an intrinsic sociolinguistic and socio-political meaning attached to it, as it most of the time relates to the combination of an event and a cause. Hence, #BLM is one of many cases of hashtag activism and other famous ones have related to similar events such as, the Arab Spring (Jansen, 2010) or more generally children and human rights (#BringBackourGirls, for a critical analysis see Loken, 2014 or the recent #metoo, adding to the many calls and actions against sexual violence).

In the specific context of Black activism, the structuration of online communities appears both generic and specific: generic as human rights and equality-based (De Choudury et al., 2016), specific when concerned with an event (Bonilla & Rosa, 2015) or an identified movement (e.g. Black feminism, see Williams, 2015). It is maintained in this chapter that the #BlackLivesMatter movement is both generic and specific, both the product and the cause of new narratives and social agencies (Campbell, 2005; Yang, 2016). Therefore, the next sections will explore the preceding social structures to the hashtag and the movement, its exportability and transferability to other national contexts, and its consequences in terms of potential new agency.

The Story of #BlackLivesMatter

George Zimmerman's Acquittal, Michael Brown's Murder and a Chronology of Publicised Cases

The hashtag #blacklivesmatter was created by Alicia Garza, Patrisse Cullors, and Opal Tometi in response to the trial and acquittal of George Zimmerman, responsible for the shooting and killing of 17-year-old Trayvon Martin in 2012.

The rise of the hashtag as a communicative method and of political identification has proliferated the cries of "Black Lives Matter!", "hands up, don't shoot", "I can't breathe" and "WhatHappenedTo-SandraBland" across the globe.

In research published by Pew Research Center (Anderson & Hitlin, 2015) from its first use mid-2013 to March 2016 #BLM has been used almost 11.8 million times on Twitter, spiking at key events in 2015, including the deaths of Eric Garner on December 1, Freddie Gray on April 27 and Sandra Bland on July 20. Its biggest spikes on Twitter since its formation have exploded at other key political events; the rejection of indictment for police officers in the case of Eric Garner, 2014 (189, 210 times: the most it has been used in a single day); the Presidential campaign debate where by Senator Bernie Sanders defended the movement, 2015 (more than 127, 000); and finally, the one-year anniversary of Michael Browns death, August 9, 2015 (120, 067 and 98, 518 the preceding day).

In 2014 #BLM was the American Dialect Society's 2014 Word of the Year (Steinmetz, 2014). Chair of the New Words Committee told TIME "it's a time to recognize that hashtags are an innovative linguistic form that deserve our attention." It was also voted into the top 12 world changing hashtags of 2014, but 'in the age of the Internet, conflict comes with corresponding online movements (Weedston, 2014). Undoubtedly this is the case for the BLM movement in relation to the emergence of #AllLivesMatter

(#ALM), a corresponding social media campaign rooted in opposition to the political statement, made specific to the state of black lives.

In June 2015, the massacre of nine Black worshippers by White supremacist, Dyllan Roof, in an African-American church sparked further outrage and protests in Charleston. The Black Liberation Movement declared what happened here was an act of terrorism, the media refuses to label this as terrorism, they want us to wait until all of the details come out, but had it been one of us, to go into a white church and gun down nine people, it would have been terrorism (Murdoch, 2016).

Social media has presented an array of online video footage to the public that has documented the murder and mistreatment of Blacks, most importantly from all different backgrounds, demographics and walks of life. Whether it be the Dallas pool party (2015), where teenagers were thrown to the ground and held at gunpoint or Sandra Bland (2015) whose death, ruled a suicide, provoked questions and interrogation into what happens behind the prison cell walls, or the shooting of Richard Ramirez (2014).

The killing of Walter Scott (2015) was a key moment in the run up to the official establishment of Black Lives Matter. Not only did the video portray a man being shot in the back but it captured police officer, Michael Slager, stating "he grabbed my taser" [conducted electrical weapon, part of the equipment of the police forces in the USA, UK and France] and whilst continuing to walk over to his body and plant the taser next to him.

The BLM movement's message has echoed, sparking solidarity protests in the UK, Ireland, Germany, The Netherlands, Amsterdam, Canada and South Africa against anti-black racism and violence worldwide, triggered by the deaths of Alton Sterling (2016) in Baton Rouge, Louisiana, and Philando Castile (2016), Minnesota.

The movement gained the backing of black elites sparking the US National Anthem protests, predominantly within the National Basketball Association (NBA) and National Football League (NFL), most notably sparked by Colin Kaepernick who sat during a national anthem whilst playing for the San Francisco 49ers in August 2016. This sparked a national campaign with other elite players joining and taking a knee before games and was backed by the former President Barack Obama as exercising his political right (Jones & LoBianco, 2016).

With over 40 chapters, worldwide, BLM was awarded with the 2017 Sydney Peace Prize, in particular for its Australian chapters and its fight for the aborigine struggle; becoming in addition, a recognised global network (Wahlquist, 2017).

America's 'Post-Racial' Proposition

The success of a minority of black elites such as the election of Barack Obama, corporate executives, government officials as well as celebrities means America, became the epitome of a "post-racial" society (Balkaran, 2015) largely attributed to the success of its first Black President. At the time, this was considered representative of a change in attitudes towards race with the success of a relative few African-Americans upheld as a vindication of the United States' color-blind ethos and a testament to the transcendence of its racist past (Taylor, 2016).

Overall statistics show, concerning education, voter turnout, number of congressional representatives and life expectancy, these have all increased in the US (Plumer, 2013). Although mass incarceration for black men has fallen over the last decade, Plumer (2013) highlights that, between 1960 and 2000, there had been a huge continual increase of the number of incarcerated blacks. Statistics published by Pew Research Centre document the incarceration rate of Black men as six times higher than White men, increasing since 1960, where it measured at five times more likely. Additionally, the poverty gap between Blacks and Whites has remained stagnant for the last fifty years (PEW, 2013). Lack of economic opportunities; particularly within the jobs market was researched: black people were half as likely to get a job offer or call back when submitting an identical resume of a White counterpart; and a Black person with no criminal convictions was not more successful than White applicants who had recently been released from Prison (Denver, 2003; Vaidyanathan, 2016).

As Murdoch points out, the Klu Klux Klan (KKK) are still very much the poster boys of White supremacy and he highlights research undertaken by The Southern Party Law Centre which claim that the number of active Klan groups increased in 2015 to 190 klans in America from 72 the year before.With KKK members declaring for a long time, that their members lie in the midst of ranks within various organisations and professions including, police officers, politicians and congressional representatives (Murdoch 2016). The #BLM has been about political action against the institutional racism reinforced within a capitalist system that stems from elite positions of power and infiltrates society throughout the remaining classes.

Footage of protests show both Black and White protestors at public marches. One benefit of social media is the opportunity to promote unity of black groups within local communities. Being unified under the hashtag allows them to relate to and present a uniformed identification for the cause and a unified message. The #BLM is not only the leading affiliate for all black movements but also the direct message to the world, which encapsulates the overall aim and the epitome of the black struggle on a global scale.

However, despite the level of global support for the BLM movement, there is still tension amongst White and Black supporters. One member of a local community group (Murdoch 2016) who faced problems with a White Trump supporter who had infiltrated the group and asked all whites to leave, explained,

...we created an African only space for a second just to re-group and think about security and who's who, and some of our European alliances who are very consistent, that we love, they felt a little upset and so we had to explain to them why there's that tension and the only example we could give them is Dylann Roof who sat in church and prayed with our elders for an hour and they welcomed him with open hands and he shot each one of them execution style in the back.

Many ask why social media is focused around the police. The BLM's focus on 'white supremacy as a system of oppression stretching through policing, politics and education gives the movement relevance in a globalised context. After all, globalisation refers mostly to the sharing of Western ideals but with white supremacist systems in practise within this, it's hard to see how Blacks will fare well.' Alternatively, without living in a globalised world driven by the developments in technology, social media campaigns such as BLM would not exist. Arguably, on both sides the #BLM may or may not survive in invoking social and political change for Blacks and only time will tell whether this campaign will accomplish the same successes as the Civil Rights Movement did but it most definitely impacts the Black demographic of political campaigning.

Trump's America: The Current Political Climate

January 20, 2017 saw Donald Trump become the 45th President of the United States and with it a tumultuous white America. Predominantly secured by a white vote, America had elected a man who openly targeted people's freedoms; endorsing a white transphobic, misogynist power who openly targeted the vulnerable within his own political audiences and the American people. A resurgence of whiteness, white power and the re-empowerment of the white American voter resurfaced in America; one rooted in anger and resentment from discontented Republican voters, a diverse class of people who felt cheated of 'their legacy: a bright, white future' (Hughes, 2017).

This was a post-Civil Rights political epoch, where we did not just see institutional controls overtly at work, but we saw white power divulged at the lower levels of society reverting to scaremongering tactics of the segregation era with localized groups mobilizing to threaten and target black minority ethnic voters. It was also one where by the New Right and neoliberal groups had previously appropriated Civil Rights political discourses, evoking empowerment and equality and accused by some of rolling back Civil Rights legislation and policies to aid colour-blind policy and a post-racial ideology; one deemed by some scholars as post-racial or colour-blind racism (Makovsky, 2017) in that it attributes racial inequality to non-racial dynamics such as cultural and biological limitations as opposed to historical enslavement and discrimination (Mullings, 2005).

Makovsky's (2017) coining of white nationalist post-racialism demonstrates this political shift well. Defined as paradoxical politics of the twenty first century; they define this term as a white resentment whose exponents aim to re-claim America for white Americans, whilst paradoxically denying ideological investment in white supremacy. Subsequently, Trump's America embodies an implosion in national identity politics, where racial identity specifically has been pushed to the forefront and the political sphere has become a black/white binary mirroring America's dominant and enforcing racial spectrum; this is backed by an establishment that counteracts BLM as a global movement; spear-headed by the anti-globalist and anti-immigrant leader convivial to white nationalist rhetoric.

An Epoch of Hate

The FBI Uniform Crime Reporting (UCR) program's 2016 hate crime statistics show a five per cent increase from the year 2015-16 with a total of 6,121 reported criminal incidents (FBI, 2017); 57.5% motivated by race, ethnicity or ancestry, 21.0% religious, 17.7% sexual orientation, with remaining incidents motivated by gender identity, disability and gender.

Trump's stance on perpetrators of terrorism as people of colour; attributed to anti-Islam and anti-Muslim sentiments in comparison to white terrorists and government policies against the black right to protest, organisations and activists have been consistently identified; most notably in the failure of the President to denounce and condemn Virginia white supremacists in the case of Charlottesville where a car ploughed into counter protestors at an organised white nationalist rally in opposition to the removal of the statue of Confederate general, Robert E Lee, killing one person dead (Jacobs and Murray, 2017).

This is in addition to an increase in mass shootings committed by white perpetrators; the most recent that of the First Baptist Church, Sutherland springs, where 26 people were gunned down by Devin Patrick Kelley and the Harvard Music Festival; 58 people were killed by Stephen Paddock who fired from the 32nd window of the Mandalay Bay Resort and Casino in Las Vegas. Reinforcement of these attacks of white terrorism of cases attributed to mental health issues as opposed to America's growing gun crisis and gun legislation (Shapiro, 2017) is in stark contrast to that of BLM; added to the FBI's terror watch list and the dedicated surveillance of black organised activism and activists declaring 'black identity extremists a violent threat and motivated to the targeting of law enforcement officers (FBI, 2017).'

Internationalisation

One media sensation that has taken both the US and Europe by storm since the Iraq war has been the concept of terrorism which has been a contributing factor to the evoking of racial hate against ethnic minorities, has driven stereotypes and swayed public opinion to be anti-immigrant and anti-refugees.

Social media has become a method of information, consumption and mobilization resulting in a demonstrable shift in power-play and the development of a collective consciousness for Blacks that adopts the movement's strategy as a cultural process. (Black Liberation Movement, Murdoch, 2016). Primary video material pertaining black injustice becomes a localised safeguarding measure and method to enforce accountability. Throughout the emergence and disappearance of periodic hashtags, #BLM has remained and from this has developed into a trans-national, socio-political movement for Black people and this is mostly attributed to the fact that it puts the issue of systemic racism at the forefront (Weedston 2014).

Taylor (2016) writes the advent of social media has almost erased the lag between when an incident happens and when the public becomes aware of it, time and geographical barriers are removed. The case of #BLM demonstrates not only a significant shift in the sharing and consumption of news but arguably as a multimedia platform operating with more freedom for social engagement, determined by the sharing of news being preliminarily in the control of the user. To some extent, it could be argued that for social movements in favour of oppressed minorities, social media is a necessity to the survival of a social movement as opposed to facing definitive barriers determined from an elite agenda (Noam Chomsky's Filters of Bias) which mainstream media operates within.

Co-founder of Black Lives Matter Toronto, Janaya Khan (2015) states that:

...the reach of anti-black racism is not confined to the borders of North America. Black Lives Matter has become a transformative outlet for all black people from different historical, cultural, socioeconomic and political identities. It is a source of solidarity for the survivors of colonization, exploitation, capitalism and police brutality.

The hashtag's international relevance and momentum has developed from its use in other international social media campaigns and as political identification with other oppressed groups such as #Palestine-2Ferguson, connecting the murders of Palestinians in Gaza to the suffering of blacks in the US (Khan, 2015). The resonance of BLM was further reinforced in Ethiopia when the Israeli police attacked a member of the Israeli army highlighting 'anti-black racist discrimination' against Ethiopians living in Israel. This protest became affiliated to the #BLM movement, with Ethiopian Jews demanding an end to discrimination and police brutality in Israel.

White supremacist society has not only been challenged within a social and political context, but an environmental one too; solidarity for the cause was also demonstrated at The annual United Nations climate summit in Lima, Peru, with the 'climate-justice movement to symbolically join the increasingly global #BLM uprising staging a "die-in" outside the convention center much like the ones that have brought shopping malls and busy intersections to a standstill, from the US to the UK' (Klein, 2014).

To some, the reasons as to why this is the case, in places such as the UK does not seem so apparent, statistics show that police in the UK have reportedly shot four people fatally in 2016 compared to 957 in the US (Mortimer, 2017). The BLM movement is at the conjunction of acute events and historical construction of racial oppression or colonial history, as American, British and French examples show

(Tharoor, 2016). The following section explores the internationalisation and re-contextualisation of the movement in two European countries.

THE RECEPTION OF BLACK LIVES MATTER IN EUROPE

To illustrate the diversity of #BLM reception, it appeared relevant to assess the responsivity to #BLM in two other structurally different but historically related Western countries. The colonial history (Cooper, 1996) and current structural differences between the French assimilative model and UK multicultural-ist are well documented (Favell, 2001; Bertaux, 2016). Both models provide different social structures leading to different social treatments of migration (Freeman, 2015), integration of cultures and faith (Brahm-Levey & Modood, 2009; Durham, 2015). Each case study focuses on ethnic and discrimination statistics to contextualise the relevance of #BLM, then analyse its public reception and media coverage.

United Kingdom

Ethnic Statistics

To provide a clearer picture of ethnic statistics within the UK, we can refer to the ethnic demographic data from the 2011 census (Office for National Statistics, 2012a). According to the official report, the population was 56.1 million people. The statistical breakdown was as follows, White: 86.0%, Mixed/ Multiple Ethnic Groups: 2.2%, Asian/ Asian British: 7.5%, Black, African/ Caribbean/ Black British: 3.3% and Other Ethnic Groups: 1.0%

In relation to specific regions of the UK and to provide an overview of ethnic demographics of the UK, the key relevant findings (2012a) were as follows:

- The most ethnically diverse region within the UK was London (2012a: 2) and contained the highest proportion of ethnic minority groups at 3.4 percent and White at 59.8 percent (2012a:7). London had above average quantities for minority groups which included African (7.0%), Indian (6.6%), Caribbean (4.2%) and other whites (12.6%), (2012a:7). This was followed by the West Midlands; the second most diverse region, which also had a higher than average of minority ethnic groups including Pakistani (4.1%), Indian (3.9%) Caribbean (1.5%) and a lower average regarding White ethnic groups (82.7%) including White British (79.2%) (2012a:7).
- In addition, relating to international migrants, the top ten local authority areas with the highest proportion of residents born outside of the UK (2012b: 15) were in London.
- The White majority ethnic group accounted for 86.0 percent (48.2 million), of this White British was the largest group at 80.5 percent (45.1 million), (2012a:2)
- Wales was found to be the least diverse area in the UK (2012a:2) followed by the South West and North East (2012a:7). The report highlights that 95% of the population in these areas identified as White.

The population of people belonging to Black groups according to statistics provided in the 2011 census would accumulate to just over 1.8 million people (mixed/multiple ethnic groups not included).

Minorities and Police Discrimination in UK

Since 1990, there has been 171 Black, Asian and Minority Ethnic (BAME) deaths in police custody or following contact with police, including 16 shootings, 155 deaths in custody and 493 deaths in prison within England and Wales (INQUEST, 2017). These include ten unlawful killing verdicts returned by juries at inquests however to date, from the point of monitoring; there have been no successful murder or manslaughter prosecutions of government agents involved in a death in police custody (this includes deaths resulting from police contact or deaths occurring whilst in prison). Restraint, use of force and mental health related issues are dominating features of deaths in custody and two times more likely to be a contributing factor in BAME cases. The research documents levels of racial disparity in relation to white counterparts and raises the issue of institutional racism as a contributing factor.

Although critics argue that the UK remains dissimilar to the USA regarding criminal justice, independent research (Prison Reform Trust, 2017) concluded that BAME groups are considerably over-represented within the prison system: prisoners are 10% Black and 6% Asian, which is significantly different from the general population of 2.8%. Overall, authors suggest Black prisoners account for the largest number of minority ethnic prisoners at 49% and add that at the end of June in 2014, 28% of minority ethnic prisoners were foreign nationals. The official statement comments that according to the Equality and Human Rights Commission, there is now greater disproportionality in the number of Black people in prisons in the UK than in the United States.

This can be explained by a racial bias in police stop and searches. The Institute of Race Relations (IRR, 2011) found that people from BAME groups are more likely than whites to be stopped and searched by police in the UK:

...police were 28 times more likely to use 'Section 60' stop-and-search powers (where officers do not require suspicion of the person having been involved in a crime) against Black people than White people. In the year 2013-2014, 59% of people stopped under Section 60 by London's Metropolitan Police Service were either Black British or Asian British.

BAME groups are still two times more likely to be stopped and searched by police; for Black people, specifically, this rises to 4.2 times the rate of white people (Stopwatch, 2016). In 2014, blacks were four times more likely to be arrested than whites were. A retrospective study of over a million court records suggested prison sentences were more likely for a black offender than a white one (44% more likely for driving offences, 38% for public order offences or possession of a weapon, 27% for possession of drugs (IRR, n.d.)

As Athwal and Burnett (2014) investigated, biases are also found in lack of legal enforcement. There have been 93 known or suspected racially motivated deaths since the death of Steven Lawrence in 1999 (preceded by the Macpherson report). They argue 'the racially motivated aspect of cases is being filtered out by the police, the CPS and the judiciary' often leaving families of victims to challenge police decisions and mobilising the media to exert pressure into recognition of the racial element (IRR, 2014).

Additionally, in a report on racial violence (IRR, 2013) in the UK, Burnett (2013) identifies that in 2011/12 there were more than 37,000 racial or religious recorded aggravated crimes, no longer predominantly found in 'urban centres' which bare a historic association. The impact of pauperisation in areas with little to no history of diversity is pointed out (IRR press release, 2013).

Disempowerment arises also from the inability to access the criminal justice system and trigger legal proceedings. The Report of the Independent Review of Deaths and Serious Incidents in Police Custody (Lindon & Roe, 2017) commissioned by Prime Minister, Theresa May highlighted a number of inequalities within the current system. These included i) imbalances within the coronial process due to family of the deceased having no automatic right to funding for legal representation despite different branches of the state having access to senior legal representation throughout the process (2017, p. 13), as well as ii) the vulnerability of individuals suffering mental health issues and the proficiency and use of NHS services in these cases as opposed to police custody (2017, p. 16).

Post EU referendum has seen an increase in racially motivated hate crimes with reports to police increasing by 42%, more than 3,000 allegations of hate crime were made across the UK in the week before and the week after the vote (Dodd, 2016). Although it is important to note that these racial experiences were encountered by a variety of people of mixed ethnicities including that of Eastern-Europeans; distinct attributions to the image of that of a refugee or immigrant were reinforced by the mainstream press that were attributed to 'blackness'. As far back as 2013, Nagarajan explored mainstream media's 'anti-immigrant rhetoric as common public opinion. Trans-national histories become lost in a country where by Black-British history is disregarded.

Organisations such as the English Defence League and right wing political parties such as the British National Party (BNP), United Kingdom Independence Party (UKIP) and some members of the Conservative Party, have powered this 'anti-British' concept. These public backers of the 'Leave Campaign', figure-headed by Nigel-Farage and Boris Johnson led a racist, anti-immigration campaign endorsing political tactics that used refugees as political targets.

Post-Brexit poses a risk to the British judicial process with regards to BAME rights and protections with the process currently enshrined and protected by Article 2 of the *European Convention on Human Rights*, which imposes a procedural obligation on the UK 'to conduct an active, impartial, independent and prompt investigation into deaths for which the State might be responsible. This Article also forms one of the Convention rights incorporated in the Human Rights Act 1998' (2017, p. 12). The UKs intention to scrap the human rights Act 1998 and Britain's sanctioning of Article 50 to withdraw as a member of the European Union means that the ramifications on legal proceedings and people's rights remain unknown and in a stagnant state of legal and societal vulnerability.

Seminal UK Case: Mark Duggan and the London Riots

On 4th August 2011, the shooting of Mark Duggan, an unarmed black man in Tottenham, London, initiated social unrest and racial tension across the country. This act triggered what is now known as 'The London Riots' which saw the spreading of rioting across the London boroughs and the continuation across the main major cities within the UK.

Starting on August 4, 2011, the riots saw thousands of people take to the streets up and down the country. The protest, which began peacefully involving 300 members of the community at Tottenham police station quickly turned into violence resulting from a confrontation between a teenager and the police (BBC, 2011). The first night saw 49 primary fires, looting, violence and clashes with police. Over the next week, two police stations were set on fire, major shopping centres were targeted and five deaths were being investigated. Across the country, 1436 arrests had been made by forces and as of August 12, 2011, 838 people had been charged (BBC, 2011). In London, Solihull and Manchester, courts stayed open throughout the night to fast track those in custody for disorder related offences (BBC, 2011).

BLM UK Today

On July 15th 2016, the official Twitter account was established for Black Lives Matter UK, the first post being "We are #BlackLivesMatterUK. In Solidarity with our black family all over the world fighting against racist violence. Join us. Follow us" (@UKBLM, posted 2016, July 15). In addition to this introductory post, early tweets relate to US events and re-tweets from prominent US Black media organisations. Alternatively, media organisations and twitter users with articles or information on race-related issues in the UK have used this as a platform to tweet @BLMUK, with latest research and news pieces directly communicating with UKBLM's following.

In the Statement of Solidarity with the UK, the message from Black Lives Matter was "We send you solidarity, as we see Mzee Mohammed. We see Sarah Reed, we see Jermaine Baker, the 1,558 people killed by police in the UK and your struggle to gain justice for them…" (@BLMUK, 2016, July 16). The March *Justice for Mohammed*, 2016, July 17, held in protest to the death of the 18 year old who died in police custody in Liverpool after being restrained by Merseyside officers at a shopping centre.

The death of Mohammed sparked BLM protests in London and Liverpool (Bulman, 2016). Traynor (2016) for the Liverpool Echo reported, "The movement, currently sweeping America and the UK - with demonstrations throughout the country since the fatal shootings of Philando Castile and Alton Sterling by police officers in the USA - came to Merseyside this afternoon. Cries of "Black Lives Matter, Mzee's Life Mattered" were shouted out as the march snaked through the city centre." The London march in the capital the next day coincided with the BLM rally in Melbourne Australia, highlighting the treatment of Aboriginal Australians.

BLMUK have circulated numerous Black cases of injustice ranging from Leon Patterson (1992), Errol McGowan (1999), Sean Rigg (2008) and Mark Duggan (2011) which continue to hold precedence for the fight for black rights evident in the more recent killings of Jermaine Baker (2015), professional footballer, Dalian Atkinson (2016) and Rashan Charles (2017).

Since the launch of UKBLM on Twitter, like the BLM in the USA, the group has mirrored an intersectional formation with the creation of localised UKBLM Facebook groups for each specific region, as are the American chapters.

In August 2016, UKBLM organised a nationwide #shutdown across the UK preceding the march *Tottenham Remembers* to mark the five-year anniversary of the killing of Mark Duggan. The shutdown included marches and rallies in Manchester (estimated at 3000 people by Pidd, 2016), Birmingham, Nottingham, Bristol and London, involving the shutdown of tramlines and road blockades throughout the city. A rally in London was led by the mother of Sean Riggs who died in police custody in 2008, after being restrained.

The organisation tweeted: #BlackLivesMatterUK@ukblm, Aug 5 "This morning we #Shutdown major transport hubs because the conventional avenues to justice have been shutdown to us". (@UKBLM, posted 2016, Aug 5)

As well as larger scale protests across major cities, local rallies for UKBLM have also taken place, most prominently on the issue of immigration and brought the attention to the treatment of migrants; with specific focus on the case of Luqman Onikosi where students did a sit in at Sussex University. Onikosi was an international student fighting deportation on the grounds no treatment for Hepatitis B was available in his country and would result in death. He eventually had his degree cancelled by the institution and was deported by the UK home office (Lentin, 2016).

One BLM protest in the UK that has created controversy has been the shutdown of London City Airport where nine environmental activists staged a protest under the BLM banner. The group faced public criticism for being a predominantly White group and were accused by anti-racist campaigners of being "white left-wing activists hijacking the Black Lives Matter banner" (Grierson, 2016). Whilst this was one perception of public opinion circulated by the mainstream, other organisations used the opportunity to inform the public on how climate change has a disproportionate effect on black people globally; re-affirmed as a 'racist crisis', by UKBLM activist, Kelbert (2016). Whilst these responses can be gauged as a reflection of mainstream media, there has not been enough research done into how people have engaged with UKBLM other than levels of physical engagement in active protests and social media metrics i.e. number of likes and followers, given above.

Additionally, collaboration between BLM and other movements has become precedent, the United Families and Friends Campaign (UFFC) annual march was promoted by BLMUK and by use of #BLM in conjunction with its news sharing of prominent deaths in custody and police killings on all of its social media platforms.

France

The French system is marked by a form of idealism, in its conception of society and identity (Favell, 2001). Indeed, the egalitarian aspiration and memories of previous labelling led to decades of a national policy preventing any ethnic and religious statistics from the state (Spire & Merllié, 1999), and so was the legal decision to ban the word race from any official documents in 2015. However, as the end of separate but equal doctrine in the USA, structural and legal equality is theoretical and differs from a social reality sometimes in denial or unable to accept its history (Nidiaye, 2008). If race can be thought of as construction to impose power, the ideal of a colour-blind French system fails to address discrimination and stigma related to cultural and ethnic background or skin-colours (Begag, 2016).

Ethnic Statistics

So far, the French system is aware of its discrepancies. On the one hand, at the structural level, banning the word race from the constitution was a symbolic attempt to promote an egalitarian ideal. On the other hand, facing reality, civil society finds ways to fight against discrimination based on ethnicity, religion or any other label. Indeed, civil society institutionalised the equality promotion through non-governmental organisations (e.g. SOS Racisme) but also consultative community groups (e.g. Representative Council of Black Associations of France - CRAN) and state-funded agency (The National Consultative Commission of Human Rights - NCCHR).

French National Institute of Statistics and Economic Studies (INSEE, 2015) do not report ethnic or religious backgrounds of the French population. However, surveys and other research could provide an estimation through side approaches. Beauchemin et al (2010a, 2010b) estimate that 10% of the people living in France are migrants, 12% of people living in France are direct descendants of at least one migrant. Main countries or areas of origin are Northern Africa with more than a million people (Morocco, Algeria, Tunisia), European Union with more than a million people, Sahel and Central Africa with over 350 000 people, other areas include Turkey, South Asia and other countries. If these statistics provide an overview of origins, no information can be deduced regarding either ethnic or religious background, even less, on how people identify.

In the same national survey (Beauchemin, Lagrange and Safi, 2011), one-third of interviewees agreed to the statement that "to be accepted in France you have to forget your origins". Authors interpret this as a reflection of the assimilationist idea and ideal therefore questioning the sense and possibility of transnational practices.

In 2006, the Representative Council of Black Associations commissioned the first poll including self-reported ethnic data to investigate experience of discrimination (CRAN, 2007); for the first time how people identify was investigated. Main categories and distribution were as follows: not belonging to any visible ethnic minority 90%, Black 3.2%, Arabo-Berber 3.2%, Mixed 1.4%, Asian 0.5%, Indian-Pakistani 0.2 and other 1%. It has been estimated that approximately 4% (including people identifying as mixed with one Black descent) over 1.8 million people, of the French population is black. 57% of the Black respondents do report experiencing discrimination. This discrimination occurs for 62% in public space or transportation and ranges from disrespectful attitude to actual violence. 61% of the Black people have reported a discriminatory event within the past twelve months. This alarming number is amplified by the very slow proportion of people engaging in legal recourse or in taking action. Other studies specified the different types of discrimination, notably regarding employment (SOS Racisme, 2016)

Minorities and Police Discrimination in France

The survey on racism (NCCHR, 2016) showed that anti-Muslim acts more than tripled and racist acts increased to 17.5% in 2015 compared to the previous year. Specific scopes also analysed anti-Semitic and anti-Romany acts. However, this refers to the analysis of justice statistics and seems far from the daily experiences of discrimination. Official statistics show an increase in the number of complaints against the police, but it is residual.

Nevertheless, the past decade saw the rise of media coverage and press releases related to police violence. One of the most prominent cases was the death of two young boys (one French-Black and one French-Arab) aged 15 and 17, who were chased by the police and hiding close to an electric substation were electrocuted and died. The teenagers were chased after information of a robbery and fled when seeing the police. This event was the trigger of French Riots in 2005 and led to the systematic focus on police officers. At the time and contingent to the riots, social reaction blamed the police. Families of the victims filed against the police but after a decade of legal procedures the sense of justice and the legal accountability of police officers remains uncertain.

This event is very similar to the UK and the USA ones, in the fact that it led to riots denouncing the ghettoization and the social inequalities suffered by the suburban population. Similarly to the UK, at the time, the lower classes and poorest people were at the heart of the French riots.

Seminal French Case: Adama Traore

From the very beginning, #BLM movement has been spread and supported in France. Discrimination of minorities and police violence has been recognised and has led to general emotional reaction and condemnation; however, it did not relegate the movement. Adama Traore died in police custody after being chased and arrested. The autopsy revealed he died of asphyxia.

This event and the secrecy around the autopsy, the absence of any criminal record gave the media grounds to question the relevance and the possibility of a French Black Lives Matter (Zappi, 2016). The first protest in the name of the BLM movement occurred on July 2, 2016, in Paris (Citiletti, 2016). Families of up to then forgotten cases joined the march. This march is the symbolic date of a French chapter of the BLM movement with the actual website http://blmfrance.com/. After this first protest, journalists started documenting more comprehensively and re-inspecting previous tragedies, such as the death of Babacar Gueye. In December 2015, the 27-year-old man, who was living undocumented in Rennes was shot with five bullets. Police invoked his aggressiveness to justify the shooting but it appeared the man was having a panic attack and dealing with mental health issues.

Indeed, the Adama Traore case highlights the French discrepancies and newspaper coverage reflects an international scope. Interestingly, French newspapers released foreign criticisms and reference to the BLM movement in the press seems to alert on police impunity (Gauthier-Faure, 2016).

During the spring and summer 2016, Facebook pages of BLM France (Facebook page and timeline can be tracked back to July 29) and BLM Paris started launching protest marches in different cities. The delocalisation of the protests to small cities, such as Bordeaux shows the concern and mobilisation out of the capital quite early on. If the number of followers on the BLM France Facebook page remains low (less than a thousand) mobilisation and media coverage shows a higher number of shares, re-tweets and global agreement.

Other events, such as the case of Theo L., a 22-year-old Black French young man who had an altercation that degenerated into a fight with four policemen. The four police officers were later charged, three of them for assault and last one for rape. The rape charge was abandoned and the four police officers were convicted for assault. This could have been the breeding ground for the rise of the BLM movement in France. Instead, it led to a social movement against police brutality and institutional investigations. The scarcity of studies on this topic raises concerns; however, French system tends to support initiatives from the civil society.

In October 2016, the first French Black Newspapers was launched, as an official response to this lack of visibility and representation in the public space and medias. Again, it seems that the social structure requires local adjusted means to reach an equality, awareness and visibility goal. The remaining question is can the #BLM movement translate into social action (McAuley, 2016) in the French context? If so, the next question is will it be a #BLM movement or a #ALM movement incorporating all discriminated minorities and fitting the colour-blind French system?

CRITICAL ANALYSIS: SHOCK WAVE, GLOBALISATION AND ADVOCACY

The power of social media is encapsulated in its ability to bypass professional journalism and sees activists able to use their own media production to mobilize the people. The circulation of visual footage has also challenged racial stereotypes and has 'erased the imaginary line between "respectability politics" - the concept that if black people are upstanding they won't experience racism and the lived experiences of black people; destroying the myth that black lives worth protecting are those of moral citizens' (Thrasher, 2015).

On a trans-national scale in relation to the BLM movement globalisation becomes about the globalised identification of being 'Black' and as well as identification with social and economic disparities, solidarity becomes also an acknowledgement of cultural hegemony across borders linked by historical references to colonization and enslavement. From a cultural perspective, trans-national relations between Blacks are further strengthened by the historic relevance to previous conquests, of which, are re-affirmed by the BLM movement, in this case through visual imagery. Take for example the Pan-African flag used in protest; this holds cultural resonance for all Africans but within a national context, for British-Blacks and French-Blacks, reflects the national significance for the movement for Blacks within the UK and France through historic association with the Pans-national congress.

Social Media Statistics and Impact

The increased usage of the smartphone worldwide has broadened possibilities of mobile social networks and this has been attributed to the development of location-based services (Statista, n.d.) Facebook is the leading social network worldwide with 1.71 billion monthly active users followed by Whatsapp and Facebook messenger, each with a billion monthly users. Twitter is 9th leading worldwide with 313 million active users (Statista, 2016). A recent report on the *number of social media network users worldwide 2010-2020* show that in 2016 there were an estimated 2.34 billion users globally; data analysis predicts these figures will increase to 2.67 billion in 2018 and 2.95 billion in 2020 (Statista, n.d.).

Collating statistics on the state of digital, mobile and social media usage on a global scale, there are 2.31 billion active social media users, 31% of the overall population of which 27% of these are mobile social users (We Are Social, 2016). Social media usage was measured around the globe, showing a stark contrast between different regions of the world. North America has the highest level of usage (59%), followed by South America (50%), Western Europe (48%) and Eastern Europe (45%). Regions with the lowest levels of usage included Central Asia (6%), South Asia (11%) and Africa (11%), (We Are Social, 2016).

To highlight the specific countries focused on within this chapter, the percentage of social media use by country were the following, USA (59%), UK (59%) and France (50%), (WAS, 2016).

Currently 59 percent of the United Kingdom have active accounts on social media (this data was specific to the top social networking site in the country, WAS, 2016). On Twitter, Black Lives Matter UK currently has 17.2K followers (Metrics: tweets: 275, following: 261, likes: 66, taken 2016, Sep 29, 18:53 GMT @UKBLM, Twitter).

Take the case of Africa, with a population of just over 1.2 billion, only 349 million are active internet users; 129 million are active social media users (WAS, 2016). One key point that must be paid attention is the BLM movement's principal focus concerning the social position of Blacks and racial injustice within a white supremacy system. Alternatively, to blacks living within these westernised systems, there are a Black population who may not relate to power structures based on a racial hierarchy, but have been exploited by it historically and are affected by it globally in relation to environmental challenges and social economic stability. Can therefore, this trans-national movement advocate a cause that will benefit the poorest of blacks?

Global Integration of Communication Technologies and Distribution of Media

Cole (2015) identifies the three main aspects of globalization as economic, cultural, social and political, which are powered by the following core areas: 'technological development, the global integration of communication technologies and the global distribution of media.'

Globalised advances in technology particularly in the 'smart-era' with the developments of the smart phone has seen a new generation of communicative methods and being connected particularly amongst young people. Technology advances have given us more power, control and access to social networking. All elements combined, ranging from video quality, to internet speed; the development of 4G and in particular the development of 'the app' has made information easier to access and faster to put out and circulate. The ranges of 'like', 'share' and 'tweet' features make accessibility and distribution an extremely fast process that spread quickly amongst online communities. Today often breaking news now comes over the internet first, followed then by TV and newspapers that cover it due to public interest.

This study however, highlighted core barriers in relation to specific varied properties of individual social media platforms (Giglietto, Rossi & Bennato, 2014). Facebook privacy settings can inhibit the circulation of news sharing and further inhibit data analysis of closed groups. On both Facebook and Twitter, originality was a major issue when identifying official BLM affiliated pages. Different variations of the hashtag i.e. #AllBlackLivesMatter led to a varied collation of circulated material; including related news. Variations on the hashtag such as this, although connected to the original hashtag, made search optimisation difficult and socio-behavioural patterns difficult to observe, further study should be done as to the effects on the overall follower demographic of the official organisation.

These advances in technology have benefited the globalised world when it comes to accountability of the state and the establishment and have developed as accessible resources to be used as protective methods. These developments in the modernised world have opened the door for resources to be made for specific groups including the minorities and the marginalised. See the example of the new ACLU Cell phone App, (Wiener, 2015) 'Mobile Justice CA app' which automatically preserves videos of police encounters and geographic information which are directly transmitted to the ACLU, so even if the phone is damaged or destroyed the footage is protected.

Patrice Cullors, the director of the Truth and Reinvestment Campaign at the Ella Baker Center, which is working with the ACLU of California explains:

People who historically have had very little power in the face of law enforcement now have this tool to reclaim their power and dignity, our vision is that this app will ultimately help community members connect and organize to respond to incidents of law enforcement violence, and then share their experiences and knowledge with others.

However, barriers to these developments are founded in state law in the US, to combat this the ACLU affiliates in other states have developed other versions for use in those states: 'residents of New York should use the "Stop and Frisk Watch" app; in New Jersey, it's the "Police Tape" app; in Oregon and Missouri it's the "Mobile Justice" app.' (Wiener, 2015) Arguably globalisation means that technology developments are equipped to be re-developed for each geographic demographic with economic interests vested in both the UK and the US. The constitutional set-up of the US makes this more difficult as unlike the UK which has one governing law, problems arise within different parts of America such as the one in Texas where 'a proposed law would make it a crime for ordinary people to videotape police actions—on the grounds that it was "interference" with police activity. In California, on the other hand, the state senate this month approved legislation providing clear legal protection to people who videotape police activity without interfering with investigations.'

This example displays the different aspects of globalisation on both a technological, economic and political scale and the implications it can present at a local level. But if we look at globalisation as a whole specifically with regards to internet users and social media, there is cause to question as to whether the #BLM can impact social and political change for the poorest people of colour.

Consequences of the Hashtag

Not all black people identify with the hashtag #blacklivesmatter (Freelon, 2016) including younger demographics of black communities. Further studies explore the breakdown of racial categories (Bonilla-Silva, 2004), and unsure Americans regarding the future distribution of power. The study presents the case for racial tension with the hashtag resulting from formal groupings aligned to on the basis of identity politics and in relation to racial categories which have formed on opposing hierarchical notions of race within what England, (2009:198) refers to as 'the logic of the colour continuum'. Although physical protests show a wide demographic of people in attendance, further exploration is needed into how individualised, categorised ethnic groups i.e. Asian, Hispanic, Latino engage with the movement. The movement has received criticism (Morrison, 2015) for its lack of coverage of other ethnic groups. Nevertheless, on a trans-national level the alliances built in the case of #Palestine2Ferguerson did progress interconnected issues of the mistreatment of people of colour across borders.

The strength of the hashtag results from its agility in use as a political statement and as a form of social identification where by Black political groups and organisations under a socially mobile political label, can capture the aims and direct message of a unified socio-political movement. Its durability arises from relevance to mirrored social justice situations and a broad resonance of socio-political issues that affect Black people (McLaughlin, 2016).

CONCLUSION: #BLM IN NON-AMERICAN CONTEXTS – RESPONSIVITY AND RETERRITORIALIZATION

Seen from a social construction approach (Hoberman, 1997; Boulle, 2002; Machery & Faucher, 2005; Steinberg, 1989); deconstructed and demystified by scientific studies (Smedley and Smedley, 2005; Sussman, 2014), race as an empirical concept is erroneous but persists as a social category. The #BLM movement is spreading widely and supported all over the world. However, its embodiment in other countries seems to depend on local contexts, local social constructions of race or ethnicity and social reality of minorities' integration.

Responsivity and the Need for a Similar Case

The French case study showed how police-related violence against minorities is not enough to embrace the cause. Indeed, if African-Americans are an important minority in the USA, historically, France has a different migration history. Moreover, terrorist attacks endured since 2015 has led to the social targeting of Arab descendants and Muslim people more than the Black community. This led to the social responsivity to what is perceived as a cold-blooded killing, as an unfair and evitable drama. Adama Traore is (rightly) becoming an archetype of the innocent, victim of a suspicious system, discriminatory state and authoritarian state.

Reterritorialization, Embodiment, and Reframing

A dominating ideal amongst Western countries has been the 'post-racial' one, whether through 'colour-blindness' as evidenced in the French system or the multiculturalist British or American ones. Currently, in these systems, nationalist ideals arise and with them a new form of White superiority. Nationalism counteracts with globalisation and reinforces the idea of an elite power structure (Sabanadze, 2010). BLM is a decentralized network with a grouping of local chapters including members from all different communities, which reflects the idea of the local first.

Regarding the French context, events are too recent to enable any interpretation. Nevertheless, the re-contextualisation of the movement in the UK shows an interesting becoming. The struggle and oppression is worse for the lower classes/ poorer people. Historically, within the UK, Black rights have been tied to working class movements. This explains why not only Black people protest against the establishment, but Whites too.

It is an example of how, counterintuitively, even ordinary white people have an interest in exposing the racist nature of US society, because doing so legitimizes the demand for an expansive and robust regime of social welfare intended to redistribute wealth and resources from the rich back to the working-class— Black, Brown and white. Conversely, it is also why the political and economic elites have such a vested interest in colorblindness and in the perpetuation of the myth that the United States is a meritocracy (Taylor, 2016).

Using the hashtag is to make a political statement. As a form of social identification under a political label Black groups and organisations can send the key and direct message of a holistic socio-political movement. From a trans-national perspective, the same capitalist system is mirrored within Europe, magnifying comparable social issues that in conjunction, oppress Blacks within that system and is embedded within key institutional elements such as politics, education and criminal justice.

One of the consequences of BLM in relation to global struggles is the perpetuated definition of racism as one confined in a black/white schema of racism; a reflection of America's racial history and structure. How then can BLM advocate for those affected by other racisms such as ethnic cleansing, religious and cultural persecution, committed by distinctive groups amongst people of colour that sit beyond the boundaries of a social reality constructed within black-white terms? Racism is a global phenomenon, with a diverse and ever-changing form (Castle, 2000). Subsequently, BLM becomes, in part, a paradox: pertaining to advocate for Black people in different national and demographical contexts whilst simultaneously reinforcing a restrictive narrative of oppression, which was created for the rights and citizens that lay within the boundaries of a Westernised context.

REFERENCES

Aboud, F. E. (2003). The formation of in-group favoritism and out-group prejudice in young children: Are they distinct attitudes? *Developmental Psychology*, *39*(1), 48–60. doi:10.1037/0012-1649.39.1.48 PMID:12518808

Allport, G. W. (1954). *The nature of prejudice*. Cambridge, MA: Addison-Wesley.

Anderson, M., & Hitlin, P. (2016). *Social Media Conversations About Race*. New York: Pew Research Center.

Athwal, H., & Burnett, J. (2014). Investigated or ignored? An analysis of race-related deaths since the Macpherson Report. *Race & Class*, *56*(1), 22–42. doi:10.1177/0306396814531694

Balkaran, S. (2015, May 27). Post Racial America in the Age of Obama. The Huffington Post. Retrieved September 27, 2016, from http://www.huffingtonpost.com

BBC. (2011). England riots: Maps and timeline. Retrieved from http://www.bbc.co.uk

Beauchemin, C., Borrel, C., & Régnard, C. (2010b). Migrations : Les immigrés et les autres. In P. Simon, C. Beauchemin, & C. Hamel, (Eds.), Trajectoires et Origines. Enquête sur la diversité des populations en France. Premiers résultats (Ch. 2). Paris: Institut national d'études démographiques, pp 19-24.

Beauchemin, C., Hamel, C., Simon, P., & Equipe Te, O. (2010a). *Trajectoires et origines : enquête sur la diversité des populations en France. Premiers résultats*. Paris: Institut National d'Études Démographiques.

Beauchemin, C., Lagrange, H., & Safi, M. (2011). *Transnationalism and immigrant assimilation in France: Between here and there?* Paris: HAL et INED.

Begag, A. (2016). La France en panne d'intégration. *Contemporary French Civilization*, *41*(2), 273–277. doi:10.3828/cfc.2016.14

Bertaux, S. (2016). Towards the unmaking of the French mainstream: The empirical turn in immigrant assimilation and the making of Frenchness. *Journal of Ethnic and Migration Studies*, *42*(9), 1496–1512. doi:10.1080/1369183X.2015.1119651

Bonilla, Y., & Rosa, J. (2015). # Ferguson: Digital protest, hashtag ethnography, and the racial politics of social media in the United States. *American Ethnologist*, *42*(1), 4–17. doi:10.1111/amet.12112

Bonilla-Silva, E. (2004). From bi-racial to tri-racial: Towards a new system of racial stratification in the USA. *Ethnic and Racial Studies*, *27*(6), 931–950. doi:10.1080/0141987042000268530

Boulle, P. H. (2002). La construction du concept de race dans la France d'Ancien Régime. *Outre-mers*, *89*(336/337), 155–175. doi:10.3406/outre.2002.3987

Brahm Levey, G., & Modood, T. (2009). *Secularism, Religion and Multicultural Citizenship*. Cambridge: Cambridge University Press.

Brand, E. S., Ruiz, R. A., & Padilla, A. M. (1974). Ethnic identification and preference: A review. *Psychological Bulletin*, *81*(11), 860–890. doi:10.1037/h0037266

Breindl, Y. (2010). Internet-based protest in European policymaking: The case of digital activism. *International Journal of E-Politics*, *1*(1), 57–72. doi:10.4018/jep.2010102204

Brown v. Board of Education of Topeka, 347 U.S. 483, 74 S. Ct. 686; 98 L. Ed. 873. (1954).

Bulman, M. (2016). Death of black teenager detained by police sparks Black Lives Matter protests in UK cities. *The Independent*. Retrieved from http://www.independent.co.uk

Burnett, J. (2013). *Racial Violence: Facing Reality*. London: Institute of Race Relations.

Caleffi, P. M. (2015). The 'hashtag': A new word or a new rule? *Skase Journal of Theoretical Linguistics, 13*(2).

Campbell, K. K. (2005). Agency: Promiscuous and prote-an. *Communication and Critical/Cultural Studies, 2*(1). doi:10.1080/1479142042000332134

Cashmore, E., & McLaughlin, E. (Eds.). (1991). *Out of Order: Policing Black People*. Routledge.

Castelliti, C. (2016, July 24). Reportage au cœur de la première manifestation "Black Lives Matter France. *Les Inrocks*. Retrieved from http://www.lesinrocks.com/2016/07/24/actualite/reportage-coeur-de-manifestation-black-live-matter-france-11855472/

Castles, S. (2000). *Ethnicity and globalization: From migrant worker to transnational citizen*. London: Sage.

Cockerham, C. (2011). The defining moment: Children's conceptualization of race and experiences with racial discrimination. *Ethnic and Racial Studies, 34*(4), 662–682. doi:10.1080/01419870.2011.53 5906 PMID:21532908

Cole, N. (2015).h What is Globalization, A Sociological Definition: About Education. Retrieved from: http://sociology.about.com/od/Ask-a-Sociologist/fl/Globalization.htm

Cooper, F. (1996). *Decolonization and African society: The labor question in French and British Africa*. Cambridge University Press. doi:10.1017/CBO9780511584091

CRAN. (2007). Les discriminations à l'encontre des populations noires de France (short report). Retrieved from le-cran.fr/document-cran-associations-noires-de-france/63-tns-sofres-premiere-enquete-statistique-sur-les-noirs-de-france.pdf

Daniel, P. (1973). *The Shadow of Slavery: Peonage in the South, 1901-1969*. London, Oxford: Oxford University Press.

Daniel, P. (1979). The Metamorphosis of Slavery, 1865-1900. *The Journal of American History, 66*(1), 88–99. doi:10.2307/1894675

De Choudhury, M., Jhaver, S., Sugar, B., & Weber, I. (2016). Social Media Participation in an Activist Movement for Racial Equality. AAAI In (Ed.), *Proceedings of the Tenth International AAAI Conference on Web and Social Media* (pp. 92-101).

Dodd, V. (2016). Police blame worst rise in recorded hate crime on EU referendum: The Guardian. Retrieved September 20, 2016 from https://www.theguardian.com

Durham, C. W. (Ed.). (2015). *Religion and the Secular State*. Madrid: International Center for Law and Religion Studies, Universidad Complutense.

England, S. (2010). Mixed and multiracial in Trinidad and Honduras: Rethinking mixed-race identities in Latin America and the Caribbean. *Ethnic and Racial Studies, 33*(2), 195–213. doi:10.1080/01419870903040169

Favell, A. (2001). Philosophies of Integration. Immigration and the Idea of Citizenship in France and Britain (2nd ed.), New York: Palgrave in association with Centre for Research in Ethnic Relations, University of Warwick. doi:10.1057/9780333992678

FBI. (2016). Hate Crime Statistics: Criminal Justice Information Services Division: Government website. Retrieved November 22, 2017 from https://www.fbi.gov/news/stories/2016-hate-crime-statistics

FBI. (2017, August 3) Black Identity Extremists Likely Motivated to Target Law Enforcement Officer. Counterterrorism Division, Government report: Retrieved November 22, 2017 fromhttps://assets.documentcloud.org/documents/4067711/BIE-Redacted.pdf

Franklin, S. M. (2014). *After the rebellion: Black youth, social movement activism, and the post-civil rights generation.* NYU Press. doi:10.18574/nyu/9780814789384.001.0001

Freelon, D., McIlwain, C. D., & Clarke, M. D. (2016). *Beyond The Hashtags: #Ferguson, #Blacklivesmatter and the online struggle for offline justice.* Washington, DC: Centre for Media & Social Impact. American University.

Freeman, G. P. (2015). *Immigrant labor and racial conflict in industrial societies: The French and British experience, 1945-1975.* Princeton University Press.

Gauthier-Faure, M. (2016, July 31). Mort d'Adama Traoré: le New York Times dénonce l'impunité de la police française. Retrieved from http://www.marianne.net/mort-adama-traore-new-york-times-denonce-impunite-police-francaise-100244747.html

Giglietto, F. A., Rossi, L., & Bennato, D. (2014). The Open Laboratory: Limits and Possibilities of Using Facebook, Twitter, and Youtube as a Research Data Source. In K. Bredl, J. Hunniger, & J. L. Jensen (Eds.), *Methods for Analyzing Social Media* (pp. 5–19). London, New York: Routledge.

Goffman, E. (1963). *Stigma: Notes on the management of spoiled identity.* London: Pelican Books.

Grierson, J. (2016). Black Lives Matter activists admit trespass after City airport protest. Retrieved from, https://www.theguardian.com

Groves, H. E. (1951). Separate but Equal--The Doctrine of Plessy v. Ferguson. *Phylon, 12*(1), 66–72. doi:10.2307/272323

Hoberman, J. M. (1997). *Darwin's Athletes: How Sport has Damaged Black America and Preserved the Myth of Race.* Boston: Houghton Mifflin Co.

Ibahrine, M. (2017). Women Hashtactivism: Civic Engagement in Saudi Arabia. *World Academy of Science, Engineering and Technology. International Journal of Information and Communication Engineering, 11*(3), 79.

INQUEST. (2017). BAME deaths in police custody. Retrieved from http://inquest.org.uk/statistics/bame-deaths-in-police-custody

IRR. (2013). Facing up to racial violence. Retrieved September from http://www.irr.org.uk/news/facing-up-to-racial-violence/

IRR. (2014). Investigated or ignored? Press Release. Retrieved from http://www.irr.org.uk/news/investigated-or-ignored/

IRR. (n.d.). Criminal justice system statistics. Retrieved from http://www.irr.org.uk/research/statistics/criminal-justice/

Jacobs, B., & Murray, W. (2017, August 13) Donald Trump under fire after failing to denounce Virginia white supremacists. *The Guardian*. Retrieved November 22, 2017 from www.theguardian.com

Jansen, F. (2010). Digital activism in the Middle East: Mapping issue networks in Egypt, Iran, Syria and Tunisia. *Knowledge Management for Development Journal*, 6(1), 37–52. doi:10.1080/19474199.2010.493854

Jausset, J. S. (2016, Aug 8). France: abattu par la police, Babacar Guèye a été accusé de tentative de meurtre par deux des policiers. Jeune Afrique http://www.jeuneafrique.com/346546/societe/abattu-par-police-babacar-gueye-accuse-de-tentative-de-meurtre/

Jones, A., & Lobianco, T. (2016, September 5). Obama: Colin Kaepernick 'exercising constitutional right'. *CNN*. Retrieved from http://edition.cnn.com

Kelbert, A. W. (2016). Climate change is a racist crisis: that's why Black Lives Matter closed an airport. *The Guardian*. Retrieved from https://www.theguardian.com

Khan, J. (2015). Black Lives Matter has become a global movement. The root. Retrieved from: https://www.theroot.com

Klein, N. (2014) Why #BlackLivesMatter Should Transform the Climate Debate. *The Nation*. Retrieved September 5, 2016 from: https://www.thenation.com

Lentin, A. (2016) Luqman Onikosi's deportation shows we are all being asked to become border guards. *The Guardian*. Retrieved from, https://www.theguardian.com

Lindon, G., & Roe, S. (2017). *Deaths in police custody: A review of the international evidence. Research Report 95*. London: Home Office, Crown Copyright.

Loken, M. (2014). # BringBackOurGirls and the Invisibility of Imperialism. *Feminist Media Studies*, 14(6), 1100–1101. doi:10.1080/14680777.2014.975442

Machery, E., & Faucher, L. (2005). Social construction and the concept of race. *Philosophy of Science*, 72(5), 1208–1219. doi:10.1086/508966

Maskovsky, J. (2017). Toward the anthropology of white nationalist postracialism: Comments inspired by hall, goldstein, and Ingram's "The hands of donald trump". *HAU*, 7(1), 433–440. doi:10.14318/hau7.1.030

Maslow, W., & Robison, J. B. (1953). Civil Rights Legislation and the Fight for Equality, 1862-1952. *The University of Chicago Law Review. University of Chicago. Law School*, 20(3), 3. doi:10.2307/1597662

McAuley, J. (2016). Black Lives Matter movement comes to France. But will it translate? Washington Post.

McLaughlin, M. (2016). The Dynamic History of #BlackLivesMatter Explained, This is how a transformed into a movement. *The Huffington Post*. Retrieved June 30, 2016, from http://www.huffingtonpost.co.uk

Moore, H. L., & Selchow, S. (2012). 'Global Civil Society'and the Internet 2012: Time to Update Our Perspective. In M. Kaldor et al... (Eds.), *Global Civil Society 2012* (pp. 28–40). Palgrave Macmillan, UK. doi:10.1057/9780230369436_2

Morrison, K. (2015, July 30). Social Media Activism: Sandra Bland, Police Brutality and #BlackLivesMatter. *Adweek.com*. Retrieved from http://www.adweek.com

Mortimer, C. (2017, January 3). M62 Shooting: Charts show difference between police shootings in the US and the UK. *The Independent*. Retrieved November 19, 2017 from http://www.independent.co.uk

Mullings, L. (2005). Interrogating Racism: Toward an Antiracist Anthropology. *Annual Review of Anthropology, 34*(1), 667–693. doi:10.1146/annurev.anthro.32.061002.093435

Murdoch, D. (2016). *Black power: America's armed resistance*. Documentary, UK: BBC; Retrieved from http://www.bbc.co.uk/programmes/p03t9g3j

Nagarajan, C. (2013). How politicians and the media made us hate immigrants (Blog post). *Open Democracy Online*. Retrieved from https://www.opendemocracy.net/transformation/chitra-nagarajan/how-politicians-and-media-made-us-hate-immigrants

NCCHR. (2016). *Report on the prevention of racism, anti-semitism and xenophobia*. Paris: CNCDH.

Ndiaye, P. (2008). *La condition noire. Essai sur une minoritéfrançaise*. Paris: Calmann-Lévy.

Nieman, D. G. (1994). *From Slavery to Sharecropping: White Land and Black Labor in the Rural South, 1865-1900*. London: Garland.

Office for National Statistics. (2012a). *Ethnicity and National Identity in England and Wales: 2011. National Identity*. London Crown Copyright.

Office for National Statistics. (2012b). *Ethnicity and National Identity in England and Wales: 2011. Migration*. London: Crown Copyright.

Pager, D. (2003). The Mark of a Criminal Record. *American Journal of Sociology, 108*(5), 937–975. doi:10.1086/374403

Painter, N. I. (2006). *Creating black Americans: African-American history and its meanings, 1619 to the present*. USA: Oxford University Press.

Pew Research Center. (2013). King's Dream Remains an Elusive Goal; Many Americans See Racial Disparities. Retrieved from http://www.pewsocialtrends.org/2013/08/22/kings-dream-remains-an-elusive-goal-many-americans-see-racial-disparities/4/

Pidd, H. (2016). Thousands attend Black Lives Matter solidarity march in Manchester. The Guardian. Retrieved from https://www.theguardian.com/uk

Plessy v. Ferguson, 63 U.S. 537, 16 S. Ct. 1138; 41 L. Ed. 256. (1896).

Plumer, B. (2013, Aug 28). Ten charts show how the U.S. has changed for the better since MLK's speech. *The Washington Post*. Retrieved August 28, 2016 from www.washingtonpost.com

Prison Reform Trust. (2016.). Projects & Research. Retrieved from http://www.prisonreformtrust.org.uk/ProjectsResearch/Race

Racisme, S. O. S. (2016, July 12). Les discriminations dans l'accès à l'emploi public: un rapport bienvenu. Retrieved from http://sos-racisme.org/communique-de-presse/les-discriminations-dans-lacces-a-lemploi-public-un-rapport-de-bienvenue/

Roche, J. P. (1951). The Future of "Separate but Equal". *Phylon*, *12*(3), 219–226. doi:10.2307/271632

Rutland, A., Hitti, A., Mulvey, K. L., Abrams, D., & Killen, M. (2015). When does the ingroup like the out-group? Bias among children as a function of group norms. *Psychological Science*, *26*(6), 834–842. doi:10.1177/0956797615572758 PMID:25888686

Sabanadze, N. (2010). Globalization and Nationalism: The Relationship Revisited. In *Globalization and Nationalism: The Cases of Georgia and the Basque Country* (pp. 169–186). Central European University Press.

Scheper-Hughes, N. (2017). Another country? racial hatred in the time of trump: A time for historical reckoning. *HAU*, *7*(1), 449–460. doi:10.14318/hau7.1.032

Shapiro, R. (2017, November 6). Trump says deadly Texas shooting isn't a guns issue, it's a mental health problem. *The Huffington Post*. Retrieved November 22, 2017 fromhttp://www.huffingtonpost.co.uk

Smedley, A., & Smedley, B. D. (2005). Race as biology is fiction, racism as a social problem is real: Anthropological and historical perspectives on the social construction of race. *The American Psychologist*, *60*(1), 16–26. doi:10.1037/0003-066X.60.1.16 PMID:15641918

Spire, A., & Merllié, D. (1999). La question des origines dans les statistiques en France. Les enjeux d'une controverse. *Le Mouvement Social*, *188*(188), 119–130. doi:10.2307/3779961 PMID:22029101

Stache, L. C. (2015). Advocacy and political potential at the convergence of hashtag activism and commerce. *Feminist Media Studies*, *15*(1), 162–164. doi:10.1080/14680777.2015.987429

Statista. (2016). UK Social Media Statistics for 2016. Leading social networks worldwide as of September 2016, ranked by number of active users (in millions). Worldwide; We Are Social; WhatsApp; Tumblr; LinkedIn; Google. Retrieved from https://www.statista.com

Statista. (n.d.). Number of social media users worldwide 2010-2020. Retrieved from https://www.statista.com/statistics/278414/number-of-worldwide-social-network-users/

Steinberg, S. (1989). *The ethnic myth: Race, ethnicity, and class in America*. Boston: Beacon Press.

Steinmetz, K. (2014) #blacklivesmatter Is the American Dialect Society's 2014 Word of the Year: TIME online. Retrieved June 19, 2016 from http://time.com

Stopwatch. (2015). Stop and Search Statistics 2014/2015. Retrieved from http://www.stop-watch.org/news-comment/story/new-stop-and-search-statistics-2014-2015

Sussman, R. W. (2014). *The myth of race: The troubling persistence of an unscientific idea*. Cambridge: Harvard university press. doi:10.4159/harvard.9780674736160

Taylor, K.-Y. (2016). *From #Blacklivesmatter To Black Liberation*. Haymarket Books Chicago.

Tharoor, I. (2016). Black Lives Matter is a global cause. *The Washington Post*. Retrieved September 5, 2016 from https://www.washingtonpost.com

Thrasher, S. W. (2015). Black Lives Matter has showed us: the oppression of black people is borderless. *The Guardian*. Retrieved March 7, 2015 from https://www.theguardian.com/uk

Traynor, L. (2016, July 16). Pleas for "justice" for 18-year-old Mzee Mohammed at Black Lives Matter march in Liverpool. Liverpool Echo. Retrieved from http://www.liverpoolecho.co.uk

@UKBLM (n.d.). Official Twitter Page Black Lives Matter UK. Twitter. Retrieved from https://twitter.com/ukblm

Vaidyanathan, R. (2016). The compass: America in black and white: Criminal Justice. *BBC*. Retrieved September 17, 2016, from http://www.bbc.co.uk/programmes/p03db7zh

Vaidyanathan, R. (2016). The compass: America in black and white: Economic Opportunity. *BBC*. Retrieved September 17, 2016, from http://www.bbc.co.uk/programmes/p03drnpt

Wahlquist, C. (2017, May 22). Black Lives Matter awarded 2017 Sydney peace prize. *The Guardian*. Retrieved November 18, 2017 from https://www.theguardian.com/uk

We Are Social. (2016). Digital In 2016. Retrieved from http://wearesocial.com/uk/special-reports/digital-in-2016

Weedston, L. (2014). 12 Hashtags That changed the world in 2014. *YES Magazine*. Retrieved from http://www.yesmagazine.org

Williams, S. (2015). Digital defense: Black feminists resist violence with hashtag activism. *Feminist Media Studies*, *15*(2), 341–344. doi:10.1080/14680777.2015.1008744

Witte, G. (2015, June 11). Do Britain's gunless bobbies provide answers for America's police? *The Washington Post*. Retrieved September 5, 2016, from https://www.washingtonpost.com

Yang, G. (2016). Narrative agency in hashtag activism: The case of# BlackLivesMatter. *Media and Communication*, *4*(4), 13–17. doi:10.17645/mac.v4i4.692

Zappi, S. (2016). Rassemblement à Paris de "Black Lives Matter France" après la mort d'Adama Traoré. Le Monde. Retrieved from http://www.lemonde.fr/police-justice/article/2016/07/23/rassemblement-a-paris-de-black-lives-matter-france-apres-la-mort-d-adama-traore_4973930_1653578.html#7zT5dvQqPYTMwEgm.99

KEY TERMS AND DEFINITIONS

Activism: The policy or action of using vigorous campaigning to bring about political or social change.
Advocacy: Individual or collective public support for or recommendation of a particular cause or policy.
Assimilationism: Doctrine of cultural integration.

Colour-Blindness: Doctrine related the social integration of minorities thought to be not influenced by racial prejudice.

Hashtactivism: Activism using online media and subversion of social media into online campaigning

Multiculturalism: Doctrine of cultural cohabitation.

ENDNOTE

[1] The Universal Negro Improvement Association was created in 1914 in Jamaica by Marcus Garvey and was settled in the USA in 1916.

Chapter 3
Rethinking Media Engagement Strategies for Social Change in Africa:
Context, Approaches, and Implications for Development Communication

Adebayo Fayoyin
UNFPA, South Africa

ABSTRACT

Media engagement is a powerful strategy of achieving development outcomes in society. This has resulted in the deployment of different media platforms and processes (including the mass media, community media, mediated media and social media) by development agencies for social change. This chapter examined the imperatives for and the diverse approaches by development organizations in mobilizing the media for social change in Africa. While such media engagement processes have contributed to influencing public and media agenda in line with organizational mandates, they also heavily integrate corporate promotion and individual organizational positioning. Our analysis demonstrates the absence of a collective media engagement strategy aligned with the overarching global and continental development goals among development agencies. Drawing on insights from contemporary development frameworks such as the United Nations Sustainable Development Goals (SDGs) and Agenda 2063 of the Africa Union, the study calls for a rethink of existing media engagement approaches in achieving social change in Africa. It also recommends actions to enhance issue positioning and advocacy journalism.

INTRODUCTION

Development organizations undertake a variety of media and communication activities to influence social, policy and political agenda. This is predicated on the inherent power of the media in addressing the information gap in the process of social change (McCombs, 2005; Waisbord, 2006) and educating

DOI: 10.4018/978-1-5225-9869-5.ch003

the public on health outcomes (Wallack et al, 1993). Media deployment by development agencies also emanates from the conviction that the mass media can either serve as a means of transferring ideas and innovation essential for change (Oxfam. (2015; Praekelt, 2012) or facilitating the creation of an enabling environment for dialogue and empowerment pivotal for sustainable development (PANOS, 2003). Also, the advent of digital media globally and in Africa has led to significant optimism on social media solutions in enhancing civic engagement and collective innovation (Green et al, 2014:208) and social and behaviour change (Fayoyin 2016:9). Undoubtedly, technological innovations have created horizontal integration of the society resulting in multipolar, multidimensional and multidirectional social interaction and information flows (Christakis & Fowler, 2011).

However, the emergence of new development frameworks at the global and continental levels presents new obligations and challenges for media's role in development. First, the United Nations Sustainable Development Goals (SGDs) adopted in 2015 enshrines the global vision for human development to be achieved by 2030 as follows:

We resolve to build a better future for all people, including millions who have been denied the chance to lead decent, dignified and rewarding lives and to achieve their full human potential. We can be the first generation to succeed in ending poverty, just as we may be the last to have a chance of saving the planet. The world would be a better place in 2030 if we succeed in our objectives (United Nations, 2015:12)

Second, the African Union Agenda 2063 for the continent contains a similar goal for social change and overall development. The aspirations for a new Africa include:

1.   A prosperous Africa based on inclusive growth and sustainable development;
2.   An integrated continent, politically united and based on ideals of Pan Africanism and the vision of Africa's Renaissance;
3.   An Africa of good governance, democracy, respect for human rights, justice, and the rule of law; and
4.   An Africa whose development is people-driven relying on the potential of African people, especially its women and youth and caring for children" (Africa Union, 2014:2).

Achieving these laudable objectives requires, among others, the full deployment of all the instruments of social change, including the media. Arguably, the voice of the people which is essential in effecting change cannot be integrated into the development agenda without effective media deployment. Implementing a coherent and comprehensive action for vulnerable people is impossible without the media holding government and other institutions accountable to the people and to the development vision.

Against this backdrop, the chapter examines the current context and approaches of engaging the media for social change in Africa. We define media engagement for development as the deployment of professional journalism skills and utilization of media products, platforms and processes in promoting social change. This perspective also describes media advocacy activities by development agencies in achieving their mandates. Chapman (2004:1) situates media advocacy within the general framework of public health advocacy as the 'strategic use of news media to advance a policy initiative, in the face of opposition' while Wallack *et al.,* (1993:35) describe it as a strategy to use the mass media "appropriately, aggressively and effectively to support the development of healthy public policies". For this paper, media engagement entails the holistic deployment of multiple media platforms to influence public opinion, mobilise community activists, and influence levels of influence and advance social change agenda. In particular, the paper examines the media mobilization activities of selected agencies - UNICEF, UNFPA and UNAIDS – and draws implications for communicating human development. Overall, the article uses the new global and continental development agenda as the interpretative lens and agenda setting as the theoretical framework to offer fresh insights for enhancing development communication practices.

The paper is divided into five sections of which this introduction is a part. Second it examines the essential contexts (conceptual and programmatic) in engaging the media for social change. Third, the paper reviews the media engagement approaches of UNICEF, UNAIDS and UNFPA to illustrate how development agencies are currently mobilizing the media in achieving development outcomes. The fourth section identifies salient issues in the utilization of media for social change based on critical highlights of the global and the continental development frameworks. Finally, the paper makes specific recommendations for both development organisations and media institutions in the last section.

CONCEPTUAL AND PROGRAMMATIC CONTEXTS OF MEDIA ENGAGEMENT IN DEVELOPMENT

Conceptual Underpinning

One of the dominant conceptual frameworks for explaining and understanding media engagement in society is agenda setting. There are several strands of agenda setting research, especially from policy science and mass media studies (McCombs, 2005). However, a brief overview is presented as the theoretical context of our analysis.

McCombs & Shaw (1972) articulated the agenda setting hypothesis into a theory based on the notion that mass media channels are critical to shaping public opinion and keeping issues on the public agenda. The implicit power of the media allows them to attract attention while the salience devoted to issues by the media determines the extent to which they become objects of public agenda and the actions they elicit. This is predicated on the underlying assumption that "the mass media have the ability to transfer salience on their news agenda to their public agenda." (Griffin, 2012: 378). Basically, agenda setting establishes that there is some correlation between media agenda and the public's agenda in that the media determines what the society considers as important (Scheufele &Tewksbury, 2007; Kim & McCombs, 2004). In addition, as Dearing & Rogers (1996:1) suggest, agenda setting "is an on-going competition among issue proponents to gain the attention of media professionals, the public and the policy elites". This conclusion is important for our study which looks at how development agencies try to influence both media agenda and public agenda for development outcomes. However, there is abundant evidence of limited causal relationship between media agenda and social change.

Kingdon (1995) expounds agenda setting from a policy prism to explain how issues get on the public and political agenda. From the Multiple Streams framework, the author identifies three independent streams in the agenda setting process: problem, politics and policy streams. According to the author, the likelihood that an issue will be given attention within the political space is when two or all streams connect, based on what is called a "policy window". In other words, the coupling of streams is what helps to attract attention to an issue (Zahariadis, 2007:66). This approach also examines the role of policy entrepreneurs which helps to build momentum for issues. From this perspective, it is observed that the process of influencing political decision making and public agenda does not take a linear stimulus-response relationship. It is also subject to political manipulation of different political influencers, images and other contextual variables. Invariably, getting issues on the public and policy agenda is a complex process involving the collective action by different stakeholders and not just the role of the mass media.

A relevant concept to agenda setting is news framing which focuses on how issues are constructed for the public through the pattern of presentation and the type of symbols used. Both agenda setting and news framing are connected to how issues are depicted in the media rather than with which issues or objects are more or less reported (Scheufele & Tewksbury 2007; Weaver, 2007). News framing deals with how symbols are used to evoke specific action from the audience. Daniel Kahneman Nobel Laureate for Economics Sciences developed the prospect theory to capture framing effect. According to him, issues can be framed in different and multiple ways and the nature of frame tends to affect public response. His research showed that the intensity of frames by any given factor can yield corresponding amount of stimulus (Kahneman, 2011). Writers such as (Castells, 2009; Weaver, 2007) agree that framing is central to influencing media discourse and public process, but as a theory of media effect, it has been criticised on a number of fronts, including theoretic vagueness, incomparable methods, fractured paradigm, scattered conceptualisation, weak definition and deficient operationalization (Weaver, 2007; Entman, 1993). Nevertheless, framing is relevant to how development agencies interact with the media through their advocacy and public communication activities. As will be demonstrated in the discussion of media advocacy practices by development agencies, issue framing is one of the main elements of their media advocacy activities.

The emergence of the digital media has added a new dimension to agenda setting and issue attention. Wilson and Murby (2010:30) postulate that the merger of social media and communication into a new media has changed the vital part of life and created a new world of possibilities. According to them, with so many people "blogging, tweeting, uploading, downloading, crowd-sourcing, wiki-ing, linking in, geo-referencing, i-chatting, skipping, flipping, videotaping and many more," the new media is contributing to the emergence of a new eco-system and social enterprise (Wilson & Murby, 2010:33). This shows that social media platforms have become a critical tool to consider in the study of media and public attention to social issues.

The African continent has in recent years, experienced significant progress and transformation in its digital technology systems. Internet penetration in Africa has been described as 'phenomenal' and the emergence of mobile technology is generally perceived as the 'second communications revolution'. A recent report on the media landscape in sub-Saharan Africa concluded as follows:

Sub-Saharan Africa is the cockpit of change in terms of global divide and changing media use; in little over a decade, it has gone from being largely unconnected to the Internet to having millions using it (Balancing Act, 2014:10).

Additionally, various digital media solutions have been deployed for different sectors of society to achieve social change. A host of country specific and multi-country social media initiatives have been designed toward addressing the multifaceted public health dilemmas confronting the continent (Green et al, 2014; Oxfam, 2015; West, 2014). An assessment by the World Health Organisation in 2012 concluded that apart from scores of interventions in existence, over 300 E-Health initiatives were being planned on the continent (WHO, 2012:1). Besides, judging by the rapidity with which development agencies are applying eHealth and social media technologies, the number of such interventions will by now have grown exponentially.

However, the digital context bodes substantial potential for health misinformation. Despite wide usage of the Internet for health information, Jessen (2008) opines that it is also a source of massive misinformation. The conclusion is validated by Fayoyin and Ngwainmbi (2014:537-538) who established specific instances of misinformation and circulation of incorrect health data nationally and internationally because of information agility and social connectivity of the digital age. This concern is further reinforced by Wahba and Roudi-Fahimi (2012) with respect to the impact of social media on young people. They submitted that Internet and social media can perpetuate misconceptions on sexual and reproductive matters for young people and can lure them into inappropriate platforms and contents.

From the foregoing, it is argued that the context for engaging the media in development is multidimensional. It entails the deployment of both mainstream and alternative media in influencing social and public discussion, and ultimately social change. Clearly, development issues cannot be elevated to policy and public agendas solely because of rational deliberation and careful consideration of evidence, but through various variables such as power play, the role of allies, the interest of advocates and how issues are portrayed (Shiffman, 2009:608; True, Jones, Baumgartner, 2007:155). Nevertheless, the mass media play a critical role in conferring salience to social issues and how they construct reality.

Programmatic Context

As already mentioned, the main mechanism through which development agencies engage the media for social and policy change is media advocacy. In this section, some of the imperatives for engaging with the media for development outcomes are explored.

First, most development agencies are dealing with long-standing and complicated issues which are susceptible to social apathy, media misrepresentation and controversy. Primarily, the context for advocacy and public communication is largely that of opposition or lack of interest (Pisanni 2008; Chapman 2004). Many development and public health interventions have experienced signification opposition, misinformation and controversies to their issues and mandates. Examples include the crisis over condom quality, supply and promotion in Kenya (Kibira 2013; IRIN 2013; Kenya Health News 2002); controversy over polio immunization in northern Nigeria (Kaufmann & Feldbaum 2009; Agbeyede 2007; Obadare 2005); and public misunderstanding on the protective effect of medical male circumcision for HIV prevention (Wang, Duke & Schmid 2009). The media also serve as the battleground for such controversies. Therefore, continuous media engagement is necessary to promote better public understanding of the issues and expected institutional or systemic changes.

Second, many development agencies have witnessed incidence of poor reporting or coverage of social, health or development issues. In particular, media coverage of science, health; development and population issues is generally considered as inadequate compared to other areas such as politics, business and sports (Fayoyin 2015:3). The causes of poor reporting of health and development include the complicated nature of health issues, poor understanding of development dynamics, desire for scoops by some journalists, gatekeeping gaffes in treating health issues, speculation as a result of inadequate information from development agencies and poor relationship between scientists and media professionals (Kaye *et al*, 2011:115-116). As will be illustrated later in the paper, the need to address these challenges has led many aid agencies to put in place a strong media education programme for better understanding of health and development issues.

Third, development agencies are under constant scrutiny to justify their existence, relevance and added-value. The contemporary development landscape is characterised by a multitude of bilateral and multilateral agencies, funds and programmes, different NGOs and INGOs and different foundations and initiatives (Steinward 2013; Aldasoro *et al* 2010) all wanting to attract attention to their issues. Critics of development aid such as Easterly (2002) have accused development agencies of performing poorly on a number of variables. In another study, Easterly and Pfutze (2008), argue that the rhetoric of aid effectiveness by development agencies is far from its reality as many of them are performing below expectation. Consequently, aid agencies are driven to communicate developments results to justify their existence and added-value. (Vollmer 2012; da Costa 2009, 2008).

The main implication of the constant scrutiny of aid agencies and their performance is the stronger desire for media advocacy and public communication. Such media advocacy activities, in part, are expected to position their issues in the public sphere, promote the work and enhance their image. The need for aid agencies to show result is not limited to regular development intervention, but also to humanitarian interventions. Hence most aid agencies have developed strategies for engaging with the media during humanitarian or emergency situations to demonstrate how they are actively involved in life-saving interventions. Undoubtedly, reputation management has become an important basis of the concerted media advocacy and public communication activities of development organisations. Image is an intangible quality which can be affected by negative publicity or poor visibility, hence the desire by development agencies to invest in organization promotion through media advocacy and issue communication (Ngwainmbi 2014:118-120) However, development agencies are also committed to ensuring social change through a variety of media engagement strategies.

MEDIA ENGAGEMENT BY UNICEF, UNAIDS AND UNFPA

This section presents an overview of the main strategies through which UNICEF, UNFPA and UNAIDS engage the media in achieving development outcomes. The information is obtained from documentary research and key informants interviews. It is followed by a review of cross cutting issues in development communication and implications for both media organisations and development agencies.

UNICEF is the global child rights organization, which strives for a world in which every child has a fair chance in life (UNICEF, 2014). The organization is also committed to a world where all children survive, thrive and fulfill their potential to the benefit of a better world. Its media advocacy programme is based on a global communication policy which is aimed at putting equity at the heart of its agenda for children (UNICEF, 2011:4). This principles applies to all media and communication activities at the regional and country levels. UNFPA is the agency for population activities with the mandate of "delivering a world where every pregnancy is wanted, every childbirth is safe and every young persons' potential is fulfilled" (UNFPA, 2015:12). The vision for communication is predicated on the organization's need to drive the desired change and ensure that its mandate is effectively understood. Ultimately UNFPA attempts to make a convincing case for its mandate in a crowded and context social and political terrain. UNAIDS is saddled with the global mandate of addressing the AIDS pandemic (Okigbo Yu, & Napakol 2013:214). The organization uses strategic media engagement and activism, among others, as a strategy for achieving change (UNAIDS, 1999; 2011). From this synopsis of the mandate of the agencies, we present a synthesis of how the three organisations deploy different media strategies for social development.

Print Media

The development and distribution of print materials is one of the modalities of public communication. Examples of print materials produced and distributed by the agencies are programme updates, situation assessment and analysis, findings from studies and research, country assessments, health assessments and many others. In particular, UNICEF has made significant investments in producing information packages including - fact sheets, press kits, photos gallery, country kit, progress of children, and the production of annual flagship publication – the state of the world's children report. As a child rights organization, the treaties that serve as the basis of its work - the Convention on the Rights of the Child and the OAU Charter on the Rights and Welfare of Children - have been popularized through various print materials. Most project areas also develop periodic updates and case studies for public education and media communication.

UNFPA supports the development of information packages including evidence briefs, stories of change, press kits, photo stories, multi-media productions, country kits, the state of the world population report and other topical publications. Print communication provides a constant stream of information for media professionals and make them informed advocates of the mandate of the international conference on population and development programme of action. Additionally, the provision of print materials is aimed at enhancing the understanding of population issues by media professionals.

Under the auspices of the UNAIDS, a clearing house was established in the 1990s to facilitate prompt information dissemination to media institutions and professionals. UNAIDS and its co-sponsors have also launched and distributed regional and global reports, the Global Plan Progress report, and World AIDS Day reports for public information. The South Africa HIV and AIDS Information Dissemination Service (SafAIDS) established in 1994 has also contributed to information collection, production, and dissemination of cutting edge information on AIDS. Targeted exhibitions, photo essays and other forms of visual communication have been organized to stimulate public attention to specific HIV issues (UNAIDS, 2011b). Other print media tactics include information packages such as best practice, case studies, investment cases, briefing notes, policy briefs, score cards, progress reports, and trend analyses.

Electronic Media

Based on the inherent advantages and characteristics of the electronic media which include larger reach, better feedback process, and the capacity for multisensory communication, development agencies actively utilize them for public information and social change communication. UNAIDS offices in East and southern Africa have supported the production of broadcast materials to stimulate public attention to different aspects of AIDS programming and interventions. Examples include videos on male circumcision, documentaries on leadership for HIV prevention, interactive programmes on key population, participatory videos and songs on HIV prevention and commercials on multiple and concurrent sexual relationships. UNICEF offices at the regional and country levels have also produced and disseminated a variety of electronic communication materials for targeted engagement. These include feature films on child survival, docudrama on equity approach to child protection, stories of change on children affected by HIV, videos on water and sanitation, feature films on child rights abuse and neglect, magazine programmes on sexual exploitation of girls and animated cartoons on hygiene practices. The various electronic media have been used with different target groups for public information and health education. Similarly, UNFPA has produced podcasts and videocasts on issues of gender based violence in Senegal, the menace of female genital mutilation in Kenya, child and forced marriage in Niger, teen pregnancy in Botswana, the impact of midwives in maternal health in South Sudan and special reports on family planning and demographic dividend in Tanzania. The combination of print and electronic communication ensures that the various audience groups are reached with appropriate information.

Community Media

Community media form a major part of media engagement by development agencies. These comprise different processes and channels of communication with and within local communities which are useful for both interpersonal communication, cultural orientation, information sharing, community dialogue and interpersonal engagement among community groups. Africa has myriads of traditional media and communication system such as folkmedia, popular arts, folklore, oral poetry, indigenous communication practices, informal communication, or community media which have been deployed for development purposes (Panford et al, 2001:1559; Ugboajah, 1985:185). In many African countries, UNICEF has used popular arts, dance, music, visuals, idioms, poetry and folktales to promote child rights. For example, to enhance community conversation on polio immunization, UNICEF Nigeria used community visualization with religious groups and community leaders in 2008 (UNICEF, 2010). In East and southern Africa, UNAIDS and its partners have also deployed forms of oramedia such as storytelling puppetry, proverbs, visual arts, drama, role-playing, concerts, dirges, drumming and dancing for health education on the AIDS pandemic. UNFPA in West and central Africa has also used stories, beliefs, folklore, songs, narratives, riddles, poems, and other channels to communicate issues around girl child marriage, female genital mutilation, and prevention of women's death during pregnancies and child birth, and promotion of family planning.

However, there is a dwindling application of community media by development organisations. UNECSO (2008) argues that safeguarding oral traditions in some East African countries is critical to avoid extinction. Also, Osho (2011) identifies several challenges faced by community media as extinction of African languages, impact of global media, the ubiquitous influence of the mass media, increasing urbanisation and the erosion of indigenous value systems. But perhaps the greatest challenge to community media use in development is the emergence of digital technology, epitomised by the existence a multitude of new media platforms.

Digital Technology and Social Media

Advancements in digital media and communications technology have generated considerable optimism on the role of social media in achieving developmental and public health outcomes globally. The unprecedented availability of digital devices and platforms has also prompted different development institutions to design and implement a range of social media interventions for social and behaviour change (Fayoyin, 2016:6). UNICEF uses social media to promote child rights agenda through various formats such as Facebook, Twitter, Instagram, Mix it and many others. This includes innovative crowd sourcing initiative such as the U- Reporters in Uganda and digital citizenship and safely project in South Africa. UNAIDS has also deployed digitally enabled social media interventions such as mobile phones, instant messaging, chat room forums, and social networking sites to mobilise different audiences for social and behavior change in Africa. UNFPA employs social media platforms for message customization, narrow casting and crowd sourcing on sexual and reproductive health, planning, gender-based violence and humanitarian response.

The engagement of staff members as social media advocates of development agencies also deserve some mention. Increasingly, the staff of UN agencies are encouraged to use social media to promote the mandate of their organisations (United Nations, 2011:1). Increased use of employee advocacy is an offshoot of the current digital explosion. Edelman's Trust Barometer (2012) affirms that the increasing credibility of employees among various publics and customers is enhancing their perception as new influencers for their organisations. Thus, the deployment of a connected, committed, engaged and empowered workforce has great potential to transform any organisation's profile and positioning in the new economy. To this end, the development agencies are promoting the engagement of their staff for development purposes.

From the foregoing, it is evident that the increasing levels of internet penetration and the pervasiveness of mobile devices and social networking services, have led to the burgeoning of digital communication and social media engagement for eHealth communication in Africa. These include a wide range of platforms comprising (i) networking sites such as Facebook, YouTube and LinkedIn, etc.; (ii) micro blogging platforms such as Twitter, Wikkis, and (iii) mobile messaging services such Instant Messaging, SMS/MMS. Some of the interventions utilise single media platforms such as Twitter or Facebook, while others adopt multi-media platforms. However, it would be essential to consider their effectiveness and sustainability. The use of social media by development agencies have largely been for 'information blast', 'message storm' or 'buzz creation' or 'noise' around specific health issues. Practical field experience seems to indicate that the deployment of social media for public health delivery is being viewed as another 'pet project syndrome' of development agencies for their branding and visibility. Many of the interventions are branded for specific agencies with limited linkages and coordination. It is thus critical for development institutions to ensure greater coordination of social media programmes to enhance their effectiveness.

Media Capacity Building

The capacity of mass media professionals to effectively report health and development is a major challenge of development organizations (Kaye *et al*, 2011:115). This necessitates the need for capacity building aimed at improving their knowledge on health and development issues. UNICEF's goal for media capacity building is to help media professionals effectively report and advocate for child rights. Examples include media training on children and women rights, effective reporting in humanitarian contexts, and issue attention for children affected by AIDS. For example, series of training workshops have been held with different media professionals – reporters, cartoonists, photojournalists, and writers - on child rights. The various articles of the Convention on the Rights of the Child have been packages for child rights education. Photo journalists have been supported to undertake photo missions on child rights abuse and violation. On the whole, the various media capacity building processes have enabled UNICEF to influence news reports and broadcasts, news analysis or commentary, entertainment pages, specialized pages, op-eds, features or even music programmes.

UNFPA and UNAIDS at country and regional levels also undertake media training, orientations sessions and institutional capacity support to enhance the knowledge of media professionals. During such sessions, project experts are invited to present current trends and issues on identified topics. The organizations have also supported media training and communication institutions in Nigeria, Malawi,

Ghana and Kenya through the establishment of courses in health reporting and development communication. The rationale is to enhance the knowledge of communication students in health and development through the development of modules in their curriculum. An additional area of media capacity building is sponsorship of project visits also to first-hand information on the projects. But many of these programmes have suffered from inconsistent support from the agencies.

Engagement with Media Gatekeepers

Gatekeeping function in media practice involves the process of in selecting, writing, editing, positioning, scheduling, repeating or otherwise massaging information to become news or programmes in the mass media (Shoemaker, Vos & Reese, 2009). In specific terms, gatekeepers are those involved in the editorial or production process such as writers, correspondents, news people and editors (Coleman *et al.*, 2009). Recognizing the critical role of media gate-keepers in the media production process, UNFPA undertakes targeted briefing and orientations sessions for senior editors, sub-editors, production management and chief executives of media organizations on various aspects of population and development issues. This is intended to facilitate their buy-in towards improving the coverage of its mandate by media gate-keepers. Tactics of engaging them include high profile visit by representatives of development organisations, study tours, special working sessions, or formal and informal workshops. One of the main approaches adopted by UNICEF to influence the editorial content of flagship publications has been periodic consultations with the Nigerian Guild of Editors and member of the editorial boards of the print media. The overall goal is to influence media gatekeepers to be more supportive of population and health topics in the face of competition with economics, politics and sports stories. Some media gate-keepers have been sent on specialized courses in population studies and advanced training in journalism abroad. With such high level engagement, development stories have been featured more in media and public discourse in influential media organizations. Nonetheless, the impact of such interventions has been short-lived.

Media Campaigns

Campaigns are an important modality of engaging the media and the public to draw attention to the social and development issues in society. All the agencies implement periodic and thematic campaigns focusing on different elements of their mandate area. UNICEF implements topical campaigns on breast feeding, child marriage, girl child education, child health immunization, bed nets promotion and roll back malaria. Some of the campaigns are also linked to specific observances such as the Day of the Africa Child, world water day, international health day, world breastfeeding week, and many others which serve as important hooks for media mobilization and public communication. UNFPA also runs thematic campaigns for the international day on zero tolerance for female genital mutilation, international women's day, international day of the midwife, international day to end obstetric fistula and international youth day. Appropriate thematic materials are prepared and distributed to relevant media organizations and professionals. Such efforts have also helped to maximise media mileage on the issues. Although campaigns are useful in galvanising public support, they are generally short-termed and their results episodic. Thus, development agencies need to invest significant energy and resources in programmes that enhance sustainable change.

Media Partnerships

Strategic networking is crucial to social transformation, policy and development results (Adam & Kriesi, 2007; Sabatier & Weible, 2007; Shiffman 2016). Therefore, media partnership is a major strategy by development agencies in attracting attention and sustaining public interest to their issues. With support from UNAIDS and other partners, media networks such as the Forum for Southern Africa Editors on AIDS, the Media Institute of Southern Africa (MISA) and Journalists against AIDSs (JAIDS) have been established to galvanise necessary momentum toward ending the pandemic. In many African countries, journalist networks on AIDS have been established which increased the level of attention to HIV issues (Komolafe-Opadeji, 2008). In the early 2000s, the co-sponsors of UNAIDS established collaborative engagements with influential media institutions such as PANOS and Inter Press Service (IPS) to publish informed and well- researched stories on the pandemic. The African Broadcast Media Partnership against HIV/AIDS (ABMP) is promoting national partnerships for an HIV-free generation. This collaboration with over 70 broadcasting networks on the continent has led to the allocation of 5% of airtime to HIV issues (ABMP 2010:10).

In Nigeria, UNICEF facilitated the formation of media alliance for children from a set of thematic groups working on children issues – such as health correspondents, children editors, education correspondents, art and life writers etc. The network has been used to promote and position children rights during the campaign to domesticate the children laws in the country. Many UNPFA country offices have also assisted in establishing Media Network on Population and Development in Malawi, Kenya, The Gambia, Burundi, Ethiopia and Madagascar. According to UNFPA (2012:5) the objectives of the network are to:

- Strengthen the capacity of journalists and their organizations, and improve pro-population and development focus of media policies and institutions;
- Raise levels and frequency of news stories and radio/TV programmes which address population and development issues;
- Reduce vulnerability of pro-population and development news to other major subjects such as politics and sport;
- Foster institutional learning through knowledge sharing/management and strategy formulation;
- Build communications partnerships with local media, to report population issues and create momentum of synergy and coordinated action;
- Support pro-population communication channels such as local and community-based media; and,
- Increase the capacity of the various key stakeholders to enhance general understanding of population and development problems of the country.

Such efforts have made UNFPA activities in the countries more visible and led to the production of media materials which promote population and development issues. For example, in Ethiopia there was an increase in the number press articles from 52 press articles in 2010 and 117 in 2011 (UNFPA, 2013:12). But the effectiveness of the network is constrained by institutional and financial challenges. Other barriers are dwindling motivation to cover health and development issues, poor attitude of media gatekeeper and lack of incentives for reporting development issues.

Use of Data

Data is an important resource in achieving development and democratic outcomes. Most advocates agree that research findings, numbers and statistical evidence are helpful to prove or disprove a belief, assertion or proposition. Data for development is thus a major intervention undertaken by different development agencies in public communication. The UN has established the Global Pulse, an initiative aimed at bringing expertise from the public, private, development and academic sectors to harnesses the power of big data for development policy and action (United Nations Global Pulse, 2013, p. 3). The three agencies have also initiated processes to make more programme data widely accessible to the public. Data sites that enable users to map, chart, and comparative indicators and statistics have been established. They have also undertaken diverse thematic analyses, budgetary allocation analysis, expenditure information, country status reports, facility utilization/data, bottleneck analysis, investment cases, return on investment analysis, cost benefit analysis, policy or programme impact analysis, or strategic modelling approaches to generate new information for public advocacy (Fayoyin & Ngwainmbi, 2014:532-533). Findings from these activities are presented in creative ways – such as interactive maps, infographics, factographs, dashboards, maps from geographic information systems, and stories of change - which can be targeted to specific decision makers and influencers.

Despite the promise of data use in development and communication, it is subject to various misuses and abuses. The democratization of information and diversity of content generation bodes significant challenges for effective data use in social development. For example, UNAIDS has been accused of data manipulation in order to convince the world to take action on HIV. According to Pisanni (2008), UNAIDS made the HIV incidence data "scream by creating a compelling picture" for the global community. The author also noted that UNAIDS undertook 'manipulative gymnastics of the Global Reports' which resulted in 'cooking up an epidemic', that finally 'hit the headlines'. Clearly, the overestimation of the AIDs situation has been a subject of recurring controversy and, in 2007 UNAIDS agreed that AIDS in Africa was overstated (GAVI Report, 2007:4; McNeil Jr, 2007:1; Timberg, 2006:2). Undoubtedly, the use and abuse of data in health and development pose significant implications for public communication and media practice.

CROSS CUTTING ISSUES

From the foregoing, development organisations deploy myriads of media approaches such as the mass media, digital platforms and community media in achieving development outcomes. Based on the analysis, the paper identifies the following implications for development communication.

Inconsistent Attention to Social Issues

Across all development agencies, the power of the media in helping to achieving social change is well recognized. Through the utilization of various media formats, development agencies have created awareness for their issues, influenced public opinion and challenged norms. However, while media mobilization approaches have contributed to improving media coverage of child, rights, population and development and HIV and AIDS in many African countries, they have not resulted in sustained media attention. In Nigeria, the development of advocacy and social mobilization for children rights have led to some level of media and public support of children and youth issues and facilitated policy and political response in some areas. However, there is overwhelming evidence that the level of attention is still wavering and insufficient (Fayoyin, 2015:3). From an analysis of 600 stories covering a five-year period coinciding with the passage of the Children's Act, Oyero (2010:35) found that there were only 193 stories published on children by two main newspapers, *Daily Times* and *The Guardian*. The study demonstrated that child rights issues were not given sustained attention by the media. The AIDS pandemic is also confronting a shrinking media attention in Africa. According to Esipisu (2013, 2014) HIV as a 'tired' story because of media fatigue and a general unwillingness among editors to approve another HIV story. In another study, (Chalk, 2014) found that HIV is no longer an engaging story for journalists or the public. Boredom with HIV also manifest in other population groups. In an article "Does anybody remember AIDS?" focusing on the situation in South Africa, Heywood, (2014) writes:

AIDS is sinking ashamedly back into the shadows, where many think it should always have been, like Tuberculosis.... AIDS points fingers at academics who romanticized and theorized 'social movements' when they were on the rise, but deserted them when they began the difficult days of staying alive. AIDS rebukes media houses who brought AIDS to (the) light and now help to put it back into the shadows; journalists who found convenient heroes but now ignore the real ones because they are poorer or darker. AIDS reviles editors who make (it) something into the past when it's still in the present.

Lack of sustained attention typifies media reportage of social issues is society. This calls for new approaches to reporting development issues in the media.

Lack of a Common Media Agenda for Change

An important finding from our study is the absence of a coherent and collective media agenda by development organizations for achieving social change in Africa. Despite the overlapping nature of their programmes, each agency develops and implements separate media interventions. Field experience in communicating development issues clearly demonstrates competitive communication by development agencies. Different agencies churn out press releases, publish different data, and promote their agenda and organizational brands. Also in empowering the media to cover health and development, they undertake disparate and uncoordinated capacity building approaches. Most media advocacy efforts results in competition for media attention and promotion of institutional image. An editorial by *The Lancet* (2010: 1) alludes to this phenomenon as follows:

Media coverage as an end in itself is too often the aim of their activities. Marketing and branding have a high profile. Perhaps worst of all, relief efforts in the field are sometimes competitive with little collaboration between agencies, including smaller, grass-roots charities that may have better networks in affected counties and so are well placed to immediately implement emergency relief.

Although the commentary was made within the context of humanitarian response of development agencies, it applies to various aspects of their programmes. With the crowded, competitive and fragmentary aid environment (Easterly, 2002), there is fragmentary and patchy media and public communication engagement. A key informant from one of the agencies said:

It is not uncommon to see the logos of various development agencies on the same project or press release. It is also not uncommon to see different reports by development agencies reflecting different statistics on the same issue and sometimes contradictory information.

To address the criticism of fragmentary approach to development and public communication, specific actions have been put. First, the Communication for Development programme for the United Nations System (2008:8) called for collaborative actions in creating an enabling environment and giving a voice to affected people. Also, the UN Communication Group at the country level helps to promote coherence in advocacy and media engagement through the philosophy of 'joint UN communication' While this has worked in some countries, it has not in others. (United Nations Communication Group, 2009; United Nations Development Group, 2008). Many agencies still continue to carry out their branded communication campaigns and aggressive promotion of their development mandates. Besides, media professionals need to contend with the overbearing posture of some individual agencies or the combined actions of multi-lateral organisations in their media relations approach. Unfortunately from the government side, there is also no national harmonized agenda or plan for media engagement. The absence of a common agenda for media engagement in development thus affects the effectiveness of their deployment for social change.

Limited Media Knowledge of Development Frameworks

A good understanding of the development frameworks is essential for development communication. But our analysis shows limited knowledge of media practitioners on the existing frameworks and resolutions that underpin development work. The Convention on the Rights of the Child serves as the context for UNICEF, while the International Conference on Population and Development Programme of Action is the framework for UNFPA. But the knowledge of the two documents by many journalists who cover their issues is weak. A straw poll of 60 journalists who participated in media advocacy workshops in 2015 revealed that most of them had not fully read the two documents. At another training session for journalists in 2016, two thirds of the 45 participants had not seen or read some of the main development documents that enshrine health and development outcomes at the international and regional levels. These documents include the Rio Declaration on Environment and Development, the World Summit on Sustainable Development, the World Summit on Social Development, the United Nations Conference on Sustainable Development, the New Partnership for Africa's Development and the AU Agenda 2063 for Africa's Development. Thus, limited or inadequate knowledge of the basis of development reporting by media professionals has significant implications on what they communicate and how they communicate. Clearly, health and development communication needs to move from merely reporting issues and events to empowering different audience groups and publics with the information that will result in social change and development outcomes.

Besides, due to limited resources in media organization, development beats have not been effectively staffed in most media houses. This implies that many reporters are not adequately equipped on the core development issues. Although development organisations have set up projects to establish development beats in many countries – e.g. family planning desk, health desk, environment desk, science desk, children desk, - this has not achieved significant result due to lack of sustainability.

Increasing Role of Citizen Journalism and Social Media

The unprecedented availability of digital devices and platforms has resulted in increased digital journalism, online advocacy, and cyber-advocacy for development issues and social causes. Developments in mobile telephony have made the sharing of health messages more interactive, more 'mobile' and almost a 24/7 phenomenon. The extensive availability of mobile phones has also accelerated the delivery of health messages and made health education more social and more interactive. However, development organisations need to be aware of the multiple discourses and engagements taking place in the digital media sphere to be harnessed for social change. The use of digital media in development communication also has specific challenges. Macpherson and Chamberlain (2013) posit that mobile telephony should not be considered a panacea for the health challenges of developing countries. Another study identifies the following constraints on the use of mobile phones for health communication: cost, limited access to mobile phones, content restriction and limited personalisation of health information (de Tolly & Benjamin, 2011). Although social media platforms are particularly useful for message customisation, narrow casting and targeted messaging, they are constrained by poor quality services and resources, violation of privacy and confidentiality, potential misuse and social isolation (West, 2014).

RECOMMENDATIONS: RETHINKING MEDIA ENGAGEMENT APPROACHES

The central thesis of this paper is the need for a reexamination of the media engagement strategies by development agencies for social change in Africa. This position is reinforced by the preceding discussion, and particularly by the imperatives of the new global and continental development agenda which calls for far reaching social transformation within specific timeframes. Consequently, the paper makes the following recommendations.

Recommendations for Development Agencies

People Based Communication

Development is about people. The SDG 2030 vision and the Africa Agenda 2063 emphasise the need to put people at the centre of development. The post-2015 HIV agenda also highlights the centrality of putting people first in the HIV response. Thus, media engagement for development should reprioritize issue-based communication and not the communication for visibility of development organizations. The affected population should not be a tool of development agencies in attracting attention to their work or organization but genuine engagement of the people for their development and empowerment. This is why their need must be at the center of media engagement and overall communication programme. With a people-focused communication strategy comes more emphasis on the voice of people, especially the marginalized ones. It also reduces or eliminates media engagement aimed at corporate promotion and organizational marketing. This will also involve systematic empowerment of multiple communicators (including health workers) with adequate information and knowledge of development issues to keep the dialogue going behind the media headlines. Development communication needs to move from just messaging, to multiple voice; and to the interactive engagement of people who are the center of development (PANOS, 2003). A new communication for development emphasis should be on the rights, risks, and responsibilities of critical audience groups.

Innovative Multi-Media Approaches

Effectively promoting human development requires more innovative communication approaches by development agencies. Africa's media landscape has changed and will continue to change. This requires new media strategies for development. As part of innovative media communication, development advocates need to engage more in dynamic storytelling, powerful issue portrayal and the empowering voice of the affected population to elicit public and political action. A good practice that needs to be enhanced is how the AIDS movement utilised creative approaches, tools, platforms, approaches and channels in communicating the severity of AIDS and attracted global, regional, and national and community attention to the pandemic. Nevertheless in an age of dwindling public and media attention and hyper competition of social issues for attention, additional creativity would be imperative. Innovative communication will enhance the plurality of voices essential for positioning issues in society. New arguments to mobilise new partnerships will be required in communicating development issues to an information fatigued audience and the media constantly driven to business and political news. Empowering consultations to generate appropriate frames for different messages and integrate fresh voice into the multiple development narratives would be critical. Also in a digital age, visual communication has become more essential than before. Hence development agencies need to prioritise a stronger visual communication and other forms of multi-sensory engagement in their media strategy. New strategies of engaging various audience groups for targeted social change would be essential for more effective communication in the new development context. The increased penetration of new media to communities will enhance the use of different formats of community media. And part of innovative multimedia communication would be the remediation of community media with digital media, thus enhancing new uses of traditional media in a digital age. Clearly, to achieve the new development agenda, development advocates would need to leverage the collective power of various media channels in order to keep development issues continuously on public agenda.

Integrated Media Engagement

The new development framework (in particular the SDGs) is based on a different development philosophy characterized by universality of goals. Therefore, a coherent and comprehensive communication agenda and a convergence of media engagement strategies would be fundamental. As a result, this paper highlights the importance of joint communication by development agencies linked to all levels of human development - international, regional and national. This approach will require a new mind-set and programme approaches which emphasize genuine collaborative advantage rather than competitive organizational positioning. An integrated approach to media engagement for development will involve strategic capacity building of media and communication professionals. Currently, many of the agencies are organizing disparate short-term training, orientation, workshops, and seminars for media professions which are not at a sufficient scale and intensity to develop a critical mass of communication and media professionals who are skilled in development communication. A coordinated approach will facilitate the establishment of centres of excellence in training and research for media and development communication. Strategic alignment of social media interventions will be more impactful than the current fragmentary efforts supported by different development agencies. This will ultimately reduce transaction cost and achieve more mileage.

Creative Deployment of Big and Small Data

Data is a major element of media engagement in development practice. All development organisations have recognized the power of deploying statistics and evidence in moving the will of policy makers and other decision makers for social change. But the use of data in development is also bedeviled with various controversies especially relating to the publication of wrong data or the deliberate use of data to influence. Therefore, both producers and disseminators of data need to embrace the vision of data as a tool of meaningful public participation and sustainable development, not for mere organizational positioning. The creative deployment of both big data and small data in development programming is also advocated.

To effectively deploy the vast area of media for social change, it is critical to continuously invest in media research. The media landscape is constantly changing. So are the needs, uses and preferences of the audiences. Development organisations need to invest more in research and evidence generation and knowledge uptake by media and other advocates. This calls for regular and ongoing research by development organisations and their partners to investigate these changing patterns. An important aspect of media research is the interface between the new media and the community media. This is crucial in view of the penetration of most communities with new and social media technologies and channels. Meta-analysis and multiple case studies designed to produce empirical information necessary for sophisticated analysis of findings of new media engagement need to be conducted. Studies based in interdisciplinary approaches would provide new insights on audience engagement through the media. Impact assessment of media use for social change will also help generate new data and information in programming for media engagement in development.

Recommendations for Media Professionals

Enhanced Knowledge of Development Issues

Development issues are complex and require a deeper knowledge by media professionals to effectively communicate them. However, as has been noted, many journalists do not have a good understanding of the issues. Media organisations must commit to strengthening health and development coverage for the life cycle of the SDG or till the achievement of Agenda 2063 vision in Africa. Communication institutions also need to incorporate various levels of training in development reporting and communication for various cadre of media professionals. This will redress the episodic approach to communication human development issues in the media. To be able educate people on development issues and hold government accountable for their commitment to the development goals, media professionals need more informed education of development issues not just through workshops, press releases or special reports. A continuous process of empowerment and education of media professionals is fundamental to effort media mobilization for social change.

A related concern is sensitivity to health and development issues. Many development issues are cultural and politically sensitive. Media professionals need to exercise discernment and sensitivity to contentious development issues. They also need to adopt a more critical approach of the use of development data. Any data to be disseminated for the public should be unpacked and appropriately interpreted. To facilitate better understanding of health and development data, media professionals should improve their skills in data appreciation, data visualisation and data communication. They need to use data and statistics more meaningful. Development journalists need to engage with more data producing institutions to enhance adequate reporting of data from health and science and development sector. Regular orientation would be required for journalists to understand emerging trends in health and development in order to communicate such issues adequately.

A Stronger Sense of Advocacy Journalism

Achieving development outcomes calls for an advocacy and activist mindset by media professionals. Human development is a new kind of struggle. It is about social justice, empowerment and requires media professionals to confront the issues. The letter and the spirit of the development agenda require far-reaching transformation and sustainable change. This calls for media professionals who will utilize their platforms and skills to promote change and social justice. This may necessitate turning media professionals into passionate and committed advocates or civic journalists for change. According to Waisbord (2009:372) civic journalism is grounded in the process of political mobilisation and uses organised groups during the struggle for liberation in Africa. Besides, the historical development of the press in many African countries was based on the advocacy and activism role of the press. This involved canvassing and editorializing for political change, mobilizing the court of public opinion, and catalyzing public dissent. To be clear, the battle for political independence was largely fought in the pages of the tabloid and many politicians were actually activists.

Overall, achieving the current development agenda for Africa requires the revival of advocacy journalism by the media professionals. Such a journalism will not be satisfied with merely reporting on issues but using journalism skills for social mobilization at all levels. It will also not be content with the surface reporting, but adopt an approach to defending the cause of humanity and making a compelling case for change. It will entail a crusading mindset as long as social injustice exists and millions of people are still in poverty and affected by underdevelopment. This approach will also enhance the accountability of various stakeholders to the development goals and agenda. Development work requires holding various stakeholders - development organisations, government institutions and the media - accountable for human development. Media professionals would therefore engage and communicate in ways that hold the various sectors accountable to public interest. It is a type of journalism which challenges traditional media ethos and strives to use the media and other communication channels in empowering the audience for social change.

CONCLUSION

The paper sought to examine media approaches for achieving social change by development agencies in Africa. Our analysis demonstrates the prospects and problems of diverse media engagement strategies of selected agencies in human development. Media platforms and processes utilized by development agencies for achieving social change include the mass media, community media mediated media and social media. However, the major challenge is the absence of a common media engagement strategy among development agencies aligned with the overarching global and continental development framework. The paper thus argues for an integrated communication programmes that focus on human development rather than the agenda of development organisations. Furthermore, the Sustainable Development Goals requires a "comprehensive far reaching, people centered set of universal and transformative goals and targets" (p.3).Thus the paper argues for a rethink of existing media practices of development agencies in line with the transformative and universal vision enshrined in the global and regional development frameworks. Development reporting needs to shift from mere media reports to a crusading mind-set and activist attitude to achieve results. However, such re-orientation may cause tensions and contradictions for contemporary journalism practice. Therefore additional research and empirical investigation on how the media can help achieve the new set of global and regional development goals would be critical.

REFERENCES

ABMP Report, . (2010, September 10). African Broadcast Media Partnership against HIV/AIDS. Presentation at *UNAIDS Workshop on Countdown to Zero Campaign*, Johannesburg, South Africa.

Adam, S., & Kriesi, H. (2007). The Network Approach. In P. A. Sabatier (Ed.), *Theories of the Policy Process* (pp. 129–154). West Press.

Africa Union. (2014). *Agenda 2063: The Africa We want*. Addis Ababa: Africa Union.

Agbeyede, L. (2007). Risk Communication: The overlooked factor in the Nigeria Polio Immunization Boycott Crisis. *The Nigerian Medical Practitioner*, *51*(3), 40–44.

Aldasoro, I., Peter, N., & Rainer, T. (2010). Less aid proliferation and more donor coordination? The Wide Gap between Words and Deeds. *Journal of International Development*, *22*(7), 920–940. doi:10.1002/jid.1645

Balancing Act. (2014). *The Sub-Saharan Africa Media Landscape*. Retrieved from http://www.balancingact-africa.com/sites/balancingact africa.com/files/products/1.%20SSA%20Media%20Landscape.pdf

Brodie, N., Hamel, E., Brady, L., Kates, J., & Altman, D. (2004, March/April). AIDS at 21: Media Coverage of the HIV Epidemic 1981-2002. *Columbia Journalism Review*, 1–8.

Chalk, S. (2014). *HIV and Stigma: The Media Challenge*. London: International Planned Parenthood Federation.

Castells, M. (2009). *Communication Power*. Oxford, UK: Oxford University Press.

Chapman, S. (2004). Advocacy for public health: A primer. *Journal of Epidemiology and Community Health*, *58*(5), 361–365. doi:10.1136/jech.2003.018051 PMID:15082730

Christakis, N., & Fowler, J. (2011). *Connected: The Amazing Power of Social Networks and How They Shape our Lives*. London: Harper Press.

Coleman, R., McCombs, M., Shaw, D., & Weaver, D. (2009). Agenda setting. In K. Wahl-Jorgensen & T. Hanitzsh (Eds.), *The Handbook of Journalism Studies*. New York: Routledge.

da Costa, P. (2009). *Study in Communicating Development Results*. Commissioned by the OECD DAC Development Co-operation Directorate and Devcom Network.

da Costa, P. (2008). *Managing for and Communicating Development Results*. Background paper prepared for the OECD Informal Network of DAC Development Communications.

Dearing, J. W., & Rogers, M. (1996). *Agenda Setting*. London: Sage.

de Tolly, K., & Benjamin, F. (2011). Mobile Phones: Opening new channels for health communication. In S. Waisbord & R. Obregon (Eds.), Handbook of Global Health Communication. Oxford, UK: Wiley-Blackwell.

Easterly, W. (2002). The Cartel of Good Intentions. *Foreign Policy*, (July–August), 40–49. doi:10.2307/3183416

Easterly, W., & Pfutze, T. (2008). *Where does the money go? Best and Worst Practices in Foreign Aid*. Brooking Global Economy and Development, Working Paper 21.

Edelman. (2012). *Edelman 2012 Trust Barometer*. Retrieved from http://www.edelmanberland.com/portfolio_item/edelman-trust-barometer-2012-2/

Entman, R. M. (1993). Framing: Toward Clarification of a Fractured Paradigm. *Journal of Communication*, *43*(4), 51–58. doi:10.1111/j.1460-2466.1993.tb01304.x

Dearing, J. W., & Rogers, E. M. (1996). *Agenda Setting*. London: Sage.

Esipisu, I. (2014). *Two Million Dead in 2013: The HIV/AIDS story today*. Retrieved from http://gijn.2014/01/31/two-million-dead-in-2013-the-hivaids-story-today

Esipisu, I. (2013). Reviving a "Tired" Story: Tips for covering HIV/AIDS. In M. H. Guerreto & S. Grillen (Eds.), *Reporters Guide to the Millennium Development Goals: Covering Development Commitments for 2015 and Beyond* (pp. 91–93). Vienna: International Press Institute.

Fayoyin, A. (2016). Engaging Social Media for Health Communication in Africa: A Synthesis of Approaches, Results and Lessons. *Journal of Mass Communication and Journalism*, *6*(6), 6. doi:10.4172/2165-7912.1000315

Fayoyin, A. (2015). *Positioning Youth Development Agenda in Public Discourse in Nigeria: An Advocacy Imperative*. Online Access Library.

Fayoyin, A., & Ngwainmbi, E. (2014). Use and misuse of Data in Advocacy, Media and Opinion Polls in Africa: Realities, challenges and Opportunities. *Journal of Development and Communication Studies, 3*(2), 528-545.

GAVI Report. (2007). *HIV Prevalence Estimates: Fact or Fiction*. Author.

Green, K., Girault, P., Wambugu, S., Clement, N., & Adams, B. (2014). Reaching Men who have sex with men through social media: A pilot intervention. *Digital Culture & Education*, *6*(3), 208–213.

Griffin, E. M. (2012). *A First Look at Communication theory* (8th ed.). New York: McGraw-Hill.

Heywood, M. (2014). *Does anybody remember AIDS?* Retrieved from http://groundup.org.za/article/does-anybody-remember-aids_2022

IRIN. (2013). *Kenya: Anger and anxiety over "leaky" condoms.* Retrieved from http://www.plusnews.org./PrintReport.asp?REportID+86090

Kahneman, D. (2011). *Thinking Fast and Slow.* New York: Farrar, Straus and Giroux.

Kaiser Health News. (2002). *'Racy' Condom Ad Spark Controversy in Kenya.* Retrieved from http://www.kaiserhealthnews.org/Daily-Report/2002/March/19/dr0010098.aspx?p=1

Kaufmann, J. R., & Feldbaum, H. (2009). Diplomacy and the polio Immunization Boycott in Northern Nigeria. *Health Affairs*, 28(4), 1091–1101. doi:10.1377/hlthaff.28.4.1091 PMID:19597208

Kaye, D. K., Bakyawa, J., Kakande, N., & Sewankambo, N. (2011). The media's and health scientists' perceptions of strategies and priorities for nurturing positive scientist media interaction for communicating health research in Uganda. *Journal of Media and Communication Studies*, 3(3), 112–117.

Kibira, H. (2013). *Controversial condom advert now withdrawn.* Retrieved from http://www.the-star.co.ke/news/article-1140093/controversial-condom-advert-now-withdraw

Kim, S. H., Scheufele, D. A., & Shanahan, J. (2002). Think about it this way: Attribute Agenda-Setting function of the Press and the Public Evaluation of a Local issue. *J&MC Quarterly*, 79(1), 7–25. doi:10.1177/107769900207900102

Kingdon, J. K. (1995). *Agendas, Alternatives and Public Policies.* New York: Harper Collins.

Komolafe-Opadeji, H. O. (2008). Promoting Public Awareness of HIV/AIDS in Africa. Follow-Up to a Pilot Study. *Library Philosophy Practice.* Retrieved from http://www.webpages.uidaho.edu/-mbolin/komolafe.htm

Klugman, B. (2011). Effective social justice advocacy: A theory of change framework for assessing progress. *Reproductive Health Matters*, 19(38), 146–162. doi:10.1016/S0968-8080(11)38582-5 PMID:22118149

McCombs, M. (2005). A Look at Agenda-setting: Past Present and Future. *Journalism Studies*, 6(4), 543-557. Retrieved from http://www.informaworld.com/smpp/title~content=t713393939

McCombs M, Shaw DL. (1972). The agenda-setting function of the mass media. *Public Opinion Quarterly, 36*(2), 176-187.

McNeil, D. G., Jr. (2007). UN to say it overstated HIV cases by Millions. *New York Times.* Retrieved from http://www.nytimes.com/2007/11/20/world/20aids.html

MacPherson, Y., & Chamberlain, S. (2013). Health on the Move: Can Mobile Phones Save the World. London: BBC.

Ngwainmbi, E. (2014). Communication for Organization Adjustment: How to position Development institutions for Enhanced Health communication. In E. Ngwainmbi (Ed.), *Healthcare Management Strategy*. Lexington, MA: Communication and Development Challenges and Solutions in Developing Countries.

Obadare, E. (2005). A crisis of trust: History, politics, religion and the polio crisis in Northern Nigeria. *Patterns of Prejudice, 39*(3), 265–284. doi:10.1080/00313220500198185

Okigbo, C. C., Nan, Yu., & Napakol, A. (2013). HIV/AIDS in Africa: Contradictions, Controversies, and Containment. In E. Ngwainmbi (Ed.), *Healthcare Management Strategy*. Lexington, MA: Communication and Development Challenges and Solutions in Developing Countries.

Osho, S. (2011). *The Uniqueness of African Means of Communication in Contemporary World*. Paper presented at Seminar on Cultural Diplomacy in Africa and International Conference on Cultural Diplomacy in Africa – Strategies to confront the challenges of the 21st Century: Does Africa Have What is Required? Berlin, Germany.

Oyero, O. (2010). Children: As 'invisible' and voiceless as ever in the Nigerian news media. *Estudos em Communicacao, 2*(7), 25–41.

Oxfam. (2015). *Using Mobile Phones for Polio Prevention in Somalia*. Retrieved from http://policy-practice.oxfam.org.uk/publications/using-mobile-phones-for-polio-prevention-in-somalia-an-evaluation-of-the-201314-552890

Solomon, Maud, Amoah, & Garbrah. (2001). Using folk Media in HIV/AIDS Prevention in Rural Ghana. *American Journal of Public Health, 91*(10), 1559-1562.

PANOS. (2003). *Missing the Message*. London: PANOS.

Pissani, E. (2008). *Wisdom from Whores*. London: Granta Publications.

Population Council. (2012). *Baseline Survey of Nigerian Media Coverage of Youth Sexual and Reproductive Health and HIV and AIDS related Issues*. Abuja: Population Council.

Praekelt, G. (2012). *Using mobile social networks to stimulate SRH service and uptake: the case of young Africa live*. Retrieved from http://www.commonwealthhealth.org/wp-content/uploads/2012/05/93-94.pdf

Sabatier, P. A., & Weible, C. M. (2007). The Advocacy Coalition Framework: Innovations and Clarifications. In P. A. Sabatier (Ed.), *Theories of the Policy Process* (pp. 189–220). West Press.

Shiffman, J. (2016). Networks and global health governance: Introductory editorial for Health Policy and Planning supplement on the Emergence and Effectiveness of Global Health Networks. *Health Policy and Planning, 31*, i1–i2. Retrieved from http://heapol.oxfordjournals.org/

Shiffman, J. (2009). A Social explanation for the rise and fall of global health issues. *Bulletin of the World Health Organization, 87*(8), 608–613. doi:10.2471/BLT.08.060749 PMID:19705011

Shoemaker, P. J., Vos, T. P., & Reese, S. D. (2009). The Journalist as a Gatekeeper. In K. Wahl-Jorgensen & T. Hanitzsh (Eds.), *The Handbook of Journalism Studies*. New York: Routledge.

Smith, J. H., & Whiteside, A. (2010). The history of AIDS Exceptionalism. *Journal of the International AIDS Society, 13*, 47. Retrieved from http//www.joascoety.org/content/13/17

Steinwand, M. C. (2013). *Compete or Coordinate? Aid Fragmentation and Lead Donorship*. Paper presented at the Department of Political Science, Stoney Brook University.

Timberg, C. (2006). *How AIDS in Africa Was Overstated*. Retrieved from www.washingtonpost.com/wp-dyn/content/article/2006/04/05/AR20060405025

The Lancet. (2010). Growth of Aid and Decline of Humanitarianism. *The Lancet, 375*.

Ugboajah, F. O. (1985). Oramedia in Africa. In F. O. Ugboajah (Ed.), *Mass Communication, Culture and Society in West Africa* (pp. 165–176). Han Zell Publishers.

UNAIDS. (1999). Communications Framework for HIV/AIDS: A New Direction. UNAIDS.

UNAIDS. (2011a). *Nations at the Crossroads*. UNAIDS.

UNAIDS. (2011b). *UNAIDS Outlook Report 2011*. Geneva: UNAIDS.

UNAIDS. (2012). Report of meeting of media professionals on Countdown to Getting to Zero Campaign. UNAIDS.

UNCG. (2009). *Delivery as One Pilot. Communication Workshop Report 11-14 December 2009*. New York: United Nations.

UNDG. (2008). *United Nations Development Group*. Background Paper for meeting of Principals, Paris, France.

UNESCO. (2008). *Safeguarding oral tradition in East Africa*. A report prepared for UNESCO, Nairobi, Kenya.

UNFPA. (2015). *Global Communication Strategy*. New York: UNFPA.

UNFPA. (2013). Concept Note on Media Network for Population and Development, Case Study of Ethiopia. Addis Ababa: UNFPA.

UNFPA. (2012). Report on Media Advocacy for the Campaign on accelerated Reduction of maternal Mortality in Africa. Kampala: UNFPA.

UNICEF. (2014). *Nigeria: Short Duration country programme document*. Abuja: UNICEF.

UNICEF. (2011). *Communication Global Strategy Communication and policy Advocacy Strategic Framework – 2012-2015*. New York: UNICEF.

UNICEF. (2010). *Situation Analysis of Women and Children*. Abuja: UNICEF.

United Nations. (2011). *Social media Guidelines for UN staff*. New York: United Nations.

United Nations Global Pulse. (2013). *Big data for Development. A Primer*. New York: United Nations.

United Nations. (2015). *Transforming our world: the 2030 Agenda for Sustainable Development*. New York: United Nations.

Urvin, P. (2010). From the right to development to rights-based approach: how human rights entered development. In A. Cornwall & D. Eade (Eds.), *Deconstructing Development Discourse – Buzzwords and Fuzz words*. Oxford, UK: Oxfam.

Vollmer, F. (2012). *Visibility Vis- a-Vis Aid Effectiveness: Looking for a Third Way*. Berlin: German Development Institute.

Waisbord, S. (2006). Advocacy journalism in a Global Context. In K. Wahl-Jorgensen & T. Hanitzsh (Eds.), *The Handbook of Journalism Studies* (pp. 371–385). New York: Routledge.

Wallack, L., Dorfman, L., Jenigan, D., & Nixon, M. (1993). *Media Advocacy and Public health: Power for Prevention*. Sage.

Wang, A.L., Duke, W., & Schmid, P. (2009). *Print media reporting of male circumcision for HIV prevention in Sub-Saharan Africa*. Academic Press.

Weaver, D. H. (2007). Thoughts on Agenda Setting, Framing and Priming. *Journal of Communication*, *57*(1), 142–147. doi:10.1111/j.1460-2466.2006.00333.x

West, D. M. (2014). *Using mobile technology to improve maternal health and fight Ebola: A case study of mobile innovation in Nigeria*. The Brookings Institution.

World Health Organisation. (2010). *An Assessment of E-Health Initiatives in Africa*. Geneva: WHO.

Wilson, E. R., & Murby, R. (2010). *Communication as Innovation in Social Enterprise*. Retrieved from http://wbi.worldbank/org/

Zahariadis, N. (2007). The Multiple Streams Framework: Structure, Limitation, Prospects. In P. A. Sabatier (Ed.), *Theories of the Policy Process* (pp. 65–92). West Press.

This research was previously published in Exploring Journalism Practice and Perception in Developing Countries edited by Abiodun Salawu and Toyosi Olugbenga Samson Owolabi; pages 257-280, copyright year 2018 by Information Science Reference (an imprint of IGI Global).

Chapter 4
With a Little Help from My Friends:
The Irish Radio Industry's Strategic Appropriation of Facebook for Commercial Growth

Daithi McMahon
Univeristy of Limerick, Ireland

ABSTRACT

Ireland has faced significant economic hardship since 2008, with the Irish radio industry suffering as advertising revenues evaporated. The difficult economic circumstances have forced radio station management to devise new and cost effective ways of generating much-needed income. The answer has come in the form of Facebook, the leading Social Network Site (SNS) in Ireland. Using Ireland as a case study, this chapter looks at how radio station management are utilising the social network strategically in a bid to enhance their audiences and revenues. Radio station management consider Facebook to be an invaluable promotional tool which is very easily integrated into radio programming and gives radio a digital online presence, reaching far greater audiences than possible through broadcasting. Some radio stations are showing ambition and are realising the marketing potential that Facebook and other SNSs hold. However, key changes in practice, technology and human resources are required to maximise the profit-making possibilities offered by Facebook.

INTRODUCTION

The Irish radio industry has undergone significant change in recent years due to the challenges posed by the economic recession and the pervasion of digital media. Irish radio stations are fighting for the attentions of modern audiences who have high demands placed on their time and attention from digital and social media. Through smartphones, individuals have the entire globe at their fingertips and this presents threats and opportunities to an older medium like radio.

DOI: 10.4018/978-1-5225-9869-5.ch004

This chapter explores how the radio industry in Ireland is incorporating the Facebook phenomenon into the traditional broadcasting business model. This ongoing development has involved modifications to radio production practices, an alteration of technology needs and additional human resources in the form of dedicated digital media managers. Management at some radio stations, particularly the youth oriented stations, are enjoying some success in using their significant social media followings to promote their commercial partners and gain revenue from these services. This chapter demonstrates that a dedicated and aggressive social media strategy can have a positive influence on audience ratings. Furthermore, the stations that are having the most success in exploiting social media for commercial gain are primarily the youth-targeted radio stations.

The main aim of this chapter is to assess the commercial impact of SNSs on Irish radio stations. First, it seeks to assess the importance of Facebook and other SNSs as conduits for communication between radio audiences and radio stations. Second, it attempts to assess how radio stations are using Facebook and other SNSs to engage with their audiences. The third objective is to gauge how SNSs are being used by radio stations for commercial gain. The hypotheses are two fold: first, that radio audiences and radio producers are spending increasing amounts of time interacting with one another on SNSs; and second that radio station management are successfully using SNSs to strategically build a strong online audience which can be sold to advertisers and sponsors, thus creating a new revenue stream to help grow their businesses.

BACKGROUND

The radio industry in Ireland has faced huge challenges since 2008 due to the economic recession that has gripped the country. The Independent Broadcasters of Ireland (IBI) is an organisation representing the interests of the thirty-four independently-owned commercial radio stations in Ireland. In 2013 IBI Chairman John Purcell revealed that revenue within the radio industry was down some forty percent compared to pre-recession figures (Purcell, 2013, np). It was in the context of these desperate economic times, that innovative minds within the industry spotted the potential to be gained from appropriating SNSs into the radio broadcaster's remit and set about exploiting the power of digital media for economic gain.

Independent commercial radio stations in Ireland are privately owned and operated enterprises which rely on commercial revenue via advertising, sponsorship and investment income. Although the four public service radio stations that are owned and operated by *Raidió Teilifís Éireann (RTÉ)* are largely supported by the television licence fee, independent stations do not receive any direct pecuniary input from the government and thus have been under severe financial pressure. *RTÉ*'s radio stations meanwhile have enjoyed the safety net provided by public funding, coupled with advertising and sponsorship revenue from the commercial market where they compete with independent radio stations.

Despite the initial threat to radio posed by digital media – namely that audiences would switch off radio in favour of online podcasts and digital streaming services – radio continues to survive, if not thrive, thanks to the emergence of one of the most pervasive of digital media, SNSs (colloquially known as social media). This is due to a number of factors. First, radio is a highly flexible and adaptable medium capable of adjusting to changes in the mediascape. Moreover, it faced down the arrival of television in the 1960s and the internet in the late 1990s, both of which, many predicted, would signal the end of radio. Instead of posing a threat to radio, SNSs have instead offered a significant opportunity, which the Irish radio industry has largely taken advantage of. This convergence of an old medium (radio) with new media (SNSs) is a significant phenomenon and has helped radio maintain its viability.

Despite having battled through over eight years of economic recession the industry has maintained its high standards of output and Irish audiences continue to listen in strong numbers with 83% of the adult population tuning in to live radio each day (Ipsos/MRBI, 2015a).

Social Network Sites (SNSs), also known as 'social networking media' or 'social media' are websites and web applications that allow users to connect and network with virtually millions of people around the world while also allowing individuals to participate in smaller networks of friends and online communities (Morris 2010, p. 13). SNSs continue to grow exponentially in popularity representing, "one of the fastest uptakes of a communication technology since the web was developed in the early 1990s" (Stefanone et al., 2010, p. 511). This makes the study of SNSs timely and relevant in modern media and communications academic studies.

Ellison et al. (2007) write, "Social network sites (SNSs)…allow individuals to present themselves, articulate their social networks, and establish or maintain connections with others" (Ellison et al., 2007, p. 1). This offers a clear and succinct description of what SNSs do, however one of the most comprehensive attempts to define and outline the phenomenon of SNSs was made by Boyd and Ellison (2007) who define them as:

Web-based services that allow individuals to (1) construct a public or semi-public profile within a bounded system, (2) articulate a list of other users with whom they share a connection, and (3) view and traverse their list of connections and those made by others within the system. The nature and nomenclature of these connections may vary from site to site (Boyd & Ellison, 2007, p. 211).

It is important to note that authors Boyd & Ellison (2007) make a key distinction between 'Social Network Sites' and 'Social Networking Sites', preferring the former to describe the computer-mediated movement in question, despite the latter existing commonly in public discourse and both terms being used interchangeably. The authors employ 'network' over 'networking' for two reasons:

… emphasis and scope. "Networking" emphasizes relationship initiation, often between strangers. While networking is possible on these sites, it is not the primary practice on many of them, nor is it what differentiates them from other forms of computer-mediated communication (CMC) (Boyd & Ellison, 2007, p. 211).

This is supported by evidence that suggests that SNSs are used to support existing offline friendships or connections rather than make new ones (Boyd & Ellison, 2007; Ellison et al., 2007; Dunbar, 2012). Dunbar argues that one of the reasons SNSs have flourished can be directly attributed to "the fact that they allow us to keep up with friends without seeing them face-to-face" (Dunbar, 2012, p. 3). Therefore, the fact that SNS users are not seeking out new connections but rather interacting with their existing network of contacts renders 'social network sites' a more apt term; this despite the prolific use of 'social networking sites' as a term in modern nomenclature. The author will thus adopt the term 'social network site' henceforth except when quoting other authors directly.

Methodology

Using the Irish radio industry as a case study, this research is based on qualitative interviews with N=10 radio industry professionals across four different radio stations. The radio stations were chosen for the diversity in programming and the geographic spread of the stations' broadcast areas. *RTÉ 2fm*, one of the four radio stations owned and operated by the state broadcaster RTÉ, broadcasts nationally to the 20-44 year old demographic. *Beat 102103* is one of three regional radio stations in Ireland targeting youth audiences and broadcasts to 15-35 year olds in the south-east of the country. *Spin South West* is also a regional station, which broadcasts to listeners aged 15-35 years in the south-west of Ireland. *Radio Kerry* is a regional radio station broadcasting to all adults in county Kerry, a rural county in the southwest corner of Ireland. Interviews were conducted during the month of July 2013.

Irish radio stations are engaging with audiences via a number of SNSs, and while this chapter discusses how Irish radio stations are using SNSs generally to promote growth, the research has focused on the use of Facebook primarily. Twitter is also commonly used by Irish radio stations but from an early stage the author decided to focus on Facebook for a number of reasons. First, preliminary research showed that Facebook offered the audience a much deeper participatory experience than Twitter. Second, the same preliminary research also showed that radio stations had significantly more audience members engaging through Facebook than Twitter. Third, Facebook is the most popular social network in Ireland with 59% of the population owning a Facebook account according to Ipsos/MRBI (2015b).

This research employed the inductive strategy of using newly sourced empirical data to develop original theory. This concept, known as grounded theory is the "discovery of theory from data systematically obtained from social research" (Glaser & Strauss, 1999, p. 2). Therefore the findings were used to inform the research and develop sound theory.

A multi-method approach was used to collect both quantitative and qualitative data for this research. The use of multiple methods allowed for a rich collection of information to be gathered and for the triangulation of data, which strengthened the veracity of the findings. The main source of qualitative data comprised of semi-structured interviews with industry professionals at the four Irish radio stations listed above. The working practices of the radio presenters and producers of three programmes were recorded by use of direct observation during the programmes' broadcast, namely *Kerry Today* on *Radio Kerry*, *Beat Breakfast* in *Beat 102103* and *Tubridy* on *RTÉ 2fm*. Finally, the content and activity on the Facebook pages of the stations in question were recorded and analysed. This textual analysis involved the recording by method of screen grabs, the entire content contained on one day of Facebook page posts from three of the radio stations involved (*Beat 102103, RTÉ 2fm* and *Radio Kerry*). This was repeated on four separate dates between July 2013 and August 2014. This material was then analysed and detailed records of the content made including types of posts, response from audience and number of likes, shares and comments made by the audience.

Three members of the *Tubridy* programme were interviewed: the programme presenter, the Producer-in-Charge and one of the researchers. Two staff members from *Beat 102013* were interviewed, the *Beat Breakfast* Producer and the station's Chief Executive Officer. At *Spin South West* the Assistant CEO/Programme Controller was interviewed. Four *Radio Kerry* staff members were interviewed: the General Manager, the Sales & Marketing Manager, the News/Current Affairs Editor and the Digital Media Manager. To protect the anonymities of those involved all names have been withheld and interviewees will be referred to by their respective job titles. The interviews were recorded, transcribed, and then analysed to identify consistent themes in their responses. These were then compared horizontally against field notes and observations to develop critical themes.

SOCIAL NETWORK SITES: A STRATEGY OF INTERACTION

This chapter investigates the use of Facebook as a conduit for communication and interaction between radio stations and their audiences. In order for this relationship to exist interaction is required from both parties. For their part audiences need to be active, meaning they need to visit radio station Facebook pages and engage with content through emoji reactions, shares or comments. Radio producers need to make efforts to draw the audience in by regularly posting stimulating or engaging material that will appeal to their target cohort.

Active/Interactive Audience

Before looking at how radio stations are using Facebook as a marketing tool, it is important to first understand how the radio audience comes to use Facebook to interact with radio stations. Recent research shows that the Irish public are using Facebook regularly and are spending significant portions of their days on the popular social medium (Ipsos/MRBI, 2015b). Furthermore, radio producers have noticed this shift and have established a presence for their brand on Facebook and are encouraging interaction by posting content that appeals to the audience's desire for information and entertainment (McMahon 2015).

McMahon's (2015) study found that audiences visit radio station Facebook pages seeking three main types of content

1. Additional information,
2. Entertainment, and
3. Opportunities to learn about and enter competitions.

These findings are in line with those of other authors analysing the motivations of Facebook use particularly the motives of seeking out information and entertainment (Park et al., 2009; Sheldon, 2008). McMahon (2015) found that audiences also want to exercise their agency by interacting and participating in the on-air and online discussions.

The evidence from the current research proposes that radio audiences operate in a cycle of broadcast and social media consumption which, if nurtured and encouraged, contributes to the building of their loyalty (Enli & Ihlebaek, 2011; McMahon, 2015). The cycle operates as follows. At the outset

1. The audience are regular listeners of a radio programme.
2. The audience visits the programme's Facebook page for an enhanced experience with more information, a wider variety of entertainment and the opportunities to enter competitions and win prizes.
3. At the third and final stage, the audience remains on the radio station's Facebook page for the opportunity to participate and contribute to the online discussions and debates.

As a result of an informative, entertaining and perhaps rewarding experience on-air and online, the audience returns to consume the on-air and online content again in the future, thus completing the cycle. As with any media product, the challenge for producers is to consistently stimulate and engage the audience, which is achieved by continually delivering quality content that is fresh and interesting, and that satiates the audience's wants.

Enli & Ihlebaek (2011) argue that audiences who are afforded the opportunities to participate in television programmes experience deeper engagement, which builds the audience's loyalty. This is precisely what the managers and producers at the commercial radio stations stated was their motivation behind using Facebook: to engage audiences in the expectation that they will return as radio listeners. Aside from the financial return achieved through improved ratings there are other ancillary benefits also. According to Chaputula et al. (2013), mass media organisations that use SNSs benefit not only through increased audiences but also constructive feedback that helps the organisation improve its product.

Social Media Strategies

The present research found that social media fits into an overall audience and revenue growth strategy for some of the radio stations involved. This strategy is made up of a four-step process which is orchestrated by radio station management and executed by presenters and producers. The process runs as follows: radio stations interact with their audience via Facebook to improve their online presence, which will create more opportunities. To promote the station, and to help increase audience interaction, which will ultimately increase listenership and create new revenue streams. Each step of the process is now discussed in detail.

Step 1: Increase Online Presence.

Digital media are a mainstay of modern society, becoming more and more prevalent as technology allows increased connectivity through mobile communication devices such as smartphones and tablets. "In the present-day radio landscape", argue Stark and Weichselbaum (2013), "one might not be wrong in declaring that a traditional radio station without a website of its own comes close to resembling radio without sound" (p. 186). This is an astute metaphor but could now be updated to read that a traditional radio station without a website and strong social media presence of its own comes close to resembling radio without sound. SNSs are the latest software to open new and exciting communication and connection opportunities, and the radio industry in Ireland has learned that it must have a strong online presence if it is to remain in the audience's daily consciousness. There are a host of new opportunities open to radio producers through simple-to-use online tools such as Facebook, which can enhance the overall entertainment package offered to the radio audience.

The CEO of *Spin South West* states that people are increasingly using Facebook to communicate and especially those within the station's key demographic, the 15-34 year old cohort. As CEO, she understands the importance of her station being present on Facebook, "we have to be there because that's where our listeners are". She further points out that being on Facebook is similar to her station being present at nightclubs and other places where young people gather in large numbers; it allows the station to get noticed and promotes the station's brand.

Beat 102103's CEO also posits that an online presence is absolutely essential "because we are a youth station and social media is so huge for our audience". She stresses the importance of all presenters and deejays being connected to the audience via social media, asserting that if the station is doing something on-air they have to be supplementing that item online, "we have to make sure it's part of what we do". Radio stations like *Beat 102103* have to embrace social media more than other companies, she believes, because the station has to be where their audience is and *Beat*'s audience is on Facebook: "they're all engaging with Facebook so it's really important that we're there" asserts the CEO.

Although *Radio Kerry*'s target audience is an older demographic than that of *Beat 102103* and *Spin South West*, the General Manager (GM) understands that her station needs to be online and active on Facebook if the station wants to reach listeners. "It's part of our listeners' world and if we want to engage with them then we have to be in their space, we have to be in their zone" according to the GM. She believes that any radio station would be foolish to ignore Facebook such is its prevalence in modern society and the strength of its relationship with modern audiences. Facebook is therefore a very useful way for stations to have a presence where audiences are spending increasing amounts of time.

The Producer-in-Charge of the *Tubridy* programme on *RTÉ 2fm* values the opportunities offered by Facebook as it provides a more vibrant, interactive and meaningful online presence compared to a radio station's website. He acknowledges that prior to the arrival of social media, a website was a radio station's only online platform and he believes the traditional website is becoming somewhat redundant today as a result of SNSs. According to the researcher on the *Tubridy* programme, having an online presence is also very useful for engaging those who cannot listen to the radio programme when it airs for whatever reason, but still want to follow the show and be involved. The *Tubridy* researcher goes on to explain how SNSs also allow her and her team to bring visual components into the radio show, thus enhancing the experience for the audience. In the case of the *Tubridy* programme, this usually comes in the form of photos or images often of the presenter in the office, in studio, with studio guests, or on an outside broadcast, thus giving the audience greater familiarity with the programme.

The presenter of the *Tubridy* programme agrees and certainly sees an advantage of being able to "bring a visual element to an aural product" by posting photos, videos and other audio visual multimedia on their Facebook page. Through such material, the production team are able to give listeners a better understanding of what the presenter is talking about on the programme or what the person he is interviewing actually looks like.

The increased online presence afforded by Facebook allows radio stations to reach new audiences and helps make the radio product more attractive. This raises the next function of Facebook for radio stations: its value as an effective promotional tool.

Step 2: Promote the Station.

According to marketing executives at *Beat 102103, Spin South West, RTÉ 2fm* and *Radio Kerry*, Facebook is an extremely useful tool for promoting the station online. The strategy being that Facebook content could drive online audiences back to the on-air product or the station's website, both of which are direct revenue generators for the stations.

Initially when radio stations started using SNSs in 2008, Facebook had imposed severe restrictions on radio stations running sponsored promotions on their Facebook pages. Recently however Facebook has softened their stance and at the time of writing (December 2015) management at *Beat 102103* had started selling integrated Facebook exposure as part of enhanced marketing packages for their clients. This is a significant development in terms of the opportunities it presents for radio stations to exploit their massive followings on Facebook. In December 2015, *Beat 102103* had more than 470,000 followers on Facebook and growing by the day. When compared to the number of daily on-air listeners, which stood at 95,000 at the time of writing, it is clear just how much more pervasive Facebook can be, as five times more people are following *Beat 102103* on Facebook than are listening to the station's radio broadcasts (Ipsos/MRBI 2015a). This is further evidence that SNSs have significant potential as digital marketing tools, not only for radio stations, but for all commercial enterprises.

According to *Beat 102103*'s CEO, Facebook is an extension of the station's brand. "If we do something on-air, we always want to see how we can make more people aware of it". The CEO hopes that Facebook posts can be shared throughout their followers' social networks and make others aware of what *Beat 102103* do, thus courting new listeners to the station.

Building brand recognition was identified as an important factor by management at *Radio Kerry* and *Beat 102103*. Branding can be reinforced by a strong Facebook presence. A radio station's brand can be pushed to the forefront of people's minds if the content is engaging and achieves a strong reach via Facebook. A popular post that goes viral could result in a listener identifying *Radio Kerry* or *Beat 102103* as their preferred station at the time a listenership survey is being conducted, thus boosting the stations listenership figures.

Spin South West's Facebook page is highly reflective of their brand and is used very much as a promotional tool to encourage people to listen to the radio station or to visit the website. For example, if the station is running a competition to win concert tickets, they will always require that the audience listen on-air for instructions on how to enter. This allows the station to encourage more listeners to sample the station's on-air product and perhaps become regular listeners.

Step 3: Increase Interaction.

The third step of the social media strategy employed by radio stations is to generate increased interaction between the audience and station producers on Facebook. Modern Irish radio listeners want to engage in two-way communication with media producers and are demanding increased agency over the radio programmes they consume (McMahon 2013). This empowers the audience and makes them media users, rather than passive media consumers. Facebook fills this need by offering the audience increased interaction opportunities including the prospect of contributing content themselves.

Until only recently text messaging was the preferred method of audience interaction but Facebook offers a much more diverse range of options for the audience to communicate with a radio station. This includes audience members sharing photos, videos, images and links with a radio station and its followers. *Spin South West*'s CEO sees Facebook as,

… a way to connect with our audience, it's a way to gauge what our audience is doing, thinking about and how they feel about issues, music and what's going on in their lives and it's a direct communication with them.

Radio Kerry's News Editor believes that Facebook offers the audience more communication options and helps the producer to "get conversation from listeners" especially those who have outgrown the other forms of audience interaction such as telephone, text or email, or those who simply find it a less formal method of communication. *Radio Kerry* management feel that the more communication channels open to the audience, the better.

The *Tubridy* team feel that Facebook is an excellent resource that provides a wealth of information about the audience including their opinions on matters, what their likes and dislikes are, and what they want to talk about, which in turn informs the team as to what they should be covering in the show.

The Head of Music at *Beat 102013* argues that Facebook is another way of "attracting interaction from the audience" and agrees that the social network is a useful tool to gauge how people feel about what is going on. The creation of content for the *Beat Breakfast* programme forms an important part of the interactivity between station and audience. Facebook provides the audience with a platform to contribute that content, be that written text, an image, a video, a photo or any multi-media content they may want to share with others. According to Enli & Ihlebaek (2013), when an individual's material or contribution is included in a programme, they feel involved and this further engages them to continue to follow the programme to find out how they have influenced the outcome of the show, thus building loyalty. Engagement with audiences through Facebook is therefore viewed by industry management as part of a cohesive strategy to build listenership.

Step 4: Increase Listenership.

All independent radio stations in Ireland are commercial organisations and as such are focused on monetary profit. Traditionally this is achieved by growing a station's audience, which in turn allows a station to increase advertising and sponsorship rates. Therefore any tool or strategy that can increase listenership is naturally likely to be exploited for maximum return. From this perspective, radio stations see Facebook as an opportunity rather than a threat.

Spin South West has been consistently growing its Facebook audience and has one of the highest followings of all the radio stations in Ireland. The station has also experienced steady growth in listeners over the last number of years. The CEO uses Facebook because it makes people aware of the *Spin South West* brand in the hope that it may help recruit new listeners and maintain existing ones. However, she is hesitant to draw a direct correlation between the number of Facebook followers and listener ratings without evidence to support it and believes there are other factors at play. She describes Facebook as "a really important tool to drive people to listen to the radio and essentially sell advertising, because that's the basis of commercial radio".

The CEO of *Beat 102103* believes there is a correlation between Facebook engagement and listener numbers. She encourages the station's staff to use Facebook to engage the audience and "drive them back to listen on-air". She believes that Facebook has helped the station grow its listenership because of the staff's effective use of the social network. She points out that the station has seen consistent audience growth since 2004 and argues that the station would have become stagnant and probably lost listeners had they not embraced technology, including SNSs, from an early stage. Furthermore because of the rapid rate at which technology is evolving, she believes that some radio stations will fall behind if they choose not to keep up with technology and embrace SNSs. The CEO continues by stating that *Beat 102103* is growing its listener base primarily because the management are listening to what the audience want to hear on the radio; and the station is using Facebook to gather this information.

In addition to the assertion that Facebook helps grow listener ratings *Beat 102103*'s CEO has also realised the marketing potential of the popular SNS. By 2015 *Beat 102103* had employed three dedicated social media managers while the marketing department had not only incorporated social media exposure into sales and marketing strategies for clients on a larger scale but also developed dedicated social media sponsorship packages. These new sponsorship packages involve the integration of the client's branding and key messages into all social media output and on-air programming. The management of *Beat 102103* foresees significant financial opportunities in social media marketing due to the ability of SNSs to reach beyond the relatively limited on-air audience and communicate using a wider variety of multi-media messages. With the *Beat 102103* Facebook page boasting nearly half a million followers in late 2015, the station has the opportunity to reach one in nine adults in Ireland.

Radio Kerry's Marketing and Events Manager believes that a station has to reach out beyond the regular listeners if it wants to expand its listenership. If a station is promoting itself on the radio only, then the station is promoting itself to people who are already listening. The station is not reaching the non-listeners, and this is the advantage of using Facebook. It presents the opportunity to promote the station to those who might not necessarily be listening on a regular basis, but who are on Facebook and may come across a station's posts. Facebook offers the opportunity to be spontaneous and engaging to grab a user's attention and give them a reason to listen to *Radio Kerry*. Facebook therefore offers radio stations the opportunity to reach out to potential new listeners and draw them in.

Radio Kerry management are hesitant to state for certain that Facebook helps the station gain listeners due to the lack of evidence to support the theory but they do believe that Facebook is of benefit to the station because it is proven to engage Kerry people. Even if it only helps to maintain the existing audience, *Radio Kerry* management believe using Facebook is beneficial. The station's GM recognises that Facebook is more often used by younger audiences. However, she feels that connecting with younger audiences today will help establish their loyalty for the future when their tastes mature and *Radio Kerry*'s output is more inline with their preferred programming.

The *Radio Kerry* GM reiterates the point made above that a radio station's bottom line is "to keep your listenership up, so the more ways you can tell people about it and engage with them the better". The argument is that Facebook helps attract potential new listeners who would not normally interact with the station via traditional methods or be aware of what is available on-air. Therefore, in terms of promotion, the GM believes that by

… teasing people, hooking them, be it towards a programme piece or a competition, Facebook can be very useful for informing people of what is on- air and hopefully appealing to their tastes or interests.

The Producer-in-Charge of *RTE 2fm*'s *Tubridy* programme does not see increasing listenership as a primary function of Facebook for his programme. Nor does he believe that the social network can help increase listenership because there is no evidence to suggest it does. The *Tubridy* presenter agrees with his Producer-in-Charge declaring, "No, is the simple answer, I don't think it's actually going to garner more listeners". He believes the only way to gain more listeners is by having a quality radio show, not by having a good Facebook page. He argues that producers should "focus on the core product of broadcasting" as a means of increasing listeners.

The *RTÉ 2fm* staff members interviewed therefore have opposing viewpoints to their counterparts working in commercial radio and are reticent to draw any positive correlation between Facebook engagement and listenership figures. This may be due to the fact that *RTÉ* relies less on audience ratings to support its business model due to the public funding it receives through the television licence fee. This allows *RTÉ 2fm* to be less reliant on advertising revenue compared to commercial radio stations. It is clear from the interviews that Facebook and other SNSs hold significant present and future value for independent commercial radio stations but limited value for the state owned *RTÉ 2fm*.

Irish radio stations were found to be incorporating social media strategies into their wider marketing plans. The youth targeted radio station *Beat 102103* is the most dynamic and forward-thinking of the stations studied and is leading the way in terms of employing SNSs for maximum benefit. Further research is required to determine whether a direct correlation exists between increased Facebook interactions and increased radio listenership.

SOLUTIONS AND RECOMMENDATIONS

Changes in Radio Production_

Along with the addition of Facebook to the radio producer's remit, there have also been a number of changes to how radio is produced. Producers now have to incorporate social media management into their daily routine meaning new practices have been incorporated, new technology has been introduced, and in some cases ancillary human resources have been added.

In radio production, the terms producer and presenter are often used interchangeably. In most instances a programme presenter is also the programme producer or co-producer. In some cases, when the budget allows, the roles of presenter and producer are separated and other positions may even exist in the team. Most often however, the presenter is also the producer and thus the term producer will be used hereafter to denote the role of the person primarily responsible for the programme's output.

Practice

Radio producers have had to alter their production practices to incorporate social media into their programmes. Producers have to constantly manage the station/programme Facebook page to ensure they are making the most of the technology. Because audiences interact with Facebook pages outside of programme transmission hours, management of social media content must continue before, during, and after each programme is aired.

Before a programme begins, the producer routinely checks the station Facebook page to review the posts other producers have published recently. This allows the producer to avoid duplication of information and bombardment of the audience with too many posts. The producer can also get an idea of what has proved popular or unpopular and generally get a feel for what is happening online at that time. Producers also regularly monitor their competitors' Facebook pages to see what content other stations are posting. The producer will often publish a post at the start of his/her programme to signal that a new programme is starting, to preview what is coming up on that programme and to encourage participation from the audience.

The *Beat Breakfast* producer will often post a *meme* (a humorous image with accompanying text) to incite a reaction from the audience. Common subject matter relates to being fatigued in the morning or a commentary regarding the general excitement felt on Fridays. These sorts of posts instil feelings of being part of an affective community of people who are all experiencing a similar feeling or emotion and thus makes the audience more engaged with the Facebook page and the radio station. Such content was found to be particularly popular amongst Facebook users as such posts would regularly receive high counts of emoji reactions, comments and shares.

A radio producer must manage a number of tasks that relate specifically to audience participation. During the programme's transmission the producer regularly monitors Facebook on one of the studio's computer monitors. S/he keeps the Facebook page open at all times to pick up on useful comments from the audience, react if something is proving popular and moderate any inappropriate comments that may be posted by the public.

The producer must also manage the flow of contributions from other communication channels including phone, text message, email and any other SNSs the station may use. These demands relate solely to the management of audience participation which is only a part of the producers remit. The producer must also continue to provide a quality on-air product to the audience, producing and presenting continuous content over several hours of broadcast. The remit of a radio producer is therefore ever-expanding due to the demands placed by SNSs. Producers often require further technological tools to carry out their duties effectively in the age of digital audience participation.

Technology

Radio stations and their producers have also had to make technological changes to adapt to social media use. Because Facebook is accessible via virtually any web browser, radio stations have not required upgrades in software or hardware to access and manage their Facebook accounts. Some producers however, have recognised that additional technology has been required in-studio to manage Facebook and other SNSs.

The most common in-studio set-up includes two computer monitors for the producer with one dedicated almost exclusively to the broadcast management system: the software used to arrange and play-out audio including ad breaks, music, sound clips, et cetera. The other computer monitor is used for researching and browsing the internet, monitoring and managing SNSs, sending/receiving email, managing incoming text messages, editing and reading word documents, communicating with colleagues via the intranet, and any other computer-based tasks the producer may need to carry out during the course of their broadcast.

This has put a great deal of pressure on the two monitors available to the producer and has led in some instances to the addition of a laptop into the studio. Such is the case at *Radio Kerry* where, during the *Kerry Today* programme, the producer now uses a laptop dedicated to Facebook and Twitter. This extra piece of hardware – only introduced into the studio in the spring of 2013 – allows the producer to constantly monitor the two social media accounts, publish posts, make comments, and read comments made by the audience.

Additional computers or monitors may not always be required, however, and some producers are finding that in fact mobile communication devices such as smartphones can be used to very good effect to manage social media. For example the *Beat Breakfast* Producer manages the station's Twitter account via his company-issued smartphone. Using a smartphone allows him more flexibility to supervise various communication channels without having a supplementary computer in studio. This is an example of a radio producer being adaptable and negates the need for additional computers, which can be costly and occupy valuable space in-studio.

In an effort to provide the audience with a deeper media experience beyond the aural radio broadcast, producers are increasingly using their mobile devices to capture images and videos and then post this content on Facebook. These images and videos provide in-studio and behind-the-scenes access to reveal to the audience more about the producers/presenters and their personalities.

Smartphones are also highly useful for producers when working on outside broadcasts. In such scenarios, producers are able to post images and other content relating to the outside broadcast in real time and offer an insight for the audience member who may be listening on-air or following online via social media.

Human Resources

The expansion of social media use by radio stations has saddled production personnel with added responsibilities and duties. Producers interviewed expressed their concerns at the time and energy required to manage numerous SNSs effectively. However they agree that it is a burden that must be adopted in order to maintain a competitive edge. This added workload, coupled with staff cut-backs during the economic downturn, has put considerable pressure or producers to do more with fewer resources.

Station managers appreciate the importance of Facebook but also accept that the SNS is a time-consuming and thus costly tool to manage. This raises an important dilemma for radio professionals: considering the value of Facebook, should stations be hiring dedicated social media managers to get the most out of SNSs or let existing staff manage it as best they can?

In some circumstances, notably *Spin South West*, *Beat 102103* and *Radio Kerry*, management have come to the realisation that bespoke staffing resources are required in order to maximise the potential of SNSs and vie with the competition in this fast-changing industry. These stations have hired dedicated social media/digital content managers, who are trained and experienced in their field, and are finding this to be a sound investment. Conversely at *RTÉ*, such a move has not been prioritised and the *Tubridy* programme's researcher has all social media responsibilities as part of her remit, despite the fact that her skills and training are in radio production. By hiring a social media/digital content manager, not only are the producers relieved of much of the burden of social media management, but those stations are now able to have a staff member apply dedicated time, energy and specific skills into improving the online content for the station. This represents a significant investment for struggling radio stations, but clearly station management are coming to appreciate that such recruitment and investment are necessary steps forward.

Spin South West's CEO affirms that she "could not afford not to employ someone" to manage the online content particularly social media as it is so important to the station's output and identity. At the time of interview (June 2013) *Spin South West* had just recently hired a Digital Media Manager. The individual is a university graduate with a master's degree in digital communications and is charged with driving content through SNSs and maintaining a vibrant and cutting edge presence across all of *Spin South West*'s online platforms.

This investment of scarce resources reiterates *Spin's South West* management's appreciation of the significance Facebook and other social media can have as a promotional tool for the station. The station's CEO sees digital marketing as the future and explains that advertising expenditure on digital media is growing significantly and is now higher in Ireland than on-air advertising. The management's strategy is to sell more website advertising because their research shows that 50% of *Spin South West*'s web traffic comes from Facebook.

The management at *Radio Kerry* feel that SNSs along with other online digital platforms such as the station's website is important enough that someone should be employed full-time to manage it but agrees that it comes down to resources. The main issue is that Facebook does not actually make any money directly for the station so it if difficult to justify the expenditure. At the time of interview (June 2013) *Radio Kerry* had only recently hired an online content editor on a trial basis to assess the effectiveness of such an appointment. The Online Content Editor's role includes managing web content, uploading podcasts, running SNS analytics and managing social media content in conjunction with programme producers and marketing staff. The trial was a success and the editor continues to work at *Radio Kerry* in 2015, thus clearly justifying the cost of his salary through the effectiveness of his digital media management.

A further interview in 2015 with the *Beat 102103* CEO revealed that the station now has three dedicated Social Media Managers. In addition the marketing department was not only incorporating social media exposure into sales and marketing strategies for clients on a larger scale but also selling dedicated social media marketing packages to its clients. This represents another significant step forwards in terms of the use of SNSs for marketing purposes and is an example of *Beat 102103*'s innovation and aggressive strategy to exploit commercial opportunities.

FUTURE RESEARCH DIRECTIONS

As there is a clear dearth of research into the use of SNSs by radio stations – not only in Ireland but globally – more research is needed in this area. Several industry professionals interviewed as part of this project argue that an effective and sustained social media strategy can have a positive affect on listener ratings. Although there are some signs that suggest this may be true, further in-depth research on a much wider scale and over a sustained period of time is required to advance this argument. Expanding this research to examine the use of SNSs in the UK radio industry and other larger European media markets would also be beneficial.

CONCLUSION

The appropriation of SNSs by the radio industry in Ireland continues to expand rapidly with each station seeking an edge over the competition. These are changing times for radio as a medium that has changed relatively little over the last number of decades is quickly adapting to the digital age. As SNSs continue to become more pervasive, it is the responsibility of marketers to look at the opportunities rather than the threats provided by these digital phenomena. In some instances the commercial opportunities and potential presented by Facebook have been realised and some radio stations have formulated social media strategies to harness the power of the social network.

Radio has been able to converge almost seamlessly with SNSs because it is such a flexible and adaptable medium that has embraced the opportunities available. Radio stations have altered production practices, installed new technological hardware and invested in skilled staff to execute their social media strategies. Management at progressive, innovative radio stations have turned Facebook into a powerful marketing tool. Furthermore, because of the far superior reach of the Facebook pages compared to radio listenership, selling Facebook exposure could soon become more lucrative than selling airtime. What is not in question is the importance being placed on social media strategies, which involve investing in dedicated and skilled digital media staff. Ignoring the opportunities provided by SNSs may soon become detrimental to radio stations in Ireland.

REFERENCES

Boyd, D. M., & Ellison, N. B. (2007). Social Network Sites: Definition, History, and Scholarship. *Journal of Computer-Mediated Communication*, *13*(1), 210–230. doi:10.1111/j.1083-6101.2007.00393.x

Chaputula, A. H., & Majawa, F. P. (2013). Use of social network sites by mass media organisations in Malawi. *Aslib Proceedings*, *65*(5), 534–557. doi:10.1108/AP-06-2012-0055

Dunbar, R. (2012). *Social Networks*. Reed Business Info. Ltd. Available: http://search.ebscohost.com/login.aspx?direct=true&db=a9h&AN=74134004&site=ehost-live

Ellison, N., Steinfield, C., & Lampe, C. (2007). The benefits of Facebook "friends:" Social capital and college students' use of online social network sites. *Journal of Computer-Mediated Communication*, *12*(4), 12–25. doi:10.1111/j.1083-6101.2007.00367.x

Enli, G. S., & Ihlebaek, K. A. (2011). 'Dancing with the audience': Administrating vote-ins in public and commercial broadcasting. *Media Culture & Society*, *33*(6), 953–962. doi:10.1177/0163443711412299

Glaser, B. G., & Strauss, A. L. (1999). *The discovery of grounded theory: strategies for qualitative research*. New York: Aldine de Gruyter.

Ipsos/Mrbi. (2015a). *Joint National Listenership and Readership: Third Quarter 2015*. Dublin: Ipsos/Mrbi.

Ipsos/Mrbi. (2015b). *Social Media Quarterly: August 2015*. Dublin: Ipsos/Mrbi.

McMahon, D. (2013). *The Role of Social Media in Audience Engagement with Irish Radio*. Paper presented at the ECREA Radio Research Conference, London.

McMahon, D. (2015). Old Dog, New Tricks: Can Social Media Help Youth Radio Stations Grow Their Audience? Presented at the *MeCCSA Conference*, Newcastle.

Morris, T. (2010). *All a twitter: a personal and professional guide to social networking with Twitter*. Indianapolis, IN: Pearson Education.

Park, N., Kee, K. F., & Valenzuela, S. (2009). Being Immersed in Social Networking Environment: Facebook Groups, Uses and Gratifications, and Social Outcomes. *Cyberpsychology & Behavior*, *12*(6), 729–733. doi:10.1089/cpb.2009.0003 PMID:19619037

Purcell, J. (2013). Keynote Address. Paper presened at the IBI Radio: Future Shock Conference, Dublin, Ireland.

Sheldon, P. (2008). Student Favorite: Facebook and Motives for its Use. *Southwestern Mass Communication Journal*, *23*, 39–53.

Stark, B., & Weichselbaum, P. (2013). What attracts listeners to Web radio? A case study from Germany. *Radio Journal: International Studies in Broadcast & Audio Media*, *11*, 185–202.

Stefanone, M. A., Lackaff, D., & Rosen, D. (2010). The Relationship between Traditional Mass Media and "Social Media": Reality Television as a Model for Social Network Site Behavior. *Journal of Broadcasting & Electronic Media*, *54*(3), 508–525. doi:10.1080/08838151.2010.498851

This research was previously published in Analyzing the Strategic Role of Social Networking in Firm Growth and Productivity edited by Vladlena Benson, George Saridakis, and Ronald Tuninga; pages 157-171, copyright year 2017 by Business Science Reference (an imprint of IGI Global).

Chapter 5
The Personalized and Personal "Mass" Media – From "We-Broadcast" to "We-Chat":
Reflection on the Case of Bi Fujian Incident

Yu Zhang

New York Institute of Technology, USA

ABSTRACT

China's two major social media, the microblog Weibo and the messaging service WeChat have played important roles in representing citizens' voices and bringing about social changes. They often grow an ordinary event into a national debate as in the case of the Bi Fujian incident. They have also turned ordinary Chinese citizens into amateur reporters, empowering them to influence on issues that matter to them. An equalizer of power and discourse opportunity, the personalized and personal social media "weapons" are delivering the much needed social justice and consolation to the Chinese citizens amid widespread injustice, inequality, hypocrisy, indifference and corruption in the Chinese society.

INTRODUCTION

In a widely circulated home video on WeChat, according to the *Guardian* (Guardian, 2015), Bi Fujian, the host of a talent show at China's flagship state television station, the CCTV (China Central Television), was entertaining his companions at a private dinner by mimicking an old Chinese revolutionary song about Communist Party-led soldiers fighting bandits in northeastern China in the 1940s. Based on media reports, to the laughter of those guests, Bi inserted improvised comments in a speaking voice between the lyrics. After the part that mentioned China's late paramount leader Mao Zedong, he used a vulgar Chinese insult, and said "he has ruined us all" (Guardian, 2015). He also mocked the soldiers' battles as meaningless and the song's claim of victory boastful. The WeChat video went instantly viral across China. The incident renewed debate both on free speech and about Mao, who many Chinese blame for the disastrous 1959-1961 famine and the decade-long (1966-1976) chaotic Cultural Revolution. However,

DOI: 10.4018/978-1-5225-9869-5.ch005

Bi's remarks also drew sharp criticisms from the state media and Mao's many loyal and vocal followers (Guardian, 2015) despite the fact that his policies have been discontinued and critiqued. The revolutionary leader, whose portrait still hangs on Tiananmen Rostrum, remains a source of legitimacy for the Chinese Communist Party (CCP). The identity of the person(s) who taped and released the video remain a mystery.

In recent years, the Chinese microblog (Weibo), the Chinese version of Twitter, and WeChat (Weixin 微信) play an increasingly important role in transforming a local or trivial event into a national issue. Chinese netizens' intensive and extensive discussion often add provoking meanings and value to that event and frequently turn a seemingly insignificant issue into major national event. With the help of WeChat and Weibo, citizen journalism and online public opinion increasingly influence the behaviors of traditional media and government. This paper investigates the Bi Fujian parody case with regard to WeChat and Weibo. It argues that this kind of "silent" or less vocal expression, which differs from Weibo's "broadcasting" style, has become an influential way for netizens to engage in civic discourse. It also makes the state censorship less effective by upsetting the media and public agenda.

Following a literature review on Chinese social media, my study will use the Bi Fujian case and the phenomena of WeChat and Weibo to examine the following areas: 1), the differences between Weibo and WeChat, and why more people began to favor WeChat as their choice of social media. 2), the paper argues that not all censorship is political in nature and some may be legitimate and beneficial to the society. 3), social media upset as well as reset public agenda and media agenda. 4), balance, responsibility and compromise between the netizens and the state are needed when it comes to information and speech liberalization and legitimate limitations. 5), WeChat and Weibo serve as an equalizer of social and political power and discourse opportunity. 6), these personalized social media deliver the much needed social justice to the Chinese citizens amid widespread injustice, inequality, indifference and corruption in the Chinese society.

LITERATURE REVIEW

In China's communication and political systems, the media are instruments through which the Party propagates its ideologies and government policies (Pan, 2000). However, with the rapid development of the social media, optimism and even excitement about its ability to derail state agenda-setting capacity and transfer some of that agenda setting power to the public has been high (Chiu, Ip, & Silverman, 2012). As the "singing" incident demonstrates, citizen-generated events on social media has become an important news source for professional media, such as the official *Xinhua News Agency, People's Daily* and *CCTV*, which all have covered this case. Some other sensitive issues, such as the sudden collapsing of residential buildings, have also attracted national media who join the social media to demand the government agencies and authorities to be more accountable and transparent.

Some studies disagree on how effective social media can be. For example, a study by Pew Research Center and Rutgers University (Center, 2014) finds that social media actually weakens instead of enhancing people's engagement in expressing their opinions especially when they differ from their friends due to a spiral of silence impact (Center, 2014). However, other scholars have argued that discourses are more than expressions of meaning or emotion, they construct or build the world, and as such can serve as a form of an empowerment or power brokering (Poster, 1995; Stockmann D., 2014). Chinese civic discourse, which has been transformed by the emergence of the social media, is citizens' collective voice on public affairs regardless of their socio-economic class (Chen, 2014; Sullivan, 2012; King,

Pan, & Roberts, 2013). It is both countering and complementary to the authoritative discourse and elitist discourse (Pell, 1995). Besides censorship, commercialization of Chinese media also deprives Chinese citizens of the opportunity for open civic discourse. Pressure from advertisers and ratings render the media programs and their contents to become hegemonic and homogenized and restrictions on length and content render making real statements near impossible (Xu, 2012).. Besides, the contents can be edited by the gatekeepers, thus distorting and degrading civic discourses.

The Chinese government's strict censorship policies, and control over Internet appear to have paradoxically resulted in a vibrant proliferation of online creative public discourse and folk narratives (Esarey & Qiang, 2011). For example, to bypass the censorship, netizens often uncensored alternative but similarly sounding Chinese words, taking advantage of the features of the Chinese language. One explanation for the paradox is that after years of censorship and suppression, Chinese citizens have finally found a discursive outlet on social media (Economist, 2013; Leibold, 2011). Citizen online discourse has become so popular even the CCP often listens to the comments, suggestions, and complaints (Luo, 2014). Weibo and WeChat articulate an individual-to-public agenda, which competes with the state agenda and expands these alternative public platforms. They also promote expression of personal emotions, concerns, and opinions on public affairs, and pushes the government for transparency and accountability (Wang, 2013; Chen, 2014). The intensive discussions on various events and accidents often triggered broader national debates on issues such as celebrity behaviors, product safety, official corruption, and government transparency (Gu, 2014; Xu, 2012). Weibo discussion on villagers' protests of local corruption, land seizure, and police power abuse have upset the state agenda in portraying a harmonious society through the mainstream media. Weibo and WeChat enable a self-organized network of contentious politics, simply by aggregating and scaling up grievances from ordinary citizens without conventional organization or a coherent collective identity (Chen, 2014). If a case trigged by social media quickly gains national attention and thus becomes more sustainable, it eventually generates discussions on the political system and development policy (Esarey & Qiang, 2011). Agenda-setting theory (McCombs, 2005) emphasizes the media's role as a central gatekeeper to construct the social reality in the public's mind and that the media can transfer the salience of issues on media agenda to the public agenda. According to Cairns (Cairns, 2013), agenda setting is a powerful tool the CCP relies on to influence public opinion. By directing toward and concentrating on reporting a particular topic, the media "help" the public find which issues and topics are important by virtue of the mere fact that they are reported on or not. While reporters do have some discretion to cover these topics, they nevertheless follow the Party line to avoid censorship or professional consequences (Cairns, 2013). It is argued that agenda setting as a form of soft-power, is superior to censorship when it comes to thought control (Cairns, 2013), as the latter often encounters resistance whereas the former can seep through people's minds and hearts to influence. Besides, while human censors can sometimes remove an online critical post almost as soon as it is created, but damaging messages may spread when a censor hesitates or consulting with their supervisors (Stockmann D., 2014; Stockmann & Gallagher, 2011). Thus, the Chinese government has realized that a more sophisticated way to exert state influence over public discourse is by allowing selective dissent that acknowledges the issue. For example, Xi's anti-corruption campaign encourages media to report on previous taboos, such as high-level CCP corruption to convince the public that this CCP leadership is very serious in curbing corruption. This serves to both dampen online rumors about a specific case and to take a preemptive strike against any criticisms. In this capacity, despite its temporary reputational costs, this proactive approach enhances the Party's long-term reputation and thus is able to influence the public in a positive way.

A TALE OF TWO SOCIAL MEDIA

The spectacular development of the Chinese social media is epitomized by the growth of Weibo and WeChat. Their unique niche and role in Chinese society lie in their abilities to reach and influence the masses in a personal way. In a society where information and media are still tightly controlled, the public quickly embraced the two "personal" and "personalized" media. Within two months of the launch of Sina Weibo in August 2009, it amassed one million users, and by its eighth month, 10 million (Millward, 2012). Within less than two years of Weibo's inception, numbers increased to 249 million in 2011 (CNNIC, Statistics report of Chinese internet development, 2012). The Sina Weibo as China's most popular "Twitter" has richer multimedia functionalities than Twitter (Chiu, Ip, & Silverman, 2012). Besides, Weibo's 140-Chinese-character limit allows more information to be transmitted than Twitter due to the nature and feature of the Chinese characters, which contain more information than the English words especially in permutation (Li J., 2014). The Twitter-like Weibo allows for immediate distribution of information from grassroots sources including photos and videos as a platform for snippets of interesting news and conversation flows on socially popular topics.

WeChat, on the other hand, resembles Facebook, but offers heightened privacy in communicating among an exclusive friend circle. Launched in 2011, WeChat, known as Weixin (微信) in Chinese, attracted 50 million users in the first year and over 400 million users globally (Hong, 2013). WeChat's identity as a private communication platform, to some degree, insulates it from censorship. Besides, the volume of explicit political discourse on WeChat is very small (Sloan, 2014). WeChat's privacy barriers has created a social networking space that respects the Chinese psyche and society against sharing some information and opinions in unlimited public (Simcott, 2014). This mobile messaging app focuses on communication among close friends and provides more intimate and private social-networking experiences than many other social media including Facebook (Millward, 2012; Zoo, 2014). However, beyond its appearance as a tool of one-on-one interaction, it is also a personal mass media. WeChat's easy-to-use feature and private nature are an efficient way to stay in touch with a personal but potentially enormous circle.

FROM TOWN SQUARES TO TEAHOUSES

Weibo, once China's major online oasis for vibrant debate, saw a drop of fifty-six million users in 2014 alone from 331 to 275 million accounts (CNNIC, Statistics report of Chinese internet development, 2014). Acting to ban posts that threatened national security, reputation or interests, the Chinese authorities closed the Weibo accounts of several prominent critics of government known as the Big Vs. One of them, Charles Xue, was arrested for soliciting prostitutes, although his role as a government critic on Weibo was a key reason he was targeted (Hatton, 2015). Another reason for Weibo's decline is the rise of WeChat, a mobile messaging platform, whose growing popularity and unmatched convenience, has quickly attracted millions of users. Its invitation-only format was disarming to government censors but its seeping power increasingly worries the authorities. If Weibo is a town square or concert stadium, WeChat resembles a chain of private tea houses, where conversation flows like tap water from home to home quietly but quickly. It thrives by filling the opinion void the government neglects and the public wants. For example, stopping local authorities from trampling citizens' rights, such as demolishing their homes or exposing hypocrisy of public figures is powerfully contagious. While these exposures constitute no threat to the CCP, the state is concerned with the power of online discourses and has implemented a new rule: Individuals could face up to three years in prison if their "rumor" posts are viewed 5,000+ times or forwarded 500+ times (Zhao, 2013).

The popularity of WeChat signifies a shift of the trend and paradigm of social media towards a more personal and private mass media model. While both Weibo and WeChat put facts and objectivity to test in a new type of social environment, where diverse incipient masses of civic discourses interpret the discourses as they are constructed and transmitted, WeChat users align themselves with their more personalized audiences to create an alternative civic and news discourse that differs from that of the dominant media. The most significant difference between WeChat and Weibo is in the convergence of their discourse production and consumption processes, which is a new participatory civic engagement model. Weibo allows users to post, share or broadcast brief and personal messages in a virtual town square where people can discuss almost anything. However, its huge user base and town-square format attract growing government scrutiny, resulting in many uncomfortable users switching to rival WeChat, which only lets people see posts from accounts they subscribe to. Because information spreads more slowly on WeChat, the platform has been less of a censorship target. The state media, which are renowned for their turgidity, especially in their print edition, now use social media to publish or promote their news in a livelier and more casual fashion, trying to broaden the party's reach by using unconventional language and popular language to appeal to the masses.

The anonymity to share one's ideas, opinions or videos, as in the Bi Fujian case, in an uninhibited manner make the netizens feel socially connected in an increasingly indifferent Chinese society. WeChat allows people to feel personal although users know that sharing within a small group always means the possibility to share with the masses outside this group--the message may even reach national masses as in the case of Bi Fujian. In the past, the Chinese citizens have few ways to be part of the media's agenda-setting process or start any collective action through the state controlled media (Gu, 2014). Therefore, when social media became available, Chinese citizens quickly realized its agenda-setting and agenda-upsetting power. As in the above case of celebrity Bi Fujian, the person who released this video does not even have to say a word to make his/her point—exposing the hypocrisy of a Party-state media host and the CCTV that made him a national celebrity, and triggered a storm. In other cases, government officials were dismissed or otherwise punished because of the public outcry on Weibo and WeChat, which have become the most dynamic personal mass media for Chinese netizens due to their agenda-setting ability. The quick communication model of Weibo and WeChat, from individual to intertwined groups and to the masses, allow them to seep and expand their boundaries to engage in civic journalism. Its many functions, from text and voice messaging to photo sharing, allow, for example, WeChat users to form a closely knit group, who might want to organize around any given idea or cause. According to *New Zoo* (2014) a social media monitoring website, Tencent, the Chinese Internet company that owns WeChat, also has a PC-based messaging app QQ, whose group chats has about 800 million active monthly users. The growth and consolidation of WeChat and QQ make its potential even more powerful.

IS STATE CONTROL ALL BAD?

The remarks by Bi Fujian, who is a public figure of the state CCTV, embarrassed both the state and CCTV and enraged millions of Chinese citizens. This and other incidents are magnified by the social media and often catch authorities and the masses by surprise. For many years, the Chinese government's dual strategies of information control target both domestic and foreign information contents and sources

(Economist, 2013). Its Great Firewall blocks foreign websites such as YouTube, Facebook and Twitter, while its Golden Shield watch Internet activity within China. Government agencies have invested heavily in manpower and software to track and analyze online behavior, both to gauge public opinion and to contain threats before they spread (Economist, 2013). The Bi Fujian case reminds the government that its "great firewall" and the "golden shield" could do nothing to prevent the release of information or image that could trigger a national debate about Chinese politics. Almost all Chinese internet users have a social media account and spend more time than netizens in other nations (Chiu, Ip, & Silverman, 2012).

China's big four internet service providers, Sina, Tencent, Sohu, and Netease were informed in March 2012 to enforce the state policy of registering users with their real identities (all four companies provide microblog or Weibo services), but the enforcement is so ineffective that the government has to remind them every year (Li, 2015; Lynch, 2015). The government outlaws anonymity in blogs, social networks, online forums and IM services, saying that fake accounts impersonate celebrity, government departments or pretend to be media organizations and release fake news (Hatton, 2015; Li J., 2014; King, Pan, & Roberts, 2013). The media and Western critics usually characterize these restrictions under the umbrella of censorship without seeing any legitimacy in this. However, what are considered unacceptable screen names by the Chinese government might not be welcome in the Western society either. These include anything harmful to the nation, fans ethnic discrimination, spreading rumor or relate to violence, etc. (Lynch, 2015). The identity of the person (s) who taped and released the video about Bi Fujian remains a mystery although the content of the video is not related to any of the banned category. It can be argued that many would like to know the identity of the person, but it can also be argued that if the person knows that he/she can be identified, the person might never have released the video. His freedom or restriction to "speak" affects the public's right to know and ability to debate about the contentious issue surrounding a public figure.

The government insists on identifying users of social media, requiring authentic names registration, and banning misleading personal handles such as "Clinton" or "Xinhua News" in blogs, microblogs, IM services, online forums, news comment sections and related services, according to the Cyberspace Administration of China (Li, 2015; Lynch, 2015). Netizens can still select their own personal usernames that do not involve "illegal, unhealthy or fake" contents and accounts that had "polluted the cyber environment, harmed the interests of the public, and seriously violated socialist values" (Lynch, 2015). The new regulations specifically ban nine categories of usernames and contents, including anything that harms or compromises national security, national secrets, incites ethnic discrimination/hatred, or harms national unity. Names that promote pornography, swindling, gambling, violence, terror, superstition, religious cults, and rumors are also banned (Lynch, 2015). CCP views the Internet as an ideological battleground it cannot afford to lose. Chinese President Xi Jinping has created and personally chairs a new high-level committee on Internet security (Annonymous, 2014).

Western media, scholars and politicians almost always view the Chinese crackdown as bad censorship by an authoritarian regime. The Chinese government has argued that identifying users and verifying their information and tracking their activities can bring increased credibility and integrity to the media and the online environment in general. Also, the Chinese government's blocking of Western social media players such as Twitter and Facebook is usually perceived in the West and academic community from the perspective of censorship only. However, the encouragement and protection of homegrown competitors are part of the reason for such blocking. For example, without the competition from Western social media, Sina Weibo has grown to be popular social network in China, with about 300 million active users and 600 million registered users (Simcott, R., February 27, 2014).. Its multimedia functions, displaying video and photos in timelines, even predated Twitter's rollout of these services. Sina Weibo's competitor Tencent Weibo has more than 230 million active users or a base of 507 million users, thanks to Tencent's instant messaging service, QQ. WeChat has become even more popular and competitive than Weibo with over 300 million users who are attracted by its combining features of Twitter, Facebook, Skype, Instagram and geo-location apps. (Simcott, R. February 27, 2014).

In contrast to the polarizing national debate about the freedom of public and private speech as indicated in the case of the video clip about Bi Fujian, a rare consensus between the Chinese masses and the Chinese government on censorship is in the area of pornography, rumor, fraud and violence. Over the years, the Chinese public have been creating social and psychological cyberspace to explore traditional taboo areas such as pornography and sexual identities as well as facilitating and promoting a porn culture, with widespread and lucrative sex entertainment across the nation (Jacobs, 2012). Ironically, even websites of state media such as the *Xinhua News* agency, *People's Daily* and *CCTV* contain links to provoking pictures and content. On the other hand, as the Bi video incident has shown, the fragmented, decentralized and anonymous nature of the social media postings and their posters makes it difficult to trace and verify their identities. As a result, unidentified and unverified malicious messages, such as rumors or computer viruses can cause harm and sabotage social integrity.

AGENDA UPSETTING

There is no doubt that the Chinese government is mixing "hard" censorship with a "soft" persuasive approach when it comes to social media. By allowing and encouraging critical views and discussion in the case of the video clip of Bi Fujian, the state actually benefits from the explosive critical comments against those who are disrespectful of Mao Zedong and the Party. On the other hand, this video exposed the hypocrisy of the politically correct image of CCTV and its host. Such silent but smart protests on Weibo and WeChat can potentially snowball from issue-specific criticisms into a sweeping denouncement of the CCP and its leadership reminiscent of the weeks leading to the 1989 Tiananmen event. While a crisis can prompt an outburst of public opinion in social media, how government responds can either alleviate or worsen an incident like this. In the Bi Fujian incident, the government took a balanced response, which has served to pacify both the Left, who criticized the defamation of Mao by a public figure, and the Right who insisted on protecting the freedom to speak. The state CCTV fired Bi but did not arrest or charge him. He could have been imprisoned or executed during the era of the Cultural Revolution.

Zhan Zhang and Gianluigi Negro argued that Weibo's roles as alternative media and new journalism foster civic engagement to achieve justice (Zhang & Negro, 2013). They believe that Weibo, as a platform for opinion leaders, maximizes individual power for social impact, and as a public administration tool, keeps netizens informed. The Weibo platform synergistically combines personal, interpersonal and mass communication elements in an intertwined way in disseminating information and creating new ways of communicating. According to Pan (2010), authoritarian regimes can, through content aggregation, generate collective opinion, turning a "private" opinion suddenly into a "public" opinion. What individuals say on the social media can ultimately contributes to and often becomes the collective opinions. Thus a few online activists can often lead or grow an army of critics to speak out on issues that matter to the public, such as corruption or environmental disaster. What is empowering is that individual Chinese citizens, whom the government usually ignores, can trigger overwhelming opinions from other netizens to collectively criticize the status quo, as in the case of the Bi Fujian incident. The state fears this phenomenon of a firestorm of criticism and commentary, especially when it is hard to identify those behind it and that the potential for those views to snowball into massive protest, online or offline, is huge and real.

Cairns (2013) argues that even without any spin, the media's ability to bring certain thoughts to the public can influence their political stances. Since media only reports on topics of which the government approves or tolerates to support CCP's claims to legitimacy, the result is to shift citizens' prioritization of issues and positions closer to the government's position. For example, two Chinese navy warships rescued 571 Chinese nationals stranded in the Yemen crisis in early 2015 (BBC, 2015). The state media reported that Chinese soldiers only ate pickles - while the citizens they rescued ate like kings. This triggered a wave of scorn on Chinese social media. Rather than being impressed, many Chinese netizens seemed furious and sarcastic about the story, calling the scenes either a misjudged publicity stunt, or simply a reflection of incompetence of navy officers. "Where is military expenditure going?" read one comment on Sina Weibo. If an eight course meal was on offer, the passengers and soldiers could have had four courses each, many pointed out. The story attracted tens of thousands of comments on Sina Weibo.

Despite the challenge, supervision and competition from the social media, the resilience of the "authoritarian" Chinese government has puzzled and impressed the world. The CCP is successful in persuading the public of its legitimacy as well as capable of balancing between censorship and producing exciting media content to keep it in power. For example, its recent state-led project, the China Dream, not only enhances CCP's political legitimization but also fosters heightened national identity and pride and cultivates a nationalistic chorus against Western ideologies and influences. It is not surprising that Bi Fujian is harshly criticized for attacking Mao, who remains a fetish, a national hero and a symbol for many Chinese. President Xi Jinping has fostered greater eagerness to cherish China's inner strength and historic glory to push for the realization of the China dream and to uncover China's historical and cultural past in a quest for a new identity and rejuvenation in the new era.

Social media as a nexus of revealed and disguised identity, ideology and people's everyday lives reflect Chinese collective inspirations for political representations. The voluminous chats surrounding the video clip of Bi Fujian on social media articulate the collective Chinese identity based on the memories of the Mao era. According to Chen Wenhong, social media reflects many contradictions and complexities of Chinese society (Chen, 2014). To resolve these social problems, WeChat and Weibo can help by pushing transparency and enhancing the visibility of oppressed groups by putting the control button in the hands of average Chinese citizens as demonstrated in a growing number of online incidents in recent years. While some studies have celebrated and praised social media, other scholars doubt whether they alone can achieve any genuine political or social changes, arguing that China has been successful in harnessing the power of the Internet without significant political changes (Whyte, 2010; Zhang, 2015; Luo, 2014).

However, the rising tide of activism and discourses on social media, despite state surveillance and control, challenge the legitimacy of the CCP's political power especially on issues that matter to the public such as livelihood, environmental, and social justice. The Chinese government has not only invested enormous technological and human resources on censorship but also on influencing public opinion, for example, using Weibo and WeChat for surveillance as well as mobilization of its citizens. Digital activism and civic engagement are safety valve (Chen, 2014) that allow people to vent their frustration and thus reduce the dangerous pressures felt by Chinese society and force a dialogue and negotiation between the state and civil community through social media. In B's case, the social media stormy discussion not only magnifies and adds fuel to the debates between conservatives and reformers, but also forces into the open the reconsideration of what constitutes private speech and what is not. While China regularly criminalizes certain political speech, it is also a nation where most people still feel they can talk freely among friends or at a dinner table. However, this case reminds the public that the pervasiveness of technology such as smartphones and social media can threaten the cozy social oasis more than state censorship. The combination of smartphones and WeChat could be a killer as well as savior. The Bi Fujian case raises the issue of behavior and speech on and in front of the social media and the consequences. In this case, it ended Bi's career with the prestigious CCTV.

LIBERALIZATION WITH LEGITIMATE LIMITATION

Chinese leaders have long been skeptical and dismissive of the Western style media freedom as trouble-inducing and damaging to China, believing that it will cause China chaos and to dissolve like the former Soviet Union. Despite still believing that complete liberalization of media, information and speech is bad for China, the Chinese leaders now also believe that a certain degree of freedom is actually needed and good for China. For example, the power of amassing public opinions to supervise officials and public figures for their misconducts and reevaluating problematic policies and practices are especially attractive to the CCP leadership who now focus on fighting rampant corruption in the Chinese society. The public's hatred and disdain towards corrupt officials and their abuse of power is a driving force that contributed to the gradual dissolving and loosening of the state monopoly of information and speech. In China's conventional media, the Party-state can easily control the information flow, and information becomes a privilege for authorities but luxury for common citizens (Shao, Lu, & Wu, 2012). Traditional media, where content are subject to extensive editorial review and political monitoring, were unlikely to release the video clip regarding Bi, which embarrasses a state media and the CCP. Gu (2014) argued that due to the lack of alternative information channels, Chinese citizens could only passively succumb to the imposed messages from state media, which usually ignore citizens' concerns and complaints. Petitioning and appealing their cases or causes further are often cost prohibitive and emotionally difficult, and protesting on the street is often not allowed or ignored. Their basic rights of being heard are frequently trampled.

Cases like Bi's video indicate that Weibo and other social media are capable of breaking the power and information asymmetry and empower citizens to collect, report, analyze, disseminate and petition information via "citizen journalism" without having to seek approval from authority (Han, 2011). Social media and their threaded comments attract users to create, repost, and comment, and public discourse of all types, topics, styles, and persuasions have blossomed and flooded the cyber space (Leibold, 2011; Xu, 2012). Paradoxically, the Chinese government's censorship and control have resulted in a vibrant proliferation of online public discourse and folk narratives (Xu, 2012). Blocking the bursting information flood may not be as effective as diverting and guiding it. Some citizens' online opinions have become so helpful and popular that even the CCP has adopted these opinions (Sullivan, 2012) to help make policy changes.

Despite its role in censorship, the Chinese government undisputedly plays a central role in driving the exponential growth of the Chinese internet, helping break its own monopoly of information, and paving the way for the social media to flourish as an influential and democratic media for political and social discourses. According to the China Internet Network Information Center survey, China had 3.2 million websites by the end of December 2013, a growth rate of 19.4% from 2012. The overall Chinese instant messaging users grew to 532 million, up by 64.4 million over the end of 2012 and with a utilization ratio of up to 86.2% (CNNIC, 2014). The Chinese government has also invested heavily in the promotion of e-government and e-commerce projects. Nearly all national and local government agencies now have Weibo and/or WeChat public accounts (CNNIC, 2014).

AN EQUALIZER OF POWER AND DISCOURSE

WeChat and Weibo have replaced one-way communication, equalizing everyone with access to the Internet, from the powerful and elite to average citizens to the same status, netizens. Citizens are motivated to carrying out their discursive discourses in a virtual space, which are facilitated by the increasing technological ease and their desire to speak their minds. They transformed the once elite power communication and put ordinary citizens on an equal footing with the elite, who either control or are favored by state or traditional media. As the video clip incident has ironically and clearly shown, that Bi and the person who released the video are reversed in their roles overnight: from envious power figure to powerless ordinary citizen, and vice versa. As such, power discourse and communication are no longer a privilege reserved just for the elite. Weibo and WeChat have equalized everyone into a writer, editor, journalist, commentator, producer and director all in one. However, as mentioned earlier, the colorful and dynamic discourses are not always matched with quality and value in some contents.

Social media exposure often forces overturn of unjust decisions and promptly investigates corruption, bureaucracy, inefficiency and waste. The only caveat is that while the state allows and encourages the media to supervise local officials and public figures, it prohibits challenging the central government and top national leaders, projecting a "nice central but bad local" image to divert public resentment (Stockmann, 2014) toward corrupt officials rather than the CCP in general. The central government such as the State Council, the CCP Central Committee and the Politburo, and other politically significant institutions are usually shielded from negative coverage. The media still serve as a propaganda tool, portraying the top political institutions and leadership as righteous and benign (Yang & Tang, 2010).

The popularization of social media such as Weibo and WeChat has led to the liberalization of public discourse and provided the Chinese citizenry with new opportunities for political advocacy. These social media spaces empowered China's netizens and diminished the state's ability to set public agenda and shape political preferences with unprecedented power to counter the might of China's propaganda state (Esarey & Qiang, 2011). The power of Weibo and WeChat to liberalize civic discourse and facilitate public supervision of the state actors has radically transformed the relationship between state and societal actors.

The above mentioned cases of the Chinese navy and the Bi Fujian incident have shown that WeChat and Weibo have effectively broken the party-state's monopoly on discourses and mobilization. According to Esarey and Xiao (2011), various exposures of social media have contributed to the abolition of the custody and repatriation system for migrant workers, the halting of environmental problematic development projects, the overhaul of the criminal justice system, the reconsideration of wrongfully convicted murder cases, and the investigation and dismissal of Party officials. As mentioned above, the CCP encourages netizens to challenge immoral practices and corrupt officials but not the power of the Party. Anytime when an online rant against the official abuses of power is about to change direction or grow bigger, the nervous attention of the censors are attracted. Because Weibo and WeChat have become a battleground where the state does not necessarily win just because they have monopoly over most resources in shaping public opinion. Moreover, the CCP's strategy to harness and guide the social media and the power of public opinion does not always work: the masses do not always think what the state wants them to think, and unintended outcomes do develop.

SOCIAL JUSTICE ON SOCIAL MEDIA

For people who despise Bi Fujian and other hypocritical public figures who "eat (Chinese Communist) Party's meals but breaks Party's Wok," the inequality and injustice in today's Chinese society has betrayed Mao Zedong's vision. The WeChat incident and Bi's firing from CCTV can be seen as an indirect revenge–that justice is carried out by a social media weapon on behalf of the disadvantaged, the marginalized and the disenfranchised. The Party-state has built its legitimacy on economic growth and political stability, but China's rapid economic growth has both alleviated and caused glaring social inequalities. The distribution of prosperity gained through decades of economic reform has become increasingly uneven. While Bi is not necessarily that rich or that bad, the netizens are just happy that they have caught red-handed another representative of a privileged group, who is part of the Party propaganda machinery. While some online protest cases have been driven by narrowly defined socioeconomic or environmental injustice rather than specific political claims, and protesters seek for solutions within the current Chinese political system, some participants are not necessarily direct victims of injustice or deprivation.

The right to freedom of speech is voraciously pursued and exercised by a population that previously had no outlet for such a type of critical public discourse (Xu, 2012). Pan (2010) argued that the competition and fight for the articulation between the state media and social media is common. Articulation on social media allows citizens to sustain, repair, or fortify as well as amend, resist, or erode an agenda. Social media's democratizing potentials to advance an agenda or a point of view, or simply coordinate some oppositional discourse or collective actions, are irresistible. Within the state-society framework, a vitalized and unofficially organized netizens strongly and creatively resist the authoritarian state to articulate their agenda or interests. To netizens, the opportunities to express is also an opportunity to impress and to make that voice matter. Viewed in this light, the persistent inequality and injustice in political and civic participation are alleviated with the help of social media such as WeChat and Weibo.

CONCLUSION

WeChat and Weibo have provided the Chinese citizens with an unprecedented ability and opportunity to challenge the dominance of the state discourses, without the limitation of time and space. As in the cases of Bi Fujian incident and the navy rescue, not only are the freedom and decisions of posting information generally controlled by posters themselves, the convenient, accessible, autonomous and interactive platform keeps citizens current on what is going on, often in real time. As an equalizer and highly grass-root technology, Weibo and WeChat allow netizens equal rights to freely narrate his/her own story and contribute to the social and civic dynamics by synergizing and combining individual voices to exert powerful impact. As a public oasis for citizens to engage in social and public affairs and vent dissatisfactions without physically protesting in the streets, they empower citizens to collect and analyze current social issues.

As a game-changer, WeChat and Weibo have turned the conventional one-way surveillance censorship into an engaging mutual monitoring, and empower Chinese citizens to supervise and comment on the conduct of public figures and officials. Despite state efforts at various censorship, WeChat and Weibo have boosted and contributed to China's democratization by breaking down the state information monopoly and providing citizens with more opportunities to access, analyze, post and exchange information. However, they defied the imagination and prediction of the Western technological determinants, who believed that information technology would compel the state toward a Western-style democracy.

The gradual shift and preference by Chinese netizens from town square styled "we broadcast" Weibo to tea-house kind of "we chat" personal, personalized and mass "conversation" are even more effective to evade and meander through censorship as in the case of Bi Fujian incident. Both the participatory and interactive nature of WeChat and Weibo force authorities to relax information censorship. Even the state news organizations now routinely leverage, publicize and rely on public comments from these social media to attract the public, which creates a new information environment where the participation of amateur citizen "journalists" are forcing the state and professional journalists to become competitive sense-makers instead of the parrots of the Party lines.

REFERENCES

Anonymous. (2014, February 28). *Xi to lead CCP group on Internet safety and information.* Retrieved from Sina News: http://news.sina.com.cn/o/2014-02-28/042029584155.shtml

Cairns, C. (2013). Air pollution, social media, and responsive authoritarianism in China. *UCLA Compass Conference.* Los Angeles, CA: UCLA.

Center, P. R. (2014, August 27). *The 'Spiral of Silence' on Social Media.* Retrieved from http://www.pewinternet.org/2014/08/27/the-spiral-of-silence-on-social-media/

Chen, W. (2014). *Taking stock, moving forward: The Internet, social network and civic engagement in Chinese societies.* Academic Press.

Chiu, C., Ip, C., & Silverman, A. (2012, April). Understanding social media in China. *McKinsey Quarterly.* Retrieved from http://www.mckinsey.com/insights/marketing_sales/understanding_social_media_in_china

CNNIC. (2012). *Statistics report of Chinese internet development.* Retrieved from China Internet Network Research Center: http://www1.cnnic.cn/

CNNIC. (2014). *Statistics report of Chinese internet development.* Retrieved from China Internet Network Research Center: http://www1.cnnic.cn/

Economist. (2013, April 6). China's internet: A giant cage. *Economist.* Retrieved from economist.com

Esarey, A., & Qiang, X. (2011). Digital communication and political change in China. *International Journal of Communication, 5,* 298–319.

Gu, Q. (2014). Sina Weibo: A mutual communication apparatus between the Chinese government and Chinese citizens. *China Media Research, 10*(2).

Guardian. (2015, April 10). *Chinese broadcaster apologizes for Mao Zedong insults.* Retrieved from The Guardian: http://www.theguardian.com/world/2015/apr/10/chinese-broadcaster-apologises-mao-zedong-insults-bi-fujian

Hatton, C. (2015, February 24). *Is Weibo on the way out?* Retrieved from BBC News: http://www.bbc.com/news/blogs-china-blog-31598865

Hong, K. (2013, July 3). *Tencent's WeChat chalks up 70 million users outside of China thanks to aggressive global marketing.* Retrieved from http://thenextweb.com/asia/2013/07/03/tencents-wechat-chalks-up-70-million-users-outside-of-china-thanks-to-agg

King, G., Pan, J., & Roberts, M. (2013). How Censorship in China Allows Government Criticism but Silences collective expression. *The American Political Science Review*, *107*(2), 326–343. doi:10.1017/S0003055413000014

Leibold, J. (2011, November). Blogging alone: China, the internet, and the democratic illusion? *The Journal of Asian Studies*, *70*(4), 1023–1041. doi:10.1017/S0021911811001550

Li, J. (2014, April 14). *'Twitter' and 'Facebook' of China are best frenemies.* Retrieved from Market Watch: http://www.marketwatch.com/story/twitter-and-facebook-

Li. (2015, January 14). *China to force social media users to declare their real names.* Retrieved from South China Morning Post: http://www.scmp.com/news/china/article/1679072/china-beefs-social-media-rules-forcing-people-use-real-name-registration?page=all

Luo, Y. (2014). The Internet and agenda setting in China: The influence of online public opinion on media coverage and government policy. *International Journal of Communication*, 8, 1289–1312.

Lynch, A. (2015, February 4). *China demanding real names be used on social media.* Retrieved from Lighthouse News Daily: http://www.lighthousenewsdaily.com/china-

McCombs, M. (2005). A look at agenda-setting: Past, present and future. *Journalism Studies*, *6*(4), 543–557. doi:10.1080/14616700500250438

Millward, S. (2012, May 30). *The rise of social media in China with all new user numbers.* Retrieved from Tech in Asia: http://www.techinasia.com/rise-of-china-socialmedia-infographic-2012/

Pan, Z. (2010). *Articulation and Re-articulation: Agenda for understanding media and communication in China.* Academic Press.

Pell, C. (1995). Civil Discourse is Crucial for Democracy to Work. *Insight (American Society of Ophthalmic Registered Nurses)*, *11*(37), 13.

Poster, M. (1995). *The second media age.* Cambridge, MA: Polity Press.

Simcott, R. (2014, February 27). *Social media fast facts: China. Social Media Today.* Retrieved from Social Media Today: http://www.socialmediatoday.com/content/social-media-fast-facts-china

Sloan, A. (2014, March 19). *China's suprise freedom of speech crackdown on WeChat.* Retrieved from https://www.indexoncensorship.org/2014/03/chinas-suprise-freedom-speech-crackdown-wechat/

Stockmann, D. (2014). *Media commercialization and authoritarian rule in China.* Cambridge University Press.

Stockmann, D., & Gallagher, M. (2011). Remote control: How the media sustains authoritarian rule in China. *Comparative Political Studies*, *44*(4), 436–467. doi:10.1177/0010414010394773

Sullivan, J. (2012). A tale of two microblogs in China. *Media Culture & Society*, 774–783.

Wang, W. Y. (2013). Weibo, framing, and media practices in China. *Journal of Chinese Political Science*, *18*(4), 375–388. doi:10.100711366-013-9261-3

Xu, Y. (2012). Understanding netizen discourse in China: Formation, genres, and values. *China Media Research, 8*(1).

Zhao, Y. (2013, September 23). *Anti-graft watchdog told to convey results*. Retrieved from China Daily: http://www.chinadaily.com.cn/china/2013-

Zoo, N. (2014). *Introduction to the Chinese games markets*. Retrieved from New Zoo: http://www.pro-elios.com/wp-content/uploads/2014/03/China-Games-Market-Newzoo-Report-2014.pdf

This research was previously published in Defining Identity and the Changing Scope of Culture in the Digital Age edited by Alison Novak and Imaani Jamillah El-Burki; pages 29-42, copyright year 2016 by Information Science Reference (an imprint of IGI Global).

Chapter 6
Radical Political Communication and Social Media:
The Case of the Mexican #YoSoy132

Lázaro M. Bacallao-Pino
National Autonomous University of Mexico, Mexico

ABSTRACT

This chapter aims to analyze the practices of radical political communication within the context of social mobilizations whose emergence and initial spreading are inherently associated to social media. On the basis of a case study -the #YoSoy132, a university student mobilization during the 2012 electoral campaign in Mexico- the text analyzes the main uses of social media as part of the mobilizations and the interrelationships between online (communication) and offline collective action. The author concludes that, despite the importance of social media and the collective actions based on their use, even the participants recognize the necessity of going beyond the online space. Although social media pluralize the actors of political communication and even force its traditional actors to participate in alternative communication spaces, collective communicative action cannot be confined to the digital space, but it must be understood within the processes of social mobilization, in all its articulations and mediations.

INTRODUCTION

The increasing role of the information and communication technologies (ICTs) in everyday practices of communication in general and, particularly, in political communication, has become a relevant topic of research in contemporary societies (Bentivegna, 2006). At the same time, social movements and mobilizations have also become a relevant issue for social theories and research. In the articulation of these two trends, the analyses on the ICTs have underlined, on the one hand, its contribution for enabling processes of participation and democratic dynamics and, on the other hand, have criticized certain tendencies to a technological determinism. Those debates have increased with the emergence of social media, associated to openness, freedom and horizontality and a richer user experience and an architecture of participation (Vickery & Wunsch-Vincent, 2007).

DOI: 10.4018/978-1-5225-9869-5.ch006

Social mobilizations put in practice a significant appropriation of ICTs as part of their collective action that has been associated to the emergence of new cyber-based repertoires of contention and the development of horizontal forms of organization by those collective actors. This tendency leads to the peculiarities of the political communication as part of this collective phenomena. In that regard, the chapter aims to critically analyze the appropriation of social media as resources for radical political communication within the context of social mobilizations by people who are not traditional political militants. Radical political communication refers to the specifically sociopolitical-oriented communicative practices by counterhegemonic groups, that aim at explicitly questioning and challenging the mainstream political communication — i.e., the political communication by institutional hegemonic groups, such as political parties.

If social movements are counter-institutions — this is, absolute negations of the institutions that try to configure another institutional regime, alternative to the modern one (Alonso, 1986) — that give a significant importance to the communicative dimension (Kavada, 2005), then these collective actors may be considered as particularly challenging agents against the practices of communication by institutional political groups. Social movements have traditionally associated with practices of alternative communication (Alfaro, 2000), a notion that has been widely discussed. From a complex perspective, alternative communication refers to a participatory communicational model and, consequently: 1) it cannot be understood in terms of a communicational or technical alternative, nor a simple alternative use of media; and 2) "true alternative political communication projects" must have "a globalizing presence at the macro-political level" (Capriles, 2006, p. 305).

In that regard, radical political communication: 1) implies a participatory model of alternative communication; 2) overcomes an understanding of the communicational practices of social mobilizations and movements that is limited to a "citizen" and "non political" nature, a tendency derived from certain simplistic conceptualizations of these collective agents that place them out from politics; 3) goes beyond traditional concepts of radical political communication that are based on a very simple communication model and accept the idea that "whomsoever possesses the senders can control the throughs of humans" (Autonome a.f.r.i.k.a gruppe, 2003, p. 87); and 4) implies also an alternative understanding of politics, not as the activity associated with the traditional political agents such as political parties, but as "a space of accumulation of social, cultural and directly political forces" (Sader, 2001).

From this perspective, the text examines the main tendencies and dimensions mediating the online practices of digital radical political communication, in particular the online/offline tension, through the study of a relevant case of use of social media in the context of an electoral campaign: the Mexican #Yosoy132 (English: #Iam132). This was a mobilization led by students from both private and public universities that took place against the then presidential candidate of the Partido Revolucionario Institucional (PRI, English: Institutional Revolutionary Party) and current Mexican President, Enrique Peña Nieto, during the 2012 electoral campaign. The analysis focuses on the period between 23 May and 1 July 2012, when the #YoSoy132 published its foundational statement and elections were held, respectively. During this period, mobilizations and the electoral campaign coincided in time.

THEORETICAL AND CONTEXTUAL BACKGROUND

Social movements and mobilizations put in practice, as part of their collective action, certain repertoires of contention (Tarrow, 1998; Tilly, 1995), a notion that firstly focused on "public display of disruptive action", while most recent works have moved towards "broader contentious performances, stressing the constant innovation in the various forms of contentious politics" (Della Porta, 2013). The uses of ICTs for collective action have lead to the configuration of an online repertoire of contention — including online sit-ins, signing online petitions, hacking, defacing web pages, email floods, etc.—, in what has been defined as cyber-activism (Van Laer & Van Aelst, 2009).

The new digital communicative scenario has fundamental effects on politics, in such a way that communication becomes the main space of politics (Castells, 2000). Discussions on the political impact of the ICTs have ranged from the analysis of the consequences of the Internet on traditional representative democracy (Davis et al., 2002), to the Internet's potential to revitalize the public sphere and produce a new regime of participatory democracy (Thornton, 2001) and a new scenario for democratic dynamics, the so-called cyberspace (Poster, 1997). As part of these debates, for instance, some approaches have discussed how the online practices contribute in advancing democratic dynamics beyond its conceptualizations within the liberal-capitalist political context (Dahlberg & Siapera, 2007), or the extension and pluralization of the public sphere as a result of cyberspace practices (Dahlgren, 2005). In a context characterized by diverse and even opposite perspectives (see Morozov, 2011; Dahlgren, 2005), these debates bring us to the impact of the ICTs —and, particularly, social media— in the current dynamics of political communication.

Social Media and Political Communication

Political communication is an extremely complex notion that refers to a vast field. In an overview of this concept and as part of an effort to operationalize it, Franklin (1995, p. 225) defines political communication as the study of "the interactions between media and political systems, locally, nationally, and internationally", arguing that it focuses on the analysis of the following dimensions: 1) the political context of the media; 2) the actors and agencies involved in the production of media content; 3) the impact of political media content on the audience and/or on policy development; 4) the impact of the political system on the media one; and 5) the impact of the media system on the political one. Norris (2004) also defines political communication as "an interactive process concerning the transmission of information among politicians, the news media and the public" that "operates down-wards from governing institutions towards citizens, horizontally in linkages among political actors and also upwards from public opinion towards authorities".

This interactive nature of political communication is relevant for the proposed analysis, since —as aforementioned— social media are associated with the increase of the enabling conditions for interactivity. At the same time, these Web 2.0 platforms emerge in a context that has been described in terms of "media malaise", a notion that refers to negative impact of the process of political communication has upon civic engagement, by considering that "common practices in political communications by the news media and by party campaigns hinder 'civic engagement', meaning citizens learning about public affairs, trust in government, and political activism" (Norris, 2000, p. 4).

Given this scenario — and in line with the shared interactive nature of social media and political communication — different authors have underlined that the emergence of the Web 2.0 — including communicational resources such as blogs, wikis and social networks — has produced relevant changes in political communication, its structures and dynamics (Feenstra & Casero-Ripollés, 2014), by providing to the citizens technological resources that enable them not only to consume but also to produce their own communicative products and spaces (Dylko & McCluskey, 2012). These technological resources empower people since they can find new spaces of autonomy on the Internet (Castells, 2009; Jenkins, 2006) and open the information environment to multiple groups that can create or incorporate new issues or topics into the public debate (Casero-Ripollés, 2010; Chadwick, 2011), fostering this way transparency as well as facilitating many-to-many communication processes and promoting citizen's interactivity (McNair, 2006).

However, there have been also some debates on the potential of social media as a source of change for political communication: while some authors consider that the role of social media in collective action generates "a new fetishism of technology", distracting people from the core contradictions of contemporary capitalism (Fuchs, 2012), others highlight that social media have generated new communicational practices, bringing new dynamism to public mobilization, fueling revolts and bringing about political transformation (Bardici, 2012).

On the one hand, previous analyses have discussed, for instance, the capacities of the Internet as community builder in a context of raising political disengagement and disenchantment (Davis et al., 2002). In this scenario, although the use of social networks — such as Twitter — for political communication has been considered as "another arena for already established societal actors", it has been noted that this use "also helps broadening the public debate, because chances for 'ordinary' citizens to get in touch and discuss with the establishment of political communication are much higher on Twitter than in traditional contexts of interaction" (Maireder et al., 2012, p. 160). But, at the same time, despite the general recognition of the increasingly important role played by social media in shaping political communication in contemporary societies (e.g., Aday et al., 2010; Tumasjan et al., 2011), other authors have noted that "until now the potentials of political discussions in social media involving political institutions could not be exploited sufficiently" (Stieglitz & Dang-Xuan, 2012). In the same line, Macnamara and Kenning (2011, p. 19) suggested that, although the raising level of use of social media and the volume of social media content used for political communication, "Web 2.0-enabled social media are being used primarily in election-related political communication for one-way transmission of messages, rather than engaging in listening, dialogue, consultation and collaboration", resembling mass media communication and the practices of journalism, advertising and public relations.

These debates add new polemic dimensions to previous debates on the communication of social movements, a dimension that, although recognized as a central one for these collective actors, has been been under-theorized and under-researched by the theories on collective action (Kavada, 2005). In that regard, the uses of social media by recent episodes of social mobilizations offer a complex view of the communicative dimension of collective action, overcoming these trends, and it also provides a relevant analytical scenario for the understanding of what can be considered as a social media-based radical political communication. While, as a result of its technological characteristics — user-generated content, architecture of participation, openness, freedom and horizontality —, there is a trend to underline the positive impact of social media in the communicational democratization, as we have seen before, a more complex perspective of it is needed.

A particularly relevant dimension of analysis is the online/offline tension within social media-based practices of radical political communication. Since these episodes of collective action are political performatives — in the sense of that "participants start to experience what they strive to become" (Arditi, 2012), in this case through the online communication — then online collective action becomes, at the same time, a space of radical political communication. In that regard, there are opposite positions regarding the interrelationships between the online and the offline dimensions of collective action. While some previous studies have shown cases in which social networks have been used to mobilize online movements that moved offline (Harlow, 2012), other researches suggested that "a significant increase in the use of the new media is much more likely to follow a significan amount of protest activity that to precede it" (Wolfsfeld, Segev, & Sheafer, 2013: 115).

From this perspective and taking into account these debates, we aim to analyze — through the case study of the #YoSoy132 — how the uses of social media mediate the configuration of collective action's practices of radical political communication. We will focus on the tension between online and offline communicative collective actions, proposing that it will mediate, in a central way, the enabling conditions for these social mobilizations to become sustained practices for citizen participation and, consequently, practices of radical political communication that challenge the mainstream one.

#YoSoy132 and the Mexican Political and Communicative Context

The emergence and initial spreading of the #YoSoy132 are inherently linked to social media. It emerged as a result of the popular support, via Twitter, to a university students' protest against the Mexican presidential candidate Enrique Peña Nieto, during the electoral campaign in 2012. A video of the protest — that took place on May 11, 2012, during his visit to the Ibero-American University, Mexico City — was uploaded onto social media, but mainstream Mexican television channels and newspapers reported that protesters were not students, in an effort to discredit the manifestation. Then, 131 students from the Ibero-American University published a video on YouTube identifying themselves by their university ID card and people showed their support to them by symbolically stating, mainly on Twitter, that they were the "132nd student," thus creating a hashtag #YoSoy132 giving birth and naming to the social mobilization.

The relevance of that mobilization for the analyses of the social media-based enabling conditions for the emergence of radical political communication is derived largely from the Mexican political system and media system context. The latter is characterized by a high level of concentration — the better example of this is Televisa, the largest Mexican multimedia mass media company and, after Organizações Globo (Brazil), the largest one in Latin America and the first of Spanish-speaking world — where social media offer new enabling possibilities for the development of autonomous dynamics of communication. Some studies have examined how the use and appropriation of ICTs — and, particularly, social networks sites — by the Mexican civil society can be considered as the basis for a process of democratization of mainstream media, fostering pluralism and triggering important processes related to political culture within the Mexican context (García & Treré, 2014).

There is a particular articulation between this media system concentration and the hegemonic Mexican politics. It has been dominated by the PRI for 71 years in the last century, being the party in power from 1929 to 2000. Due this, the PRI has been described by some scholars as a "state party" (MacLeod, 2005; Russell, 2009), a term that describes both the non-competitive history and character of the party itself, and the inextricable connection between the PRI and the Mexican nation-state for much of the 20th century. It configured an authoritarian system characterized by PRI's anti-democratic practices such as vote buying, electoral fraud and clientelism (Gómez Vilchis, 2013).

In the context where previous studies (LAPOP/Barómetro de las Américas 2010; Latinobarómetro, 2009) have noted that the Mexicans are profoundly disappointed of their democratic regime, different authors (Vázquez, 1997; Villamil, 2012) have analyzed the complicity among the media system — in particular the Televisa Group — and the PRI, describing it as "the perfect dictatorship", an institutional one where media groups defined themselves as "soldiers of the PRI" (Vargas Llosa, 1990). In this scenario, some authors have underlined the increasing importance of social media for political and social activism in Mexico, highlighting in particular the role of Twitter in influencing government decision-making and shaping the interrelationships between different socio-political actors, including governments, politicians, citizens and other stakeholders. In that regard, the #YoSoy132 has been considered a new influential actor within Mexican politics that have shown how, based on social media, political movements can emerge and evolve, by using those technological resources to communicate certain concerns and organize protests (Sandoval-Almazan & Gil-Garcia, 2013).

In that scenario, the #YoSoy132 becomes a relevant case for the analysis of the specificities of social media as sources for radical political communication both in content and form, since, on the one hand, it is a social media-based mobilization and, on the other hand, its primary and foundational claim was the democratization of communication and the freedom of expression. Besides this, it emerged in the context of an election campaign, that can be considered the most densely political communication scenario. Although some authors have proposed the notion of political marketing for the analysis of communicative processes "in the context of political communication in the immediate pre-election period" (Lock & Harris, 1996, p. 27), we prefer to notion of radical political communication since, although the #YoSoy132 was a social mobilization that emerged in the context of an election campaign and one of its goals was to avoid the election of the PRI's candidate, the objective of a democratization of communication points out to a social actor aiming for cultural change and a general process of transformation of the political communication.

In that regard, although the #YoSoy132 is understood here — following the Norris' (2000) typology — as a specific campaign organization in the context of the short-term period of election campaign, which is characterized by purposive political communication with the aim of struggle for power, its general goal of a political communication transformation becomes a relevant underlying mediation that must be taken into account from the analytical perspective of the social media-based radical political communication.

METHODS AND DATA

The case study research uses a qualitative methodological perspective, involving mainly the discourse analysis of texts linked to the #YoSoy132 (declarations, interviews, speeches and other texts). If, as Castells (2004) affirms, social movements are what they say they are, then discourse analysis is an appropriate method for examining the issue. Discourse analysis has become a significant method for understanding social movements (Taylor & Whittier, 2004), as part of an increasing concern about the processes of meaning construction, "aware of this complexity and try to creatively approach the multiplicity of levels implied in a collective discourse" (Melucci, 2004, p. 57), and tend to focus on movement-related texts in the effort to identify patterns, linkages and structures of ideas related to these collective agents (Jonhston, 2002).

From a complex perspective of discourse analysis that is adequate for the proposed research, Franzosi (1998, p. 527) suggested to focus on the narrative dimension of discourse since it provides a point of view centered on actors as well as on discourse structures. This perspective transcends the focus on the search for the meaningful and moves on to the meanings contained in the structure and the narrative sequences of texts, in a transition "from variables to actors, away from regression-based statistical models to networks, and away from a variable-based conception of casualty to narrative sequences".

In the discourse analysis we included three types of texts, all from secondary sources and from 23 May to 1 July 2012. These three types of discourse are: 1) interviews with participants in the movement, taken from both mainstream and online alternative media (a total of 5 interviews with participants of the movement, published by 7 different media, were included in the analysis); 2) texts that appeared on social network sites (Facebook) and microblogging sites (Twitter) associated with the #YoSoy132 (these texts include tweets, posts, videos, pictures, etc. published during the analyzed period); and 3) public declarations and other documents by the #YoSoy132 (it includes the First Declaration of the #YoSoy132, its public declaration about the occupation of Televisa and the Counter-report of September 1st, 2012). We focussed particularly on three dimensions of the discourse: 1) references to mainstream political communication and other social dimensions associated with it (democracy, citizen participation, etc.); 2) comments on social media and its role as part of the emergence of a radical political communication; and 3) reflections on the tensions between online and offline actions as part of collective action.

The following section discusses the main findings of the study, aiming at provide a thorough understanding of some of the main characteristics, challenges, tensions and complexities of the interrelationships between social media and the emergence of practices of radical political communication, taking into account some of the main aforementioned theoretical tensions, in particular the online/offline one. Although a case study does not allow to obtain statistically representative results that can be generalized, it provides a thorough analysis of the more relevant characteristics of social media-based radical political communication. Despite the pros and cons of the discursive analysis approach (Paltridge, 2012), the study is relevant given the analytical significance of the #YoSoy132, a social media-based mobilization that emerges in the context of an election campaign focuses on the democratization of communication, challenging the mainstream political communication.

POLITICAL COMMUNICATION AND SOCIAL MEDIA-BASED MOBILIZATION: #YoSoy132

Democracy and Participation: Criticism and Alternatives from the Perspective of the Social Mobilization

The #YoSoy132 is defined as "a nonpartisan movement, with no leaders or ringleaders, a horizontal one" (Teyve de Lara, participant in the #YoSoy132, in Moraga, 2012) and, as part of these characteristics, social media are regarded by the participants as an enabling condition that allows "that now we do not depend on nothing nor nobody for communicating between us, as citizens" (Comment, #YoSoy132's profile on Facebook, 3 June 2012). Consequently, participants put in practice singular repertoires of contention, both online and offline ones, that has a special communicational nature and symbolical dimension —such as protest, manifestations and occupations— making an important effort for putting in practice participatory and horizontal forms of organization and decision-making.

In line with this tendency, democracy and participation have been central notions on the discourses of the movement and its participants. From the first declaration, the #YoSoy132 claimed for "the empowerment of common citizens through information," since it was considered as a "necessary condition" that allows citizens to "demand and criticize —based on arguments— their government, political actors, entrepreneurs and society". The #YoSoy132 "makes the right of information and freedom of expression to be its main demands", by considering that social democratization and a conscious and participatory citizenship requires "the democratization of the mass media of communication" (#YoSoy132, 28 May 2012).

The Mexican democracy was qualified as a "farce", given the absolute divorce between politicians and citizens, questioning a political dynamic that is limited to "vote every six years, [and] although even that is not respected", according to (Attolini, 2012), another participant in the #YoSoy132. Participants in the protests explained the mobilization as a result of "being full of indignation" about what the presidential candidates' in particular the PRI's one, represent (Protester, in Attolini, 2012). In that regard, the mobilization sets a radical opposition between this questioned representative democracy and what is considered as a real democracy, but also between two different practices of political communication associated to each one of these typologies of democratic regimes. In that oppositeness, social media and mobilizations are considered as core and articulated dimensions, since protests — resulting from, and inherently linked to online collective action — are seen as "healthy expressions for any democracy" (Teyve de Lara, in Moraga, 2012).

Comments by the users in the social network sites underline, on the one hand, the immediate purpose of avoiding that "the television channels impose me a candidate" (Comment, #YoSoy132's profile on Facebook, 24 May 2012), given advices about the strategies for their communicative practices: "instead of shouting insults to the candidates (…), we should give real facts about their frauds" (Comment, #YoSoy132's profile on Facebook, 25 May 2012). But, on the other hand, users also highlight "the marvelous opportunity given by social networks and the Internet in general for the organization and diffusion of this authentic and important movement" (Comment, #YoSoy132's profile on Facebook, 20 May 2012). From a more long-term perspective, the goal of the radical political communication developed by the social media-based mobilization is "to reassess the symbolic dimension of politics" against a political communication that is based on "empty figures and oxidized speeches", as part of the process of building "an authentic democracy, just right know" (Attolini, 2012). In the new democratic order, and as part of renewed scenario of political communication, the main objetive of the #YoSoy132 is associated with a certain practice of radical political communication, as agents of permanent political questioning: to become "the shadow of those one who would be the decision-makers" (Alina Rosa Duarte, participant in the #YoSoy132, in Moraga, 2012).

The Tension among Online and Offline Collective Action

Offline collective action is seen as a space for this new democratic regime, thanks to the radical political communication that is made possible by the appropriation of social media. In that regard, social networks sites are considered as "a fabulous way for fostering social mobilizations" (Diego Dante, participant in the #YoSoy132, in Goche, 2012), but also a space for a different model of political communication, since in these Web 2.0 platforms "no one is more important than another; we are all 140 characters" (Rodrigo Serrano, participant in the #YoSoy132, in Goche, 2012). The interrelationship between online and offline collective action —given the appropriation of social media as resources for spreading the protests, as well as their association with a horizontal and netlike structure— is underlined in tweets and comments in Facebook: "IMPORTANT - Let's spread this WARNING! # YoSoy132 – RT!" (@ElPsicosofo); "A decentralized movement is impossible to be cancelled or infiltrated" (@anonopshispano); "we must communicated through social media or mobile phones, so one can inform all the other people if one sees something rare during the election" (Comment, #YoSoy132's profile on Facebook, 27 June 2012); "we are organizing us in such a way that we can have an online platform ready for all the areas of work, so we can join ourselves in groups throughout the whole country" (Post, #YoSoy132's profile on Facebook, 1 July 2012).

In line with the role of social media in the emergence of the #YoSoy132, the participants give a particular importance to the online collective action, to the extent that the participation of some individuals in the mobilizations "takes place completely in the social networks" (Tania, participant in the #YoSoy132, in De Mauleón, 2012). However, despite the importance of the online dimension of radical political communication, participants also underlined the necessity of taking the mobilization from social networks sites into the streets, by putting in practice offline practices of radical political communication. Although individuals identify a trend to the decrease of the number of people attending the offline meeting spaces once online activity diminishes, in what is considered a prove of the capacities of online social networks "as a tool for organization and diffusion" (Diego Dante, in Goche, 2012), at the same time they also recognize that there is the need of creating offline communicational spaces, considered as sources for reinforcing the organizational capabilities of the movement and its national spreading. In that regard, even the online spaces, the users highlight that "we have to go to the streets, squares, restaurants, and all available places, and hand out leaflets" (Comment, #YoSoy132's profile on Facebook, 27 May 2012).

There are callings to "create informative groups that bring all what we know and share here in social networks to those people that only see Televisa" (Comment, #YoSoy132's profile on Facebook, 19 May 2012), since "we must take into account that, unfortunately, few people have access to the Internet, so each one of us must replicate and spread all what we comment here among the people around oneself" (Comment, #YoSoy132's profile on Facebook, 10 June 2012). The digital divide is also included as a main topic in the public declarations of the movement. The #YoSoy123 demands that "the access to Internet has to become an effective constitutional right" (#YoSoy132, 28 May 2012), denouncing the failure of the commitments regarding the bridging of the digital divide, underlining the hight costs of the access, the lack of telecommunication infrastructure and the inefficient computer literacy (#YoSoy132, 1 September 2012).

The offline spaces of radical political communication are important, in the view of the participants, because "what we want is not only to complain about what is not currently happening, but also to begin to make proposals about what we want to happen" (José Miguel Barberena, participant in the #YoSoy132, in Notimex, 2013). Although the radical political communication associated to the online collective action through social media has certain organizational dimension, the individuals underline, above all, its importance as resource of visibility. The tension between online and offline collective action mediates, in a central way, the enabling conditions for the continuity of the collective action after the end of the cycle of protest (Tarrow, 1995).

In that regard, the offline political communicative actions are considered as a step that goes beyond the online ones, a guarantee for the configuration of permanent spaces of radical political communication and the inclusion of the transformation of the mainstream communicative system in the public agenda. Participants underline that the #YoSoy132 "has [also] a very specific agenda, for example with regard to media law" (Teyve de Lara, in Moraga, 2012). The long-term goal, after the end of the election campaign, is to organize and consolidate the movement, in order "to become something like a citizen oversight, very active politically speaking, to propose agendas on issues of reforms" (Alina Rosa Duarte, in Moraga, 2012), underlining this way the objective of becoming a permanent collective action focused on the development of a radical political communication.

Social Media and Mobilization: Towards a Radical Political Communication?

As above-mentioned, the #YoSoy132's main and foundational claim was the democratization of communication. Traditional political communication in Mexico was put into question from the very beginning of the mobilizations, particularly through their spaces in social media. Participants frequently claim a new political communication in their posts and comments in social media: "Those who are not prepared to listen, have the reward of not learn anything", "I want a free Mexico, where my voice is heard", "Why keep quiet if I was born screaming?" (Post, #YoSoy132's profile on Facebook, 16 May 2012). There is a narrative in social media that associates this new political communication with a change in democracy: "Fair media, free minds," "Truth will make us free" (Post, #YoSoy132's profile on Facebook, 27 May 2012).

As we have seen before, social media are considered main sources for sharing information in a participatory way. There is a permanent concern about "spreading and forwarding all this information to those who did not have access to it during these elections", a demand of accurate information and a request for media "to stop the manipulation and the imposition of a candidate" (Post, #YoSoy132's profile on Facebook, 23 May 2012) and an explicit purpose of developing communicative spaces by "us, the people from below, against those ones above" (@Soy132MX).

However, both the context of electoral campaign and the sense of radicalness centrally mediate the development of this communicational collective action through social media. On the one hand, participants underline their apolitical position, denying any commitment with Mexican political parties and describing the #YoSoy132 as a movement from below, "without any party, without [political] colors, without violence" (Post, #YoSoy132's profile on Facebook, 23 May 2012). But, on the other hand, the use of social media is not an apolitical one: for instance, there are many complaints about the efforts made by political parties for co-opting the mobilization for their own electoral advantage. In that regard, previous analyses have noted that what was new during the 2012 electoral campaign, was the creation of "digital armies, responsible for opening electoral fronts in the Internet" that included false profiles, paid twitterers or the use of bots for creating trending topics in Twitter or placing topics in the public agenda (De Mauleón, 2012).

During the analyzed period, participants continuously denounce those trends through social media, in what are considered as "attempts to hijack the movement and use it by political parties for their own political capital" (@Soy132MX). Social media are regarded as resources for opposing these tendencies, since these Web 2.0 platforms can be used to "share, communicate, inform, criticize, participate" (@Soy132MX). Consequently, social media are considered main resources for the "transformation of the Mexican society" towards "a real democracy" where "the conscious, informed, active and purposeful participation defines the political life of the country" (Comment, #YoSoy132's profile on Facebook, 15 June 2012).

Social media become a relevant resource for a new democratic scenario, given its contribution for the configuration of practices of radical political communication. During the analyzed period, there is an intense activity in the both the Facebook's profile and the Twitter's account of the #YoSoy132. Most of the posts in Facebook are marked as "Like", commented and shared hundreds and even thousands of times. The profile is used for six surveys and the creation and diffusion of events (manifestations, assemblies, occupations), or asking celebrities and leaders for supporting the mobilizations. There are tweets that underline the emotional dimension — "I have already joined the movement! What are you waiting for?", "Hey! Do you follow @Soy132MX? It is the account of all of us!" (@Soy132MX) — and the hashtag #YoSoy132 became a trending topic for six days, occupying the first place within global trends from May 17-19, 2012.

The participants in the mobilizations organized an alternative debate among the presidential candidates and, during the debate, the three main hashtags on Twitter were: #debate132 (10225 tweets and 8152 users), #YoSoy132 (7659 tweets and 6031 users) and #DebateYoSoy132 (4389 tweets and 3590 users). The last one remained as global trending topic for more than 14 hours after the end of the debate (Capital Social Investigaciones, 2012). Many tweets also underline the importance of social media as resources for processes of communication from below: "What we do know is that a tweet replicated by key people will reach virtual media and then the traditional media too, continuing from there to television and reaching the people without access to networks. The elections showed us this chain. How we can fill a square. How we can trust unknown people who, nevertheless, have our same interests. There is no censorship in the Internet; nothing can stop the spreading of messages" (@lvloon, in De Mauleón, 2012).

Previous studies on the #YoSoy132 (De Mauleón, 2012; Salgado Andrade, 2013) agree in considering that some of the trending topics determined the media agenda during the electoral campaign. These analyses have highlighted that mobilizations made the Twittersphere to become an electoral thermometer, arguing that, for instance, the online collective action forced the mainstream media —particularly the television stations — to include the protests in their agenda and also made three of the candidates —all of them but Enrique Peña Nieto, to participate in the citizen debate organized and moderated by university students. This shows that social media did not only pluralized the actors of the political communication by giving voice to the students, but also became platforms from where the traditional actors of the political communication, i.e. the presidential candidates, were compelled to participate in spaces of radical political communication, such as a citizen debate. At the same time, since the participants "don not accept the representation that the power tries to impose to us as reality" (Comment, #YoSoy132's profile on Facebook, 5 June 2012), the social media-based radical political communication also include the transmission of offline collective actions, such as occupations and debates, through the technological resources available (streaming or Youtube).

But the objetive of developing a radical political communication goes beyond the period of election campaign. In that regard, the #YoSoy132 denounce the criminalization of "the citizen efforts for the creation of their own media", spaces that are considered main resources for the democratization of communication and the emergence of a radical political communication since these communicative experiences "give voice to the less favored groups in the society, bringing them information in line with their needs", becoming "an excellent tool for the communities to exercise their right to the information and freedom of expression" (#YoSoy132, 1 September 2012). Even the #YoSoy132 has an expression of continuity in an alternative communicational space: Colectivo Másde131 (English: CollectiveMoreThan131; see it at http://www.colectivo131.com.mx/). Created on May, 2014, it is defined as a space of alternative communication working for "the empowerment of the voice —from citizen to citizen— through projects aiming to strengthen our social networks", with the objective of developing "complaints accompanied by conscious actions, through the participation of all the Mexicans" in order to achieve "well informed citizens" and "an authentic democracy" (Colectivo Másde131, 2014).

SOLUTIONS AND RECOMMENDATIONS

The analysis sets a number of issues with regard to the practices of radical political communication associated to social mobilizations that are particularly based on social media. In particular, the case provides some relevant perspectives in the context of the debates regarding the impact of the uses of the ICTs in political communication. The Internet has been considered as a source of destabilization of political communication systems from a positive perspective, associated with the dispersion of older patterns of political communication and the extension and pluralization of the public sphere (Dahlgren, 2005). The ICTs are regarded as the cause of a new age of political communication, characterized by the reshaping of it through five trends: the intensification of professionalizing imperatives, the increase of competitive pressures, the emergence of anti-elitist populism, a process of "centrifugal diversification", and significant changes in how people receive politics (Bloomer & Kavanagh, 1999).

The #YoSoy132 shows that the appropriation of social media as part of collective action may destabilize traditional political communication, particularly in the scenario of a highly concentrated media system that is inherently articulated with an institutional politics characterized by corruption, clientelism and the hegemony of only one political party. Social media provide the technological resources for, on the hand, generating spaces of radical political communication from below and, on the other hand, forcing the traditional political communicative practices to open its agenda, by including the collective action on it and even compel their actors (such as presidential candidates) to participate in spaces of radical political communication.

Previous studies on social media have analyzed the increasing use of these technological resources during political campaigns and its impact on contemporary political communication, as well as the use of social media by some specific social groups, specifically in relation to political self-efficacy and situational political involvement in certain particular scenarios, such as election campaigns (Kushin & Yamamoto, 2010). The analysis of the #YoSoy132 shows that, as part of this process, the online/offline tension should be considered a central mediation, at least in the case if social mobilizations that emerge from the cyberspace. On the hand, this tension mediates aspects underlined by previous studies, such as the need of moving beyond the informational functions of social media on contentious politics, towards their roles as organizing mechanisms for collective action (Segerberg & Bennett, 2011). On the other hand, it also mediates the development of the collective action itself, in particular the weight given to the creation of spaces of alternative communication that are sources of radical political communication.

While the analysis proves that we are far from the days when initial studies spoke in terms of a cyber-diffusion of contention and it is clear that the cyberspace has become an autonomous scenario for specific cyber-repertoires of action, the online/offline tension remains as a core aspect of the configuration of a radical political communication as part of online-based social mobilizations. This tension will mediate the development of the social mobilization and its communicative dimension. Since the online dimension is particularly important during the emergence and initial spreading of collective action, this will increase the importance of the radical political communication as a dimension in the long-term development of collective action and its continuity beyond the period of greater activity of protest.

But, at the same time, participants in social mobilizations also believe that communicative collective action through social media is not enough for guaranteeing the continuity of the mobilizations. The transition from social media into the streets is regarded as a necessity and this becomes an important challenge to be borne in mind for a complex analysis of the radical political communication associated with social media-based collective action. In particular, it must take into account that the radicalness of this political communication is associated with both its content, i.e. the criticisms towards mainstream political communication, and its form, i.e. horizontality and participatory dynamics enabled by the characteristics of social media, but also with its inherent and crucial interlinkage between radical political communication and collective action.

FUTURE RESEARCH DIRECTIONS

Radical political communication articulates multiple dimensions and tensions. In particular, the centrality of the online/offline tension and the way in which it is managed as part of the development of collective action, are core aspects for a complex understanding of the issue. The study of this tension and its mediation is a relevant topic of research for future analyses of the consequences of social media for political communication. Another significant dimension of analysis is the articulation of radical political communication within the general collective action, in order to examine how being part of these social media-based mobilizations mediate these communicative practices, in particular their radicalness. This analytical perspective would be relevant for overcoming technology-centered approach to the re-configuration of political communication as a consequence of the use of social media, by including the socio-political context of these uses and the general aims of the collective action within which this technological appropriation takes place.

CONCLUSION

Radical political communication is a significant and core dimension of social media-based collective action. For the participants, given their interactivity and participatory architecture, social media enable the pluralization of the political communicative actors, challenge the manipulation and concentration of media system and open the public sphere to people from below, a relevant trend particularly in scenarios characterized by high levels of media concentration and complicity among the hegemonic institutional politics and mainstream media, as well as in contexts of electoral campaigns.

However, the importance of the online dimension in the case of social media-based episodes of collective action, there is a remaining technological determinism finds it expression in the online/offline tension. Although social media are used for a wide number of purposes — emotional mobilization, diffusion of information, denouncement of manipulation by mainstream political communication, share of resources for collective action, or pushing traditional political actors for them to participate in alternative spaces of communication — there is certain trend to underline the use of these Web 2.0 platforms as resources of visibility. At the same time, despite the importance given by the participants to the articulation between online and offline action — an even the transition from the former to the latter — it is hard to achieve this articulation/transition.

Although there is an explicit recognition of the need of putting into practice offline spaces of radical political communication, the prevailing trend is towards online radical political communication through the use of social media. On the one hand, the necessity of this transition from social media into the streets shows the limits — at least in the imaginary of the individuals — of the use of these technological resources for the transformation of the general practices of political communication. On the other hand, this online/offline tension can be understood in the light of the processes of social change that collective action tries to develop and its context. In the case of the #YoSoy132, the long-term main goal is precisely the democratization of communication but the immediate objective is to avoid the election of the PRI's candidate.

Consequently, the radical political communication will be mediated, in the short-term period of the election campaign, by the necessity of achieving the greatest possible influence and, in a very concentrated mainstream media system, social media are the most important channel available for this. However, the digital divide that characterizes the Mexican context forces to take into account the people who does not have access to the Internet. From a long-term perspective, the goal of the democratization of communication will find expression in the relevance of the communicative dimension as part of the continuity of the collective action, in particular through the creation of spaces of alternative communication that can be considered as experiences of radical political communication. While the impact of the short-term and social media-based radical political communication seems to be limited in the case analyzed, given the victory of the PRI's candidate in the election, the long-term consequences of these spaces of alternative communication — as radical political communication — in the mainstream political communication will need further research.

REFERENCES

Aday, S., Farrel, H., Lynch, M., Sides, J., Kelly, J., & Zuckerman, E. (2010). *Blogs and bullets: New media in contentious politics. Technical report.* U.S. Institute of Peace.

Alfaro, R. M. (2000). Culturas populares y comunicación participativa. *Revista Caminos*, *20*, 13–20.

Alonso, L. E. (1986). La mediación institucional y sus límites en el capitalismo avanzado. *Revista Espanola de Investigaciones Sociologicas*, *35*(35), 63–79. doi:10.2307/40183154

Arditi, B. (2012). Insurgencies don't have a plan – they are the plan: Political performatives and vanishing mediators in 2011. *Journalism, Media and Cultural Studies, 1*, 1-16. Retrieved from http://www.cardiff.ac.uk/jomec/jomecjournal/1-june2012/arditi_insurgencies.pdf

Attolini, A. (2012, September 19). Por una democracia auténtica, #YoSoy132. *ADN Político*. Retrieved from http://www.adnpolitico.com/opinion/2012/09/19/antonio-attolini-por-una-democracia-autentica-yosoy132

Autonome k. a. gruppe. (2003). What is Communication Guerrilla. In J. Richardson (Ed.), Anarchitexts: Voices from global digital resistance (pp. 86-91). New York: Autonomedia.

Ayres, J. M. (1999). From the streets to the Internet: The cyber-diffusion of contention. *The Annals of the American Academy of Political and Social Science*, *566*(1), 132–143. doi:10.1177/0002716299566001011

Bardici, M. V. (2012). *A Discourse Analysis of the Media Representation of Social Media for Social Change - The Case of Egyptian Revolution and Political Change. (Master dissertation).* Malmö University. Retrieved from http://muep.mah.se/handle/2043/14121

Bentivegna, S. (2006). Rethinking politics in the world of ICTs. *European Journal of Communication*, *21*(3), 331–343. doi:10.1177/0267323106066638

Blumler, J. G., & Kavanagh, D. (1999). The third age of political communication: Influences and features. *Political Communication, 16*(3), 209–230. doi:10.1080/105846099198596

Capital Social Investigaciones. (2012, June 20). *Algunos datos sobre la actividad en Twitter del debate de YoSoy132.* Retrieved from http://capitalsocialmexico.com/2012/06/20/algunos-datos-sobre-la-actividad-en-twitter-del-debate-de-yosoy132/

Capriles, O. (2006). Alternative communication, horizontal communication, alternative use of media, participant communication: Which is the paradigm? In A. Gamucio-Dragon & T. Tufte (Eds.), *Communication for Social Change Anthology: Historical and Contemporary Readings* (pp. 302–305). Communication for Social Change Consortium.

Casero-Ripollés, A. (2010). El despertar del público?: Comunicación política, ciudadanía y web 2.0. In M. Martin Vicente & D. Rothberg (Eds.), *Meios de comunicaçao e cidadania* (pp. 107–122). São Paulo: Cultura Académica.

Castells, M. (2000). Materials for an exploratory theory of the network society. *The British Journal of Sociology, 51*(1), 5–24. doi:10.1080/000713100358408

Castells, M. (2004). *The network society: A cross-cultural perspective.* Northampton, MA: Edward Elgar Publishing. doi:10.4337/9781845421663

Castells, M. (2009). *Communication power.* Oxford, UK: Oxford University Press.

Chadwick, A. (2011). The political information cycle in a hybrid news system: The British prime minister and the "bullygate" affair. *The International Journal of Press/Politics, 16*(1), 3–29. doi:10.1177/1940161210384730

Colectivo Másde131. (2014). *Sobre nosotros* [About us]. Retrieved from http://www.colectivo131.com.mx/

Dahlberg, L., & Siapera, E. (Eds.). (2007). *Radical Democracy and the Internet: Interrogating Theory and Practice.* Basingstoke, UK: Palgrave Macmillan. doi:10.1057/9780230592469

Dahlgren, P. (2005). The Internet, public spheres, and political communication: Dispersion and deliberation. *Political Communication, 22*(2), 147–162. doi:10.1080/10584600590933160

Davis, S., Elin, L., & Reeher, G. (2002). *Click on Democracy: The Internet's Power to Change Political Apathy into Civic Action.* Boulder, CO: Westview Press.

De Mauleón, H. (2012, September 1). De la red a las calles. *Nexos.* Retrieved from http://elecciones2012mx.wordpress.com/2012/09/01/de-la-red-a-las-calles-hector-de-mauleon-blog-nexos-en-linea/

Della Porta, D. (2013). Repertoires of contention. In D. A. Snow, D. Della Porta, B. Klandermans, & D. McAdam (Eds.), *The Wiley-Blackwell Encyclopedia of Social and Political Movements.* Malden, MA: Blackwell; doi:10.1002/9780470674871.wbespm178

Della Porta, D., & Diani, M. (2006). *Social movements: An introduction.* Malden, MA: Blackwell Publishing.

Dylko, I., & McCluskey, M. (2012). Media effects in an era of rapid technological transformation: A case of user-generated content and political participation. *Communication Theory*, *22*(3), 250–278. doi:10.1111/j.1468-2885.2012.01409.x

Feenstra, R., & Casero-Ripollés, A. (2014). Democracy in the Digital Communication Environment: A Typology Proposal of Political Monitoring Processes. *International Journal of Communication*, *8*, 2448–2468. Retrieved from http://ijoc.org/index.php/ijoc/article/view/2815

Franklin, B. (1995). A bibliographical essay. *Political Communication*, *12*, 223–242. doi:10.1080/105 84609.1995.9963067

Franzosi, R. (1998). Narrative analysis -Or why (and how) sociologists should be interested in narrative. *Annual Review of Sociology*, *24*(1), 517–554. doi:10.1146/annurev.soc.24.1.517

Fuchs, C. (2012). Social media, riots, and revolutions. *Capital and Class*, *36*(3), 383–391. doi:10.1177/0309816812453613

García, R. G., & Treré, E. (2014). The# YoSoy132 movement and the struggle for media democratization in Mexico. *Convergence (London)*, *1354856514541744*. doi:10.1177/1354856514541744

Goche, F. (2012, September 11). Yo soy 132, movimiento del siglo XXI. *Contralínea*. Retrieved from http://contralinea.info/archivo-revista/index.php/2012/09/11/yo-soy-132-movimiento-del-siglo-xxi/

Gómez Quintero, N. (2014, May 15). ¿Qué ocurrió con #YoSoy132? *El Universal*. Retrieved from http://www.eluniversal.com.mx/nacion-mexico/2014/historias-que-ocurrio-con-39yosoy132-39-1010493.html

Gómez Vilchis, R. R. (2013). El regreso del dinosaurio: Un debate sobre la reciente victoria del PRI en la elección presidencial de 2012. *Estudios Politicos*, *28*, 45–161. doi:10.1016/S0185-1616(13)71443-4

Harlow, S. (2012). Social media and social movements: Facebook and an online Guatemalan justice movement that moved offline. *New Media & Society*, *14*(2), 225–243. doi:10.1177/1461444811410408

Jenkins, H. (2006). *Convergence culture: Where old and new media collide*. New York, NY: NYU Press.

Jonhston, H. (2002). Verification and proof in frame and discourse analysis. In B. Klandermans & S. Staggenborg (Eds.), *Methods of social movement research* (pp. 61–91). Minneapolis, MN: University of Minnesota Press.

Kavada, A. (2005). Exploring the role of the internet in the 'movement for alternative globalization': The case of the Paris 2003 European Social Forum. *Westminster Papers in Communication and Culture*, *2*(1), 72-95.

Kushin, M. J., & Yamamoto, M. (2010). Did social media really matter? College students' use of on-line media and political decision making in the 2008 election. *Mass Communication & Society*, *13*(5), 608–630. doi:10.1080/15205436.2010.516863

LAPOP/Barómetro de las Américas. (2010). *Consolidación democrática en las Américas en tiempos difíciles: Informe sobre las Américas*. Retrieved from http://lapop.ccp.ucr.ac.cr/pdf/ReportontheAmericasSpanish2.pdf

Latinobarómetro. (2009). *Encuesta Latinobarómetro 2009*. Retrieved from http://latino-barometro.org/latino/LATDatos.jsp

Lock, A., & Harris, P. (1996). Political marketing - vive la difference. *European Journal of Marketing, 30*(10-11), 21–31.

MacLeod, D. (2005). *Downsizing the state: Privatization and the Limits of Neoliberal Reform in Mexico*. Pennsylvania, PA: Penn State Press.

Macnamara, J., & Kenning, G. (2011). E-electioneering 2010: Trends in social media use in Australian political communication. *Media International Australia, 139*, 7–22.

Maireder, A., Ausserhofer, J., & Kittenberger, A. (2012). Mapping the Austrian Political Twittersphere. How politicians, journalists and political strategists (inter-)act on Twitter. In P. Parycek, N. Edelmann & M. Sachs (Eds.), *CeDEM12. Proceeding of the International Conference for E-Democracy and Open Government* (pp. 151-163). Krems: Edition Donau-Universität Krems.

Melucci, A. (2004). The process of collective identity. In H. Jonhston & B. Klandermans (Eds.), *Social movements and culture* (pp. 41–63). Minneapolis, MN: University of Minnesota Press.

Moraga, S. (2012, July 24). #YoSoy132 busca ser la sombra del poder en México. *ADN Político*. Retrieved from http://www.adnpolitico.com/2012/2012/07/21/el-yosoy132-busca-ser-la-sombra-del-poder-en-mexico

Morozov, E. (2011). *The Net Delusion: The Dark Side of Internet Freedom*. New York: PublicAffairs.

Norris, P. (2000). *A Virtuous Circle: Political Communication in Post-Industrial Democracies*. New York: Cambridge University Press. doi:10.1017/CBO9780511609343

Norris, P. (2004). Political Communications. In *Encyclopedia of the Social Sciences*. Retrieved from http://www.hks.harvard.edu/fs/pnorris/Acrobat/Political%20Communications%20encyclopedia2.pdf

Notimex (2013, February 11). Afirman que movimiento "Yo Soy 132" carece de fecha de caducidad. *Crónica*. Retrieved from http://www.cronica.com.mx/notas/2012/664356.html

Paltridge, B. (2012). *Discourse analysis: an introduction* (2nd ed.). London: Bloomsbury.

Pérez de Acha, G. (2012, September 19). La democracia de #YoSoy132. *Animal Político*. Retrieved from http://www.animalpolitico.com/blogueros-blog-invitado/2012/09/19/la-democracia-de-yosoy132/#ixzz33PD7zyBc

Poster, M. (1997). Cyberdemocracy: Internet and the public sphere. In D. Porter (Ed.), *Internet culture* (pp. 201–218). New York: Routledge.

Russell, J. W. (2009). *Class and Race Formation in North America*. Toronto: University of Toronto Press.

Sader, E. (2001). Hegemonía y contra-hegemonía para otro mundo posible. In J. Seoane & E. Taddei (Eds.), *Resistencias Mundiales* [De Seattle a Porto Alegre] (pp. 23–45). Buenos Aires: CLACSO.

Salgado Andrade, E. (2013). Twitter en la campaña electoral de 2012. *Desacatos, 42*, 217–232.

Sandoval-Almazan, R., & Gil-Garcia, J. R. (2013, January). Cyberactivism through Social Media: Twitter, YouTube, and the Mexican Political Movement I'm Number 132. In *Proceedings of the 46th Hawaii International Conference on System Sciences (HICSS)* (pp. 1704-1713). Wailea, HI: IEEE. 10.1109/HICSS.2013.161

Segerberg, A., & Bennett, W. L. (2011). Social media and the organization of collective action: Using Twitter to explore the ecologies of two climate change protests. *Communication Review*, *14*(3), 197–215. doi:10.1080/10714421.2011.597250

Stieglitz, S. & Dang-Xuan, L. (2012). Social media and political communication: a social media analytics framework. *Soc. Netw. Anal. Min.*, published online 25 August 2012. doi:10.100713278-012-0079-3

Tarrow, S. (1995). Cycles of Collective Action: Between Moments of Madness and the Repertoire of Contention. In M. Traugott (Ed.), *Repertoires and Cycles of Collective Action* (pp. 89–116). Durham, NC: Duke University Press.

Tarrow, S. (1998). *Power in Movement: Social Movements and Contentious Politics*. Cambridge, UK: Cambridge University Press. doi:10.1017/CBO9780511813245

Taylor, V., & Whittier, N. (2004). Analytical approaches to social movements culture: The culture of the women's movement. In H. Jonhston & B. Klandermans (Eds.), *Social movements and culture* (pp. 163–187). Minneapolis, MN: University of Minnesota Press.

Thornton, A. L. (2001). Does the Internet create democracy? *Ecquid Novi: African Journalism Studies*, *22*(2), 126–147. doi:10.1080/02560054.2001.9665885

Tilly, Ch. (1995). *Popular Contention in Great Britain, 1758-1834*. Cambridge, MA: Harvard University Press.

Tumasjan, A., Sprenger, T., Sandner, P., & Welpe, L. (2011). Election forecasts with Twitter: How 140 characters reflect the political landscape. *Social Science Computer Review*, *29*(4), 402–418. doi:10.1177/0894439310386557

Van Laer, J., & Van Aelst, P. (2009). Cyber-protest and civil society: the Internet and action repertoires in social movements. In Y. Jewkes & M. Yar (Eds.), *Handbook on Internet Crime* (pp. 230–254). Portland, OR: Willan Publishing.

Vargas Llosa, M. (1990, September 1). México es la dictadura perfecta. *El País*. Retrieved from http://elpais.com/diario/1990/09/01/cultura/652140001_850215.html

Vázquez, J. J. M. (1997). *La televisión y el poder político en México*. Madrid: Diana.

Vickery, G., & Wunsch-Vincent, S. (2007). *Participative web and user-created content: Web 2.0 wikis and social networking*. OECD.

Villamil, J. (2012). *El sexenio de Televisa: conjuras del poder mediático*. México: Random House Mondadori.

Wolfsfeld, G., Segev, E., & Sheafer, T. (2013). Social Media and the Arab Spring. Politics Comes First. *The International Journal of Press/Politics*, *18*(2), 115–137. doi:10.1177/1940161212471716

#YoSoy132. (2012a, May 28). *Manifiesto del #YoSoy132*. Retrieved from https://www.youtube.com/watch?v=igxPudJF6nU

#YoSoy132. (2012b, September 1). *Contrainforme presidencial*. Retrieved from http://www.sinembargo.mx/01-09-2012/352855

KEY TERMS AND DEFINITIONS

Electoral Campaign: In representative democracies, refers to the period previous to election, wherein representatives are chosen or referendums are decided, characterized for an intense activity of political communication. In modern politics, the highest electoral campaigns are focused on candidates for head of state or government.

Mainstream Media System: The prevailing current media (or media groups) in a given country or region, often associated to the hegemonic economic and political groups.

Offline Collective Action: A notion that has been defined from many areas of the social sciences (psychology, sociology, anthropology, political science and economics), it refers, in a general sense, to any action taken together by a group of people, aiming at enhance their status and achieve some common objectives.

Online Collective Action: ICTs-based actions, which is commonly referred as cyberactivism, held by some collective or social group, as part of its strategies for demanding some kind of resources or changes.

Online Social Networks: Web-based platforms that allow individuals to create a public profile as well as a list of users with whom to share connections and interact through Internet-based resources such as email and instant messaging, viewing and crossing the connections within the online system. Online social networks connect people who share interests, activities, backgrounds or real-life connections, through different tools, including mobile connectivity, photo/video/sharing or blogging.

Radical Political Communication: Practices of communication generally developed by people out of traditional political structures, which have a political nature, opposing mainstream political communication, and propose radical changes in politics and society.

Social Mobilization: Also known as mass or popular mobilization, it refers to the mobilizations of civilian population, often used by social movements, as part of their strategies of contentious politics, usually by meetings, marches, protests and demonstrations.

Uses (of ICTs): It refers to the diverse kind of actions made by individuals or groups for some purpose, by employing the ICTs as technological resources associated to some function.

This research was previously published in (R)evolutionizing Political Communication through Social Media edited by Tomaž Deželan and Igor Vobič; pages 56-74, copyright year 2016 by Information Science Reference (an imprint of IGI Global).

Chapter 7

The Resistance of Memories and the Story of Resistance:
July 15 Coup Attempt and Social Movement in Turkey

Fadime Dilber
Karamanoğlu Mehmet Bey University, Turkey

ABSTRACT

This study focused on the relationship of cross-media and social movements. The role of the new media in social mobility has gained a universal qualification though not directly but with the function as a communication platform between individuals by informing and guiding them all. Coup attempt on July 15, 2016 is one of the most important events in the history of the Republic of Turkey. In this coup attempt, the media, contrary to other coups, moved with the people who went out to the streets as an anti-coup. President Recep Tayyip Erdoğan invited the public to social movement by using the mass media and new media in the prevention of the coup attempt of July 15th. When the attitude of the national media is supported by citizens and mass media, new media and those struggling against the coup have gained strength and helped to make the coup attempt unsuccessful. This chapter examines the story structure of struggle exhibited against the July 15 coup attempt in the transmedia.

INTRODUCTION

We are witnessing a period that economic, political, and social structures are changing rapidly and that world is experiencing fundamental change and transformation. Particularly with the process of industrialization, urbanization, modernization accelerated from the middle of the 20th century, the changes in the communities can affect both their own geography and other continents. In all these changes and transformations, the position and role of social events, social actors are coming up and are being argued (Demircioğlu, 2014).

DOI: 10.4018/978-1-5225-9869-5.ch007

The media is accepted as the fourth pillar in addition to three known pillars of democracy: legislature, executive and judiciary. Media is the name given to mass communication tools such as newspapers, magazines, TV, radio, internet which can send messages to the masses to inform them about the events, and can create platforms for people to be informed, educated and to discuss social problems. Media is a powerful guidance tool. Media functions as the fourth pillar of democracy in democratic countries. It is also possible to control societies more easily through media. However, the development and widespread use of new media technologies has reversed this situation. As seen in the recent popular movements, people who are aware of the developments in the world thanks to social network and internet were organized on social networks and by 3G and they took to the streets. New media technologies have now taken place in every aspect of daily life and have had a great influence on the development of social, cultural, political and economic life. The world is aware of the power of new media technologies. New media technology is action oriented and requires organizing in order to make the right use of it, and the structure of this technology makes it possible (Türk, 2013).

The coups that are considered as social movements in Turkey's political life, poses an important place. Many times in the history of 94 years, it has been faced with social movements such as junta, coup, postmodern coup, memorandum or e-memorandum, declaration, insurrection and attempt. The coup attempt on July 15, 2016 is one of them. It is separated from other coups in terms of the quality of new media, the point of view of information and orientation, the failure of the attempt, the awareness of the public about attempt.

While it is seen that the coups in the past were announced to the public through traditional mass media; the coup attempt of July 15, 2016 was carried out through new media. News about important strategic areas was attacked by the coupists such as military vehicles, bridges, airports, military bases and Grand National Assembly was spread. Within the context of social movements for the prevention of 15 July coup attempt, President Recep Tayyip Erdoğan invited public to a social movement by using mass media and new media with live broadcasts. The number of tweets, from 10 pm on the night of the coup attempt on July 15 has continuously increased, and this increase rate reached 223 percent on 16 July. The maximum number of tweets was reached after President Recep Tayyip Erdoğan's connection to CNN Türk TV via FaceTime. It is possible to say that the effect of the social media on the failure of 15 July coup attempt. On the 15th and 16th of July, the number of tweets surpassed millions (Miş et al. 2016, pp. 7-71).

In the end, how effectively changing and evolving technology is used to prevent dangerous social movements such as coups; the response of the people to this call with sensitivity has turned into social movement and success was achieved against the dangerous coup attempt. It is possible to say that the fact that the power of new media and mass media to create perception in society resulted in a social movement for this coup is undeniable. The transformation of the media, the pluralization and the development of communication technology has made the work of the coupists difficult. Although they had a plan to leave TRT open and close other channels, they could not get the result they wanted (Miş et al. 2016, pp. 7-71).

In this study, the role of the new media on the transformation of the 15 July coup attempt to collective movement, guidance of people to each other against the attempt, establishment of resistance platform and movement of people to act together with national unity and solidity is examined. We can say that ordinary citizens and the important people in the administration of the country like the president and the prime minister turn out to be broadcasters and reveal the importance of the new media for the organization of the people.

The transformation of the July 15 coup attempt into social movement has cost many of the citizens' lives. 248 martyrs and 2194 veterans (Adalet Bakanlığı, 2017). The subject of the study is to examine the story structure of struggle exhibited against the July 15 coup attempt in the trans-media. It was theoretically supported by literature search during this study. The level of use of new media during and after the coup attempt was addressed.

NEW MEDIA AND ITS ROLE ON SOCIAL MOVEMENTS

The media is an effective means of communicating first and foremost in the development of democratic regimes and democratic consciousness in terms of their functions and position. The influence of the media on people and community life has reached substantial level today. The media is an informative and guiding force in all areas of life. Media is seen as the most powerful tool in our everyday life, to transmit information, to entertain, to form social synergy. It is known by everyone that media in Turkey is an important factor in the creation of agenda and has great influence on people or societies (Yılmaz, 2013).

The new millennium started in the context of new media formations. In a very short time, different systems from the usual mass media and tools are included in the routine of our lives. New media draws attention by its functions such as sharing information, cooperation, organization, decision making, educational features, and action. In these communication environments, which are open to the access of a large population, various movements are able to spread their messages to different segments in order to realize their political goals. The Internet does not only simply provide a technological base for computer-aided social movements. It strengthens organization mentality and the network topology is being networked. Decentralized, local / global networks increase dominant organizational forms in computer-assisted movements and new digital technologies increase the formation of radical, decentralized networks in a significant way and facilitate multinational coordination and communication among current movements (Özel, 2012, Kalafatoğlu, 2015).

Social networks, powered by the widespread use of the Internet and at the highest level of information flow on a global scale, provide the reinterpretation of individual and social life by breaking down the concepts of time and space. In the society that Castells defines as "the network society", "the individuals now live in globally and locally interconnected (relevant) networks." New media (digital technologies, social networks, mobile phones, etc.) are alternatives for the recreation of civil society. It is observed that the Internet now provides many advantages to social movements as well as other new communication tools that contribute to these advantages. Activists are using digital technologies to organize and plan mass action. Media which is the number one effect of the formation of social structures, mass media which is the number one effect of the formation of social structure in public spaces, have gained power over time and with the help of this power it played active roles to establish new equilibriums in society (Türk, 2013, Kalafatoğlu, 2015, Kaya, 1985, Yılmaz, 2008).

The effective use of social media as a new form of 'new' communication tools in the last decade we are living causes a new structural transformation of new social movements, resulting in a much more atomized, more "new" structure. Social media tools have recently come to the fore in the context of new local and global social movements. In this context, social media can function as a tool that facilitates the communication and organization of an organized social movement in real life. With the rise of the social media, it has increased and has begun to make people feel it more in every field. The determination of social convictions has also had the power to affect the social trust that is attached to institutions (Babacan, 2014, Damlapınar, 2007).

The internet, which uses simple communication techniques like getting news in the past, has now become a social communication and interaction tool with the widespread use of especially social media tools, facebook, twitter etc., and it has proven its power in terms of transformation and guidance. With the social media concept affecting the lives, the relations, actors, size, function and discourse within the social structure have begun to change (Yağmur, 2015).

The presence of developments in computer and internet technologies have changed and transformed social movements in many ways. With the computer and the internet with computer hardware, does not only turn the communication adventure into an ontological transformation but it changes the direction of all the horizontal and vertical passages by touching all the elements of the social structure. In this respect, despite its late existence in the history of mankind, the internet has made it possible to create a new environment that cannot be limited by any field or subject, but can across the borders of the whole world (Babacan, 2014). The virtual world opened by Internet technology is built on a space framework independent of the physical, spatial and temporal boundaries of the physical world (Alemdaroğlu & Demirtaş, 2004).

The news produced in the new media can be created and published by anyone in public, and the purpose here is not always tangible. Motivation may succeed by making the presented news to become a current issue *"The media may not be successful in telling us what to think, but it is extremely successful in telling us what to think about"* (Cohen, 1963). Communication with new media is characterized as "information flow" rather than product or meta-valuation, and the nature of communication is at a global level (as far as possible) in a democratic structure (Timisi, 2003).

Generally, social movements are defined as "collective actions developed by individuals who have solidarity and common goals with constant interaction with factors and other groups against elites, authorities, other groups or cultural codes" (Demircioğlu, 2014). These changes on the social level have also altered the reasons for the emergence of social movements, the characteristics of their participants, their goals and their forms of movement (Demircioğlu, 2014). Chomsky argues that new media technologies are the media of large media monopolies and of citizen controlled media that outside the control of the state (Türk, 2013).

In the first months of 2011, the popular movements that started in the Middle East and North Africa started to use the social media tools as a means of organization and communication, followed by definitions of 'social media revolution' etc. and the debate on the importance and effect of social media continues to increase (Babacan, 2014).

The recently emerging dimension of "communicative action" of social movements has gained importance. The common ground in the emergence and success of social movements is the perfect interaction between people. In this direction, social movements are effective in bringing people's knowledge, ideas, experiences and wishes together in a common ground and collectively embracing the products that they create (Sungur, 2017).

New media technologies now allow individuals to have the information they need in a very short time. Thus, individuals become able to search, get informed, reach information quickly, and become conscious, query. In addition, new media technologies also provide an easy-to-organize environment for people. The media, which has entered our lives as a means of mass communication, has become one of the greatest forces in terms of effectiveness on people through change, transformation and development (Türk, 2013, Arslan, 2001).

New social movements and activist initiatives are now common in our democracy. They take full advantage of social networks and new media environments, and they stand out with their performance. The most important role of the new media is to create new representations and to announce dissident political voices. As a result of these developments, the world is actually closer to become 'global village'. In particular, the free and wide environment brought by the internet media has enabled passive masses to announce their voices. Civil society movements have left the attention of television channels to announce their voices and now have managed to establish communities through their own social media (Karagöz, 2013).

With social movements are being realized in squares, the organization and the starting point of massive encouragement is social media. Social media allows the masses who use it to form public opinion. Social media comes to the front in terms of instant updating by users, enabling multi-use, and so forth (Sungur, 2017).

Social media can serve as a means of facilitating the communication and organization of an organized social movement in local and global scale in real life. However, unlike the structural nature of social media tools and other traditional means of communication, openness to all interactions makes it possible to become an easily manipulated, provoked and misleading tool. As with the e-memorandum issued by the General Staff on April 27, 2007, governments could be warned even via the internet and large-scale media organizations could be secondary. Similarly, mass actions such as those in the Violence Actions of Gezi Park could be managed and manipulated with internet based social networks (Babacan, 2014, Demir, 2016).

The facts that new media tools provide the ability to act in a horizontal plane to individual and social movements, and the ability to be active in everyday life and politics lead to new possibilities for social opposition/struggling (Babacan, 2014).

Social media in the "Wall Street occupation", "London rebellion", "Arab rebellion" and similar mass movements; to organize individuals, to reach wider masses and to maintain the flow of information. It was emphasized that the role of social media emerged in these rebellions and the term "Twitter Revolution" was spoken everywhere. On the other hand, the rise in regional and global actions is unprecedented in some of the different cultural, political and economic outlooks, and believes that social media plays an important role for most Arab revolutionaries for local, national and international development. Social media is not one of the causes of mass movements, and users only use this platform as a means of organizing and communicating in mass movements (Joseph, 2012).

Since 2000, the power of visual media has gained different dimensions with the development of mobile communication technologies and rapid spread in society. This rapid change in means of communication has provided new possibilities in terms of the coup method and the fight against it, even though the established relations and dogmas behind the coup culture have not been deeply shaken (Demir, 2016).

Today, new social movements and activist protests are no longer a surprise for the public and the media, and are becoming commonplace in our democracy. The new media plays an important role in the digital organization of such activist protests. The most important role of the new media is the capacity to create new representations and to announce dissenting political voices. In study entitled 'Activism and New Media' (Morozov, 2007, as cited in Meriç 2012), Morozov collected activists' new media utilization strategies under eight main topics:

1. Accessibility and correct information;
2. Attract public attention to a specific problem;

3. Analyzing the data to help voters and making it easier to find;
4. Establish direct contact with politicians and voters;
5. Reach new members;
6. Mobilize the activities and help to provide logistical support;
7. Find creative methods for collective actions and produce innovations;
8. Providing information exchange between other non-governmental organizations and activists and printing those (Karagöz, 2013).

COUPS IN TURKEY AND 15 JULY COUP ATTEMPT

The military coup is to illegally overthrow the government and seize power with secret plans and programs by official military institutions under the control of the state. In order to prevent the radical changes in the current administration, coups mainly include elements of violence. In the Turkish political life, coups and the military tutelage system became a tradition (Akıncı, 2014, Sungur, 2017).

May 27, 1960 coup was the first military coup in Turkey. It set an example for the March 12 memorandum and the September 12 coup. From 27 May 1960 until October 15, 1961, the National Unity Committee held the country administration. The coup was announced to the public through printed media and the public was informed through radio in the morning of May 27th. This day, coup was announced through radio. Staff Colonel Alparslan Türkeş, who read the declaration that started with the sentence of "Turkish Armed Forces invite Turkish citizens to listen to their radios", mentioned that the army seized power in a "joint cooperation" and "bloodless" manner. After this coup concluded with the execution of Adnan Menderes, the second coup that took place after the March 27, 1960 memorandum of March 12, 1971. Unlike the previous coup, the memorandum did not completely remove civilian power from the government, so it was described as a memorandum. The memorandum period can also be described as a semi-military regime. Memorandum was announced to the public through TRT radio and a copy of it was announced by reading in Grand National Assembly of Turkey (Demir, 2016, Sungur, 2017).

On September 12, 1980, the third military coup was carried out by the Turkish Armed Forces under the leadership of Kenan Evren. The September 12, 1980, coup was held in the "chain of command" of the generals. It was announced to the public by Kenan Evren in the visual and written press by TRT and newspapers (Sungur, 2017). On September 12, 1980, similar remarks were repeated by the TRT spokesman, Mesut Mertcan, via radio: The Turkish Armed Forces have completely seized the state administration in chain of command. The September 12 coup, in which radio technology was used effectively, was also supported by television, which has just begun to enter the houses. Kenan Evren has appeared on the TRT and has underlined that they aim to place the democracy that is unable to control itself on solid foundations. With these messages spreading from the screen to the public, the coup was not only "text" and "voice", but also has acquired a majestic and fearful "visuality" (Demir, 2016, Emiroğlu, 2011).

Republic of Turkey's democracy efforts have been disrupted army's management to bring peace to the people on May 27, 1960 March 12, 1971, and September 12, 1980 and it is possible to say that the wounds opened in democratic life that even cannot be closed today. Generally social movements, "The resources that social movements can benefit are quite diverse". Within this diversity, moral, cultural, social, organizational and material resources are at the forefront. In the name of social movements to gain an identity; structural eligibility (general social conditions), structural tension (injustice or anger) and belief need to be developed and shared by the masses. Military interventions are the deterioration and moral decay of the concept of freedom that is caused by personal relations (Sungur, 2017, Böğrekci, 2013).

As we have witnessed in the publication of Wikileaks documents worldwide, the Arab Spring, Gezi Park events, December 17 Investigations and 15 July Coup attempt in Turkey, social media has a strong influence on community. People are starting to use social media, which is faster and more massive, in social activities. 2016 Turkey military coup or the name given by the coupists as Peace at Homeland Operation, between 15-16 July 2016 by a group of soldiers within the Turkish Armed Forces that identifies themselves as Peace at Homeland Council made a military coup attempt. The declaration published in the official website of the Turkish Armed Forces and in the TRT stated that the army had taken control of the management and a martial law and curfew was declared. The flow of information provided through calls made through online platforms, news and live broadcasts played an important role in the failure of the coup attempt (Halıcı, 2011).

Because of the social movement against the 15 July coup attempt in our country, there is mass and organization in both. It is possible to say that the information shared through the media and the sharing of this information by the users, the formation of the spirit of stance against the coup, the emergence of democracy in the forefront lead to spread of consciousness and strength of this awareness. The end result is that the media is a force on its own. At this point that exhibiting common attitudes, especially in events that concern the general public, develops within this issue. In the 15th of July coup attempt the citizens laid in front of the armored vehicles and this reflex was shown by the general population, and the social media had a great influence in spreading the mass. Social media has played a critical role in the coup attempt of July 15. Tweets that were sent by President Recep Tayyip Erdoğan, who is the head of the state administration and from Presidential Twitter account that remove panic were the important elements that constitute the spirit of resisting the coup. The social media provided shared information and the sharing of this information by the users, the formation of the spirit of stance against the coup, the emergence of democracy in the forefront lead to spread of consciousness and strength of this awareness (Sungur, 2017).

The July 15 coup attempt is based on "image" centered coup that of was directed and changed by media and communication technologies without ignoring the military dimension. It also suggested that smart phones, which are thought to be limited to the opportunities of individual entertainment and group interaction in everyday life, have transformed the coup into a "popular revolution", as facilitated the coup attempt. 17 minutes after the announcement of the coup in TRT, President Erdoğan's image, which was connected to CNN Türk via FaceTime, was reflected on the screen via the smart phone. Immediately afterwards, President Erdoğan's personal and Presidential calls to resist against the coup from official Twitter and Facebook accounts were repeated. As a result, although it was forbidden to go out until a second order within the scope of martial law enforcement, people organized through television programs, social media and smart phone applications and went out to protest. In fact, the motivation of the public is the trauma of the text that was read on TRT, and perhaps the first time that a trauma is a constructive function in a mass event. In Turkey "Electronic communication" platforms like this and the innovations made in that field in recent years in communication technologies and has prepared the ground for the necessary mass and collective cooperation to failure of the coup attempt. They have faced the resistance of the civilian people who effectively used communication technologies. The people exposed to the attack continued to encourage each other by "visual sharing", and in this way they disabled the coup attempt. In addition to the security forces, the biggest share in neutralizing the coup attempt belongs to the Turkish society who undoubtedly showed supreme sacrifice. However, the media have played a vital role both in the strategy development of the security units and in the anti-coup resistance of the people. The media, which often acted prior or on top of the public until the day of the coup attempt on July 15, acted like a "character" from public with the rise of coup probabilities. This is a considerable change in terms of sociology of media. Especially in events that can affect the whole of the country, such reflexes of common attitude development should be developed in a sustainable way. However, this attitude was made possible by the use of internet-oriented communication tools to spread the collective the courage (Demir, 2016, Halıcı, 2011).

After 22:00, the first and most important time of the coup attempt, there was no access to Twitter, Facebook and YouTube without any court decision. Twitter made an official statement at 00:53 and stated that their services were deliberately slowed down. Social media services, which have been somewhat more eased after midnight, have been used extensively by the public as it was understood that events are a "coup attempt". Millions of people who meet around the tags of #NoToCoup and #WeAreAtSquaresNationally have exhibited a common stance against the coup. News organizations continued to convey statements from the authorities and updates related to detentions and operations and without any problem on social media platforms where social media access has returned to normal. In addition to the news organizations, people who went out to protest the coup instantly conveyed the situation throughout the country by live broadcasts via Facebook and Periscope. Every image and message transmitted from the scene in the night of the coup attempt was also purposefully shared by some certain "virtual groups" other than the instant broadcast systems, and these shares provided the basis for the common action development of the nation. The July 15 coup attempt has shown that every innovation in the field of communications hardware and software is now one of the most decisive variables of social change. As a matter of fact, social and political events as well as everyday life are becoming increasingly media-oriented and communication policies have very dominant visual values (Demir, 2016).

The new media is not one of the causes of mass movements, and users are using this platform as a means of organizing and communicating in mass movements. Social media was used to organize individuals to reach wider masses and to maintain the flow in different cultures such as "Wall Street occupation", "London rebellion", "Arab rebellion" and similar mass movements. The same usage of this platform for mass movements in societies which have different social norms, beliefs, forms of governance, wealth levels, reveals the universality of the social media (Sungur, 2017). The coup attempt carried out in Turkey on July 15, 2016, there were 248 martyrs and 2194 veterans (Ministry of Justice, 2017).

It is possible to say that the present development level of technology and the spread of new media tools proved once again that it is an important platform for finding fast and effective solutions for individuals. These innovations have become an example of the fact that they will be sensitive to any movements that can occur in the social order and that they have gained a global dimension in moving, guiding and informing people together. The Turkish society has shown a very clear attitude towards the coup attempt. Turkish society whose mind is filled with quite tragic memories stood as a whole for the first time against the ones who are against democracy. In the wake of this struggle, where hundreds of martyrs were given, the coup attempt of a terrorist organization has been succumbed to failure. The value that dominates this struggle has been the homeland love that brings democracy and all elements of this country together (Miş et al. 2016, pp. 7-71).

Many stories written after the coup attempt are texts based on memory or testimony. Most are similar to stories written during the years of National Struggle. These stories are written according to the axis of the testimonies of the authors or their own memories. For stories written in extraordinary situation in the first phase of the 20th century, the determination of "a little lack of art but full of sincerity" can be made for many stories written after July 15th. (Kaya, 2017).

Of course, there are many individuals who lost their lives in the coup attempt of July 15th. However, Sergeant Ömer Halisdemir, who was one of the most influential people in the country's agenda and who was the most influential at the beginning of these social movements, shot Brigadier General Semih Terzi in the Special Forces Command, was at the forefront of those heroes. The twin brothers Ahmet and Mehmet Oruç, who were martyred in the Security Special Operations Center, and the martyr police Demet Sezen were the martyr symbols. It can be said that there are more stories to say and more stories to tell with related to the events on July 15th and the following period (Erdem, 2017, Kaya, 2017).

CONCLUSION

The disappearance of the importance of geographical boundaries in the world and the widespread use of mass media has gained a new dimension in the livable environment. Individuals have the chance to be able to instantly observe and to be aware of events happening in the world, no matter where they are. As a result of the globalization movement that has emerged at an unprecedented rate in recent years, there is an important and rapid change in the social sense. The focal point of this change is improvements in new communication technologies. These developments in communication technologies have also transformed social movements. They have started to use new media to react to events that have occurred in society with the opportunities created by new media technologies. It is possible to say that the new technological revolution started a new social period with these developments. New communication technologies can be regarded as a medium to realize participatory democracy in society because of its strong characteristics such as possibilities of information transfer, personal communication, interaction between individuals and accessibility to universal dimension.

Today's social movements are based on problems like social environment, rights, political practices, education, freedoms rather than appearing as ideological thoughts as they are in the past. Thanks to new media and developing social networking groups, there is an easy organization platform and a mobility that has the opportunity to convey voice to wider masses and interact with wider masses. While rapid flow of information by the Internet brings an important effect, accessibility of individuals to social media through new media tools with mobile and online features give them the opportunity to reach information and broadcast at any time. Social media can be a means of public information and organizing together with information sharing. We can say that the use of cross media by large masses at a national and international level causes changes in attitudes in societies.

The new media is directing the masses in a short period of time, organizing the public over these networks, offering the possibility of self-expression, introduction and organization to individuals and institutions. With the contribution of the social media, individuals have an idea about every event in the community. It presents the form of rapid organization by solving the causes of social events by bringing forward the individual plan in social movements. While contributing to the formation of social movements in the new media; it is aimed to create and direct the perception necessary for the formation of these movements, and to draw the masses to the streets. It is generally realized that the activity of the new media is used and the social movements are designed.

Individuals use new communication technologies more and more every day in the processes of communicating, managing, directing, informing, and organizing social movements. Especially internet has become the basic communication medium. People have begun to use the new media in social activities that enable them to reach larger masses faster. The new media has enabled social movements to reach individuals, while making democracy more functional.

Technological developments in the mass media can be said to be effective in accelerating globalization, which we define as the impact on societies across borders from everywhere in the world the with technological developments, use of these tools by individuals and influence on economies, politics, societies and culture. The new media allow individuals to have the information they need in a very short time. Thus, individuals become able to search, get informed, reach information quickly, and become conscious, query. As a result of the development and popularization of new media, people become aware of the issues at national and global level and show their reactions by organizing through social networks.

The new media accelerates the sharing of information on an individual basis, creates an agenda, and provides the ability to quickly organize and implement social movements. The fact that the new media is a democratization tool can't be denied. There are also harmful aspects of the technological development of new media as far as it is beneficial. However, when openness of the new media environment is considered, it can act as a proper tool for democratization and organization of people and serve for right purposes if controlled environment could be established.

The coups that are considered as social movements in Turkey's political life, poses an important place. Many times in the history, it has been faced with social movements such as junta, coup, postmodern coup, memorandum or e-memorandum, declaration, insurrection and attempt. The coup attempt on July 15, 2016 is one of them. We can conclude that one of the reasons for the failure of the coup attempt is that the public was informed, guided and aware of this attempt through new media and mass media. When the coup attempt of July 15, 2016 is considered, it is different from past coup structures and is separated from other coups in terms of the effectiveness of new media. The coups that is one of the social movements in Turkey's political life, poses an important place. It is possible to say that written and verbal means of communication are used in the announcement of all social movements up to the July 15 coup, however people are informed about the social movement by the use of new media and mass media in the attempt 15th of July. The most important element that distinguishes this attempt from others emerged through the new media after the speech of President Recep Tayyip Erdoğan on CNN Turk. He invited people to social movement. This message reached to the public in a short period of time and this situation allowed the public to participate with sensitivity to events. We can state that social media played critical role during the coup attempt on 15 July and acted as tool and means of communication to organize people, to make people to protect democracy.

Tweets that were sent by President Recep Tayyip Erdoğan, and from Presidential Twitter account that remove panic were the important elements that constitute the spirit of resisting the coup We can say that it contributes to the formation of social movement by triggering the public's reaction to the coup as well as the tendency to have democracy. It is possible to say that critical steps in the struggle against the coup in the 15 July coup attempt were made through visual and social media messages from new media and mass media.

Social Media is not one of the causes of political action, whereas societies use social media as a platform for organizing and communicating during political actions. The social media was used to organize people, to reach more people and to communicate, in political actions in different societies such as the "Wall Street occupation, London rebellions and Arab rebellions. Internet usage in Turkey and the world continues to grow rapidly and in the context of media and communication of July 15 coup attempt, we can say that it has an important effect on regulation or prevention of social movements. Besides the fact that it is effective in the prevention of social movements; we cannot ignore the fact that it is also an effective platform for the planners of this coup.

Today's social networks represent an important role in transformation of representative democracy to participatory democracy, and will open up new roles every day, thus the 15 July coup attempt has revealed that there is a need for new media and communication technologies to be controlled for the country's permanence. The formation of a national media communication policy seems to be the most important problem to be solved. People directly experience or get updates of information of the social events that occur through media or indirectly through trans-media. Particularly in the process of informing individuals, the importance and effectiveness of the trans-media has become more apparent. Differences in the way people are influenced by trans-media types in terms of political and social awareness can be better demonstrated and compared.

REFERENCES

Adalet Bakanlığı. (2017). 15 Temmuz: Yüzyılın ihaneti-Yüzyılın zaferi. Ankara: Ertem.

Akıncı, A. (2014). Türkiye'nin darbe geleneği: 1960 ve 1971 müdahaleler. *Eskişehir osmangazi üniversitesi İİBF dergisi, 9*(1), 55-72.

Alemdaroğlu, A., & Demirtaş, N. (2004). Biz Türk erkeklerini böyle bilmezdik!: Mynet'te erkeklik halleri. *Toplum ve bilim dergisi, 101*, 206-224.

Arslan, A. (2001). Türk medya elitleri: Bir durum tespiti. *Sosyoloji araştirmalari dergisi, 8*, 135-164.

Babacan, M. E. (2014). Sosyal medya sonrasi yeni toplumsal hareketler. *Birey ve toplum, 4*(7), 135-160

Böğrekçi, Ü. A. (2013). Siyaset, medya ve ordu üçgeninde 27 Mayıs atmosferi: "Karanlığa direnen yildiz" üzerinden bir bakiş. *Turkish Studies, 8/9*, 1913–1932.

Cohen, B. C. (1963). *The press and foreign policy.* Princeton, NJ: Princeton University Press.

Damlapınar, Z. (2007). Medya okuryazarliği dersi öğretmen el kitabi. Ankara: RTÜK Araştırma Geliştirme Daire Başkanlığı.

Demir, S. T. (2016). 15 Temmuz darbe girişiminde medya. *SETA Analiz, 161*, 8–9.

Demircioğlu, E. T. (2014). Yeni toplumsal hareketler: Bir literatür taramasi. *Marmara üniversitesi siysal bilgiler dergisi, 2*(1), 133-144.

Emiroğlu, A. (2011). 27 Mayıs 1960 ihtilali ve Demokrat Parti'nin tasfiyesi. *Selçuk üniversitesi kadinhani faik içil meslek yüksekokulu sosyal ve teknik araştirmalar dergisi, 1*(1), 13-27.

Erdem, S. E. (2017). *15 Temmuz direnişinin en genç şehidi.* Retrieved from 15.07.2017, from https://www.memurlar.net/haber/681096/15-temmuz-direnisinin-en-genc-sehidi.html

Halıcı, C. Y. (2011). Toplumsal hareketlere etkisi bakimindan sosyal medya. *Akademik incelemeler dergisi, 6*(2), 1-10.

Joseph, S. (2012). Social media, political change and human rights. *Boston College International and Comparative Law Review, 35*(1), 45–188.

Kalafatoğlu, Ş. T. (2015). Toplumsal hareketler ve politik oluşumlar bağlaminda yeni medya araciliğiyla politik aktivizm. *Sobiad, 5*(11), 126–145.

Karagöz, K. (2013). Yeni medya çağında toplumsal hareketler ve dijital aktivizm hareketleri. *İletişim ve diplomasi, 1*, 131-157.

Kaya, R. (1985). Kitle iletişim sistemleri. Ankara: Teori.

Kaya, S. Z. (2017). 15 Temmuz hakkinda yazilmiş hikâyelerden Güray Süngü'nün "gece"sini tahlil denemesi. *İnsan ve toplum bilimleri dergisi, 9*, 267-280.

Miş, N., Gülener, S., Coşkun, İ., Duran, H., & Ayvaz, M. E. (2016). *15 Temmuz darbe girişimi toplumsal algı araştırması*. İstanbul: SETA.

Özel, S. (2012). Yeni medyanin temelleri üzerine bir tartışma. *Online academic journal of information technology, 3*, 31-45.

Sungur, S. A. (2017). 15 Temmuz darbe kalkişmasini engellenmesinde sosyal medyanin rolü. *Akademik sosyal araştirmalar dergisi, 47*, 597-612.

Timisi, N. (2003). Yeni iletişim teknolojileri ve demokrasi. Ankara: Dost.

Türk, G. D. (2013). *Demokrasinin dördüncü kuvveti yeni medya teknolojileri. In XVIII. Türkiye'de internet konferansı* (pp. 55–60). İstanbul University.

Yağmur, H. (2015). *Sosyal medyanin siyaset ve kamuoyunu yönlendirmedeki rolü* (Master's Thesis). Available from Council of Higher Education Thesis Center. (No. 422422)

Yılmaz, M. (2013). Medyanın, toplumsal ve siyasal yaklaşim üzerindeki önemi, siyasal görüşün medya üzerindeki rolü. *2. İnternational Conference on Communication, North Cyprus, Media Technology and Desing*, 365-370.

Yılmaz, R. (2008). *Toplumsal gerçekliğin kurulumunda gazetelerin edimsözel etkileri* (Master's Thesis). Available from Council of Higher Education Thesis Center. (No. 229523)

KEY TERMS AND DEFINITIONS

Cross Media: Investors who want to take advantage of all the media's integrations and produce in all aspects have invested in multiple mediums and have grown in the cross direction.

FaceTime: It was firstly introduced in 2010 with the iPhone 4 and is a video call service.

Internet: It is a constantly growing communication network that is widespread around the world, where many computer systems are interconnected.

Military Coup Attempt: The military coup means the fact that armed forces take control of the administration of the country.

Social Media: Digital platforms where you can follow people based on your interests, get simultaneous information, and share that information called social media.

Social Movements: The movements of revolt, rebellion and resistance are the rise of the social relationship based on conflict. Although all these movements have different forms and appearances, they may be said to have acted with similar rejection and opposition. Rebellions sometimes have a social, cultural, or political goal but often base on a sense of rejection. Here, the basis is objection against social or cultural order that is perceived as injustice and inequality.

Storytelling: Along with the emergence of new media tools, storytelling has become a universe expanding with faster and more narrative contribution. The story telling method, which is also shaped by today's new communication tools, is confronted with the concept of "trans-media storytelling."

This research was previously published in Handbook of Research on Transmedia Storytelling and Narrative Strategies edited by Recep Yılmaz, M. Nur Erdem, and Filiz Resuloğlu; pages 436-448, copyright year 2019 by Information Science Reference (an imprint of IGI Global).

Section 2
Media and Social Platforms

Chapter 8
We the New Media:
The Disruption of Social Media in Interpersonal and Collective Communication

Miguel del Fresno
Universidad Nacional de Educación a Distancia (UNED), Spain

ABSTRACT

The Internet have led to the emergence of a new communication ecosystem that is not restricted to the online context and in which professional and social media intersect and cohabitate to compete for the attention of audiences. This ecosystem occurs in cyberspace; a placeless space where new forms of power, influence, control, and management of collective perceptions have developed. These emerging macro social platforms are giving rise to a new paradox: people need social media to express their opinions and creativity, while the major platforms tend to view users as products. A new model is presented to describe and explain this new communication ecosystem that has put an end to the mediating exclusivity of professional media and maximizes collective interpersonal communication on one and the same social continuum. It is a new interpersonal and collective communication ecosystem whose deep logic is necessary to understand and in which academics must compete.

INTRODUCTION

Communication can be understood as the act of sharing "meaning through the exchange of information", which is defined "by the technology of communication, the characteristics of the senders and receivers of information, their cultural codes of reference and protocols of communication, and the scope of the communication process" (Castells, 2009, p. 88). Communication is also defined as "a binding force in social relationships without at the same time being visible or having tangible and permanent forms…within a given structure of relationships and have consequences for this structure without being readily open to observation" (McQuail & Windahl, 1993, p. 4). Communication is therefore a property of collective interpersonal action rather than of those who engage in it, although anyone may be a potential communicative agent.

DOI: 10.4018/978-1-5225-9869-5.ch008

The *Era de la información* (the Information Age) (Castells, 2001), or the *Société de l'information* (the Information Society) (Mattelart, 2003), is characterized by the social changes that have occurred since the late twentieth century as a result of the evolution of digital information and communication technologies as well as the emergence of a social network structure that has affected all areas of human activity on a global scale. Social changes brought about by technological innovations have always given rise to "changes in the order of interpersonal relationships" (del-Fresno, 2011a, p. 20). The uninterrupted technological spans have been presented as a gradual extension of our senses. As McLuhan (1964) stated, "we have extended our central nervous system in a global embrace, abolishing both space and time as far as our planet is concerned" (p. 3), thus leading to the growing technologization of reality (Virilio, 1991). This means that new media and technologies are transforming not only the "*how*" of communication, but the "*meaning*" of what is being communicated.

The Internet is one of the most disruptive technological phenomena for communication in history, especially collective interpersonal communication. The Internet, even in the second decade of the twenty-first century, is the result of decisions taken regarding its architecture and code in the early 1990s. Indeed, "the first generation of these architectures was built by a noncommercial sector—researchers and hackers, focused upon building a network" (Lessig, 2009, p. 7). As William Mitchell (1996) put it, the "code is cyberspace's law" (p. 111) or as Joel Reidenberg (1998) called it, "*Lex Informatica*" or "*control of code is power*" (Lessig, 2009, p. 79). As regards the social media in particular, the code is "the unavoidable boundary around which no detour exists in order to participate fully in modern life. It is ubiquitous" (Berry & Pawlik, 2008, p. 58).

The code has a performative function because it is the condition for allowing communication on the Internet, and the means by which the expressive capacities of people are enhanced or restricted, and which facilitates, or not, the diversity of communicative practices in cyberspace. Thanks to the Internet, the previous communication ecosystem has been reabsorbed and a new one comprised of numerous and diverse players (both professionals and non-professionals) has emerged that enables the constant production and exchange of exponential amounts of data and information anytime and anywhere.

Early on, it was anticipated that this phenomenon would be a collective problem in the form of *information overload* (Toffler, 1970; Toffler & Toffler, 1994; Lewis, 1999) or an *accident*: "the damage caused by the explosion of unlimited information" will be "the great accident of the future, the one that comes after the succession of accidents that was specific to the industrial age" (Virilio, 1995, para. 14), where each technology entails its own accident. It is estimated that, thanks to technological development, more information was available in the second half of the twentieth century than ever before in the history of humankind (Feather, 2008) and that the Internet has played a key role in information overload since its entry into society (Swash, 1998).

Following the expansion of the Internet at the global scale, there emerged a "new form of interactive communication, characterized by the capacity of sending messages from many to many, in real time or chosen time, and with the possibility of using point-to-point communication, narrowcasting or broadcasting depending on the purpose" (Castells 2009, p. 55), what Castells referred to as *mass self-communication*. It is, at one and the same time, "mass self-communication because it can potentially reach a global audience" and "self-communication because the production of the message is self-generated, the definition of the potential receiver(s) is self-directed, and the retrieval of specific messages or content… is self-selected" (Castells, 2009, p. 55). This process "has broadened the collective interpersonal communication system, which has had an effect on the reconfiguration of social reality itself" (del-Fresno, 2015, p. 75). Therefore it makes perfect sense to examine the communicative practices arising from the intersection of sociability and communication in the Internet, whose result is understood as an intentional, interpersonal and collective, global and local social action around communication that is not restricted to the digital ecosystem.

These new forms of communication marked a break with the dominant communication model imposed by the mass media prior to the emergence of the Internet. In the mass media, people were relegated to being receptive and more or less passive audiences. In contrast, social media have facilitated the emergence of audiences with the ability and capacity to be senders and receivers, the *micromedia* (del-Fresno, 2011b), thus causing a growing process of disintermediation of professional media. A micromedium can be any individual or entity that, through a simple technological device with Internet access and increasing code, web or mobile applications, can choose at will to change their role as active/passive receivers/senders in the symbolic distribution of content and information to other micromedia or professional media. In the Internet age, where "real time is prevailing over real space" (Virilio, 1996) and "the idea of time can be reduced to a point of view" (Virilio, 1991, p. 105), audiences are no longer stable, homogeneous and passive masses, but rather fragmented, reshaped and (re)presented in interchangeable roles.

This chapter explores how the Internet, as well as its architecture and code, has enabled the emergence of social media—Web 2.0 social platforms (O'Reilly, 2005)—which come and go according to the same market logic as professional media. This has sped up the development of a new communication ecosystem that is not restricted to the online context, and which is characterized by the intersection and cohabitation of professional media and social media, that is, professional communicators and micromedia. It is a new social ecosystem and communicative *placeless space* where there have arisen new forms of power, influence, control and collective management of perceptions on any relevant topic in societies at the local and global scale. As a result, "the communication ecosystem can simultaneously contain without any trace of contradiction noise and signal, truth and lies, virtue and vice, news and rumors, the original and duplicate, voyeurism and exhibitionism—all within the same bold universe of inclusiveness" (del-Fresno, 2015, p. 76).

From the viewpoint of communication, it has always been an easy task to identify senders and receivers. Since the emergence of the Internet and social media, however, these concepts are no longer so obvious or explanatory. The rise of social media communication is "another example of the exceptional ability of people to collectively communicate meaning and ideas" (del-Fresno, 2015, p. 75). We are witnessing a paradigm shift in communication where the media and professional communicators must cohabitate, form part of and compete with social media and micromedia. Following in the path of the traditional models used to study mass communication (McQuail & Windahl, 1993), a new model has arisen to describe and explain this new communication ecosystem that has put an end to the mediating exclusivity of professional media and maximizes collective interpersonal communication on the same social continuum, where the notion of offline and online have lost their traditional explanatory power. In terms of accident, as understood by P. Virilio, in exchange for greater resources and opportunities for global and local, synchronous and asynchronous, and interpersonal and collective communication we must accept that the boundaries between communication and pseudo-communication, between signal and noise, between the relevant and the irrelevant are being blurred as a sign of our times.

This is the social and communicative context in which individuals and academics seek to build their identity and position themselves in the online environment. A proper understanding of this reality is critical for individuals and organizations to successfully undertake projects, as the social media is another example of the extraordinary ability of individuals to generate, disseminate and exchange meanings in a massive network system in real time.

BACKGROUND

Throughout human history, communication has always been tied to a specific technology through drawing, painting, writing, printing, etc. up to Internet and smartphones. In the late nineteenth and early twentieth century, communication occurred as a result of technological changes (sped up by printing and distribution), the dissemination of written press and the break from a dominant localist, elitist and minority type of information with ideological-political, economic-financial and religious intentions. In 1883, Benjamin Day, the editor of the *New York Sun*, decided to lower the price of the daily by reducing printing costs in exchange for advertising to make written press accessible to the working classes, thus founding *The Penny Press*. In the 1990s, the owners of mass media viewed the Internet, above all, as a new advertising medium, but did not fathom the extent to which collective interpersonal communication would be reorganized globally or let alone how their business model and mediation exclusivity would be plunged into crisis.

From N. de Condocert, L. Mumford, H. Innis and M. McLuhan to the cyberpunk authors, there has been a long tradition of receiving newly emerging media in society as the bearers of a new civilization, thus "the utopian, as well as dystopian, terms in which new media have been received have caused several media historians to record a sense of déjà vu, the feeling that we have been here before" (Lister, Dovey, Giddings, Grant, & Kelly, 2009, p. 65)

The sociologist A. Mattelart (2003) associated this sense of déjà vu with the telegraph in as early as the eighteenth century, claiming that it is possible to identify a recurring "prophetic discourse on the democratic virtues of long-distance communication" although such emancipatory expectations "would soon be contradicted by the continuation of the embargo on codes and encrypted language of signs and by the refusal to authorize their use for civilian purposes in the name of domestic security and national defense" (p. 23). He added that each new technology generation "revived the discourse of salvation, the promise of universal concord, decentralized democracy, social justice and general prosperity. Each time, the amnesia regarding earliest technology would be confirmed" (Mattelart, 2003, p. 23). If each technology is presented, at least in its initial stages, as a door to a new era and those expectations are repeated with each new media, it should come as no surprise that this also occurred with the Internet.

In the dawn of the Internet, cyberpunk authors encountered the metaphorical and life-saving hybridization of man and machine in computing and technology. Cyberpunks envisioned different scenarios in which the established social order would breakdown and an ideal community would emerge around a techno-emancipatory cyberculture where human capacities are enhanced by technology or, alternatively, machines are created and evolve to finally overcome the contradictions of society and pave the way to a new one. Some of the most important topics related to the notion of overcoming previous stages of human development include gender contradictions (Haraway, 1989; Franck, 1995), the evolution of our consciousness or identity parallel to technological development (Turkle, 1984, 1994), the broadening of our cognitive capacity to gain a better understanding of our place in the world and access a larger reality (Heim, 1998), or the cyberspace experienced in religious terms as the spiritual realm of the non-physical space, a new *soul space* (Wertheim, 1999). Thus, since the early 1990s, the Internet has been welcomed and defended—in the same spirit of its researcher and hacker founding fathers—as the door to a new era. Although these notions have undergone successive revisions on a par with the rapid development of technology (Sirky, 2009; Bertot, Jaegar, & Grimes, 2010; Li & Bernoff, 2008), to some extent they still prevail today and continue to conceive of the Internet as an exceptional space for social emancipation, frictionless horizontal communication, mass collaboration (Tapscott & Williams, 2006), participatory culture and collective intelligence (Jenkins, 2006). The Internet is so far removed from both the techno-utopian and dystopian visions (Nie & Erbring, 2002) that they have tended to accuse the Internet of being a new form of social isolation where contact with the social environment is lost, even more so than television.

More than two decades after the dawn of the Internet, the analysis of its effects has shown that the Internet has had a greater capacity for eroding or destroying business models than for creating new ones; a promise of *creative destruction* (Aghion & Howitt, 1992, 1997; Foster & Kaplan, 2001; Cowen, 2004) that has been repeatedly postponed and unfulfilled (Lanier, 2011). This phenomenon of erosion or destruction of business models brought about by the Internet (film, music, travel, the hospitality industry, commerce, publishing, etc.) is also evident even with regard to classic mass media that have adapted and evolved since *The Penny Press*.

The triangulation of sociability, communication and technology means that we are immersed in a dense web of social interactions forming an aggregate and vast social network that "connects people, information, events and places, thus facilitating or restricting the flow of information, ideas and perceptions in an instant and massive network communication system" (del-Fresno, 2014, p. 246). The importance of the Internet and its evolving code does not lie so much in its potential as an emancipatory lever or its accidents but in the evidence that it has both reorganized mass communication and deeply modified the conditions that enable collective interpersonal communication.

The Internet has given rise to a triple hybridization: 1) between offline and online sociability where "an ontological and phenomenological distinction between the online and offline world is no longer timely or meaningful" (del-Fresno, 2011a, p. 61) "as part of the same social continuum" (del-Fresno, 2014, p. 247); 2) between professional media and social media in a single and inclusive macromedium with all types of information and content; and 3) between individual and collective communicative practices in one macro communication ecosystem.

The most significant effects of the social media on the professional media forced to cohabit with them are:

1. The introduction in the communication ecosystem of the capacity for feedback and the circularity of social media insofar as audiences have the potential—regardless of whether they use it for good or bad purposes or do not use it at all—to create, modify, share, accept or reject and redistribute their own or others' information and content in an autonomous and immediate way.
2. The loss of the mass media's exclusivity to mediate vertically with audiences, symbolically control meanings and manage the social synchronization of perceptions.
3. The radical reorganization of the advertising market where the battle once waged by professional media to capture attention translated into advertising revenue is now focused on social media, which have become a competitor with a high potential for the cannibalization of revenues.

The result is not a communication model restricted to the digital context, nor is it a utopian or dystopian one from the viewpoint of emancipatory expectations. The information circulating in the new communication ecosystem remains as relevant and/or as trivial as before and suffers from the same problems of veracity as in the previous model, but is of a greater complexity in terms of understanding how information is produced and distributed and how opinions and behaviors are shaped and spread at an unprecedented scale.

Social Media

A definition of social media must incorporate two concepts dating from its origins: the Web 2.0 and UGC (user-generated content). The term "Web 2.0" was coined by Tim O'Reilly at the Web 2.0 Conference in 2004 (O'Reilly, 2005; Graham, 2005). The Web 2.0 is considered the ideological and technological platform for the development of what is now known as social media. From a technical standpoint, the Web 2.0 as a governing social media refers to the group of code applications that exploit the ideological and technological foundations of Internet architecture to facilitate the creation and exchange of UGC (Kaplan & Haenlein, 2010). Web 2.0 research takes a user perspective, the expression of the online identity and reality (Turkle, 1995) that gives full meaning to social media.

However, the communication enabled by social media goes considerably beyond the mechanics of how it is produced. Although SixDegrees (1997) is often claimed to be the first social network (Boyd & Ellison, 2007), the Bulletin Board System (BBS), USENET newsgroups, the first CompuServe and later America Online (AOL) forums could be considered the first social media although they were not referred to as such in the early days of the Internet.

Social media can be organized into different categories which include, although not exclusively, social networking platforms (Facebook, LinkedIn), microblogging (Twitter, Weibo), photography (Flickr, Instagram, Pinterest), video (YouTube, Vimeo, MetaCafe), social news (Menéame, Digg, Reddit), live broadcasts (Livecast, Ustream), social gaming (World of Craft), bookmarking (Delicious, StumbleUpon), blogs (WordPress, Blogger), and many more. Social media have become the source of an enormous amount of data produced ubiquitously, relentlessly and massively known as *big data* (Mayer-Schönberger & Cukier, 2014). This type of data, which is studied using social media mining techniques to uncover meaningful patterns, offers numerous opportunities and challenges for researchers, the most interesting of which is not the sheer amount of the data, but what can be done with them that cannot be done with small amounts.

In the scientific literature (Pérez, Portilla, & Sánchez, 2011), social media are understood as spaces for *mass collaboration* (Tapscott & Williams, 2006) and media convergence, participatory culture and collective intelligence (Jenkins, 2006), which gives way to a growing social component in individual decision-making processes (del-Fresno, 2012 a). Similarly, social media and the new forms of social interaction via technology have changed the way people form groups and how they coexist without the need for traditional organizational structures, which ultimately has profound economic and social effects (Shirky, 2009). Social media enable forms of communication in which the one-way control of information is weakened and reduced, when precisely the rigid model to control the emission and distribution of information has been one of the key functions and policies of mass media (Li & Bernoff, 2008). Social media can also be understood as the age of instant communication, transparency, narcissism and participation, calling into question organizations' one-way communication towards people (Qualman, 2009). Moreover, the potential of social media is recognized as a means of communication and expression to promote openness, transparency, combat corruption and improve cultural attitudes about government transparency (Bertot et al., 2010). From a sociopolitical perspective, it is a space where new battles for power and counter-power are waged and "shows the direct link between politics, media politics, the politics of scandal, and the crisis of political legitimacy in a global perspective" (Castells, 2007, p. 238). In short, from the viewpoint of collective communication, *social media* competitively cohabitate with traditional media in terms of immediacy, coverage, scope, visibility and relevance due to their circularity, marketability and open communication practices.

As subjects of social media, micromedia have the "dual property of being both part of the medium as well as part of the message" (del-Fresno, 2015, p. 76) insofar as other peers grant varying degrees of credibility to their individual (one to one) or social (one to many and many to many) communications in a synchronous or asynchronous manner. Thanks to the code applications of social media, micromedia are able to create, modify, share and discuss or reject all kinds of information from any source, while at the same time they can provide late-breaking or redundant information live, thus resulting in a collective and informative narrative that is not subject to an agenda of unilateral interests and generating relevant and/or trivial information and content with the same problems of veracity that already occurred with mass media.

The originality of the new communication ecosystem following the emergence of social media lies in:

1. **Who Sends:** The hegemony and mediation exclusivity of professional media with audiences has been broken; they are now forced to cohabit with social media, which entails the growing deinstitutionalization of mass media.
2. **What is Sent:** The volume of data and information in circulation—signal and noise on an unprecedented scale—requires new ways of capturing, storing, analyzing and producing knowledge that has led to the emergence of social media techniques such as mining.
3. **In Which Channel:** The control of channels by major media groups undergoing constant merger processes continues to exist on a par with the explosion of social media channels and the multiplication of individuals as potential micromedia broadcasters or narrowcasters.
4. **To Whom:** The media are based on a one-way, vertical communication from professional media owners—and their agenda setting—towards audiences understood almost as a property of professional media, thus commercializing attention in the form of advertising. This aspect must also coexist with the new, major social media players that are capturing increasing shares of the advertising market.

The definition of social media proposed here is therefore: media resulting from collective and interpersonal communication thanks to Internet architecture and the creation of web or mobile code applications that enable synchronous and/or asynchronous communication by (multi)decentralized, (de)localized, (co)generative micromedia with the capacity to provide constant feedback to audiences in an ongoing process of reconfiguration, without a predefined geographical scope of a non-recurring, non-normalized and heterogeneous set of symbolic content or messages (their own or of others) that is not subject to a performative agenda.

Thus, it is not a question of somehow reformulating the theory of meaning such as that derived from the sentence *the medium is the message* (McLuhan, 1964). The novelty stems from the fact that the new communication ecosystem has emerged as a result of both the technology that enables the expansion of innovative communication practices and that, for the first time in the history of communication, people as micromedia play the simultaneous and interchangeable role of audience (passive or active) and sender (narrowcaster and broadcaster) with the capacity of response; a phenomenon that has led to profound changes in the democratization of communication (Kietzmann, Hermkens, McCarthy, & Silvestre, 2011). Indeed, this is how the shift from "other" the media to "we" the media has occurred.

The emergence of social media has resulted in the reorganization of the ecosystem of influence and collective management of perceptions once monopolized by the mass media, particularly large global communication groups. The traditional system of influence oriented towards the massive-scale

Figure 1. Professional and social media: New communication ecosystem
Source: Author

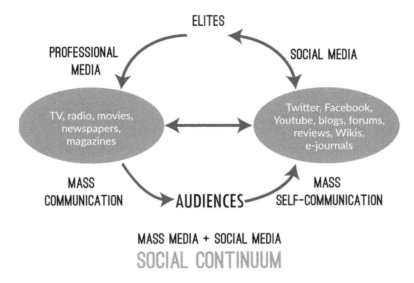

synchronization of perceptions has been disrupted by social media and the mass self-communication of micromedia, giving rise to a new media ecosystem (Figure 1).

The mass media's ecosystem of vertical, one-way influence survives embedded in the emerging system, forcing professional media to take part in an uncomfortable—and undesired—cohabitation with social media. Social media and thousands or millions of micromedia have taken a leading role in the battle for the management of social perceptions by influencing beliefs and the dissemination of opinions and behaviors, thus unifying interpersonal and collective practices on one and the same continuum. This "hybrid, all-media space forms a labyrinth linking people who share information, news, perceptions, beliefs, and rumors in a real-time, immense, networked communication system" (del-Fresno, 2015, p. 77).

COMMUNICATION MODELS

Models for Studying Collective Communication

With the emergence of mass consumption in the 1920s, the first "notions of opinion management and engineered consent began to circulate, pointing to an infatuation with the new method of governing mass democracy, involving a carefully calculated combination of information and censorship" (Mattelart, 2003, p. 38) at the hands of pioneering researchers such as W. Lippmann (1922) and H. Lasswell (1938). Coinciding with the pre-war and wartime evolution of World War II in the 1940s, the written press and other mass media, such as radio, film and later television, showed increasing interest in the systematic research of figures like P. Lazarsfeld and R.K. Merton (1940 and 1943). At that time, there came a need for concise models to explain the phenomenon of mass communication in a historical context and how communication was changing on a par with the social and technological changes of the time. Models are useful as tools depending on how effective they are in simplifying complex, abstract or ambivalent phenomena and help to reflect on changes in communication practices. The speed with which social changes are occurring requires simple communication models that provide maximum explanatory power.

According to McQuail and Windahl (1993), a model of collective communication is always "a consciously simplified description in graphic form of a piece of reality [that] seeks to show the main elements of any structure or process and the relationships between these elements" (p. 30). However, because mass communication is an abstract and dynamic process, there is no multipurpose model that can give a definitive analytical, heuristic or epistemological answer.

For McQuail and Windahl (1993), a model for studying collective communication is useful if it provides:

1. An *organizing function* and presents an overall picture to explain the whole phenomenon of communication at a given moment;
2. A *heuristic function* that allows communication researchers to focus on key aspects of communicative processes and practices;
3. A *predictive function* of how results can be achieved and which facilitates the presentation of research hypotheses; and
4. A *descriptive function* if communicative practices can be explained in terms of "forces and their direction, the relations between parts and the influence of one part on another" (p. 3).

The most relevant models are those which have the ability to be explanatory and address the key conceptual core of collective communication.

Harold D. Lasswell was the first to propose a model for the study of mass communication, which was based on the effects of propaganda on World War II fighters (Lasswell, 1948). Lasswell's classic model sums up communication as: *Who–says what–in which channel–to whom–with what effect*. The most significant aspect of Lasswell's model is that it revealed the keys of mass media early on: one-way communication, the highly passive assumption—especially from the advertising point of view—of receiving the message and the absence of feedback from audiences. All the models developed after Lasswell's have a common purpose: to show how a privileged sender tries to influence a large audience in a one-way and intentional manner.

Theodore M. Newcomb's ABX model offered a different approach in assuming that "communication among humans performs the essential function of enabling two or more individuals to maintain simultaneous orientation toward one another as communicators *and* toward objects of communication" (Newcomb, 1953, p. 393). However, the model was naïve in two ways:

1. It assumed a natural tendency for consensus in communication, and
2. Extrapolated communicative processes between individuals or small groups to society as a whole.

In their co-orientation model, J. McLeod and S. Chaffee (1973) incorporated the concept of conflict as a variable of mass communication together with those of accuracy, congruency and the search for informative support. The co-orientation model exerted considerable influence in the twentieth century as it provided strong heuristic and descriptive power in mass media by incorporating a new technology: television. Since then, the most widely accepted definition of mass communication is:

The transmission from a single or centralized (and organized) sender to all or most of a population of a recurring and standardized set of messages (news, information, fiction, entertainment and spectacle), without there being much possibility of responding or answering back…Mass communication enabled the symbolic and informational dominance of a whole society by those with control of the means of dissemination. (McQuail, 2002, p. 5)

Countless models for the study of collective communication in relation to the media have been proposed, but there is a gap in the literature (Lister et al., 2009) as models that include the collective interpersonal communication of the Internet, especially social media, are lacking.

Model for Studying Collective Interpersonal Communication in the Internet Age

We have seen how mass media channels and messages were the only game in town and they owned both the message and the means of communicating that message. Within a mass self-communication system, micromedia are able to extend messages through social media from and to others (peers or professional media) via a multidirectional communication system. "This system reflects individual (one to one) or social (one to many and many to many) interactions without the imposition of any agenda from the larger professional media" (del-Fresno, 2015, p. 76). The model proposed here (Figure 2) (del Fresno, 2012 b) to study collective interpersonal communication incorporates elements of mass media collective communication models together with new post-Internet elements.

The lines connecting the concepts in the figure indicate one-way or two-way relationships (direct or indirect), attitudes, perceptions and a feedback process. The traditional one-way communication of mass media is indicated by a continuous line on the left; while the dotted line on the right represents social media communication.

The *ELITES* are interest groups that may be in conflict or in competition with each other (political parties, corporations, lobbies, governments, brands, etc.) for the symbolic and informational dominance of the largest possible set of audiences. These groups defend their interests by exerting their influence (ideological or economic pressure as advertisers) on the *PROFESSIONAL MEDIA* or through the direct ownership of them. The professional media have lost their classic mediating exclusivity and have also been forced to a renounce a key aspect of their history: to be the first in breaking the news. Indeed, there are countless cases where the micromedia offer exclusive or breaking information and news before the mass media (Ibáñez & Baraybar, 2011; Weaver, Johnson, Sweetser, & Howes, 2009).

Since the elites have recognized *SOCIAL MEDIA* as significant collective interpersonal channels of communication, they have begun to deploy ownership strategies (by purchasing stocks), thus incorporating the social media corporate layer into their communication and public relations strategies in a direct (Verhoeven, Tench, Zerfass, Moreno, & Verčič, 2012; Bajkiewicz, Kraus, & Yeon Hong, 2011; Eyrich, Padman, & Sweetser, 2008) or indirect manner (del-Fresno & López-Peláez, 2014) in addition to investing in advertising in major social media platforms.

Topics on any matter that are susceptible to social exchange in both professional media and social media circulate in the communication ecosystem. *AUDIENCES* interested in or related to any of the topics circulating in the informational ecosystem are the target group to be impacted upon.

The relationship between professional media and social media is two-way since the former draw on information from the latter as sources to (re)elaborate the content and information (Hong, 2012; Canavilhas & Ibars, 2012; Weaver et al., 2009). Information considered interesting or of value is filtered from social media and selected by the micromedia (blogs, forums, information and opinion aggregators, etc.) of professional media to be (re)sent and spread virally among (micro)audiences in constant reconfiguration.

Figure 2. Collective interpersonal communication model
Source: Author

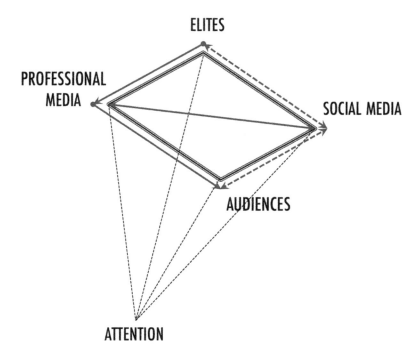

Cohabitation between the professional media and the social media is therefore 1) a feedback process related to the flow of data and information circulating in the ecosystem and 2) a competitive cohabitation in the battle to capture audiences' *ATTENTION*. As information grows exponentially, the audience's *attention* becomes an increasingly scarce resource (Goldhaber, 1997; Lanham, 2007). The purpose of all media is to attract and retain the attention of the audience, since it has both a symbolic and economic value. Unlike mass media, social media attention is not merely passive, but can be monetized in the market in the form of both advertising or e-commerce through online behavior data, private and personal data, private aggregated metadata, etc.

While media, brands, companies, organizations and others compete for the attention of citizens and consumers, other individuals tend to develop cognitive mechanisms and strategies of defense against the excessive demand for attention (Datchary, 2005; Pashler, 1998). The ability to reconcile these two aspects is a challenge for the media and a competitive advantage in the digital economy (Kessous, Mellet, & Zouinar, 2010).

From the cognitive point of view, the novel contribution of social media is the new emphasis on sensory impressions integrated into a new perception regime (Styhre, 2009). This has led to new forms of perception and attention-action due to the multimedia integration of text, sound, images or tactile impressions characteristic of virtual media called *haptic sense-impression*s (Prentice, 2005).

The relevance of introducing attention as a scarce resource within the collective communication model presented here is how the tension between two logics are depicted: protecting individuals' attention against the risk of cognitive overload versus the *market value* of attention that all media tend to saturate with advertising and calls-to-action.

The value of *attention* in the proposed communication model is manifold as it is presented as:

1.   A scarce resource;
2.   As something to capture, win, retain and capable of being monetized;
3.   The variable ensuring strong competition between media; and
4.   The cornerstone of the economic viability of both professional media and large social media platforms based on a market logic with their IPOs (Facebook, Twitter, LinkedIn, Yelp, Zinga, etc.).

Finally, the model includes social change in its heuristic. This is because while collective communication in the mass media occurred through information flows *towards* people (as in all classic models of collective communication), by including social change, the model captures the quality of the communication and extends it to the interpersonal collective scale, thus reflecting communication as a flow *of* people as micromedia at an unprecedented scale.

In short, the model also reflects the difficulty of drawing the boundaries between media. Thus, as McQuail and Windahl (1993) predicted, "we anticipate a future in which existing boundaries will become even less clear than they are at present and when communication technology and new expressions of communication needs will produce different structures and relationships" (p. 2).

Both individually and collectively, we are facing a new context of collective interpersonal communication at the local and global scale as a result of the emergence of the Internet; the most disruptive technological phenomenon in recent decades, which has led to a radical reorganization of communicative practices. In this chapter, a definition of social media has been proposed that contrasts with the classic notion of media, as well as a new model to study the collective interpersonal communication of our time, where all media and micromedia are exposed to new technological developments, new competitors, new options for audiences and new challenges that also define them as they unfold.

The proposed communication model unifies and explains the cohabitation of the mass media and social media, thus uniting the vertical, one-way communication typical of mass media with the multidirectional communication of social media. An additional key contribution is the incorporation of the variable *Elites'* fight for the *Attention* of local and global audiences in the model, where elites are understood as interest groups that may be in conflict or in competition with each other for the symbolic and informational dominance of the largest possible set of audiences through the direct or indirect control of classic and competing broadcasting channels or new global digital corporations at the local or global scale such as Facebook, Google, Apple, Amazon, Twitter, and others.

Micromedia can take an active part in the whole communication process by creating, distributing and disseminating content and information through multidirectional interaction. The tension between senders and audiences is reflected in two distinct logics: the protection of individual privacy versus the *market value* of their attention.

FUTURE RESEARCH DIRECTIONS

As a result of increasing computational capacity and the development of ad hoc technologies and Internet architecture, it is possible to capture, represent and analyze online relational data in order to broaden our knowledge. The new communication ecosystem presented via a model entails new challenges for researchers who must deal with large amounts of information. What is of interest, however, is not only the amount of data generated, but what can be done with such large amounts that cannot be done with small ones. In this regard, the two major challenges for researchers are:

1. The *challenge of complexity* or how to capture and consistently aggregate multidimensional data that are not homogeneous, unstructured and massive and produced *ad infinitum* in any time or place, as well as heterogeneous and unstable media (which may come and go), while maintaining the central objective of seeking out and identifying significant patterns.
2. The *challenge of n=all* or how to develop methods to work with all the data that is produced, that is, how to investigate with complete universes which are now accessible thanks to big data and data mining. Sampling is a technique that was developed two centuries ago to respond methodologically to times of scarce information, something which no longer seems to be the problem.

CONCLUSION

Online sociability is defined by the code, which according to Berry and Pawlik (2008), "…harmonised with the language of machines, our life history, tastes, preferences and personal details become profiles, mailing lists, data and ultimately markets. Societies of control regulate their population by ensuring their knowing and unknowing participation in the marketplace through enforced compatibility with code" (p. 58). Thus, the code of major social platforms like Facebook imposes some very specific forms of normative sociality and tends to hide a "logic of connectivity imbued in the commercial drives and coercive formats" (Van Dijck, 2013, p. 155). This has given rise to tensions and, to a large degree, the paradox between the original meaning of the social media's communicative community and the market-oriented connectivity of large platforms aimed at gaining revenues.

As has occurred throughout the history of the media, much of the global market share (attention, audience, etc.) is in the hands of a small number of social media platforms. These large platforms not only monetize attention via advertising, but also through the commercialization of the aggregate metadata derived from audience activity and the personal data that they capture or are provided by users (socio-demographic data, friendships, likes, images, videos, etc.). In this way, privacy becomes a monetized product. If platforms like Facebook are free it is because people are invariably understood as a product due to the capturing of both attention—which generates advertising revenues—and individual and aggregate data and metadata on audience participation and activity. The fact that social media fall under the *freemium* umbrella does not mean that users have to pay nothing: through the transfer of private data they become part of the product, thus opening up a new mass commercial market.

Whether media users have control over their data or not (private, behavioral, etc.) or are the property of major media appears to be a battle dominated by corporate forces, which take advantage of their global presence and local laws to impose privacy policies or, more commonly, unilateral and ever-changing terms of service (ToS) at their whim, which is practically the same as saying that de facto privacy policies do not exist.

As mentioned above, an additional effect of major social media social platforms is that they frequently impose a particular form of online sociality through the code. One example is the Facebook timeline changes that allow the users themselves to enrich (enrichment) databases (basic demographic data, friendships, preferences, complete biographies, photos, interests, etc.). In this regard, the cover of the *MIT Technology Review* (2012) stated that Facebook "has collected more personal data than any other organization in human history. What will it do with that information?" and that "the company's social scientists are hunting for insights about human behavior. What they find could give Facebook new ways to cash in on our data—and remake our view of society" (Simonite, 2012, p. 42). What the big social media platforms are pursuing is "to lure and lock users into their chairs of platforms" (Van Dijck, 2013, p. 156) and "discipline their users into particular roles and modes of behavior" (Van Dijck, 2013, p. 157) by restricting to the largest possible degree any attempt to opt-out of them. This implies a clear ideological vision of the mainstream platforms based on a corporate market logic as opposed to the original Web 2.0 ideas based on the sharing, community, freedom and egalitarian interaction of liberal democratic ideology.

The accident of social media, in P. Virilio's terms, is not only a question of contributing vast amounts of new data, but an increasing loss of privacy, the gilded cages of lock in and opt-out restrictions and what is possible or not for the people restricted by the code; a code that was not developed by the successors of those scientists and hackers in the dawning of the Internet but by brilliant corporate programmers. A growing number of users and some governments are beginning to see the risks of a few big social media corporations engaging in the privacy trade as a threat to public and private democratic principles.

We are now faced with technologies of the self, which for M. Foucault had a positive rather than a negative meaning, as the development of such technologies entailed the improvement of the self. That is, they are techniques that allow individuals to construct and change themselves in an effort to develop their own potential "in order to attain a certain state of happiness, purity, wisdom, perfection or immortality" (Foucault, 1988:18). Like all technology, however, the new technologies of the self cause their own accidents. Among the negative effects technologies of the self have on redefining the interpersonal and mass communication ecosystem is the need for greater personal branding, which entails the risk of progressively reducing researchers to a mere market product or service through the social marketing of the self. Yet communicating and promoting oneself to gain visibility is not the same as being a brand or explicitly waiving growing areas of privacy. The private has been made public in the form of a social conquest and can be viewed as a new step towards the expropriation of privacy, which due to increasing corporate concentration, reveals the potential of the technological accidents arising from the new technologies of the self.

The paradox becomes increasingly evident: people need social media to express their opinions and creativity, while the major platforms tend to lock-in and understand users as products to generate revenues, which are two opposing ideological premises. Nonetheless, the dominant position of some mainstream platforms are more precarious than would seem, as evidenced by the rise and fall of other online giants (AOL, Yahoo, Second Life, MySpace, etc.). Just as Google defended itself against antitrust charges, there can be no monopoly if the competition is just a click away. One click today can be a great act of dissent because, ultimately, we are the new media.

REFERENCES

Aghion, P., & Howitt, P. (1992). A Model of growth through Creative Destruction. *Econometrica*, *60*(2), 323–351. doi:10.2307/2951599

Aghion, P., & Howitt, P. (1997). *Endogenous Growth Theory*. Cambridge, MA: MIT Press.

Anderson, C. (2008). The end of theory: the data deluge makes the scientific method obsolete. *Wired, 16*(7). Retrieved June 15, 2015, from http://archive.wired.com/science/discoveries/magazine/16-07/pb_theory

Bajkiewicz, T. E., Kraus, J. J., & Yeon Hong, S. (2011). The impact of newsroom changes and the rise of social media on the practice of media relations. *Public Relations Review*, *37*(3), 329–333. doi:10.1016/j.pubrev.2011.05.001

Berry, D. M., & Pawlik, J. (2008). What is code: A conversation with Deleuze, Guattari and code. In *Libre culture. Meditations on free culture*. Winnipeg: Pygmalion Books. Retrieved June 15, 2015, from http://sro.sussex.ac.uk/46287/1/BERRYMOSS-LibreCulture2008.pdf

Bertot, J., Jaeger, P., & Grimes, J. (2010). Using ICTs to create a culture of transparency: E-government and social media as openness and anti-corruption tools for societies. *Government Information Quarterly*, *27*(3), 264–271. doi:10.1016/j.giq.2010.03.001

Boyd, D., & Ellison, N. (2007). Social network sites: Definition, history, and scholarship. *Journal of Computer-Mediated Communication*, *13*(1), 210–230. doi:10.1111/j.1083-6101.2007.00393.x

Canavilhas, J., & Ivars, B. (2012). Uso y credibilidad de fuentes periodísticas 2.0 en Portugal y España. *El profesional de la información*, *21*(1), 63-69.

Castells, M. (2001). *La era de la información: economía, sociedad y cultura*. Madrid: Alianza editorial.

Castells, M. (2007). Communication, Power and Counter-power in the Network Society. *International Journal of Communication*, *1*, 238–266.

Castells, M. (2009). *Communication and power*. Oxford, UK: Oxford University Press.

Cowen, T. (2004). *Creative Destruction: How Globalization Is Changing the World's Cultures*. Princeton, NJ: Princeton University Press.

Datchary, C. (2005). Se disperser avec les tics une nouvelle compétence? In *Le travail avec les technologies de l'information* (pp. 157-173). Paris: Hermès-Lavoisier. Retrieved June 15, 2015, from http://hal.archives-ouvertes.fr/docs/00/33/17/82/PDF/_Datchary.pdf

Del Fresno, M. (2011a). *Netnografía*. Barcelona: UOC.

Del Fresno, M. (2011b). Infosociabilidad: monitorización e investigación en la web 2.0 para la toma de decisiones. *El profesional de la información*, *20*(5), 548-554.

Del Fresno, M. (2012 a). *El consumidor social. Reputación online y social media*. Barcelona: UOC.

Del Fresno, M. (2012 b). Comprendiendo los social media y mass media un modelo para el estudio de la comunicación interpersonal colectiva en tiempos de Internet. *Derecom*, *11*, 99–109.

Del Fresno, M. (2014). Haciendo visible lo invisible: Visualización de la estructura de las relaciones en red en Twitter por medio del Análisis de Redes Sociales. *El profesional de la información*, *23*(3), 246-252.

Del Fresno, M. (2015). We are the media: the ongoing disruption of social space via social media. In *#Commoncore Project. How social media is changing the politics in education.* Consortium for Policy Research in Education Pennsylvania. Retrieved June 15, 2015, from http://www.hashtagcommoncore.com

Del Fresno, M., & López-Peláez, A. (2014). Social work and Netnography: The case of Spain and generic drugs. *Qualitative Social Work: Research and Practice, 13*(1), 85–107. doi:10.1177/1473325013507736

Eyrich, N., Padman, M., & Sweetser, K. (2008). PR practitioners' use of social media tools and communication technology. *Public Relations Review, 34*(4), 412–414. doi:10.1016/j.pubrev.2008.09.010

Feather, J. (2008). *In The information society: A study of continuity and change.* London: Library Association.

Foster, R., & Kaplan, S. (2001). *Creative Destruction: Why Companies that are Built to Last Underperform the Market – And how to Successfully Transform Them.* New York: Crown Business.

Foucault, M. (1998). *Technologies of the Self. A seminar with Micher Foucault.* The University of Massachussets Press.

Franck, K. (1995). When I Enter Virtual Reality, What Body Will I Leave Behind? *Architectural Design, 65*(118), 20-22. Retrieved June 15, 2015, from digitalarts.bgsu.edu/faculty/wmadsen/.../in_VR_Where_is_my_body.pdf

Goldhaber, M. (1997). The attention economy on the net. *First Monday, 2*(4). doi:10.5210/fm.v2i4.519

Graham, P. (2005). *Web 2.0 Want to start a startup?* Retrieved June 15, 2015, from http://www.paulgraham.com/web20.html

Haraway, D. (1989). *The Cyborg Manifesto.* Retrieved June 15, 2015, from http://faculty.georgetown.edu/irvinem/theory/Haraway-CyborgManifesto-1.pdf

Heim, M. (1998). *The virtual reality of the tea ceremony.* Retrieved June 15, 2015, from http://www.mheim.com/files/vrtea.pdf

Hong, S. (2012). Online news on Twitter: Newspapers' social media adoption and their online readership. *Information Economics and Policy, 24*(1), 69–74. doi:10.1016/j.infoecopol.2012.01.004

Ibáñez, J.A., & Baraybar, A. (2011). Fuentes 2.0 y periodistas. Transformaciones en la comunicación museística. *El profesional de la información, 20*(6), 634-638.

Jenkins, H. (2006). *Convergence Culture: Where Old and New Media Collide.* New York: New York University Press.

Kaplan, A., & Haenlein, M. (2010). Users of the world, unite! The challenges and opportunities of Social Media. *Business Horizons, 53*(1), 59–68. doi:10.1016/j.bushor.2009.09.003

Kessous, E., Mellet, K., & Zouinar, M. (2010). L'économie de l'attention: Entre protection des ressources cognitives et extraction de la valeur. *Sociologie du Travail, 52*(3), 359–373. doi:10.1016/j.soctra.2010.06.009

Kietzmann, J., Hermkens, K., McCarthy, I., & Silvestre, B. (2011). Social media? Get serious! Understanding the functional building blocks of social media. *Business Horizons*, *54*(3), 241–251. doi:10.1016/j.bushor.2011.01.005

Lanham, R. (2007). *The Economics of Attention: Style and Substance in the Age of Information.* Chicago: University Of Chicago Press.

Lanier, J. (2010). *You are not a gadget: A manifesto.* New York: Vintage.

Lasswell, H. D. (1938). *Propaganda techniques in the world war.* New York: Peter Smith. Retrieved June 15, 2015, from http://babel.hathitrust.org/cgi/pt?id=mdp.39015000379902,view=1up,seq=9

Lasswell, H. D. (1948). The structure and function of communication in society. In *The communication of ideas.* New York: Harper. Retrieved June 15, 2015, from www.irfanerdogan.com/dergiweb2008/24/12.pdf

Lazarsfeld, P. (1940) *Radio and the Printed Page: An Introduction to the Study of Radio and Its Role in the Communication of Ideas.* New York: Duell, Sloan and Pearce. Retrieved June 15, 2015, from https://archive.org/stream/radiotheprintedp00lazarich/radiotheprintedp00lazarich_djvu.txt

Lazarsfeld, P., & Merton, K. (1943). *Studies in radio and film propaganda.* Retrieved June 15, 2015, from http://onlinelibrary.wiley.com/doi/10.1111/j.2164-0947.1943.tb00897.x/abstract

Lessig, L. (2009). *Code: versión 2.0.* Retrieved June 15, 2015, from http://codev2.cc/download+remix/Lessig-Codev2.pdf

Lewis, D. (1999). *Information Overload.* London: Penguin.

Li, C., & Bernoff, J. (2008). *Groundswell: Winning in a World Transformed by Social Technologies.* Boston: Harvard Business Press.

Lippmann, W. (1922). *Public opinión.* London: Allen and Unwin. Retrieved June 15, 2015, from http://monoskop.org/images/b/bf/Lippman_Walter_Public_Opinion.pdf

Lister, M., Dovey, J., Giddings, S., Grant, I., & Kelly, K. (2009). *New Media: A Critical Introduction.* London: Routledge.

Lycett, M. (2013). Datafication: Making Sense of (Big) Data in a Complex World. *European Journal of Information Systems*, *22*(4), 381–386. doi:10.1057/ejis.2013.10

Mattelart, A. (2003). *The Information Society: An Introduction.* London: Sage.

Mayer-Schönberger, V., & Cukier, K. (2014). *Big Data: A Revolution That Will Transform How We Live, Work, and Think.* London: John Murray Publishers.

McLeod, J., & Chaffee, S. (1973). Interpersonal approaches to communication research. *The American Behavioral Scientist*, *16*(4), 469–500. doi:10.1177/000276427301600402

McLuhan, M. (1964). *Understanding media: The extensions of man.* Cambridge, MA: MIT Press.

McQuail, D. (Ed.). (2002). *McQuail's reader in mass communication theory.* London: Sage.

McQuail, D., & Windahl, S. (1993). *Communication Models for the Study of Mass Communications*. New York: Longman.

Mitchell, W. (1996). *City of Bits: Space, Place, and the Infobahn*. Cambridge, MA: MIT Press.

Newcomb, T. (1953). An Approach to the Study of Communicative Acts. *Psychological Review*, *60*(6), 393–404. doi:10.1037/h0063098 PMID:13112341

Nie, N., & Erbring, L. (2002). Internet and Society: A Preliminary Report. *IT & Society*, 275-283. Retrieved June 15, 2015, from www.stanford.edu/group/siqss/itandsociety/v01i01/v01i01a18.pdf

O'Reilly, T. (2005). *What Is Web 2.0*. Retrieved June 15, 2015, from http://oreilly.com/web2/archive/what-is-web-20.html

Pashler, H. (1998). *The Psychology of Attention*. Cambridge, MA: MIT Press.

Pérez, F. J., Portilla, I., & Sánchez, C. (2011). Social Networks, Media and Audiences: A Literature Review. *Comunicación y Sociedad*, *24*(1), 63–74.

Prentice, R. (2005). The anatomy of surgical simulations: The mutual articulation of bodies in and through the machine. *Social Studies of Science*, *35*(6), 837–866. doi:10.1177/0306312705053351

Qualman, E. (2009). *Socialnomics: How Social Media Transforms the Way We Live and Do Business*. New York: John Wiley.

Reidenberg, J. (1998). Lex Informatica: The Formulation of Information Policy Rules Through Technology. *Texas Law Review*, *76*(3), 553–593.

Shirky, C. (2009). *Here Comes Everybody: The Power of Organizing Without Organizations*. New York: Penguin.

Silver, N. (2013). *The signal and the noise: why so many predictions fail — but some don't*. New York: Penguin Books.

Simonite, T. (2012). What Facebook knows. *Technology Review*, (July-August), 42–49.

Styhre, A. (2009). The cinematic mode of organizing: Media and the problem of attention in organization theory. *Information and Organization*, *19*(1), 47–58. doi:10.1016/j.infoandorg.2008.06.001

Swash, G. (1998). UK business information on the Internet. *New Library World*, *99*(1144), 238–242. doi:10.1108/03074809810236793

Tapscott, D., & Williams, A. (2006). *Wikinomics: How Mass Collaboration Changes Everything*. New York: Portfolio.

Toffler, A. (1970). *Future shock*. New York: Bantam Books. Retrieved June 15, 2015, from http://goo.gl/KDGWwn

Toffler, A., & Toffler, H. (1994). Surfing the third wave. *Microtimes*, *118*. Retrieved June 15, 2015, from http://www.yoyow.com/marye/tofflers94.html

Turkle, S. (1984). *The Second Self. Computers and the human spirit.* Cambridge, MA: MIT Press. Retrieved June 15, 2015, from http://mitpress.mit.edu/books/chapters/0262701111intro1.pdf

Turkle, S. (1994). *Constructions and reconstructions of the Self in Virtual Reality.* Cambridge, MA: MIT Press. Retrieved June 15, 2015, from http://web.mit.edu/sturkle/www/constructions.html

Turkle, S. (1995). *Life on the Screen: Identity in the Age of the Internet.* New York: Simon and Schuster.

Van Dijck, J. (2013). *The Culture of Connectivity: A Critical History of Social Media.* New York: Oxford University Press. doi:10.1093/acprof:oso/9780199970773.001.0001

Verhoeven, P., Tench, R., Zerfass, A., Moreno, A., & Verčič, D. (2012). How European PR practitioners handle digital and social media. *Public Relations Review, 38*(1), 162–164. doi:10.1016/j.pubrev.2011.08.015

Virilio, P. (1991). The aesthetics of disappearance. New York: Semiotext(e).

Virilio, P. (1995). *Speed and Information: Cyberspace Alarm!* Retrieved June 15, 2015, from http://www.ctheory.net/printer.asp?id=72

Virilio, P. (1996). Speed Pollution. *Wired.* Retrieved June 15, 2015, from http://archive.wired.com/wired/archive/4.05/virilio.html

Weaver, R., Johnson, E., Sweetser, K., & Howes, P. (2009). An examination of the role of online social media in journalists' source mix. *Public Relations Review, 35*(3), 314–316. doi:10.1016/j.pubrev.2009.05.008

Wertheim, M. (1999). *The pearly gates of cyberspace. In Cyber_reader. Critical writtings for the digital era.* New York: Phaidon Press.

KEY TERMS AND DEFINITIONS

Communication: To share meanings through the exchange of information where the technology used, the characteristics of the senders and receivers, the cultural codes of reference, the protocols used and the scope of the process are significant.

Information Society: The era characterized by social changes occurring since the late twentieth century as a result of the evolution of digital information and communication technologies alongside the emergence of a social network structure, which has affected all areas of human activity on a global scale.

Micromedia: Any individual or entity which, through a simple technological device with Internet access and increasing web or mobile code applications, can choose to change their role as active/passive receivers/senders in the symbolic distribution of content and information with other micromedia or professional media.

Social Media: The media resulting from Internet architecture and the creation of code-based web or mobile applications which enable synchronous and/or asynchronous communication by people who, as micromedia, acquire the ability to provide constant feedback to audiences in constant reconfiguration and without a predefined geographical scope of a non-recurring, non-normalized and heterogeneous set of symbolic content or messages (their own or of others) not subject to a performative agenda.

156

Social Media Mining: The process of extracting, storing, representing, visualizing, and analyzing massive amounts of user-generated data in order to uncover meaningful patterns from interactions within social media.

Web 2.0: The group of code applications that exploit the ideological and technological foundations of the original architecture of the Internet to facilitate the creation and exchange of user-generated content.

This research was previously published in Digital Tools for Academic Branding and Self-Promotion edited by Nuria Lloret and Marga Cabrera; pages 11-30, copyright year 2017 by Information Science Reference (an imprint of IGI Global).

Chapter 9
Social Media as Public Political Instrument

Ikbal Maulana
Indonesian Institute of Sciences, Indonesia

ABSTRACT

Due to its large number public cannot gather in one place and speak as a single voice, and consequently it cannot represent itself. However, public is always needed as political legitimation, therefore political forces compete to make their own definitions of public and use them as the basis of political claims. To make their definition of public close to the real people, democratic mechanisms have been developed. Once in a number of years, people elect candidates who will represent and govern them. But, most of the time they will be silent and ignored by the changing dynamics of politics. Conventional media does not help the public much to express its voice. Most often it becomes the tool of the elite for indoctrination or the mobilizing of bias. However, social media might empower people, because it allows them to voice their own concerns and to have conversation with each other. But, to have a real impact, the conversation must be directed to solve a real problem. Leadership is required to mobilize people's voice virtually and then turn it into a real political pressure.

INTRODUCTION

The recent intensive uses of social media in social and political activisms indicate that it has a great potential to reshape modern democracy by giving people their voice back which previously must be delegated to their political representatives. Social media might take the practice of democracy back to its original form as in Ancient Athens in which it was practiced directly by citizens without any representative mediation (Ober, 1996). Theoretically practicing democracy on social media would be more inclusive than that of the Ancient Athens which excluded women and slaves, because social media allows everyone to speak out their opinions without the limitation of gender, social status and, even, space and time.

The optimism regarding the positive impact of social media on democracy is supported by the recent social movements, from Occupy Wall Street to Arab Spring. Just as in the pre-social media era, in order to have a real political impact a social movement needs to manifest itself in public urban spaces, such

DOI: 10.4018/978-1-5225-9869-5.ch009

as streets or squares. Prior to the mobilization of the masses, activists need to do various efforts, from having coordination among themselves to raising issues to public. Most of these activities are conducted through the networks of acquaintances and contacts, and social media can best facilitate such activities by enhancing the speed of information exchanges and broadening the participation of people. During the Arab Spring, for example, Howard *et al.* (2011) found out that:

1. Social media played a central role in shaping political debates in the Arab Spring,
2. A spike in online revolutionary conversations often preceded major events on the ground, and
3. Social media helped spread democratic ideas across international borders.

The Arab Spring has been hailed as a political change forced by people who organized themselves using social media. It has increased the rhetoric of the impact of social media on democratization. However, after years of turmoil, the expectation of democratization has steadily faded away as the old political players get back to the center of power, disappointing those who want a radical change in politics. While social media still facilitates people to express any political view, it cannot prevent the return of the unwanted political power despite the many refutations against them can always be expressed freely on social media. This indicates that the impact of technology, including social media, on democratization is not deterministic. There is no unique correlation between technological progress and distribution of power (Feenberg, 1999, p. 76). Social media gives the opportunity to advance democracy, but, it is also possible, that this technology is used to preserve the existing hierarchy of power.

This chapter will discuss the extent to which social media can be used by citizens to promote and advance their political interests. It will also discuss if its extensive and intensive use will lead to democratization.

THE POLITICAL CONSTRUCTION OF PUBLIC

Politicians often speak on behalf of public as if it is a single concrete entity. But, does public really exist? If yes, then why it needs others to speak on its behalf? Can public not speak by itself? Habermas asserts that the main character of public is the existence of interactive speaking among its members, "A portion of the public sphere comes into being in every conversation in which private individuals assemble to form a public body" (Habermas, 1974, p. 49). Public, as well as society, consists of individuals who interact with each other. While society, by definition, can emerge in any condition, free or oppressed, under totalitarian or democratic regime, whereas "Citizens behave as a public body when they confer in an unrestricted fashion - that is, with the guarantee of freedom of assembly and association and the freedom to express and publish their opinions - about matters of general interest" (Habermas, 1974, p. 49).

It is hardly imaginable that populations of a town, moreover of a country, mostly strangers to each other, through conversations could converge into a single entity called public. The notion of public is abstracted from a society by reducing its complexity and variety that makes public to have only specific attributes and aspirations in accord with the interests of power holders which determine it. Therefore, public can be perceived as a political construction having weak correspondence with the reality, even though "those, who do possess power can only claim legitimacy by speaking in its name and acting in its interests" (Coleman & Ross, 2010, p. 8). Even strong dictators need to claim everything they do is on behalf of the public.

Most often people inhabiting a vast area may have fragmented and sometimes conflicting interests. Without a leader or a spokesperson, it is hard for them to come up with a single voice. Democratic mechanisms have been developed to make the "public" claimed by the spokesperson legally correspond with people having flesh and blood. Democracy is supposed to ensure that representatives well represent the voters who have elected them. Indeed, democratic system does not guarantee that people's aspirations will be fulfilled, but, so far the system has provided a fair procedure to select representatives then "the people can have no complaint because their rights have been safeguarded.... If the properly chosen representatives create policies not of their liking, it is the fault of the people. And the remedy is also at hand: at the next election, the people can choose other representatives" (Markovitz, 1999, p. 49).

Representation in modern democracy is the solution as well as the source of problems. For it is impossible to involve all adult people in every political decision making process, a political representative system is needed. Public is then represented by the representatives who are selected in an election. Even though the representative mechanism is considered as the most fair solution but it cannot eliminate the following problems. First, there is no guarantee that each voice of the representatives represents the interest of their constituents, because when they were still the representative candidates they did not inquire about people's interests. They just proposed a political position which they considered might attract people. There is unlikely a negotiation between the candidate and the people about the appropriateness of the former's political positions and the latter's interests. People only select a candidate who is most acceptable to them. Second, election is held once every four or five years, while, over time, politics most likely will be changing for various reasons, and politicians often resolve their differences by compromising their opinions, which in turn diverting them from their constituents.

The diversion of representatives from their constituents is often unavoidable, and the former compensate it by redefining new public interests which are in accord with their new political orientation. People who do not know each other are transformed by their representatives into a new public. They cannot prevent it, because "Never meeting in one place or speaking with one voice, the public is unable to represent itself. It is doomed to be represented" (Coleman & Rose, 2010, p. 8 – 9). Therefore, "the public is always a product of representation. There is no a priori public that is "captured" or "recorded" by the media. The public is invoked through processes of mediation that are dominated by political, institutional, economic, and cultural forces" (p.3).

As a political construction, "public" has always been the target of determination by competing political forces each of which has its own ideas of what public is, what its interests are, and to whom it refers. So, public is not a fixed defined entity, but "a space to be filled in" (Coleman & Rose, 2010, p. 2). Since there are competing interests, it becomes a space of contention around which innumerable institutional devices and discursive strategies have been deployed. Media have always been important instruments to influence and shape public. By transmitting messages through media, elites persuade ordinary people to identify themselves as the public which the elites has defined.

Those in power of course do not like the statement that public is a mere political construction, because it questions the legitimacy of their position. Democratic institutions and mechanisms have been developed to make public as close as possible to real people so that it can be claimed as the source of legitimacy. If an ideal democratic system cannot be realized, then the working system should be considered as the most fair of all possible systems by all parties, especially by those to be represented. Since 'the public is doomed to be represented', the controversy emerging from the representative system should be prevented or minimized. One important way to do this is by measuring the degree of representation, that is by counting the number of those being represented. Numbers are important to legitimize political system,

"... numbers determine who holds power, and whose claim to power is justified... Numbers, here, are part of the mechanism of conferring legitimacy on political leaders, authorities and institutions" (Rose, 2004, p. 197). Indeed, numbers trim the complexity of the people's aspirations, but they are the best solution that we can have right now.

People participating in current democratic systems are divided into two mutually exclusive categories: the representatives and the represented. While the former play active role in political debates and decision making, the latter can only judge the former and select them in an election. However, the election occurs every certain period of time, and in between the latter have no formal influences on politics, because the election has legitimately transferred the right of political decision making to the former.

Innovations have been developed to let the voice of people be heard outside an election period. For example, opinion polls are run to calibrate and quantify public feelings on political matters and social surveys are conducted "to transform the lives and views of individuals into numerical scales and percentages" (Rose, 2004, p. 197). However, the above political innovations only reveal public voice on questions raised by the opinion polls or surveys, while unquestioned issues will remain silent. And these kinds of questions only collect simplified answers and avoid the complexity of public problems.

Complex questions and answers are better accommodated by conventional media which can present complex narratives of people's stories and problems. However, most conventional media whose contents are created or selected by a group of organized people who have a collective interest tend to have certain discursive characteristics, which in turn simplify the picture of public as a single entity, with clear and non-conflicting attributes. Therefore, when they have to make public correspond to real people, they refer it to the groups which fit their created picture. And those that do not fit will be excluded. This inclusion and exclusion of people into politically defined public is conducted through the selection and exclusion of issues from political discourses. It is achieved by

... crucial reporting omissions or over-emphases on a systematic basis and so contribute to a subtle, long-term 'mobilisation of bias' in media reporting. This excludes certain groups in society. More significantly, it also ensures that chronic, long-term problems, many of which contribute to power imbalances, remain a minor part of public sphere discussions until they reach crisis point. Such tendencies have become all the more exacerbated by rising competition. Thus, the very discursive practices that are supposed to reveal the world as it is also, unwittingly, serve to leave crucial causal elements of inequality and crisis uncovered. (Davis, 2007, p. 36).

FIGHTING FOR PUBLIC EXISTENCE THROUGH CITIZENSHIP

Public is more often an object of definition and is manipulated to legitimize those who define it. It is claimed to be abstracted from the largest majority of real people, but is given specific attributes determined by particular interest. So, when its needs are satisfied, it will be the needs who define it which are satisfied.

Public does not have to be the object of definition of elites. Citizens, even though they are strangers to each other, still have an opportunity to constitute public by themselves. It can be achieved if they can be "regularly thrown into contact with one another and there had to be newspapers and pamphlets to provide a common focus of discussion and conversation. The public, then, was a society of conversationalists, or disputants if you prefer a more aggressive term, dependent upon printing" (Carey, 1995, p.381). Press or media in general provide focus on public conversation as well as preserve the conversation to be part of public memory.

Conventional media, especially printing media which has had a long history, is a constituting factor of public, because normatively "it exists to inform the public, to serve as the extended eyes and ears of the public. The press protects the public's interest and justifies itself in its name" (Carey, 1995, p. 381). The press does not just facilitate public conversation but also enriches the conversation by, for example, providing experts' opinions and investigative reporting. However, the power behind the press can also influence or dictate public discourse. Opinions of public or experts and investigative reporting are selected to frame public discourse in accord with the interests of power holders. This condition may result in journalism which "justifies itself in the public's name but in which the public plays no role, except as an audience" (Carey, 1995, p. 391).

On conventional media people do have the choice, not to determine the content of media, but to choose the media itself, such as which newspaper to read or which radio station to listen. As they choose the media, they have to accept the whole packages given by it. They may have impact on content, their preferences will be accommodated by the media, but more due to marketing considerations rather than democratic reasons of media owners. Media tends to become the stage of propaganda of which public is only the spectators and ratifier of decision made elsewhere (Carey, 1995). During the rise of broadcasting in the early twentieth century, the public was conceived as something to be molded and tamed. The media was given the task "to provide the public with what it needs, and indeed to reshape its needs so that it wants what is normatively better for it" (Coleman & Ross, 2010, p. 29). The public was seen as less intelligent than people of the media and therefore should be educated by the latter.

The Internet, especially its social media, has brought radical change to the constitution of public. It is partly due to the global operation of social media of which the owners are not interested in local politics. What they want are merely the maximum number of users and user generated contents which can be sold to advertisers. This profit motivated purpose has led to the development of increasingly user-friendly and widely accessible social media which provides users easy access to voice their concerns and ideas. Public can express their political opinions without conflicting with the interest of social media owners.

The practice of citizenship, which consists of making political judgment about public matter in relation to and with others (Barney, 2007), can be easily carried out on social media by anyone. Citizenship should be practiced in public sphere so that it can be watched by and affects others, and on social media a user's informational act is instantly visible to others who are online at the same time. Therefore social media has a great potential to achieve the ultimate end of citizenship, which is to make individual cause shared by public and trigger the intended change.

The level of democracy is closely related to the level of citizenship which "depends upon a series of rights of entry, ranging from the polling station to town squares to cyberspace where much contemporary interaction now occurs. In the absence of these rights of public access, democratic citizenship becomes a pious aspiration rather than a practicable commitment" (Coleman & Ross, 2010, p. 24). Ideally legitimate political decision requires a rational agreement among all citizens, which may only be achieved if all of them exercise active citizenship. "Thus the rationality proper to the communicative practice of everyday life points to the practice of argumentation as a court of appeal that makes it possible to continue communicative action with other means when disagreements can no longer be repaired with everyday routines and yet are not to be settled by the direct or strategic use of force" (Habermas, 1984, p. 17-8).

The above ideal has never been realized in practice, because involving all citizens in decision making is very costly, impractical and, most often, impossible. Only in a few rare cases all citizens are asked to make a direct political decision, such as in a secessionist referendum or a referendum for the adoption of a new constitution. In these cases they are only asked a very important but simple question that has been formulated by parliament and requires only yes or no answer. It is politically impractical to ask people with an open question. It would even be impossible to engage all people to seriously discuss political matters and make a political decision. Members of parliament, whose number is limited but legitimately represent people, can much more effectively achieve political consensus.

Democracy is developed by imperfect humans to collectively deal with their imperfection. The problems caused by the imperfection can never be removed, but it gives legitimation which can minimize or prevent dangerous conflicts. Measures are implemented to overcome particular imperfection lasting too long. For example, periodical election is held to prevent representatives from ignoring their constituents for too long. They have to keep paying attention to the people's interest if they want to keep their position in the next term. However, even the period between two consecutive elections is considered too long when people can no longer tolerate the representatives ignoring their voices and concerns on an important issue. Under this circumstance, they may feel the need to engage in extra-parliamentary activity to force their representatives to listen to their voice. But this activity rarely happens because it requires a lot of cost and time to mobilize a sufficient number of people to represent public interest.

As democracy does not emerge instantly just because people choose to adopt it, people also do not practice active citizenship just because they are not satisfied with the politics. Citizenship is something which develops and needs to be developed. It is "a habit motivated by circumstance and obligation, cultivated through education and experience, consistently performed" (Barney, 2007, p. 39). While its effectiveness "rests not only on equality before and under the law but also upon relatively equal access to the social and material resources that allow people to act on these entitlements" (p.39).

Not everyone can readily practice citizenship if we regard that "The practice of citizenship is, at its core, the practice of political judgment" (Barney, 2007, p. 40). The views of some scholars which emphasize the important of argumentation also imply that not all people can involve in political decision making. Habermass (1984) suggests that only through the force of better argument we can make a cooperative search for the truth. Beiner also emphasizes the use of speech in politics. "Political experience as a specific mode of being in the world, is constituted by speech, by the capacity of human beings to humanize their world through communication, discourse and talk about what is shared and thus available for intersubjective judgment" (Beiner, 1983, p. xiv). Since the practice of citizenship relies on the practice of political judgment and the judgment should rely on and be expressed in rational argumentation, then elites have better skill than average people to make political judgment.

The views of Habermas or Beiner are too optimistic to be found in real politics in which people do not alway want to win the truth or to humanize the world. It is often the winning itself that matters the most. Relying citizenship only on rational argumentation will exclude and subordinate people who are not capable to make a good argumentation. Anyone can make a political judgment, and anyone is the best person to express a judgment which is related to her own problem. Therefore, to be just to all citizens it is necessary to acknowledge "the multiplicity of modes in which citizens might make political judgments, and the contribution made to the struggle for justice by these modes of expression and the people who use them" (Barney, 2007, p. 43). Peaceful political protest do not have to be expressed in speech, and people participating in a political rally are not to engage in a political debate.

TECHNOLOGICAL EMPOWERMENT OF PUBLIC

In contrast to instrumentalist view, which believes in the neutrality of technology, a small but growing number of scholars regard technology as having political quality (e.g. Mumford, 1964; Ellul, 1980; Feenberg, 2002; and Winner, 1986). They argue that technology has a political impact, that is influencing power relations in society in which the technology is used, and the design and use of technology are also influenced by the power relation. Mumford, for example, suggests that technology is not politically neutral,

... from late neolithic times in the Near East, right down to our own day, two technologies have recurrently existed side by side: one authoritarian, the other democratic, the first system-centered, immensely powerful, but inherently unstable, the other man-centered, relatively weak, but resourceful and durable. If I am right, we are now rapidly approaching a point at which, unless we radically alter our present course, our surviving democratic technics will be completely suppressed or supplanted, so that every residual autonomy will be wiped out, or will be permitted only as a playful device of government, like national ballotting for already chosen leaders in totalitarian countries (Mumford, 1964, p. 2).

Following Mumford's division of technology, broadcasting technology, such as radio and television, can be regarded more as an authoritarian technology, whereas the Internet is a more democratic one. On the Internet users can be both receivers and senders of information, while radio listeners can only receive what is broadcasted by a radio station. It does not mean that democracy cannot grow out of a society whose mainstream media is radio technology. As long as there is no one who controls public information, and people have enough choices of media to select from, then people can avoid being dictated by a single media.

Regardless of the used technology, "Communication, whether through speech, manuscript, print, broadcast, or digital media has always been a crucial resource for political resistance, influencing cultural norms in the process" (Waite, 2013, p. 18). The more people get the opportunity to communicate, the more they can exercise power, and the more difficult for elites to dominate them. It does not imply that the development of communication technology will deterministically advance democracy. It depends on who can better utilize technology for their own benefits. Today, communication technologies, including the Internet, have been widely used in either democratic or undemocratic countries. Nevertheless, there is a reasonable optimism regarding the potential of social media to empower people, because it gives the opportunity to anyone to express and share her views with others.

The relationship between the representative and the represented and the power relation between the ruler and the ruled have been challenged by Internet technologies which have given voice to those who were previously voiceless. While most technologies are "reducing individuals to mere appendages of the machine, computerization can provide a role for communicative skills and collective intelligence" (Feenberg, 2002, p.89). In the past, if there was a controversial government's policy or a controversial opinion raised by a politician, only public figures could participate in the polemics on conventional media. The majority of the people could only watch or discuss it in coffee shop without any influence on the politics. Social media has now given average people the opportunity to discuss it even at the national level. It proves that "evolving communication technologies have always altered who can say what to whom" (Waite, 2013, p. 18). Today politics is not only fought out in parliamentary building or on conventional media, social media has increasingly become political battlefield and instrument of the people to achieve their political goals. Even many people in developing countries, such as Indonesia

(Lim, 2004) and some Arab countries (Howard *et al.,* 2011), have benefited from the empowerment of social media. It shows that people are able to exert political pressure on parliamentary members or governments through raising issues on social media.

The political impacts of social media is not deterministic. Different countries having different local contexts experience the technology differently. "Consequently, what surfaces as a serious challenge for one country may not be the most important challenge for a country with different social norms" (Waite, 2013, p. 18). However, no country will remain unaffected by the transformative power of social media. Elites and general public will increasingly take advantages from the different kinds of use of social media. Some people may try to make others well-informed, while some other people may misinform and mislead others. The cooperative search for the truth as suggested by Habermas (1984) is not guaranteed, because even untruth can benefit some people and be the source of power.

The relatively easy access of social media makes it an inexpensive but effective instrument either to mobilize bias or organize social movement. The interactivity on social media can involve much more people than that in actual life using the combination face-to-face communication and conventional communication technologies. An important characteristics of social media is the use of number as the indication of the strength of information. The technology of social media can easily count the number of people who click "Likes" or share a message. This number may indicate the strength of a message, and it cannot be given by conventional media.

THE SIMPLICITY IS THE POWER

It seems counter-intuitive that complex social movements, such as Arab Spring, are supported by a very simple-to-use technology. Practically no significant technical and writing skills are required to be an active user of social media. The essential feature of social media is its simplicity which makes it more suitable for making social contact rather than having sophisticated dialogues. The limited number of characters for each message makes trivial messages look normal. While the difference between a dumb and a smart blog is clear and impress readers differently, the difference between a dumb and a smart message on social media is much less clear. On social media users normally do not need to think a lot to post a message. There are much higher number of simple messages circulating on social media than sophisticated ones which require a lot of thought to digest. Therefore social media attracts a much broader range of people, and link them to unprecedented social network.

The large number of social media users, most of whom exchange only unimportant messages to each other, has attracted those who want to benefit from that great number. Business people, social activists, intellectuals and politicians develop the skills to repackage a complex message into many small simple ones to be sent to the mass of social media users. Through a series of short messages a marketing campaign can be conducted, a social cause can gain massive support, and even people can be mobilized to take action on street. The user-friendliness of social media has eased and enhanced human contact and "...any technology that enhances human contact has democratic potentialities" (Feenberg, 2002, p. 92).

Social media has eased people's participation in a political discourse which was previously only the domain of elites. Technological development increasingly gives public what they most need, from products to information, and, ultimately to voice which in turn allows freedom to flourish (Grant, 1974). Does this development indicate that technology will take us to the future which will be better, wealthier, and, especially, more democratic? Will the development of the technology confirm the expectation of the utopianists like Negroponte (1995, p. 230) that "Digital technology can be a natural force drawing people into greater world harmony"?

Some thinkers - e.g. Marx, Marcuse (1964), and Feenberg (1999, 2002) - have explored the relationships between technology, public and power. The history of technology often shows that not all people benefit from technology equally. There are those who gain initial control and appropriate it to their interest. Those in power can take advantage of the development of technology, and secure the already existing social hierarchy. But, sometimes the development of technology challenges their existing power, "new technology can also be used to undermine the existing social hierarchy or to force it to meet needs it has ignored" (Feenberg, 1999, p. 76). The impact of technology cannot always be anticipated, "there is no unique correlation between technological advance and the distribution of social power" (p.76). This is what Feenberg calls the ambivalence of technology: it might be used to support the conservation of hierarchy, but it could also push for the democratic rationalization of society.

COMPETING INTERESTS IN MEDIA

According to an optimistic view, affordable media technology which allows for easy access to information opens the door for "an educated and participatory democracy" (William, 2003, p. 156). Indeed, widely available information may improve the quality of public participation, but it does not necessarily make a society more democratic. People in many undemocratic countries also have access to various media technologies, from radio to television to the Internet, but "quite a lot of discursive energy is required to get from computers to data to information to democracy" (Saco, 2002, p. xiii). Media can be used for good or evil, either for democratic engagement or for indoctrination of people. People may not be aware of the undemocratic practices of media, that they cannot really distinguish between the mass media as instruments of information and entertainment, and as agents of manipulation and indoctrination (Marcuse, 1964).

There might be support as well as resistance coming from media owners whose interest is not ideological but financial profit. Democracy is not in their agenda. If making public well-informed is profitable, they will do it, if not, they will do something else. If the exploitation of public sentiment gives them more profit, then they will do it as well. They have been increasingly stronger in influencing our lives, that they "could reach farther into our lives, at every level from news to psychodrama, until individual and collective response to many different kinds of experience and problem became almost limited to choice between their programmed possibilities" (William, 2003, p. 157).

The industrialization of media does not necessarily deter democratization. If the source of profit can only be maximally exploited by satisfying the information need of the majority of people rather than the much smaller number of elites, then the industry will serve the people even though it does not have democratic agenda. History shows that "the demise of the bourgeois public sphere relates to the commercially transformative dynamic of the capitalist political economy" (Coleman & Ross, 2010, p. 31). The growth of media industry since the early of nineteenth century has enabled media institutions to become large-scale businesses "delivering news as a commodity with a view to profit" whereas "Ownership of the press was consolidated into the hands of business tycoons with little interest in the cultivation of bourgeois chatter" (p. 31).

Commercialization of media has put profit over public interest, which leads to change the social function of journalism. Conventional media no longer serves public to gain empowering information and reach social consensus, "but to produce entertainment and information that can be sold to individual consumers. And it clearly contributes to homogenization, undercutting the plurality of media systems rooted in particular political and cultural systems of individual nation states that characterized Europe through most of the twentieth century, and encouraging its replacement by a common global set of media practices" (Hallin & Mancini, 2004, p. 277).

The subtle domination of media over public is realized through the mobilization of bias. People may not be aware that the discourse in which they engage has been directed to particular direction. Media has become one of the sophisticated instruments of exercising power which prevent the raising of issues which are detrimental to the power holder's set of preferences (Bachrach & Baratz, 1970). Through the creation and reinforcement of social and political values and institutional practices, which are partly best facilitated by media, potential conflicts are prevented even before they arise. It is natural for people or political organization to favor some issues over others to be discussed openly, as Schattschneider (1960: 71) states that "All forms of political organization have a bias in favour of the exploitation of some kinds of conflict and the suppression of others, because organization is the mobilization of bias. Some issues are organized into politics while others are organized out." By mobilization of bias, not only leaders can control what issues can be raised, but also shape others' desires. Political leaders "do not merely respond to the preferences of constituents; leaders also shape preferences" (Dahl, 1961, p. 164). And "... is it not the supreme exercise of power to get another or others to have the desires you want them to have - that is, to secure their compliance by controlling their thoughts and desires? .... thought control takes many less total and more mundane forms, through the control of information, through the mass media and through the processes of socialization" (Lukes, 2005, p. 27).

Conventional media is a powerful instrument to mobilize bias because it can pretend to report the world objectively. It can dictate political discourse by letting others to speak freely. But not all speeches will be published, only those which are in accord with their political agenda. "If we accept the existence of even the most benign form of agenda-setting on the part of the press, then who is allowed to speak in the news is just as important as which stories are selected for inclusion. Who speaks matters because access to the media is access to persuasive influence" (Coleman & Ross, 2010, p. 50).

Social media is not immune from the influence of business and political interests. Politicians and businesses can mobilize an army of social media users to mobilize bias, for example, by raising particular issues or directing attention of public to more acceptable problems. However, social media is much harder to control than conventional media because everyone is also an information provider even though anyone has different capability to influence others.

SOCIAL MEDIA AS A SOCIAL SPHERE

On social media anyone is simultaneously a producer, consumer, and distributor of information. Social media is even no longer media in traditional sense. It has become a social sphere, the world of its own, in which the exchanges of information can be conducted instantly as if people meet face-to-face with each other. Social media is even more 'social' in the sense that the interaction can involve more people each of whom has the opportunity to express her voice. One of the main differences between virtual world constructed on social media and the actual world is that the former will record everything that happens inside it. Every interaction in virtual world is automatically preserved and can be examined by anyone anytime later, while any event in the actual world needs people and media to record and report it.

Social media is more than just a world containing virtual versions of anything in the actual world. There are differences between what happen in both world. The social interactions on social media have their own characteristics and dynamics.

First, on social media all users have equal access to its technological services. There is no such thing as 'the rich has better access than the poor'. What makes users different from each other is the social network which they have built by themselves. Having different social networks, people may have access to different information, or participate in different types of interactions. But, it is the activeness, not the material wealth of users, which determine the extent of their social networks.

In the actual world, whether in democratic or undemocratic countries, political inequality can always be found. The main difference is that in democratic countries the inequality is not institutionalized but resulted from a political game which is not against the laws or constitutions of the countries. For example, the concerns of the majority of people tend to dominate public discourses, because they have more people who raise their concerns. It can be claimed as the consequence of liberal democratic systems in which equal access of individuals to public sphere is given as the foundational principle and is secured by their constitutions (Peleg, 2007). In undemocratic countries the inequality is institutionalized to give privilege to dominant groups.

Conventional media may preserve inequality in a society, since it does not attempt to serve every individual or group of people equally. It is even impossible or, at least, impractical to serve every social group equally. Due to its limited space it is only targeted to a particular market segment. The inequality is also influenced by unequal position between journalists and audiences of media. The former can control the content of media, whereas the latter can only select the media which best represent their interest.

On social media each user is both the producer and consumer of information. And the owners of social media mostly do not have interest in dictating discourses circulated on their platform. Their main business is to increase the number and activities of users in generating content, and then to sell them to advertisers.

Second, you do not have to be smart to be an active social media user. The limited length of information that you can send in a single message forces you to post only simple messages which do not require much thought. You can send any message spontaneously about anything serious, funny, or totally unimportant. It is not the content, but the contact you make, which is important. Social media equalizes everyone by lowering the technical and writing skill barriers to create its content. It is different from earlier Internet technologies, such as Webs or blogs which discriminate average users from those who have technical and/or writing skills. In the early history of the Web, people were required to have the knowledge of HTML to create a Web page. With the availability of blog services, technical skills have no longer been prerequisite to write a Web page, but users must have writing skills and commitment, because a blog post is normally written as a long essay. Therefore average or busy people had to wait until social media being invented to be active information producers on the Internet.

Third, the possibility of anonymous interaction on social media has enabled a more equal position among its users. In a country where the minority is under-represented or their interests do not have opportunity to be voiced, social media which allows fake identity has become the only public sphere in which anyone can voice any opinion without fearing of the judging eyes of others or, even, physical threats. However, there is the negative side of anonymity too: it allows irresponsibility which can make a virtual space become a battlefield of hatred rather than a place of practicing rational argumentation. In this case, virtual sphere is no longer a public sphere in which social consensus can be developed through communicative rationality.

Fourth, a virtual society can be different from an actual one due to the elimination of actual identity and space and time barriers to social interaction. With social media the same-minded people who are geographically dispersed or socially hidden can easily find one another and form a social group. The accessibility of social media through mobile technologies also allows geographically dispersed people to keep in touch with each other anytime and anywhere. In the physical world in order to make conversation with other people you firstly have to match your place and time with theirs, and ask their permission too. On social media you can send a message or respond to others' message anytime without the worry of bothering others.

Fifth, social media may cause the weakening of power distance. Hofstede *et al.* (2010, p. 61) defines power distance "as the extent to which the less powerful members of institutions and organizations within a country expect and accept that power is distributed unequally." A low-power distance society tend to be democratic in which they have leaders, but they elect them and can contradict them, and their leader have consultative style of decision-making. In high-power distance, submission to someone who has an authority is expected not only from those under her authority, but also from other people whose position in social or organizational hierarchy is similar to her subordinates. This submission becomes a social norm to which every member of a society has to comply. In high-power distance society, people tend to mingle only with those of the same social class. In real life overcoming power distance is no less difficult than overcoming geographical distance. But, on social media this power distance has been weakened. In the actual life the place where you work and socialize will determine the people who will become your friends, while on social media you are given the keys to the doors to any social group including those whom you do not have the chance to meet in actual life. This possibility is open because it is difficult to determine the social class to which an unknown person you meet online belongs. But, since it will not do any harm, you can expand your social network beyond your immediate friends or contacts.

Sixth, the equal access and the elimination of space and time barriers will in turn open the opportunity for any social media user, not just elites, to participate in the mobilization of political participation or the mobilization of bias. Users do not have to be aware that they engage in the mobilization. On social media something unplanned can develop into something surprising anyone, a simple message can develop and mutate into a complex set of ideas as it diffuses across many social media users (Shifman, 2014). A simple message responding to an event can trigger chains of responses which develop into a set of political opinions and even a mobilization of the masses. Therefore it is often difficult to trace who firstly triggers the raising of political issues. Most people do not need to know that, since on social media public does not need to appoint a spokesperson, because it can easily represent itself.

Seventh, just as in the actual world, on social media the formation of the opinion of a citizen is influenced to some extent by her social network. The difference is that on social media a user can create her own social network deliberately. She can select anyone she likes and deselects and blocks the one she does not. Theoretically, on social media anyone can create the social network whose opinions are in accord with hers. It leads to the development of a virtual world consisting many diverse social groups each of which is much more homogeneous than an actual one. So, social media allows the plurality of public.

PRACTICING CITIZENSHIP THROUGH SOCIAL MEDIA

Democracy is supposed to provide citizens, not only elites, with the opportunity to influence the decision making processes that affect their life. The ideal of democracy, according to Habermas (1984), is that it enables a political problem – the problem concerning the organization of society in common – to be resolved through the force of better argument. He is optimistic that, despite their different interest, people are able to find the best way to resolve their disputes through communicative reasons: the critical reflexive dialogues to find the most reasonable consensus to solve political problems. The question to be explored here is how social media can be used to practice collective communicative reasons.

A collective problem, either social or environmental, will be perceived differently by individuals from different positions. Victims and unaffected individuals will have different attitudes toward the problem due to different experiences with the problem. Individuals who suffer and bound together by a shared problem, such as the threat of pollution to their neighborhood or unintended result of policy implementation, develop a situated knowledge as they confront the problem (Feenberg, 1999). Such situated knowledge normally cannot be obtained unless you have real experience with the problem. All possible problems resulted from a development project cannot be anticipated in advance, because experts, bureaucrats, and politicians cannot have foreknowledge about all of them. With the emergence of social media, all ignored situated knowledge can easily be raised by the victims themselves.

Another important concern is Habermas' emphasis on the force of better argument in practicing citizenship. This kind of practice of citizenship will exclude people who have their own political preferences and judgments but cannot express them in reasoned speeches (Barney, 2007). That the best political solution can be found through political debate is only possible if the participants have no other interest than finding the truth. In practice, it is rarely the case. If better argument becomes the only mode of democratic decision making practice, then lay people can never compete against professional politicians. People who participate in political rally do not want to have arguments with the government, but just want to protest or to show their disappointment to them. They do not want to argue, but they support their political statement with the showing up of the many people who participate in the rally. On social media, citizenship is expressed in information, either in text or picture or video. You can create the information by yourself, or you can do the least effort by clicking just a single button of "Share", "Retweet" or "Like".

Social media has facilitated the practice of citizenship by easing the making of political judgments in a public sphere. In actual life, when an average citizen without access to conventional media wants others to know about her opinion, then she must personally come to them and tell her opinion. And she will face the risk of being rejected or even socially sanctioned if her opinion contradicts theirs. On social media she does not have to face such risk. She can write anything on her virtual wall and her virtual friends who are online will read it without being asked to do so, and even they can share her message to other people. Her message is communicated automatically without specifically being addressed to them.

When social media was first invented no one expected that it could be used to topple a dictator. The constraints to have a long and deep argumentation in a single message seems to make it only suitable for trivial communications. At first sight its short message seems to be its limitation. But the simplicity of social media is the very reason that makes it attractive to many people, including those who have neither the technical knowledge of the Internet nor the capability nor time to write a long essay such as that on a blog service. Social media appears to be intended to facilitate to build a social network rather than to exchange serious content (Maulana, 2014). However, no social group can be developed without contents, without shared meanings and interests. Therefore, many users also develop the capability to decompose a complex idea into several simpler ones which enables any idea, including social or political cause, to be communicated to the virtual masses.

CRITIQUES AGAINST SOCIAL MEDIA

According to Hefner (1999, p. 158), "prospects of democratization increase with the development of multiple centers and power and a plurality of public discourses in society" because "a multiplicity of ideas and authorities makes it difficult for any single group to win a clear monopoly of power," therefore the competing parties come to agree to some kind of power sharing compromise. So democracy can also be perceived as a pragmatical solution when no one nor group can dominate or convince other political actors or groups, even though there are well people who pursue democracy due to ideological reasons.

On social media there is no monopoly of power. It can also accommodate unlimited plurality of public discourses, because anyone, especially if she has anonymous identity, can express anything without the fear of social or physical sanctions. If she is expelled from a particular virtual community, she can switch to another one or even finds other same-minded people to form a new one. On social media people can easily avoid discursive confrontation by isolating themselves in their own virtual community. Under this condition people may take no effort to develop a healthy democracy, because they can easily avoid engaging in rational argumentation or making consensus with others. Social media may lead to the fragmentation of society in which anyone only interacts with other same-minded people.

Social media has been hailed to be an important instrument behind the success of some social activisms (Howard *et al.*, 2011; Lim, 2004). We need to critically check our optimism about the potential of social media. To mobilize people virtually is much easier than to do it in real life. We may be able to gain support for a cause from thousands of people if what we ask them to do is only to click "like" or "yes" button. But, would this kind of click activism lead to real social change which often requires strong commitment, including willingness to face the risk? Gladwell argues that social network that we have on social media is built around weak ties.

This is in many ways a wonderful thing. There is strength in weak ties, as the sociologist Mark Granovetter has observed. Our acquaintances—not our friends—are our greatest source of new ideas and information. The Internet lets us exploit the power of these kinds of distant connections with marvellous efficiency. It's terrific at the diffusion of innovation, interdisciplinary collaboration, seamlessly matching up buyers and sellers, and the logistical functions of the dating world. But weak ties seldom lead to high-risk activism. (Gladwell, 2010).

Social media can be a world of its own, but if we expect it to have a real impact to change the actual world, then we need people who are willing to translate what happen virtually into real activities. Real social activisms often demand people to spend their money, time, and even willingness to risk their life which not everyone is ready to do. Without the fulfillment of the demands, the practice of citizenship on social media is just a discursive game.

CONCLUSION

Social media has given voice to the public which has been most of the time voiceless. The technology, which was initially developed to help people to make contact rather than content, has evolved to be a powerful public political instrument. Its simplicity and ubiquitousness have enabled lay people without technical and writing skills to develop extensive social networks without the limitation of geographical distance and social class distinction. Social media eases the development of the network of people having the same concerns and the mobilization of bias to support their concerns. Public which was previously doomed to be represented ultimately can, to some extent, to represent itself on social media. There have been cases of how social media is being used to mobilize social movement that can even topple powerful dictators. However, it requires a lot of energy to translate what have been achieved virtually into a real impact in the actual world.

In the current democratic system there is inevitable separation between the representative and the represented. Normatively the former should always represent the latter. In practice, those who claim to represent their constituents in an election may change their opinions later. The dynamics of parliamentary politics may cause politicians to compromise with one another, which in turn may change their political stances over time. Therefore it is not easy for them to stick to the promises they made to their constituents during the election. Even though it may disappoint the latter, most often they cannot do anything but wait until the next election, because within the current democratic system it often takes too much efforts for the represented to correct the changing opinions of the representatives.

Social media may change the above situation. Any social media user is both a producer and consumer of information. While conventional media make public the target of indoctrination and the mobilization of bias, social media allows public not only to counter but also to participate in its own mobilization of bias. Even though not belonging to any political organization a user has the opportunity to raise an issue to the public and strengthen the issues raised by others. A political disappointment, if it is felt by many people, can easily be shared and blown up on social media. Through chains of simple messages people can confirm one another's disappointment.

There is also reason to be critical of the impact of social media on democratization. Social media stimulates the plurality of public which is good and necessary for maintaining a healthy democracy. But, democracy is an attempt at coexistence which requires people to resolve their conflicting interests and views. On the contrary, social media eases people to avoid confronting each other and interact only with the same-minded others, and therefore constraining them to make consensus with others who have conflicting interests. Even worse, the abundance of information does not prevent them to have prejudice toward others. On social media many people send and resend messages of hateful prejudice without checking their accuracy. Overcoming information overload, they select only information that suits their prejudice and ignore the other. Since social media can readily facilitate the formation of a virtual community among geographically dispersed people, consequently it may lead to social fragmentation of people within a particular geographical area. A virtual community may also gives an illusion that they are as real as an actual community, while they are indeed built around weak ties without real commitment other than sending information to each other.

REFERENCES

Bachrach, P., & Baratz, M. S. (1970). *Power and Poverty: Theory and Practice*. New York: Oxford University Press.

Barney, D. (2007). Radical Citizenship in the Republic of Technology: A Sketch. In L. Dahlberg & E. Siapera (Eds.), *Radical Democracy and the Internet*. New York, NY: Palgrave Macmillan. doi:10.1057/9780230592469_3

Beiner, R. (1983). *Political Judgment*. Chicago, IL: University of Chicago Press.

Carey, J. (1995). The press, public opinion, and public discourse. In T. Glasser & C. Salmon (Eds.), *Public Opinion and the Communication of Consent*. New York: Guilford.

Coleman, S., & Ross, K. (2010). *The media and the public: "them" and "us" in media discourse*. Oxford, UK: Wiley-Blackwell. doi:10.1002/9781444318173

Dahl, R. A. (1961). *Who Governs? Democracy and Power in an American City*. New Haven, CT: Yale University Press.

Davis, A. (2007). *The Mediation of Power: A Critical Introduction*. London: Routledge.

Ellul, J. (1980). *The Technological System* (J. Neugroschel, Trans.). New York, NY: The Continuum Publishing Corporation.

Feenberg, A. (1999). *Questioning Technology*. London: Routledge.

Feenberg, A. (2002). *Transforming Technology: A Critical Theory Revisited* (2nd ed.). Oxford: Oxford University Press.

Gladwell, M. (2010). *Small Change: Why the revolution will not be tweeted*. Retrieved June 20, 2014, from http://www.newyorker.com/reporting/2010/10/04/101004fa_fact_gladwell?currentPage=all

Grant, G. (1974). *English-Speaking Justice*. Toronto: Anansi.

Habermas, J. (1974). The Public Sphere: An Encyclopedia (1964). *New German Critique, NGC, 3*(Autumn), 49–55.

Habermas, J. (1984). *The Theory of Communicative Action – Reason and the Rationalisation of Society* (Vol. I). (T. McCarthy, Trans.). Boston, MA: Beacon Press.

Hallin, D. C., & Mancini, P. (2004). *Comparing Media Systems: Three Models of Media and Politics*. Cambridge: Cambridge University Press. doi:10.1017/CBO9780511790867

Hefner, R. W. (1999). Civic Pluralism Denied? The New Media and *Jihadi* Violence in Indonesia. In D. F. Eickelman & J. W. Anderson (Eds.), *New Media in the Muslim World: The Emerging Public Sphere*. Bloomington, IN: Indiana University Press.

Hofstede, G., Hofstede, G. J., & Minkov, M. (2010). *Cultures and Organizations: Software of the Mind* (3rd ed.). New York: McGraw-Hill.

Howard, P. N., Duffy, A., Freelon, D., Hussain, M., Mari, W., & Mazaid, M. (2011). Opening Closed Regimes: What Was the Role of Social Media During the Arab Spring? In *Project on Information Technology & Political Islam*. Retrieved from: http://pitpi.org/wp-content/uploads/2013/02/2011_Howard-Duffy-Freelon-Hussain-Mari-Mazaid_pITPI.pdf

Lim, M. (2014). Seeing spatially: people, networks and movements in digital and urban spaces. *IDPR, 36*(1).

Lukes, S. (2005). *Power: A Radical View* (2nd ed.). New York: Palgrave McMillan.

Marcuse, H. (1964). *One-Dimensional Man*. Boston: Beacon Press.

Markovitz, I. L. (1999). Constitutions, The Federalist Papers, and the Transition to Democracy. In L. Anderson (Ed.), *Transitions to Democracy*. New York: Columbia University Press.

Maulana, I. (2014). Social Media for Knowledge Workers. In V. Benson & S. Morgan (Eds.), *Cutting-Edge Technologies and Social Media Use in Higher Education*. Hershey, PA: IGI Global.

Mumford, L. (1964). Authoritarian and Democratic Technics. *Technology and Culture, 5*(1).

Negroponte, N. (1995). *Being Digital*. London: Hodder and Stoughton.

Ober, J. (1996). *The Athenian Revolution: Essays on Ancient Creek Democracy and Political Theory*. Princeton, NJ: Princeton University Press.

Peleg, I. (2007). *Democratizing the Hegemonic State: Political Transformation in the Age of Identity*. Cambridge: Cambridge University Press. doi:10.1017/CBO9780511611254

Rose, N. (2004). *Powers of Freedom: Reframing Political Thought*. Cambridge, UK: Cambridge University Press.

Saco, D. (2002). *Cybering democracy: public space and the Internet*. Minneapolis, MN: University of Minnesota Press.

Schattschneider, E. E. (1960). *The Semi-Sovereign People: A Realist's View of Democracy in America*. New York, NY: Holt, Rhinehart & Winston.

Shifman, L. (2014). *Memes in Digital Culture*. Cambridge, MA: The MIT Press.

Waite, C. (2013). *The Digital Evolution of an American Identity*. New York, NY: Routledge.

William, R. (2003). *Television: Technology and cultural form* (2nd ed.). London: Routledge Classics.

This research was previously published in Handbook of Research on Citizen Engagement and Public Participation in the Era of New Media edited by Marco Adria and Yuping Mao; pages 231-247, copyright year 2017 by Information Science Reference (an imprint of IGI Global).

Chapter 10

The Politics of Immersive Storytelling:
Virtual Reality and the Logics of Digital Ecosystems

Christian Stiegler
Brunel University London, UK

ABSTRACT

This article applies and extends the concept of social media logic to assess the politics of immersive storytelling on digital platforms. These politics are considered in the light of what has been identified as mass media logic, which argues that mass media in the 20th century gained power by developing a commanding discourse that guides the organization of the public sphere. The shift to social media logic in the 21st century, with its grounding principles of programmability, popularity, connectivity, and datafication, influenced a new discourse on the logics of digital ecosystems. Digital platforms such as Facebook are offering all-surrounding mediated environments to communicate in Virtual Reality ('Facebook Spaces') as well as immersive narratives such as Mr. Robot VR. This article provides an understanding of the politics of immersive storytelling and of its underlying principles of programmability, user experience, popularity, and platform sociality, which define immersive technologies in the 21st century.

INTRODUCTION

On October 6, 2016, Facebook CEO Mark Zuckerberg gave a glimpse of his vision of social networking through Virtual Reality (VR) technology. When he took the stage at Oculus Connect in California to present a demo version of the company's ideas for VR, the announcement did not only include the launch of Facebook's '360° Spatial Workstation', a mainstream platform allowing users to upload and share 360° videos. But it also showcased the launch of 'Facebook Spaces', which enables users to connect with others in a VR environment. Zuckerberg's demo imagines Facebook's social media platform as a three-dimensional space, in which users can move and interact, feel involved, and engaged with

DOI: 10.4018/978-1-5225-9869-5.ch010

others. User's profiles on Facebook will be enhanced by the creation of three-dimensional digital avatars, which are able to fully interact with each other. In addition, 'Spaces will be able to allow users to view 360° content by literally becoming surrounded by content productions such as videos, and to meet friends via their digital animated avatars, share information and watch streamed entertainment content together. Users will be able to have a feeling of presence, the immersive sense of actually being inside an immersive space.

At the heart of 'Spaces' lies the utopian desire to be fully immersed in an all-surrounding mediated environment, 'transporting' users to unusual and hard-to-visit locations (a tropical island, under the sea, the surface of a far-away planet, or Mark Zuckerberg's office). At these places users are able to have real-time video calls through Facebook's messenger VOIP (named 'Parties'), share images and play multiple-player online games such as Chess. Spatial audio gives the impression of location-based conversations. Through controllers and other haptic embodiments of the virtual environment, users are able to connect the real with the virtual, and increase the level of interactivity and connectivity (van Dijck, 2012). What Marie-Laure Ryan described as 'digital wonderland' almost twenty years ago seems like an accurate description of current developments in VR technology:

…[a] computer-generated three-dimensional landscape in which we would experience an expansion of our physical and sensory powers; leave our bodies and see ourselves from the outside; adopt new identities; apprehend immaterial objects through many senses; including touch; become able to modify the environment through either verbal commands or physical gestures; and see creative thoughts instantly realized without going through the process of having them physically materialized. (Ryan, 2001, p. 1)

With Facebook's \$2 billion acquisition of start-up company Oculus and its VR head mounted display-technology (HMD) Rift in 2014, and multiple new platforms such as Google (Daydream VR), Sony (Playstation VR), Samsung (Gear VR) and HTC (Vive), the idea of immersive digital ecosystems is already very much part of our cultural landscape. Oculus is part of Facebook's strategy to expand its digital ecosystem to full sensory technology and fully immerse users on its social media platform. According to Facebook's full year results (Facebook, 2017), monthly active users (MAU) were 1.86 billion in 2016, which is an increase of 17% year-over-year. Much more relevant are mobile MAU's, which were 1.74 billion with an increase of 21% to the year before. Mobile advertising revenue represented approximately 84% of the advertising revenue. Immersion ((*lat. immersio*: dive under, dive in) is the key: Facebook claims its users already spend more than 50 minutes a day across Facebook's suite of apps globally, a number that grows if you include communication on instant messenger service WhatsApp. A figure that, along with ad impressions and average price per aid, is about to increase with the mass market implementation of VR HMD technology and a wider range of content productions.

One strategy to the challenge of digital ecosystems to be sustainable, desirable environments is the extension of their platforms. Facebook sees its social media platform 'Facebook' as the foundation for the growth of its business (see Figure 1), with additional services Video, Messenger, Search, Groups and communication tools Instagram and WhatsApp as the most influential assets to reach a mass market audience through mobile devices. However, immersive technologies are the next step as outlined in its 10-year roadmap, most importantly through connectivity (drones, satellites, lasers, terrestrial solutions, telco infra and free basics) as well as artificial intelligence (AI) including communication through vision, language, reasoning, and planning. Augmented reality (AR) and VR technologies are as well in

Figure 1. Facebook 10-Year Roadmap. (© [2016], [Facebook]. Used with permission.)

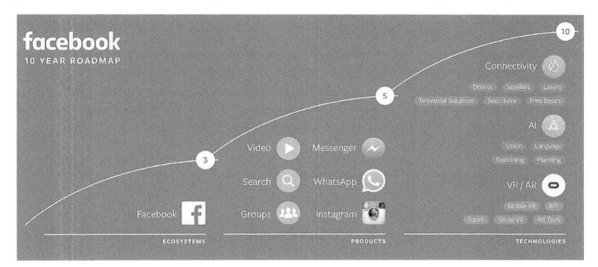

the focus of Facebook's strategy, such as AR tech, mobile VR, Rift, Touch (Rift's haptic controller) and Social VR (incl. 'Spaces', 'Parties', and other all-surrounding mediated environments).

Major digital companies are investing in VR technology and their influence spans across entertainment, games, journalism, film and TV. The result is what is called a 'console or platform war', in which the most accessible hardware with the most appealing software and content solutions still have yet to find its audience. On the hardware side, high-end market competitors Oculus, HTC and Sony are linking their own individual headsets to premium content products (such as games or VR experiences) to compete with cheaper cardboard and mid-range plastic solutions for mobile phones (Samsung, Google). On the content side, the language of VR storytelling is about to be explored with widely recognised VR productions such as the *Mr. Robot VR* experience (2016), the Academy Award nominated short *Pearl* (2017) and ILMxLAB's forthcoming *Darth Vader VR Experience*. VR now fulfils the long promise of being fully surrounded in mediated narratives such as the *Mr Robot* and *Star Wars* story universes, but also poses fundamental questions of uncertainty in relation to dramaturgical structures, the role of audiences and their ability to interact, move and communicate in fully immersive 360° narratives. Cardboard-compatible headsets offer limited interactivity, and most of them are suited for watching 360° video content only. However, smartphones contain the sensors and positioning systems to accurately track movements, and Google's cardboard solution is one way to connect to Google's Daydream VR platform, on which Daydream partners such as Hulu, Netflix, CNN and HBO Now offer premium content as well as Google services such as YouTube, Street View, Play Movies and Play Store.

Nearly 89 million VR headsets have been sold in 2016, 98% of them for mobile devices (Korolov, 2016). Forecasts expect Virtual and Augmented Reality products to hit the $120 billion mark by the year 2020 (TMT Predictions, 2016). With the extension of mobile 360° platforms such as Facebook's 'Spaces' and 'Parties', and Google's Daydream VR, mass market VR will increase in the foreseeable future, and pose fundamental questions of how immersive technologies with emerging virtual communities, new democracies, and new economies will shape the future of digital ecosystems. This new frontier of immersion can be also discussed from a more pessimistic and dystopian angle with warnings against the digital divide, information glut, and extensive surveillance. Both outlooks are rooted in the general idea of new media technologies, with terms such as hypertext, virtual reality, and cyberspace, determining the shift from the material to the immaterial, from atoms into bits (Negroponte, 1995) and matter into mind (Barlow, 1996).

VR is in the centre of immersive technologies and therefore a culmination of recent developments in regard to digital ecosystems. This article provides an analysis of the hidden strategies and politics of immersive storytelling in VR by looking at the logics of digital ecosystems, in which they are embedded. By analyzing USA Network's *Mr. Robot VR* it understands the rise of VR technology within the shift from mass media logic in the 20th century to social media logic in the 21st century.

THE RISE OF IMMERSIVE TECHNOLOGIES

Virtual reality is a technology that convinces the participant that he or she is actually in another place by substituting the primary sensory input with data received produced by a computer ... the virtual world becomes a workspace and the user identifies with the virtual body and feels a sense of belonging to a virtual community. (Heim, 1998, p. 221)

Heim's definition of virtuality refers to the notion of replacing the primary sensory input of reality with a new, virtual, alternative, digitally produced, and most importantly immersive reality. By looking at VR as a part of the extension of digital ecosystems, immersion becomes the key characteristic to define the new era of new media technologies. Immersion underlines the feeling of presence and the illusion of 'being there' in a mediated environment, the 'make-believe' of being involved, engaged and attached to mediated narratives as a psychological and physiological sensation. Murray describes immersion as the pleasurable "experience of being transported to an elaborately simulated place" which results from the "sensation of being surrounded by a completely other reality, as different as water is from air, that takes over all of our attention, our whole perceptual apparatus" (Murray, 1997, p. 98). While VR does not literally transport you to any other place, the shift of attention is crucial when defining immersive technologies and environments.

With the growing importance of the internet, social media platforms, and digital communication tools, immersive technologies can be found in all kinds of industries. We're living our lives in the design of their mediated spaces. Over the past decade, the medialization of the self has affected people's informal interactions, as well as institutional processes, and professional routines. By creating digital avatars of our perceived identity (often referred to as the 'ideal self') on social media platforms such as Facebook and Instagram, distributing selfies to craft the digital self as a substitutive reality, and by offering forms of involvement, engagement, and interactivity (user-generated content) in participatory (mobile) communication (social media debates, collective knowledge on wikis, etc.), the conditions and rules of social interaction depend on the grade of immersion in our performance and management of the self within digital ecosystems. How we make others and ourselves believe what we think we are, what we seem to know of the world, and how we communicate this knowledge, has much to do with how immersive the dynamics are between the digital management of the self, mass media, and consumption. Through the creation of virtual platforms, which are connected with each other to form digital ecosystems, we are recreating and embodying our identities in virtual spaces and are consuming information, knowledge and entertainment on immersive spaces. May it be posting images on Instagram, texting on WhatsApp, or reading newsfeeds on Facebook, we are navigating our time on Facebook's ecosystem. Our perception of mediated knowledge has much to do with how this knowledge can be distributed, accessed, and processed on and through digital platforms. The definition of digital ecosystems reshapes entire markets by including new digital business models, digital consumers, and digital technologies. What Jenkins sees as a shift from old to new consumers could be considered as one of the reasons why companies such as Facebook or Google currently invest in VR technologies:

If old consumers were assumed to be passive, the new consumers are active. If old consumers were predictable and stayed where told them to stay, then new consumers are migratory, showing a declining loyalty to networks or media. If old consumers were isolated individuals, the new consumers are more socially connected. If the work of media consumers was once silent and invisible, the new consumers are noisy and public. (Jenkins, 2006, p. 18-19)

Facebook is not the only corporation, which extends its ecosystem through an immersive approach. Digital platforms such as Amazon and Netflix are implementing digital technologies to offer their products as part of immersive experiences. These platforms are designed to be immersive and to create profiles of their users based on their tastes, trends and social fragmentation. Phenomena such as the algorithmic flow of binge-watching illustrate the constellation of power relationships between media texts, algorithms, and immersion, as VoD platforms modify the reception of serial storytelling by skipping intros and 'previously on'-segments to fully engage audiences and make them forget about the underlying principles and tactics of entertainment platforms (Stiegler, 2016). Amazon is applying the same tactics of algorithms to link individual shopping behaviouristics with entertainment consumption on Amazon Prime Video. Digital companies such as Google (Cardboard, Daydream VR), Facebook (Oculus), Sony (PlayStation VR), Samsung (Gear VR) and HTC (Vive) are major competitors in the global cultural industries, and they will continue to influence our understanding of knowledge, heritage, and identities through VR technologies (Hesmondhalgh, 2013). Cultural production, however, did experience a drastic change in the last two decades, with the process of digitalisation being the most immediate impact on technologies of cultural production. This has much to do with a rise of virtual and immersive technologies and a shift from mass media logic of the 20th century to social media logic of the 21st century. However, how do immersive technologies fit in the framework of social media logic with its grounding principles of programmability, popularity, connectivity, and datafication, or are they closer to the concept of mass media logic? Are immersive technologies such as VR an extension of social media, such as both the majority of digital business strategies, as well as Facebook's 10-year road plan, would suggest or are the politics of immersion influencing the extension of digital ecoystems on the basis of different parameters?

THE SHIFT FROM MASS MEDIA TO SOCIAL MEDIA LOGIC

Mass media logic argues that mass media in the 20th century gained power by developing a commanding discourse that guides the organization of the public sphere while its principles increasingly invade all areas of public life, hence fully immersing users and audiences within mass media consumption and the tactics of mass media ecosystems. The influence of mass media logic became increasingly important in relation to mass media institutions, which were able to cement their institutional status through their influence on politics, economy, and social life. Over thirty years ago, David Altheide and Robert Snow (1979) defined the influence of media institutions by emphasizing their logic as a set of principles that penetrate and dominate the public sphere and its organisational structures: "The present-day dominance of media has been achieved through a process in which the general form and specific formats of media have become adopted throughout society ... media are the dominant force to which other institutions conform" (Altheide & Snow, 1979, p. 15). They argued that through discursive strategies and performative tactics the power of mass media could be diffused and exercised. While defining which strategies and tactics make up mass media logic, Altheide and Snow singled out elements that related to the media's ability to frame reality and claim neutrality and independence. For instance, by referring to Raymond Williams, they argue broadcast media create a programming flow, which "saturate[s] coverage of events over a short period of time, slack off, and eventually turn to something else (Altheide & Snow, 1979, p. 238). The quick turnover creates a certain perception of reality in relation to the rhetorical power of language, and therefore dominates the selection of content itself, like a commodity principle. Television cameras and broadcast techniques add a certain sense of intimacy and intensity to the content, as can be seen in the ability to live-broadcast events. In addition, mass media has the tendency to present themselves as neutral platforms through standardized procedures such as neutral presentation by anchors, subjective commentaries by authoritative voices (experts), and the coverage of events by objective reporters, while in fact they operate as filters through which some people get more exposure than others. As a result, the authors argue that so-called public values are influenced by mass media and have a significant impact on institutional spheres. "In short, people may adopt a media logic as the interpretive framework through which definitions of reality are developed and problems solved." (Altheide & Snow, 1979, p. 44) While the authors never use the term 'mediated reality', they are constantly referring to the concept as an alternate reality shaped by the rules and conditions of mass media, and perceived through mass media technologies. Also, even though the authors do not mention the term 'immersion', it is evident that alternate realities achieve their potential through the adoption of immersive content strategies, may it be through presenting themselves as neutral and objective, or as the filter to interpret and understand the world.

However, as the general transformations described by the authors have taken place in the 1980s, there are a number of developments that have reshaped media logic to an extent that questions most of its characterstics. With computer mediated interaction, mobile communication and social media platforms, various cultural and technological trends have changed the media landscape with a set of new economic, technological and sociocultural implications. Van Dijck and Poell (2013) therefore coin the term 'social media logic' to add new elements and transform existing mechanisms. Van Dijck and Poell are focusing on the social traffic on social media platforms, which they recognise as a drastic change in the way mass media logic could be defined. For them, 'social media logic' consists of four main elements: programmability, popularity, connectivity, and datafication. They argue that social media logic remains to be entangled to a certain degree with mass media logic, when it comes to shape private, corporate and state forces.

Programmability for instance consists of two parts: technology and human agency. While scheduling and programming for mass media are often visible, the technological mechanism through algorithms, protocols, interfaces, and platform organisation on social networking sites are not: "While algorithms are nothing but sets of coded instructions, it is important to observe how social media platforms shape all kinds of relational activities, such as liking, favoriting, recommending, sharing and so on. [...] The power of algorithms [...] lies in their programmability: programmers steer user experiences, content, and user relations via platforms." (van Dijck & Poell, 2013, p. 5) While the authors are mainly referring to Facebook and the way the platform is engaging its users by 'friending' other users, their definition also applies to other digital ecosystems, which do not operate as social media platforms. Netflix's way of distributing content to its audiences has much to do with this principle of invisible programmability based on algorithms and recommendations. Its premium content is actually very limited, but carefully planned and researched to maximize its appeal to a targeted section of the audience, exemplified in the recent relaunch of *Gilmore Girls* (a popular and missed TV show, with a strong fanbase) and the science fiction show *Stranger Things* (which exploits nostalgia for the 1980s among today's 30-40 year olds, who grew up with films such as *E.T.*, *The Goonies* and *Stand by me*). All of those are based on data and preferences provided by its users through ratings, searches and algorithms. The phrase 'You might also like…' at the end of an episode is more than just a recommendation; it's a way to collect data from the audience: "Although today's television climate provides viewers with a more personalized experience, creating a sense of choice and freedom users are constantly being conditioned by those very same recommendation systems, which thereby focus the range of choices and limit potential content diversity", therefore "[d]igital television integrates social media logic." (Groshek & Krongard, 2016, p. 5) Amazon even offers its customers pilot episodes for some of its planned shows on Amazon Prime Video, greenlighting whatever pilots get the best ratings.

At the same time, streaming platforms feed the audience's desire for more. Netflix gives users exactly 20 seconds between episodes to decide, if they want to continue to stay in their ecosystem. If they refuse to make a decision, the platform will do it for them: it not only plays the next episode, it also skips the intro to resume the narrative world without further interruption. That way programmability merges with immersive technologies and provides non-stop entertainment based on underlying principles and tactics of digital platforms. What van Dijck and Poell therefore describe as 'human agency' is "the mix of crowdsourcing principles of social media with the editorial values expected of mass media." (van Dijck & Poell, 2013, p. 6)

Popularity as another grounding principle is strongly intertwined with programmability. Mass media logic already established how popular people are achieving the status of celebrities, as Altheide and Snow point out: "(1) the illusion of the images on television as 'bigger than life' phenomena; (2) the legitimizing role of television in establishing the importance of people and characters we see on television; (3) the extent to which viewers become personally involved with television personalities." (Altheide & Snow, 1979, p. 51) Social media logic however does contain the same principles, as it was transformed from being more egalitarian and democratic than mass media to having "distinct mechanisms for boosting popularity of people, things, or ideas, which is measured mostly in quantitative terms." (van Dijck & Poell, 2013, p. 7) The like-mechanism and 'like-economy' (Gerlitz & Helmond, 2013) become profound strategies for these platforms publishing popularity scores and rankings across the board.

The third grounding principle of social media logic is connectivity. While for a long time social media platforms were aiming for the pursuit of human connectedness or participation, the term connectivity as "socio-technical affordance of networked platforms to connect content to user activities and advertisers" (van Dijck & Poell, 2013, p. 8) seems more encompassing and accurate to capture the logic of digital platforms: "The shifts from analog [sic] to digital, from centralized to dispersed, from mass media to social media, from information transmission to collective intelligence, from old statistical extrapolations to new data feeds, all point to media use that is social by design, not social by default." (Uricchio, 2009, p. 138) The 'platform apparatus' is able to track individual connections and behaviouristics, while deemphasizing the power of platform agency as a way to connect users, platform and advertisers through and within immersive environments. The quality of content is crucial and is one of the biggest concerns of the platform owners: "… if the wires get clogged with sexually explicit messages or spam, the site will quickly become unfit for the purposes it was designed for. Protocols – both technical and regulatory – are thus put in place to keep platforms clean from polluting traffic." (van Dijck, 2012, p. 148) In relation to this, van Dijck referred to 'automated personalization' as the alliance between consumers, content and advertisers to entail a strategic deployment of recommendations (van Dijck & Poell, 2013, p. 9). Even though there is a strong sense of the individual performing itself on the platform, there are still patterns of personalization governed by social media profiles. It becomes evident that connectivity is not so much about how and which people are connected, but rather through which sort of content, as can be seen in the recent debate about 'fake news' and 'alternative realities' distributed on social media platforms.

The final principle of social media logic is datafication, a term coined by Mayer-Schoenberger and Cukier to describe the ability of networked platforms to render into data many aspects, which have never been quantified before, such as metadata from smart phones, GPS locations, or the preference of music, books, films, games etc. (Mayer-Schoenberger & Cukier, 2013). Van Dijck and Poell include as well the possibility to add real-time data to social media platforms in forms of polls or surveys, which results in data gathering becoming sort of a premium content itself that is not only consumed but actively influenced by users: "An important aspect of datafication is the invisibility or naturalness of its mechanics: methods for aggregation and personalization are often proprietary and thus often inaccessible to public or private scrutiny." (van Dijck & Poell, 2013, p. 10)

While programmability, popularity, connectivity, and datafication build complex dynamics, which not only unfold on one particular platform, but on the whole range of platforms within a distinctive ecosystem, the role of VR and other immersive technologies are still unclear. The politics of immersion complement the logics and tactics of both mass media and social media by adding extra dimensions, which need to be analysed further.

THE POLITICS OF IMMERSIVE STORYTELLING

Content productions distributed on immersive technologies such as streaming platforms, social media platforms, and AR/VR applications are influenced by a specific sustaining logic and widespread dissemination, which need to be scrutinized to understand their impact in various fields. Immersive technologies indicate an immaterial context of interaction between the user/audience and the mediated environment, meaning a kind of intangible architecture, which supports the mediated perception. Netflix is such a digital ecosystem, which uses an immersive technology, as it applies a platform full of keywords, genres, and ratings to create profiles of its users to keep them on the platform. The users on the other hand interact with the environment through the popularity of content (binge watching) and the wish to recommend and rate. In that sense 'Spaces' becomes another communication tool on Facebook through VR technology, as it is now possible to speak through a digitally animated avatar rather than just language and emoticons, voice messages, images (including memes), and video. VR content productions, which can be experienced through Rift, are connected through this intangible architecture by providing links to the existing ecosystem. This means immersive technologies create an organized field of relations that people navigate through by channeling their stream of awareness to the logics of the mediated environment. This leads to a splitting of consciousness such as the audience's focus is on the mediated rather than the non-mediated aspects of their perception. Immersive content productions take advantage of creating a mediated environment, which gives users the opportunity to connect with an already established story universe, as well as with the different channels of a digital ecosystem.

Figure 2. Mr. Robot VR Experience. (© [2016], [USA Network]. Used with permission.)

One of the major VR content productions in recent years, which is also a legitimate narrative experience, is USA Network's *Mr. Robot Virtual Reality Experience* (*Mr. Robot VR*). The VR production was launched in July 2016 as part of a transmedia marketing campaign to promote the second season of the network series about Elliot Anderson, an engineer with social anxiety disorder and clinical depression, who is recruited by an insurrectionary anarchist known as 'Mr. Robot' to join a group of hacktivists. The TV series has won multiple awards including the Golden Globe for Best Television Drama Series. See Figure 2.

For *Mr. Robot's* second season, the network managed to reactivate the shows' audience with a transmedia marketing campaign using Facebook Live and various other social media platforms. Around two months before the season premiered, USA Network shared a video of a faux press conference, in which President Barack Obama addresses the activities of the fictional hacker group 'fsociety', which is known from the series. The clip appeared to be authentic through a fake authenticity-approach, known from feature films such as *The Blair Witch Project* (1999) and *Cloverfield* (2008). In cooperation with Facebook Live as a platform, USA Network let 'fsociety' spread its anti-capitalist message around the globe, including various live streams targeted at 13 regions in the course of 24 hours. Live streams were followed by a teaser clip to the next season with a much-discussed cliffhanger. The network even surprised fans with an unexpected turn by hacking itself and leaking the first episode of the second season within one of its livestreams. The stream was interrupted by 'fsociety', who leaked the episode, which was then immediately removed from the page after the stream ended. After that, the episode was made available in staggered succession and for a limited time on Twitter, BuzzFeed's Discover channel on Snapchat, YouTube, and USANetwork.com. With 31,000 tweets from 20,000 unique users on Twitter the leak created excitement and anticipation for the show.

Mr. Robot VR is a 13-minute VR narrative as part of the same campaign and was premiered at San Diego Comic-Con 2016 (see Figure 3). The audience experienced a flashback journey with lead character Elliot as he remembers an early encounter with his dealer and love interest Shayla. As the first global VR simulcast, fans were invited to a Baseball stadium to watch the experience together with the cast at

Figure 3. Mr. Robot VR, Comic-Con. (© [2016], [USA Network]. Used with permission.)

a specific time, since the content would disappear afterwards from the Within app, the VR start-up that distributed the experience created by VR production company Be Here Dragons. Even though fans were able to watch the production later on platforms Samsung Gear VR, Oculus Rift, HTC Vive, or Google Cardboard/Daydream VR, it created another hype for the premiere of the second season.

VR narratives such as *Mr. Robot VR* are very much an integral part of the 21st century as they are intertwined with the development of new media technologies, which include a shift from the material to the immaterial, and the extent in which they are embedded in society and everyday life (Lievrouw, 2004; Bakardjieva, 2005). While immersive storytelling in VR is still in a phase of development and therefore cannot be assessed to its full extent yet, it is possible to refer to the underlying tactics of already established immersive productions such as *Mr. Robot VR* to better understand the complexity of how immersive VR productions are embedded in the logics of digital ecosystems. Building up on the grounding principles of social media logic, immersive storytelling on digital ecosystems is defined by programmability, user experience, popularity, and platform sociality.

Programmability

The main grounding principle of the politics of immersive storytelling on digital ecosystems is programmability. As van Dijck and Poell argued, programmability is a key element to understand social media logic though technology and human agency, and they defined it as "the ability of a central agency to manipulate content in order to define the audience's watching experience as a continuous flow." (van Dijck & Poell, 2013, p. 5) Programmability on immersive technologies therefore consists of two parts, technology and content.

Programmability refers to immersive content itself (mainly 360° videos, interactive storytelling, transmedia storytelling, games, etc.), which can be distributed through VR technology. *Mr. Robot VR* is an example of transmedia storytelling, as the narrative of the experience can only be understood in relation to season one of the series on USA Network. Without this knowledge, it would not be possible to build up an emotional connection with the characters or understand the storyline portrayed in the VR narrative. However, by attaching the VR production to the already established story universe of the show, trademark narrative elements such as characters (the main character), settings (his apartment) and key features (voice over) can be used without further introduction to the audience. In that sense, *Mr. Robot VR* is very much part of the continuous flow of narrative experiences, even though the second season of the show can be still watched and understood without watching the VR narrative.

In terms of technology, programmability for immersive technologies also means the ability to benefit from a diverse product portfolio and synergy effects within a media conglomerate. USA Network is owned by the Cable division of NBCUniversal. With a set of subsidiaries and joint ventures, NBCUniversal is able to reach out to other partners such as Here Be Dragons, Facebook, and Samsung to achieve the biggest reach for its *Mr. Robot VR* production. "The idea behind [it] was that different parts of a corporation should relate to each other in such a manner as to provide cross-promotion and cross-selling opportunities, so that sales would exceed what was possible when divisions acted separately." (Hesmondhalgh, 2013, pp. 195-197)

Other examples are The Sony Group, Alphabet, and Facebook. The Sony Group (PlayStation VR) for instance is not only a multinational conglomerate, that offers both hardware and software solutions, it also engages business through four operating and connected components: electronics, motions pictures, music and financial services. By being able to provide cross-selling opportunities between entertainment content and VR technology, Sony offers long-established franchises on PlayStation VR such as *Batman: Arkham VR*. Players can wear the Batsuit and experience how it feels to be the Dark Knight. While the technology itself establishes immersive environments, it builds on past experiences with the *Batman* universe (films, comics, series) and associated sociocultural immersive phenomena such as fandom and theme parks. Alphabet Inc. on the other hand, the multinational conglomerate which owns Google (Daydream VR), also owns a wide range of subsidiaries, such as the research and development facility X, the self-driving car project Waymo, the research and development biotech company Calico, and the broadband internet and cable television provider Google Fiber, among others. Alphabet is offering a diverse range of other products, which are integrated within its VR solution Daydream, such as YouTube, Street View, Play Movies and Play Store. Facebook as another example owns not only its social media platform, but also Oculus VR, Instagram, WhatsApp and a wide range of technology businesses in the fields of augmented, virtual and artificial intelligence sectors. Programmability in that regard does not refer solely to the platform's algorithms and interfaces to influence data traffic and content, but also to the aspects of cross-promotion and cross-selling opportunities within a multinational conglomerate. Netflix, which does have a comparable small portfolio in comparison to its competitors, relies more strongly on its ability to assess the data traffic on its platform to make sure it is able to provide immersive content ideas.

User Experience

Immersive storytelling on digital ecosystems requires a different view on user experience, as user perception consists of two crucial dimensions: the representation of individuals and the nature of their interpersonal interactions. As an individual experiencing immersive productions, the user's representation in the immersive environment is most commonly passively integrated in a story: as a person, who is present, but not recognised by other characters of the narrative ('0th person'); or as a person, who is present, and is recognised by other characters of the narrative, but is not able to interact with them ('3rd person'); or as a person, who is present and as well defined as a character, who is recognised by other characters, but not able to interact with them ('2nd person'). The most interactive approach is an emergent position in an immersive environment inspired by games design ('1st person'), meaning the user is a character in the story and able to direct the narrative to a certain degree, as well as interact with other characters or users. Although not strictly as a narrative design, Facebook offers this '1st person' experience by creating different immersive environments with 'Spaces: "As we move into global interaction models, our technology must enable us to be natural, adapting to communication, navigating with our physical bodies, and interacting effortlessly with objects that self-assemble and allow us to easily create them using our imagination as the technology." (Damer & Hinrichs, 2014, p. 27)

However, non-social network-based experiences such as VR productions also need to consider user experience on a different level. The narrative experience of *Mr. Robot VR* connects immediately with the story universe of *Mr. Robot*. The narrative design establishes a 3rd person perspective: the user is present and recognised, but is not able to interact with other characters in the narrative. As viewer, the audience sits next to Elliot in his apartment, getting addressed by the show's trademark voiceover. Together with various looks straight into the camera and breaking the fourth wall, the viewer is able to feel a sense of presence, which is further supported by subtle camera movements. As Elliott is answering a knock at the door, the user gets smoothly pushed into the right direction. Even though there is a still the opportunity to look in all directions, the narrative implements a directive element to guide the viewer in his or her perception. Further scenes in a ferris wheel car, or on the boardwalk take advantage of both VR technology as well as the notion of intimacy, which has been already established through the emotional connection fans have with the characters of the show.

Even though 0th and 3rd person are most commonly used in current VR productions, the possibility to interact within digital ecosystems increases with the use of haptic embodiments such as remote controls (Google Daydream VR, HTC Vive, PlayStation VR, among others) and body tracking systems. By giving audiences the possibility to (inter)act as users or characters in a mediated environment, the chances of feeling engaged and attached to increase, which then also intertwines with programmability, popularity, and platform sociality strategies. Platforms obviously also have the ability to exploit the interactive potential of participatory cultures in VR:

[T]he contemporary deployment of interactivity exploits participation as a form of labor. Consumers generate marketable commodities by submitting to comprehensive monitoring. They are not so much participating, in the progressive sense of collective self-determination, as they are working by submitting to interactive monitoring. The advent of digital interactivity does not challenge the social relations associated with capitalist rationalization, it reinforces them and expands the scale on which they operate. (Andrejevic, 2004, p. 197)

Popularity

Individual user experiences are essential currencies for digital ecosystems to deploy complex algorithms and attract advertisers. Van Dijck and Poell point out that this grounding principle of social media logic has a profound influence on the user's perception by implementing ways to manipulate, influence and measure audiences through popularity figures (van Dijck & Poell, 2013, p. 7). This principle is essential for digital platforms, as they are keen on creating popularity hypes and fandom. *Mr. Robot VR* for instance implements its storyline through the story universe of an already popular TV show on the same network, making it a significant contribution to programmability strategies. Van Dijck and Poell also mention the individual approaches of platforms to boost popularity of characters, things, or ideas, and Facebook's mechanisms to measure which topics are discussed most. Immersive content productions on digital ecosystems are a result of this measurement, as these platforms are able to create content based on the data provided by its users, but also through the exchange with traditional mass media: "Popularity becomes enmeshed in a feedback loop between mass and social media, and, as was argued in the case of programmability, becomes part of a larger cultural arena where different institutional discourses and counter-discourses engage in a struggle to make their logics more pressing." (van Dijck & Poell, 2013, p. 8) For social media platforms such as Facebook, 'Spaces' becomes another way to promote social experience and popularity figures through immersive technologies. However, social media platforms already established standardized metrics to measure data and make it meaningful in social life. Tools such as Google Analytics and Facebook Memology help to measure aggregated popularity and influence on digital ecosystems. These established metrics would need to be transferred to VR technology, so advertisers would have an understanding of the potential revenue of their investment.

Platform Sociality

The fourth grounding principle of immersive storytelling on digital ecosystems is platform sociality. Sociologists and media scholars have investigated the behaviour of users on social media platforms (Boyd & Ellison, 2007), as well as how platforms such as Facebook help users to maintain relations (Ellison et al., 2007). Immersive technologies such as VR take a distinct position within that research, as they can be used to further support platform sociality (e.g. 'Spaces'), even though VR technology is often perceived as an isolated, individual process of consuming content. Certainly, the way in which platforms can be viewed as an intermediary between users is about the change with the introduction of VR technology on social media platforms. Online sociality is strongly attached to the creation of avatars and digitally mediated environments, as the user's focus is on the mediated rather than the non-mediated aspects of their perception. The architecture of digitally created environments needs to be designed in a way that invites users to spend time in these spaces and comfortably interact with others. However, also VR content productions are about to become part of platform sociality, as they soon will have to compete with other entertainment experiences, such as cinema and concerts, which both allow a higher level of social interaction. In addition, participatory experiences through television content is becoming much more relevant as well, for example "to engage via Twitter while viewing a real-time televised event, using a shared hashtag to participate in a broader, synchronous conversation with other users." (Groshek & Krongard, 2016, p. 2) At the moment it is still not possible to integrate these engagement activities as part of VR experiences, because users have to wear heatsets. However, there are efforts to apply a social element to VR experiences, such as can be seen in the way *Mr. Robot VR* was presented in a baseball stadium. Also, recent developments in establishing an infrastructure of VR cinemas (Wong, 2016) to enable cinematic experiences in VR are offering another way to engage users with each other.

CONCLUSION

The battle for supremacy over the future of immersive technologies is taking place between the Hollywood studios and Silicon Valley tech industries (e.g. Google, Apple, Facebook, Amazon, etc.) in the increasingly fragmented digital media economy where content has emerged as its most valuable currency. All major studios and global digital industries are working on their own technological solutions to further immerse audiences in their digital ecosystem. This is not always an advantage: at the moment, the current marketplace for immersive technologies is too fragmented to have global impact. Also, the range of current VR technologies is still too diverse, and offers everything from low-end cheap cardboard-solutions (Google Cardboard) to mid-range products with additional features (Samsung Gear VR, Google Daydream VR), and expensive high-end headsets, which run off external computers or game consoles (Oculus Rift, HTC Vive, PlayStation VR). However, they are all embedded within an already existing ecosystem, which offers the possibility to spread content across different platforms and to reach audiences through various channels.

This article argued that the grounding principles of immersive storytelling on digital ecosystems are intertwined with social media logic and its elements of programmability, popularity, connectivity, and datafication. The politics of immersive technologies are strongly influenced by these principles, as they are embedded in and connected through already established digital ecosystems. Programmability, user experience, popularity, and platform sociality define the way these ecosystems operate through immersive technologies and immersive content productions. *Mr. Robot VR,* as one of the most recent examples of this type of content, displayed the importance of an existing story universe. In a transmedia storytelling approach the VR narrative has been intertwined with an already established franchise, making it easier for users to feel emotionally attached and engaged. Through programmability, digital ecosystems are able to position their formats not only in a story universe, but also integrate them within the strategy of a multinational conglomerate. This becomes more efficient when taking popularity into consideration and offering possibilities of platform sociality. The most crucial grounding principle for immersive storytelling though is user experience. While passive involvement remains dominant in current immersive narratives, social media platforms such as Facebook with its strategy to integrate interactive immersive components as part of its digital communication tools ('Spaces') will challenge immersive technologies to become as interactive as possible. This will give platforms the ability to collect and exploit user data to attract advertisers and increase commercial success. However, the market for immersive technologies is still too fragmented to ensure that VR will penetrate deeply into the mechanics of everyday life, and affect all sorts of social interactions and routines. Without a global platform, universal narratives, as well as accessible and affordable technology solutions, immersive storytelling on digital ecosystems will remain in its experimental phase for a longer time.

REFERENCES

Altheide, D., & Snow, R. (1979). *Media logic.* London: Sage.

Andrejevic, M. (2004). The webcam subculture and the digital enclosure. In N. Couldry & A. McCarthy (Eds.), *MediaSpace: Place, scale and culture in a media age* (pp. 193–208). London, New York: Routledge.

Bakardjieva, M. (2005). *Internet society: The Internet in everyday life.* London: Sage.

Barlow, J. (1996). *A declaration of the independence of cyberspace.* Retrieved from http://www.eff.org/~barlow/Declaration-Final.html

Boyd, D., & Ellison, N. B. (2007). Social network sites: Definition, history, and scholarship. *Journal of Computer-Mediated Communication*, *13*(1), 210–230. doi:10.1111/j.1083-6101.2007.00393.x

Damer, B., & Hinrichs, R. (2014). The virtuality and reality of avatar cyberspace. In M. Grimshaw (Ed.), *The Oxford Handbook of Virtuality* (pp. 17–41). Oxford: Oxford University Press. doi:10.1093/oxfordhb/9780199826162.013.032

Deloitte (2016). *Technology, Media & Telecommunications Predictions 2016. Virtual Reality: A billion dollar niche.* Retrieved from https://www2.deloitte.com/global/en/pages/technology-media-and-telecommunications/articles/tmt-pred16-media-virtual-reality-billion-dollar-niche.html

Ellison, N. B., Steinfield, C., & Lampe, C. (2007). The benefits of Facebook friends: Social capital and college students use of online social network sites. *Journal of Computer-Mediated Communication*, *12*(4), 1143–1168. doi:10.1111/j.1083-6101.2007.00367.x

Facebook. (2017). *Reports Fourth Quarter and Full Year 2016.* Retrieved from https://investor.fb.com/investor-news/press-release-details/2017/Facebook-Reports-Fourth-Quarter-and-Full-Year-2016-Results/default.aspx

Gerlitz, C., & Helmond, A. (2013). The Like Economy: Social buttons and the data-intensive web. *New Media & Society*, *11*(6), 985–1002.

Groshek, J., & Krongard, S. (2016). Netflix and engage? Implications for streaming television on political participation during the 2016 US presidential campaign. *Social Sciences 5*(4), 65, 1-18.

Heim, H. (1998). *Virtual Realism.* New York: Oxford University Press.

Hesmondhalgh, D. (2013). *The Cultural Industries* (3rd ed.). London: Sage.

Jenkins, H. (2006). *Convergence culture: Where old and new media collide.* New York: New York University Press.

Korolov, M. (2016). Report: 98% of VR headsets sold this year are for mobile phones. *Hypergrid Business.* Retrieved from http://www.hypergridbusiness.com/2016/11/report-98-of-vr-headsets-sold-this-year-are-for-mobile-phones/

Lievrouw, L. (2004). Whats changed about new media? Introduction to the fifth anniversary issue of New Media & Society. *New Media & Society*, *6*(1), 9–15. doi:10.1177/1461444804039898

Mayer-Schoenberger, V., & Cukier, K. (2013). *Big Data. A Revolution that Will Transform How We Live, Work and Think.* London: John Murray Publishers.

Murray, J. (1997). *Hamlet on the Holodeck. The Future of Narrative in Cyberspace.* New York: The Free Press.

Negroponte, N. (1995). *Being digital.* New York: Knopf.

Ryan, M.-L. (2001). *Narrative as Virtual Reality. Immersion and Interactivity in Literature and Electronic Media.* Baltimore, MD: John Hopkins.

Stiegler, C. (2016). Invading Europe. Netflix's expansion to the European market. In K. McDonald & D. Smith-Rowsey (Eds.), *The Netflix Effect. Technology and Entertainment in the 21st Century* (pp. 235–247). New York: Bloomsbury.

Thon, J. (2008). Immersion Revisited. On the Value of a Contested Concept. In F. Amyris, O. Leino & H. Wirman (Eds.), Extending experiences. Structure, analysis and design of computer game player experience (pp. 29-43). Rovianemi: Lapland University Press.

Uricchio, W. (2009). Moving beyond the artefact: Lessons from participatory culture. In M. van den Boomen, S. Lammes, A.-S. Lehmann, J. Raesssens, & M. Schäfer (Eds.), *Digital Material. Tracing new media in everyday life and technology* (pp. 135–146). Amsterdam: Amsterdam University Press.

van Dijck, J. (2012). Facebook and the engineering of connectivity: A multi-layered approach to social media platforms. *Convergence*, *19*(2), 141–155. doi:10.1177/1354856512457548

van Dijck, J., & Poell, T. (2013). Understanding Social Media Logic. *Media and Communication*, *1*(1), 2–14. doi:10.17645/mac.v1i1.70

Wong, R. (2016). World's first permanent VR cinema opens in Amsterdam, and it's very weird. *Mashable.com*. Retrieved from http://mashable.com/2016/03/07/vr-cinema-amsterdam/#pYrP9IXHjgqY

This research was previously published in International Journal of E-Politics (IJEP), 8(3); edited by Sofia Idris; pages 1-15, copyright year 2017 by IGI Publishing (an imprint of IGI Global).

Section 3
Media Credibility

Chapter 11
Modeling Rumors in Twitter:
An Overview

Rhythm Walia
Netaji Subhash Institute of Technology, India

M.P.S. Bhatia
Netaji Subhash Institute of Technology, India

ABSTRACT

With the advent of web 2.0 and anonymous free Internet services available to almost everyone, social media has gained immense popularity in disseminating information. It has become an effective channel for advertising and viral marketing. People rely on social networks for news, communication and it has become an integral part of our daily lives. But due to the limited accountability of users, it is often misused for the spread of rumors. Such rumor diffusion hampers the credibility of social media and may spread social panic. Analyzing rumors in social media has gained immense attention from the researchers in the past decade. In this paper the authors provide a survey of work in rumor analysis, which will serve as a stepping-stone for new researchers. They organized the study of rumors into four categories and discussed state of the art papers in each with an in-depth analysis of results of different models used and a comparative analysis between approaches used by different authors.

1. INTRODUCTION

Social networks are very powerful means of communication where information can flow fast and has deep penetration. Any user can both generate and consume content which is provided to wider audience when compared to conventional media. Social media has power to affect user behavior and emotions as shown by Robert M. Bond et al. (2012) in an experiment conducted over 61 million subjects, where they found that 2% more users have voted when associated with friends who have voted and shared on Facebook. Facebook Scientist Adam Kramer et al. (2014) has shown direct impact of a Facebook post on the emotion of a user. It also showed flow of an emotion over the social networks. Engaging topics like politics, religion, race and etc. have even higher effect on the users. Egyptian revolution is one such

DOI: 10.4018/978-1-5225-9869-5.ch011

case, which distinctly depicts the impact of Facebook (Bradly, 2008). Video of Khaled Said an Egyptian businessman who was beaten to death by police in June 2010 was leaked on YouTube and a page named '*We are all Khaled Said*' was created on Facebook to protest. The page was joined by hundred thousand citizens and played prominent role in spreading the discontent among public. The page called for protest on 25th January, which witnessed 400,000 participants. The revolution ended with resignation of the president. Trends on social networks are extracted using Data Mining algorithms. The study, which extracts meaningful content from large datasets, is called data mining. Data mining has its roots penetrated to different segregated sectors like data mining is used with Rough Set Theory to extract meaningful knowledge from large databases (Rana & Lal, 2016), data mining is used to mine medical data (Banu et al., 2015; Dey et al., 2014), it can be used with steganography techniques (Bhattacharya et al., 2012) and it is also used in systems proposing frameworks for firms dealing customer management relationship (Ranjan & Bhatnagar, 2009).

Cross border operation and granularity of Internet makes it impossible to monitor the content on social networking sites. Since its inception, social networking sites have been used by antisocial elements for illegal activities. Due to scale and feasibility social networking sites doesn't provide verification of the accounts, so it is hard to link a user profile with a person in society especially when user chooses to hide his personal details. Many countries have outdated laws where there is no provision to accept content on Internet as an evidence. This battle against miscreants is thereby need to be carried online by identifying such rumormongers and associated patterns. Most of the work on rumors in social media is carried on Twitter which is another popular social networking site. Twitter has second biggest user base next to Facebook (Curtis, 2013) but every post (tweet) on twitter is public. This gives twitter even bigger width and spread. The impact of twitter is well understood by public relation agencies, which spread all sorts of propaganda against their competitors. David M. Cook et al. (2014) showed the use of bots by the two leading parties in the Australian Elections, 2013 to affect the voters through twitter. Apart from propaganda, Twitter has been extensively used by antisocial elements to propagate false information. The Guardian newspaper (Procter, 2011) showed multiple rumors being tweeted during UK riots which include fake news of police brutality to the burning of London eye. These rumors were diffused into twitter to fuel the discontent among public. Boston marathon bombing case presents a perfect case study to analyze the impact of rumors spread on society. Boston marathon met with twin bombings on April 15, 2013 killing 2 civilians and injuring 200 more. Soon after the bombings a post on Reddit, claims to identify the culprit and shared the pictures. This post went viral and it was soon picked pace on twitter. The culprit, identified as Sunil Tripathi was soon met with abuses, hate everywhere until his name was cleared by police three days later. But the damage was done, Sunil Tripathi was found dead on 23th April, 2013(Alexander, 2013). Gupta et al., (2013) showed that 29% of the tweets regarding the bombings were spreading rumors. The authors identified that 32,000 accounts were created within three days of the bombings out of which 20% of the accounts were suspended by twitter later. These accounts shared status regarding the bombings, most of which were rumors. Timely detection of such rumors and a counter strategy could have saved the life of an innocent student.

In this paper we have structured the study of rumors on Twitter into following four different classes - (1) Classification of statement as fact or rumor (2) Diffusion patterns of rumors (3) Limiting the spread of rumors (4) Finding the source of rumors. Each study has its relevance and output from one study could bootstrap the study for other classes. Figure 1 shows the relationship between the class of problems and their significance.

Figure 1. Four classes of problems in rumor analysis

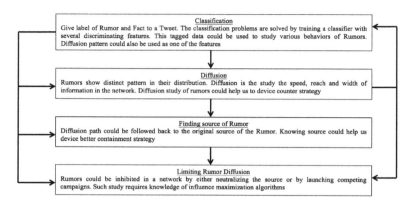

2. CHARACTERISTICS OF A TWEET

Before proceeding further, it is essential to understand the basic building block of twitter - *Tweet*. A tweet is a micro-blog of maximum 140 characters shared by writer with the world. Apart from text a tweet has several other characteristics, which are briefly discussed below.

2.1. Content Based Characteristics

These are the properties present in the text of the tweet written by the user. These characteristics are useful when classifying tweets into rumors and fact as we will see later in next section.

1. **Text:** Text of tweet itself presents enough information to study. We could mine context of the tweet (Cagliero & Fiori, 2013) and sentiments (Hassan et al., 2010), which can be useful in predicting about positive/negative attitude of the user about a topic.
2. **Hash-Tag:** Hash-tag is an alphanumeric word (often concatenation of the words) starting with a '#'. Hash-tag was a feature introduced in twitter in year 2008. Since then users are tagging their post to present context, brief summary or feelings. In 2009, twitter has started giving search options, trends on the bases of Hash-tags.
3. **URL:** Users sometimes share URLs in their tweet to either overcome the world limit twitter has imposed, or to share the source of the tweet. In general URL is related to the content of the tweet and it could be followed to retrieve context and sentiments.
4. **User-Tags:** Users sometimes tag other users by using @ [username] tag in their tweet to draw attention of a particular user towards the context in the tweet.

2.2. Network Based Characteristics

These properties are derived from the follower – followed relationship on twitter. Such characteristics help us to find position of a user in the network and determine its influence. Studies employing Influence Maximization algorithm at their core could utilize these features. Following are the two characteristics used extensively by the studies discussed later in the paper.

1. **Follow Graph:** This is a directed graph where each user is a node and the edges represent the following. For e.g. if a user u follows user v, then:
   G(V,E): Follow Graph G with V and E as vertex set and edge set
   u∈V, v∈V, e(u,v)∈ E where e(u,v): u follows v
2. **Retweet Graph:** This is a directed graph where each user is a node and the edge between users is added when a user re-tweets the status of another user. Each tweet has its own Retweet Graph.
   G(V,E): Retweet Graph, u∈V, v∈V, e(u,v)∈ E where e(u,v): u retweets the tweet written by v

2.3. Twitter Metadata Based Characteristics

Twitter provides some metadata about each tweet which is not directly visible on the site but could be retrieved by using the API exposed by twitter. Some of them are discussed below:

1. **User Description:** The description entered by user sharing the tweet. This information could be used to model user interests.
2. **Created at:** The date-time when the tweet was created by the user.
3. **Followers count:** Number of followers of the user sharing the tweet.
4. **Favorite count:** Number of times the tweet has been tagged favorite by distinct users.
5. **Coordinates:** The latitude-longitude position of the user at the time of tweet generation. If this data is not present, then the location of the user profile will be returned.
6. **Status Count:** The total count of the status shared by the user generating the tweet
7. **Retweeted status:** If the current status is retweeted by the user, then the original tweet is also returned with all the metadata.
8. **In reply:** If the current status was in reply to a tweet, then the targeted tweet is returned.

All of these characteristics make a tweet unique. Researchers process these characteristics to extract features, which could have correlation with the target variable in a machine-learning problem. For example, network-based features could be used to create time series model could depict the flow of a tweet in the twitter network.

3. IDENTIFYING RUMORS

A lot of information is disseminating on social media. Such information ranges from blogs, posts, advertisements, news and rumor. Each of the information has its own key characteristics or features unique to them, useful in distinguishing it from other information. Classification of statements into facts and rumor is basically mining the social networking sites for real cases of such information spreading and finding features which are unique to rumors.

3.1 Rumor Has It

Qazvinian et al., (2011) identified both rumors and the users believing in them. Authors proposed following features:

3.1.1. Features

1. **Lexical Pattern:** Twitter text is tokenized by taking space as the delimiter. Authors made two features from each text - Unigram and Bigram. These features are obtained by removing all the stop words like - 'is,' 'he,' 'their,' etc. These words have little significance to the context. Then the words are normalized by removing tense forms for e.g. 'running' is changed to 'run.' Now the text is suitable for the text analysis. Unigram features are obtained by taking each space-separated word. Such feature gives the context of the text. In Bigram each consecutive word is joined as a token. Bigrams are useful in extracting sentiment, adjective about an object. (**TXT**)
2. **Part of Speech Pattern:** Twitter text is also tagged manually to tag the part of the text, which represents nouns, verb, and adjective etc. Same words of a tweet could represent different meaning in different tagging. Adding such tags helps to mine the proper context of the text. After adding tags, modified text is again tokenized into unigrams and bigrams. (**POS**)

So, total authors extracted four features from the content of the tweet. Authors used sentiment analysis by Hasan et al. (2010) on these features to predict whether the user believes or rejects the rumor contained in the text. Following is an example of the feature extraction from twitter text.

"#Latest Barack Obama is Muslim URL / www.anyinfo.com"

Above is an example of rumor making rounds on the Twitter. Here firstly all the words are separated by spaces. Than # symbol is removed and word is preceded by its part of speech tag as adjective /latest. Then part of speech tag is added before all words. Like: Noun/Barack Obama, noun/Muslim. All single words are features called unigrams and all combination of two words is bigrams

1. **Retweet:** Users can retweet the tweet of another user. Suppose a user *i* tweeted tweet of user *j* then there could be two possibilities - user (1) x or (2) y have history of sharing/re-tweeting a rumor. Here we will have two user models from the training data - positive and negative, which are the probability distribution over the users under positive or negative instance. (USR)
2. **Hashtags:** Context derived from hashtags in the training data can also be used to build positive and negative training models. (TAG)
3. **URL:** URLs can also be followed to retrieve text. Again from this text unigram and bigram features are made and positive/negative training model is constructed. (URL)

Bayes classifier is built for each feature under positive and negative training data retrieved above. It is calculated how many times a tweet comes in positive model with respect to a feature. Log likelihood ratios are used to avoid dealing with extremely small numbers and are calculated as shown below:

$$\ln \frac{P\left(\theta_i^+/t\right)}{P\left(\theta_i^-/t\right)} = \ln \frac{P\left(\theta_i^+\right)}{P\left(\theta_i^-\right)} + \ln \frac{P\left(t/\theta_i^+\right)}{P\left(t/\theta_i^-\right)} \tag{1}$$

$\theta_i^+ and \theta_i^-$: Probabilistic models built on feature i using positive and negative instances respectively

$P(\theta_i \neg^+ / t) / P(\theta_i \neg^- / t)$: Likelihood ratio of tweet t to belong in the positive class to negative class with feature i.

$P(\theta_i \neg^+)$: Probability estimate (frequency) of a feature i to lie in the positive class in the training data.

$P(t / \theta_i \neg^+)$: Probability estimate (frequency) of a feature i to lie in the positive class for the data in Tweet

3.1.2. Results

Equation (1) gives the likelihood of a tweet under positive model to the negative model. Right hand side is calculated from the training data to calculate the likelihood for the testing data in the left hand side. Both training and testing data are collected using regular expressions from twitter. Websites like urban legend and snopes.com are used for finding rumors and then regular expression for that rumor is submitted to search API. Authors collected 10,000 tweets belonging to 5 different controversial stories. However, the tweets returned, had great number of false positives where some users, instead of endorsing were actually denying the rumor. So the authors annotated the tweets to have two annotations - (1) Tweet is related to be a rumor or not, (2) User believes or discard the rumor.

Two experiments are performed one for rumor retrieval and other for testing the effectiveness of features in predicting rumors. Regex Queries are built for each set of topics. Rumor related tweets are annotated as relevant if it is rumor and non-relevant otherwise. Cross validation testing is used to predict the relevance of tweets. Regex is compared with two other methods of data retrieval - random and uniform. Results show that that *regex* shows improvement over other methods in rumor retrieval. To test effectiveness of features, cross validation testing is performed with all queries for each feature. Content based features have high precision and recall but twitter based features have high precision but low recall. Cross validation testing showed the effectiveness of the features in identifying the people who spread rumors. Experiment is also performed to find the generality of algorithm to identify new rumors. The accuracy and precision of classifier trained with the features increases as the labeled data increases.

3.2 Epidemiological Modeling of News and Rumors on Twitter

Jin et al., (2013) discussed various characteristics of rumors as:

3.2.1. Features

1. **The number of tweets of news is greater than rumors**: The paper showed that the number of tweets in case of news is higher than rumor at the inception phases. However news dies quickly, but rumors live for a longer period of time. Rumors have spikes in the volume. They die and they rise again sharply.
2. **Follower-Followed ratio:** The paper also showed that there is no significant difference in the number of people following others and also who are followers of others.
3. **Response Ratio:** All the replies and retweets are counted as response. Response ratio is calculated as

Figure 2. Tweet Volume with time

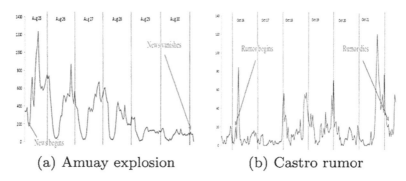

(a) Amuay explosion   (b) Castro rumor

$$\text{Response Ratio} = [(N_{tweets} + N_{replies}) / N_{total})] \tag{2}$$

3.2.2. Results

Authors reported that the response ratio of the news is higher if compared with that of rumors. For experiments, authors collected tweets related to the eighth stories, which include four rumors and news each. Figure 2 are the graphs taken from (Jin et al., 2013) belonging to the two of the stories:

1. **News Story**: When Amuay Explosion, blast that happened in Venezuela on 25th august 2012 was declared on Twitter, there was an outburst in the number of tweets which went to as high as 49,015 which can be seen from Figure 1. The number of tweets decreased with each passing day which we can see that by August 30, the number of tweets decreased to as low as 20.
2. **Rumor Story:** On 16 October 2012, rumor was spread about the ill health of political leader Fidel Castro, which was later denied and declared to be a rumor on October 22, 2012. As shown in Figure 1, it found that for the rumor there was no activity burst. The rumor began with as few as 20 tweets, which increased by the time it was officially denied. But still the number of tweets was not comparable to news.

The paper was more focused on the diffusion pattern of rumors, hence discussed further in the next section, where authors have modeled the diffusion in one of the information diffusion model.

3.3 Aspects of Rumors

Kwon et al., (2013) identified the differences in diffusion of rumor and non-rumor on the basis of social psychological literature and social media study. Four hypotheses are studied from social physiological literature:

1. Rumors are more liable to propagate from low-degree users to high-degree users and rumor diffusers are likely to be new based on registration time and have fewer followers.
2. Rumors are less successful as conversation topics and contain more words related to skepticism and doubts.

3. Compared to other types of information, rumors contain several characteristic sentiments (e.g., anger).
4. Rumors will more likely contain words related to social relationships (e.g., family, mate) and actions like hearing.

To support their hypothesis, authors proposed following features:

1. **Personal Features:** (a) Registration age and (b) number of followers.
2. **Topological Features**
    a. **Friendship Network:** The sub-graph of original graph where all users are linked and have posted a tweet to each other.
    b. **Diffusion Network:** It represents the flow of information from one user to another. From diffusion set two measures are taken, one is flow, which is the information diffusion from users with low degree to users with high degree. And other is singleton which is the number of users whose none of the influences have posted about a topic
3. **Linguistic Features**: Linguistic enquiry and word count (LIWC) (Pennebaker et al., 2003 & Tausczik et al., 2010) is used to detect meanings, thinking styles, individual difference in experiment data. A group of words is given as input to LIWC and it outputs the sentiment of the group.

Discriminating power of each feature supports the viability of the corresponding hypothesis. Table 1 lists all the features with their Mean Decrease Accuracy (MDA) score calculated by training the Random Forest classifier. Higher MDA means more discriminative power of the feature. Table 2 summarizes the various classification studies.

4. ANALYZING THE DIFFUSION PATTERN OF RUMOR

Social media is a very dense network which each user being both consumer and producer of a content. A piece of information in such a network could reach a larger audience in a lesser time. In this section we will discuss how rumors spread with time and other patterns visible in the spread. We will see how number of followers, time, and a node affect the diffusion of rumors. As discussed the section 1, diffusion patterns could be used to identify rumors, which will be discussed in this section as well.

4.1 Epidemiological Modeling of News and Rumors on Twitter

Jin et al., (2013) proposed a diffusion characteristic of rumors called retweet topology. It shows how information propagates on Social media. The retweet topology is the collection of retweet graphs, where each node denotes a user and the edge is made when a user retweets from the other user. As shown in Figure 3 (Jin et al., 2013) we see that both news and rumor has a subtle start but with the time, difference become prominent. Rumors are limited closer to the source, whereas news has wider reach. Rumors in the *retweet* topology spawn a graph closer to star topology whereas news presents a mesh topology. This again shows that users post news from multiple sources but in case of rumors one source infect multiple nodes. The graph is plotted with 6 hours interval.

Table 1. Variable importance by Random Forest

Rank	Variable	Hypothesis	Characteristic	MDA
1	Negate	3	linguistic	18.46
2	Affect	3	linguistic	17.67
3	Flow	1	Topological	16.16
4	Singleton	2	topological	11.63
5	Hear	4	linguistic	10.94
6	Tentative	2	linguistic	10.20
7	Exclusive	2	linguistic	10.14
8	Posemo	3	linguistic	9.29
9	Cogmech	2	linguistic	9.10
10	Social	4	linguistic	5.52
11	Sad	3	linguistic	4.73
12	Insight	2	linguistic	2.84
13	Anxiety	3	linguistic	2.66
14	Follower	1	Personal	1.45
15	Negemo	3	Linguistic	1.34
16	Age	1	Personal	1.20
17	Anger	3	linguistic	0.30

Table 2. Comparison of Rumor Classification studies

Study	Algorithm	Data Set	Comments
Rumor has it	1. Tweets are tagged by taking user sentiments into consideration 2. Text Features by making Unigrams & Bigrams. 3. Other metadata like URL etc. are also taken as features. 4. Naïve Bayes is trained by taking combinations of the features.	1. 10000 Tweets related to 5 preselected topics. 2. Tweets are tagged manually into rumors or facts. 3. User sentiments about the rumors are captured and an automated system whose accuracy is verified by manual tagging	1. Diverse range of features and each of them is separately evaluated by training Naive Bayes. 2. User's belief is also considered instead of plainly taking the text as feature. 3. The topics related to rumors and facts are not related to each other and there is no overlapping in the context. This left untested by the authors when the both rumors and facts are dealing with same context
Aspects of Rumor	1. Authors proposed 4 hypotheses, which are tested by taking various features, which are categorized, into personal, linguistic and topological. 2. These features are tested for their accuracy by training a Random Forest classifier individually	1. Websites like Snopes and Urban Legends are probed for rumor topics 2. 70,000 tweets were collected related to the topics selected above which includes 47 topics for rumors and 55 non-rumors	1. Extensive list of features ranging across various domains like social network, language etc. 2. P-value is calculated to check for any role of chance in the results obtained from Random Forest. 3. Each of the features is ranked separately as done by *rumor has it.*

Figure 3. Re-tweet cascades. Each node is user id and each edge connects re-tweet user to original user

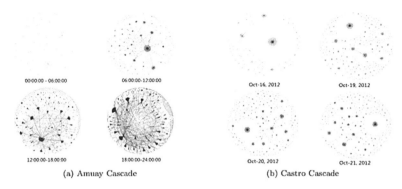

(a) Amuay Cascade   (b) Castro Cascade

The authors also used epidemiological models to analyze diffusion patterns of news and rumors. Epidemiological model provides understanding to how information diffuses on social networking sites in terms of how an epidemic spread in a society by taking rumor as an epidemic. SIR (susceptible – infected – recovered) model (Newman, 2002) explains variety of diffusion behaviors where a user is *susceptible* for infection could be *infected* and could be *recovered*. There are some problems, which could not be described by SIR. In such problems a user could be affected multiple times for the same information. SIS (susceptible – infected – susceptible) model (Kimura, 2009) explains such cases well, where a user can never be fully recovered.

However (Jin et al., 2013) showed that these models were not able to capture the diffusion on Twitter and instead proved SEIZ (susceptible – exposed – infected – skeptic) model to be better suited which was first used in adoption of Feynman diagrams (Bettencourt, 2006). SEIZ model better explains the diffusion on Twitter because of its states skeptics (Z) which demonstrates users who do not wish to tweet about a topic even after hearing it and exposed (E) which shows the users who take some time after hearing a topic and prior to posting about it. All epidemiological models are modeled mathematically with ordinary differential equation to show the change in state of the population in a time interval (dt). For e.g. in the below SIS model with states - S and I respective probabilities of attaining the states are changed as shown in Figure 4 and Equation (3).

$$\frac{dS}{dt} = -P_1 SI + P_2 I; \frac{dI}{dt} = P_1 SI - P_2 I \tag{3}$$

Figure 4. State Diagram for SIS model

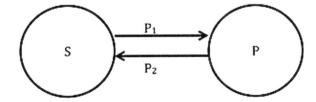

Now the parameters like P_1, P_2, S and I are known. Authors performed least square fit of the model with twitter data to estimate the parameters and found SEIZ to have lower mean square error than SIS model. The authors also made the hypothesis that the ratio of sum of probabilities to enter exposed state via susceptible to the sum of probabilities exiting from exposed state to infected state will be larger for news as compared to rumors. In other words, rate of users to turn infected from exposed is higher for rumors.

4.2 Prominent Features of Rumors

Kwon et al., (2013) extended the previous paper (Kwon et al., 2013) discussed in previous section of rumor with the introduction of the diffusion temporal features and proposed PES (periodic external shock) model which shows how rumors fluctuate with time. A data set comprising all of tweets on twitter for 3.5 years is used. The periodic external shock model can capture the burst nature of rumors. It showed that rumors have multiple spikes in their course of spread whereas non-rumors have a single prominent spike. It can be seen in the Figure 5 taken from (Kwon et al., 2013).

PES model is an extension to SpikeM model first proposed by Matsubara et al. in (Matsubara et al., 2012). SpikeM model is extension to traditional Susceptible-Infected (SI) model by adding a power law decay term to lower the infection rates of nodes and periodic interaction function to show people spend different time on social media on different times of day. The structural and linguistic features are same as discussed in (Kwon et al., 2013).

To classify a topic as rumor or non-rumor three classifiers based on decision tree, random forest, and SVM are built, given the set of tweets about the topic. Classifiers based on the temporal, structural, and linguistic features provide high precision and recall in the range of 87% to 92%. Features with high predictive power are periodicity of rumors, flow and singletons. Table 3 summarizes the rumor diffusion studies.

5. LIMITING THE SPREAD OF RUMORS

In the previous sections we discussed the techniques to identify rumors on social media and its diffusion pattern. However, we need to device a counter strategy to stop the further diffusion of the rumors. In this section we will study papers which will limit the spread of rumors. These papers solve *Influence*

Figure 5. # tweet verses time graph showing rumors to have multiple periodic spikes whereas news have one prominent spike

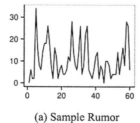
(a) Sample Rumor

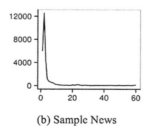
(b) Sample News

Table 3. Comparison of Rumor diffusion studies

Study	Algorithm	Data Set	Comments
Epidemiological Modeling of News and Rumors on Twitter	Modeled twitter data using SEIZ and SIS epidemiological model. Proved that SEIZ fits the data better with lower mean error deviation. Also proposed a ratio R_{SI} as the indication of a topic being a rumor	4 topics, each of rumors and facts were selected with number of tweets ranging from 100 to 45,000	1. This paper presents the study of rate of conversion of users from *susceptible* to *infected* from via *skeptics* and *exposed* states. Such study could be useful to estimate the reach of a recent rumor. 2. Authors used hash tags and search keywords to extract the data related to a topic however no discussions were made regarding the cases where user might be discarding a rumor, or the tweet containing similar keywords has no relation with the rumor
Prominent feature of Rumors	PES model for temporal data, which captures the periodic spikes in the tweets related to the rumors. Diffusion graph is similar to the (Jin et al., 2013. It combines temporal features modeled by PES with the features in (Kwon et al., 2013) and trained three classifiers – *Decision Tree, SVM, Random Forest*	1.7 Billion tweets collected for 3.5 years belonging to 54 million users.	1. Huge dataset to support the experimental results. 2. Very detailed annotation process. Only the topics with interclass correlation coefficient of 0.992 and p-value zero were selected. So topics with poor agreements were removed to remove the noise from learning. 3. Also uses epidemiological model to study diffusion. 4. Extension of (Kwon et al., 2013) by adding temporal feature 5. Authors could use a feature selection algorithm Yudong Zhang et. el.(2014)

Maximization problem, which is to find *K* initial nodes in a social network, which will affect maximum numbers of nodes with given information. Each study used various respective diffusion models, which they determined characteristic to the rumors.

5.1. Least Cost Rumor Blocking

Fan et al., (2013) investigated Least Cost Rumor Blocking (LCRB) problem. In LCBR the rumors are assumed to originate from a community. In the problem, authors proposed to launch a competing opposite campaign cascaded by a subset of nodes called protectors against rumors (R) cascading. Each node could exist in one of the three states – *Inactive, Rumored, Protected*. Inactive is the state when the node is not affected by any of the competing campaigns, Rumored and Protected being the states when the node is affected by Rumor or Protector Campaigns respectively. The problem is to find the initial subset of Protector nodes such that at least α fraction of bridge nodes is protected from the Rumor. The problem is modeled on two diffusion models: -

- **Opportunistic One Activate One (OPOAO):** In this diffusion model the active node could choose only one of the neighboring nodes to activate. So probability of selecting a node is 1/degree (u). Where *u* is the current active node and degree is its number of neighboring nodes.
- **Deterministic One Activate Many (DOAM):** An active node *u* could activate all the neighboring so the probability to activate a node is 1

For each of the above model, an algorithm was proposed to solve the LCRB problem. Both the algorithms find and protect the bridge nodes.

1. **LCRB-P for OPOAO:** A greedy approach where we select the best node every time to maximize the influence of Protector Campaign. This is done by defining an influence function

$\sigma(A)$ = number of nodes to be rumored if nodes in set A are not selected at initial protectors.

Algorithm runs for all nodes until $\alpha \times B$ bridge nodes are protected, where at each step we select node v from set of all nodes V such that the influence function is maximized for the current selection, Mathematically shown in Equation (4):

$$A = \bigcup_{v \in V, \max(\sigma(A+v)-\sigma(A))}^{\sigma(A)<\alpha|B|} v \tag{4}$$

2. **LCRB-D for DOAM:** For DOAM models there is no polynomial time solution to the problem. So a greedy algorithm called set cover based greedy algorithm (SCBG) is proposed which gives polynomial time efficiency. Two real world networks are used as datasets: - (1) Enron Email Communication network, also used in (Nemhauser et al., 1978 & Klimt 2004) which covers email communication of millions of mails. Nodes represent email address and edges if two people send a mail to each other. This dataset contains 36692 nodes connected by 367662 edges with an average node degree of 10.0, (2) Collaboration Network previously used in (Leskovec et al.,2005) covering scientific collaboration between authors with papers submitted in High Energy Physics. In this network, the nodes stand for authors and an undirected edge *e(i,j)* represent node *i* co-authors a paper with node *j*. This dataset contains 15233 nodes connected by 58891 edges with an average node degree of 7.73. The performance of the proposed algorithm is compared with two heuristics
   1. **Max Degree:** It chooses the protectors with descending order of node degrees.
   2. **Proximity:** A simple heuristic algorithm, in which the direct out-neighbours of rumors are chosen as the protectors.

The experiments results showed that that SCBG algorithm outperforms other two in selecting protector nodes. The proposed approach protects the network better than other heuristics.

5.2. β I/T Node Protector

Nguyen et al. (2012) tried to limit the spread of rumor by solving β I/T node protector problem, where β is the desired decontamination threshold, i.e. β percent of the nodes in the network are protected from rumor at the end of the process, I is initial set of contaminated nodes and T is the time-frame under which we need to achieve the desired result.

Similar to LCRB, a small set of influential nodes is found, whose infection with good information helps to contain the spread of rumor. Rumor starts from less influential nodes and spread further in the network according to the trust rating of the intermediate nodes and their reach. The authors in the paper find the smallest set of highly influential nodes to start diffusing good information, which will have the desired effect on the rumor diffusion. Based on the initial set I and time window T we could further have following sub-problems:

1.   β-NP: I is unknown and T is unconstrained (T = ∞)
2.   βI-NP: I is known and T is unconstrained (T = ∞)
3.   βI/T-NP: I is known and T is constrained (T< ∞)
4.   β /T-NP: I is unknown and T is constrained (T< ∞)

The authors proposed two algorithms to solve the above problems. Due to NP-Hard nature of the problems, we cannot have a deterministic solution but only approximate solution.

1.   **Greedy Viral Stopper (GVS):** The greedy viral stopper (GVS) algorithm is modified Hill-Climbing algorithm (Bharathi et al., 2007), where it greedily adds nodes with the best influence gain, to the current solution. Let $\sigma(v)$ expected number of nodes to be affected by a node $v \in V$. Kempe et al., (2005) proved that $\sigma(S)$ function is sub-modular under both IC and LT models, and thus the problem of selecting the set S of k nodes that maximizes $\sigma(S)$ admits an $(1 - 1/e)$−approximation guarantee. Each iteration includes adding a node v to the current set S, such that the $\sigma(S + v) - \sigma(S)$ is positive until we have achieved β ratio of safe nodes. This algorithm could be applied to all the three problems; however, run time varies as the search space varies with each problem.

The results are verified on NetHEPT, NetHEPT WC and Facebook networks. GVS algorithm provides very better solutions for both β-NP and βI/T-NP problems in comparison with other methods. However, one of its down sides is the extremely slow execution due to the expensive task of estimating the marginal influence when a node is added to the current solution.

2.   **Community Based Heuristic Algorithm:** Due to its high runtime GVS is impractical for larger social graphs, this led the authors to given an heuristics based approach find community and solve the problem independently in each community. Authors used the fact that people tend to interact more with members of community then the outside world. The proposed method contains two phases-
     ◦   **Community Detection Phase:** Use Blondel's et al., (2008) algorithm to find communities in the given social graph G(V,E).
     ◦   **Influence Node Selection Phase:** In each community GVS algorithm is applied to find influential nodes.

Therefore, problem can be regarded as the selection of nodes in each community to decontaminate so that β percent of inactive nodes is achieved within each community, and hence achieving the total β percent on the whole network. Because of smaller size of community with respect to whole network selection of influential nodes inside community is not expensive.

Both the above algorithms are compared with random, high degree, discount IC and pagerank algorithms. In all experiments, the Monte Carlo simulation for estimating expected influence is averaged over 1000 runs for consistency. GVS algorithm gives the smallest number of influential nodes for all datasets compared to the other mentioned algorithms. However, community based algorithm was much

Table 4. Running time of 5 Algorithms

	NetHEPT	**NetHEPT_WC**	**Facebook**
GVS	33.1 min	36.1 min	5 hours
Community	10 sec	11 sec	2.4 mins
High Deg	41.8 sec	44.2 sec	4.3 mins
Discount IC	4.3 min	4.3 min	20.3 mins
Page rank	14.4 min	14.4 min	21 mins

faster at the cost of returning more nodes, which are equal to the number of communities returned by (Blondel et al., 2008).

Dataset used: NetHEPT, NetHEPT WC and Facebook networks. Probability of edges is added uniformly for NetHEPT network and as reverse of in-degree for NetHEPT WC network. The Facebook network contains friendship information among New Orleans region from September 2006 to January 2009. To collect the information, the author created several Facebook accounts, joined each to the regional network, started crawling from a single user and visited all friends in a breadth-first-search fashion. Results taken from Nguyen et al. (2012) are given in the Table 4. Where we can see that community based algorithm is significantly faster than other.

In Figure 6 (Nguyen et al., 2012), we could see that both proposed algorithms give less number of nodes when compared with other state of the art algorithm at that time. So overall community-based algorithm achieves best accuracy in the least execution time.

Figure 6. Number of nodes returned when applied to Facebook dataset

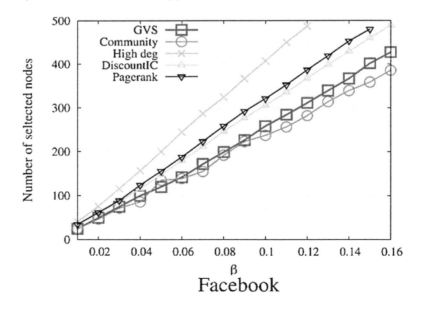

5.3. γ − k Rumor Restriction Problem

Li et al., (2012) gave an extension to β I/T node protector problem (Nguyen et al., 2012) and proposed a new problem called γ-k rumor restriction problem. In Nguyen et al. (2012) as discussed above, the seed nodes are chosen only from the decontaminated nodes, but Li et al. (2012) made an assumption that even the contaminated nodes could be turned decontaminated if it comes in contact with official denial of the rumor, thus protector nodes are chosen not only from decontaminated set but also from contaminated set so that number of decontaminated nodes is maximized. The rumor restriction problem is studied with both LT and IC models. The objective function of problem is monotone and sub-modular so a greedy algorithm guarantees a performance ratio of 1-1/e.

Given a social network represented by a directed graph G = (V, E, w), an underlying diffusion model (either LT or IC model), a time duration T, and a contaminated set I that holds the rumor information, to find a set S $\subseteq$ V, |S| = k, where $\gamma * k$ nodes are from contaminated nodes and $(1-\gamma)*k$ nodes are from decontaminated set. Providing good information to this set can maximize the expected number of decontamination nodes in the whole network when this time duration ends. It is assumed that once good information reaches a decontaminated node, the bad information will never influence it any more. Good information threshold is chosen randomly for each contaminated node in Linear Threshold model. It represents the threshold for contaminated node to trust good information. When the weight $w(u, v)$ is larger than the good information threshold the good information will take over the bad one on a node. In Independence Cascade (IC) model, a trust factor (q) is defined which indicates the probability that a contaminated node becomes decontaminated after it is activated by a decontaminated neighbor u ($u \in S$). Experiments are performed on three datasets to analyze the performance of algorithm under both IC and LT models. Datasets used are Nethept which is collaboration n/w of high energy physics having 15K nodes and 62K edges, Wiki vote which contains Wikipedia voting data having Wikipedia data since January 2008 and Slashdot a technology website having $77K$ nodes and $905K$ edges. The probability and threshold values for IC and LT models are chosen. The results show that that a high value of y gives more decontaminated nodes. It is also shown that the effect of trust level of nodes on its neighbors in influencing. As the trust threshold increases the number of decontaminated nodes increases as well but outperforms the trust threshold in achieving more decontamination under both IC and LT models.

6. FINDING THE SOURCE OF RUMOR

Identifying the source of a rumor could provide the vital information to device a counter strategy. It could provide us the motive or influence could be estimated, by extracting the position of source in the graph. Knowing the source, counter strategies could better target the rumor taking all the metadata about the source in consideration. We will discuss some papers, which have addressed the problem of detecting source of the rumors in this section.

6.1. Identify Rumors and their Sources

Seo et al., (2012) intend to find the source of rumor and detect whether a particular piece of information is rumor or not. To achieve this some *monitor* nodes are injected into the network. The purpose of monitor nodes is to report the data they received, by which algorithm detects rumors sources. There are two types of monitors m+ and m-, which receive and do not receive the information respectively. Rumor source is likely to be close to the positive monitors as previously shown by previous rumor diffusion papers (Jin et al., 2013 & Kwon et al., 2013) where we saw that the rumors stay close to the source in the retweet topologies. So for all nodes likely to be the source these four metrics are calculated:

1. Reachability of the node to all positive monitors.
2. Distance to positive monitors.
3. Reachability to negative monitors
4. Distance to negative monitors.

The node with smallest distance to positive monitors is chosen. If tied, number of reachable positive monitors, sum of distances to reachable positive monitors, number of reachable negative monitors, sum of distances to reachable negative monitors is used in decreasing priority. Following methods are used to choose monitors:

1. Random: Select any k nodes of the vertex set V randomly.
2. Inter monitor distance (Dist): Any pair of k selected monitors should be at least d distance away
3. Number of incoming edges (NI): k Nodes with largest in-degrees are chosen as monitors
4. NI$^+$ dist: nodes with largest in-degrees are sorted and then 'Dist' is used to select k nodes
5. Betweenness centrality (BC): Indicate how central the node is in a graph. It is the number of shortest paths from all vertices to all others that pass through that node. Calculate BC and select top k nodes.
6. BC$^+$ dist: Nodes are sorted by their BC number and then Dist is applied to select k nodes.

Authors proposed following two metrics which is characteristics of each graph. Following two metrics are used to find the source and rumors.

1. **Greedy Sources Set Size:** Most frequent node leading to M$^+$ node is selected as candidate for being source node. C is the candidate list of the sources of the rumor. Initially it is empty. Choose x node with reach to the maximum reach to the positive monitors as the candidate source. Remove other positive monitors, which are reachable from x and put them in P$_x$. At every step we remove 1 or more positive monitor from the set, so algorithm will stop when all the monitors are removed and C is the set of sources. Size of set C is called Greedy Sources Set Size. Algorithm is given in Figure 7.
2. **Maximal Distance of Greedy Information Propagation (MDGIP):** In the previous algorithm, maximum numbers of positive monitors are assigned to a single source x. so the resulting greedy information propagation trees tend to become larger than the real ones. To calculate the difference between the actual propagation tree and the one returned in GSSS, take another metric as - Maximal Distance of Greedy Information Propagation (MDGIP), which is given as: max d(x,y), for $x \in C$ and $y \in P_x$

Both GSSS and MDGIP metrics increase with increase in the number of sources. Authors hypothesized that rumors corresponds to lower number of sources, so low values of the above metrics signifies if the information is rumor.

Figure 7. Algorithm 1

Algorithm 1: Greedy Sources Set Size (GSSS)

```
C ← {};
for each m ∈ V:
    P_m ← {};
    for each m ∈ M⁺:
        S_m ← the set of nodes which have a path to m;
        while M⁺≠{}:
            let x be one of the most frequent elements in all S_m, where m ∈ M⁺;
            add x to C;
            for each m ∈ M⁺:
                add m to P_x and remove m from M⁺ if d(x, m) ≠ ∞;
            end for;
        end while;
    end for;
end for;
```

6.1.1. Dataset

Twitter data set is used and tweets about a particular topic are extracted using keywords. A network graph is made having edges between two nodes if they reply or re-tweet each other's message. To simulate rumor diffusion, process a random rumor source is selected and the reachability of rumor from that node is observed. Among the four methods compared, the Dist selection method has the highest ratio followed by random. Dist and Random have higher ratios compared to other methods (NI, NI⁺Dist, BC, BC⁺Dist) as shown in Figure 8. It is very hard to find the source accurately when no monitor hears the rumor. Experimental data shows that logistic regression can classify rumor and non-rumors accurately. The first half of experimental data is used as training set and the other half as test set. For GSSS and MDGIP to be estimated accurately, monitors should be inserted in various places in rumor propagation trees. Finding a monitor selection algorithm that is good for both tasks is left as future work.

Figure 8. Average distance between top suspect and actual source by all methods

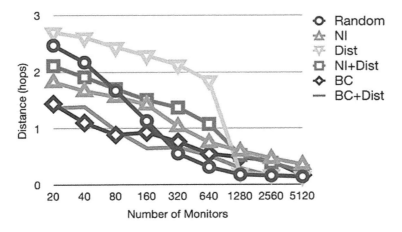

6.2. K-Suspect Problem

Nyugen et al., (2012) studied the k-suspector problem, which is to find k most influential users from a set of users who are fatality of rumor. Users who are commonly known as attackers spread this rumor. Main aim is to use reverse diffusion process and influence based algorithms to find the source of rumor. Independent cascade model is used in which each active node has a single chance to activate its inactive neighbors. The process continues till inactive nodes are left. A social network G(V,E,p) and a set of active nodes A is used. Reverse diffusion process chooses nodes from set of active nodes but in reverse order. For each node either the node is the source or some other node has infected it. If the node has some active neighbors it must be infected by it. The process stops when a node with no neighbors is left. That node can be estimated to be the source. In Influence based algorithm, the nodes that can influence maximum number of other nodes and make them infected are found. And to compute the influence in this method the Monte Carlo simulations is used.

K influence problem in independent cascade model is NP- hard. Therefore, an $(1-1/e)$ approximation algorithm is proposed that provides a set of suspected nodes while guaranteeing the quality of the solution to be close to the optimal one. For experiments 4 social networks are used ranging from minute to enormous size. In experiments the activation probability of each edge is reverse of in degree of a node. 10 nodes are chosen as attackers from top most influential nodes and nodes infected by these are found out using independent cascade model and Monte Carlo simulations. The average detected nodes and running time of algorithm is also computed. Influence-opt algorithm finds the optimal solution for k-influence problem and distance-opt algorithm finds influential k nodes efficiently on Zachary network. In this case, the numbers of sources and suspected nodes are set equal and ranging from 1 to 6. As the number of suspect nodes k increases, the detection rates of all methods increase linearly. The best detection ratio is achieved by Influence-Opt Algorithm while Influence-Sort and Imeter-Sort Algorithm follow up immediately with competitive results. The Table 5 taken from (Nyugen et al., 2012) shows the results.

Table 5. Performance of all 5 algorithms

		Epinions	*Facebook*	*Slashdot*
Influence-greedy	Single	81.5%	64%	67.6%
	Multiple	79.6%	81.9%	80.1%
Influence-Sort	Single	50.2%	37.5%	43.5%
	Multiple	76%	78.9%	80.7%
Distance-Sort	Single	58.2%	49.4%	60%
	Multiple	67.3%	48.7%	60.1%
Imeter-Sort	Single	76.9%	49.7%	57.6%
	Multiple	76.1%	49.9%	64.5%

7. CONCLUSION

In this paper we discussed state of the art papers to analyze rumors on social networks. Most of the work in this domain has been produced in the last decade only, after the boom of online social networks. In this section we will summarize all the papers we have discussed, with comparative analysis and conclude the paper with the future scope of research in this domain.

We started our discussion with real life examples of the impact cause by some of the rumors on the society and established a workflow to handle the problem. Identifying the rumor itself lies in the center as core strategy. Qazvinian et al., (2011) Extracted unilateral and bilateral text features from tweet text. URL, hash tags and user believe are also taken as other features. Kwon et al., (2013) however took completely different set of features. The features were based on network topology, personal data and linguistic features. Authors proved rumors to be related to some linguistic features and topology while being independent to personal features. However, no classifier was proposed by combining the features. But in (Kwon et al., 2013) authors trained SVM, Decision Tree and Random Forest on the features in (Kwon et al., 2013) along with additional features to get a prediction accuracy more than 80% in cross validation tests.

Similar network topology was studied by Jin et al., (2012) which also proved rumor time series graph to have multiple spikes. Authors showed the rumors to be spreading from less individual nodes to higher ones. However, majority of the paper was based on diffusion studies where information diffusion was modeled on epidemiological models with SEIZ model giving lest curve fitting errors. It is a modification of SIS model where the user now has an exposed state, a state where user waits before posting on the rumor. Table 6 summarizes the different characteristics of News and Rumor discovered by the papers discussed here

Next we saw some studies to limit the spread of the rumors. In essence every one of them launches a competing opposite campaign in the social network. These studies differ in the process to select initial

Table 6. Summary of News and Rumor characteristics

Feature	News	Rumor
Source	Many known sources	Fewer (2 or 3), unknown sources
Network area	Dense and more populated	Sparse and less populated
Flow	Can start from anywhere generally from high degree nodes	Low degree users to high degree users
Response ratio	High	Low
No. of tweets	Large no. of tweets immediately after it is declared	It has large number of tweets around time when it is officially declined
No. of re-tweets	High	Less
Spikes	Single prominent spike in a time series graph	Multiple Spikes
Conversational Topics	More successful	Less successful
Social Ties	Diffuse widely through a lot of channels like news agencies	Word of mouth, friends, acquaintances
Sentiments	All sentiments depending upon topic	Contrary to expectations, rumors have low correlation with sentiments

nodes to infuse with good information. The problem itself is NP-Hard in nature thus approximate solutions were provided. Li et al., (2013) assumes rumors to be originating from a community, so authors proposed to initialize only the bridge nodes with good information. So the problem reduced to selecting α ratio of bridge nodes to activate to have maximum containment whereas Nyugen et al., (2012) simply selected the most influential nodes following the greedy approach. The author gave another heuristic based approach, which is much faster than the greedy one while compromising on the quality i.e. giving higher number of nodes for same containment factor. (Li et al., 2013) Further extends (Nyugen et al., 2012) by assuming that good information could actually make a node to change state permanently from infected to protecte

Reversing the diffusion could allow us to reach the source of the rumor in a network, this assumption is used by (Nyugen et al., 2012) to find k suspects. Author considered diffusion to follow IC model, so each active node must have been activated by one of the neighboring nodes. Nyugen et al., (2012) also did reverse diffusion from an active node, however instead of choosing any node as initial nodes, authors selected some nodes deciding basis of various heuristics and start retracing from there.

8. FUTURE WORK

This paper has provided a clear picture of the state of the art studies and presents a base to start for the researchers new to the domain. As we have seen, most of the work has been limited to Twitter only, mostly because of its widespread and easy API interface, rumors need to be studied on other social networks which provide different features to identify, and different diffusion models owing to the difference in audience and nature of the connectivity. Another study is possible to find more generic features to identify rumors. Most of the studies discussed here have taken a set of known rumors to extract features. Performance of such features in any new rumor is still not tested. Lastly, papers regarding limiting the rumors and finding sources have made assumptions regarding the diffusion model. We could attempt to find a diffusion model in a social networking site and take it further to limit the spread.

REFERENCES

Alexander, H. (2013). Boston bombings: Sunil Tripathi found dead. *Telegraph*. Retrieved from: http://www.telegraph.co.uk/news/worldnews/northamerica/usa/10018632/Boston-bombings-Sunil-Tripathi-found-dead.html

Banu, P. N., & Andrews, S. (2015). Performance analysis of hard and soft clustering approaches for gene expression data. *International Journal of Rough Sets and Data Analysis*, 2(1), 58–69. doi:10.4018/ijrsda.2015010104

Bettencourt, L. M., Cintrón-Arias, A., Kaiser, D. I., & Castillo-Chávez, C. (2006). The power of a good idea: Quantitative modeling of the spread of ideas from epidemiological models. *Physica A: Statistical Mechanics and its Applications, 364*, 513-536.

Bharathi, S., Kempe, D., & Salek, M. (2007). Competitive influence maximization in social networks. In *Internet and Network Economics* (pp. 306–311). Springer Berlin Heidelberg. doi:10.1007/978-3-540-77105-0_31

Bhattacharya, T., Dey, N., & Chaudhuri, S. R. (2012). A session based multiple image hiding technique using DWT and DCT. arXiv preprint arXiv:1208.0950.

Blondel, V. D., Guillaume, J. L., Lambiotte, R., & Lefebvre, E. (2008). Fast unfolding of communities in large networks. *Journal of Statistical Mechanics*, *2008*(10), P10008. doi:10.1088/1742-5468/2008/10/P10008

Bond, R. M., Fariss, C. J., Jones, J. J., Kramer, A. D., Marlow, C., Settle, J. E., & Fowler, J. H. (2012). A 61-million-person experiment in social influence and political mobilization. *Nature*, *489*(7415), 295–298. doi:10.1038/nature11421 PMID:22972300

Bradly, J. R. (2008). The Land of the Pharaohs on the Brink of a Revolution.

Cagliero, L., & Fiori, A. (2013). *Twecom: topic and context mining from twitter* (pp. 75–100). Springer Vienna.

Cook, D. M., Waugh, B., Abdipanah, M., Hashemi, O., & Abdul Rahman, S. (2014). Twitter Deception and Influence: Issues of Identity, Slacktivism, and Puppetry. *Journal of Information Warfare*, *13*(1), 58–71.

Curtis, A. (2013). Social media history, mass communication dept. University of North Carolina. Retrieved from http://www2.uncp.edu/home/acurtis/NewMedia/SocialMedia/SocialMediaHistory.html

Dey, N., Samanta, S., Chakraborty, S., Das, A., Chaudhuri, S. S., & Suri, J. S. (2014). Firefly algorithm for optimization of scaling factors during embedding of manifold medical information: An application in ophthalmology imaging. *Journal of Medical Imaging and Health Informatics*, *4*(3), 384–394. doi:10.1166/jmihi.2014.1265

Edwards, C., Edwards, A., Spence, P. R., & Shelton, A. K. (2014). Is that a bot running the social media feed? Testing the differences in perceptions of communication quality for a human agent and a bot agent on Twitter. *Computers in Human Behavior*, *33*, 372–376. doi:10.1016/j.chb.2013.08.013

Fan, L., Lu, Z., Wu, W., Thuraisingham, B., Ma, H., & Bi, Y. (2013, July). Least cost rumor blocking in social networks. *Proceedings of the 2013 IEEE 33rd International Conference on Distributed Computing Systems (ICDCS)* (pp. 540-549). IEEE. 10.1109/ICDCS.2013.34

Giles, J. (2011). Social-bots infiltrate Twitter and trick human users. *New Scientist*, *209*(2804), 28. doi:10.1016/S0262-4079(11)60614-3

Gupta, A., Lamba, H., & Kumaraguru, P. (2013, September). $1.00 per rt# bostonmarathon# prayforboston: Analyzing fake content on Twitter. Proceedings of eCrime Researchers Summit (eCRS), 2013 (pp. 1-12). IEEE.

Hassan, A., Qazvinian, V., & Radev, D. (2010, October). What's with the attitude?: identifying sentences with attitude in online discussions. *Proceedings of the 2010 Conference on Empirical Methods in Natural Language Processing* (pp. 1245-1255). Association for Computational Linguistics.

Jardin, X. (2007). More on Orkut and law enforcement: Brazil. *Boing Boing*. Retrieved From http://www.boingboing.net/2007/03/13/more-on-Orkut-and-la.html

Jin, F., Dougherty, E., Saraf, P., Cao, Y., & Ramakrishnan, N. (2013, August). Epidemiological modeling of news and rumors on twitter. *Proceedings of the 7th Workshop on Social Network Mining and Analysis* (p. 8). ACM. 10.1145/2501025.2501027

Kempe, D., Kleinberg, J., & Tardos, É. (2005). Influential nodes in a diffusion model for social networks. In *Automata, languages and programming* (pp. 1127–1138). Springer Berlin Heidelberg. doi:10.1007/11523468_91

Kimura, M., Saito, K., & Motoda, H. (2009, July). *Efficient Estimation of Influence Functions for SIS Model on Social Networks*. Proceedings of *IJCAI* (pp. 2046–2051).

Klimt, B., & Yang, Y. (2004, July). *Introducing the Enron Corpus*. CEAS.

Kramer, A. D., Guillory, J. E., & Hancock, J. T. (2014). Experimental evidence of massive-scale emotional contagion through social networks. *Proceedings of the National Academy of Sciences of the United States of America*, *111*(24), 8788–8790. doi:10.1073/pnas.1320040111 PMID:24889601

Kwon, S., Cha, M., Jung, K., Chen, W., & Wang, Y. (2013a). Aspects of rumor spreading on a microblog network. In *Social Informatics* (pp. 299–308). Springer International Publishing. doi:10.1007/978-3-319-03260-3_26

Kwon, S., Cha, M., Jung, K., Chen, W., & Wang, Y. (2013b, December). Prominent features of rumor propagation in online social media. *Proceedings of the 2013 IEEE 13th International Conference on Data Mining (ICDM)* (pp. 1103-1108). IEEE. 10.1109/ICDM.2013.61

Leskovec, J., Kleinberg, J., & Faloutsos, C. (2005, August). Graphs over time: densification laws, shrinking diameters and possible explanations. *Proceedings of the eleventh ACM SIGKDD international conference on Knowledge discovery in data mining* (pp. 177-187). ACM. 10.1145/1081870.1081893

Li, S., Zhu, Y., Li, D., Kim, D., & Huang, H. (2013, December). Rumor Restriction in Online Social Networks. *Performance Computing and Communications Conference (IPCCC), 2013 IEEE 32nd International* (pp. 1-10). IEEE.

Matsubara, Y., Sakurai, Y., Prakash, B. A., Li, L., & Faloutsos, C. (2012, August). Rise and fall patterns of information diffusion: model and implications. *Proceedings of the 18th ACM SIGKDD international conference on Knowledge discovery and data mining* (pp. 6-14). ACM. 10.1145/2339530.2339537

Nemhauser, G. L., Wolsey, L. A., & Fisher, M. L. (1978). An analysis of approximations for maximizing submodular set functions—I. *Mathematical Programming*, *14*(1), 265–294. doi:10.1007/BF01588971

Newman, M. E. (2002). Spread of epidemic disease on networks. *Physical Review E: Statistical, Nonlinear, and Soft Matter Physics*, *66*(1).

Nguyen, D. T., Nguyen, N. P., & Thai, M. T. (2012, October). Sources of misinformation in Online Social Networks: Who to suspect? *Proceedings of the Military Communications Conference, 2012-MILCOM 2012* (pp. 1-6). IEEE. 10.1109/MILCOM.2012.6415780

Nguyen, N. P., Yan, G., Thai, M. T., & Eidenbenz, S. (2012, June). Containment of misinformation spread in online social networks. *Proceedings of the 4th Annual ACM Web Science Conference* (pp. 213-222). ACM. 10.1145/2380718.2380746

Pennebaker, J. W., Mehl, M. R., & Niederhoffer, K. G. (2003). Psychological aspects of natural language use: Our words, our selves. *Annual Review of Psychology*, *54*(1), 547–577.

Procter, R., Vis, F., & Voss, A. (2011). How riot rumours spread on Twitter. *Reading the Riots, Guardian.co.uk*.

Qazvinian, V., Rosengren, E., Radev, D. R., & Mei, Q. (2011, July). Rumor has it: Identifying misinformation in microblogs. *Proceedings of the Conference on Empirical Methods in Natural Language Processing* (pp. 1589-1599). Association for Computational Linguistics.

Rana, H., & Lal, M. (2016). A Rough Set Theory Approach for Rule Generation and Validation Using RSES. *International Journal of Rough Sets and Data Analysis*, *3*(1), 55–70. doi:10.4018/IJRSDA.2016010104

Ranjan, J., & Bhatnagar, V. (2009). A framework for analytical CRM: A data mining perspective. *International Journal of Business Excellence*, *3*(1), 1–18. doi:10.1504/IJBEX.2010.029484

Rivlin, G. (2005). Hate Messages on Google Site Draw Concern. *NY Times*. Retrieved From http://www.nytimes.com/2005/02/07/technology/hate-messages-on-google-site-draw-concern.html

Seo, E., Mohapatra, P., & Abdelzaher, T. (2012, May). Identifying rumors and their sources in social networks. *Proceedings of SPIE Defense, Security, and Sensing* (pp. 83891I-83891I). International Society for Optics and Photonics. doi:10.1117/12.919823

Tausczik, Y. R., & Pennebaker, J. W. (2010). The psychological meaning of words: LIWC and computerized text analysis methods. *Journal of Language and Social Psychology*, *29*(1), 24–54. doi:10.1177/0261927X09351676

Zhang, Y., Wang, S., Phillips, P., & Ji, G. (2014). Binary PSO with Mutation Operator for Feature Selection using Decision Tree applied to Spam Detection. *Knowledge-Based Systems*, *64*, 22-31.

This research was previously published in International Journal of Rough Sets and Data Analysis (IJRSDA), 3(4); edited by Nilanjan Dey; pages 46-67, copyright year 2016 by IGI Publishing (an imprint of IGI Global).

Chapter 12
Contribution of Mindfulness to Individuals' Tendency to Believe and Share Social Media Content

Peerayuth Charoensukmongkol

National Institute of Development Administration, Thailand

ABSTRACT

The objective of this research was to explore the effect of mindfulness on individuals' tendencies to believe social media content and share it without realizing the potential consequences. The sample used in this study comprised 300 participants in Bangkok, Thailand, of whom 157 were full-time employees and 143 were college students. Results from partial least squares regression analysis supports the hypothesis that individuals who exhibit higher levels of mindfulness tend to be skeptical of the validity of information to which they are exposed. In addition, skepticism is linked to a decreased tendency to believe social media content and to share content on social media. The findings further support a direct link between mindfulness and a decreased tendency to share social media content. Overall, these findings confirm the positive contribution of mindfulness as a quality that may allow individuals to question the validity of social media content before they decide to believe it and share it with others.

1. INTRODUCTION

The term social media has been widely defined in literature as "Internet-based services that allow individuals to create, share and seek content, as well as to communicate and collaborate with each other" (Lee & Ma, 2012, p. 332). It is evident that social media have begun to replace traditional media, such as television and newspapers (Kaplan & Haenlein, 2010). Currently, people tend to rely heavily on social media, such as Twitter and Facebook, to gain access to news and information (Talcoth, 2015). Advances in smartphone technology also provide access to news and information from anywhere through mobile social media applications. Information posted on social media often disperses rapidly across geographic boundaries (Suh et al, 2010). These platforms not only allow individuals to obtain a wide coverage of information faster and easier than traditional media do, but also facilitate information sharing among

DOI: 10.4018/978-1-5225-9869-5.ch012

members (Li et al, 2014). In contrast to traditional media where individuals passively receive information provided by content editors, social media promote the active participation of users in producing content, thereby empowering people (Lee & Ma, 2012).

Despite the benefits of social media, which significantly facilitate information diffusion, problems can arise when people increase their reliance on these applications for information consumption without questioning the accuracy of the content (Carlos et al, 2013; Gundecha & Liu, 2012). In addition, some users share posts with others without considering the potential consequences of sharing invalid or distorted information. Literature has shown that rumors tend to be pervasive in social media (Diakopoulos et al, 2012; Mendoza et al, 2010; Ratkiewicz et al, 2011). According to Oh et al (2010), a major criticism of social media is that they can be used for propagating misinformation, rumors, and, in extreme cases, propaganda. Similarly, they can be used as channels for spreading biased information, tribal prejudices, and hate speech (Mäkinen & Wangu Kuira, 2008). The viral spreading of political misinformation in social media is one example of social media abuse (Ratkiewicz et al, 2011). Furthermore, hoaxes, such as Hollywood rumors, tend to spread via social media from time to time (Dewey, 2014). Given the negative effects of overreliance on social media for news and information and the tendency to share misinformation on social media, which can cause suspicion and fear among the public (Chen et al, 2015; Oh et al, 2010; Stieglitz & Dang-Xuan, 2013), it is important to understand some of people's personal characteristics that explain these social media behaviors. Gaining this body of knowledge is crucial because it can offer some recommendations to help prevent this behavioral tendency. In practice, it is generally difficult and somehow controversial for policy makers to resort to legal actions to strictly monitor and control contents that citizens post and share on social media (Sakawee, 2013). However, if policy makers understand some key personal characteristics that can restrain such behavior and are able to provide proper intervention or campaign to promote these characteristics, this can serve as a more effective solution to reduce the spread of misinformation in society.

In particular, this study focuses on the role of mindfulness, which is defined as a state of bringing a certain quality of attention to moment-by-moment experiences (Kabat-Zinn, 1990). The concept of mindfulness, which originates from the practice of meditation, has been applied extensively in the fields of clinical study, psychology, and management over the past decade (Gärtner, 2013; Shonin et al, 2014; Zhang et al, 2013). However, little is known about its benefits in use of technology, particularly with regard to behaviors concerning the use of social media. Although the benefits of mindfulness during use of social media were previously proposed (Deschene, 2011), its contribution has not been empirically tested in academic research. The main reason mindfulness is the focus of the study is that research extensively supports that it is a characteristic that significantly helps individuals reduce a wide array of unhealthy behaviors that result from uncontrolled emotions and impulses (Hafenbrack et al, 2013; Shonin et al, 2014). Given some empirical evidence that shows that the tendency to share contents on social media is also significantly driven by emotions (Oh et al, 2010; Stieglitz & Dang-Xuan, 2013), the quality of mindfulness might be an important personal characteristic that can tackle social media behaviors.

Because the main goal of mindfulness is to cultivate awareness of internal and external stimuli that individuals experience moment-to-moment (Brown & Ryan, 2003), the objective of this research was to explore whether the degree of mindfulness individuals exhibit explains the tendency to believe information posted on social media platforms without questioning content validity and to share content without considering the consequences of doing so. Because mindful individuals typically are constantly aware of their thoughts, feelings, and actions, this research postulates that mindfulness may make individuals aware of the accuracy of social media information before they believe it or decide to share it.

2. BACKGROUND AND HYPOTHESES

2.1. Information Sharing on Social Media

Individuals not only post personal information on social media, but also re-share information their friends posted. Today, many leading social media Web sites make it easy to share content in just one click. On the positive side, this sharing feature speeds the diffusion of information, thus allowing people to gain access to major news and events that happen in their communities or around the world faster than they would when using traditional media. In addition, social media can serve as an alternative channel for citizen communication and participatory journalism when traditional media are inaccessible (Mäkinen & Wangu Kuira, 2008).

However, given the growing number of people increasing their reliance on social media to consume news and information, the accuracy and trustworthiness of information shared on social media platforms is the main issue individuals need to consider. Overreliance on news or information from social media without questioning the validity of the content can be harmful to people and society, particularly when individuals decide to share content that lacks validity or is simply a rumor or hoax. The danger of careless sharing is that the shared content not only exist between members of the sharer's social media group, but also can be re-shared to other social media groups, rapidly multiplying as an increasing number of people in different groups share the content. In this regard, information shared by one person can spread nationwide or even worldwide in a short time.

Generally, any social media user can generate unverified information, which can be either true or false (Aula, 2010). Literature has shown that rumors and hoaxes spread through social media Web sites are extremely common (Diakopoulos et al, 2012; Oh et al, 2010; Ratkiewicz et al, 2011). Rumors can gradually obtain credibility as a growing number of users acquire and re-share them, and these rumors can be harmful under some circumstances. For example, Oh et al (2010) indicate that misinformation spread on Twitter during the 2010 Haiti earthquake increased anxiety and caused informational ambiguity for communities during the crisis. Similarly, Mendoza et al (2010) report that false rumors spread quickly on Twitter during the 2010 earthquake in Chile, contributing to general chaos in the absence of first-hand information from traditional sources.

Given the potential negative effects of information sharing on social media, understanding people's motivations for sharing social media content is a major focus of current research. For example, scholars argue that sharing news on social media enhances personal status within the social media community (Burke et al, 2009; Lee & Ma, 2012; Lin, 1999). Stieglitz and Dang-Xuan (2013) found that people who have positive sentiments towards Twitter messages tend to retweet more frequently and quickly compared to people who had neutral sentiments. Other scholars focused on how the content characteristics of social media information influence content sharing (Nagarajan et al, 2010; Suh et al, 2010). It can be expected that individuals' perceptions about the believability of content should be a fundamental motivator for sharing the content. Simply put, when individuals perceive that the content is true (although it may be false in reality), they are more likely to share it without hesitation. Therefore:

Hypothesis 1: Individuals who believe in the validity of content posted on social media have a greater tendency to share this content.

2.2. Mindfulness and Social Media Behaviors

In this study, mindfulness is proposed as a personal characteristic that can regulate individuals' tendencies to believe social media content without taking into account its validity and to share content without considering the consequences. In literature, mindfulness is conceptualized as a psychological state and a personality trait (Dane, 2011). According to Leroy et al (2013, p. 27), mindfulness represents one's ability to "bring one's complete attention to the experiences occurring in the present moment, in a nonjudgmental or accepting way." This definition suggests that mindfulness comprises two main characteristics, namely self-awareness and nonjudgmental evaluation of stimuli. First, mindful individuals are inclined to be aware of internal stimuli, such as thoughts and feelings, and external stimuli, such as objects and their environment, moment-to-moment. Simply put, mindful individuals tend to be aware of what they are thinking, feeling, doing, perceiving, or experiencing now.

Another characteristic of mindfulness, nonjudgmental evaluation of stimuli, makes individuals acknowledge any thoughts, feelings, or sensations they experience from stimuli without labeling them as favorable or unfavorable experiences. In other words, they avoid seeing things through their own filters. A combination of attentiveness and non-judgmental evaluation of stimuli allows individuals to avoid the habitual and routine interpretation of stimuli and information. According to Reb et al (2012), mindful individuals typically perceive and process stimuli and information in a more creative and differentiated manner, thereby allowing the creation and refinement of categories, connections, and perspectives. In research, mindfulness was found to promote a variety of psychological wellbeing (Brown & Ryan, 2003; Shonin et al, 2014), improve decision making (Gärtner, 2013; Hafenbrack et al, 2013), and enhance performance outcomes (Glomb et al, 2011; Zhang et al, 2013). Mindfulness was used recently to explain the effects of social media use behaviors. For example, Charoensukmongkol (2015) asserts that being mindful when using social media is important to help individuals to obtain benefits from using social media while preventing some negative consequences that may occur from social media misuse. In the next section, the author discusses in detail how mindfulness influences social media behaviors.

The researcher proposes that being attentive to one's internal stimuli and behaviors in the moment while maintaining non-judgmental evaluation are important characteristics of mindfulness that prevent people from acting without thought or on impulse, which may lead to negative consequences when using social media. In this regard, Wells (2005, p. 337) asserts that mindfulness "can be equated with effortful attentional processing and is seen as the opposite of mindlessness, a state of automatic processing." When individuals are not mindful when receiving information from social media, they can make hasty judgments to believe the content they see and re-share it without thinking. Being mindful of one's thoughts, emotions, and actions not only raises awareness of the accuracy of information before a person decides to believe it, but also makes one appreciate some of the consequences that may arise from sharing the information before doing so. For example, before deciding to share content, mindful individuals may stop to consider whether the content is valid and reliable or can harm themselves and others after they share it. The opposite of this action is mindless sharing, which happens when individuals simply share content without comprehending what they are doing.

Moreover, being aware of one's own social media behaviors while maintaining non-judgmental evaluation of the social media experience prevents a person from being affected by favorable or unfavorable sentiments when exposed to content that seems believable or to share content impulsively (Charoensukmongkol, 2015). For example, the careless sharing of rumors on Twitter and Facebook about the spread of Ebola infection across the United States caused tremendous fear and anxiety in many states.

People exposed to that type of content may believe in it quickly and share it right away due to fear and their concern for others. Because evidence supports that emotions can affect social media sharing significantly (Stieglitz & Dang-Xuan, 2013), being mindful prevents individuals from being influenced by their feelings about information that may persuade them to share the content carelessly and without regard for content validity and the consequences of sharing. Therefore:

Hypothesis 2: There is a negative relationship between degree of mindfulness and individuals' tendency to believe content posted on social media.

Hypothesis 3: There is a negative relationship between degree of mindfulness and individuals' tendency to share content posted on social media.

In addition to the direct contribution of mindfulness, the researcher further proposes that individuals who exhibit high levels of mindfulness are more likely to develop some degree of skepticism, which, in turn, causes them to question the accuracy of social media content before they decide to believe or share it. Generally, skeptics do not easily believe any information to which they are exposed until they have researched it or obtained solid evidence to support the validity of the information (Glick et al, 1989). In fact, skepticism can benefit information processing because it facilitates the development of critical thinking abilities. Because of these characteristics, skeptics spend more time reasoning; consequently, this helps them to make fewer errors in decision making (Pennycook et al, 2013). Therefore, without sound and adequate evidence to affirm that information on social media can be trusted, it is difficult for these people to believe the information.

Because a number of studies have shown that mindfulness can improve the quality of decision making and information-processing capabilities (Gärtner, 2013; Hafenbrack et al, 2013), a linkage between mindfulness and skepticism can be expected. In particular, research suggests that mindfulness represents the quality of the metacognitive capability individuals exhibit (Bishop et al, 2004; Wells, 2002, 2005). For example, Bishop et al (2004) asserted that mindfulness can be considered a metacognitive skill as it allows individuals to effectively control cognitive process and to monitor stream of consciousness. Metacognition is the higher cognitive capability that helps individuals effectively monitor and control their own thought processes (Flavell, 1979). First, individuals with this capability typically have cognitive flexibility, constantly question the accuracy of their preexisting knowledge whenever they encounter new information, and are willing to adjust their preexisting knowledge when it is proven to be inaccurate (Thomas, 2006). Second, cognitive complexity is another characteristic that supports the capability to process information more profoundly (Garofalo & Lester, 1985; Mevarech, 1999). For example, a study by Brown and Krishna (2004) provides evidence that metacognition makes consumers more skeptical about marketing schemes. Considered this evidence, the characteristics mindful individuals with metacognitive capabilities exhibit may make them more likely to have reservations about social media information. Instead of quickly concluding information is true, these people may pause to question and evaluate the legitimacy of the information (Brown & Krishna, 2004). As a result, they typically withhold the decision to believe or re-share the content until they can be confident or obtain additional proof from other sources to support the validity of the information (Gärtner, 2013; Karelaia & Reb, 2014). Therefore:

Hypothesis 4: A positive relationship exists between level of mindfulness and the degree of skepticism an individual exhibits.

Hypothesis 5: Degree of skepticism negatively affects an individual's tendency to believe content posted on social media.

Hypothesis 6: Degree of skepticism negatively influences an individual's tendency to share content posted on social media.

3. METHODS

3.1. Samples and Data Collection

The sample used in this study comprised 300 participants in Bangkok, Thailand, of whom 157 were full-time employees and 143 were college students. The employee sample was selected from two leading corporations, whereas the student sample was obtained from one private university. A self-administered questionnaire survey was developed to collect data, and respondents were informed that participation in the study was voluntary and anonymous. For respondents who were full-time employees, questionnaires and cover letters were distributed in person, and completed questionnaires were collected in person within one week. For respondents who were college students, a research assistant distributed questionnaires to a random selection of students on campus. After students completed the questionnaires, they returned them to a research assistant on the same day. Table 1 summarizes the characteristics of the sample.

Table 1. Demographic characteristics of the sample

Age	Under 18 years: 48 (16%) 18-25 years: 128 (42.7%) 26-33 years: 61 (20.3%) 34-41 years: 33 (11%) 42-49 years: 25 (8.3%) 50 years or over: 5 (1.7%)
Gender	Male: 128 (42.7%) Female: 172 (57.3%)
Education	Below bachelor's degree: 97 (32.2%) Bachelor's degree: 163 (54.3%) Master's degree or higher: 40 (13.3%)
Occupation	Student: 143 (47.6%) Full-time employee: 157 (52.4%)
Social media use intensity (measured as the percentage of total leisure time)	Less than 10 percent: 16 (5.3%) 10-20 percent: 27 (9%) 21-30 percent: 47 (15.7%) 31-40 percent: 36 (12%) 41-50 percent: 66 (22%) More than 50 percent: 108 (36%)
Major source of news and information	Mostly from other media: 40 (13.3%) From social media and other media equally 126 (42%) Mostly from social media: 134 (44.7%)

3.2. Measures

Mindfulness was measured by the mindfulness attention and awareness scale (MAAS) developed by Brown and Ryan (2003), which is a fifteen-question scale widely used in research to measure trait mindfulness. Sample items include "I could be experiencing some emotion and not be conscious of it until sometime later" and "I break or spill things because of carelessness, not paying attention, or thinking of something else." All questions in the original scale were scored on five-point Likert items, ranging from 5 (almost always) to 1 (almost never). Subsequently, the scores were reversed to make low scores represent low levels of mindfulness and high scores represent high levels of mindfulness.

The researcher developed the measures for the tendency to believe social media content, the tendency to share social media content, and skepticism. The tendency to believe social media content was measured by four questions that required respondents to assess to what extent they generally thought content posted or shared by others on social media could be trusted. The tendency to share social media content was measured by four questions that requested respondents to assess the extent to which they thought sharing content posted or shared by others on social media would not cause any negative consequences. Skepticism was measured in terms of the likelihood that respondents would normally question the validly of information to which they are exposed daily before believing it. This construct was measured by three questions. All questions that measured these three constructs were rated on five-point Likert items ranging from 1 (strongly disagree) to 5 (strongly agree). The appendix contains the questions employed in data collection.

In addition, control variables that can affect the dependent variables were incorporated in the analysis. These include age, education, gender, collectivistic attitude, social media use intensity, and the degree to which respondents access other media, such as television and newspapers. Generally, younger people typically are less mature and more likely to believe and share social media content (Correa et al, 2010). Those with higher levels of education are more knowledgeable, with more developed critical thinking skills (Pithers & Soden, 2000), so they are more skeptical of social media information and are less likely to share it carelessly in comparison to their less educated counterparts. Moreover, females tend to emphasize social relationships more than males do (Pujazon-Zazik & Park, 2010), which increases the possibility that they believe the content shared and are more prone to share it with others (Chen et al, 2015). Age and education were measured on an ordinal scale, while gender was measured on a nominal scale.

Collectivistic attitude was considered as a control variable because collectivists are usually strongly connected to their social group; thus, they might easily believe the content their friends post and are more prone to share it with others (Singelis et al, 1995). Collectivistic attitude was measured by the scale developed by Singelis et al (1995). For social media use intensity, it is likely that individuals who experience greater exposure to social media content are more inclined to believe and share it (Lee & Ma, 2012). This variable was measured on an ordinal scale by asking respondents to estimate what percentage of their leisure time they spend using social media. Finally, the degree of access to other media was included as a control variable because information obtained from multiple sources can facilitate verification (Tran, 2013). This variable was measured on an ordinal scale by asking respondents to rate the degree to which they access news and information via traditional rather than social media.

3.3. Statistical Analysis

Partial least squares (PLS) regression was used to analyze the data. PLS combines principal component analysis, path analysis, and a set of regressions to generate estimates of the standardized regression coefficients for the model's paths and factor loadings for the measurement items (Chin & Newsted, 1999). PLS provides greater flexibility than other structural equation modeling (SEM) techniques because it does not require data to be normally distributed and requires a smaller sample size (Kline, 2005). PLS was suitable for this study because the results from the Shapiro-Wilk test indicated that all main constructs proposed in the hypotheses are not distributed normally. PLS estimation was performed using WarpPLS version 4.0.

4. RESULTS

4.1. Construct Validity and Reliability

Before the PLS model was assessed, a series of analyses was performed. First, the researcher determined the convergence validity and discriminant validity of all reflective constructs including mindfulness, the tendency to believe social media content, the tendency to share social media content, skepticism, and collectivistic attitude. Convergence validity was assessed using factor loadings, which need to be greater than .5 to support adequate convergence validity (Hair et al, 2009). Two items related to the mindfulness construct fail to meet the minimum requirement; therefore, they were removed from the analysis. Factor loadings of other reflective constructs are above this threshold. Discriminant validity was assessed by comparing the average variance extracted (AVE) to the squared correlation coefficient. According to Fornell and Larcker (1981), the square root of the AVE must be greater than the correlations between the constructs for discriminant validity to exist. Table 2 shows that all AVEs meet this requirement. Second, the researcher examined construct reliability by evaluating the Cronbach's alpha coefficient and composite reliability coefficient. For the constructs' reliability to be satisfactory, these two coefficients should be higher than .7 (Nunnally, 1978). The results in Table 2 indicate that most reflective constructs have coefficients that meet the minimum requirement. However, the construct that measures the tendency to share content on social media has a Cronbach's alpha coefficient of .65, which is still acceptable.

4.2. Multicollinearity and Common Method Bias

Multicollinearity between latent variables was evaluated using full variance inflation factor (VIF) statistics. Petter et al (2007) recommended that full VIF should be lower than 3.3 to confirm that multicollinearity is not a serious issue. The results indicate that the maximum full VIF is 1.866, which is lower than the maximum threshold. Furthermore, Kock and Lynn (2012) argue that the full collinearity test can serve as a technique that captures the possibility of common method bias (CMB) in the PLS model analysis. They propose that full collinearity VIF lower than the critical value of 3.3 can provide some evidence that CMB may not be a major threat for the analysis.

Table 2. Correlation between variables and square root of average variance extracted

Variable	Composite reliability coefficients	Cronbach's alpha coefficients	SMS	AM	SMUI	MALE	AGE	EDU	MFN	SKPT	COL	SMB
SMS	.789	.65	(.699)									
AM	-	-	-.018	(1)								
SMUI	-	-	.235**	-.399**	(1)							
MALE	-	-	.055	-.127*	.098	(1)						
AGE	-	-	-.22**	-.051	-.176**	.02	(1)					
EDU	-	-	-.269**	-.141*	.045	-.033	.54**	(1)				
MFN	.84	.804	-.209**	.053	-.179**	.01	.276**	.179**	(.547)			
SKPT	.877	.789	-.256**	-.111	-.062	-.038	.37**	.498**	.188**	(.839)		
COL	.87	.815	.006	-.173**	.105	-.044	.121*	.355**	.002	.469**	(.757)	
SMB	.815	.804	.31**	-.318**	.365**	.069	-.144*	-.162**	-.112	-.165**	-.052	(.724)

Notes:** $p<.01$; * $p<.05$;

Square roots of average variance extracted from latent variables are shown in parentheses;

SMS=tendency to share information posted on social media websites, AM=degree of access to other media, SMUI=social media use intensity,

MALE=male dummy variable, AGE=age, EDU=education, MFN=mindfulness, SKPT=skepticism, COL=collectivistic attitude,

SMB=tendency to believe information

4.3. Social Desirability Bias

Because self-reported measures were used in data collection, the social desirability bias (SDB) test is required to assess whether the respondents answered the survey questions truthfully or misrepresented themselves in order to manage their self-presentation (Crowne & Marlowe, 1960). SDB was detected by using the recommendation suggested by Barger (2002). SDB scale items were developed by the author to make them applicable to Thai culture. Respondents were asked to indicate whether they have ever engaged in ten aspects of activities that seem to be socially undesirable in Thai culture, but people tend to display in normal life (e.g., displaying selfishness, having dirty thoughts, telling lie, gossiping, swearing, covering up wrongdoings, stealing, breaking rules, littering, and blaming others). The response was coded '1' if a respondent reported that they have never engaged in an activity; and was coded '0' otherwise. These scores are intended to measure how likely the respondent is to give answers that sound good instead of answers that are true (Crowne & Marlowe, 1960). The total SDB scores were then correlated with four outcome variables in the model. According to Barger (2002), if the answers to the question are not related to respondents' SDB scores, the correlation coefficient should be near 0. The results show that the SDB variable weakly correlates with mindfulness ($r=-.065$; $p=.249$), the tendency to believe social media content ($r=.045$; $p=.438$), the tendency to share social media content ($r=.097$; $p=.095$), and skepticism ($r=-.038$; $p=.516$). These findings mitigate the concern that SDB bias the key measures.

4.4. Hypothesis Testing

Results from PLS analysis are summarized in Figure 1. All control variables were included together in the model. Standardized path coefficients and p-values are reported. All fit indices of the PLS model, including the average path coefficient (APC=.126; p=.003), average r-squared (ARS=.276; p<.001),

Figure 1. PLS results

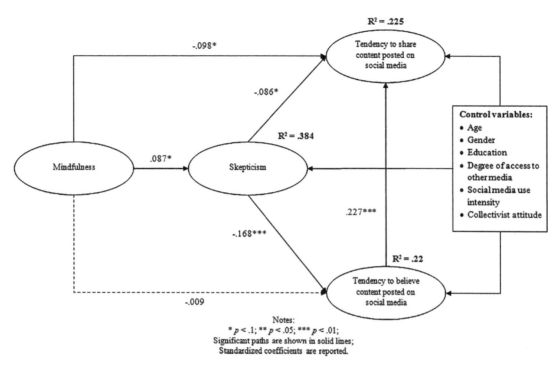

average full collinearity (AFVIF=1.413), Sympson's paradox ratio (SPR=.792), r-square contribution ratio (RSCR=.991), and statistical suppression ratio (SSR=.875) are satisfactory.

Hypothesis 1 predicts that individuals who believe information posted on social media typically have a greater tendency to share information posted on social media, and the result statistically supports this hypothesis (β=.227; p<.001). Hypothesis 2 predicts a negative relationship between mindfulness and individuals' tendency to believe information posted on social media. Although the result shows that these two constructs negatively associate, it is not statistically supported (β=-.009; p=.429). Hypothesis 3 predicts a negative relationship between mindfulness and individuals' tendency to share information posted on social media, and the result statistically supports this hypothesis (β=-.098; p=.024). Hypothesis 4 predicts a positive relationship between the level of mindfulness and the degree of skepticism; the result statistically confirms this hypothesis (β=.087; p=.039). Hypothesis 5 predicts a negative association between the degree of skepticism and individuals' tendency to believe information posted on social media, which is statistically supported by the result (β=-.086; p=.042). Finally, hypothesis 6 predicts a negative association between degree of skepticism and individuals' tendency to share information posted on social media without considering the consequences. The result also statistically supports this hypothesis (β=-.168; p<.001).

The relationships between control variables and each dependent variable are as follows. The tendency to believe social media content positively associates with social media use intensity (β=.278; p<.001) and age (β=.014; p=.391); but it negatively associates with education (β=-.169; p<.001), the degree to which individuals access media (β=-.239; p<.001), male dummy variable (β=-.002; p=.486), and collectivistic attitudes (β=-.029; p=.275). The tendency to share social media content positively associates with social media use intensity (β=.158; p<.001), the degree to which individuals access other media (β=.118; p=.009), collectivistic attitudes (β=.165; p<.001), male dummy variable (β=.036; p=.236), and age (β=.018; p=.357); however, it negatively associates with education (β=-.199; p<.001). Finally, skepticism was found to associate positively with age (β=.134; p=.003), education (β=.280; p<.001), and collectivistic attitude (β=.354; p<.001); but negatively with social media use intensity (β=-.089; p=.036), the degree to which individuals access media (β=-.045; p=.179), and male dummy variable (β=-.014; p=.387).

5. DISCUSSION

5.1. General Discussion

The objective of this research was to explore the effect of mindfulness on individuals' tendency to believe social media content and share it without realizing the potential consequences. The demographic characteristics and other social media behaviors of the respondents were controlled, and the results support the hypothesis that those who believe a social media content are more likely to share it. This finding is consistent with the argument that suggests that individuals' perceptions of the believability of a content can be an influential factor that leads to content sharing (Nagarajan et al, 2010; Suh et al, 2010). The more individuals feel positive about a content, the higher the tendency they will share it (Stieglitz & Dang-Xuan, 2013). Moreover, the analysis supports the hypothesis that individuals who exhibit higher levels of mindfulness tend to be skeptical of the validity of information to which they are exposed. This finding supports the role of mindfulness proposed in prior research as a characteristic that helps individuals enhance information processing capabilities (Bishop et al, 2004; Wells, 2002). It is also consistent with the results of a study that suggest that mindful individuals tend to constantly question the accuracy of information (Thomas, 2006). In addition, skepticism is found to be linked to a decreased tendency to believe social media content and share it on social media. The findings further support a direct link between mindfulness and a decreased tendency to share social media content. This is also consistent with the findings of a prior research that suggest that skeptics tend to spend more time reasoning out to avoid making errors in their decision making (Pennycook et al, 2013). Although the hypothesis regarding the direct link between mindfulness and tendency to believe social media content is not supported, it can be explained that a skeptic attitude associated with mindfulness may serve as a mechanism that makes individuals not easily believe in a social media content. Overall, these findings confirm the positive contribution of mindfulness as a quality that may allow individuals to question the validity of a social media content before they decide to believe it and share it with others.

Because the role of mindfulness in social media behaviors has not been widely investigated in literature, results from this research offer additional evidence that supports the importance of mindfulness in determining the degree to which users evaluate information on social media before they decide to share it. Specifically, results from this research are consistent with the findings of a study conducted by Charoensukmongkol (2015), which emphasizes the role of mindfulness in helping individuals regulate their social media behaviors to avoid negative consequences that may arise through mindless use. It has been shown in the present study that mindful individuals are generally more likely to evaluate the validity of social media content before they decide to trust and share information. Moreover, this research contributes to existing research regarding factors that motivate individuals to share social media content

(Lee & Ma, 2012; Nagarajan et al, 2010; Stieglitz & Dang-Xuan, 2013; Suh et al, 2010). While existing research focuses on personal motivations, social factors, and content characteristics, this study suggests that mindfulness should be another key characteristic that needs to be considered when studying social media use behaviors. Specifically, evidence about the contribution of mindfulness is closely congruent with prior studies that support the influential role of emotions (e.g. fear, anxiety) that can trigger a social media sharing behavior (Chen et al, 2015; Oh et al, 2010; Stieglitz & Dang-Xuan, 2013). Considering the role of mindfulness that helps individuals effectively regulate their own emotions and prevent them from engaging in impulsive behaviors like in the case of careless social media sharing, the present study extends these prior studies by adding that being mindful when exposed to a social media content can be an essential characteristic that can help prevent this behavioral tendency.

5.2. Limitations and Suggestions for Future Research

Although most of the hypotheses are supported, the study contains several limitations that need to be considered. First, the data do not capture the types of social media content to which the respondents typically are exposed or share. Sharing general content, such as news and entertainment, from well-known sources may not cause harmful consequences compared to sharing sensitive content from unknown sources. For the former, believing or sharing the content may not be a serious matter because individuals can verify it easily. Additionally, the study did not consider the possibility that individuals may be inclined to believe content shared by a trusted person although the original source of that content may be unidentified. Given these gaps in the study, future research needs to focus on specific content that makes careless sharing on social media platforms a critical issue, and should consider the role of the trustworthiness of the person who shared the content and may influence others to believe or to re-share it.

Second, the results were interpreted from cross-sectional data, thereby making the causality between key variables difficult to confirm. Third, the data were collected from respondents from three institutions in Bangkok; thus, the results cannot be generalized to an entire population. Future research that collects data in a broader scope is required to generalize the findings. Nevertheless, given the scant amount of research currently published that tests the role of mindfulness in social media behaviors, future research may replicate the study in different cultural contexts to explore whether the effects of mindfulness on social media behaviors are similar in different cultures. In addition, future studies may consider some culture-specific factors or cultural values that possibly moderate the role of mindfulness on social media behaviors.

5.3. Practical Implications

Based on the overall findings, this research provides some solutions that could mitigate the potential problems caused by the careless sharing of information on social media platforms. Given the power of social media technology to disperse information rapidly across geographical areas, it is crucial for individuals to consider validity before they decide to trust or share content. When people carelessly share false information on social media, it creates rumors that quickly become pervasive. Although people may not perceive the information as harmful, in some circumstances it can be ambiguous and cause anxiety. Thus, the researcher recommends that individuals be mindful when accessing information via social media. Being mindful in this sense can help raise awareness and promote skepticism about the legitimacy of social media content. When people are mindful about the accuracy of information, they do not allow their emotions to influence their judgment about its reliability (Stieglitz & Dang-Xuan, 2013) until they can obtain evidence to support the trustworthiness of the information. This approach supports the careful evaluation of information to determine its trustworthiness before sharing it. Being mindful with using social media is especially important when people rely extensively on social media to receive news and information. As indicated by the data, the majority of respondents reported that they not only spent more than half of their leisure time on social media, but also that they relied more heavily on social media than traditional media as a source of news and information. Without carefully evaluating the validity of social media content, people are highly susceptible to embracing false information spread on social media platforms.

The overall findings also offer policy implications to reduce the spread of rumors and misinformation in society caused by careless social media sharing. As mentioned previously, policy makers experience difficulty in resorting to legal actions to regulate and control social media contents, so they will have to provide appropriate interventions that target some personal characteristics that influence such behaviors. Given the role of mindfulness that negatively relates with the aforementioned behavioral tendency, a policy maker may need to initiate a campaign to educate and encourage their citizens to be mindful when they are exposed to social media information. In Thailand, for example, the government and the press have continuously communicated to the public to encourage the citizens to exercise mindfulness before they believe, share, or reshare social media contents (Doman, 2015; Raksaseri, 2015). While some scholars propose that individuals differ inherently in the quality of their mindfulness, it has been proven that one's state of mindfulness can be enhanced with proper training (Wells, 2005). When individuals are trained adequately to cultivate their state of mindfulness, self-regulation abilities usually improve, thereby helping them to be less prone to processing information and performing tasks on autopilot. This allows them to evaluate social media contents effectively and to regulate behaviors concerning the use of social media to avoid problems that arise from careless content sharing.

In addition to the implications obtained from the hypotheses testing, some significant effects of the control variables provide further implications. First, the result indicating that respondents with higher education not only exhibited more skepticism but also showed a lower tendency to believe and share social media contents suggests the crucial role of education, which can help individuals develop their critical thinking skills, which can make them more cautious before they believe information from social media. This finding suggests that policy makers need to provide proper education to the citizens to make them be aware of the accuracy of a social media content before they believe it, and make them realize the negative consequences of carelessly sharing content. In addition, the results that indicate that older respondents tend to exhibit more skepticism than younger respondents do imply the essential role of mental maturity, which facilitates rational information processing. Because younger adults and teenagers are more prone to believing information they are exposed to without being skeptic about their accuracy and trustworthiness, it is important for policy makers to focus more on this group of citizens and educate and persuade them to evaluate information from social media critically. Lastly, the results indicating that respondents with collectivistic values tended to report a higher tendency to share social media contents also provide a useful implication. Generally, people with strong collectivistic values tend to share social media contents because they believe that doing so will benefit their social group (Singelis et al, 1995). However, if they realize that sharing inaccurate information on social media can be harmful to society, they might refrain from doing so. Therefore, if policy makers effectively inform this group of people about the harmful effects of careless sharing, this behavioral tendency can be reduced.

6. CONCLUSION

It is critical for individuals to evaluate the accuracy of information before they believe or share it. Once information is shared and then reshared by others on social media, it cannot be reversed. In fact, this behavior should not be ignored because in some circumstances not only does it cause harmful effects to society, but also a person who carelessly shares misinformation may face legal consequences. For example, during the recent political instability in Thailand, the panic caused by rumors spread on social media that mentioned the possibility of a military coup and urged the public to hoard food and water prompted the Thai government to prosecute anyone who shared and reshared misinformation (Sakawee, 2013). Similarly, in the United Arab Emirates, jail terms and fines are among the penalties that the government has implemented to counter false rumors circulated on social media (McGinley, 2015). Therefore, being aware of ones' own behaviors when exposed to social media information is important in order to avoid any negative consequences.

In an attempt to propose some personal characteristics as helpful in preventing this behavioral tendency, the present research illustrates the contribution of mindfulness, which can enhance people's tendency to question the validity of information posted on social media when they are deciding whether or not to share it. Subsequently, if social media users are mindful when receiving news and information, the spread of inaccurate information could be reduced. Given this concern on the negative effects of sharing misinformation, finally, the present study suggests that a campaign that aims to encourage citizens to be mindful when they are exposed to information on social media may be a solution that policy makers should consider in order to prevent the spread of misinformation in society.

ACKNOWLEDGMENT

This research was supported by the International College of National Institute of Development Administration.

REFERENCES

Aula, P. (2010). Social media, reputation risk and ambient publicity management. *Strategy and Leadership*, *38*(6), 43–49. doi:10.1108/10878571011088069

Barger, S. D. (2002). The Marlowe-Crowne affair: Short forms, psychometric structure, and social desirability. *Journal of Personality Assessment*, *79*(2), 286–305. doi:10.1207/S15327752JPA7902_11 PMID:12425392

Bishop, S. R., Lau, M., Shapiro, S., Carlson, L., Anderson, N. D., Carmody, J., ... Devins, G. (2004). Mindfulness: A Proposed Operational Definition. *Clinical Psychology: Science and Practice*, *11*(3), 230–241. doi:10.1093/clipsy.bph077

Brown, C. L., & Krishna, A. (2004). The Skeptical Shopper: A Metacognitive Account for the Effects of Default Options on Choice. *The Journal of Consumer Research*, *31*(3), 529–539. doi:10.1086/425087

Brown, K. W., & Ryan, R. M. (2003). The benefits of being present: Mindfulness and its role in psychological well-being. *Journal of Personality and Social Psychology, 84*(4), 822–848. doi:10.1037/0022-3514.84.4.822 PMID:12703651

Burke, M., Marlow, C., & Lento, T. (2009). Feed Me: Motivating Newcomer Contribution in Social Network Sites. *Paper presented at the Proceedings of the 27th international conference on human factors in computing systems.* 10.1145/1518701.1518847

Carlos, C., Marcelo, M., & Barbara, P. (2013). Predicting information credibility in time-sensitive social media. *Internet Research, 23*(5), 560–588. doi:10.1108/IntR-05-2012-0095

Charoensukmongkol, P. (2015). Mindful Facebooking: The moderating role of mindfulness on the relationship between social media use intensity at work and burnout. *Journal of Health Psychology.* doi:10.1177/1359105315569096 PMID:25680915

Chen, X., Sin, S.-C. J., Theng, Y.-L., & Lee, C. S. (2015). Why Students Share Misinformation on Social Media: Motivation, Gender, and Study-level Differences. *Journal of Academic Librarianship, 41*(5), 583–592. doi:10.1016/j.acalib.2015.07.003

Chin, W. W., & Newsted, P. R. (1999). Structural equation modeling analysis with small samples using partial least squares. In R. Hoyle (Ed.), *Statistical strategies for small sample research* (pp. 307–341). Thousand Oaks, CA: Sage.

Correa, T., Hinsley, A. W., & de Zúñiga, H. G. (2010). Who interacts on the Web?: The intersection of users' personality and social media use. *Computers in Human Behavior, 26*(2), 247–253. doi:10.1016/j.chb.2009.09.003

Crowne, D. P., & Marlowe, D. (1960). A new scale of social desirability independent of psychopathology. *Journal of Consulting Psychology, 24*(4), 349–354. doi:10.1037/h0047358 PMID:13813058

Dane, E. (2011). Paying attention to mindfulness and its effects on task performance in the workplace. *Journal of Management, 37*(4), 997–1018. doi:10.1177/0149206310367948

Deschene, L. (2011). Ten Mindful Ways to Use Social Media. *Tricycle.com.* Retrieved from http://www.tricycle.com/feature/ten-mindful-ways-use-social-media

Dewey, C. (2014). The 15 worst Internet hoaxes of 2014 – and where the pranksters are now. *Washington Post.* Retrieved from http://www.washingtonpost.com/news/the-intersect/wp/2014/12/18/the-15-worst-internet-hoaxes-of-2014-and-where-the-pranksters-are-now

Diakopoulos, N., Choudhury, M. D., & Naaman, M. (2012). Finding and assessing social media information sources in the context of journalism. *Paper presented at the SIGCHI Conference on Human Factors in Computing Systems*, Austin, TX. 10.1145/2207676.2208409

Doman, G. (2015). Think before you Tweet: Thailand's updated copyright laws. *VivaldiPR.com.* Retrieved from http://www.vivaldipr.com/vivaldi_blog/think-before-you-tweet-thailands-updated-copyright-laws/

Flavell, J. H. (1979). Metacognition and metacognitive monitoring: A new area of cognitive-developmental inquiry. *The American Psychologist, 34*(10), 906–911. doi:10.1037/0003-066X.34.10.906

Fornell, C., & Larcker, D. (1981). Evaluating structural equation models with unobservable variables and measurement error. *JMR, Journal of Marketing Research*, *18*(1), 39–50. doi:10.2307/3151312

Garofalo, J., & Lester, F. K. (1985). Metacognition, Cognitive Monitoring, and Mathematical Performance. *Journal for Research in Mathematics Education*, *16*(3), 163–176. doi:10.2307/748391

Gärtner, C. (2013). Enhancing Readiness for Change by Enhancing Mindfulness. *Journal of Change Management*, *13*(1), 52–68. doi:10.1080/14697017.2013.768433

Glick, P., Gottesman, D., & Jolton, J. (1989). The Fault is not in the Stars: Susceptibility of Skeptics and Believers in Astrology to the Barnum Effect. *Personality and Social Psychology Bulletin*, *15*(4), 572–583. doi:10.1177/0146167289154010

Glomb, T. M., & Michelle, K. (2011). Mindfulness at work. *Research in Personnel and Human Resources Management*, *30*, 115–157. doi:10.1108/S0742-7301(2011)0000030005

Gundecha, P., & Liu, H. (2012). Mining Social Media: A Brief Introduction. *Tutorials in Operations Research*, 1-17. doi:10.1287/educ.1120.0105

Hafenbrack, A. C., Kinias, Z., & Barsade, S. G. (2013). Debiasing the Mind Through Meditation: Mindfulness and the Sunk-Cost Bias. *Psychological Science*. doi:10.1177/0956797613503853 PMID:24317419

Hair, J. F., Black, W. C., Babin, B. J., & Anderson, R. E. (2009). *Multivariate data analysis* (7th ed.). Upper Saddle River, NJ: Prentice Hall.

Kabat-Zinn, J. (1990). *Full catastrophe living: Using the wisdom of your body and mind to face stress, pain, and illness.* New York, NY: Delacorte Press.

Kaplan, A. M., & Haenlein, M. (2010). Users of the world, unite! The challenges and opportunities of Social Media. *Business Horizons*, *53*(1), 59–68. doi:10.1016/j.bushor.2009.09.003

Karelaia, N., & Reb, J. (2014). Improving Decision Making Through Mindfulness. In J. Reb & P. Atkins (Eds.), *Forthcoming in Mindfulness in Organizations. INSEAD Working Paper No. 2014/43/DSC. Available at SSRN.* Cambridge University Press. Retrieved from http://ssrn.com/abstract=2443808

Kline, R. B. (2005). *Principle and Practice of Structural Equation Modeling* (2nd ed.). New York, NY: The Guiford Press.

Kock, N., & Lynn, G. S. (2012). Lateral collinearity and misleading results in variance-based SEM: An illustration and recommendations. *Journal of the Association for Information Systems*, *13*(7), 546–580.

Lee, C. S., & Ma, L. (2012). News sharing in social media: The effect of gratifications and prior experience. *Computers in Human Behavior*, *28*(2), 331–339. doi:10.1016/j.chb.2011.10.002

Leroy, H., Anseel, F., Dimitrova, N. G., & Sels, L. (2013). Mindfulness, authentic functioning, and work engagement: A growth modeling approach. *Journal of Vocational Behavior*, *82*(3), 238–247. doi:10.1016/j.jvb.2013.01.012

Li, Z.-N., Drew, M. S., & Liu, J. (2014). Social Media Sharing. *Fundamentals of Multimedia*, 617-643. doi:10.1007/978-3-319-05290-8_18

Lin, N. (1999). Social Networks and Status Attainment. *Annual Review of Sociology, 25*(1), 467–487. doi:10.1146/annurev.soc.25.1.467

Mäkinen, M., & Wangu Kuira, M. (2008). Social Media and Postelection Crisis in Kenya. *The International Journal of Press/Politics, 13*(3), 328–335. doi:10.1177/1940161208319409

McGinley, S. (2015). Dubai Police issue warning over 'social media misuse'. *Arabian Business.* Retrieved from http://www.arabianbusiness.com/dubai-police-issue-warning-over-social-media-misuse--606548.html

Mendoza, M., Poblete, B., & Castillo, C. (2010). Twitter under crisis: can we trust what we RT? *Paper presented at the First Workshop on Social Media Analytics*, Washington D.C, DC. 10.1145/1964858.1964869

Mevarech, Z. R. (1999). Effects of Metacognitive Training Embedded in Cooperative Settings on Mathematical Problem Solving. *The Journal of Educational Research, 92*(4), 195–205. doi:10.1080/00220679909597597

Nagarajan, M., Purohit, H., & Sheth, A. (2010). A Qualitative Examination of Topical Tweet and Retweet Practices. *Paper presented at the Fourth International AAAI Conference on Weblogs and Social Media*, Washington, DC.

Nunnally, J. C. (1978). *Psychometric Theory* (2nd ed.). New York, NY: McGraw-Hill.

Oh, O., Kwon, K. H., & Rao, H. R. (2010). An Exploration of Social Media in Extreme Events: Rumor Theory and Twitter during the Haiti Earthquake 2010. *Paper presented at the Thirty First International Conference on Information Systems*, St. Louis, MO.

Pennycook, G., Cheyne, J., Koehler, D., & Fugelsang, J. (2013). Belief bias during reasoning among religious believers and skeptics. *Psychonomic Bulletin & Review, 20*(4), 806–811. doi:10.375813423-013-0394-3 PMID:23397237

Petter, S., Straub, D., & Rai, A. (2007). Specifying Formative Constructs in Information Systems Research. *Management Information Systems Quarterly, 31*(4), 623–656.

Pithers, R. T., & Soden, R. (2000). Critical thinking in education: A review. *Educational Research, 42*(3), 237–249. doi:10.1080/001318800440579

Pujazon-Zazik, M., & Park, M. J. (2010). To Tweet, or Not to Tweet: Gender Differences and Potential Positive and Negative Health Outcomes of Adolescents' Social Internet Use. *American Journal of Men's Health, 4*(1), 77–85. doi:10.1177/1557988309360819 PMID:20164062

Raksaseri, K. (2015). Don't believe everything you see and read on social media. Retrieved from http://www.nationmultimedia.com/politics/Dont-believe-everything-you-see-and-read-on-social-30264714.html

Ratkiewicz, J., Conover, M. D., Meiss, M., Gonçalves, B., Flammini, A., & Menczer, F. (2011). Detecting and Tracking Political Abuse in Social Media. *Paper presented at the Fifth International AAAI Conference on Weblogs and Social Media.*

Sakawee, S. (2013). As 4 Summoned Over Coup Rumors on Facebook, Is Thailand Stepping Back From Democracy? *Tech In Asia.* Retrieved from https://www.techinasia.com/thailand-coup-romour-facebook/

Shonin, E., Gordon, W. V., & Griffiths, M. D. (2014). Mindfulness as a Treatment for Behavioural Addiction. *Addiction Research & Therapy, 5*(1). doi:10.4172/2155-6105.1000e122

Singelis, T. M., Triandis, H. C., Bhawuk, D. P. S., & Gelfand, M. J. (1995). Horizontal and vertical dimensions of individualism and collectivism: A theoretical and measurement refinement. *Cross-Cultural Research, 29*(3), 240–275. doi:10.1177/106939719502900302

Stieglitz, S., & Dang-Xuan, L. (2013). Emotions and Information Diffusion in Social Media—Sentiment of Microblogs and Sharing Behavior. *Journal of Management Information Systems, 29*(4), 217–248. doi:10.2753/MIS0742-1222290408

Suh, B., Hong, L., Pirolli, P., & Chi, E. (2010). Want to be retweeted? Large scale analytics on factors impacting retweet in Twitter network. In A. Pentland (Ed.), *Proceedings of the 2nd IEEE International Conference on Social Computing,* Los Alamitos, CA, USA (pp. 177–184). IEEE Computer Society. 10.1109/SocialCom.2010.33

Talcoth, R. (2015). Thailand's social media battleground. *Asia Pacific.anu.edu.* Retrieved from http://asiapacific.anu.edu.au/newmandala/2015/03/26/thailands-social-media-battleground/

Thomas, D. C. (2006). Domain and Development of Cultural Intelligence: The Importance of Mindfulness. *Group & Organization Management, 31*(1), 78–99. doi:10.1177/1059601105275266

Tran, H. (2013). Does Exposure to Online Media Matter? The Knowledge Gap and the Mediating Role of News Use. *International Journal of Communication, 7,* 831–852.

Wells, A. (2002). GAD, Meta-cognition, and Mindfulness: An Information Processing Analysis. *Clinical Psychology: Science and Practice, 9*(1), 95–100. doi:10.1093/clipsy/9.1.95

Wells, A. (2005). Detached Mindfulness In Cognitive Therapy: A Metacognitive Analysis And Ten Techniques. *Journal of Rational-Emotive & Cognitive-Behavior Therapy, 23*(4), 337–355. doi:10.100710942-005-0018-6

Zhang, J., Ding, W., Li, Y., & Wu, C. (2013). Task complexity matters: The influence of trait mindfulness on task and safety performance of nuclear power plant operators. *Personality and Individual Differences, 55*(4), 433–439. doi:10.1016/j.paid.2013.04.004

This research was previously published in International Journal of Technology and Human Interaction (IJTHI), 12(3); edited by Anabela Mesquita and Chia-Wen Tsai; pages 47-63, copyright year 2016 by IGI Publishing (an imprint of IGI Global).

APPENDIX

Measurement Items and Factor Loadings

Tendency to Believe Content Posted on Social Media

- I think all content posted on social media can be trusted (.84).
- I normally believe all content posted on social media (.854).
- I think all content posted on social media is accurate enough to be trusted (.842).
- There is no need for me to verify the accuracy of the content posted on social media (.744).

Tendency to Share Content Posted on Social Media

- I normally share content posted on social media without any concern about its accuracy (.786).
- I normally share content posted on social media quickly without considering the consequences it may cause if the information is invalid (.884).
- I normally share all content I like on social media quickly without thinking because I feel it will cause no harm to anyone (.839).
- I normally share all content I like on social media quickly without thinking because I believe it will not cause any negative outcome (.804).

Skepticism

- I seldom believe anything I have not proven myself (.735).
- I always search for additional information to verify the accuracy of what I have heard before I decide to believe it (.762).
- I always evaluate the trustworthiness of sources of information before I believe any information (.76).

Mindfulness (Brown & Ryan, 2003)

- I could be experiencing some emotion and not be conscious of it until some time later (.91).
- I break or spill things because of carelessness, not paying attention, or thinking of something else (.854).
- I find it difficult to stay focused on what's happening in the present (.893).
- I forget a person's name almost as soon as I've been told it for the first time (.84).
- It seems I am "running on automatic," without much awareness of what I'm doing (.819).
- I rush through activities without being really attentive to them (.901).
- I get so focused on the goal I want to achieve that I lose touch with what I'm doing right now to get there (.878).
- I do jobs or tasks automatically, without being aware of what I'm doing (.845).
- I find myself listening to someone with one ear, doing something else at the same time (.934).
- I drive places on 'automatic pilot' and then wonder why I went there (.848).

- I find myself preoccupied with the future or the past (.748).
- I find myself doing things without paying attention (.885).
- I snack without being aware that I'm eating (.792).

Collectivism (Singelis et al, 1995)

- My happiness depends very much on the happiness of those around me (.799).
- I like sharing things with others (.904).
- To me pleasure is spending time with others (.799).
- I feel good when I cooperate with others (.888).
- It is important for me to maintain harmony within my group (.841).

Chapter 13
Arabic Rumours Identification By Measuring The Credibility Of Arabic Tweet Content

Ahmad Yahya M. Floos
King Saud University, Saudia Arabia

ABSTRACT

Twitter enjoys the fame of the most popular and widely used as a platform for socializing, including all aspects of life current affairs, religious ideas, political issues, scientific research, and general knowledge. Every single activity of day to day life and human behavior and values is lodged at this platform. Sending and receiving messages on Twitter (tweets) with is limited to 140 characters, In this research the author attempts to understand the characteristics of those Arabic rumour (falsified information stream) patterns. False tweets could be a rumour which is mostly recognized as a representative whose legitimacy, authenticity, precision and significance is either unverifiable or unreliable. Arabic rumours may propagate misinformation on social networks. In this research, the author illustrates the difficulty of Arabic rumour identification in twitter social platform by studying the impact based on Arabic tweet content. Furthermore, the author explains how these content features are too influential in measuring the credibility of those Arabic tweets.

1. INTRODUCTION

This is evident that internet has become the most significant player for news in the last decade. This can be judged from the fact that only in United States of America, internet is the most popular source of news for the people under the age of thirty (30) while it is the second most popular medium for news after the television (TPR Center, 2008). Online Social Networks also called as OSNs like twitter and facebook are the recent innovative applications of this decade that influenced the humans largely. With the every passing day, the number of their users are growing. In 2011 only, the number of twitter users were more than 100 millions while the population of facebook users were more than 955 millions in

DOI: 10.4018/978-1-5225-9869-5.ch013

2012 (Securities and Exchange Commission, 2012). OSNs have totally change the way of communication among the people. People now can easily share their point of views and opinions to colleagues and friends and also spread the information to the community.

The popularity of social media like facebook and twitter has very greatly and deeply affected the journalism landscapes and news reporting. So, social media is not only used for the purpose of every day chat but also a very significant source of news and information sharing (Java, Song, Finin, and Tseng, 2007; Naaman, Boase, and Lai., 2010). Now, people refer towards social media as the major source of news (Laird, 2012). In breaking news situation, role of social media is even more prominent as the public crave for quick updated on the events and incidents in real time. Kwak et al. (2010) through his study showed that more than 85% topics on twitter are regarding news and current affairs. In addition, the accessibility, ubiquity, ease of use and speed of this social media has made it the invaluable and most important source of first hand information regarding news. In some cases, twitter also proved to be very useful in disaster and emergency situations specifically for recovery and response (Vieweg, 2010).

In this work, we focused on measuring the credibility of Arabic News content published in Twitter. This study can be considered a first attempt to explore the credibility of Twitter content targeted for the Arabic language. For this purpose, we used the natural language processing and machine learning. Language is capability to talk, write and communicate and is one of the primary characteristic of human activities. As the learning of human languages progressed the perception of contact among machines was conceptualized, this served as the fundamental idea behind the natural language processing (NLP). The concept of natural language processing is to resolve and develop software that will examine, learn and produce natural human-languages. There are numerous software of natural language processing build through the long term. One of these softwares is Romurs Identifications, current users are searching through the major samples from every twitter microblogs (tweets) they read, people have no time to verify the authenticity of news. Given the extremely busy day to day lives and notherefore it be converted into a software for présent-days.

There is two ways to perform text representation; indexing and term weighting. Indexing is the method of assigning indexing terms for a document, while terms weighting is the method of assigning weight to each term in the document. In this research, we use TF-IDF (Term frequency- inverse document frequency) to determine the weights for the terms contained in the document to determine the terms relevant the documents. We use documents that contain tweets for news and rumors, our job is to identify any new tweet to be defined as news or rumors according to the methods using tf-idf.

2. RELATED WORK

Related work has included the research related to the different roles of twitter in emergencies, researchers from the fields of network sciences about the propagation and diffusion of different information in social media networks, research from the fields of language processing about confining the propagation and diffusion of information in social media networks. We have also discussed different twitter credibility surveys, credibility of Arabic content and measurement of credibility of twitter information:

1. **Credibility Definition:** For the current study, the definition of credibility is taken from Reih (2010). Reih defines credibility as people's assessment of whether information is trustworthy based on their own expertise and knowledge.

Table 1. Assessing information credibility automatically

Model Used	Used by - Examples
Classifier-based feature: different features	Kang et al. (2013); Kang, O'Donovan, & Höllerer (2012); Castillo, Mendoza, & Poblete (2011); Yang et al. (2012); Gupta & Kumaraguru (2012); Xia et al. (2012);
Classifier-based feature: mainly linguistic features	Bhattacharya et al. (2012); Qazvinian et al. (2011)
Graph-based / Hybrid (Classification with Graph)	McKelvey & Menczer (2013); Ratkiewicz et al. (2011); Ulicny & Kokar (2013); Ravikumar, Balakrishnan, & Kambhampati (2012); Gupta,Zhao, & Han (2012)
Weighting-based feature/ Content similarity with credible source: mainly linguistic features	Assigning of the scores by some certain algorithms or mathematical functions to every feature. Al-Khalifa & Al-Eidan (2011); Al-Eidan, Al-Khalifa, & Al-Salman (2010)
Statistical analysis	Features distributions conducted by ODonovan et al. (2012)

2. **Measurement of information Credibility:** In the assessment of credibility of information automatically, different approaches have been adopted by different researchers. For instance, machine learning supervised by learning methods, graphic analysis, statistical analysis and feature distribution have been potentially used to check the credibility. For the conveneience, the famous and most used techniques are presented in the Table 1.

3. **Credibility of Online News in Traditional Media and Blogs:** The In general, the users' perception regarding the credibility of news published online appears to be positive. Usually, people trust the net as the major source of reading the news in comparsion with other media except newspapers (Flanagin and Metzger, 2000). This is fact now that internet has become the most significant player for news in the last decade. This can be judged from the fact that only in United States of America, internet is the most popular source of news for the people under the age of thirty (30) while it is the second most popular medium for news after the television (TPR Center, 2008). Online Social Networks also called as OSNs like twitter and facebook are the recent innovative applications of this decade that influenced the humans largely. With the every passing day, the number of their users is growing. In 2011 only, the number of twitter users were more than 100 millions while the population of facebook users were more than 955 millions in 2012 (Securities and Exchange Commission, 2012).

4. **Credibility of News on Twitter:** In a study conducted by Schwarz and Morris (2011), it was found that information that was being provided to users on twitter is quite valuable and useful to them. The perception regarding the credibility of a news is also gender specific (Flanagin and Metzger, 2007; Armstrong and Mcadams, 2009). An experiement regarding the credibility of the content was conducted by Schmierbach and Oeldorf-Hirsch (2010). In the experiment, headlines of news were given to the users in some different ways such as posted in conventional news media websites, posted on twitter and posted in different blogs. The user (Shahzad, 2014; Alwagait, 2014; Shahzad 2014; Alwagait 2013; Alohali, 2011) found the news less credible when was presented on twitter. Some major search engines have started to display results of the search from real time web (micro

blog and blog postings), specifically for prominent topics. This, in return, has attracted spammers that use twitter to attract the visitors to their websites that offers services and products. This function has also been used to spread misinformation and lies (Benevenuto, Magno, Rodrigues, and Almeida, 2010).

5. **Arabic Content Credibility:** In Two studies have been conducted by Eidan, Al-Khalifa, & Al-Salman (2010) and Al-Khalifa & Al-Eidan (2011) to check the content credibility in Arabic. The both studies have proposed a specific system to assess the credibility of Arabic news on twitter by using a weighting based feature approach. The given system has used two main approaches for the assigning of credibility levels. These are as follows.

   a. An evidence based method that has its basis on likeness between verified news sources and tweets.

   b. The evidence based method that has its basis on the similarities with the verified contents.

In addition, to propose new features, a specific formula was used for the calculation of the credibility of news content by assigning specific score. The formula is given as

Credibility Score = 0.6 (Similarity) + 0.2 (Inappropriate Words) + 0.1 (Linking to authoritative source) + 0.1 (Author feature).

Evaluating the system has showed that first approach was found more credible and effective for assessing the credibility of tweets. But this system only has two levels that is high and low. But these studies had many limitation as this method is useful in assessing tweets that has combination with external source and doesn't have very prominent features such as emoticons, retweets and hash tags.

6. **Twitter Credibility Surveys:** Table 2 comprises all the surveys to measure the credibility of twitter with specific twitter features.

7. **Evidence from Previous Work:** Castillo et al (2010), in their work presented a categorizer (for classification) used to sorting (classifying) a group of characteristics to distinguish each twitter-topic. This involves a number of characteristics exclusive to online twitter network, the first feature of this set of features is twitter-account-feature of the online twitter-user who posts the tweet also termed as tweet author. The primary focus was to assess the credibility of micro blogs (messages) spread over the online micro bloggers media network (social media) and to be able to detect the repetitions. Moreover, it also captures the micro blogs concerning instance-critical micro blogs and

Table 2. Twitter credibility surveys

Survey Used	Twitter Features Considered
Kang, ODonovan, & Hollerer (2012)	Re-tweets, Users' information and followers
Canini, Suh, & Pirolli (2011)	Word factors, expertise and social status
Pal & Counts (2011)	Author name
Morris et al. (2012)	Message topic, user name and user image.
Yang et al. (2013)	Gender, profile image, name style, network overlap, location and message topic
Westerman, Spence, & Van Der Heide (2012)	Ratio between followees and followers and Number of followers.

topics. Also is able to divide automatically interesting micro blogs-topics from chat sessions. With a variety of online social network-features, interesting micro blogs-topics contain links and have broadcast-trees. Additionally it also is capable of evaluating the degree of online social-network interested-topics and their credibility.

8. **Twitter Credibility of Contents:** Apart from this research, Kasyoka et al. (2014) proposed a framework for aggregating and retrieving relevant maize information using Term Frequency Inverse Document Frequency and Term Proximity. Also, they implement a term proximity scoring approach that will be able to improve relevance in the top-k documents returned by TF-IDF. The approach for term proximity score uses both the span-based method and pair-based method to ensure effective proximity scoring. User preference profile is based on keywords which form user query while text documents are composed of RSS description content and RSS title tag content.

If we discuss specifically Arab content, Fedaghi and Al-Anzi's algorithm aim to place an additional word at the beginning or at the End of root, stem and word to change its meaning and get the Arabic root is the main theme. In Al-Kharachi system (P. Kasyoka, W. Mwangi, and M. Kimwele, 2005). Article headlines are used, composer uses three preferences for indexing: words, stems, and roots. Three (3) Interrelation extent were used; the cosine measure, the Dice, and the Jaccard coefficient. A simiar Research work was conducted by Abu-Salem,et al.(1994), to boost the Performance of Arabic knowledge improvement by balancing a query string is derived from the priority of the word (the stem) the root of the query being the taxonomy in the compilation. The measurements were computed by applying the standard TFIDF measures. The expected technique, called mixed stemming, produced an advancement over the word indexing method, practicing both exclusive in the case of binary weighting schemes. Renovation over the stemming index approach was achieved for Arabic documents.

Benajiba et al. (2007) analyzed the importance of the Passage Retrieval (PR) on the achievement of the Question/Answer (QA) system. The fundamental outcome being that it is achievable to access a first Arabic paragraph improvement system conforming JIRS on preprocessed text to a light-stemmer. Beesley (1998) represent a morphological analyzer system of the latest Arabic common taxonomy. Al-Shalabi et al's (1998) morphology system practices various algorithms to examine the roots and its patterns. This algorithm eliminates the lengthy achievable prefix, and then isolates the root by verifying the first five letters of the word. This algorithm is established on a hypowork that the root must occur in the first five letters of the word. Khoja (1999) developed an algorithm that eliminate prefixes and suffixes, continuously investigates that the segment of the roots are not eliminated and compares the remaining word against the original string to the corresponding length to extract the root.

3. DATA COLLECTION

For the current study, the researcher has gathered two kinds of tweets (Rumors and News).

1. **Rumors:** The Initially, the researcher has focused at the rumors (Arabic rumors) topics and its propagation in all different kinds of media for the sensitive topics like crisis news, business, politics and health, the presence of inaccurate, questionable and misleading information might have harmful and negative effect in the believes of people, decision making and most importantly create disturbance in people, then using those topics as keywords we tend to find the tweets rumors

Table 3. Sample of the selected rumors

Tweet (Rumors)
شركة ارامكو السعودية تعثر على مقبرة "قوم عاد" في صحراء الربع الخالي.. سبحان الله ولله في خلقه شؤون
شركة ارامكو# السعودية تعثر على مقبرة "قوم عاد" في صحراء السعودية# حقيقة اثناء التنقيب عن الغاز. #الربع_الخالي اثناء التنقيب عن الغاز #حقيقة
مقابر قوم عاد اكتشاف شركة ارامكو السعودية
علمة السعودية قرية ابها فيها جديدة 1000 . . .
شاب برازيلي يفني حتى لا الدولار فالا يتحول الى كلب الحمادله على نعمة الاسلام
اشجع سيلفي يلتقط "فلسطيني باش سيلفي" #سيلفي# أثناء ملاحقته من قبل جنود صهاينة

Table 4. Sample of the selected news

Tweet (News)
#أوغل: مصافحة #الأسد كمصافحة #هتلر
#تنظيم_الدولة يخفخ كل شيء في #تكريت: مسؤول عراقي:
ظنام #الأسد يقتل مزيدا من الأطفال السوريين بغاز الكلور #سوريا #سام
#الذين ملهم المنشقين من جماعة من #الإخوان في #مصر
إحالة 16 متهما بأحداث مجزرة #الدفاع_الجوي زرة #الدفاع_الجوي أغلبهم من #الإخوان للمحاكمة في #مصر

related to the topics over twitter. This way the data of 700 tweets was collected as shown in Table 3. Samples of those tweets collected are classified as rumors.

2. **News:** The second type of data we collected for the study is news from the twitter. The news was collected from various official and verified Twitter news accounts such as @cnnarabic, and @ AJArabic. Table 4 has pointed out a snapshot of this data, The researchers selected focused on Arabic critical news topics that diffusion in various types of media.

4. METHODOLOGY APPLIED

Component heads the methodology applied for the current study is used to satisfy the requirement of the results. The study used two different files containing news and rumors separately collected from several twitter accounts. All the news is collected from official accounts. The methodology applied is explained in the steps given below.

1. First, we have split the word in all documents.
2. We removed the stop words from the documents like (من ، إلى، عن ،على...).
3. We found the distinct term from each document and delete the redundant data.
4. We calculated tf-idf (term frequency- inverse document frequency) for the distinct terms. After that we got vector for each document, in our case we have two vectors that contain the term and it's tf-idf ; one for the news document and another for rumors document.
5. For each new tweet we match each term with the term in news document and calculate the tf-idf for it, which results in vector for the whole tweets. Then, do dot product is applied to the news vector and the tweets vector, the resultant set will be scalar. The same steps are repeated for the rumors vector. Finally, we compared both the scalars and the largest scalar will be taken, e.g. (if the largest scalar for the dot product by news vector, then the tweet is a news, otherwise it's a rumor). Figure 1 gives a snapshot of the methodology applied.

Figure 1. Phase of methodology

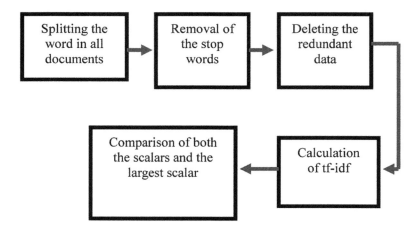

1. **Calculations:** TF-IDF (Term Frequency_ Inverse Document Frequency) are calculated according to equation (1), term with high tf-idf weight value has a stronger relationship to the document they appear in(Singh, J. N., & Dwivedi, S. K., 2014):

$$TF\_IDF=TF*IDF \tag{1}$$

where is the TF (Term Frequency) is calculated by the number of the term appears in a document. Equation 2 shows the TF calculation:

$$TF = \frac{\#\,of\,time\,term\,appearance\,in\,document}{\#\,of\,all\,terms\,in\,the\,document} \tag{2}$$

While IDF (Inverse Document Frequency) is a measurement of words' importance, it is defined as the logarithm (the ratio) of the number of all documents to the number of documents containing the terms. Equation 3 shows the IDF calculation:

$$IDF = Log\left(\frac{\#\,of\,all\,documents}{\#\,of\,documents\,contains\,the\,term}\right). \tag{3}$$

2. **Ethical Considerations:** The study has applied all the ethical consideration of the study. All the ethical standards were followed. This was assured that data collected is only used for the research purposes and is not used for any other purpose.

5. EXPERIMENTATION AND CORE FINDINGS ANALYSIS

Figure 3 have shown the interface of implementation of the classifier retrieval. The screen shot of the interference of implementation of the classifier is given below.

Figure 2. Screenshot of the interface of the classifier implementation

During the experiments that involved about 200 tweets as test sets, that were classified manually into two categories that includes 100 news and 100 rumors. Table 5 reflects retrieval, accuracy, measurement for the rumors category test set.

Moreover, it was found that the out of 100 rumors tweets the classifier's return 67% of those rumors as a result. The results are described in figure 4 mentioned below.

As it is evident from Table 6, an example of retrieval, accuracy, measurement for the 100 news tweets test set is given.

Figure 4 mentioned below describes the classifier's return i.e. 80% as news.

6. CONCLUSION

We initiated a novel mechanism to measure the Arabic tweets credibility and a novel technique to ensure the legitimacy of the tweets. Distinguishing with the primary purpose of illustrating a group of rumors(false tweets) and also examining the tweets related to the rumors. This method contains analysis of the twitter tweets to select the tweet that involves rumors and classify these tweets as rumors. This confirms the efficient use of a measuring the credibility of Arabic tweets content on Twitter. It is supposed that the design of such collected dataset of rumors allows to build tools, which utilize to credibility measurement tweets over the twitter.

Table 5. Example of rumors test sets results

Tweet (rumors)	Cosine measurement News%	Cosine measurement Rumor%	Near To
تحذير من شموع الخنزير في مكامع أطعمة مكدونالدز	3.318562845	96.68144	Rumor
سعود الفيصل رادار علي دعوة علي عبد الله صالح للحوار:ام يحصل نالا نوع من أنواع الحوار	29.8187491	70.18125	Rumor
بالصور ا مقيم صومالي يكتشف هائل زنك في مغارة بتبوك ويسلم هلم لهيئة الأثار	59.11777694	40.88222	News

Figure 3. Classifier result of rumors test set

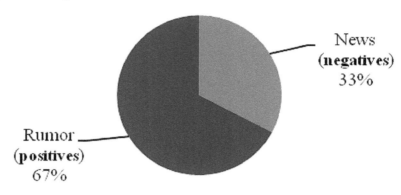

Table 6. Example of news test sets results

Tweet (news)	Cosine measurement News%	Cosine measurement Rumor%	Near To
ناس العاصمة تغلب وردها "توريايا" بركان "توريايا" روثان بركان :كوستاريكا خروسيه	78.60013	21.39987	News
على حزب الجبهة الوطنية الفرنسي عضوة زعيم التاريخي ومؤسس حزب جان مارام يدري لوبان	90.6374	9.362596	News
السابعة صباحة توقيت باريس، الطقس ممطر وبارد، متمنين لكم يوما سعيدا وموفقا أينما كنتم	12.92646	87.07354	Rumor

Figure 4. Classifier result of news test set

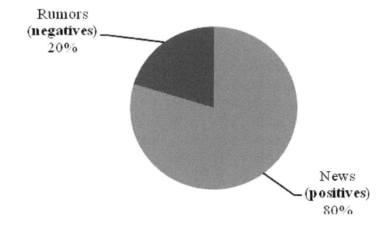

An extending perspective of application of rumors identification tool is to assess news, events, and ensure the publication of correct information to aide the peaceful conditions. Also, mitigate the propagation of false tweets (rumors) as well as confirm true tweets which also aide the reporters to publish the authentic information over the twitter.

In this research we have used the machine learning technique to verify the tweets on Twitter as news or rumors. Our model, based on the cosine similarity method to measure the Twitter tweets credibility. Our model succeeds to detect 67% of the rumors out of 100 confirmed rumors test set, Also the measurement model succeeds to detect 80% of the rumors out of 100 confirmed news test set. During the development of the model, all risk management concerns (Shahzad, 2006; Shahzad,2009; Shahzad 2010; Shahzad, 2014; Shahzad, 2011) were taken care of.

REFERENCES

Al-Khalifa, H. S., & Al-Eidan, R. M. (2011). An experimental system for measuring the credibility of news content in Twitter. *International Journal of Web Information Systems*, 7(2), 130–151. doi:10.1108/17440081111141772

Al-Ohali, Y., Al-Oraij, A. A., & ... (2011). KSU News Portal: A Case Study. *Proceedings of the International Conference on Internet Computing (ICOMP'11)*.

Alwagait, E., Shahzad, B., & ... (2014). Impact of social media usage on students academic performance in Saudi Arabia. *Computers in Human Behavior*.

Armstrong, C. L., & McAdams, M. J. (2009). Blogs of information: How gender cues and individual motivations influence perceptions of credibility. *Journal of Computer-Mediated Communication*, 14(3), 435–456. doi:10.1111/j.1083-6101.2009.01448.x

Basit Shahzad, E. A. (2013). Smartphone's Popularity Measurement by Investigating Twitter Profiles. *Proceedings of the 2013 Third World Congress on Information and Communication Technologies (WICT)*. IEEE. 10.1109/WICT.2013.7113093

Benevenuto, F., Magno, G., Rodrigues, T., & Almeida, V. (2010, July). Detecting spammers on twitter. In *Collaboration, electronic messaging, anti-abuse and spam conference* (Vol. 6, p. 12). CEAS.

T. Blog (2009). One hundred million voices. Retrieved from http://blog.twitter.com/2011/09/one-hundred-million-voices.html

Canini, K. R., Suh, B., & Pirolli, P. L. (2011, October). Finding credible information sources in social networks based on content and social structure. *Proceedings of the 2011 IEEE Third International Conference on Privacy, Security, Risk and Trust (PASSAT) and 2011 IEEE Third Inernational Conference on Social Computing (SocialCom)* (pp. 1-8). IEEE. 10.1109/PASSAT/SocialCom.2011.91

Castillo, C., Mendoza, M., & Poblete, B. (2011, March). Information credibility on twitter. *Proceedings of the 20th international conference on World wide web* (pp. 675-684). ACM.

Castillo, C., Mendoza, M., & Poblete, B. (2011). Information credibility on twitter. *Proceedings of the 20th international conference on World wide web* (pp. 675– 684). ACM.

Flanagin, A. J., & Metzger, M. J. (2000). Perceptions of Internet information credibility. *Journalism & Mass Communication Quarterly*, 77(3), 515–540. doi:10.1177/107769900007700304

Flanagin, A. J., & Metzger, M. J. (2007). The role of site features, user attributes, and information verification behaviors on the perceived credibility of web-based information. *New Media & Society*, *9*(2), 319–342. doi:10.1177/1461444807075015

Gupta, A., Kumaraguru, P., Castillo, C., & Meier, P. (2014, May). Tweetcred: A real-time Web-based system for assessing credibility of content on Twitter. *Proc. 6th International Conference on Social Informatics (SocInfo)*.

Java, A., Song, X., Finin, T., & Tseng, B. (2007, August). Why we twitter: understanding microblogging usage and communities. *Proceedings of the 9th WebKDD and 1st SNA-KDD 2007 workshop on Web mining and social network analysis* (pp. 56-65). ACM. 10.1145/1348549.1348556

Java, A., Song, X., Finin, T., & Tseng, B. (2007, August). Why we twitter: understanding microblogging usage and communities. *Proceedings of the 9th WebKDD and 1st SNA-KDD 2007 workshop on Web mining and social network analysis* (pp. 56-65). ACM. 10.1145/1348549.1348556

Java, A., Song, X., Finin, T., & Tseng, B. (2007, August). Why we twitter: understanding microblogging usage and communities. *Proceedings of the 9th WebKDD and 1st SNA-KDD 2007 workshop on Web mining and social network analysis* (pp. 56-65). ACM. 10.1145/1348549.1348556

Java, A., Song, X., Finin, T., & Tseng, B. (2007, August). Why we twitter: understanding microblogging usage and communities. *Proceedings of the 9th WebKDD and 1st SNA-KDD 2007 workshop on Web mining and social network analysis* (pp. 56-65). ACM. 10.1145/1348549.1348556

Java, A., Song, X., Finin, T., & Tseng, B. (2007, August). Why we twitter: understanding microblogging usage and communities. *Proceedings of the 9th WebKDD and 1st SNA-KDD 2007 workshop on Web mining and social network analysis* (pp. 56-65). ACM. 10.1145/1348549.1348556

Kang, B., O'Donovan, J., & Höllerer, T. (2012, February). Modeling topic specific credibility on twitter. *Proceedings of the 2012 ACM international conference on Intelligent User Interfaces* (pp. 179-188). ACM. 10.1145/2166966.2166998

Kohut, A., & Remez, M. (2008). *Internet overtakes newspapers as news outlet*. Pew Research Centre.

Kwak, H., Lee, C., Park, H., & Moon, S. (2010, April). What is Twitter, a social network or a news media? *Proceedings of the 19th international conference on World wide web* (pp. 591-600). ACM. 10.1145/1772690.1772751

Kwak, H., Lee, C., Park, H., & Moon, S. (2010, April). What is Twitter, a social network or a news media? *Proceedings of the 19th international conference on World wide web* (pp. 591-600). ACM. 10.1145/1772690.1772751

Kwon, K., Cho, J., & Park, Y. (2009). Multidimensional credibility model for neighbor selection in collaborative recommendation. *Expert Systems with Applications*, *36*(3), 7114–7122. doi:10.1016/j.eswa.2008.08.071

Laird, S. (2012). How social media is taking over the news industry. Retrieved from http://mashable.com/2012/04/18/social-media-and-the-news/

Mendoza, M., Poblete, B., & Castillo, C. (2010, July). Twitter Under Crisis: Can we trust what we RT? *Proceedings of the first workshop on social media analytics* (pp. 71-79). ACM. 10.1145/1964858.1964869

Mendoza, M., Poblete, B., & Castillo, C. (2010, July). Twitter Under Crisis: Can we trust what we RT? *Proceedings of the first workshop on social media analytics* (pp. 71-79). ACM. 10.1145/1964858.1964869

Naaman, M., Boase, J., & Lai, C. H. (2010, February). Is it really about me?: message content in social awareness streams. *Proceedings of the 2010 ACM conference on Computer supported cooperative work* (pp. 189-192). ACM. 10.1145/1718918.1718953

Naaman, M., Boase, J., & Lai, C. H. (2010, February). Is it really about me?: message content in social awareness streams. *Proceedings of the 2010 ACM conference on Computer supported cooperative work* (pp. 189-192). ACM. 10.1145/1718918.1718953

O'Donovan, J., Kang, B., Meyer, G., Hollerer, T., & Adalii, S. (2012, September). Credibility in context: An analysis of feature distributions in twitter. *Proceedings of the 2012 International Conference on Privacy, Security, Risk and Trust (PASSAT) and 2012 International Confernece on Social Computing (SocialCom)* (pp. 293-301). IEEE.

Ratkiewicz, J., Conover, M., Meiss, M., Gonçalves, B., Flammini, A., & Menczer, F. (2011, July). *Detecting and Tracking Political Abuse in Social Media*. ICWSM.

Ratkiewicz, J., Conover, M., Meiss, M., Gonçalves, B., Patil, S., Flammini, A., & Menczer, F. (2010). Detecting and tracking the spread of astroturf memes in microblog streams. arXiv preprint arXiv:1011.3768

Ratkiewicz, J., Conover, M., Meiss, M., Gonçalves, B., Patil, S., Flammini, A., & Menczer, F. (2011, March). Truthy: mapping the spread of astroturf in microblog streams. *Proceedings of the 20th international conference companion on World wide web* (pp. 249-252). ACM. 10.1145/1963192.1963301

Rieh, S. Y. (2002). Judgment of information quality and cognitive authority in the Web. *Journal of the American Society for Information Science and Technology*, *53*(2), 145–161. doi:10.1002/asi.10017

Schwarz, J., & Morris, M. (2011, May). Augmenting web pages and search results to support credibility assessment. *Proceedings of the SIGCHI Conference on Human Factors in Computing Systems* (pp. 1245-1254). ACM. 10.1145/1978942.1979127

Shahzad, B. (2014). Identification of Risk Factors in Large Scale Software Projects: A Quantitative Study. *International Journal of Knowledge Society Research*, *5*(1), 1–11. doi:10.4018/ijksr.2014010101

Shahzad, B., & Al-Mudimigh, A. S. (2010). Risk identification, mitigation and avoidance model for Handling software risk. *Proceedings of the 2010 Second International Conference on Computational Intelligence, Communication Systems and Networks (CICSyN)*. IEEE 10.1109/CICSyN.2010.82

Shahzad, B., Al-Ohali, Y., & ... (2011). Trivial model for mitigation of risks in software development life cycle. *Int. J. Phys. Sci*, *6*(8), 2072–2082.

Shahzad, B., & Alwagait, E. (2014). Best and the Worst Times to Tweet: An Experimental Study. *Proceedings of the 15th International Conference on Mathematics and Computers in Business and Economics (MCBE '14)*. World Society of Engineering and Applied Sciences.

Shahzad, B., & Alwagait, E. (2014). Maximization of Tweet's Viewership with respect to Time. *Proceedings of the World Symposium on Computer Applications & Research*, Tunisia. IEEE.

Shahzad, B., Iqbal, J., & ... (2006). Distributed risk analysis using relative impact technique. *Proceedings of the 3rd Asian Conference on Intelligent Systems and Networks* (pp. 433-439).

Shahzad, B., Ullah, I., et al. (2009). Software risk identification and mitigation in incremental model. *Proceedings of the International Conference on Information and Multimedia Technology ICIMT'09*. IEEE. 10.1109/ICIMT.2009.104

Starbird, K., Palen, L., Hughes, A. L., & Vieweg, S. (2010, February). Chatter on the red: what hazards threat reveals about the social life of microblogged information. *Proceedings of the 2010 ACM conference on Computer supported cooperative work* (pp. 241-250). ACM. 10.1145/1718918.1718965

Starbird, K., Palen, L., Hughes, A. L., & Vieweg, S. (2010, February). Chatter on the red: what hazards threat reveals about the social life of microblogged information. *Proceedings of the 2010 ACM conference on Computer supported cooperative work* (pp. 241-250). ACM. 10.1145/1718918.1718965

Vieweg, S. (2010). Microblogged contributions to the emergency arena: Discovery, interpretation and implications. In *Computer Supported Collaborative Work* (pp. 515-516).

Vieweg, S. (2010). Microblogged contributions to the emergency arena: Discovery, interpretation and implications. In *Computer Supported Collaborative Work* (pp. 515-516).

Vieweg, S. (2010). Microblogged contributions to the emergency arena: Discovery, interpretation and implications. In *Computer Supported Collaborative Work* (pp. 515-516).

Vieweg, S., Hughes, A. L., Starbird, K., & Palen, L. (2010, April). Microblogging during two natural hazards events: what twitter may contribute to situational awareness. *Proceedings of the SIGCHI conference on human factors in computing systems* (pp. 1079-1088). ACM. 10.1145/1753326.1753486

Xia, X., Yang, X., Wu, C., Li, S., & Bao, L. (2012). Information credibility on twitter in emergency situation. In *Intelligence and Security Informatics* (pp. 45–59). Springer Berlin Heidelberg. doi:10.1007/978-3-642-30428-6_4

Yang, F., Liu, Y., Yu, X., & Yang, M. (2012, August). Automatic detection of rumor on sina weibo. *Proceedings of the ACM SIGKDD Workshop on Mining Data Semantics* (p. 13). ACM. 10.1145/2350190.2350203

Yang, F. L., Yu, Y., & Yang, X., Min. (2012). Automatic detection of rumor on Sina Weibo. *Paper presented at the ACM SIGKDD Workshop on Mining Data Semantics*.

This research was previously published in International Journal of Knowledge Society Research (IJKSR), 7(2); edited by Miltiadis D. Lytras and Linda Daniela; pages 72-83, copyright year 2016 by IGI Publishing (an imprint of IGI Global).

Section 4
Media Representation and Bias

Chapter 14
Exploring the Complexities Associated to Victimization:
Addressing Media Sensationalism and Race

Erica Hutton

Hutton Criminal Profiling and Associates, USA

ABSTRACT

The following chapter addresses both the presence and complexities that are associated to the reports of victimization within the media in direct correlation to the element of how racial disparities sensationalize certain incidents of crime. The terminology pertaining to news coverage is also identified and described in regards to the modality of planning in the report of the news; in addition, the perspectives of racial conflict is expounded upon to include the sociological influences, ecological effects, and the criminological theories that best describe the cyclical reactions of race-related bias in the media. The discussion explores previous literature centered upon racial bias in media coverage and the areas that appear to be sensationalized more so than not. The goal of news broadcasting and narrowcasting are delineated upon as well as correlating measures associated to the perception of unequal treatment and fear of crime.

INTRODUCTION

It is no secret or surprise that certain types of crime appear to receive more concentration within the media; furthermore, the broadcasting is typically perceived to be somewhat true as the reporting is authenticated as "news". There are many avenues associated to media to include any of the following circuits:

- Wiki,
- Blogging,
- Google,
- Wikipedia,
- iPod,

DOI: 10.4018/978-1-5225-9869-5.ch014

- MySpace,
- Facebook,
- Youtube,
- Twitter, and
- Instragram (Surette, 2014).

However, for the purpose of this chapter, the discussion will center upon news coverage within the media, specifically, news coverage and victimization. What makes something sensational? Attention, popularity, and innovation. Such a phenomenon directly effects societal perceptions of victimization, narrowing the realm of what the public is aware of. Media and public reaction to high profile cases directly form stereotypes based upon the racialized assumptions of the public (Johnson, Warren, & Farrell, 2015). The intriguing aspect to consider in exploring the bias that subsists throughout media reporting is that not only does this effect the types of crime that society believes to occur, but this also effects the types of crime that victims are subjected to, as well as the types of perpetrators that typically participate in crime commission. These are three very disparate measures to consider, but they are all interrelated based upon the result of bias media reporting of victimization, based upon the singular notion of race.

For example, the majority of the world is under the impression that serial killers are predominantly White; however, Blacks now comprise one out of every two serial killers (Hickey, 2015). Subsequently, it could be stated that maybe one of the reasons that society is under the impression that Black serial killers are rare is due to the lack of media concentration and/or reporting of such incidents. In addition, Black victims of serial killers have the propensity to go unrecognized or at best receive substantially less media-related attention than White victims of serial killers (Hickey, 2015). Americans tend to sensationalize serial killers in general, due to the glorification of the heinous incidents that occur in such cases. Furthermore, another reason that society may hear more about White serial killers could be based on the fact that their victims are also typically White. One may believe that murder occurs all the time; however, this is false. Murder is classified as a Type I crime which means that this type of crime is perceived to be violent; therefore, the FBI classifies it as such. In addition, although murder is heard on the news quite often, it is actually the smallest Type I crime in regards to incident, meaning that this type of crime does not occur very often in regards to other Type I crimes, such as rape or robbery.

Another example pertains to the occurrence of police brutality; rarely is there news coverage in which White victims fall prey to police brutality but they certainly do, as well as Latinos. Usually, the shootings are found to be high-profile incidents with exponential news coverage and reporting alike. With this type of reporting, there is a correlation of accompanying inquiries into policing, social response of race, and criminal justice policy (Kahn & Martin, 2016). An interesting area to explore in regards to compliance or cooperation is that if we examine the crime of robbery, Blacks are less likely to cooperate with their perpetrator, when they are the victim; likewise, they are also less likely to cooperate with police as well. Future areas of research include the investigation of the variables associated to trust and the various reasons that Blacks do not wish to cooperate with police (Felson & Lantz, 2016).

Bias reporting in the media directly correlates with society's perception of what, how, and why in the realm of victimization. The media reports, through various claims, who is typically most likely to be victimized as well as who is most likely to be the perpetrator of certain types of crime; however, the correlates associated to crime are much more complex than this. The remainder of this chapter aims to address the various complexities in detail with the goal of illustrating the level of distortion in reporting claims of victimization based upon racial disparities that directly reflect such assertions.

Applicable Constructs of Perspective

Theoretical tenets are applied to the investigation of crime to assist in the comprehensive assessment of what causes crime, why it occurs, why certain victims are selected, and even the variables associated to the prevention of crime. For the purpose of this discussion, there are four perspectives that have been selected to exemplify how racial bias subsists in the media in regards to the reporting of victimization and crime. The following perspectives will be explored and delineated upon in correlation to the occurrence and effects of bias that is widespread within the media in regards to the reporting of victimization:

- Sociological.
- Ecological.
- Criminological.

Sociological Construct

The exploration of social equality purports that all individuals within society have the right to a social status that is considered to be equivalent to one another; this realm thrives as an ideology for individuals to relate to one another in social settings (Servaes & Oyedemi, 2016). The sociological perspective is addressed first in this discussion due to the fact that racial disparities and the perception of bias of this type is rather sociological in nature; in addition, these assumptions are based upon the level of subjectivity associated to such issues. For example, there are many that would state that they do not believe that race is an issue within society in regards to bias media coverage or inequality within the punitive system at all. This perspective could be based on the fact that they are not of a minority race or classification and have never had to personally face such measures; therefore, within their reality, race is not an issue for how they are treated and so forth. However, this would be erroneous. Race is most certainly a division that not only subsists throughout our nation but also categorically ploys the perspective of behavior, expectations, and even consequential actions based upon bias associated to certain racial categorizations.

When considering the effect of racial bias on society, it is important to inquire as to both self and group perceptions of race in intergroup relationships in correlation to media influence and identification alike (Tukachinsky, 2015). Social stratification is the occurrence of uneven or imbalanced distribution within society; this reaction is what results in varying social classes (Healey & O'Brien, 2015). The negative connotations of perception and racial bias does not only affect minorities and their perception of their placement within society, this consequence also modifies the perception of the majority, encouraging the bias received through media confirmation. One of the largest issues in the criminal justice system today pertains to the occurrence of racial profiling by the police. Police prejudices, whether individually based or community based, initiates with attitudinal perceptions that are established, based upon what is heard of these incidents within the news (Weitzer & Tuch, 2005). When considering the ecological results of implicit bias in race, both Forscher and Devine (2015) purport that such a complex issue within our communities may result in a public health problem. In addition, derogatory measures or perceptions that are either implicit or intentional appear to fuel community cohesiveness, whether the communities are being broken down and the system ultimately diminished, or strengthened, with the system improving (Surette, 2014). When we hear the term Muslim, we automatically divert to a specific classification based upon perception of what is known about this culture and ethnicity; this type of deduction is based upon the association that is socially conditioned. This association is not diminished when we hear Whites or

Blacks either; each race/ethnicity is subjected to judgment, which is not an innovative concept of course, but again, what we know socially about various races is based on the social placement and well-being of each group within society in general. A national research study conducted by Charles, Kramer, Torres, and Brunn-Bevel (2015) revealed Black identity and racial ideologies are a result of childhood experiences of segregation and disorganization that was experienced on a sociological level.

Different types of crime symbolically convey fear, concern, and vigilance from society; however, reports of crime have the power to condition societal awareness of who is most likely to play the role of the victim versus the role of the perpetrator. These associations are also based upon various types of crime and supports the correlation that certain individuals are more likely to commit certain types of crime. This social transference is conditioned based upon how many times it appears in the news. There is a component of competition associated to social construction and when there is a sense of winning the competition, ownership is the result. Therefore, in regards to the social construct of media coverage, the dominate pattern fuels the development and conditioning process of the construction (Surette, 2014). Societal treatment can also have an impact on trust as a study revealed that Blacks have a greater distrust towards the health care system than Whites (Shoff & Yang, 2012).

Ecological Construct

Racial bias is a concept that is behavioral and continues to progress within a cyclical manner throughout every level of society. Ultimately, minor implicit racial associations have major influences over social population pockets based upon interpretation and effect (Greenwald, Banagi, & Nosek, 2015). Ecological tenets contemplate the presence and functionality of how individuals interrelate with one another. The analysis of social inequalities from the media and communicative perspectives encompasses both a cultural and transcultural association (Appadurai, 2013; Hepp, 2015); subsequently, the concept of market value in the news represents an implicit undertone of divide, based upon the message reported and/or received (as cited in Servaes & Oyedemi, 2016). When exploring cultures outside of the United States, Hungarians reveal that there are similar associations regarding the presence of racial bias received by the media with particular focus centered upon Latinos and Blacks, with attitudinal positions that White's hold towards these groupings (Tukachinsky, 2015). While many claim that racial bias divides societal pockets, there is research that asserts that there are advantages with societal multiplicity.

There are two predominant forms of diversity:

1. Disunion that subsists within groups that thrive in our communities.
2. The removal of obstacles that limit the presence of diversity and opportunity (Galinsky, Todd, Homan, Phillips, Apfelbaum, Sasaki, Richeson, Olayon, & Maddux, 2015).

Another ecological association applicable to our discussion is the transaction that takes place between an individual's responses to the environment; therefore, one's environment contributes to one's adjustment and approach to societal reaction alike (Pardeck, 2015). When racial bias is sensationalized within the media, these effects translate over into the schools as children begin to test their boundaries, based upon the suggestive measures that are initiated in these communities and further confirmed by the news (Davis, Lyubansky, & Schiff, 2015).

Criminological Construct

The criminological construct explores the lens of behavior based upon the criminality of racial bias; this section will investigate the applications associated to motive of racial bias, how this phenomenon is conditioned, and why this cycle of prejudice and discrimination is associated to crime and criminal justice. The first perspective to address is the labeling theory. According to Merton (1967), an individual's social identification fuels behavior; therefore, when a particular label has been applied, the goal is to meet the standards of that behavior (as cited in Gabbidon, 2015). The label may be derogatory in nature or encouraging, the cycle flourishes either way. In regards to race, there are many negative associations and terms that are utilized as deprecating labels; likewise, such labels are confirmed through behavior, proving that this occurrence is tautological in nature. Goffman (1963) asserted that in regards to the labeling perspective, society was the predominant determinant for those populations that are labeled and those populations that subsist under the radar, remaining unlabeled (as cited in Gabbidon, 2015).

Many identifications are a direct result of assumptions that are constructed by individuals or groups of individuals; as a result, such prejudices have the power to influence variables of what is known in the criminal justice arena to include the occurrence of crime, fear of crime, configurations of criminality, and even patterns that are prevalent within the punitive system, all based upon a race related label.

The next perspective contemplated for the discussion is conflict theory. Conflict theory is also known as critical theory with credence afforded to Karl Marx, George Simmel, and Max Weber (Gabbidon, 2015). The conflict theory explores the behaviors that occur as a result of differential associations in power, and the various struggles that ensue as a direct product of such discriminatory engagements. The characteristics and features associated to this type of influence pertain to race, socioeconomic status, gender, and political affiliation. The assembly of power in society acts as a foundation to the disparate behaviors that exist and continue to thrive which ultimately results in conflict between the varying populations.

Discrimination and Division

According to Law (2016), discrimination is the inequity of treatment for those that have been formally or informally grouped into a specific classification and therefore, subjected to critical responses. Not only does media coverage result in the prolongation of various stereotypes and discriminatory beliefs, but the content regarding the reporting of victimization towards minorities is biased (Geschke, Sassenberg, Ruhrmann, & Sommer, 2015). Such incidents ultimately cultivate and foster erroneous levels of prejudicial responses due to the measure and modality in which media coverage is reported. The age of the viewer may also contribute to the measure of perception. For example, a study conducted by Watt, Fitzpatrick, Derevensky, and Pagani (2015) revealed that children that have daily viewing of the television were at an increased risk for being victimized by their classmates by the end of sixth grade due to lower self-esteem, traces of depression, mental health concerns, and the overall effects of underachievement. It is highly suggested that there is parental monitoring in television viewing, even when children are simply watching the news.

Significant divisions pertaining to race is not a sociological anomaly; however, such prejudicial standards shape and implement racial disparities within the justice system based on the preservation of bias in media reporting (Hutchings, 2015). Moreover, the Sentencing Project (1986) was ultimately established for the purpose of introducing reformation within the punitive process as a non-profit organization, primarily sponsoring alternatives and reductions in sentencing due to plausible unwarranted racial reinforcements (Hutchings, 2015). In addition, these said reinforcements are complex due to a broad level of application that appear to be multifaceted in nature, based upon concepts that are sociological, psychological, political, and even cultural; the perception of crime is effected by each of these categorizations, as societal perception is a compound phenomenon.

A study conducted by Dixon and Linz (2000), revealed that Latinos and Blacks have higher rate of being affiliated with breaking the law versus being a victim of crime; nevertheless, the opposite is realistic for Whites. Likewise, the fear of crime is directly a result of what the media portrays as being dangerous; mass media is responsible for the highest correlating source in regards to encouraging such fear (Weitzer & Kubrin, 2006). While comprehending that the manner in which the media presents the reporting of either perpetration or victimization, such reports do influence the perception of racial disparities within the realm of crime and/or fear of crime; however, it should be noted that this concept is a bit tautological in nature due to the fact that the criminal justice system reports can also directly fuel the media coverage and the presence of bias related responses to crime commission (Hayes, 2016).

What is the Problem?

Many could state that racial bias has always been an issue within society and most likely will always be an issue; in addition, the sensationalism associated to the reports of victimization within news coverage not only affects the perception of crime occurrence but also affects the perception of the criminal justice system and the response to social stratification. The problematic concern regarding the presence of racial bias in media coverage would seem to be elementary and obvious at best. However, the problem is generated by so many elements that the issue is quite complex. There is a synergistic component in which the variables of societal response, criminal justice policy, and the fear of crime all interlock with one another (Kahn & Martin, 2016). The sociological aspects of racial inequality have always existed; however, there has been a significant shift within this arena as the social inequalities are considered to be somewhat secondary and the punitive inequalities have now taken the forefront (Drakulich, 2015). The inherent approach of exploring the racial effects on a national level illustrate that racial bias is a concept that most are aware of and yet this issue continues to infect our society. Elements that first and foremost need to be considered is centered upon the areas that negate racial tension and the presence of various biases that are reflective within the media.

The Effects of the Problem

Attitudes that members of society hold towards the criminal justice system are extremely influential. There is a cycle that subsists within society in which the criminal justice system represents order, equality, and union; subsequently, when the decree of cases that have received heavy media reporting reveal an antagonistic ruling, respect and appreciation are deprecated on a vast level, locally and nationally. Skepticism and the role of the punitive system is not a new issue or concern; however, this phenomenon continues to illustrate problematic measures that directly disturbs the relationship between society and the media, society and the fear of crime, society and the perception of violence, and even society and the role of the criminal justice system.

Colorism is the differential treatment and or discriminatory reaction based on the color of one's skin; although this is not the same as racism, there are racial constituents present within the interpretation of colorism (Burch, 2015). Colorism is alive and well within society and always has been. There are so many individuals that are currently incarcerated, completely innocent of their conviction. Black Lives Matter is somewhat of an innovative movement in addressing the unification of Blacks within communities; the goal is to address the authorization of liberation for the purpose of modifying social identity based upon a collectivistic effort (Kahn & Martin, 2016). Black males are in the news more so than Black females and it is obvious that news coverage in regards to racial teetering concentrates more so on minorities with the manipulation of facts resulting in a skewed ecological perspective (Johnson, Warren, & Farrell, 2015). Black males that are darker in skin color are more likely to have a history of criminal behavior than their lighter counterparts (Burch, 2015). According to Tukachinsky (2015), racial disparity is only one avenue of classification in regards to the plausible presence of bias with other areas encompassing age, social economic status, gender, and sexual orientation.

Knoxville, Tennessee

In 2007, Channon Gail Christian and Hugh Christopher Newsom Jr. were killed in a heinous manner; they were both raped, tortured, and murdered. Their vehicle was carjacked and they were subsequently forced into a rental home by five individuals. What makes the actions heinous are the characteristics regarding the attacks that won't be delineated upon for the purpose of this chapter but include:

- Sodomization,
- Set on fire, and
- The drinking of bleach.

This crime did not make national news reports; claims were made that this was due to the race of the victims. In this case, the victims were White and the 5 assailants were Black; moreover, this crime was not deemed to be racially motivated or classified as being a hate crime. Murder is the smallest Type I offense with the FBI Uniform Crime Report (2013) reporting that approximately 83% of Whites were killed by White perpetrators and 90% of Blacks were killed by Black offenders (as cited in Lee, 2014).

Logan County, West Virginia

In 2007, Megan Williams, Black, was kidnapped, raped, and endured torturous acts while held captive in a shed on the property of five White perpetrators. Although her case was not deemed to be a hate crime on a local level, the case was said to have racial undertones of being a hate crime on a federal level with one defendant being charged with a hate crime for the attack. The injurious elements that occurred in this case include:

- A rape,
- Burning with hot water,
- Stabbing the victim,
- Pulling out chunks of hair,
- Eating human, rat, and dog feces,
- And at times racial slurs were used during such acts.

This case received national attention and news coverage was devoted to revealing her experience and survival.

It is unrealistic for every incident of crime to receive news coverage; however, national coverage is often based upon the sensationalism in regards to the races involved in the incident. Popular areas in which racial bias appears to be present within the criminal justice system range from racial profiling by officers, favorable verdicts made by jurors that are not minorities, and the assessment of the presence of racial disparity among the death penalty (Hunt, 2015).

Varying Effects of Bias in the Media

According to Surettte (2014), narrowcasting, the opposite of broadcasting, pertains to the type of news that occurs in the media in which there are a large number of reports with minimal content within the information recounted. Narrowcasting is a popular phenomenon within the criminal justice arena due to the concentrated details asserted in certain types of crime; for example, it is rare to hear of an obese rapist or of female perpetrators in domestic violence crimes, but both can certainly occur, and do. Who controls the news and the reports that are perceived to be intriguing? Society. The consumer is the most commanding participant in regards to media sensationalism due to the fact that demand and scope are determined by those that are viewing the news; furthermore, if the news is not deemed to be thought-provoking or stimulating, there is a chance that the consumer will change the channel or falsely exaggerate the reports made (Surette, 2014).

The elements in regards to shaping the manner in which individuals fear crime are composite and appear to be rather multidimensional, based upon the sensationalism of victimization. Societal reactions are formulated as demographic factors and location correlate with one another, demonstrating that there is a relationship between those that are criminals and those that are victims (Weitzer & Kubrin, 2006). Fear of crime may be a result of such reports, cultivating a sense of catastrophe that not only is unrealistic but at times unwarranted altogether. Racial composition effects the perception of crime, epitomizing societal reactions, beliefs, and political perspectives of fear and crime commission. Dixon and Williams (2014) proffer innovative research to assert that television media reports are no longer over-representing Blacks as criminals and Whites as victims and officers; oftentimes, Blacks are now less visible within the news and are under-represented as violent predators or victims of crime. Latinos and Muslims are over-represented as terrorists on both the network and cable news media reports with half the crimes that are even reported on network news classified as being violent crime (Dixon & Williams, 2014). There have been innovative measures enforced to address racial bias and equality. The Black and Missing Foundation was established in 2008 for the purpose of bringing additional awareness and concentration to the occurrence of missing person's that are Black (BAMFI, 2015). The End Racial Profiling Act of 2015 has been assigned to a committee within the congressional arena for the purpose of national attention to be afforded to the termination of racial profiling within policing. The Puerto Rican Legal Defense and Education Fund initiated in 1972, founded for the purpose of addressing the Latino injustice within America.

Historically speaking, racial and ethnic disparities as well as journalism-related politics have a direct impact on the bias present within the media. It may be surprising to note that accuracy in news reporting is not the most important area of concentration or importance; moreover, focus and concern is more so devoted to those programmers that persistently rake in higher ratings in effort to increase revenue. Another area of awareness is the availability of accurate data; for example, do police tend to kill more

Blacks or Whites? The answer appears to be transparent and even obvious; however, if your perception is that police tend to kill more Blacks than Whites, you would be wrong. Therefore, the question that must be considered or contemplated is why do we think that police tend to kill more Blacks? In fact, the 2015 United States Census Bureau reported these figures to be 77% to 13% in regards to the number of Whites that are killed by police officers versus Blacks; in addition, population size must be taken into account to accurately measure such occurrences (Kahn & Martin, 2016).

Media coverage extends more concentration upon the deaths of minorities that fall prey to victimization by the hands of the police versus reporting and that is why society is under the impression and even epitomizes erroneous reports. Recent motives have positioned upon the absorption of interfaith conflicts and interracial issues, resulting in the over-representation of Latinos as being a population reflective of undocumented immigrants and Muslims over-represented as terrorists (Dixon & Wallace, 2014). An innovative lens to explore the perception and effects of bias within the media is the guard dog perspective. This lens is contemplative, focusing on the constrictions and limitations of journalism and the insensible level of bias that fuel such outlooks. Dixon and Wallace (2014) assert that this lens is utilized to focus on a threat to encourage concern towards national security and those that are the least in power within the nation, are the ones that typically receive the majority of the bias within news coverage.

The perception of news coverage can result in negative influences based upon the unconscious or indirect bias toward the rights of immigrants and the threat theory that is implied to accept members of this population into our communities (Seate & Mastro, 2015). A study conducted by Dixon (2015), asserts that Latinos are under-represented in regards to being victims with Whites over-represented. According to Hayes (2016), the media directly shapes the perception of the public in regards to who is most likely to fall prey to victimization and who is most likely to be found the perpetrator of crime.

CONCLUSION

In conclusion, this chapter delineated upon the complexities associated to the prevalence of racial bias in the reporting of victimization and crime within the media. Although the problem prevalent within the discussion should be obvious, it actually is not as simplistic and congruent as one would expect due to the fact that the level of harm is really immeasurable and there are so many influential concepts that contribute to the complexities in addressing this topic as a whole. The elements that encourage the complexities associated to racial bias is not solely purposed on media coverage but rather one's peers, families, neighborhoods, and school-related dynamics all compound together for the purpose of creating racial perceptions of youth and these attitudes continue to be fostered as they are confirmed in social reactions (Tukachinsky, 2015). It is suggested that future research efforts should be devoted to the measurement of implicit racial bias and use of force (Fridell & Lim, 2016).

There are several different perspectives that pertain to defining the effects and impact that encourages the cyclical reaction of racial bias throughout society that include the sociological, ecological, and criminological aspects of behavior. Colorism is not synonymous with racism; however, the aspect of race and the exploration of differential treatment is the predominant principality of colorism. What is known is that race directly effects the media that is portrayed in news coverage, narrowcasting, and broadcasting alike. These disparities are also influential within the criminal justice system with various efforts devoted to the establishment of initiatives that support and represent the rights of minorities within the justice system.

REFERENCES

Black and Missing Foundation. (2015). Retrieved from http://www.blackandmissinginc.com/cdad/about.htm

Burch, T. (2015). Skin color and the criminal justice system: Beyond Black-White disparities in sentencing. *Journal of Empirical Legal Studies*, *12*(3), 395–420. doi:10.1111/jels.12077

Charles, C. Z., Kramer, R. A., Torres, K. C., & Brunn-Bevel, R. J. (2015). Intragroup heterogeneity and blackness: Effects of racial classification, immigrant origins, social class, and social context on the racial identity of elite college students. *Race and Social Problems*, *7*(4), 281–299. doi:10.100712552-015-9157-2

Davis, F. E., Lyubansky, M., & Schiff, M. (2015). *Restoring racial justice. Emerging Trends in the Social and Behavioral Sciences: An Interdisciplinary, Searchable, and Linkable Resource*. Hoboken, NJ: John Wiley & Sons. doi:10.1002/9781118900772.etrds0288

Dixon, T. L. (2015). Good guys are still always in white? Positive change and continued misrepresentation of race and crime on local television news. *Communication Research*. doi:10.1177/0093650215579223

Dixon, T. L., & Linz, D. (2000). Race and the misrepresentation of victimization on local television news. *Communication Research*, *27*(5), 547–573. doi:10.1177/009365000027005001

Dixon, T. L., & Williams, C. L. (2014). The changing misrepresentation of race and crime on network and cable news. *Journal of Communication*, *65*(1), 24–39. doi:10.1111/jcom.12133

Drakulich, K. M. (2015). The hidden role of racial bias in support for policies related to inequality and crime. *Punishment and Society*, *17*(5), 541–574. doi:10.1177/1462474515604041

Felson, R. B., & Lantz, B. (2016). When are victims unlikely to cooperate with the police? *Aggressive Behavior*, *43*(1), 97–108. doi:10.1002/ab.21626 PMID:26602192

Forscher, P. S., & Devine, P. G. (2015). *Controlling the influence of stereotypes on one's thoughts. In Emerging Trends in the Social and Behavioral Sciences: An Interdisciplinary*. doi:10.1002/9781118900772.etrds0054

Fridell, L., & Lim, H. (2016). Assessing the racial aspects of police force using the implicit-and counter-bias perspectives. *Journal of Criminal Justice*, *44*, 36–48. doi:10.1016/j.jcrimjus.2015.12.001

Gabbidon, S. L. (2015). *Criminological perspectives on race and crime* (3rd ed.). New York, NY: Taylor & Francis Group.

Galinksy, A. D., Todd, A. R., Homan, A. C., Phillips, K. W., Apfelbaum, E. P., Sasaki, S. J., ... Maddux, W. W. (2015). Minimizing the gains and minimizing the pains of diversity: A policy perspective. *Perspectives on Psychological Science*, *10*(6), 742–748. doi:10.1177/1745691615598513 PMID:26581729

Geschke, D., Sassenberg, K., Ruhrmann, G., & Sommer, D. (2015). Effects of linguistic abstractness in the mass media: How newspaper articles shape readers' attitudes toward migrants. *Journal of Media Psychology*, *22*(3). doi:10.1027/1864-1105/a000014

Greenwald, A. G., Banaji, M. R., & Nosek, B. A. (2015). Statistically small effects of the implicit association test can have societally large effects. *Journal of Personality and Social Psychology*, *108*(4), 553–561. doi:10.1037/pspa0000016 PMID:25402677

Hayes, R. M. (2016). *Media and crime. In The Encyclopedia of Crime and Punishment.* Hoboken, NJ: John Wiley & Sons; doi:10.1002/9781118519639.wbecpx108

Healey, J. F., & O'Brien, E. (2015). *Race, ethnicity, gender, & class: The sociology of group conflict and change* (7th ed.). Thousand Oaks, CA: Sage Publications.

Hickey, E. W. (2015). *Serial murderers and their victims* (7th ed.). Boston, MA: Cengage Learning.

Hunt, J. S. (2015). Race in the justice system. In APA handbook of forensic psychology: Criminal investigation, adjudication, and sentencing outcomes (vol. 2, pp. 125-161). Washington, DC: US American Psychological Association. doi:10.1037/14462-005

Hutchings, V. (2015). Race, punishment, and public opinion. *Perspectives on Politics*, *13*(3), 757–761. doi:10.1017/S1537592715001310

Johnson, D., Warren, P. Y., & Farrell, A. (2015). *Deadly injustice: Trayvon Martin, race, and the criminal justice system.* New York University Press.

Kahn, K. B., & Martin, K. D. (2016). Policing and race: Disparate treatment, perceptions, and policy responses. *Social Issues and Policy Review*, *10*(1), 82–121. doi:10.1111ipr.12019

Law, I. (2015). *Discrimination, categorical and statistical. In The Wiley Blackwell Encyclopedia of Race, Ethnicity, and Nationalism.* Hoboken, NJ: Wiley Blackwell; doi:10.1002/9781118663202.wberen022

Lee, M. Y. H. (2014). Giuliani's claim that 93 percent of black murder victims are killed by other blacks. *The Washington Post.* Retrieved from, https://www.washingtonpost.com/news/fact-checker/wp/2014/11/25/giulianis-claim-that-93-percent-of-blacks-are-killed-by-other-blacks/

Pardeck, J. T. (2015). An ecological approach for social work practice. *Journal of Sociology and Social Welfare*, *15*(2), 133–142.

Seate, A. A., & Mastro, D. (2015). *Media's influence on immigration attitudes: An intergroup threat theory approach.* Communication Monographs. Taylor Francis Group.

Servaes, J., & Oyedemi, T. (2016). *Social inequalities, media, and communication: Theory and roots.* Lanham, MD: Lexington Books.

Shoff, C., & Yang, T. C. (2012). Untangling the associations among distrust, race, and neighborhood social environment: A social disorganization perspective. *Social Science & Medicine*, *74*(9), 1342–1352. doi:10.1016/j.socscimed.2012.01.012 PMID:22425069

Surette, R. (2014). *Media, crime, and criminal justice: Images, realities, and policies* (5th ed.). Stamford, CT: Cengage Learning.

Tukachinsky, R. (2015). Where we have been and where we can go from here: Looking to the future in research on media, race, and ethnicity. *The Journal of Social Issues*, *71*(1), 186–199. doi:10.1111/josi.12104

Watt, E., Fitzpatrick, C., Derevensky, J. L., & Pagani, L. S. (2015). Too much television? Prospective associations between early childhood televiewing and later self-reports of victimization by sixth grade classmate. *Journal of Developmental and Behavioral Pediatrics*, *36*(6), 426–433. doi:10.1097/DBP.0000000000000186 PMID:26075581

Weitzer, R., & Kubrin, C. E. (2006). Breaking news: How local TV news and real-world conditions affect fear of crime. *Justice Quarterly*, *21*(3), 497–520. doi:10.1080/07418820400095881

Weitzer, R., & Tuch, S. A. (2005). Racially biased policing: Determinants of citizen perceptions. *Social Forces*, *83*(3), 1009–1030. doi:10.1353of.2005.0050

Chapter 15
Racial Spectacle and Campus Climate:
Media Representations and Asian International Student Perceptions at U.S. Colleges

Kenneth Robert Roth
California State University, USA

Zachary S. Ritter
University of Redlands, USA

ABSTRACT

Media spectacle has become an important way countries, culture, and commerce is expressed in the global marketplace. Media spectacle is a combination of power and capital and in its final form produces ideology. The U.S. is the global leader in the production and distribution of media, accounting for one-third of more than $90 billion annually in worldwide film distribution alone. U.S. media representations can be distinctive due to their racial dialogue and International college students with little exposure to the U.S. outside of media depictions arrive in America with perceptions that may be detrimental to campus climate. Supported by two independent qualitative studies, this chapter interrogates implications media representations may have for cross-cultural interactions. We identify ways U.S. colleges and universities are addressing campus climate issues, and how these efforts may not be enough. We call for increased diversity training across curricula to promote greater tolerance.

INTRODUCTION

When rising pop star Bruno Mars was named the headliner for the half time show of Super Bowl 48 in 2014, many of America's biggest and most influential media outlets wondered out loud whether the Hawaiian-born singer-songwriter was sufficiently luminary to stand among America's gridiron gladiators and wow the crowd (Atkinson, 2013; D'Addario, 2014; Ryan, 2014). After all, the Super Bowl is arguably

DOI: 10.4018/978-1-5225-9869-5.ch015

the most celebrated annual media spectacle in America, and inclusion in its halftime festivities signals entrée into the pantheon of the globe's great performers. The reason why Mars accepted the gig should be obvious, since already he has been characterized as the likely successor to the once and previous King of Pop, Michael Jackson (Benhaim, 2013; Levin, 2013). But what these media pundits didn't mention was Bruno's cross-racial appeal in light of his racially mixed heritage as a Puerto Rican-Filipino-American. This appeal plays well, both domestically and internationally, and may signify a cultural acknowledgement of the ascendancy of a mixed America. Mars' spectacular performance also offers a glimpse into how positive representations in media spectacles have implications for career trajectories, promoting racial acceptance, and portraying an egalitarian inclusivity. For days after the Super Bowl, a widely circulated social media meme flipped the spectacle by proclaiming, "Apparently there was a football game at the Bruno Mars concert" (Nicotheory: So...Apparently There Was A... 2014).

Alternately, as Lou Jing took a bow after her performance on China's version of the U.S. talent show, *American Idol*, viewers flooded social media outlets with comments such as, "she never should have been born," and she should "get out of China" (Chang, 2009). The 20-year-old Chinese-born woman, who was referred to by show hosts as *Chocolate Girl*, was the daughter of a Chinese mother and African American father. Her nationally televised performance and the subsequent reaction by viewers sparked a countrywide debate on race.

Depictions of people of African descent in East Asia are often problematic and fraught with stereotypes (Dikotter, 1997; Fujioka, 2000; Johnson, 2007; Russell, 1991; Talbot, 1999). These stereotypes are likely framed by imported media representations of race, and may have implications for cross-cultural interactions. As more East Asians, particularly Chinese, become a larger portion of the United States' higher education landscape as international students, it is likely campus relations between them and African American students may be strained, due in large part to stereotypes they've formed based on other examples of U.S. media spectacle that are not as racially accepting and inclusive as the Bruno Mars example.

The circulation on the Internet of an image of the uncovered dead body of 17-year-old Trayvon Martin, an unarmed teenage black male who was fatally shot by a neighborhood watch vigilante (Alvarez, 2013) comes to mind. Like front page newspaper accounts of the lynching of black men and women in the U.S. well into the middle of the 20th century, where bodies were shown hanging from trees or lying bloody on the ground (Chandler, 2013), Martin's body was splayed out on a lawn, his legs and arms akimbo, and his lifeless eyes staring upward into the night (Nyasha, 2013). Images of non-black males subjected to any similar fate are almost never seen, with the possible exception of Reginald Denney, who was not killed but beaten during broadcast coverage of rioting in South Los Angeles following the acquittal of LAPD officers who had savagely beaten an unarmed Rodney King, a black man, during a traffic stop videotaped by a witness and distributed globally (Cannon, 1997; Los Angeles Riots Fast Facts, 2014; Mydans, 1992).

In these ways, U.S. media representations of race may flavor international student views and interactions with black students on U.S. college campuses, complicating campus diversity initiatives and contributing to a less-than-ideal campus climate (Cuyjet, 2006; Hanassab, 2006; Lee, 2007b; Rankin, 2005). These tensions also may have implications for how black students view themselves (Roth, 2011, 2015a) and, if left unaddressed in the spaces and places of higher education, will persist and be reproduced in the globalizing workplace.

Supported by two recent independent qualitative studies conducted principally at the University of California, Los Angeles (cite removed), this chapter looks at how media representations can flavor cross-cultural interactions, and what implications these interactions may have for campus climate. Recent examples of diversity initiatives at U.S. colleges and universities speak to these cross-cultural issues and have identified that examination and deconstruction of media representations and stereotypes are often the core of these efforts (Althen, 2009; Chow, 2013; Gordon, 2010; Zuniga, 2002). Given the ever-increasing role media consumption plays in our lives (Horn, 2003; Stack, 2006), and the ever-increasing sophistication and potency of media culture and its associated spectacles (Kellner, 1995, 2010, 2011), strongly suggests educators need to find more ways to integrate and interrogate media representations across the curriculum. To that end, we envision a greater focus and emphasis by educators on media literacy through the examination and deconstruction of media representations, media culture and media spectacles. These interrogations should and, in our opinion, must begin upon students entering higher education, given by and through globalization, U.S. college campuses will only become more diverse, creating the very real potential for racial tensions to become very real impediments to effective, peaceful and collaborative learning spaces. We argue here for increased diversity awareness workshops and courses interrogating media representations of race, class, gender, and nationality for both incoming domestic and international students.

PROBLEM STATEMENT

The United States is home to some of the most widely known and prestigious universities in the world. According to one international ranking system, 14 of the world's top 20 universities based on reputation are U.S. schools (World Reputation Rankings, 2015). Students travel from everywhere on the globe to study in America. In many cases, these international students have had limited exposure to American culture outside of perceptions drawn from U.S. news, film, and pop culture, including television, music, dance, dress, and demeanor (Fujioka, 2000; Kim, 2008). As a result, they often arrive with negative racial stereotypes, particularly in relation to African Americans and specifically males (Ritter, 2013; Roth, 2015b). Due to these perceptions, many international students tend to fear and avoid contact with African American males on college campuses and elsewhere (Talbot, 1999).

At these same universities are African American male students who, because of years of living in the U.S., are often painfully aware of their marginalization and stereotypification (Harper, 2009, 2010; Roth, 2011, 2015a). They also have real world experience with outcomes associated with this marginalization: in classrooms (Carter, 2006), in lunchrooms (Tatum, 1997), in courtrooms (Alexander, 2010; Harris, 2003), on elevators (Solórzano, 2000), and in a multiplicity of other venues. One 21-year-old UCLA student described how popular media representations stereotypically portray black males and he questions whether these images have implications for his interactions with others:

"On different shows there's always – like the MTV's *Real World* – there's always a token black person and people sorta see that and think that every black person must be like that person. I know, right now, there's a *Real World Update* where they have a black guy; he's like a big, strong, like a *Big* black guy. And I think that – to myself like you know – does everyone see him as what every black guy is? What he shows on TV, do they think of me as that same person?" (Roth, 2011, 2015a).

Similarly, when an undergraduate Korean international student was asked whether she would date an African American male, she said: "They will hurt me because they are so big and I don't like their curly hair and big lips…it's not my style. It may come from Western aesthetics of blond and white" (Ritter, 2013).

These seemingly consistent perceptions across continents may collide on college campuses and hamper both international and domestic students' ability to interact positively (Talbot, 1999). They may also have long term negative implications for college going experiences among black students (Cha, 1992; Cuyjet, 2006; Dixon, 2003; Fujioka, 2000; Roth, 2015a; Smith, 2007a; Smith, 2007b, 2011; Talbot, 1999). Research shows black males are the most vulnerable U.S. racial-gender group for almost every health condition monitored by medical researchers (Smith, 2011). What still seems to be lacking among social, educational and professional institutions, as well as society at-large, is the understanding that gendered racism has significant emotional, psychological and physiological costs, and these costs have significant implications for the rise and presence of black males in higher education and beyond (Smith, 2011). Those who do succeed do so because they are truly exceptional. Implicit in this argument is the realization that due to racial battle fatigue (Smith, 2007b), black men are held to a higher standard than expected from any other U.S. gendered or racial group, and this standard is in conflict with the precepts on which this nation was founded.

However, when individuals meet other individuals and engage with them equally, many although not all of the racial issues present on America's college campuses today tend to disappear. Allport's (1954) contact hypothesis posits frequent contact with *out group members* – a racial/ethnic group outside of one's own race (Talbot, 1999) – can foster positive intergroup attitudes. This hypothesis identifies a number of features that contact experiences must have in order to lessen prejudice: equal status between groups, common goals, intergroup cooperation, and the support of authorities, laws or customs (Allport, 1954). Prior contact and understanding of an out group is an important step in prejudice reduction, as illustrated in Jeffries and Ransford's (1969) study which found in the aftermath of the 1965 Watts Riots, middle-class whites who had prior cross-racial contact were less fearful of blacks. In addition, Gaertner and Dovidio (2000) assert building communities of 'we' (rather than 'us' and 'them') can decrease prejudice. Forming new identities that go beyond race and ethnicity, such as superordinate groupings (international students, basketball enthusiasts, history majors), have aided in stereotype and prejudice reduction (Dovidio, 2009; Gaertner, 1989). It is clear cross-racial interaction can have positive effects on individuals' feelings toward racial out groups (Chang, 2010; Hurtado, 2001; Hurtado, 1999; Roth, 2015b), but it also appears international students and domestic students are currently missing opportunities to positively interact with one another due to cross-cultural misunderstandings (Gareis, 2012; Hechanova-Alampay, 2002; Lee, 2007b).

The picture painted at the institutional level is international students who are not versed in American racial dynamics or multicultural history are coming to the U.S. at an increasing rate (Gordon, 2010). At the same time, campuses are seeking ways to admit more African-American and Latino students (Hoxby, 2012), in an effort to live up to America's promised meritocracy. What this means for college campus climates as these students find themselves rooming with one another in residential halls and taking classes together, despite neither side possessing a firm grasp of the other's communication styles and cultural backgrounds, is at the very least a question seeking an answer.

BACKGROUND

Steele (1997, 2010) talks about "A Threat in the Air," referring to the negative outcomes experienced by individuals who are stereotyped based solely on their membership in a particular group. For instance, female students perform poorly on math exams when told in advance women in general test poorly in math (Fogliati, 2013). Too, women suffer no loss of self-esteem as a result of their poor performance because poor performance already is anticipated due to stereotype threat (Fogliati, 2013; Steele, 1997). For young Black men, their depiction in media as thugs, pimps, dope dealers, hip hoppers and gang bangers who disrespect and often abuse women tend to serve as the stereotypical representations of *all* African American men (Bjornstrom, 2010; Entman, 2008; Jackson, 2005; Kitwana, 2002). So, when black men do act out and mirror these stereotypes, there is never any discussion about psychological wounding (hooks, 2004; Smith, 2011). When young white males, especially those of privilege, act violently, media discussions invariably turn to exploring psychological issues as a partial explanation for their crimes, representing them as not inherently evil but as disturbed (hooks, 2004). However, when media interrogates reasons behind black male crime, the perpetrators are not seen as troubled but as inherently defective, "always the killer in the making," (hooks, 2004, p. 92), reinforcing the racist assumption all black men are inherently evil.

These portrayals in television news, blockbuster films, on the internet, in music videos, and newspaper crime reports paint black men as a social threat (Bjornstrom, 2010; Chiricos, 1997, 2001; Harper, 2008); and perceived as such, black men have experienced differential treatment in general (Harper, 2009), and in campus interactions specifically (Smith, 2007b, 2011), especially when interacting with international students (Kobayashi, 2010).

MEDIA REPRESENTATIONS

Representation is a central practice in the production of culture. In the context of the study of social science, the word *culture* is used to describe "whatever is distinctive about the *way of life* of a people, community, nation or social group" (Hall, 2003, p. 2). Culture also is used to describe the *shared values* of a group or of a society. In addition, there is the notion of culture as a referent to globally distributed forms of music, publishing, art, design, literature, and entertainment, as well as other visual and cultural artifacts. This definition usually is referred to as the anthropological definition of culture (Hall, 2003), and this description of culture as a producer and distributor of media messages is of central interest to this paper.

Making meaning is both a daily and lifetime routine for individuals. When engaged in conversation, for instance, the current present, the current past, and the current future, of the dialogue occupy most of our information processing capability in *real time* (Erickson, 2004). We often have a sense of where a conversation is going based on previous conversations with the same or a different person about the same or a slightly different topic. But speaking and listening "are reflexively related in an ecology of mutual influence" (Erickson, 2004, p. 4), and as hearers and speakers, we are constantly engaged in the interpretation of and adaptation to the sights and sounds associated with a communicative encounter.

It is no stretch of the imagination, then, to assume what a person is saying may be shaped by physical and spoken information received from the listener, and that these responses from the listener, in terms of movement, such as head nods, smiles or frowns, even rocking back and forth as if listening to music, also may be shaped by the activity and words of the speaker (Kendon, 1990).

The point is myriad information is transmitted between and to individuals, even if unintended, when more than one person is engaged in the consideration of a topic, notion, scene, description, visual enactment or other manifest moment of perception (Erickson, 2004).

Consider, then, mass media as one participant in a dialogue. While the day has not arrived that the *media text* can be altered or can alter itself in real time in response to verbal or physical cues from viewers or listeners, mass media are polysemic (Condit, 1989; Fiske, 1986) and capable of carrying and transmitting multiple meanings simultaneously. The importance of these various meanings is dependent on where the viewer or listener is *situated* (Harding, 2004) in relation to the content of the media text, in terms of its representation of the world and the affinity of that representation to the receiver (Bourdieu, 1984; Condit, 1989; Fiske, 1986).

Du Gay (1997) conceived six moments in the development of culture in which the meanings of cultural products are determined, negotiated and if necessary subverted during interaction between producers and consumers. This *circuit of culture* (Du Gay, 1997) also has been used to focus on how the value and meaning of culture are created, sustained, transmitted, and ultimately altered at sites of interrogation, in particular moments of changing perceptions, and as a result of certain practices (Taylor, 2002). Further, this model is derivative, in that it has foundations in Marx' earlier concept of the circuit of capital, which linked production with distribution (Taylor, 2002).

In the current instance, we have the construction of cultural meanings, or representations, by and through the movement of language, perception or other understanding through a field or set of domains – representation, identity, consumption, access, regulation, and production –, with each field or domain having potential for mediating the meaning of the language, perception or other understanding as it moves through the circuit of culture (Hall, 2003). As a result, it is not enough merely to interrogate representations of black men, but how are these representations produced and consumed and within what parameters are they produced and consumed and once produced what implications do they carry for black male identity, both internally and externally (Roth, 2015a)? Further, what supports the ongoing production and consumption of certain types of representations, some of which may be more mythological than actual?

Gray (2005) argues contemporary media representations of blackness continue to be shaped discursively by representations of race and ethnicity that began in the early years of television. The formative years of television and its representations of race and ethnicity served to define the cultural and social terms in which representations of blackness appeared and continue to appear in media and popular culture. Television in the 1950s presented blacks in stereotypical and subservient roles whose origins lay in 18th and 19th century characterizations, primarily as cooks, *mammies* and other servants, or as hustlers and deadbeats (Gray, 2005). These representations were necessary for the ongoing legitimization of a social order built on racism and white supremacy (Gray, 2005; Harris, 1993).

Additionally, Kellner (2011) sees in media representations the materials from which individuals define themselves. Media representations and *media culture* – the assemblage of representations and their culturally shared codes that are used in the process of manufacturing and distributing meaning – can provide individuals with their sense of self, their concept of gender, their understanding of class, race and ethnicity, their perceptions of sexuality and nationality, and their notions of 'us' and 'them' (Kellner, 2011). hooks (2009) adds like it or not, cinema and other visual representations assume a pedagogical role, and even though audiences have the ability to pick and choose, some messages are rarely mediated by the will of audiences.

In its most simple form, then, representation is a key ingredient in the process of meaning making and how, once determined, meanings are shared and exchanged between members of a particular culture (Hall, 2003). What is significant here is cultural meanings, derived from shared language and potentially shared interpretation of events, do not reside only in the head, or even in the text themselves. They tend to take on a *liveness* (Couldry, 2000) all of their own. As a result, these cultural meanings tend to organize and regulate behavior and have real and tangible outcomes (Hall, 2003). In effect, they are frameworks of interpretation that have implications for action, in part because of the way we give meanings to and represent experiences, perceptions and other daily practices (Hall, 2003).

However, the notion of mass media as a social monolith has been contested for some time. Ang (1996) noted the shift in critical media studies in the 1980s, during which Hall (1981), as a member of The Birmingham School of Cultural Studies, was configuring and elaborating his encoding/decoding model. Prior to that, the critical discourse, mostly out of Europe, primarily about visual texts, including film and television, centered on what Morley (1980) referred to as a preoccupation with an "abstract text/subject relationship." The role of the viewer was locked and inscribed by the text (Ang, 1996). There was little or no room for a dialogic relationship between media texts and consumers. In short, media consumers were thought to get what they got, based on what the maker made, and what as viewers they perceived, with little opportunity to interrogate or challenge content (Roth, 2015a).

As a more constructionist view (Patton, 2002) emerged, representation took on the role of forging links between people, events and experiences (Hall, 2003), and in effect became a contested terrain (Kellner, 1995, 2010, 2011), where interpretation by decoders of texts can be delimited or otherwise mediated by socio-economic status, gender, politick or race (Morley, 1980, 1992, 1993). Bourdieu (1984, 1977) examined the addition of power relations and how most of the time, though not all of the time, the message or purpose of both media and other public pedagogies corresponds with the interests of dominant groups and classes, "both by (their) mode of imposition and by the delimitation of what and on whom, it (is) impose(d)" (p. 7).

Culture primarily is concerned with the production and exchange of representations between members of a society or group in order to make meaning. As a result, meaning can define who we are, and where we belong, and is constantly being produced and shared in all personal and social interaction in which people take part (Hall, 2003; Kellner, 2011).

This concept of culture, then, depends on participants to interpret what is happening around them by making sense of the world in broadly similar ways. But these actions and reactions are often constrained by social forces in advance of individuals enacting their interpretations.

Boyd (1997) has claimed hip-hop and "gangsta" culture, as popularized in mass media, may contribute to a greater sentiment of apathy and alienation among young African American males in a misdirected attempt at reaffirming their culture and identity.

Visual media, such as television, film, online parodies and other representations, arguably are the principal window from which most world citizens develop their perceptions of each other and the world in general (Roth, 2015a). America is a global leader in the production and export of media, generating one-third of the revenue from film distribution, which in 2011 totaled $32.6 billion (Theatrical Market Statistics, 2011). The representations of the world produced by these exports often define, supplant or augment global citizens' perceptions of the U.S. beyond their on-the-ground personal experience, or the personal experiences of family and friends (Cornbleth, 2002; Hunt, 2011; Rodriguez, 2012). In the U.S., due to competition for viewership, local news organizations have focused on an action news format, which centralizes attention on crime, accounting for as much as 75% of all news coverage in some cities (Bjornstrom, 2010; Gilliam, 2000; Henkin, 2008). These local images are often transmitted worldwide due to global fascination with their sensationalized content (Bjornstrom, 2010; Chiricos, 1997; Dixon, 2003). Given the visuality of these media, and the importance of a suspect in the standard crime news "script", reportage or filmic depictions of crime stories are often imbued with racial imagery. Of the two essential elements of crime news – degree of violence and the presence of a suspect –, Gilliam

(2000) found it was the presence of a suspect that had more influence on public opinion, and served to substantiate negative attitudes about racial minorities, since African Americans comprised the largest percentage of minority suspects depicted in news media despite not having committed the majority of violent crime (Alexander, 2010).

Given this back-story, the standard crime news script used by U.S. media is "no mere journalistic device; instead it is a powerful filter for observing daily events" (Gilliam, 2000, p. 564). Further, the predilection for sensational examples of criminal human experience and activity also has permeated entertainment media, the largest of America's media exports (Theatrical Market Statistics, 2011), and while there are positive examples of men of color in blockbuster American films – the like of Will Smith and his son, Jaden Smith, Denzel Washington, Morgan Freeman, Danny Glover, Cuba Gooding, Jr., Sidney Poitier, Laurence Fishburne, and Samuel L. Jackson, among others – there are an equal or greater number of roles portraying black men as gangsters, thugs, drug dealers, pimps and murderers (Roth, 2015a). In fact, many of the actors cited for playing positive roles can be and often still are cast in films as good people caught up in serious wrongdoing. Morgan Freeman as the character, "Red", a convicted murderer serving a life sentence behind bars in *The Shawshank Redemption* (King, 1994), is just one such example. Wesley Snipes as a fugitive from alleged corrupt government in *U.S. Marshalls* (Baird, 1998) is another. *Enemy of the State* (Scott, 1998), starring Will Smith as an attorney targeted by a corrupt federal bureaucrat, is yet another.

Part of the reason for this deficit portrayal of black men is due to racial stereotypes that grew from a social construct of race (Feagin, 2006; Mills, 1997; Winant, 2000) and a general neglect to bother with viewing black men as a heterogeneous group (Celious, 2001; Harper, 2008). Both Nelson (2003) and Gatewood (2000) have chronicled known heterogeneity among African Americans since the formation of the United States. So, in order for stereotypes to remain prescient, their representation must be reified by and through institutional and cultural agents, the latter including mass media (Roth, 2015a). This black-white racial framework provides a way to assign social meaning to otherwise arbitrary physical differences based on the surface of the human body, such as skin color and curly hair (Hunt, 2005). In the case of black men, these and other physical features historically have been used to signify a social threat (Bjornstrom, 2010; Chiricos, 2001). This notion of threat has been used to justify heightened police patrols (and concomitant negative news coverage) in black communities, a practice of racial profiling (Davis, 1997; Durlauf, 2006; Gross, 2002; Harcourt, 2004; Risse, 2004; Rose, 2002; Wu, 2005), and a report in broadcast news of a black man being killed by police or other security personnel somewhere in the U.S. every 28 hours (Hudson, 2013).

This hyper-vigilance in the monitoring of African American communities and, particularly black men (Smith, 2007b), has resulted in more than one million black men incarcerated in U.S. prisons, and approximately one-third of all African American men, ages 20-29, under some correctional system supervision (Alexander, 2010; Kitwana, 2002). No other racial group in America faces as many obstacles to the benefits of full citizenship than black men.

While current media representations of blackness in general seem to be moving toward a more heterogeneous view – depicting successful outcomes in a variety of social situations, including a twice-elected U.S. President – many of these images continue to support stereotypes, particularly those linking black men with violence and crime. For Asian international students, these highly circumscribed representations indelibly constrain their perceptions of African American males (Ritter, 2014).

Previous perception studies of visual media suggest they don't simply convey information about events, and individuals take in and interpret information selectively (Blackman, 1977). These findings are consistent with Kretch and Crutchfield (1973) who assert individuals perceive and interpret information in terms of their "own needs, own emotions, own personality, own previously formed cognitive patterns" (p.251). Blackman et al. conceived of a model of the individual as social actuary wherein both good and bad information is processed and these perceptions imbue flexible attitudes and beliefs, resulting in modest and continual changes in an individual's attitudes and beliefs. Newscasts and filmic narratives, then, can act as a kind of surrogate for personal contact, and supply individuals with information they use to assess and judge their social worlds (Blackman, 1977). Amid the specter of *bad news*, or negative portrayals of others, Blackman et al. (1977) found individuals discriminated both perceptually and behaviorally in favor of others who were presented as being more like them. Conversely, those perceived to be different were avoided or viewed negatively. Hornstein (1976) reported *good news* caused the boundaries of *We* to expand and individuals are less likely to gratuitously judge others as *They*. Both this outward looking aspect of the individual as social actuary and the inward looking one of altering thoughts and behaviors based on what we may perceive from media representations can have significant implications for cross-racial and cross-cultural relations, as well as overall campus climate at U.S. colleges and universities (Chang, 2010; Cuyjet, 2006; Hurtado, 2000; Ritter, 2014; Roth, 2015b; Solórzano, 2000).

Further, there is little doubt these media representations present particular codings in the public space (Hall, 2003). While British researchers previously focused on the variety of decoding possible from a single text or message, American researchers, such as Kellner (1990, 1995, 2010, 2011), have emphasized the ideology of messages, characterizing the interpretive landscape of media representations as a kind of contested terrain, where viewers defuse particular representations by accepting, countering or disregarding them. Kellner (2010) also argues not all media representations of blackness are negative. Hollywood may in fact have facilitated the ascendancy of President Barack Obama by and through its positive and presaging depictions of a not-completely dissimilar looking Will Smith (Kellner, 2010). Still, even if there are an equal number of positive and negative media representations of blackness, positive representations of White America significantly outnumber negative representations, and negative representations are generally constrained by class and criminality (Callinicos, 1993).

All of this becomes particularly salient in the realm of media consumption, given the media role in framing the public and the private, the global and the local, as well as articulating global processes with locally-situated consumption – "where local meanings are so often made within and against the symbolic resources of global media networks" (Morley, 1993, p. 17).

While media scholarship has moved away from monolithic interpretations of what media texts *mean* and how they are read, there appears consensus on the pervasive nature of mass media, particularly visual media, and its ability to facilitate pleasure (Ang, 1985), to set agenda and define issues (Morley, 1992), to teach (Horn, 2003; Postman, 1979; Tobolowsky, 2001, 2006), to reify its own power, and to maintain a distinction between itself and ordinary people (Couldry, 2000), all the while being "inexhaustible, and coextensive with reality itself" (Houston, 1994).

CAMPUS CONTEXTS

Let's turn now to how these representations may directly or indirectly have implications for the learning enterprise in the increasingly multicultural setting of the U.S. university. Research shows diversity and a sense of acceptance of difference are tantamount to a positive learning environment (Bowman, 2010a; Chang, 2010; Cuyjet, 2006; Denson, 2009; Gurin, 2004; Hurtado, 1992, 2000, 2003, 1998; Smith,

2009). In addition, the U.S. university is thought to be the place where America's promise of equality, global citizenship values (Green, 2012), and democratic principles are enacted and instilled in future generations (Gutmann, 1999). These are some of the very reasons American campuses are so attractive to international students. Still, if these campuses do not address antagonistic perceptions among incoming students, then black men and international students will be part of a growing number of education seekers who suffer from an institutional silence on race, especially in light of the globalization of the education project (Lieber, 2002; Locke, 1987; Morey, 2004; Torres, 2006; Torres, 2002; Van Heertum, 2009), the increasing diversity of U.S. student bodies (Bowman, 2010b; Locks, Hurtado, Bowman, & Oseguera, 2008; McMurtie, 2012), and the identified cognitive and educational benefits of interactions with racial diversity (Bowman, 2012; Chang, 1996, 1999, 2010; Denson, 2009; Lee, 2004). But we believe these concerns are but a few of the potentially adverse effects associated with antagonistic cross-cultural encounters on college campuses. The increasing rapidity with which human action and interaction is globalizing begs for an associated increase in cultural sensitivity across a growing multicultural community and work force (Dillard, 2001; Kellner, 2011; Leonardo, 2005; Nemetz, 1996).

Given the likelihood many future jobs and professions have not even been conceived of as of yet, the need for increased cooperation across continents, culture, and color has never been greater, and preparation for these changes and challenges most likely need to be addressed within the portals of higher education.

Examples of campus conflict between international and African-American students exist (Ritter, 2014). In 2008, at Columbia University, at the Chinese Scholars and Students Association play entitled, Finding Li Wei, one actor said that America was a nice place, but that "We need to get rid of those Black people in Harlem. I'm terrified by Black people!" (The Blaaag: Official Tumblr of Columbia University's Asian American Alliance, 2012; Cheng, 2011). This comment was met with a great deal of laughter, causing some black organizations and bloggers to question the racial equity and sensitivity in China (Cheng, 2011). The racist dialogue was in reference to a Columbia incident in which Ming-Hui Yu, a graduate student in statistics, was fatally struck by a car after fleeing a fourteen-year-old African-American assailant near Columbia University (*The Columbia Spectator*, 2008) .

Other examples of discrimination against international students exist, as evidenced by a video rant by a white female student at UCLA deploring how the university has admitted "hordes" of Asian students who she felt were not exhibiting "American manners" (Ritter, 2013, 2014). She also went on to mock the Chinese language by saying, "ching, chong, ling, long, ting, tong" (Gordon, 2011; Parkinson-Morgan, 2011). We believe these instances have implications for future interactions well beyond the college campus.

The campus climate literature has explored racial tensions between various groups on campuses (Cuyjet, 2006; Hurtado, 1992, 2000, 1998; Locks, Hurtado, Bowman, & Oseguera, 2008; Solórzano, 2000), but almost no research has been conducted on how international students perceive and interact with racial diversity on American campuses. There are generally thought to be four dimensions that make up campus climate: 1) An institution's historical legacy, 2) The structural diversity, or the statistical representation of diverse groups on campus, 3) The psychological climate, namely perceptions and attitudes between groups, and 4) The behavioral climate, to include types of intergroup relations (Hurtado, 1998).

When structural diversity is increased (by increasing the number of international students) without considering how this structural change may engage the other three dimensions of campus climate, problems are bound to arise (Milem, 2001). As international student populations increase on American college and university campuses, these students' racial attitudes undoubtedly will affect their interactions with others, while also having implications for campus climates (Gareis, 2012; Hanassab, 2006; Lee, 2007a, 2007b). For example, with the increase in international students in the U.S., it has become apparent

European international students adjust more easily to American life and have more American friends than do East Asian international students (Gareis, 2012). Neo-racism, discrimination based on culture and national order (Barker, 1981; Hervik, 2004), may be responsible for some of the cultural insensitivity arising as structural diversity on American college campuses becomes more prevalent (Lee, 2007). Lee and Rice (2007b) assert American colleges must internationalize their students, staff, and faculty to a new globalized student body, so discrimination based on accent and national origin does not persist (Lee, 2007b). While an increase in campus diversity may raise issues of intergroup relations, there is little doubt greater diversity is both important and desired and, given the globalization of the education enterprise, inevitable (Astin, 1993; Bowman, 2010b; Chang, 1999; Denson, 2009; Gurin, 2004; Locks, Hurtado, Bowman, & Oseguera, 2008).

Importance of Campus Diversity

The educational benefits of college campus diversity and cross-racial interaction are myriad. High levels of cross-racial interaction are linked to greater cognitive development (Astin, 1993; Chang, 2010; Cuyjet, 2006; Hurtado, 1992), more positive academic and social self-concept (Chang, 1999), positive intergroup attitudes (Chang, 2002), greater cultural awareness (Antonio, 2001), the promotion of racial tolerance, and increased college satisfaction (Astin, 1993). The college years are critical ones in which cognitive, social, and academic growth take place (Pascarella, 2005). Interactions with diverse peers can be a considerable catalyst for growth (Astin, 1993), and with an increased presence of diversity on campus, students are more likely to have interaction with racial out groups (Hurtado, 1994).

However, in order to reap the benefits of this diversity, institutions must make concerted efforts to not only increase structural diversity but also interaction across culture among students. The University of California in general, and UCLA in particular, has made significant efforts to bolster structural diversity by and through the increase of international student populations. At UCLA, international students comprise 10.35% of the total student population of 41,341, including graduate students (Quick Facts – UCLA Undergraduate Admissions, 2012). But such a rapid increase in structural diversity without accounting for implications to the other dimensions of campus climate can be fraught with unforeseen problems (Hurtado, 1999; Milem, 2001). An increase in minority group populations increases the likelihood of conflict with majority group members (Blalock, 1967; Olzak, 2011). There also is the potential for conflict with and between minority populations.

So, not only is campus climate a structural issue, it also can influence the psychology and behavioral patterns of those on campus (Chang, 2010; Smith, 2007b, 2011). Faculty, staff, and students tend to view campus racial climate differently, based on their level of power within the institution, and their sense of belonging within specific communities (Hurtado, 1998). Studies have shown that white students (68%) often think their universities are supportive of minority students, while only 28% of African-American and Latino students consider their campuses supportive (Loo, 1986; Rankin, 2005). This disparity between white and minority student responses may be attributed to the fact most white students grew up in predominantly white communities and consequently had limited exposure to racism prior to college, while minority students have more than likely had previous encounters with racism (Radloff, 2003). Just as structured racism in other domains can have deleterious effects, a discriminatory campus climate can negatively impact minority student grades and lead to feelings of alienation (Ancis, 2000; Cabrera, 1994; Cuyjet, 2006).

But perceptions of discrimination are not limited to students of color. White students' college persistence also can be influenced by negative racial/ethnic campus climates (Nora, 1996). Perceptions of discrimination affect all students (Chang, 2010); therefore, it's incumbent on institutions to make special efforts to create a campus climate that is fair, tolerant, and peaceful (Hurtado, 1998). Further, social psychology literature points out the significant role on-campus peer groups play in cross-racial interaction (Carter, 2006; Ford, 1996; Harper, 2006; Milem, 1998). All too often, universities do not have policies and programs in place that generate cross-racial interactions, and these interactions, if and when they do occur, do so by happenstance (Hurtado, 1998; Pascarella, 2005; Ritter, 2014; Roth, 2015b). White students who have had limited social interaction with students of different racial backgrounds are less likely to have positive attitudes about or to support multicultural efforts on campus (Globetti, 1993). On the other hand, white students who attend diversity workshops, discuss racial/ethnic issues with other students, or simply interact with a racially diverse mix of students, are more likely to value racial tolerance (Milem, 1998).

Beyond these personally valuable attributes of racial diversity, studies show interaction with ethnic out groups has positive outcomes for student retention, satisfaction with college, and intellectual development (Allen, 2002, 2009; Chang, 1996, 2010; Hurtado, 2001; Smith, 2009). If American public institutions are to truly live up to their diversity mission statements, they must not leave cross-racial learning and interaction to chance (Hurtado, 2005). Diversity requirements in the form of living situations and intergroup dialogue must not only be encouraged, but may need to be added to requirements for matriculation. In deciding the outcome of *Grutter v. Bollinger* (Grutter v. Bollinger (02-241) 539 U.S. 306, 2003), a case challenging affirmative action practices at the University of Michigan, Supreme Court Justice Sandra Day O'Connor wrote for the majority and cited a "compelling interest" in assuring the diversity of law schools since many future leaders are derived from law schools. Further, there is no doubt campus diversity leads to a variety of positive outcomes (Astin, 1993; Denson, 2009; Herzog, 2010; Hurtado, 1998; Hurtado, 1999; Milem, 2001; Zuniga, 2005), and we recommend more research to tease out the role international students play or can play in the larger arena of diversity on U.S. campuses. Given their increasing presence, there seems to be no better time than the present to engage this empirical question.

Discrimination on Campus

Several scholars have found the increase of international students on U.S. campuses has led to an increase in rates of discrimination on campuses. International students themselves are stereotyped and mistreated based on their cultural background (Hanassab, 2006). Students have reported perceptions of, "Asian women are still viewed as exotic creatures in Los Angeles" (Ritter, 2013); and one Chinese student reported: "Chinese, and in general Asians, are immediately assumed to be hard working, smart, and submissive" (Hanassab, 2006, p. 167). Often, these stereotypes are thrust upon unsuspecting international students, causing them to internalize and adopt American racial categories (Lee, 2007b). These racial dynamics encourage international students to seek and understand their place in the context of the U.S. racial hierarchy (Lee, 2007b). These students also keenly observe European international students face less discrimination, which can be explained by the historical dominance of whiteness in America, the legacy of colonialism, and the privilege associated with white skin (McIntosh, 2008). Instead of focusing on biological racism, Lee (2007b) utilizes a neo-racist approach, which may be more fitting for an international context. Neo-racism is defined as discrimination based on culture and national order (Barker, 1981; Hervik, 2004). Neo-racism does not replace biological racism; instead, it masks it by encouraging exclusion based on national origin (Lee, 2007b). It is apparent some domestic students hold prejudices about international students that often lead to verbal assaults, sexual harassment, and even physical attacks (Lee, 2007b). These experiences coupled with imported perceptions of threat driven by mass media representations have the potential to create volatile cross-cultural interactions, leading to substantive disruptions to positive campus climate (Ritter, 2013, 2014).

While the higher Education literature explores domestic students' stereotypes and prejudiced behavior toward international students, it is significantly more muted when it comes to international students' racial attitudes and prejudices toward domestic students. However, one study reported Asian international students view African-American people as *violent hoodlums* and *second-class citizens* (Talbot, 1999). In another instance, Asian international students said they avoided interaction with African-American students because of fear, negative stereotypes, and prejudice (Ritter, 2013). These findings are troubling for a number of reasons.

First, international students are not only members of U.S. college communities, but they also are likely future leaders and policy makers (Locke, 1987). Second, these micro aggressions (Solórzano, 2000) by international students against black students can be a powerful deterrent to black male success at college (Harper, 2008; Smith, 2007b, 2011). Stereotype ossification persists for African American men, who also may view Asian international students as *foreign others* and as a result may not develop personal relationships that can lead to professional partnerships in the future (Ritter, 2013). Additionally, Asian international students may leave the U.S. with continued negative impressions of African Americans, and will not develop the cross-racial communicational toolkit that is increasingly necessary to succeed in today's globalized workplace.

The Growing Presence of International Students

International students are defined as individuals who temporarily reside in a country other than their country of citizenship in order to participate in international education exchanges (Forest, 2006; Paige, 1990). The number of international students in American colleges and universities has nearly doubled in the past two decades, from 366,354 in 1988-89 to 886, 052 in 2013-14 (Ritter, 2014). East Asian students comprise the largest segment of this increase in international students, with Chinese students leading the field, followed by Indian, South Korean and Japanese (Institute of International Education: Open Doors Data, 2011). The University of Southern California (USC) has the nation's highest enrollment of international students with 8,615 international students, followed by University of Illinois at Urbana-Champaign with 7,991, while UCLA ranked sixth with 6,249 (Institute of International Education: Open Doors Data, 2011).

The most recent generation of international students has been referred to as *students of the new global elite* (SONGEs) (Vandrick, 2011). These students often come from higher socio-economic backgrounds and can easily afford the tuition costs associated with attending American universities as international students. They often have previously attended international schools, have already lived, studied and vacationed in various parts of the world and, as a result, are thought to be familiar with American culture and speak English with ease. They have developed a particular global awareness and could be considered global citizens, due to the ease with which they move from one cultural setting to another. SONGEs' backgrounds, attitudes, and beliefs have implications for the college classrooms they attend, their interactions with instructors, and their eventual position in the global workforce after graduation (Vandrick, 2011). As a result, it is important to understand their racial attitudes and stereotypes, so institutions, faculty, staff, and policy makers can adjust to the needs of this population, as well as assist them to integrate into long-established patterns of university practice and evolving patterns of practice to aid in prejudice reduction and to promote tolerance within the campus community.

While Vandrick (2011) has asserted many of these students are global citizens and as a result are racially tolerant, this isn't necessarily the case (Ritter, 2013). Less than half of the international students in a recent UCLA study attended international schools, and many had not traveled outside of their province or prefecture (Ritter, 2013). Those who fit the profile of Vandrick's (2011) SONGEs, were indeed more-traveled, culturally aware, and racially tolerant. But just because a students' family has the financial wherewithal to afford a U.S. college or university does not mean they are sufficiently aware of U.S. cultural mores or they are racially tolerant. When it comes to East Asian international students, there are a variety of attitudes and experiences associated with cultural and racial diversity (Ritter, 2012, 2013). However, one outcome is certain: the rapid rise in the number of international students at U.S. institutions will have implications for the American college campus.

FUTURE RESEARCH DIRECTIONS

To address these long-established and structural stereotypes that continue to be reproduced in mass media representations and then exported to the rest of the world, education institutions must turn to innovative ways to broaden cross-racial/ethnic interactions between African American and Asian international students. For instance, The University of Michigan (UM), Syracuse University (SU), University of Texas-Austin (UTA), UCLA, and other institutions have begun *intergroup dialogue* programs (Pettigrew, 2000; Special Issue: Intergroup Dialogue: Engaging Difference, Social Identities and Social Justice, 2012; Zuniga, 2012), where students study structural racism in society, dissect media images, and examine the dynamics of privilege and oppression through collaborative team building exercises. Let's look more closely at these institutional efforts to reduce campus racial tensions.

Intergroup dialogue programs work to make positive cross-national and cross-racial communication a reality. This social justice education program promotes interaction and dialogue across identities of gender, class, religion, ability, race, and nationality (Pettigrew, 2000; Special Issue: Intergroup Dialogue: Engaging Difference, Social Identities and Social Justice, 2012; Zuniga, 2012). One class focuses on race and ethnicity, both through an international as well as domestic lens. But these programs do not have traditional lecture pedagogy and require different approaches to engagement. Student facilitators are trained to lead undergraduate and graduate students in creating a safe environment where peer discussions, interactive games, listening activities, and personal narrative sharing leads to a greater understanding of societal oppression and privilege across race and culture. Students also are tasked with creating social action projects to assist them to develop skills as social change agents (Zuniga, 2012). In these settings, international and African American students can interact and become familiar with each other in a safe environment that affords a forum for the discussion of issues of difference *and* similarity.

Intergroup dialogue is a good place to start, but there is also a need for diversity courses (Ritter, 2014; Roth, 2015b). At the University of California, undergraduate and graduate international students are exempted from taking a general education American history requirement so that they can participate in a diversity course specifically for international students (Ritter, 2012). To effectively combat racial stereotypes learned from media or other cultural representations, international students need to learn more about the racial diversity in the U.S. and its historical racial hierarchies. Offices of International Student

Services could partner with multicultural affairs programs on campus, to foster the development of safe places where international and domestic students can interact and examine their racial questions together.

At Central Connecticut State University, an English as a Second Language (ESL) course utilizes film and writing exercises to spur thinking about race (Althen, 2009). Gonzaga University has added African-American history to its ESL orientation (Chow, 2013). But geographical barriers persist in the eradication of negative racial views, as evidenced in the American South. At the University of Southern Alabama, Director Brenda Hinson explains why international students are not taught about race in their programming or materials: "Here in the South we spend so much time trying to overcome our past images that we wait until [foreign students] arrive and answer questions they might have about race at that time" (Althen, 2009, p. 90). Ignoring racial misunderstandings is problematic, given the history of slavery in America and only a cursory understanding of the history of slavery and civil rights movements in the U.S. on the part of international students (Ritter, 2013). But not all universities in the South approach international student education this way. At the University of Mississippi, the *Planet Partner Program* and the *Omazing Race* (Ole Miss Alumni Association: The Omazing Race, 2013) activity bring domestic and international students together in cooperative hay wagon rides, roller skating, and team building cross-cultural activities (Althen, 2009).

However, throughout the nation, such programming for undergraduates is sporadic at best, and even sparser for graduate students. Tuft University's International Center director Jane Etish-Andrews explains graduate students "do not have the issue of race on their radar screen...they are only interested in doing well academically and do not want to address issues that are outside of their academic performance" (Althen, 2009, p. 92). This is not a productive posture, nor would we consider it an accurate one. Clearly, race is on the radar of international students, given when asked they express concern, fear, and threat when discussing interaction with black males (Ritter, 2013, 2014). Further, while graduate students may be focused on academics, these same graduate students may eventually be global leaders, and to shortchange their recognition, understanding, and tolerance of others does not bode well for future improvement in global race relations. While we believe institutions must direct resources to racial understanding and international tolerance as their campuses become more structurally diverse, the addition of a monthly one-hour seminar offered through campus international or multicultural centers that deconstructs topical filmic images, provides a forum for discussion of micro aggressions, and a safe venue for students to engage in cross-cultural interaction is a cost-effective first measure. International students need to learn about racial diversity in the U.S. and create meaningful relationships with other students because these connections with the campus community stave off homesickness, depression, cultural anxiety, create a greater satisfaction with the college experience, result in higher GPAs, reduce attrition, and place students' U.S. experiences in a more positive light (Brown, 2009; Gareis, 2012; Glass, 2012; Hendrickson, 2011; Sakurai, 2010).

Washington State University (WSU) has seen a 61% increase in international student enrollment from 2007 to 2012 (WSU International Population Statistics, 2013). In response to this rapid increase of international students, WSU was awarded a grant from the American Council on Education (ACE) entitled, "At Home in the World Initiative." The initiative, funded by The Henry Luce Foundation, the Inclusive Excellence Group, and the Center for Internationalization and Global Engagement, strives to promote more inclusive and internationalized environments for students, faculty and staff, while improving campus climate through internationalization of curriculum (American Council on Education: At Home in the World Institutions Meet, Reflect on Lessons Learned, 2013). WSU also created the Global Leadership Certificate, exposing international and domestic students to the necessity of understanding different races, cultures, and religions. Students apply to the program and choose their own curriculum, exploring civic engagement from a global perspective, how cultural differences influence communication, and developing potential leadership capabilities through internships that aid in hunger eradication, sustainability, anti-poverty initiatives, and community development (WSU Global Leadership Certificate, 2013). While these efforts at WSU are not solely focused on the development of racial tolerance, they are focused on internationalizing the university, which in turn helps promote a culture where international and domestic students respect and understand one another.

University of Southern California has created a free, non-credit, 12-week course in American culture. Students from Hong Kong, Shanghai, Tokyo, Turkey, and Saudi Arabia are taken to the California African American Museum to learn about racial and cultural diversity in Los Angeles (Gordon, 2010). These students also learn to improve their cross-cultural communication skills, how to acculturate to American life, and develop an understanding of American idioms and slang. UCLA's Dashew International Center also has a course entitled, *American Culture and Communication*, wherein international students learn about the Civil Rights Movement, dissect hip-hop images and prejudices associated with them, and deconstruct stereotypes they may have toward different racial groups at UCLA. The center also encourages students to examine the racial climate of greater Los Angeles.

At the University of Iowa, the *Bridging Domestic and Global Diversity Program*, brings together underrepresented domestic students and international students to develop intercultural competencies they later use to plan and present an on campus Global Diversity Forum (University of Iowa: Bridging Domestic and Global Diversity, 2013). Twenty-five graduate and undergraduate students are selected for participation each year. They are required to complete an *Intercultural Development Inventory* and the Intercultural Conflict Styles Inventory to assist them to tease out and better understand their own values, beliefs, and approaches to other cultures. The highlight of the program is the Forum, where participants create presentations to share with the campus community on topics such as undocumented immigration, gay marriage, and the historical underpinnings of racial stereotypes.

Another example of developing sensitivity to cross-racial difference are the *African Diaspora Communities* at the University of California, Berkeley, UCLA, New York University and Rutgers University, to name just a few. These self-selected living-learning environments within residential halls provide students the opportunity to investigate and engage the relationship between the African continent and the United States. These programs are coupled with themed residential housing that provides a safe space to delve more deeply into the issues and history associated with race in America, as well as local opportunities to dispel common misunderstandings by engaging in meaningful interactions with roommates and other residents regarding identities.

Prolonged engagement between individuals from different identity groups has been shown to be strong tonic for reducing prejudice and building mutual understanding (Allport, 1954). These are some of the more established programs cropping up on college campuses nationwide but more efforts in such program development are needed. Student affairs officers must view residential halls and student clubs as vital sites where African American and Asian international students can learn to cooperatively combat cultural and media-driven stereotypes that can disrupt effective and tranquil campus climates.

While these examples show needed and appropriate interest by U.S. colleges and universities to address existing or emerging campus climate issues, their efficacy is largely unknown, which strongly suggests this is an area in need of further study.

CONCLUSION

College campuses remain both bastions for social change and stalwarts for the status quo, and for these reasons they are important sites for addressing the implications of globalization in raced relations and acceptance of difference in a multicultural world community that seems to be shrinking almost daily in terms of difference, opportunity and communication. But there's good reason to believe the forecast for our global future is favorable. Younger cohorts, such as *Millennials* – born between the early 1980s and 2000 – have demonstrated their willingness to be more racially tolerant than previous generations, portending a likely easing of America's racial divisions. Still, institutions of higher learning must be among the vanguard in pursuit of the dissolution of difference along racial lines. The acceptance of difference and the innovative practices to achieve acceptance shown here are just a few of the institutional ways U.S. colleges and universities can address America's deeply embedded racist structures due to centuries of practiced racism. In doing so, U.S. colleges and universities not only improve their campus racial climate and the learning opportunities for students, but also pave the way for greater understanding and practice in society, potentially with the result of a more peaceful and just version of the world we all must learn to live in.

REFERENCES

Alexander, M. (2010). *The New Jim Crow: Mass Incarceration in the Age of Colorblindness*. New York: The New Press.

Allen, W. R., Bonous-Hammarth, M., & Teranishi, R. (2002). *Stony the Road We Trod: The Black Struggle for Higher Education in California*. Academic Press.

Allen, W. R., Jayakumar, U. M., & Franke, R. (2009). *Till Victory Is Won: The African American Struggle for Higher Education in California: CHOICES*. UCLA.

Allport, G. W. (1954). *The Nature of Prejudice*. Cambridge, MA: Addison-Wesley Publishing Company, Inc.

Althen, G. (2009). Education International Students About 'Race'. *International Educator, 18*(3).

Alvarez, L., & Buckley, C. (2013). Zimmerman Is Acquitted in Trayvon Martin Killing. *The New York Times*. Retrieved from Zimmerman is Acquitted in Trayvon Martin Killing - NYTimes.com website: http://www.nytimes.com/2013/07/14/us/george-zimmerman-verdict-trayvon-martin.html?pagewanted=all&_r=0

American Council on Education. (2013). *At Home in the World Institutions Meet, Reflect on Lessons Learned*. Retrieved April 10, 2013, from http://www.acenet.edu/news-room/Pages/At-Home-in-the-World-Institutions-Meet-Reflect-Lessons-Learned.aspx

Amzallag, D., Peacocke, A., & Pianin, A. (2008, April 5). Grad Student Fled Assault before Killed by Car; Suspect Arrested for Manslaughter. *The Columbia Spectator*. Retrieved from http://www.columbiaspectator.com/2008/04/05/grad-student-fled-assault-killed-car-suspect-arrested-manslaughter

Ancis, J. R., Sedlacek, W. E., & Mohr, J. J. (2000). Student Perceptions of Campus Cultural Climate by Race. *Journal of Counseling and Development, 78*(2), 180–185. doi:10.1002/j.1556-6676.2000.tb02576.x

Ang, I. (1985). *Watching Dallas: Soap Opera and the Melodramatic Imagination.* London: Methuen.

Ang, I. (1996). *Living Room Wars: Rethinking Media Audiences for a Postmodern World* (1st ed.). New York: Routledge. doi:10.4324/9780203289549

Antonio, A. L. (2001). The Role of Interracial Interaction in the Development of Leadership Skills and Cultural Knowledge and Understanding. *Research in Higher Education, 42*(5), 593–617. doi:10.1023/A:1011054427581

Astin, A. W. (1993). Diversity and Multiculturalism on the Campus: How Are Students Affected? *Change, 23*(2), 44–49. doi:10.1080/00091383.1993.9940617

Atkinson, K. (2013). Bruno Mars Is Not Jersey Enough to Play Super Bowl Halftime Say Twitter. *Entertainment Weekly.* Retrieved from EW.com website: http://music-mix.ew.com/2013/09/08/bruno-mars-super-bowl-twitter-reaction/

Baird, S. (1998). *U.S. Marshals.* Hollywood, CA: Producer.

Barker, M. (1981). *The New Racism: Conservatives and the Ideology of the Tribe.* London: Junction Books.

Benhaim, M. (2013). Six Reasons Why Bruno Mars Is the Next Michael Jackson. *Metro Canada.* Retrieved from Metro News Canada website: http://metronews.ca/voices/backbeat/628929/six-reasons-why-bruno-mars-is-the-next-michael-jackson/

Bjornstrom, E. E. S., Kaufman, R. L., Peterson, R. D., & Slater, M. D. (2010). Race and Ethnic Representations of Lawbreakers and Victims in Crime News: A National Study of Television Coverage. *Social Problems, 57*(2), 269–293. doi:10.1525p.2010.57.2.269 PMID:20640244

Blackman, J. A., Hornstein, H. A., Divine, C., O'Neill, M., Steil, J., & Tucker, L. (1977). Newscasts and the Social Actuary. *Public Opinion Quarterly, 41*(3), 295–313. doi:10.1086/268389

Blalock, H. M. (1967). *Toward a Theory of Minority-Group Relations.* New York: Wiley.

Bourdieu, P. (1984). *Distinction: A Social Critique of the Judgment of Taste* (R. Nice, Trans.). Cambridge, MA: Harvard University Press.

Bourdieu, P., & Passeron, J. C. (1977). *Reproduction in Education, Society and Culture.* Beverly Hills: Sage Publications.

Bowman, N. A. (2010a). College Diversity Experiences and Cognitive Development: A Meta-Analysis. *Review of Educational Research, 80*(1), 4–33. doi:10.3102/0034654309352495

Bowman, N. A. (2010b). Disequilibrium and Resolution: The Nonlinear Effects of Diversity Courses on Well-Being and Orientations toward Diversity. *The Review of Higher Education, 33*(4), 543–568. doi:10.1353/rhe.0.0172

Bowman, N. A., & Denson, N. (2012). What's Past Is Prologue: How Precollege Exposure to Diversity Shapes the Impact of College Diversity Experiences. *Research in Higher Education, 53*, 406–425. doi:10.100711162-011-9235-2

Boyd, T. (1997). *Am I Black Enough for You? Popular Culture from the 'Hood and Beyond*. Bloomington, IN: Indiana University Press.

Brown, L. (2009). An Ethnographic Study of the Friendship Patterns of International Students in England: An Attempt to Recreate Home through Conational Interaction. *International Journal of Educational Research*, *48*(3), 184–193. doi:10.1016/j.ijer.2009.07.003

Cabrera, A. F., & Nora, A. (1994). College Student Perceptions of Prejudice and Discrimination and Their Feelings of Alienation: A Construct Validation Approach. *Review of Education, Pedagogy & Cultural Studies*, *16*(3-4), 387–409. doi:10.1080/1071441940160310

Callinicos, A. (1993). *Race and Class*. Chicago: Bookmarks Publications, Ltd.

Cannon, L. (1997). *Official Negligence: How Rodney King and the Riots Changed Los Angeles and the LAPD* (1st ed.). New York: Times Books/Random House.

Carter, P. L. (2006). Straddling Boundaries: Identity, Culture, and School. *Sociology of Education*, *79*(4), 304–328. doi:10.1177/003804070607900402

Celious, A., & Oyserman, D. (2001). Race from the Inside: An Emerging Heterogeneous Race Model. *The Journal of Social Issues*, *57*(1), 149–165. doi:10.1111/0022-4537.00206

Cha, J., & Choi, I. (1992). College Students' Attitude toward Foreigners. *Psychological Science*, *1*(1), 1–23.

Chandler, D. L. (2013). Brutal Lynching at Moore's Ford Bridge Took Place on This Day in 1946. *News One for Black America*. Retrieved from Brutal Lynching at Moore's Ford Bridge Took Place On This Day In 1946 | News One website: http://newsone.com/2642271/

Chang, E. (2009). TV Talent Show Exposes China's Race Issue. *CNN World*. Retrieved from http://www.cnn.com/2009/WORLD/asiapcf/12/21/china.race/index.html

Chang, M. J. (1996). *Racial Diversity in Higher Education: Does a Racially Mixed Student Population Affect Educational Outcomes?* (Dissertation). University of California, Los Angeles, CA.

Chang, M. J. (1999). Does Racial Diversity Matter? The Education Impact of a Racially Diverse Undergraduate Populations. *Journal of College Student Development*, *40*(4), 377–395.

Chang, M. J. (2002). Preservation or Transformation: Where's the Real Educational Discourse on Diversity. *Review of Higher Education*, *25*(2), 125–140. doi:10.1353/rhe.2002.0003

Chang, M. J., Milem, J. F., & Antonio, A. L. (2010). Campus Climate and Diversity. In J. H. Schuh, S. R. Jones, S. R. Harper, & ... (Eds.), *Student Services: A Handbook for the Profession*. San Francisco: Jossey-Bass.

Cheng, Y. (2011). From Campus Racism to Cyber Racism: Discourse of Race and Chinese Nationalism. *The China Quarterly*, *207*, 561–579. doi:10.1017/S0305741011000658

Chiricos, T., Eschholz, S., & Gertz, M. (1997). Crime, News and Fear of Crime: Toward an Identification of Audience Effects. *Social Problems*, *44*(3), 342–357. doi:10.2307/3097181

Chiricos, T., McEntire, R., & Gertz, M. (2001). Perceived Racial and Ethnic Composition of Neighborhood and Perceived Risk of Crime. *Social Problems*, *48*(3), 322–340. doi:10.1525p.2001.48.3.322

Condit, C. M. (1989). The Rhetorical Limits of Polysemy. *Critical Studies in Mass Communication*, *6*(2), 103–122. doi:10.1080/15295038909366739

Cornbleth, C. (2002). Images of America: What Youth "Do" Know About the United States. *American Educational Research Journal*, *39*(2), 519–552. doi:10.3102/00028312039002519

Couldry, N. (2000). *The Place of Media Power: Pilgrims and Witnesses of the Media Age*. New York: Routledge.

Cuyjet, M. J. (2006). *African American Men in College* (1st ed.). San Francisco: Jossey-Bass.

D'Addario, D. (2014). From Beyoncé to Bruno Mars: Why No Super Bowl Halftime Will Satisfy Everyone. *Salon.com*. Retrieved from Salon.com website: http://www.salon.com/2014/02/01/from_beyonce_to_bruno_mars_why_no_super_bowl_halftime_will_satisfy_everyone/

Davis, A. J. (1997). Race, Cops and Traffic Stops. *University of Miami Law Review*, *51*(425).

Denson, N., & Chang, M. J. (2009). Racial Diversity Matters: The Impact of Diversity-Related Student Engagement and Institutional Context. *American Educational Research Journal*, *46*(2), 322–353. doi:10.3102/0002831208323278

Dikotter, F. (1997). *The Construction of Racial Identities in China and Japan: Historical and Contemporary Perspectives*. Honolulu, HI: University of Hawaii Press.

Dillard, A. D. (2001). *Guess Who's Coming to Dinner Now? Multicultural Conservatism in America*. New York: New York University Press.

Dixon, T. L., Asocar, C. L., & Casas, M. (2003). The Portrayal of Race and Crime on Television Network News. *Journal of Broadcasting & Electronic Media*, *47*(4), 498–524. doi:10.120715506878jobem4704_2

Dovidio, J. F., Gaertner, S. L., & Saguy, T. (2009). Commonality and the Complexity of 'We': Social Attitudes and Social Changes. *Personality and Social Psychology Review: An Official Journal of the Society for Personality and Social Psychology*, *13*(1), 3–20. doi:10.1177/1088868308326751 PMID:19144903

Du Gay, P. (1997). *Production of Culture/Cultures of Production*. Academic Press.

Durlauf, S. N. (2006). Assessing Racial Profiling. *The Economic Journal*, *116*(515), F402–F426. doi:10.1111/j.1468-0297.2006.01129.x

Entman, R. M., & Kimberly, A. Gross. (2008). Race to Judgment: Stereotyping Media and Criminal Defendants. *Law and Contemporary Problems*, *71*(4), 93–133.

Erickson, F. (2004). *Talk and Social Theory: Ecologies of Speaking and Listening in Everyday Life*. Cambridge, MA: Polity Press.

Essay on How Colleges Should Respond to Racism against International Students. (2012). Retrieved September 4, 2013, from http://www.insidehighered.com/views/2012/10/26/essay-how-colleges-should-respond-racism-against-international-students

Feagin, J. R. (2006). *Systemic Racism: A Theory of Oppression.* New York: Routledge.

Fiske, J. (1986). Television: Polysemy and Popularity. *Critical Studies in Mass Communication, 3*(4), 391–426. doi:10.1080/15295038609366672

Fogliati, V. J., & Bussey, K. (2013). Stereotype Threat Reduces Motivation to Improve: Effects of Stereotype Threat and Feedback on Women's Intentions to Improve Mathematical Ability. *Psychology of Women Quarterly, 37*(3), 310–324. doi:10.1177/0361684313480045

Ford, D. Y., Harris, J., & John, I. I. I. (1996). Perceptions and Attitudes of Black Students toward School, Achievement, and Other Educational Variables. *Child Development, 67*(3), 1141–1152. doi:10.2307/1131884 PMID:8706514

Forest, J. J., & Altbach, P. G. (2006). *International Handbook of Higher Education.* Dordrecht: Springer.

Fujioka, Y. (2000). Television Portrayals and African American Stereotypes: Examination of Television Effects When Direct Content Is Lacking. *Communication Abstracts, 23*(1), 3–149.

Gaertner, S. L., & Dividio, J. F. (2000). *Reducing Intergroup Bias: The Common Identity Model.* Hillsdale, NJ: Psychology Press.

Gaertner, S. L., Mann, J., Murrell, A., & Dividio, J. F. (1989). Reduction of Intergroup Bias: The Benefits of Recategorization. Journal of Personal and Social Psychology, 57, 239-249.

Gareis, E. (2012). Intercultural Friendship: Effects of Home and Host Region. *Journal of International and Intercultural Communication, 5*(4), 309–328. doi:10.1080/17513057.2012.691525

Gatewood, W. B. (2000). *Aristocrats of Color: The Black Elite, 1880-1920.* Fayetteville, AK: University of Arkansas Press.

Gilliam, F. D., & Iyengar, S. (2000). Prime Suspects: The Influence of Local Television News on the Viewing Public. *American Journal of Political Science, 44*(3), 560–573. doi:10.2307/2669264

Globetti, E. C., Globetti, G., Brown, C. L., & Smith, R. E. (1993). Social Interaction and Multiculturalism. *NASPA Journal, 30*(3), 209–218.

Gordon, L. (2010, January 12). UC Freshman to Include Record Number of out-of-State and International Students. *Los Angeles Times.* Retrieved from http://www.latimes.com/news/local/la-me-uc-enroll-20100715,0,2160250.story

Gordon, L., & Rojas, R. (2011). UCLA Won't Discipline Creator of Controversial Video, Who Later Withdraws from University. *Los Angeles Times.* Retrieved from http://articles.latimes.com/keyword/education

Gray, H. (2005). The Politics of Representation in Network Television. In D. M. Hunt (Ed.), *Channeling Blackness: Studies on Television and Race in America* (p. ix). New York: Oxford University Press.

Green, M. F. (2012). *Global Citizenship – What Are We Talking About and Why Does It Matter.* Retrieved from https://globalhighered.wordpress.com/2012/03/11/global-citizenship/

Gross, S. R., & Livingston, D. (2002). Racial Profiling under Attack. *Columbia Law Review*, *102*(5), 1413–1438. doi:10.2307/1123676

Grutter v. Bollinger (02-241) 539 U.S. 306 (U.S. Supreme Court 2003).

Gurin, P., Nagda, B. R. A., & Lopez, G. E. (2004). The Benefits of Diversity in Education for Democratic Citizenship. *The Journal of Social Issues*, *60*(1), 17–34. doi:10.1111/j.0022-4537.2004.00097.x

Gutmann, A. (1999). *Democratic Education with a New Preface and Epilogue*. Princeton, NJ: Princeton University Press.

Hall, S. (1981). Encoding and Decoding in Television Discourse. In S. Hall, D. Hobson, A. Lowe, & P. Willis (Eds.), *Culture, Media, Language* (pp. 128–138). London: Hutchinson.

Hall, S. (Ed.). (2003). *Representation: Cultural Representation and Signifying Practices*. London: Sage Publications.

Hanassab, S. (2006). Diversity, International Students, and Perceived Discrimination: Implications for Educators and Counselors. *Journal of Studies in International Education*, *10*(2), 157–172. doi:10.1177/1028315305283051

Harcourt, B. E. (2004). Rethinking Racial Profiling: A Critique of the Economics, Civil Liberties, and Constitutional Literature, and of Criminal Profiling More Generally. *The University of Chicago Law Review. University of Chicago. Law School*, *71*(4), 1275–1381.

Harding, S. G. (2004). *The Feminist Standpoint Theory Reader: Intellectual and Political Controversies*. New York: Routledge.

Harper, S. R. (2006). Peer Support for African American Male College Achievement: Beyond Internalized Racism and the Burden of "Acting White". *Journal of Men's Studies*, *14*(3), 337–358. doi:10.3149/jms.1403.337

Harper, S. R. (2009). Niggers No More: A Critical Counternarrative on Black Male Student Achievement at Predominantly White Colleges and University. *International Journal of Qualitative Studies in Education*, *22*(6), 697–712. doi:10.1080/09518390903333889

Harper, S. R. (Ed.). (2010). *An Anti-Deficit Achievement Framework for Research on Students of Color in Stem*. San Francisco: Jossey-Bass.

Harper, S. R., & Nichols, A.H. (2008). Are They Not All the Same? Racial Heterogeneity among Black Male Undergraduates. *Journal of College Student Development, 49*(3), 199-214. doi: 10l1353/csd.0.0003

Harris, A., & Allen, W. (2003). Lest We Forget Thee …: The under- and over-Representation of Black and Latino Youth in California Higher Education and Juvenile Justice Institutions. *Race and Society*, *6*(2), 99–123. doi:10.1016/j.racsoc.2004.11.008

Harris, C. I. (1993). Whiteness as Property. *Harvard Law Review*, *106*(8), 1707–1791. doi:10.2307/1341787

Hechanova-Alampay, R., Beehr, T. A., Christiansen, N. D., & Van Horn, R. K. (2002). Adjustment and Strain among Domestic and International Student Sojourners: A Longitudinal Study. *School Psychology International*, *23*(4), 458–474. doi:10.1177/0143034302234007

Hendrickson, B., Rosen, D., & Aune, R. K. (2011). An Analysis of Friendship Networks, Social Connectedness, Homesickness, and Satisfaction Levels of International Students. *International Journal of Intercultural Relations*, *35*(3), 281–295. doi:10.1016/j.ijintrel.2010.08.001

Henkin, D. M. (2008). On Forms and Media. *Representations (Berkeley, Calif.)*, *104*(1), 34–36. doi:10.1525/rep.2008.104.1.34

Hervik, P. (2004). Anthropological Perspectives on the New Racism in Europe. *Ethnos*, *69*(2), 140–155. doi:10.1080/0014184042000212830

Herzog, S. (2010). *Diversity and Educational Benefits*. San Francisco: Jossey-Bass.

hooks, b. (2004). *We Real Cool: Black Men and Masculinity*. New York: Routledge.

hooks, b. (2009). *Reel to Real* (Routledge Classics ed.). New York: Routledge.

Horn, R. A. Jr. (2003). Developing a Critical Awareness of the Hidden Curriculum through Media Literarcy. *The Clearing House: A Journal of Educational Strategies, Issues and Ideas*, *76*(6), 298–300. doi:10.1080/00098650309602024

Houston, B. (1994). The Metapsychology of Television Reception. *Quarterly Review of Film Studies*.

Hoxby, C. M., & Avery, C. (2012). *The Missing 'One-Offs': The Hidden Supply of High-Achieving, Low Income Students*. National Bureau of Economic Research. Retrieved from http://www.nber.org/papers/w18586

Hudson, A. (2013). 1 Black Man Is Killed Every 28 Hours by Police or Vigilantes: America Is Perpetually at War with Its Own People. *Alternet*. Retrieved from ALTERNET.ORG website: http://www.alternet.org/news-amp-politics/1-black-man-killed-every-28-hours-police-or-vigilantes-america-perpetually-war-its

Hunt, D. M. (2005). Making Sense of Blackness on Television. In D. M. Hunt (Ed.), *Channeling Blackness: Studies on Television and Race in America* (p. 320). New York: Oxford University Press.

Hunt, D. M. (2011). *The Cosby Show: U.S. Situation Comedy*. Retrieved from http://www.museum.tv/eotv/cosbyshowt.htm

Hurtado, S. (1992). The Campus Racial Climate: Contexts of Conflict. *The Journal of Higher Education*, *63*(5), 539–569. doi:10.2307/1982093

Hurtado, S. (2000). The Campus Racial Climate: Contexts of Conflict. In M. C. Brown (Ed.), *Organizational Governance in Higher Eduation* (pp. 182–202). Boston, MA: Pearson.

Hurtado, S. (2001). Linking Diversity and Educational Purpose: How Diversity Affects the Classroom Environment and Student Development. In G. Orfield, & Kurlaeder (Eds.), Diversity Challenged: Evidence on the Impact of Affirmative Action (pp. 187-203). Cambridge, MA: Harvard Publishing Group.

Hurtado, S. (2003). Institutional Diversity in American Higher Education. In S. R. Komives, D. B. Woodward Jr, & ... (Eds.), *Student Services: A Handbook for the Profession* (4th ed., pp. 23–44). San Francisco, CA: Jossey-Bass.

Hurtado, S. (2005). *Higher Learning for Citizenship. Presented at 28th Annual Earl V. Pullias Lecture.* Center for Higher Education Policy Analysis, University of Southern California.

Hurtado, S., Clayton-Pedersen, A. R., Allen, W. R., & Milem, J. F. (1998). Enhancing Campus Climates for Racial/Ethnic Diversity: Educational Policy and Practice. *The Review of Higher Education, 21*(3), 279–302. doi:10.1353/rhe.1998.0003

Hurtado, S., Dey, E. L., & Trevino, J. G. (1994). *Exclusion or Segregation? Interaction across Racial/ Ethnic Groups on College Campuses.* Paper presented at the American Educational Research Association, New Orleans, LA.

Hurtado, S. M. J., Clayton-Pederson, A., & Allen, W. (1999). *Enacting Diverse Learning Environments: Improving the Campus Climate for Racial/Ethnic Diversity. ASHE/ERIC Higher Education Reports Series 26, No. 8.* Washington, DC: George Washington University/ERIC Clearinghouse on Higher Education.

Institute of International Education. (2011). *Open Doors Data.* Retrieved from http://www.iie.org/ Research-and-Publications/Open-Doors/Data/International-Students.aspx

Jackson, D. Z. (2005). Stereotyping Black Men. *The Boston Globe.* Retrieved from http://www.boston. com/news/globe/editorial_opinion/oped/articles/2005/05/27/stereotyping_black_men/

Jeffries, V., & Ransford, E. (1969). Interracial Social Contact and Middle Class White Reactions to the Watts Riot. *Social Problems, 16*(3), 312–324. doi:10.2307/799665

Johnson, D. (2007). *Race and Racism in China: Chinese Racial Attitudes toward Africans and African Americans.* Bloomington, IN: AuthorHouse.

Kellner, D. (1990). *Television and the Crisis of Democracy.* Boulder, CO: Westview Press, Inc.

Kellner, D. (1995). *Media Culture.* New York: Routledge. doi:10.4324/9780203205808

Kellner, D. (2010). *Cinema Wars: Hollywood Film and Politics in the Bush-Cheney Era.* Malden, MA: Wiley-Blackwell.

Kellner, D. (2011). Cultural Studies, Multiculturalism, and Media Culture. In G. Dines, & J. M. Humez (Eds.), Gender, Race and Class in Media (3rd ed.; pp. 7-18). Thousand Oaks, CA: Sage Publications, Inc.

Kendon, A. (1990). *Conducting Interaction: Patterns of Behavior in Focused Encounters.* Cambridge, UK: Cambridge University Press.

Kim, N. (2008). *Imperial Citizens: Koreans and Race from Seoul to L.A.* Palo Alto, CA: Stanford University Press.

King, S., & Darabont, F. (1994). *The Shawshank Redemption* [Film]. L. Glotzer, D. Lester, & Niki Martin (Producer). Hollywood, CA.

Kitwana, B. (2002). The Hip Hop Generation: Young Blacks and the Crisis in African American Culture. New York: Basic Civitas Books.

Kobayashi, Y. (2010). Discriminatory Attitudes toward Intercultural Communication in Domestic and Overseas Contexts. *Higher Education, 59*(3), 323–333. doi:10.100710734-009-9250-9

Kretch, D., & Crutchfield, R. (1973). Perceiving the World. In W. Schramm (Ed.), *Men, Messages and Media*. New York: Harper and Row.

Lee, J., & Bean, F. D. (2004). America's Changing Color Lines: Immigration, Race/Ethnicity, and Multiracial Identification. *Annual Review of Sociology, 30*(1), 221–242. doi:10.1146/annurev.soc.30.012703.110519

Lee, J. J. (2007a). Bottomline: Neo-Racism toward International Students. *About Campus: Enriching the Student Learning Experience, 11*(6), 28–30. doi:10.1002/abc.194

Lee, J. J., & Rice, C. (2007b). Welcome to America? International Student Perceptions of Discrimination and Neo-Racism. *Higher Education, 53*(3), 381–409. doi:10.100710734-005-4508-3

Leonardo, Z. (2005). Through the Multicultural Glass: Althusser, Ideology and Race Relations in Post-Civil Rights America. *Policy Futures in Education, 3*(4), 400–412. doi:10.2304/pfie.2005.3.4.400

Levin, J. (2013). Bruno Mars: New Pop Prince. *MiamiHerald.com*. Retrieved from MiamiHerald.com website: http://www.miamiherald.com/2013/08/31/3598303/bruno-mars-new-pop-prince.html

Lieber, R. J., & Weisberg, R. E. (2002). Globalization, Culture, and Identities in Crisis. *International Journal of Politics Culture and Society, 16*(2), 273–296. doi:10.1023/A:1020581114701

Locke, D. C., & Valesco, J. (1987). Hospitality Begins with the Invitation: Counseling Foreign Students. *Journal of Multicultural Counseling and Development, 15*(3), 115–119. doi:10.1002/j.2161-1912.1987.tb00386.x

Locks, A. M., Hurtado, S., Bowman, N. A., & Oseguera, L. (2008). Extending Notions of Campus Climate and Diversity to Students' Transition to College. *The Review of Higher Education, 31*(3), 257–285. doi:10.1353/rhe.2008.0011

Loo, C. M., & Rolison, G. (1986). Alienation of Ethnic Minority Students at a Predominantly White University. *The Journal of Higher Education, 57*.

Los Angeles Riots Fast Facts. (2014, May 3). Retrieved March 21, 2015, from http://www.cnn.com/2013/09/18/us/los-angeles-riots-fast-facts/

McIntosh, P. (2008). White Privilege: Unpacking the Invisible Knapsack. In P. S. Rothenberg (Ed.), *White Privilege: Essential Readings on the Other Side of Racism*. New York: Worth Publishers.

McMurtie, B. (2012). China Continues to Drive Foreign-Student Growth in the United States. *The Chronicle of Higher Education*.

Milem, J. (2001). Increasing Diversity Benefits: How Campus Climate and Teaching Methods Affect Student Outcomes. In Diversity Challenged: Evidence on the Impact of Affirmative Action. Cambridge, MA: Harvard Education Publishing Group.

Milem, J. F. (1998). Attitude Change in College Students: Examining the Effect of College Peer Groups and Faculty Normative Groups. *The Journal of Higher Education, 69*(2), 117–140. doi:10.2307/2649203

Mills, C. W. (1997). *The Racial Contract*. Ithaca, NY: Cornell University Press.

Morey, A. I. (2004). Globalization and the Emergence of for-Profit Higher Education. *Higher Education, 48*(1), 131–150. doi:10.1023/B:HIGH.0000033768.76084.a0

Morley, D. (1980). *The 'Nationwide' Audience: Structure and Decoding*. London: BFI.

Morley, D. (1992). *Television, Audiences, and Cultural Studies*. London: Routledge.

Morley, D. (1993). Active Audience Theory: Pendulums and Pitfalls. *Journal of Communication, 43*(4), 13–19. doi:10.1111/j.1460-2466.1993.tb01299.x

Mydans, S. (1992, Apr. 30). Los Angeles Policemen Acquitted in Taped Beating. *The New York Times,* p. 1. Retrieved from http://www.nytimes.com/learning/general/onthisday/990429onthisday_big.html

Nelson, H. V. (2003). *The Rise and Fall of Modern Black Leadership: Chronicle of a Twentieth Century Tragedy*. Lanham, MD: University Press of America, Inc.

Nemetz, P. L., & Christensen, S. L. (1996). The Challenge of Cultural Diversity: Harnessing a Diversity of Views to Understand Multiculturalism. *Academy of Management Review, 21*(2), 434–462.

Nicotheory: So...Apparently There Was A... (2014). Retrieved March 24, 2014, from https://twitter.com/NicoTheory/status/430209850736271361

Nora, A., & Cabrera, A. F. (1996). The Role of Perceptions of Prejudice and Discrimination on the Adjustment of Minority Students to College. *The Journal of Higher Education, 67*(2), 119–148. doi:10.2307/2943977

Nyasha, K. (2013). The Acquittal of a Murderer. *San Francisco Bay View*. Retrieved from San Francisco Bay View >>> The acquittal of a murderer website: http://sfbayview.com/2013/the-acquittal-of-a-murderer/

Ole Miss Alumni Association. (2013). *The Omazing Race*. Retrieved September 4, 2013, from http://olemissalumni.com/news/default.aspx?page_id=322&nb=yes

Olzak, S. (2011). Does Globalization Breed Ethnic Discontent? *The Journal of Conflict Resolution, 55*(1), 3–32. doi:10.1177/0022002710383666

Paige, R. M. (1990). International Students: Cross-Cultural Psychological Perspectives. In R. W. Brislin (Ed.), *Applied Cross-Cultural Psychology* (pp. 161–185). Newbury Park, CA: Sage. doi:10.4135/9781483325392.n8

Parkinson-Morgan, K. (2011). *Updated*: UCLA Student's Youtube Video 'Asian in the Library' Prompts Death Threats: Violent Responses Criticized as Equally Damaging. *The Daily Bruin*. Retrieved from http://dailybruin.com/2011/03/14ucla_student039s_youtube_video_039asians_in_the_library039_prompts_death_threats_violent_re-sponses_c/

Pascarella, E. T., & Terenzini, P. T. (2005). *How College Affects Students: A Third Decade of Research* (Vol. 2). San Francisco: Jossey-Bass.

Patton, M. Q. (2002). *Qualitative Research & Evaluation Methods* (3rd ed.). Thousand Oaks, CA: Sage Publications.

Pettigrew, T. F., & Tropp, L. R. (2000). Does Intergroup Contact Reduce Prejudice? In S. Oskamp (Ed.), *Reducing Prejudice and Discrimination: Social Psyhological Perspectives* (pp. 93–114). Mahwah, NJ: Erlbaum.

Postman, N. (1979). The First Curriculum: Comparing School and Television. *Phi Delta Kappan, 61*(3), 163–168.

Quick Facts – UCLA Undergraduate Admissions. (2012). *Campus Profile*. Retrieved from http://www. admissions.ucla.edu/campusprofile.htm

Race, Racism and International Students in the United States. (2013). *NACADA Academic Advising Today: Voices from the Global Community*. Retrieved from http://www.nacada.ksu.edu/Resources/ Academic-Advising-Today/View-Articles/Race--Racism--and-International-Students-in-the-United-States.aspx#sthash.Tgew30Vv.dpuf

Radloff, T. D., & Evans, N. J. (2003). The Social Construction of Prejudice among Black and White College Students. *NASPA Journal, 40*(2), 1–16. doi:10.2202/0027-6014.1222

Rankin, S. R., & Reason, R. D. (2005). Differing Perceptions: How Students of Color and White Students Perceive Campus Climate for Underrepresented Groups. *Journal of College Student Development, 46*(1), 43–61. doi:10.1353/csd.2005.0008

Risse, M., & Zeckhauser, R. (2004). Racial Profiling. *Philosophy & Public Affairs, 32*(2), 131–170. doi:10.1111/j.1088-4963.2004.00009.x

Ritter, Z. (2012). Essay on Dealing with Racist Ideas of International Students. *Inside Higher Ed*. Retrieved from InsideHigherEd website: http://www.insidehighered.com/views/2012/10/26/essay-deadling-racist-ideas-international-students

Ritter, Z. (2013). *Making and Breaking Stereotypes: East Asian International Students' Experience with Cross-Racial Interactions*. (Ph.D. Dissertation). UCLA, Los Angeles, CA.

Ritter, Z., & Roth, K. (2014). Realizing Race: Media Representations and the Uneasy Adjustment of Asian International Students and African American Males on U.S. College Campuses. In N. D. Erbe (Ed.), *Approaches to Managing Organizational Diversity and Innovation* (p. 387). Hershey, PA: IGI Global. doi:10.4018/978-1-4666-6006-9.ch006

Rodriguez, D. (2012). De-Provincializing Police Violence: On the Recent Events at UC Davis. *Race & Class, 54*(1), 99–109. doi:10.1177/0306396812444831

Rose, W. (2002). Crimes of Color: Risk, Profiling, and the Contemporary Racialization of Social Control. *International Journal of Politics Culture and Society, 16*(2), 179–205. doi:10.1023/A:1020572912884

Roth, K. (2011). *The Other Curriculum: How Mass Media Can Shape Perceptions of College Going for African American Males*. Paper presented at the Association for the Study of Higher Education (ASHE), Charlotte, NC.

Roth, K. (2015a). *The Other Curriculum: Media Representations and the College Going Perceptions of African American Males*. (Ph.D. Dissertation), UCLA, Los Angeles, CA.

Roth, K., & Ritter, Z. (2015b). Diversity and the Need for Cross-Cultural Leadership and Collaboration. In N. D. Erbe & A. H. Normore (Eds.), *Cross-Cultural Collaboration and Leadership in Modern Organization*. Hershey, PA: IGI Global.

Russell, J. (1991). Race & Reflexivity: The Black Other in Contemporary Japanese Mass Culture. *Cultural Anthropology*, 6(1), 3–25. doi:10.1525/can.1991.6.1.02a00010

Ryan, P. (2014). Will Bruno Mars 'Wow' with Super Bowl Halftime Show? *USA Today*. Retrieved from USA Today website: http://www.usatoday.com/story/life/music/2014/01/30/will-bruno-mars-wow-with-super-bowl-halftime-performance/4977173/

Sakurai, T., Mccall-Wolf, F., & Kashima, E. (2010). Building International Links: The Impact of a Multicultural Intervention Programme on Social Ties of International Students in Australia. *International Journal of Intercultural Relations*, 34(2), 176–185. doi:10.1016/j.ijintrel.2009.11.002

Scott, T. (1998). *Enemy of the State* [Film]. J. Bruckheimer (Producer). Hollywood.

Smith, D. G. (2009). *Diversity's Promise for Higher Education: Making It Work*. Baltimore, MD: The Johns Hopkins University Press.

Smith, T. B., Bowman, R., & Hsu, S. (2007a). Racial Attitudes among Asian and European American College Students: A Cross-Cultural Examination. *College Student Journal*, 41(2), 436–443.

Smith, W. A., Allen, W. A., & Danley, L. L. (2007b). Assume the Position...You Fit the Description. *The American Behavioral Scientist*, 51(4), 551–578. doi:10.1177/0002764207307742

Smith, W. A., Hung, M., & Franklin, J. D. (2011). Racial Battle Fatigue and the Miseducation of Black Men: Racial Microaggressions, Societal Problems, and Environmental Stress. *The Journal of Negro Education*, 80(1), 63–82.

Solórzano, D., Ceja, Miguel, & Yosso, Tara. (2000). Critical Race Theory, Racial Microaggressions, and Campus Racial Climate: The Experiences of African American College Students. *The Journal of Negro Education*, 69(1/2), 60–73.

Special Issue: Intergroup Dialogue: Engaging Difference, Social Identities and Social Justice. (2012). *Equity & Excellence in Education*, 45(1).

Stack, M., & Kelly, D. M. (2006). Popular Media, Education, and Resistance. *Canadian Journal of Education*, 29(1), 5–26. doi:10.2307/20054144

Steele, C. M. (1997). A Threat in the Air: Stereotypes Shape Intellectual Identity and Performance. *The American Psychologist*, 52(6), 613–629. doi:10.1037/0003-066X.52.6.613 PMID:9174398

Steele, C. M. (2010). *Whistling Vivaldi: How Stereotypes Affect Us and What We Can Do*. New York, London: W. W. Norton and Company.

Talbot, D., Geelhoed, R., & Ninggal, M. T. (1999). A Qualitative Study of Asian International Students' Attitudes toward African-Americans. *NASPA Journal*, 36(3). doi:10.2202/0027-6014.1081

Tatum, B. D. (1997). *Why Are All the Black Kids Sitting Together in the Cafeteria? And Other Conversations About Race*. New York: Basic Books.

Taylor, B. C., Demont-Heinrich, C., Broadfoot, K. J., Dodge, J., & Jian, C. (2002). New Media and the Circuit of Cyber-Culture: Conceptualizing Napster. *Journal of Broadcasting & Electronic Media, 46*(4), 607–629. doi:10.120715506878jobem4604_7

The Blaaag: Official Tumblr of Columbia University's Asian American Alliance. (2012). Retrieved from http://theblaaag.tumblr.com/post/4415598604/cucssas-finding-li-wei

Theatrical Market Statistics. (2011). Retrieved from www.bumpercarfilms.com/assets/downloads/movies.pdf

Tobolowsky, B. F. (2001). *The Influence of Prime-Time Television on Latinas' College Aspiration and Expectations.* (Ph.D Dissertation), UCLA, Los Angeles, CA.

Tobolowsky, B. F. (2006). Beyond Demographics: Understanding the College Experience through Television. *New Directions for Student Services, 2006*(114), 17–26. doi:10.1002s.204

Torres, C. A., & Rhoads, R. A. (2006). Introduction: Globalization and Higher Education in the Americas. In *The University, State, and Market: The Political Economy of Globalization in the Americas.* Stanford, CA: Stanford University Press.

Torres, C. A., & Schugurensky, D. (2002). The Political Economy of Higher Education in the Era of Neoliberal Globalization: Latin America in Comparative Perspective. *Higher Education, 43*(4), 429–455. doi:10.1023/A:1015292413037

University of Iowa. (2013). *Bridging Domestic and Global Diversity.* Retrieved June 15, 2013, from http://international.uiowa.edu/cultural-training/bridging-domestic-and-global-Diversity

Van Heertum, R., & Torres, C. (2009). Globalization and Neoliberalism: The Challenges and Possibilities of Radical Pedagogy. In M. Simons (Ed.), *Re-Reading Education Policies: Studying the Policy Agenda of the 21st Century.* Netherlands: Sense Publishers.

Vandrick, S. (2011). Students of the New Global Elite. *TESOL Quarterly: a Journal for Teachers of English to Speakers of Other Lanugages and of Standard English as a Second Dialect, 45*(1), 160–169. doi:10.5054/tq.2011.244020

Winant, H. (2000). Race and Race Theory. *Annual Review of Sociology, 26*(1), 169–185. doi:10.1146/annurev.soc.26.1.169

World Reputation Rankings. (2015). *The Higher Education World University Rankings.* Retrieved 8/17, 2015, from https://www.timeshighereducation.co.uk/world-university-rankings/2015/reputation-ranking#/sort/0/direction/asc

WSU Global Leadership Certificate. (2013). Retrieved September 3, 2013, from http://ip.wsu.edu/resources/statistics/intl-students.html

WSU International Population Statistics. (2013). Retrieved August 30, 2013, from http://ip.wsu.edu/resources/statistics/intl-students.html

Wu, S. (2005). The Secret Ambition of Racial Profiling. *The Yale Law Journal, 115*(2), 491–499.

Zuniga, X., Lopez, G. E., & Ford, K. A. (2012). Intergroup Dialogue: Critical Conversations About Difference, Social Identities, and Social Justice: Guest Editors' Introduction. *Equity & Excellence in Education*, *45*(1), 1–13. doi:10.1080/10665684.2012.646903

Zuniga, X., Nagda, B. A., & Sevig, T. D. (2002). Intergroup Dialogues: An Educational Model for Cultivating Engagement across Differences. *Equity & Excellence in Education*, *35*(1), 7–17. doi:10.1080/713845248

Zuniga, X., Williams, E. A., & Berger, J. B. (2005). Action-Oriented Democratic Outcomes: The Impact of Student Involvement with Campus Diversity. *Journal of College Student Development*, *46*(6), 660–678. doi:10.1353/csd.2005.0069

This research was previously published in Handbook of Research on Race, Gender, and the Fight for Equality edited by Julie Prescott; pages 142-171, copyright year 2016 by Information Science Reference (an imprint of IGI Global).

Chapter 16
Portrayal of Women in Nollywood Films and the Role of Women in National Development

Suleimanu Usaini
Covenant University, Nigeria

Ngozi M. Chilaka
Covenant University, Nigeria

Nelson Okorie
Covenant University, Nigeria

ABSTRACT

This study investigates how women are portrayed in Nollywood films, as well as the interpretation of their representations. It aims at understanding how the images of women are reflected in films, with a focus on investigating the influence of such portrayals on their role in national development. The methods adopted were Quantitative Content Analysis (five Nollywood films were content analysed) and Focus Group Discussion (three sessions of FGD were organised). Data collected and analysed show that over two-thirds of major female characters analysed were portrayed as dependent, 80% were depicted in such situations of physical, sexual, and emotional abuse, while only 30% of the major female characters were portrayed as career professionals and intellectuals. It was observed from the analyses that portrayals and representations of women have negative influences on their contributions towards national development. The study concludes, therefore, that positive portrayal of women in Nollywood films should be encouraged. This can only be made possible through changing the narrative style of the film scripts. This is a call for more female script writers and directors to be involved in charting the narratives that will adequately give women a voice, new roles, and the right representation in Nollywood films.

DOI: 10.4018/978-1-5225-9869-5.ch016

INTRODUCTION

The media has become inevitable in this present society. From newspapers to magazines, radio to television, the Internet to films, these various media outlets influence their audience in one way or another. The media inform, entertain, and educate us. Fischer (2010, p.1) says that "the impact of the media on our daily lives is tremendous, and most of the time we are not aware of this huge influential factor". The media can "move our emotions, challenge our intellects, and insult our intelligence. They can also influence people's beliefs, values, attitudes, behaviours, perceptions and opinions on various issues without them even realising it" (Baran, 2010). Furthermore, the mass media, beyond the three core functions of providing information, education and entertainment, play a significant role in shaping the perceptions and worldviews of the audience through the messages they communicate and the interpretation they also give to the messages. It, therefore, comes as no surprise that, due to its especially powerful and pervasive nature, the media contributes to shaping people's perception and opinion on issues having to do with social relationships and gender relations in the society.

Among the mass media of communication, television is seen as the most influential. By combining pictures and sound, TV can communicate messages which are impossible to convey as effectively by radio and or print. Television is the central cultural arm of society, as a culture's primary story teller. It is the chief creator of entertainment and information for heterogeneous mass publics (Baran, 2009).

Jonah (2011, p.1) points out that "Film is one of the channels of mass communication which is transmitted via the television which has grown over the years. It started as cinema and later grew into home video which many Nigerians patronize today". Sambe (2008, p.142) defines film as series of motionless images projected into a screen so fast as to create in the mind of anyone watching the screen an impression of a motion. Nigerian films industry otherwise known as Nollywood films has come of age.Nigerian films daily flood the global channels with series of films which dwell on various aspects of life (Jonah, 2011).

Nigerian films are deeply rooted in the Nigerian cultural traditions and social texts that focus on Nigerian community life (Onuzulike, 2007). Daramola (2008) supports this that the Nigerian film industry holds up a mirror to the society and projects what is seen in the society.

As the twentieth century ended, research evidences showed that Nigerian films were filled with negative and stereotypic images of women. This is done to the disadvantage of women as these images promote continuous domination by men and subordination and subjugation of women (Okunna, 2002). "Given the great influence that Nollywood has over African culture, such effect is reinforced by a massive consumption of Nigerian films by Africans living in Africa and off the shores of Africa" (Onuzulike, 2007, p. 237).

According to Amobi (2010, p.1), the treatment of women in films has occupied the realm of discourse for several decades now. Feminist scholars, critics and women's movements have relentlessly challenged the stereotypical representations of women in Hollywood films (the American film industry), criticising their sexist depictions as whores, jilted mistresses, emotional cripples, sex-starved spinsters and psychotics. The Nigerian film industry, Nollywood, is no different as this entrant to the world of cinema has also been criticised for its portrayal of women as sex objects, weak, cold-hearted, materialistic, vengeful, vicious, diabolical, and scheming.

This study investigates why women's roles are mostly captured in domestic spaces which shows them as a marginalised group whose functions in some of the films cannot go beyond those of being mothers, housewives, and other related roles. In contrast, men are depicted mostly as leaders both in military and civilian spheres of rulership and as successful businessmen.

The portrayal of women in these films demands great scrutiny to identify the image of women which can have adverse effects on women viewers and the extent to which it can with a view to reordering the trend. This study, therefore, investigates the portrayal of women in Nigerian films and how their representations influence perceptions of the roles they play in the society as the backbone of the family.

LITERATURE REVIEW

The Nigerian film industry is fast growing and its global reach is quite phenomenal. It is said that Nollywood has become the third largest film industry in the world after Hollywood and Bollywood (Eke, 2012). Aladese (2013) agrees that Nollywood is one of the foremost filmmaking industries in the world and has earned a reputation for being one of the most prolific filmmaking industries in the world. Despite the success story of Nollywood, a lot of critics are concerned about the themes reflected in the films. Some researchers have argued that Nollywood films portray negative themes that damage the way other countries perceive Nigeria.

Akinfeleye and Amobi (2011, p. 6) opine that Nollywood films are internationally dismissed for their low production quality while scholars posit that they defy all theoretical explanations to phenomenon. Osofisan (2006) adds that most Nollywood films portray cultural and ideological deficiencies, promoting alien customs and inferiority complex among the people. He criticises the financiers and script writers for their interest in filmmaking as business to make quick money, and consequently ignoring the aesthetic or ontological dimensions of film production.

Akpabio (2007, p. 95) conducted a study that revealed that, "A majority of respondents (53.6%) expressed the view that there is glorification of negative themes and storylines in Nollywood films. Respondents who expressed disagreement accounted for 22.5% while close to a fifth of the respondents (18.7%) preferred to remain neutral on this score. Based on this finding, the study concluded that there is indeed glorification of negative themes and storylines in some home video productions". Akpabio (2003) enlists some themes portrayed in Nollywood films such as: evils of polygamy, extra marital affairs, different forms of evil rituals, cultism, occultism and witchcraft, conflict between western and indigenous cultures, religious divergence and complexities of the Nigerian society, just to mention a few.

Ebewo (2007) has a different view as he sees nothing wrong with a film dealing with any of these themes. He opines that critics frown at the fact that they recur, film after film. Aladese (2013, p. 20) argues that while some believe the themes that recur in Nigerian films are negative, others believe that it is these very themes that allow viewers to be aware of the society a part of which they are. She also claims that some researchers are of the opinion that Nigerian films do not portray the country in a negative light by showcasing negative themes but reflect the culture of the society they emanate from. The argument thus is that the films are reflections of the society. They capture our cultural make-ups and differences. The contents of the films are indigenous and they address issues that relate to the day-to-day lives with which the audience can relate.

Therefore, what is the role of women in or their contribution to national development? Women make useful contributions to the development of society. Obi (2001) opines that one of the ways they do this is through their ability to keep neat homes and environments, produce smart and healthy children and also cook neatly. She further expatiated on this that women can contribute to the development efforts of their country, improve their families' health, diet, productive ability, socio-cultural status and also be able to discharge responsibilities as mothers, wives and members of the society effectively. According to Sani (2001, p. 139), women more often than not derived their social status from performing dual roles of wife and mother. As a mother, the woman is the primary custodian of the cherished values of the society. This she does by devoting her valuable time and energy to teaching and inculcating societal values into the growing babies, caring for the well-being of all other members of the family, which earned her a high social status. Haralambos & Holborn (2008, p. 83), citing Goldthorpe (1983), do not believe that a male where present should automatically be considered head of a household. They believe that the head should be defined as "the family member who has the greatest commitment to and continuity in the labour market".

Therefore, husbands and wives should be allocated to classes as individuals rather than as part of a family unit. Igwesi (2012, p. 218) further posits that developing countries such as Nigeria need not only understand and emphasise the importance of gender equity in national development but also to ensure that at all levels in the society females are given the opportunity to harness their in-built potentials and are able to contribute immensely to national development. National development in this context refers to the plans, policies and actions of a nation to improve the lives of its citizens. This presupposes that national development is not just the responsibility of the government or political representatives of the people, but the responsibility of all and sundry. This development can be social, economic, political, educational, quality health care, reducing poverty, providing job opportunities, etc. Therefore, the goal of every national development agenda is to improve the lives of the citizens within the context of a growing economy, and an emphasis on the good of the community at large.

Igwesi (2012) recalls that there are many women who have contributed immensely to the socio-economic, political and human development of the society. Some are politicians, academics, entrepreneurs, leaders of different organisations, career professionals and bread winners. Examples are Professor Alele Williams, former Vice-Chancellor of University of Benin; Dr. Ngozi Okonjo-Iweala, Nigeria's former Minister of Finance and former Vice President, World Bank, who contributed to the economic growth and development of Nigeria, and late Professor Dora Akunyili, former Director General of National Agency for Food Drug Administration and Control (NAFDAC) and former Minister of Information also contributed to the fight against fake drugs and rebranding campaign of Nigeria's image in the international community. This is just to mention few Nigerian women who have made their marks in the country as Ministers, members of the National Assembly, Deputy Governors, etc, and have contributed useful ideas to the growth, development and sustainability of their immediate communities and the country at large.

According to Sani (2001, p. 4), historical records show that there were situations where women not only contributed to the socio-economic development of their communities, but were also involved in the territorial struggles. Examples of such women were Queen Amina of Zazzau, Queen Kambasa of Bonny, Chief (Mrs.) Olufunmilayo Ransome-Kuti, Nana Asma'u, and Queen Emotan of Benin Kingdom. Their positions were not merely passive, supportive roles, but powerful, constructive, sometimes self-sacrificing roles. Some of these historical women, especially the legendary figures, sacrificed themselves in the service of their communities.

Onwubiko (2012, p. 69) states that, "in Nigeria today, the women folk have come a long way; in business, politics, education, sports and other professions. Women have made an indelible mark in their effort to conquer the limitations of the past which have sought to place them permanently in the kitchen and bedroom". Sani (2001, p. 221) argues that in order to further strengthen the effort of women in national and international development, policy makers, international organisations and non-governmental organisations, should continue to do the following:

- Promote women's access to economic resources.
- Encourage women to acquire both formal and informal education.
- Increase women's access to appropriate, affordable and qualitative health care and related services.
- Eliminate all forms of violence against women.
- Encourage the media to always portray positive images of women.
- Increase women's participation in decision-making.
- Establish national mechanism towards the emancipation of women.
- Integrate women into environmental management.

Empowering Nigerian women towards national development should be a matter of national top priority which demands the attention and genuine commitment of every responsible member of the society. The Nigerian nation owes the women folk the responsibility of removing those artificial and institutional barriers based on religion, culture or traditional considerations which have incapacitated the ability of Nigerian women to participate effectively and freely in national affairs particularly at the political and economic levels (Onwubiko, 2012).

Theoretical Framework

The theory adopted for this study is the Cultural Norms Theory. Folarin (2005, p. 96-97) in his view states that, through selective presentation and emphasis on certain themes, the mass media created the impression among their audience that such themes were part of the culture or clearly defined cultural norms of society. As a result, some members of the society tend to pattern their behaviour along the line of such media presentations.

This theory of mass communication suggests that the mass media selectively presents, and emphasises certain contemporary ideas or values. According to this theory, the mass media influences norms by reinforcing or changing them. For example, the cultural norm theorists argue that television programmes presenting an active lifestyle for women as promiscuous and dependent on their male counterparts can change the attitudes of viewers in that direction (Ballack, 2009). According to Okenwa (2000, p. 22), the cultural norms theory postulates that the mass media through selective presentations and emphasis on certain themes create impressions among the audience that common cultural norms concerning the emphasized topics are structured or defined in specific ways. Furthermore, the media can potentially influence behaviour by reinforcing existing norms; creating new norms; and modifying existing norms.

Okenwa (2000, p.22), states that, "the media can be adequately utilised for the transmission of culture both internally and externally". Oyero (2011) opines that cultural norms theory offers a broad range of interesting ideas about how media can affect culture and provide many different views concerning the long-term consequences of the cultural changes affected by media. The theory directly addresses questions about the way media might produce profound changes in social life and argued that media might have the power to intrude into and alter how we make sense of ourselves and our social world. This theory posits that through the presentations and depictions of women, Nigerian films have created an impression among their audience that such portrayals are part of the culture of the society and as a result they begin to mould their behaviour in line with the film's depictions. Therefore, it might likely influence the perceptions of the audience towards the roles of women in their active participation towards national political, socio-economic and human development.

Research Questions

1. What specific roles are assigned to women in the selected Nollywood films?
2. How is the ability of women to contribute to national development portrayed in the selected Nollywood films?
3. What behavioural traits are female characters assigned in the selected Nollywood films?
4. To what extent do these representations of women in the selected Nollywood films showcase their active participation in the process of national development?

Methodology

The researchers adopted a quantitative and qualitative approach to the study. Quantitative content analysis was used to collect data concerning how women were portrayed in the selected Nollywood films. The researchers got access to the list of some Nollywood films approved for distribution and viewership in the year 2012 by the National Film & Video Censors Board (NFVCB). A total of Eighty (80) films produced in English were got. The sample for the study was drawn from the list of films. The list formed the sampling frame for the sampling process, and the sampling method used to select the five films examined was systematic sampling with a random start, adopting an interval of five. The researchers decided to study only five out of the 80 films (over five per cent of the total number). The five selected films were: *Mr. & Mrs.*, *Damage*, *Ties that Bind*, *Fazebook Babes*, and *Midnight Whispers*. The conclusions reached in this study were based mainly on the five selected and analysed films.

Also the researchers went further to do a Focus Group Discussion (FGD) on the perceived influence these films have on women's participations in national development. Three (3) sessions of FGD involving a representative sample of viewers of Nollywood films from different socio-economic groups were conducted. The participants ranged according to age, sex, and educational level, and were drawn from undergraduate and postgraduate students of University of Lagos, Akoka, and some selected residents of Akoka community.

The participants in the first group (18-25 years) consisted of participants who were in their third and fourth years of their first degree at the University of Lagos. The second group (26-34 years) were postgraduate students studying at Masters Level on part-time basis also at the University of Lagos. Participants in the third group (35-45 years) were predominantly less educated people including artisans, traders, and shop owners who were residents of Akoka at the time this study was conducted.

Results

For results, see Tables 1 and 2 and Figures 1 and 2.

DISCUSSION

Nollywood films are deeply rooted in Nigerian cultural traditions and social contexts that focus on Nigerian community life (Onuzulike, 2007). "Given the great influence that Nollywood has over African culture, such effect is reinforced by a massive consumption of Nigerian films by Africans living in Africa and off the shores of Africa" (Onuzulike, 2007, p. 237). As the twentieth century ended, research evi-

Table 1. Distribution of major female characters in the films

Film Title	Major Female Characters
Mr & Mrs.	5
Damage	2
Ties that Bind	3
Fazebook Babes	3
Midnight Whispers	2
Total	n=15

Table 2. Frequency of behavioural traits attributed to females

Feminine Traits	Percentage
Caring/ Loving	67%
Childlike	40%
Crying/Whining	53%
Dependent	73%
Fearful	33%
Happy	53%
Scared/ Desperate	47%
Total	n=15

Figure 1. Percentage of stereotypical and non-stereotypical female professional role

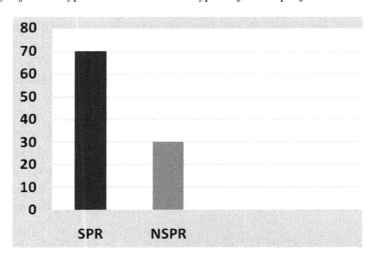

Figure 2. Percentage of stereotypical and non-stereotypical female behavioural traits

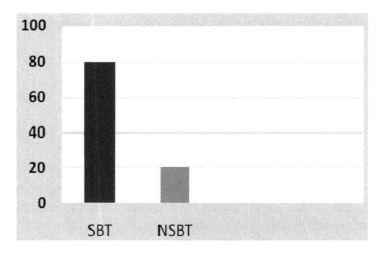

dences showed that some Nollywood films were filled with negative and stereotypic images of women. This is done to the disadvantage of women as these images promote continued domination by men and subordination and subjugation of women (Okunna, 2002).

The researchers, therefore, sought to analyse and evaluate the portrayal of women in some selected Nollywood films, the interpretations given to their roles in the films, and audience perception of such roles in relation to women's contribution to national socio-economic, political and human development. For the five (5) Nollywood films selected and analysed, the unit of analysis used was every major female character in each film. A total of 5 major characters were analysed. See Table 1 which presents the number of female characters in each film analysed.

What specific roles are assigned to women in the selected Nollywood films?

From the data analysed, only 30% of the female characters were portrayed in high ranking positions, career professionals and intellectuals while 70% of the female characters in the films were not portrayed as career professionals and high ranking positions (see Figure 1). Rather, they were portrayed as being dependent and subordinates. It was also observed that assigning high ranking positions in film mostly to men leaves female characters as the inferior gender, lacking the ability to intellectualise. It is no wonder that scholars such as Signorielli (2001) agree that independence and intelligence are highly recognised traditional values of boys.

Thompson and Zerbinos (1995) posit that if women were portrayed in high occupations or intellectual roles such as lawyers and doctors they were often sexually objectified. This can be seen in the film, *Mr. & Mrs.* as Linda, a dedicated banker is seen wearing extremely tight fitting clothes that expose sensitive parts of her body and portrays her as sexually attractive.

Consequently, in previous studies males were more likely portrayed in more leadership positions than the females (Baker and Raney, 2007), and this can be seen in the analysed Nollywood films. For example, in *Mr. & Mrs.*, Ken Abbah plays the part of a rich and influential son of a minister, who heads the family business and is married to a lawyer whom he insists that she becomes a full-time house wife. *Damage* has Taiwo a successful businessman who loves to be in control of his wife.

Also, Figure 4.2 clearly reveals that 70% of the female characters in the films were depicted in stereotypical domestic roles (taking care of the family and other home management chores) and contexts. About 25% of female characters were not portrayed performing domestic activities. Based on this statistical presentation it is clear that female characters in Nigerian home videos are assigned to more of domestic roles than professional or high ranking positions.

Durkin and Nugent (1998) opine that in the popular media, women are more often shown in the domestic setting, as housewives than their male counterparts. This can be clearly observed in films such as *Mr. & Mrs, Ties that Bind, Damage,* and *Midnight Whispers,* in which female characters were constantly depicted in domestic roles such as cooking, washing, taking care of the children and the home.

How is the ability of women to contribute to national development portrayed in the selected Nollywood films?

Oyinade, Daramola, and Lamidi (2013, p. 100) state that, "Nigerian women had contributed enormously to what is known as the family unit as they specialised in maintaining their households, rearing children and emotionally supporting their respective husbands." Responses from both the male and female members of the Focus Group Discussion conform to the ideal of mass culture, agreeing that Nollywood, as a cultural industry, has some filmmakers who produce films that portray women perpetually in negative lights, using stereotypic roles, and the narratives do not represent the ideals that women are active participants in the growth and development of their immediate communities that translate into national development.

Chisom Agugua who was a participant in the first group is of the opinion that women take up exceptional roles in the society. She goes further to mention women such as Dora Akunyili and Ngozi Okonjo-Iweala who have or are still making marks in relation to how they have used their position to transform Nigeria politically. Osaze Ezodaghe also from the first group was of the opinion that socially, women nurture the children even in schools; women are mostly in charge of training the children both in school and at home and this helps the children to learn more from the women while growing up. The way they are trained determines the way they grow up to become and how much they can impact in their society.

Blessing Ume says that it was observed that women were more than men statistically and this makes them form a larger percentage of workforces in the country. She also says in her own words, "You educate a man, you educate a man; you educate a woman you educate a generation". Joy Eze (second group) says that because men are hardly around, women have more responsibilities in taking care of the children. It is this nurturing and upbringing that determines what they turn out to be in the society. She also observed that school teachers are more of women because they have an exceptional ability and skill in raising children. Chima Ohameze, one of the participants in the third group agrees to this fact by saying that his wife gives him strength and supports both emotionally and physically. He goes further to say that he does not know what he would have done with his children if his wife was not there. In his words, 'I no sabi cook, I no sabi change napkin, I no dey even get chance carry my pikin go school...na my wife dey do all those ones, my own na to hustle for money'. Shola Akinwunmi (Third group) states that, "A child is relevant to the society if he or she is properly trained and mothers have an upper hand in this aspect of child development".

Contrary to the views of the FGD participants so far, the films selected for the study were few of the many Nollywood films that do not give women a good image in the society as mothers and homemakers. The films have also been criticised for their portrayal of women as sex objects, weak, cold-hearted, materialistic, vengeful, vicious, diabolical, and scheming. This has in no way presented them as agents of development in all spheres of the society.

Angela Olusanya (First group) says that Nollywood has not succeeded in showcasing women as contributors to national development because there are just few or no films where a woman is seen taking up an important role that contributes to the society politically, culturally, or socially. Rather, they are underrated and subjugated by the opposite sex. Osaze says that the reason why women cannot be assigned important roles in a film, especially political role. In his own words, "you cannot be watching a film and a woman plays the role of a president; this is because when a president is mentioned no one thinks of a woman first. Everyone assumes it is the role of a man so it is only realistic a man plays that part in the film".

Seun Balogun (Second group) was of the opinion that the portrayal of women in Nollywood films is in contrast with what they actually contribute to national development and these representations have in no way showcased them as agents of social change. Blessing Ume gives examples of Nollywood actresses Mercy Johnson and Ini Edo who act vulgar and obscene roles; she says that such actresses might not be taken seriously as contributors to national development or agents of social change as the roles they play in films are negatively influencing youths rather than empowering them to be useful in the society.

She also mentions that though the blame is not solely the actors' but also film producers'. But being realistic, the audience do not think of the film producer first but the actors who play these roles. It is the role they play that people get to watch and it is what people see that people believe. If they portray women in a negative light, the impression lasts in the minds of the audience. Rather than see women as agents of social change which they really are, they are rather influenced by the unfavourable narratives concerning women portrayed in the films.

It can be concluded from the analyses of the selected films and the responses of the participants of the Focus Group Discussion (FGD), that women arenot adequately presented in the selected Nollywood films as being actively involved in national development through the roles they play in the films.

What behavioural traits are female characters assigned in Nollywood films?

In order to analyse the behavioural traits female characters are assigned in Nigerian home videos, it was important to identify the behavioural traits that are stereotypically assigned to women. The behavioural traits for this study were derived from Fischer (2010) who gathered these measures from Thompson and Zerbinos (1995) and the Bem Sex Role Inventory (Bem, 1974). The behavioural traits coded as stereotypically feminine are: caring/loving, childlike, crying/whining, dependent, fearful, happy, and scared/desperate.

From Figure 2, almost all the female characters with a total of 80% were recorded as having exhibited the identified stereotypical behavioural traits (SBT) in film while less than 20% of them did not exhibit such behavioural traits (NSBT). It was also realised after analysing the female characters in each film that 11 out of 15 female characters possessed at least four (4) of these behavioural traits and so were described as having stereotypical feminine behavioural traits. By virtue of these results, it is clear that, except for some insignificant others, most female characters in Nigerian home videos are assigned specific behavioural traits. The data presented in Table 4.3 elucidate the results further.

To what extent do these representations of women in the selected Nollywood films showcase their active participation in the process of national development?

Drawing from the tables, a large percentage of the women play subservient roles. They are mostly portrayed as victims of abuse, always dependent on the opposite sex. From the analyses of these films, it was observed that it was to a low extent that the representations of women in the selected Nollywood films showcased their active participation in the process of achieving national development.

Women were not portrayed as diverse personalities and with active roles in the changing world. It even reinforces the stereotypical image of women as sex objects, consumers and slaves (Ali and Khan, 2012). Helen John, a participant in the first group says that this is where the media is important to changing people's orientation. When home videos start to give women important roles to play in a film, people's perspective begin to change and they begin to see women in a different light. Amarachi Arinze agrees by saying that the media should project what is ideal rather than carrying on with what seems to be the status quo. Seun Balogun (Second group) is of the opinion that these portrayals have made women see themselves as the weaker vessel and this has affected their role in national development as they have become reluctant and docile towards decision making even in their respective homes and the society at large. Rather they have become over dependent on the men like the films portray them. Joy Eze was of the opinion that women are beginning to lose their identity because if they understand that they are agents of social change they will be selective in the roles they play in the film industry. Titus Johnson says that some films portray women as agents of social change, but Mabel Okafor negates that by saying that Nollywood films do more of promoting the patriarchal society by showcasing the man's domineering attitude over a woman, and the women are left with no choice but submission. She adds that instead of showcasing women as home builders which they really are, they showcase women as society spoilers. Chima Ohameze agreed by saying that the kind of films women act does not portray them as homemakers and bearers of future leaders. He also compared the kind of films women act abroad to that of Nigeria saying that women are highly respected abroad than in Nigeria".

Future research endeavour in this area should investigate the role of the filmmakers in the portrayal of women in Nollywood films. There are few women who are actively involved in film production in Nigeria. Some of them are: Emem Isong, Stephanie Okereke Idahosa, Uche Jumbo, Monalisa Chinda, Ini Edo, and Funke Akindele. It is important to carry out a research into what strategies they are adopt to correct the negative portrayal and to ensure that women get favourable depictions in the Nollywood films, taking into cognizance societal and cultural expectations of the female folks.

CONCLUSION

Based on the findings of this study, the researchers conclude that women were not well represented in the selected Nollywood films and this has created doubt in the minds of the audience if women are actually capable of contributing to national development. It was clear that the audience are influenced by the films they are exposed to. When the films continuously position women as dependent, sex symbols, the weak gender incapable of carrying out certain tasks, these images begin to stay in the minds of the audience as they start to see women in that light. Nwabudike (2012, p.82) agrees with this when she states that "repeated exposure to certain stereotypes may cause people, especially people of impressionable age, such as youths, to believe that what they view in these films are actually realistic".

Furthermore, because of the images these films have created in the minds of the audience, they do overlook the efforts women make as agents of social change in their communities, and women are given little or no chance to contribute to national development. Though these portrayals sometimes depict reality but the media should rather change this trend and project the ideal because these negative gender stereotypes are not necessarily created by the Nollywood films; they are projected and reinforced by them.

The Nollywood industry is a veritable aspect of the Nigerian media and so, it is certain that Nigerian films form a crux of the Nigerian media (Aladese, 2013). This is why their negative representations of females are being given adequate attention as such representations are also affecting their roles as change agents.

The role of a woman starts from the family, and the family is an agent of socialisation. A woman's role in the family cannot be overemphasised. Women occupy important positions in the home and therefore play a crucial role in home management and training of the children. Fischer (2010) notes that socialisation, specifically gender socialisation, begins with the family as the primary agent and later other agents of socialisation become more influential, e.g. peers, school, and media. It is no wonder then that Nollywood films serve as channels through which gender stereotypes are projected and maintained. As was stated earlier, these Nollywood films are not necessarily responsible for creating these gender stereotypes but they play a major role in projecting and sustaining them. It can be deduced that Nigerian films seem to be reinforcing some of the negative images resident in the minds of the audience concerning the roles of women in promoting national development.

From the data analysed and discussed in this study, there is need to change the narratives of the inadequate representation of women in Nollywood films. Stereotypes can be positive or negative, and they are inevitable as part of film narratives. Therefore, positive stereotypes of women in Nollywood films should be encouraged. This can only be made possible through changing the narrative style of the film scripts. There seems to be a lot of dynamics when it comes to film production, especially in Nollywood, and it begins with the narrative the script writer wants to tell. The script serves as the map for the film production which the director and the actors/actresses follow. The script, therefore, determines the roles the female talents are to play. If the storyline does not provide a narrative that will aptly capture and represent women as valuable assets and active participants in nation building, there is no way the female talents can play contrary roles in the films. This, therefore, calls for more female script writers and directors to be involved in charting the narratives that will adequately give women a voice, new roles, and the right representation in Nollywood films.

NOTE

According to the Zonal Director, National Film and Video Censors Borad (NFVCB), South-West Zone, Ikoyi, Lagos, Mr. Edward Edion, the eighty films approved for viewership in the year 2012 is not the sum total of all films in circulation in the Nollywood market, becuase not all the films go through the NFVCB for censorship and approval due to sharp practices in the industry. Therefore, even the board does not have a complete record of all films or home videos released into the market.

REFERENCES

Akinfeleye, R., & Amobi, I. (2011). Nollywood video films as a medium for reconstructing the African cultural identity. *Communication Review*, *5*(1), 1–23.

Akpabio, E. (2003). Themes and content of Nigerian home video films. *Unilag Sociological Review*, *4*(October), 138–139.

Akpabio, E. (2007). Attitude of audience members to Nollywood films. *Nordic Journal of African Studies*, *16*(1), 90–100.

Aladese, T. (2013). *Gender stereotyping in Nigerian home videos* (Unpublished undergraduate thesis). Department of Mass Communication, College of Development Studies, Covenant University, Ota, Ogun State, Nigeria.

Ali, G., & Khan, L. (2012). A language and construction of gender: A feminist critique of Sms Discourse. *British Journal of Arts and Social Sciences*, *4*(2), 342–360.

Amobi, I. (2010). *Audience interpretation of the representation of women in Nigerian Nollywood films: a study of women from different social contexts in Nigeria.* Retrieved from http://profteri.wordpress.com/2010/11/12/online-journalism-syllabus/

Baker, K., & Raney, A. A. (2007). Equally super?: Gender-role stereotyping characters in childrens animated programs. *Mass Communication & Society*, *10*(1), 25–41. doi:10.1080/15205430709337003

Ballack, X. (2009). *Cultural norms theory*. Retrieved from http://ballack.xomba.com/cultural_norm_theory_mass_communication

Baran, S. J. (2009). *Introduction to mass communication: Media literacy and culture* (5th ed.). New York: McGraw Hill.

Baran, S. J. (2010). *Introduction to mass communication: Media literacy and culture* (6th ed.). New York: McGraw-Hill.

Bem, S. L. (1974). The measurement of psychological androgyny. *Journal of Consulting and Clinical Psychology*, *42*(2), 155–162. doi:10.1037/h0036215 PMID:4823550

Daramola, Y. (2008). Mass media and society in Nigeria: Selected functional perspectives. In R. Akinfeleye (Ed.), *Mass Media and Society: A Multi-perspective approach* (pp. 31–45). Lagos: Department of Mass Communication, University of Lagos.

Durkin, K., & Nugent, B. (1998). Kindergarten childrens gender-role expectations for television actors. *Sex Roles*, *38*(5), 387–402. doi:10.1023/A:1018705805012

Ebewo, P. (2007). The emerging video film industry in Nigeria: Challenges and prospects. *Journal of Film and Video, 59*(3), 46-57.

Eke, M. (2012). *Nollywood, women, and cultural identity*. Paper presented at the International Conference on Nollywood, Women, and Cultural Identity. Retrieved from http://www.cfplist.com/default.aspx

Fischer, S. (2010). *Powerful or pretty: A content analysis of gender images in children's animated films. Graduate faculty*. Auburn University. Retrieved from http://etd.auburn.edu/etd/bitstream/handle/10415/2065/ThesisSabrinaFischer.pdf?sequence=2

Folarin, B. (2005). *Theories of mass communication*. Ibadan: Bakinfol Publications.

Haralambos, M., & Holborn, M. (2008). *Sociology: Themes & Perspectives*. London: Collins Educational.

Igwesi, B. N. (2012). Enhancing women participation in national development through a change in the gender system of Nigeria. *Asian Social Science*, *8*(1), 217–223.

Jonah, A. A. (2011). *Film as a vehicle for cultural promotion and unity in Nigeria*. Department of mass communication, The Federal Polytechnic, Bida, Nigeria. Retrieved from www.imim- ng.org/downloads/Alice%20Jonahacticle.doc

Nwabudike, N. (2012). *Stereotyping in Nigerian movies and social interaction among students of Bells University of Technology* (Unpublished undergraduate thesis). Department of Mass Communication, College of Development Studies, Covenant University, Ota, Ogun State, Nigeria.

Obi, C. (2001). Women's political participation through economic empowerment. Lagos: Human Development Initiatives.

Okenwa, S. A. (2000). *The mass media: Uses and regulations*. Enugu: Bismark Publications.

Okunna, C. S. (2002). *Gender and communication in Nigeria: Is this the twenty-first century?* Department of Mass Communication, Nnamdi Azikiwe University, Akwa, Nigeria. Retrieved from www. portalcommunicacion.com/bcn2002/n_eng/programme/prog_ind?papers/o/pdf/o005se04_okunn.pdf

Onuzulike, U. (2007). Nollywood: The influence of the Nigerian movie industry on African culture. *The Journal of Human Communication, 10*(3), 231-242.

Onwubiko, C. P. (2012). Empowerment of Nigerian women towards national development. *Journal of Resourcefulness and Distinction*, 2(1), 68–78.

Osofisan, F. (2006). *From Nollywood to Nollyweight? Or reflectons on the possiblities of literature and the burgeoning film industry in Nigeria.* Retrieved from http://www.africultures.com/index.asp

Oyero, O. S. (2011). *Theories of mass communication. Unpublished lecture notes, Department of Mass Communication.* Ota, Nigeria: College of Development Studies, Covenant University.

Oyinade, R., Daramola, I., & Lamidi, I. (2013). Media, gender, and conflict: The problem of eradicating stereotyping of women in Nigeria. *Kuwait Chapter of Arabian Journal of Business and Management Review*, 2(12), 100–114. doi:10.12816/0001275

Sambe, J. A. (2008). *Introduction to mass communication in Nigeria.* Ibadan: Spectrum Books Limited.

Sani, H. (2001). *Women and national development: The way forward.* Ibadan: Spectrum Books Limited.

Signorielli, N. (2001). Television's gender role images and contribution to stereotyping: Past, present and future. In D. Singer & J. Singer (Eds.), *Handbook of children and the media* (pp. 341–358). Thousand Oaks, CA: Sage.

Thompson, T. L., & Zerbinos, E. (1995). Gender roles in animated cartoons: Has the picture changed in 20 years. *Sex Roles*, 32(9/10), 651–673. doi:10.1007/BF01544217

KEY TERMS AND DEFINITIONS

Behaviour Trait: An action and attitudinal composition commonly observed in a person or group of people. It captures and defines the person's or group's identity and peculiarities.

Culture: The sum total way of life a people in a community, and it includes their values, norms, mores and artefacts. It is their identity and it defines who they are.

Feminism: A movement in all ramifications (social, political and economic) that has at the base of its ideology, advocacy for women's rights with the belief in equality of all sexes.

National Development: A concept that explores how the socio-economic living standards of the citizens in a nation or country can improve greatly through valuable and positive changes orchestrated by the government in partnership with the people.

Nollywood: The name used to refer to the Nigerian film industry after the likes of Hollywood in United States of America, and Bollywood of India.

Portrayal: The act of depicting or representing a person, a place or thing in a work of art and literature, for example a film. In this context, it refers to the depiction or representation of women as a group in Nollywood films.

Stereotype: A widely held or accepted belief, idea, or image about a person or particularly a group of people.

Theme: The central idea or message that recurs or permeates a film as well as other works of arts.

This research was previously published in Impacts of the Media on African Socio-Economic Development edited by Okorie Nelson, Abiodun Salawu, and Babatunde Raphael Ojebuyi; pages 126-140, copyright year 2017 by Information Science Reference (an imprint of IGI Global).

Chapter 17
The Digital Politics of Pain:
Exploring Female Voices in Afghanistan

Mary Louisa Cappelli
Globalmother.org, USA

ABSTRACT

After 9/11, the upsurge of the Internet and intensification of mass media has provided Afghans with access to a global information highway of new perspectives, narratives, ideas, and images. Global connectivity has likewise brought with it cultural challenges over meaning. Within these digital spaces, the politics of ideological warfare ensue for the battle of representation and signification, which are inevitably interlinked to questions of power and powerlessness. Within this digital space of ideological contestation, I explore the power of the Afghan Women's Writing Project and its ability to empower women to bear witness and share their geographies of pain. Moreover, I demonstrate how AWWP operates as a social media democratizing campaign meticulously employing Western feminist rhetoric to shape Afghan cultural and social systems and subvert opposing Islamic forces that attempt to undermine protections against women and principles of free market democracy.

INTRODUCTION

In her poem "Letter to an Orphan," Sharifa (2015) writes, "Dear Orphan, / I know you lost your father and mother / To war, to suicide attacks / And bomb blasts. / I know you wish / it had been you who died / Instead of them" (AWWP, Workshop 108). Sharifa, like many other women of the *Afghan Women's Writing Project* shares her history of suffering and loss while at the same time gathering strength and courage with other women in her community and with a larger collective of global women across international borders. In this article, I explore the power of the *Afghan Women's Writing Project* and its ability to empower women to bear witness and share their geographies of pain. Within this digital space of ideological contestation, female identities are described, inscribed, and re-inscribed in a dialectical pattern of power, struggle, and resistance. In "reading otherwise," I examine questions of power and patterns of resistance and female agency in a digital space that has provided a global media platform

DOI: 10.4018/978-1-5225-9869-5.ch017

for Afghan women to re-insert their voices into history. As a mentor for the project for three months, I argue while this digital community offers a space to "empower Afghan women to tell their own stories and truths," it is important to consider how the painful memories and "truths" are constructed, politicized, and used as ideological weapons of war against entrenched patriarchal systems. This includes an examination of the rhetoric of spreading democracy across geopolitical borders and liberating "women of cover" with Western ideals of civilization and human rights. In so doing, I interrogate AWWP's mission and its similarities to First Lady Laura Bush's rationalization for military invasion in which she said, "The fight against terrorism is also a fight for the rights and dignity of women" (Oliver, 2007, p. 56). In examining the discursive dialectic of the mentor prompts and writer responses, I demonstrate that AWWP operates as a social media democratizing campaign that spreads its message of socio-cultural and political values across geographical borders. In effect, the cultural production is intrinsically linked to international struggles around gender rights and free market justice. By meticulously employing Western feminist rhetoric to shape Afghan cultural and social systems, AWWP subverts opposing Islamic forces that attempt to undermine protections against women and principles of free market democracy.

Historical Context

Because of Afghanistan's geographical location between continents and countries it is a vital bridge for transnational commerce and a battleground of different political forces vying for control of its geopolitical position. Its historical trajectory of the Soviet invasion, Jihadism, Talibanism, the rise of ISIL and other ethnic militias, signaled a US response to "to bring the hope of democracy, development, free markets, and free trade to every corner of the world" (Their, 2009, p. 3). For decades, Afghanistan has experienced an unprecedented degree of socio-cultural and political change, which has also spawned destabilizing effects at both the individual and community level. "For many Afghans, this new regime looks like a Western ideological expansion not so different from the stillborn Communist revolution in the 1980s" (Rubin, 2009, p. 17). Economic and political destabilization has resulted in the estrangement and marginalization of Afghans living in rural villages and increased recruitment of Afghans into national ethnic or ideological politics.

While the upsurge of the internet and intensification of mass media has provided Afghans with access to a global information highway of new perspectives, narratives, ideas, and images, global connectivity has likewise brought with it cultural challenges over meaning. Within these digital spaces, the politics of ideological warfare ensue for the battle of representation and signification, which are inevitably interlinked to questions of power and powerlessness. Media offer a venue to facilitate nation building and reconstruct a historical narrative; yet, media freedoms in Afghanistan are precarious. Built within the passage of the 2004 Afghan Constitution exists directly opposing legal frameworks on Mass Media Law. According to Article 34, "freedom of expression is inviolable ... [and] every Afghan has the right to express his thought through speech, writing, or illustration or other means, by observing the provisions" of the constitution (Afghan Embassy, 2002, p. 9). Under Article 34, Afghans can publish without "prior submission' to state authorities" (Afghan Embassy, 2002, p. 9). Article 7 strengthens the provisions of Article 34 by stipulating that the state "shall observe" accords made in international conventions, including the Universal Declaration of Human Rights (UDHR) (Afghan Embassy, 2002, p. 9). Article 34 further stipulates even broader freedom of expression stating: "Every Afghan shall have the right to express thoughts through speech, writing, illustrations as well as other means in accordance with provisions of this constitution. Every Afghan shall have the right, according to provisions of law, to print and publish on subjects without prior submission to state authorities" (Afghan Embassy, 2002, p. 11). These constitutional protections come to a complete ideological roadblock with the presence of Article 3, which works to undermine all previous safeguards. Article 3 states: "No law shall contravene the tenets and provisions of the holy religion of Islam in Afghanistan," as pursuant to Article 1, "Afghanistan shall be an Islamic Republic," that under Article 2 follows "the sacred religion of Islam" (Afghan Embassy, 2002, p. 5). The legal dynamic between freedom of expression and Islamic law appears to be a hotbed of ideological contradictions. According to Amin Tarzi (2009), Afghanistan's history with mass media is complicated by Islamic fundamental beliefs:

Despite efforts to put in place laws guaranteeing inviolable rights to freedom of expression and opinion, some exercising these rights via the media have been killed or have been charged with violating those very laws. Because Afghanistan is a nascent democracy, many of the institutions established to protect democratic principles are not fully developed. The security forces have not been able to fully protect those reporters who have challenged warlords, narco-traffickers, and neo-Taliban forces. (p. 50)

The increase in violence against journalists has intensified with impunity since 2014 with women once again bearing the brunt of political violence from both the domestic and social sphere. According to Amnesty International, women who appear to defy "cultural, religious and social norms" are increasingly vulnerable to gender-specific violence" (Amnesty International, 2015, p. 10). Caught between a resurgence of the Taliban and the rise of domestic violence, women have little in the way of social protections. The redrafting of criminal procedural codes that benefit patriarchal structures has further undermined what legal protections that did exist. The passage of article 26 provides protections for domestic abusers stating that in criminal proceedings on domestic abuse "relatives of the accused" cannot be called to provide testimony or interrogated as witnesses (Amnesty International, 2015, p. 10). Former President Hamid Karzai amended article 26 by decree to state that relatives of the accused may testify on a voluntary basis, but are still not required to do so under law.

It is against this backdrop of rising Taliban and ISIL forces and patriarchal political and juridical systems that favor the rule of the Islamic Father that Afghan female writers risk their lives to share their stories. Prompted by Western feminist journalists and mentors to come "Out of the Burqua" and "Into the World," AWWP gathers women writers to challenge deep-rooted patriarchal structures, that can often times render women vulnerable to sectarian violence. According to Deputy Minister at Afghanistan's Ministry of Labor and Social Affairs Seema Ghani (2015) men "don't believe in women's rights at all" and believe that Afghanistan's cultural identity is under siege by external propaganda forces (Dogan, Today's Zaman, np). The remainder of this essay explores this area of concern interrogating the degree to which AWWP balances women's rights alongside the political agenda of a privileged sector materially invested in the development of a free market society.

AWWP Perspective

Masha Hamilton a US journalist and former Director of Communications and Public Diplomacy for the US Embassy in Kabul, founded AWWP in 2009 in memory of Zarmeena who was killed by the Taliban in 1999 "without ever being able to tell her own story" (AWWP np). Because of Zarmeena's execution and ultimate silencing, the AWWP encourages women to share their stories in order to help women "take control of their own lives and make the changes that feel right to them" (AWWP np). Women writers share their stories under a pseudonym to safeguard their identities and, more importantly, to protect them from possible gender specific punishment because of their writings. The encouragement of women to develop and share their voices and lived experiences on its online platform is key to its stated mission. AWWP believes that the online writing community fosters "greater economic independence" and promotes "the inclusion of women's voices in Afghanistan's national dialogue" and does so "without the filter of the media or other influences" (AWWP np). During my time mentoring Workshop 108, I discovered that while AWWP encourages women "to take control of their own lives," it constructs and shapes an imaginary social ontology. Through its mediated workshops, AWWP encourages women to write about their gendered subordinate conditions within the structured ideological frameworks of the mediated prompts.

The establishment of US military operated "Culture and Language Centers" to understand and to negotiate "culture" and cultural differences is not new. According to Maj. Gen. David Hogg, head of the Adviser Forces in Afghanistan, the military must familiarize itself with the culture in order to use it to "fight its enemies along with more conventional armaments" (Rochelle, 2010, p. 8). Culture is a "weapon system" in which strategic openings can be found to facilitate cross-cultural communication and spread Western epistemologies. The concept of media culture as a post-September 11 political strategy can be found in the 2006 Army's Counter-intelligence *Field Manuel* which, "posits that the weaponization of culture can be a crucial element of military intelligence, used to influence others, to attack their weak spots and, more benignly, to understand the others the military is trying to help" (Rochelle, 2010, p. 8). I believe this is certainly the case with the AWWP, which occasions numerous discourses to highlight women's socio-historical and cultural position. These writings focus on the daily rhythm of women's life living in the combat zone and capture the raw sentiment of negotiating these vulnerable spaces of violence and terrorism.

Though it is correct that the social media platforms have the promise to enrich Afghan culture, "the Internet can also have a negative impact and is viewed by many Afghans who fear that their cherished cultural identity—and the established norms and behavior that this implies—could be lost in a welter of external influences" (Leslie, 2009, p. 73). Employing Edward Herman and Noam Chomsky's (2002) principles of manufacturing consent, I examine, how AWWP, while it undoubtedly provides Afghan a women a creative space to voice their concerns, emotions, and social and political conditions, moreover acts as a propaganda platform, which benefits US foreign interests. This is evidenced from the "the selection of topics, distribution of concerns, framing of issues, filtering of information" and the editorial suggestions—all which construct and manufacture debate "within the bounds of acceptable premises" of AWWP's purpose and mission" (Chomsky & Herman, 2002, Loc. 7552-7559).

Out of the Burqa, Into the World

As a mentor, I was directed to seek responses about what it is like to be a subjugated woman in Afghanistan and to specifically engage women in their personal politics of pain living in a country that affords its women precarious freedoms. Adding to the inquiry of the previous mentor who had recently inquired about a series of car bombs in Kabul in July and August of 2015 linked to the Taliban, I directed my mentees to take on a feminist standpoint point and write from their vantage positions of living under the burqa, hoping to elicit textual frames in which women distinguished their position in society and challenged those complex material forces that created their subjected positionality. Thus, I intentionally asked my mentees to unveil their deepest fears and concerns and to address the truth of their lived realities. Nahid Walizadda (2015) responded to this prompt by painting a watercolor portrait of a girl in which half of her face is covered by a blue burqa, while the other side depicts a tearful eye overflowing with pain. Her poem is superimposed on the watercolor and reads: "I burned under the Burqa / No one can see my Tear / No one can hear my Voice / No one can feel my Pain / No one can give me Rights / No one can give me Respect / No one can lead me to gain Knowledge /What is my sin? Is this answer that Because I am a Girl?" (AWWP np).

Nahid's poem captures what John Beverly refers to as "the intentionality of the recorder," portraying a personal glimpse at the patriarchal social structures that cast women as invisible second skins. Her statement "I burned under the Burqa," employs a double entendre implying both physical discomfort and socio-cultural alienation in which her "pain," her "voice" and her "rights" are concealed and muted. Nahid's anaphoric use of "No one," constructs a geography of pain in which girls flounder with little access to hope and education. Nahid answers her own rhetorical inquiry: "Is this answer that Because I am a Girl?" Thematically and textually, the answer is a resounding yes. Nahid's poem creates an oppressive world in which "women of cover" beg to be unveiled and liberated from an Afghanistan that imprisons women behind the burqa. Yet, as both Kelly Oliver and Leila Ahmed argue the burqa has long been a "contested symbol within Western imperialistic discourses and within discourses of resistance to westernization" (Oliver, 2007, p. 50). Western preoccupation with unveiling "woman of cover" is countered by new attempts to "re-veil" women to signify "resistance to Western imperialist forces" and reestablish reliable "values against modernization, democratization, and westernization, whose evil is epitomized by women's sexual freedom" (Oliver, 2007, p. 50). The unveiling of Afghan women must consider these socio-political and disciplinary ramifications. As vice president of the Afghan Women's Mission, Sonali Kolhatkar, observes: "While Oprah Winfrey provides touching vignettes of Afghan women finally able to don high heels and lace dresses, politically Afghan women have been marginalized and promised more Sharia law" (Oliver, 2007, p. 54).

During the course of mentorship with Nahid (2015) she wrote two more poems one entitled "Peace" in which she writes that peace will never happen "when half of us are uneducated," and "I am Powerful," articulating how her quest of knowledge is stronger than your gun" (AWWP np). About her writing, Nahid concedes to the fear and danger most women have about sharing their stories with the world. In light of Nahid's recognition of the danger of writing, she courageously does so anyway under her burqa—under a pseudonym to protect her identity. This is in stark contrast to the American Board of Directors, who like me and the other mentors, sit within our cozy internet connected suburban homes and direct the starting point of articulation as well as the range of acceptable expressions within this saturated electronic space.

Women risk their lives to share their stories, and with the "rebirth" of the Taliban, they do so in fear of retaliation. Consider an excerpt from Pari's poem, "Taliban, Leave My Country," in which she employs the burqa as a vile emblematic symbol of gender specific cruelty. Once again, we hear the voice of the veiled Muslim women subjugated and imprisoned by the burqa.

Taliban!
You make women your slaves
You hide us under the worst thing
The burqa
I am free from that burden now
Free of slavery now
And I care for my people and my country

My country is not for you
You don't deserve Afghanistan
You deserve hell
As you make us live in hell
Taliban!
As long as I and the Afghan people are alive
We will fight against you
We won't sit silent
We want our freedom
You do not belong in Afghanistan
Go away Taliban!
You hid me under the blue burqa. (Pari, 2015)

In Pari's poem we witness the repressive association of the burqa with the Taliban in the form of a deductive syllogism suggesting that if the Taliban regains political power, women will once again be "covered" and silenced under the burqa—an articulated site of resistance and possibility. Pari directly addresses the Taliban stating that while she is "free now," from the burqa's constrictions, "You make women your slaves/You hide us under the worst thing/ The burqa" (AWWP np). Her poem recalls the Time photo-essay "Kabul Unveiled" in which women in burqas stride though a destroyed urban section of Kabul to the market suggesting that the responsibility for social reconstruction after the Fall of the Taliban will rest on women uncovering their bodies in order to move freely forward (Stanmeyer, 2015, np). Pari captures the dialectic between freedom and oppression, the veiling and the unveiling. "I am free from that burden now," she writes; at the same time, she is fearful of returning to "hell" once again "under the blue burqa" (AWWP, np).

Another poet, Balquis, continues the uncanny metaphor of the burqa as a form of imprisonment in her poem in which she compares it to being locked in a cage powerless to fly to freedom and see the world. Balquis writes:

I am arrested, I am in prison
Like a bird without wings
Homeless, in the prison of my blue burqa
With its small window like an empty cage
But I am used to it, used to its smell
Wearing it, the sky falls on my shoulders
I am bored, tired of looking at the sky
I search my way in darkness
I can't feel, I don't know what life is
I am arrested in this prison, I have to stay
In my burqa prison.
It is always cold with stale air
I always see the same thing
I have dreams in my prison
Don't limit me!
How long do you want me to stay like this? (AWWP, 2015)

What is curious about this poem is the image juxtaposed with it is a photo credit from the *Institute for Money, Technology, and Financial Inclusion,* a University of California research institute dedicated to money and technology and creating communities in poor countries that understand "the practice and inquiry in the everyday uses and meanings of money" (UCI School of Social Sciences). This uncanny juxtaposition reaffirms AWWP's position–to enlist Afghanistan women to fight against the tyranny of fashion—the burqa the symbolic barrier to free market democracy.

As Lila Abu-Lughod (2002) clarifies, the political and cultural confusion surrounding the burqa existed long before the Taliban and has its history in the Pashtun tribes of Northern Afghanistan in which Pashtun women wore the garment as a form of conventional covering to symbolize "modesty or respectability" (p. 785). Hanna Papanek (1982), who worked in Pakistan, described the burqa as a "portable seclusion" enabling women to move freely through social spaces without non-family male surveillance (Abu-Lughod, 2002, p. 785). Contrary to AWWP's cultural production, Abu-Lughod, Papanek, and Oliver admonish that the burqa must be understood within its historical and cultural trajectory and should not represent an absence of personal agency or an affront to democracy; yet, the myriad poetic articulations of burning under the burqa circulate through the media where they are contested as symbols in direct opposition to Western democracy and free dress/free market Eurocentric values. Reading Nahid, Pari's and Balquis's poetic sentiments it appears as if the struggle against Militant Islam is ultimately one for cultural control in which American mentors of the AWWP represent the burqa as a symbol of the "weaponization of culture" to manufacture consent and to do battle not only against the Taliban extremism but, more importantly, restrictions on free fashion democracy. It is important to note that even with the rise, fall, and reemergence of the Taliban, some women have maintained their burqas and do not seem to be throwing them off any time soon—much to the surprise of Western feminists.

Saving Brown Women from Brown Men

As a privileged symbolic space, AWWP translates gendered subordination and violence into a representational textual frame, which when viewed and interpreted by Western feminists can grant a grander significance to their (our) lives. Judicious espousal of feminist rhetoric against gender specific violence has become an essential political weapon of imperialist warfare tactics. In "Can the Subaltern Speak," Gayatri Spivak (1988) refers to these representational discourses as "saving brown women from brown men" (p. 271). Poets, artists, essayists writing for the AWWP provide discourse after discourse of women in need of protection from the disciplinary hand of the Islamic Father. In this cultural production, we witness Middle Eastern women who are not given the same Western freedom of "free choice" and "right to choose." Instead, they are subjugated by Islamic patriarchy and in need of liberation from their traditional social and family structures—which according to Oliver makes Western women feel freer with their own subordinate status living in America's patriarchal paradigms.

20 year-old Shama (2015), from the American University in Kabul, a university that claims to be "modeled on American Curriculum and standards," writes in her essay entitled, "Girls Should Not Be Forced For Marriage," that "young girls often face physical beatings from patriarchal family members if they refuse to marry whom they're told. This means they are forced to begin their marriage from a place of hatred and violence rather than love and compassion" (AWWP Workshop 108). Directed to call on societal reform by her mentors, Shama goes on to lobby Islamic scholars, political leaders and the media including television and advertisement "to help to inform the parents who are unaware about the horrible drawbacks of forced marriages according to both our religion and country's constitution"(Workshop

108). She claims that forced marriages are the axles of all social woes and calls on the education of all females to "more importantly, bring the magic back to marriage" (Workshop 108). Shama's narrative on forced marriage went through several edits and directive narrative changes with three different American mentors to assist (influence) her artistic vision.

When Shama writes: "For some of these girls, their wedding night is simply the first night they are forced to spend with their new, life-long tormentors," the mentor who took over from me adds her own voice to the narrative inserting "— A NEW, UNHAPPY REALITY." The dash here serves as a grammatical tool to amplify the horror of forced marriage. Shama is further directed to add specific descriptive detail to substantiate her claim. The mentor asks: *"DO YOU KNOW ANY UNWILLING BRIDES? WHAT THEY HAVE EXPERIENCED? OR WERE YOU YOURSELF PROMISED TO BE MARRIED TO SOMEONE?"* (Workshop 108).

Specific detail substantiates and propagandizes claims, thereby validating the need for military interference to liberate women from the abuse of the Islamic father. "And it is still used by Western governments when it is convenient to justify sending in freedom fighters to liberate" (Oliver, 2007, p. 51). This is especially true of societies that subordinate women into medieval roles of second-class citizens. Zahra continues the interrogation of brown man's treatment of brown women in her essay "The Crime of Being Female," in which she writes how in Afghanistan women "live as slaves" (Workshop 108). Her mentor, recalling the mandate of Virginia Woolf's a room of one's own and 500 pounds, instructs Zahra in bold capital letters that "SOME WOMEN IN UNHAPPY OR ABUSIVE MARRIAGES CANNOT LEAVE THEIR HUSBANDS' HOMES BECAUSE THEY HAVE NO MONEY OF THEIR OWN AND NOWHERE TO GO" (AWWP, 2015, Workshop 108). Zahra goes onto write how women who dress in Western values of independence are considered to be "fancy women" who prostitute themselves to men. Her poem proceeds through a propaganda model of cultural production to inculcate the barbarity of male behavior toward women:

Men, shipwrecked in sin and blame, judge innocent and sinless women and punish THEM as they want, SIMPLY for THE crime of being FEMALE. They burn women, stone women, and trespass woman. (CAN YOU EXPLAIN WHAT YOU MEAN BY "TRESPASS WOMEN"? DO YOU MEAN RAPE?) I'm wind broken being A woman in this land. (AWWP, 2015, Workshop 108)

While Zarha's prose purports to be a first person testimony of the lived experiences of female gender inequality, what the editorial comments reveal is something quite different. What we witness are ideological articulations of assigned cultural values at play in producing the cultural material of prescriptive testimonial expressions. Within these articulations, words are deleted, replaced, arranged, and assigned values that organize and shape affective responses and sensations. These discourses and their inherent values then circulate throughout the global media spaces in different geopolitical locations, which opens them up to contestation and struggle. For example, the replacement of the word "trespass" for "rape," has a harsher gender specific connotation that connotes sexual violence by force—a political hand grenade in the social arsenal against gendered inequity. Rape produces a gut level response and is a rhetorical appeal to pathos to produce an empathetic response in the reader, which can lead to advocacy, monetary contributions and other forms of political involvement, including military intervention, to support a campaign (Hennessey, 2013, p. 74). Rape, abuse, forced marriage, and burdensome clothing regulations act as political stimuli and cultural currency for gendered advocacy and change against conservative fundamentalists like the Mujahideen and Taliban who want to preserve traditional structures and "punish women" for perceived infractions that undermine Islamic notions of "honor" (Azarbaijani-Moghaddam, 2009, p. 67).

The Taliban

The proliferation of media culture throughout Afghanistan has opened up a wide range of ideologically competing multimedia programming from Tolo TV channel's *Afghan Star* a pop idol reality contest that searches for the most talented singers in Afghanistan to programs that encourage the principles of the Koran. These combating discourses have increased the cultural conflict leading to a rise in human rights abuses with women bearing the brunt of the attacks. According to Nader Nadery 2009) Taliban insurgents have spared no effort to attack schools setting fire to "42 percent of girls schools in Kandahar and Uruzgan provinces, 49 percent in Paktika, 69 percent in Zabul, and 59 percent in Helmand in the last three years" (p. 58). As mentors we are encouraged to inquire about how the women feel about the resurgence of Taliban terrorism and share these narratives across geo-political boundaries.

Specifically, we are directed to inquire about the Sept. 28, 2015, Taliban take over of Kunduz in the north, which displaced close to 100,000 residents. The Blog editor encourages the women to share their thoughts and opinions urging women to express their concerns about the rebirth of the Taliban—have their lives gotten harder? Manizha responds to what I refer to as the Taliban Prompts in two separate poems capturing the Taliban's violent assault on Kunduz.

Free Kunduz from the Taliban!
I sigh and feel pity for Kunduz
Pain of Kunduz is my pain
I feel sad for my country
My sighs burn in my chest
What a disaster
It strangles our throats
This selfishness
Kunduz is burning
We are in Kabul thinking about food
While children die from hunger without even a piece of naan
Who is responsible in this country?
Who are the supporters of my country?
National Unity
I don't believe in it any more
I want to escape from this city
I am tired of this country of war and tears
I feel pity for my country
For the hungry people
Who have no clothes
And cannot even find water to drink
God! My greatest lord!
I want justice
Remove these pains from my country
Free Kunduz from the Taliban! (AWWP, 2015, Workshop 108)

Manizha's poem responds to the dominant impression set forth in the mentor's inquiry in a sad and passionate tone that reproaches the Taliban for its stranglehold over the city. Kunduz's people suffer from food and water insecurity in a world where "children die from hunger without even a piece of naan." Her imagery "of war and tears" serves as both an indictment and an appeal to Western women to help right these wrongs and "remove these pains from my country. "In her final line, she demands: "Free Kunduz from the Taliban!" Manizha's call to arms, enlists, and entreats Western forces to "remove" the Taliban. In so doing, she deploys the global currency of human rights to emphasize her rallying position.

Mahnaz adds another poem to AWWP's cultural production on the Taliban in which we witness the substitution between the Taliban and Monsters in which the Taliban and Monsters become one in the same.

When the Monsters Come

People in Kunduz lock their doors
Praying that no one knocks
Women shiver; hide in basements and behind walls
Crying for their honor and safety
Children call for food
The electricity is gone
The heart of Kunduz bleeds
The monster is reborn
The Taliban, those scorpions
In black turbans
They sting our nation
With their poison
Father is afraid to go out
Grandmother warns him from death
Mother is searching for a burqa
Sister is cutting her long hair
She wants to dress like a man
She must avoid being raped
The younger sister cries
Her school has been closed for three days
She cradles her books
Thinking of her teachers
The neighbor's screech echoes in the yard
Her son was beheaded by the Taliban
The scorpions swarm
The streets of Kunduz
As they shout Sharia, Sharia
The monster is reborn. (AWWP, 2015, Workshop 108)

Mahnaz's slippage from Taliban to scorpions that poison the city, to monsters that behead children, advances a definite societal purpose—the rhetorical justification for military intervention. Her selective imagery detailing the gut-wrenching fears of living under Sharia law unleashes a visceral response in its mostly female readers making a military invasion of freedom fighters more legitimate for Western feminists both conservative and liberal. In Mahnaz's poem, we witness once again the currency of incitements to engage Western feminist support and entangle them in a cultural war of power relations. The attack on education, the threat of rape, abuse, imprisonment, child death— all act as a form of cultural counter-politics and weapononized system to enlist global support against human rights abuses. The rhetorical result is an effective ideological discourse of persuasion and power that carries forth its propaganda function across global borders.

CONCLUSION

In these works, I have witnessed what John Beverly refers to as "the intentionality of the recorder" magnified by "an urgency to communicate a problem" by placing issues of gender violence oppression, poverty, and social injustice "on the agenda" (Beverly, 2004, p. 37). While resistance narratives critically challenge dominant master narratives seeking to "expose the connection between knowledge and power," what is at stake is the poetic claim of bearing witness to truth (Harlow, 1987, p. 116). When attacked on principles of falsehood and fabrication, AWWP's discourses lose their validity and resistant urgency. As a mentor, I was disturbed at how much we, as mentors, shaped and constructed the poetic and narrative responses, and, in effect, fashioned the cultural production. This is not to say that Afghan Women's voices are not urgent and courageous acts of resistance against their oppression. The writers indeed risk their lives to find their voices. The question arises, however, as to how do we truly "honor" Afghan women's voices and their own autonomous discovery without dictating to them *what* their stories are and *how* their stories should be told.

To remove the "intentionality" of the AWWP mentors, we must develop the interdisciplinary praxis between theory and social activism informed by Spivak's admonishment of the importance of "unlearning one's privilege" so that first world academics do not simply focus on commonalities at the expense of differences, as the colonized subaltern subject is "irretrievably heterogeneous" (Spivak, 1988, p. 284). In this way, we, as mentors, theorists and social activists can elude epistemic violence and the fetishization of the other by unmasking hidden agendas and discerning the intricate operations involved in representation so that we do not simply construct "totalizing representations of women in the Third World" (Mohanty, 2004, p. 335). In attending to and engaging with the subaltern voice, it is important to recognize our own role as oppressors in positions of hierarchical power structures.

We must recognize how AWWP's narrative framework constructs a chain of cognitive connections and power relations between different global actors involved in nation-building in Afghanistan. In this sense, AWWP's cultural production is the political space of social activism and political resistance against a privileged patriarchal power structure that persistently subordinates women's reproductive lives to years of injustice and gendered impoverishment. It is within this recognition that the memory of the "other" is vital; however, what we have witnessed in the AWWP cultural production is the rhetoric of "war footing" to fight against the imposition of Islamic Rule and Sharia Law, which establishes again the dialect of "saving brown women from brown men." As an alternative, we need a recognition that acknowledges and accepts Islamic cultural and religious systems that are themselves influenced by geopolitical transformations. What is at stake is the sovereignty of individual Afghan female voices, free from western ideological impositions and political agendas. My experience with AWWP demonstrates that this has not been the case. Instead of encouraging Afghan women to write meaningful stories about their lives and lived experiences, I, we, have scripted them with Western mediated responses. Rather than "saving brown women from brown men," and imposing our western feministic presuppositions and perceptions, we must accompany Islamic women on their own individual journeys of liberation—something that might look completely different from Western feminist eyes.

REFERENCES

Abu-Lughod, L. (2002). Do Muslim Women Really Need Saving? Anthropological Reflections on Cultural Relativism and Its Others. *American Anthropologist, 104*(3), 783–790. doi:10.1525/aa.2002.104.3.783

Afghan Women's Writing Project (AWWP). (2015). Retrieved from http://awwproject.org/discover-awwp/history-mission/

Amnesty International LTD. (2015). *Their Lives on the Line: Women Human Rights Defendres Under Attack in Afghanistan*. London: Peter Benenson House.

Athique, A. (2013). *Digital Media and Society: An Introduction*. Cambridge, UK: Polity Press.

Azarbaijani-Moghaddam, S. (2009). The Arrested Development of Afghan Women. In A. Thier (Ed.), *The Future of Afghanistan* (pp. 63–72). Washington, DC: United States Institute of Peace.

Balquis. (2015). *In My Burqa Prison. Workshop 108*. Afghan Women's Writing Project. Retrieved from http://awwproject.org/?s=Balquis

Beverly, J. (2004). *Testimonio: On the Politics of Truth*. Minneapolis, MN: University of Minnesota Press.

Boulianne, S. (2015). Social media use and participation: A meta-analysis of current research. *Information Communication and Society, 18*(5), 524–538. doi:10.1080/1369118X.2015.1008542

Chua, A. (2003). *World on Fire: How Exporting Free Market Democracy Breeds Ethnic Hatred and Global Instability*. New York: Anchor.

Couldry, N. (2012). *Media, Society, World: Social Theory and Digital Practice*. Cambridge, UK: Polity Press.

Davis, R. (2010). Culture as a Weapon. *MER 255 Weapons of the Strong,* 40.

Dogan, S. (2015, May 24). *Violence against women in Afghanistan. Today's Zaman.*

Harlow, B. (1987). *Resistance Literature*. New York: Routledge.

Hennessy, R. (2013). *Fires on the Border: The Passionate Politics of Labor Organizing on the Mexican Frontera*. Minneapolis, MN: University of Minnesota Press. doi:10.5749/minnesota/9780816647583.001.0001

Herman & Chomsky. (2002). *Manufacturing Consent: The Political Economy of Mass Media*. New York: Pantheon.

Institute for Money, Technology & Financial Inclusion. (2015). UCI School of Social Sciences. Retrieved from http://www.imtfi.uci.edu/

International Labor Law Organization, Presidential Decree amending Article 26 of the Criminal Procedure Code, no. 137, 23/01/1393, 2014.

Leslie, J. (2009). Culture and Contest. In A. Thier (Ed.), *The Future of Afghanistan* (pp. 73–80). Washington, DC: United States Institute of Peace.

Mahnaz. (2015). *When the Monsters Come.* Afghan Women's Writing Project. Workshop 108. Retrieved from http://awwproject.org/2015/10/when-the-monsters

Manizha. (2015) *Free Kunduz from the Taliban!* Afghan Women's Writing Project. Workshop 108. Retrieved from http://awwproject.org/?s=manizhahttp

Nadery, N. (2009). A Human Rights Awakening? In A. Thier (Ed.), *The Future of Afghanistan* (pp. 55–62). Washington, DC: United States Institute of Peace.

Nahid. (2015). *Under Burqa is a Girl.* Women's Writing Project. Workshop 108. Retrieved from http://awwproject.org/?s=nahidh

Oliver, K. (2007). *Women as Weapons of War: Iraq, Sex, and the Media.* New York: Columbia University Press.

Pari. (2015). *Taliban! Leave My Country.* Afghan Women's Writing Project. Workshop 108. Retrieved from http://awwproject.org/page/2/?s=parihttp://test2.awwproject.org/2015/05

Rubin, R. B. (2009). The Transformation of the Afghan State. In A. Thier (Ed.), *The Future of Afghanistan* (pp. 13–22). Washington, DC: United States Institute of Peace.

Sharifa. (2015). *Letter to an Orphan.* Afghan Women's Writing Project. Workshop 108. Retrieved from http://test2.awwproject.org/2015/05/letter-to-an-orphan/Available

Spivak, G. C. (1989). Can the Subaltern Speak? In *Marxism and the Interpretation of Culture.* Urbana, IL: University of Illinois Press.

Stanmeyer, J. (2015). Kabul Unveiled. *Time.* Retrieved from http://content.time.com/time/photogallery/0,29307,1947784,00.html

Tarzi, A. (2009). The Politics of Mass Media. In A. Their (Ed.), *The Future of Afghanistan* (pp. 45–54). Washington, DC: United States Institute of Peace.

The Afghan Embassy. (2002). *The Afghan Constitution.* Retrieved from http://www.afghanembassy.com.pl/afg/images/pliki/TheConstitution.pdf

Thier, A. (2009). *The Future of Afghanistan.* Washington, DC: United States Institute of Peace.

Thier, A. (2009). Building Bridges. In *The Future of Afghanistan.* Washington, DC: United States Institute of Peace.

This research was previously published in Ideological Messaging and the Role of Political Literature edited by Önder Çakırtaş; pages 160-176, copyright year 2017 by Information Science Reference (an imprint of IGI Global).

Chapter 18
Islamaphobic Discourse and Interethnic Conflict:
The Influence of News Media Coverage of the ISIS Beheadings on Identity Processes and Intergroup Attitudes

Bobbi J. Van Gilder
University of Oklahoma, USA

Zachary B. Massey
University of Oklahoma, USA

ABSTRACT

This chapter examines the Islamaphobic discourse that is perpetuated by the news media coverage of the ISIS beheadings to explain the potential influence of news media on viewers' dissociative behaviors, and the justifications made by social actors for such behaviors. Specifically, this chapter seeks to explore the ways in which intragroup identities are strengthened (ingroup bias) through outgroup derogation. The authors conducted a thematic analysis of news coverage from five major news sources. Findings revealed four themes of problematic discourse: (1) naming the enemy, (2) establishing intergroup threat, (3) homogenizing Islamic peoples, and (4) accentuating the negative. The authors then describe several ways in which media can function as a buffer to alleviate intergroup hostilities through the creation of positive contact situations.

INTRODUCTION

In the aftermath of September 11, 2001, we have witnessed a significant growth in outgroup derogation and discrimination aimed at the Muslim community (Abdo, 2005). Further, in light of the recent conflicts erupting in the Middle East, and after the beheadings of two American journalists, a similar pattern of prejudice and discrimination has begun to resurface in the United States and abroad. Islamaphobia,

DOI: 10.4018/978-1-5225-9869-5.ch018

defined here as the fear of Islam or Muslims (Abbas, 2004), has permeated recent cultural and political discourses, particularly those discourses advanced by the media coverage of ISIS, which has, in turn, fostered intergroup prejudices and interethnic conflict in the United States and abroad.

In the United States, a consensus exists that individuals should not be penalized for their differences (e.g., religion, ethnicity, gender, etc.). Further, freedom of religion is a central feature of American democracy and is one of the most basic human rights guaranteed by the United States Constitution. However, some Americans continue to derogate members of the Muslim community for not fitting into the mainstream. Despite the guarantee of religious freedom, many continue to classify the United States as a Christian nation thus condemning those who do not identify as Christian. This tension between tolerance and intolerance prompts several questions. First, why are dissociative (i.e., negative/unfriendly) behaviors enacted against the Muslim community? Second, how do social actors justify such behaviors? Finally, what role does mass media play, particularly news media, in this process?

By integrating the contact hypothesis, social identity theory, integrative threat theory and the contextual theory of interethnic communication, we seek to describe and explain the role of identity in interethnic conflict and examine the ways in which mass media influences these identity processes. Specifically, this chapter focuses on the media coverage of the ISIS beheadings to understand the ways in which intragroup identities are strengthened (i.e., ingroup bias) through outgroup derogation. Of course, media has the capacity to potentially reshape and refine consumers' understandings of particular social groups, such as Muslims or Muslim Americans. Thus, this essay also seeks to identify several ways in which media can function as a buffer to alleviate intergroup hostilities through the creation of positive contact situations.

BACKGROUND: IDENTITY PROCESSES AND INTERETHNIC CONFLICT

As explained by Kim's (2005) contextual theory of interethnic communication, ethnic identification becomes especially salient in instances of environmental stress. Kim (2005) conceptualizes *ethnicity* as "a social category defined by membership that is differentiated from other groups by a set of objective characteristics, qualities, or conditions such as national origin, language, religion, race, and culture" (p. 327). *Environmental stress* includes any factor that places strain on a social system. Such factors include economic hard times, war, or acts of terrorism. Relevant to the present chapter, the recent acts of ISIS have undoubtedly created environmental stress in the United States. As Kim (2005) explains, interethnic tension "is likely to increase at the individual level when the environment is under duress due to events that are linked to a particular group" (p. 339). As such, we define the current tensions in the United States, specifically the prejudice and discrimination targeting Muslim Americans, as *interethnic* conflict stemming from environmental duress.

In the post-911 era, interethnic conflicts related to environmental stress can be evidenced by the violent acts directed against Middle-Easterners, by the growth of anti-Arab and Anti-Muslim hate groups (Rubenstein, 2003), and by the derogatory language used by politicians, media personalities, and social elites to justify such discrimination (Allen, 2004). To further exacerbate the anti-Muslim sentiment, and add to an already tense social environment, the terrorist group ISIS executed two American journalists on camera in 2014. The public execution of these journalists was reported extensively by news media sources. To better understand the myriad of identity processes at the intersection of ethnicity, conflict, and media, we outline several relevant theories in the proceeding paragraphs.

Social Identity

Social identity is a key concept within the framework of social identity theory (SIT) and refers to the psychological link between one's self-concept and social group membership. Per SIT, knowledge of belonging to a social group combined with the emotional value/significance of group membership comprises one's social identity (Tajfel, 1972). Further, the groups to which an individual belongs (e.g., social class, family, ethnic group, sports team, organization, etc.) make up an important facet of a person's identity. Following this logic, an affront on one's social group represents a threat to one's self-concept. By linking personal identity to group status, SIT provides a rationale, or justification, for many of the seemingly irrational behaviors (e.g., ingroup favoritism, outgroup bias, intergroup conflict, etc.) associated with strong group allegiance and intergroup conflict.

SIT also explains how group identification influences intergroup prejudice and discrimination. Allport (1979) defines prejudice as "antipathy based on faulty or inflexible generalizations. It may be felt or expressed. It may be directed toward a group as a whole, or toward an individual because he is a member of that group" (p. 9). Put simply, prejudice is an affective response that involves pre-judging an entire group or class of people (Allport, 1979). Alternatively, discrimination refers to the acting out of prejudice.

As explained by Turner and his colleagues (1987) prejudice stems from the process of *social categorization*, which refers to the cognitive mechanism underpinning social identity processes. According to SIT, people cognitively represent a category or group as a *prototype*. Prototypes capture similarities within the group and differences between the group and other groups (or those that are not in the in-group) (Hogg, 2006). Prototypes describe categories, evaluate them and prescribe membership-related behavior. Additionally, prototypes maximize perceptions of group cohesiveness and group distinctiveness. In overview, prototyping accentuates in-group similarity and out-group differences. Thus, categorizing social information leads to the prototyping of individuals and groups. Further, assigning individuals to social categories is an act of pre-judgment that de-emphasizes individual uniqueness in favor of category compatibility.

Categorizing an outgroup member as belonging to a specific social group transforms the way individuals evaluate or "see" that member (Hogg, 2006). By definition, the act of categorization involves simplifying social information (Billig, 1992). Through categorization, idiosyncratic characteristics are streamlined, transforming an outgroup member into a representative of a group-based category, thus depersonalizing them. If the attributes within the category are positive (attributes ascribed to one's in-group are often positive) depersonalization produces favorable perceptions (e.g., in-group favoritism). However, if the category attributes are negative (attributes ascribed to outgroups are often negative), then perceptions will be unfavorable (e.g., outgroup derogation). Thus, social categorization can become problematic when certain outgroups (e.g., Muslims) are frequently viewed in terms of negative attributions (e.g., violent, brutal, etc.).

For social categorization to affect behavior, the social identity must be psychologically salient as the basis for perception and self-conception. Social identity salience is governed by accessibility and fit. People draw on readily accessible categorizations (e.g., race, gender, profession), particularly categorizations that are valued, important, and frequently employed. Relevant to this essay, ethnic identity becomes especially salient during interethnic conflict. In fact, as Tajfel and Turner (1986) explain, the more intense an intergroup conflict, the more likely that members of each group will view the other in terms of group-based categories (e.g., religious and ethnic identifications). In the context of extreme intergroup conflict, an attack on the group (e.g., Christians, Americans, Caucasians) is viewed an attack on the individual. Further, individuals often go to extreme lengths to defend their ingroup identities, as group identities and individual identities overlap with one another. In sum, intergroup conflict can promote ingroup favoritism and outgroup derogation. However, research also shows the nature of contact between individual group members plays a significant role in intergroup relations.

Intergroup Contact and Intergroup Threat

In 1954, Gordon Allport proposed the influential *contact hypothesis* in his book *The Nature of Prejudice* (Pettigrew & Tropp, 2005). Allport's (1979) hypothesis argued that under favorable conditions, intergroup contact has the potential to reduce prejudice and ameliorate intergroup conflict. Conversely, under unfavorable conditions, intergroup contact can increase prejudice and exacerbate conflict. The nature of interpersonal contact between individual group members thus influences intergroup relations (Allport, 1979). As such, intergroup contact represents an opportunity to either decrease prejudice *or* encourage conflict. The directionality of the contact effects depends on (a) the conditions surrounding the contact and (b) the associations that occur from such contact (Allport, 1979). So, when members of different ethnic or religious groups meet, the context of that encounter frames future encounters and plays a crucial role in the formation of negative affect in both present and future encounters (Paolini, Harwood, Rubin, Husnu, Joyce, & Hewstone, 2014).

One common affective response to perceptions of intergroup threat is anxiety (Gudykunst, 2005). When groups are in conflict, and the perceived threat is salient, individuals tend to see one another in terms of their group-based categories. In the case of ISIS, perceptions of threat generate anxiety, which creates a set of conditions that are *not* conducive to positive intergroup contact. As such, contact under this type of environmental duress may lead to further conflict. Such a reaction is predicted in Stephan and Stephan's (1993) integrated threat theory (ITT), which argues that perceptions of threat can predict prejudice and other negative attitudes toward a minority group. Stephan and Stephan (1993) identify four types of threats: (a) realistic threats, (b) symbolic threats, (c) stereotypes, and (d) intergroup anxiety. Combined, perceived threats, hostilities, violence, and conflict work together to create a negative contact situation. That is, whether triggering anxiety or fostering prejudice or negative attitudes, intergroup threat—real or symbolic—is a corrosive force in intergroup relations.

Important to the present investigation, many non-Muslim Americans have never had physical contact with an individual who identifies as Muslim. That is to say, for many Americans the only opportunity for contact with the Muslim community is through exposure via mediated communication channels. However, given the negative context of war in the Middle East, international terrorism, and "the War on Terrorism," many mediated representations of Muslims on television (particularly on televised newscasts) amplify intergroup prejudices. In other words, when a minority group (e.g., Muslims) is perceived as responsible for environmental stress (e.g., terrorist acts) we can expect the deterioration of interethnic relations. We now turn our attention to depictions of Muslim/Non-Muslim relations in mass media. Specifically, we examine the ways media representations of the ISIS beheadings may motivate specific emotions and behaviors such as prejudice, discrimination, perceptions of threat, and intergroup anxiety.

ANALYSIS: "THE THREAT OF ISLAMIC EXTREMISM"

In recent months, many Americans have come to encounter the term "ISIS." The acronym stands for the "Islamic State in Iraq and Syria." For most, however, the word provokes a psychological and emotional response, as we have come to associate the term ISIS with terror, murder, hostility, and hatred. Unfortunately, ISIS has also become symbolically connected to ethnic identity (particularly African and Middle Eastern identities) and religious identity, namely Islam. As such, the denotative meanings of ISIS, and Islam, have become inseparable from the connotative meanings exemplified previously (e.g., hostile, brutal, inhuman), and media representations of the ISIS threat have played some role in the development and reinforcement of these negative connotations. Important to this book chapter, news media sources frequently frame the threat of ISIS, as the "threat of Islamic extremism." For example, dating back to August and September of 2014, when James Foley and Steven Sotloff were beheaded on camera, stories covering this event centered Islam and religious extremism as a *cause*. This was observed on many of the major U.S. news networks (i.e., CNN, CBS, FOX News, ABC, and NBC).

Similar to the News coverage of al Qaeda following the terrorist attacks of September 11th, 2001, Media coverage of the ISIS beheadings have provoked fear and hatred toward the terrorist group in the United States and abroad. However, this fear and hatred has extended beyond the actual terror group to other *non*-ISIS affiliated Muslims. In this chapter, we focused on news segments covering the ISIS beheadings of James Foley and Steven Sotloff that were aired in August and September of 2014. Specifically, we examined eleven televised news segments, broadcasted by five prominent U.S. news sources: (1) CBS News, (2) CNN, (3) FOX News, (4) MSNBC, and (5) ABC News. All news segments were televised between August 19th and September 2nd of 2014 (see Table 1 for list of news segments included in the analysis).

We conducted a thematic analysis of the news representations of ISIS to explore the discursive constructions of the ISIS organization and its members. In conducting our thematic analysis, we used two of Owen's (1984) criteria: (1) recurrence and (2) repetition. Recurrence is observed when a particular meaning or theme emerges more than once in communication, which allows salient meanings to be

Table 1. Sources of news media coverage

Source	Title of Article	Date
CNN	*Video shows ISIS beheading U.S. journalist James Foley*	August 19, 2014
CNN	*ISIS claims to behead second American*	September 2, 2014
FOX News	*ISIS claims to have beheaded American journalist James Foley*	August 19, 2014
FOX News	*The hunt for James Foley's killers*	August 22, 2014
FOX News	*Beheading of American journalist by ISIS a game-changer?*	August 20, 2014
FOX News	*Will Muslims denounce terrorists who beheaded James Foley?*	August 21, 2014
NBC News	*Kidnapped American James Foley Apparently Executed by ISIS*	August 19, 2014
NBC News	*ISIS Beheads American Journalist Steven Sotloff, Monitoring Group Says*	September 2, 2014
CBS News	*ISIS' foreign fighters: James Foley's killer reportedly a British citizen.*	August 21, 2014
ABC News	*ISIS Claims It Beheaded American James Foley*	August 19, 2014
ABC News	*Jihadist in James Foley Execution Video Has British Accent*	August 20, 2014

discovered (Owen, 1984). Repetition includes the repetition of key words, phrases, or sentences (Owen, 1984). From our analysis, four key themes were identified inductively.

Segments were watched and re-watched, and dominant and recurring themes were documented. Then, themes were grouped together on the basis of similarities to produce fewer, larger, thematic categories. Upon completion of our thematic analysis, we observed four discursive strategies employed by news media sources that potentially strengthen intergroup hostilities: (1) *naming the enemy*, (2) *establishing intergroup threat*, (3) *homogenizing Islamic peoples*, and (4) *accentuating the negative*. Based on this analysis, we argue that the media coverage of the ISIS beheadings of James Foley and Steven Sotloff were problematic, as such representations advance Islamaphobic views of the Muslim community. These four themes are described and analyzed in the following paragraphs.

Naming the Enemy

The first theme we will discuss is *naming*. Within each News segment we observed processes of naming, labeling, and categorizing the "enemy." In fact, in News segments televised by ABC, FOX News, and CNN, we frequently observe naming practices categorizing ISIS as "a violent Islamic group," "extremists," and "a terror group" among others. Along with the labeling of the organization, we also observe the naming of their acts. Some of the labels employed include "crimes against humanity," "brutality," "murder," "brutal executions" and others. While naming and categorizing is an important and necessary process for communication to be functional, we must consider the implications of such categorizations.

As Allport (1979) explains, with approximately two and a half billion separate entities making up the category of "human race," human beings cannot possibly deal with the amount of information they encounter, nor can they individualize the hundreds of entities they confront on a daily basis. So, in an effort to comprehend our social world, we must group entities together and form clusters. To help us accomplish this task, we employ names or labels (Allport, 1979). However, "a noun *abstracts* from a concrete reality some one feature and assembles different concrete realities only with respect to this one feature" (Allport, 1979, p. 178). The mere act of classifying thus forces us to overlook all other features, which can be problematic. Some labels are especially salient and powerful, such as those employed to describe ISIS. Labels such as these tend to prevent alternative classification (or even cross-classification). Allport (1979) described this as the basic law of language. He explains that every label applied to a person refers to only one aspect of that person (Allport, 1979). Thus, labels often distract us from the complexity of the human identity. In the case of terrorism news coverage, as it relates to the Muslim identity, the lines between who *is* and *is not* supporting terrorist behavior is confused due to overly simplistic labeling and sensationalism.

Further, social cognition research demonstrates that the frequent pairing of a neutral stimulus (e.g., Middle-Easterner) with an aversive stimulus (e.g., terrorism) works to produce an automatic emotional (e.g., fear) response (Davis, 1992). For example, given the consistent pairing of black men to criminality, violence, and other emotionally charged stereotypical representations from the media, we find that many individuals react to the once neutral stimulus with a conditioned fear response (Phelps, 2006; Cargile, 2011). Similarly, in the news media coverage of ISIS, we find a frequent pairing of the term "Islam" with "terror" and "violence." In this processes of labeling then, we must also consider the ways in which language shapes our perceptions of reality. If Islam is frequently described as a violent religion, individuals may come to view all practitioners of this religion as potentially violent. As a consequence of the frequent pairing of Islam with violence then, exposure to a real Muslim person may prompt an automatic fear response, which could then result in a potentially harmful physical response (e.g., hate crime, violence, discrimination) as we have observed frequently in the United States over the past year.

In sum, the linguistic choices made by media sources, such as framing the ISIS threat as a "threat of Islamic extremism," shape perceptions and understandings of the conflict as whole, and of those members who are engaged in this conflict. That is, through simplified naming, media depictions of the conflict between the United States and ISIS discursively framed the threat of Islamic extremism as a threat from Islam as a religion.

Establishing an Intergroup Threat

The second theme that emerged in our analysis was the establishment of an intergroup threat. News media coverage of ISIS established an "us versus them" dynamic. This can be exemplified by FOX News coverage, as several segments indicated that ISIS had the primary goal of "killing Christians." Several additional news segments asserted that that ISIS seeks to kill *all* Americans (e.g., CNN and FOX news). This is further explicated by one segment that described the actions of ISIS as "a crime against all Americans."

As explained by SIT, a threat to our social group can be interpreted as a threat against our individual identity. Viewed from this framework, news coverage claiming that the actions of ISIS are a crime against all Americans draws a stark ingroup-outgroup distinction defined by intergroup threat. Such a distinction implies that ISIS—in the name of Islam—is personally attacking the viewing audience. In reality, while the actions of ISIS are notoriously brutal, and have been directed at Americans, a majority of ISIS attacks have been directed at Arab and Middle East populations, many of which are Muslim (Amnesty International, 2014).

Another especially powerful example of establishing intergroup threat was observed in a segment televised by FOX News, where the actions of ISIS were referred to as "a threat to democracy." This particular example is powerful, as the ISIS threat is not simply described as a threat to the American people, but, instead a threat to the ideology of the American republic. Such a framework implies to the viewer that the actions of ISIS represent an attack on American values and that the entire fabric of American democracy is under threat. Using Stephan and Stephan's ITT framework, the threat to democracy can thus be recognized as a symbolic threat, and can therefore have a profound influence on intergroup attitudes and behaviors.

As Stephan, Ybarra, and Morrison (2009) explain, when members of one group (e.g., Americans, Christians, etc.) perceive that another group (e.g., Muslims) may be in a position to cause harm to their ingroup, an intergroup threat is experienced. As stated earlier in this chapter, four types of threats are explained by ITT: (1) realistic threats (i.e., economic, physical, and political issues/threats), (2) symbolic threats (i.e., perceived dissimilarities with regard to values, beliefs, and norms), (3) stereotypes (i.e., expectations of out-group behaviors), and (4) intergroup anxiety (i.e., the fear people experience when interacting with out-group members) (Stephan & Stephan, 1993; Croucher, Homsey, Buyce, DeSilva, & Thompson, 2013). Stephan et al. (2009) further differentiate realistic and symbolic threats, noting that a fear about physical harm or loss of resources is a realistic threat while a fear relating to the integrity or validity of the in-group's meaning system is a symbolic threat. Importantly, the effects of perceived intergroup threats on intergroup relations are largely destructive. So, while ISIS is characterized as a threat to our nation, this global conflict is largely portrayed in intergroup terms. Thus, media coverage works to create and enhance perceptions of intergroup threat, and fear of Islam, through simplistic us versus them depictions.

Homogenizing Islamic Peoples

Another theme that emerged from our analysis was the homogenization of Islamic peoples. Homogenization refers to the ways in which news media sources discursively homogenized outgroup members (i.e., Muslims). Through processes of labeling, and through the focus on the threat of "Islamic extremism," news media coverage tends to blend all Muslims into a single non-distinct category. One of the most obvious examples of this gentrification was a segment televised on FOX News, in which the newscaster, along with an expert interviewer, asked non-ISIS affiliates (i.e., Muslims who are not part of the terrorist group) to somehow prove their allegiances. In this news segment, sources call on the Muslim Brotherhood, and other Islamic organizations to denounce ISIS. One of the media sources even said, "If they are moderate, as they say, come on let's hear you condemn ISIS" (FOX News). As this example shows, some media outlets promote a homogenized depiction of Muslims wherein each individual member of the group is responsible for the whole. To provide a counter-example, imagine a television host asking an Anglo-European member of Congress to apologize for the actions of the Klu Klux Klan. While such an example seems outlandish, we found a similar trend occurring towards Muslims in the United States regarding the actions of ISIS.

Another way Islamic peoples are homogenized by the news coverage of ISIS is through the de-individualization of each separate organization. Other Islamic "terror groups" are lumped in with ISIS. For instance, in an ABC news segment covering the beheading of James Foley a speaker highlights the threat of ISIS, but emphasizes a much larger threat of "Jihadists, and ISIL, and other extremist organizations." Further examples from CNN, CBS, NBC and FOX News also refer to the terror group as "Islamic extremists," failing to define, differentiate, and identify different extremist groups. Here, the failure to identify each organization as a separate entity, works to homogenize Islamic peoples, as there is a lack of clarity as to what constitutes "extremism," and to what type of "extremism" constitutes a threat. Similarly, very little, if no mention is made to the existence of moderate Muslims or the differentiation between Sunni-Shia ideological divides. Thus, we see with both individuals and groups, Muslims are homogenized into one group where each member is responsible for the group as a whole.

Accentuating the Negative

The final emergent theme was an accentuation of the negative. In the news media coverage of ISIS, we observed an overwhelming focus on the negative, without any recognition or acknowledgment of any positive attribute of the Muslim community. Of course, this trend extends beyond the ISIS news media coverage to nearly all news media. An article published by *Psychology Today* points out that "Most news we see and hear is negative, and replete with disasters, terrorism, crime, scandals and corruption" (Williams, 2014, para. 1). Patterson (1996) makes a similar point, stating, "the notion that 'bad news makes good news' has long been a standard of American journalism, but the media have raised it to new heights in recent decades" (p. 17). In fact, "since the 1960's, bad news has increased by a factor of three and is now the dominant tone of national politics" (Patterson, 1996, p. 17). While focusing on negative news is a common theme in media coverage generally, such a focus can have harmful consequences with regard to intergroup relations.

In the news segments analyzed for this essay, we found repeated emphases on hostility, violence, and brutality as it relates to the Muslim religion. These representations can advance negative affective responses toward all Muslims, despite their connections, or lack thereof, to ISIS. For example, Veitch and Griffitt (1976) conducted a study in which news segments were played for research participants conveying "good news" or "bad news." After viewing the news segments participants were instructed to make evaluative responses of anonymous others. The news broadcasts were found "to elicit positive and negative affective responses and to affect subjects' evaluations of others" (p. 69). Moreover, a positive relationship was observed for reported affect and interpersonal evaluations.

Important to the present study, of all of the news segments analyzed, not one segment mentioned a single positive attribute connected to the Muslim community. Rather, every broadcast highlighted negative attributes in connection to the Muslim identity. This frequent pairing of Islam with "terror-ism," "violence" and "brutality" can function as a means of enhancing intergroup hostility, as negative attributions can often result in discrimination.

SOLUTIONS AND RECOMMENDATIONS

As evidenced by the analysis above, we find that media plays a significant role in shaping perceptions through processes such as defining events, engaging in naming practices, sensationalizing stories in a negative way, and appealing to national ethos, among others. As such, media has the potential to reshape and reframe interethnic relations and therefore motivate action, thoughts, feelings, and behaviors. In fact, Ting-Toomey (2005) notes that the media is a significant socializing agent and influences the formation of identities as well as understandings of others in relation to one's own social identity. So, how can media work to alleviate intergroup hostilities and potentially reduce intra-national intergroup conflict?

According to Allport's (1979) contact hypothesis, under optimal conditions, intergroup contact can decrease prejudice. Conversely, negative intergroup contact has been found to increase prejudice in a number of contexts (Bobo, 1996; McGarry & O'Leary, 1995). Thus, intergroup contact can increase or decrease prejudicial thinking depending on the nature of the contact. While a great deal has been written about the role of direct intergroup contact (see Pettigrew & Tropp, 2011), little has been written about the role of *mediated* intergroup contact. As a new line of inquiry, intercultural, interpersonal, and mass media scholars have begun to examine the role of mediated contact on intergroup relations and have found that even *mediated* contact, can significantly influence perceptions of outgroup members.

Mediated contact (e.g., contact with television characters or persons who represent a particular outgroup) has recently been explored within an intercultural context. For example, Shim, Zhang, and Harwood (2012) conducted a study in which they examined the attitudes of Korean viewers' towards U.S. Americans. The researchers found that both direct and mediated contact were predictors of intergroup attitudes. This correlation was even evident for Koreans who had no personal contact with Americans, as mediated contact still played a "significant" role in their attitudes towards Americans. Additionally, Shim et al. (2012) found that quality of the interactions, as opposed to quantity, was a better predictor of intergroup attitudes in mediated contact situations. This means that media sources have the power to potentially reframe content in a way that evokes positive change in the community. Given the role of media in the development of intergroup attitudes, we make two suggestions for the development of positive contact situations: (1) define and differentiate group membership identities, and (2) present balanced coverage of positive and negative news stories.

Define and Differentiate

As noted in our analysis, through processes of categorization and homogenization, news media has a tendency to conflate intragroup similarities, thus perpetuating notions that all Muslims are a threat to American ideals and to the American people. Therefore, we argue that news media sources should modify their terminology and make strategic and communicatively competent linguistic choices when covering news on ISIS. To more accurately describe the existing conflict between ISIS and the Unites States, media sources could begin by defining and differentiating groups on the basis of their beliefs, values, symbols, etc.

In our analysis, we found that news media sources frame ISIS as a "threat of Islamic extremism." Instead, we argue that media sources should avoid ambiguous language such as "extremism" and instead engage in the following practices: (1) define such terminology so as to clearly identify what branch of Islam is being practiced by ISIS, (2) explain what exactly distinguishes this group from other Islamic groups, (3) explain how this does *not* relate to, or represent, traditional practices or notions of Islam, and (4) identify, explicitly, the actual threat the United States is experiencing.

By engaging in the practices outlined above, media sources would no longer reinforce stereotypes through perpetuations of sweeping generalizations in their news coverage. Instead, media consumers are afforded an opportunity to critically evaluate the validity of existing stereotypes, and may therefore be more open to alternative representations of Muslim group members. Further, media sources could create a positive contact situation by providing additional representations of Islamic peoples who do not associate with ISIS; that is, show Muslim Americans as real people with whom all Americans share a similar national identity. More complex and multidimensional representations of Muslims, and specifically Muslim Americans, could disrupt the pattern of pairing Islam with terrorism, and thus enable viewers an opportunity to explore alternative representations of the Muslim identity.

Accentuate the Positive

Our second recommendation is to accentuate examples of positive behavior and/or positive identity attributes. With so much negatively dominating news coverage, individuals find it easier to view outgroup members in a negative light. However, news media can make framing decisions that instead accentuate the positive, particularly with regard to non-ISIS Muslims. So, rather than simply differentiating the many separate Muslim entities, we argue that effort should be made to enhance the positive attributes so rarely associated with specific minority groups and to challenge viewers to look beyond the negative stereotypes. By re-framing media coverage to highlight the positive, people may be less inclined to rely on automatic processes (i.e., stereotyping) and instead engage in critical reasoning. Positive and varying representations may enable the development of cognitive complexity, and prevent intergroup hostilities.

FUTURE RESEARCH DIRECTIONS

The analysis presented here is designed to highlight some of the key issues surrounding ethnic identity and news media coverage. We recognize that the intersection of ethnic identity, religion, international terrorism, and mass media is an infinitely complex web of social behaviors. Our goal is not to capture the entire spectrum of behavior within this web, but, instead, to illuminate some of the prominent factors underpinning mediated depictions of interethnic conflict. Towards this end, one area of future research is additional study of the connection between mediated depictions of terrorism and prejudicial attitudes. There exists, for instance, some research in the Terror Management paradigm that uses terrorism news as a stimulus that elicits mortality salience (see Landau, Arndt, Solomon, Greenberg, Pyszczynski, Miller, Cohen, & Ogilvie, 2004). Such research has found that terrorism news elicits ingroup favoritism and outgroup derogation (Das, Bushman, Bezemer, Kerkhof, & Vermeulen, 2009). Following this line of thinking, an intriguing avenue of research would be to further explore the connection between mediated depictions of terrorism and increased prejudice towards Muslims in general. Despite the connections between environmental stress and ingroup favoritism/outgroup derogation, there exists relatively little research into the connection between mediated depictions of terrorism and intergroup conflict. Given the rise of 24-hour news cycles, and the increasing presence of Islamic terrorism in the American psyche, we expect the constant presence of environmental stress related to a well-defined outgroup would strain intergroup relations.

Along with further explorations of the connection between mediated depictions of terrorism and prejudicial attitudes, other interethnic tensions have become salient in light of recent events as well. Specific examples include recent incidents of police violence targeting African Americans. Additionally, the recent massacre in a South Carolina church warrants further investigation. These specific tensions are occurring intra-nationally and are not connected to global terrorism or international politics.

Finally, moving away from news media, future research might also examine how police cameras and bystander recordings are influencing interethnic tensions and the debates surrounding racism and interethnic conflict. How does citizens' media work to shape and define interethnic conflict and how can such resources encourage dialogue and spark social change?

CONCLUSION

As the current analysis demonstrates, American news media may be strengthening feelings of Islamophobia by accentuating negative stereotypes of Muslims through reporting on international terrorism. Specifically, through thematic analysis we identified the following four themes: (a) *naming the enemy*; (b) *establishing intergroup threat*; (c) *homogenizing Islamic people*; and (d) *accentuating negativity*. Combined, we feel that these themes strain the tense intergroup relationships between minority Muslim-Americans and the predominately Anglo-Christian majority. Such tensions often manifest in the form of outright behavior, including anti-Muslim rhetoric or even violence. We recognize that the intersection of ethnic identity, news media, and conflict is certainly a complex set of factors. Our aim is not to describe the entirety of such a complex web, but, instead to illuminate the relationship between news media and identity during a time of conflict.

In sum, this essay offered a thematic analysis of the news media coverage of the ISIS beheadings while providing a critical, theoretical examination of the discursive strategies employed by prominent news sources. Importantly, in this chapter we problematize the current approaches of news media sources to highlight news media's influence on identity processes and intergroup behaviors. We conclude by offering suggestions for change. Media has a profound influence on intergroup attitudes and behaviors, which also means that news media can and should work to alleviate intergroup conflict through the deliberate creation of positive intergroup contact situations. Two possible strategies for the creation of positive mediated contact situations include the defining and differentiating of groups and the accentuation of the positive. Our hope is that more varied representations of Muslims, and specifically Muslim Americans, might promote more mindful and competent communication in intergroup situations.

REFERENCES

Abbas, T. (2004). After 9/11: British South Asian Muslims, Islamophobia, multiculturalism, and the state. *The American Journal of Islamic Social Sciences, 21*(3), 26–38.

Abdo, G. (2005). Islam in America: Separate but unequal. *The Washington Quarterly, 28*(4), 7–17. doi:10.1162/0163660054798717

Allen, C. (2004). Justifying Islamophobia: A post-9/11 consideration of the European Union and British contexts. *The American Journal of Islamic Social Sciences, 21*(3), 1–25.

Allport, G. W. (1979). *The nature of prejudice*. Cambridge, MA: Persus Books.

Amnesty International. (2014). *War crimes committed in the battle for Mosul*. Available from http://blog.amnestyusa.org/middle-east/war-crimes-committed-in-the-battle-for-mosul/

Billig, M. (1992). *Categorization and particularization. In Readings on Communicating with Strangers* (pp. 56–66). New York: McGraw-Hill.

Bobo, L. D. (1999). Prejudice as group position: Microfoundations of a sociological approach to racism and race relations. *The Journal of Social Issues, 55*(3), 445–472. doi:10.1111/0022-4537.00127

Cargile, A. C. (2011). Being mindful of the habitus of culture. *China Media Research, 7*(3), 11–20.

CBS News. (2014). *ISIS' foreign fighters: James Foley's killer reportedly a British citizen*. Available from http://www.cbsnews.com/videos/isis-foreign-fighters-james-foleys-killer-reportedly-a-british-citizen/

CNN. (2014) *Video shows ISIS beheading U.S. journalist James Foley*. Available from http://www.cnn.com/2014/08/19/world/meast/isis-james-foley/index.html

CNN. (2014). *ISIS claims to behead second American*. Available from http://www.cnn.com/videos/world/2014/09/02/wolf-sot-steven-sotloff.cnn

Croucher, S. M., Homsey, D., Buyce, C., DeSilva, S., & Thompson, A. (2013). Prejudice towards American Muslims: an integrated threat analysis. *Journal of Intercultural Communication, 32*. Retrieved from http://www.immi.se/intercultural

Das, E., Bushman, B. J., Bezemer, M. D., Kerkhof, P., & Vermeulen, I. E. (2009). How terrorism news reports increase prejudice against outgroups: A terror management account. *Journal of Experimental Social Psychology, 45*(3), 453–459. doi:10.1016/j.jesp.2008.12.001

Davis, M. (1992). The role of the amygdala in fear and anxiety. *Annual Review of Neuroscience, 15*(1), 353–375. doi:10.1146/annurev.ne.15.030192.002033 PMID:1575447

Gudykunst, W. B. (2005). An anxiety/uncertainty management theory of effective communication. In W. B. Gudykunst (Ed.), *Theorizing about Intercultural Communication* (pp. 323–349). Thousand Oaks, CA: Sage.

Hogg, M. A. (2006). Social identity theory. *Contemporary Social Psychological Theories, 13*, 111-1369.

Kim, Y. Y. (2005). Association and dissociation: A contextual theory of interethnic communication. In W. B. Gudykunst (Ed.), *Theorizing about intercultural communication* (pp. 323–349). Thousand Oaks, CA: Sage.

Landau, M. J., Arndt, J., Solomon, S., Greenberg, J., Pyszczynski, T., Miller, C. H., ... Ogilvie, D. M. (2004). Deliver us from evil: The effects of mortality salience and reminders of 9/11 on support for President George W. Bush. *Personality and Social Psychology Bulletin, 30*(9), 1136–1150. doi:10.1177/0146167204267988 PMID:15359017

McGarry, J., & O'Leary, B. (1995). Five fallacies: Northern Ireland and the liabilities of liberalism. *Ethnic and Racial Studies, 18*(4), 837–861. doi:10.1080/01419870.1995.9993893

McLeod, S. (2008). *Social identity theory*. Simply Psychology.

ABC News. (2014a). *ISIS Claims It Beheaded American James Foley*. Available from http://abcnews.go.com/WNT/video/isis-claims-beheaded-american-james-foley-25045729

FOX News. (2014a). *ISIS claims to have beheaded American journalist James Foley*. Available from http://video.foxnews.com/v/3738849288001/isis-claims-to-have-beheaded-american-journalist-james-foley/?#sp=show-clips

NBC News. (2014a). *Kidnapped American James Foley Apparently Executed by ISIS*. Available from http://www.nbcnews.com/watch/nightly-news/kidnapped-american-james-foley-apparently-killed-by-isis-319842371631

ABC News. (2014b). *Jihadist in James Foley execution video has British accent*. Available from http://abcnews.go.com/International/video/international-hotspot-jihadist-james-foley-execution-video-british-25055652

FOX News. (2014b). *The hunt for James Foley's killers*. Available from http://video.foxnews.com/v/3744599887001/the-hunt-for-james-foleys-killers/?#sp=show-clips

NBC News. (2014b). *ISIS Beheads American Journalist Steven Sotloff, Monitoring Group Says*. Available from http://www.nbcnews.com/storyline/isis-terror/isis-beheads-american-journalist-steven-sotloff-monitoring-group-says-n193936

FOX News. (2014c). *Beheading of American journalist by ISIS a game-changer?* Available from http://video.foxnews.com/v/3739983082001/beheading-of-american-journalist-by-isis-a-game-changer/?#sp=show-clips

FOX News. (2014d). *Will Muslims denounce terrorists who beheaded James Foley?* Available from http://video.foxnews.com/v/3741706588001/will-muslims-denounce-terrorists-who-beheaded-james-foley/?#sp=show-clips

Owen, W. F. (1984). Interpretive themes in relational communication. *The Quarterly Journal of Speech, 70*(3), 274–287. doi:10.1080/00335638409383697

Paolini, S., Harwood, J., Rubin, M., Husnu, S., Joyce, N., & Hewstone, M. (2014). Positive and extensive intergroup contact in the past buffers against the disproportionate impact of negative contact in the present. *European Journal of Social Psychology, 44*(6), 548–562. doi:10.1002/ejsp.2029

Patterson, T. E. (1996). Bad news, period. *PS: Political Science & Politics*, *29*(01), 17–20. doi:10.1017/S1049096500043997

Pettigrew, T. F., & Tropp, L. R. (2005). Allport's intergroup contact hypothesis: Its history and influence. *On the Nature of Prejudice*, 262-277.

Pettigrew, T. F., & Tropp, L. R. (2011). When groups meet: The dynamics of intergroup contact. New York, NY: Psychology Press.

Phelps, E. A. (2006). Emotion and cognition: Insights from studies of the human amygdala. *Annual Review of Psychology*, *57*(1), 27–53. doi:10.1146/annurev.psych.56.091103.070234 PMID:16318588

Rubenstein, W. B. (2003). Real Story of US Hate Crimes Statistics: An Empirical Analysis, The. *Tulane Law Review*, *78*, 1213–1246.

Shim, C., Zhang, Y. B., & Harwood, J. (2012). Direct and mediated intercultural contact: Koreans' attitudes toward U.S. Americans. *Journal of International and Intercultural Communication*, *5*(3), 169–188. doi:10.1080/17513057.2012.670715

Stephan, W. G., & Stephan, C. W. (1993). Cognition and affect in stereotyping: Parallel interactive networks. In D. M. Mackie & D. L. Hamilton (Eds.), *Affect, cognition, and stereotyping: Interactive processes in group perception* (pp. 111–136). Orlando, FL: Academic Press. doi:10.1016/B978-0-08-088579-7.50010-7

Stephan, W. G., Ybarra, O., & Morrison, K. R. (2009). Intergroup threat theory. In T. Nelson (Ed.), *Handbook of prejudice, stereotyping, and discrimination* (pp. 43–59). New York, NY: Psychology Press.

Taifel, H., & Turner, J. (1986). The social identity theory of intergroup behavior. In S. Worchel & W. Austin (Eds.), *Psychology of intergroup relations* (2nd ed.; pp. 7–24). Chicago: Nelson-Hall.

Tajfel, H. (1972). Experiments in a vacuum. In J. Israel & H. Tajfel (Eds.), *The context of social psychology: A critical assessment* (pp. 69–122). London: Academic Press.

Ting-Toomey, S. (2005). Identity negotiation theory: Crossing cultural boundaries. In W. Gudykunst (Ed.), *Theorizing about Intercultural Communication* (pp. 211–233). Thousand Oaks, California: Sage Publications.

Turner, J. C., Hogg, M. A., Oakes, P. J., Reicher, S. D., & Wetherell, M. S. (1987). *Rediscovering the social group: A self-categorization theory*. New York: Basil Blackwell.

Veitch, R., & Griffitt, W. (1976). Good News-Bad News: Affective and Interpersonal Effects1. *Journal of Applied Social Psychology*, *6*(1), 69–75. doi:10.1111/j.1559-1816.1976.tb01313.x

Williams, R. (2014). Why we love bad news more than good news: Does the current news negativity bias reflect media or public preferences? *Psychology Today*. Retrieved form https://www.psychologytoday.com/blog/wired-success/201411/why-we-love-bad-news-more-good-news

KEY TERMS AND DEFINITIONS

Environmental Stress: Any factor that places strain on a social system.

Ethnicity: A social category defined by membership that is differentiated from other groups by a set of objective characteristics, qualities, or conditions such as national origin, language, religion, race, and culture.

ISIS: Islamic State in Iraq and Syria.

Islamaphobia: The fear of Islam or Muslims.

Mediated Contact: Contact with television characters or persons who represent a particular outgroup.

Social Categorization: The cognitive process of categorizing an outgroup member as belonging to a specific social group or social category.

Social Identity: The psychological link between one's self-concept and social group membership.

This research was previously published in Impact of Communication and the Media on Ethnic Conflict edited by Steven Gibson and Agnes Lucy Lando; pages 147-161, copyright year 2016 by Information Science Reference (an imprint of IGI Global).

Section 5
Media Transparency and Press Freedom

Chapter 19
The Uses of Science Statistics in the News Media and on Daily Life

Renata Faria Brandao
University of Sheffield, UK

ABSTRACT

Statistical information as part of news reports of science is intended to legitimate the accounts of evidence based on peer-reviewed data. Indeed, the persuasive power of numbers can be seen in newsrooms as it supports and validates arguments (Boyle, 2000; Eberstadt, 1995; Goldacre, Bad Science, 2009; Hacking, 1965; Livingston & Voakes, 2005; Lugo-Ocando & Brandão, 2015). Nonetheless, these mathematical abstractions can also be used as a means to misinform the public (Huff, 1954; Moore, 1997). This chapter, thus, seeks both to understand how journalists use scientific statistics as a means to communicate current scientific research as well as how the public decodes this information. It proposes to address the construction of scientific statistics by journalists and its deconstruction by the public at large through a cross-Atlantic comparison of the uses of mathematics in science news and on daily life.

INTRODUCTION

The structure of our society would be unthinkable without a mathematical language. The idea that mathematics, statistics and its variants are on a pedestal above all other knowledge, however, has long been the subject of scrutiny of theorist, academics and philosophers. Current scholarship tells us that objectivity is central to the agency of journalism (Mindich, 1998; Koch, 1990; Kovach & Rosenstiel, 2001; Sparks & Dahlgren, 1991; 1992). Since the beginning of the 20th century, objectivity has been present in most newsroom guidelines and greatly consumed by journalists everywhere. Inferring that news articles should present facts independently of biases, the notions of objectivity claims that news pieces should be based instead on neutral grounds and when possible depict all sides. Key scholars suggest that statistics is extensively considered one of the most prominent validating tools in the construction of

DOI: 10.4018/978-1-5225-9869-5.ch019

this objective ground (Boyle, 2000; Davis & Hersh, 1986; Desrosieres, 1998; Eberstadt, 1995; Hacking, 1965; Koch, 1990; Livingston & Voakes, 2005; Zuberi, 2001). Indeed, the persuasive power of statistical data can be seen in newsrooms as it supports and validate arguments. In spite of this, few scholars have examined how this language is used in the newsroom. There are few studies that examine the origins of statistics as an objectifying tool when writing about science. This piece, thus, seeks to look at the uses of statistics in science news and evaluate the manipulation of data when gathering and disseminating news stories with reference to science. It focuses on media representations of statistics across media outlets, while examining the usage of statistics in science communication and news coverage. More specifically, it examines how statistics are used to articulate the narratives and shape discourses of science in the news media as well as how the public deconstructs these statistical information. In doing so, it looks at The Guardian and Folha de S. Paulo news production of science in 2013, how journalists in newsrooms access and interpret quantitative data when producing stories related to science and how the public decodes it. It investigates the nature of statistical news sources regularly used by journalists while also assessing how they are used as a means to articulate news stories. And produces a comparative study on how the British and Brazilian news media gather, handle and most importantly articulate statistics when writing about science. Furthermore, it looks at social networks as to assess the ways in which the public decoded this mathematical language. Results show a clear need of better education of statistical knowledge throughout the existing news processes. Focusing on science news while scrutinizing the uses of statistics in the articulation of news, it elucidates the power of statistics as a means to access truth and achieve journalistic objectivity if used properly. With the foreseeable outcome that these news processes works as a Chinese whisper, this study can potentially enlighten the possibility of changing the ways in which scientific statistical information is communicated.

LITERATURE REVIEW

Current scholarship argues that to understand the world it is imperative to think mathematically as no modern society can exist without a mathematical language (Butler, 1895; Davis & Hersh, 1986; Desrosieres, 1998; Devlin, 1998; Nikolakaki, 2009; Porter, 1997; Zuberi, 2001). Prominently, we live in a rational society dominated by numbers and logical-mathematical thought (Zuberi, 2001) where most people could survive with understanding some basic mathematical terms (Nikolakaki, 2009). Indeed, as far as mathematics and society is concerned, its relationship has always been a subtle but obvious one. "Numbers saturate the news, politics, life. For good or ill, they are today's pre-eminent public language – and those who speak it rule" (Blastland & Dilnot, 2008, p. 1). Nonetheless, in spite of numbers conquering facts, they have also been abused and even created distrust among the general public. "Potent but shifty, the role of numbers is frighteningly ambiguous" (Blastland & Dilnot, 2008, p. 1). To elaborate, one of the foremost reasons for this ubiquitous presence of mathematics in modern society, it is its applicability – i.e. 'the laws of nature' and science can be described with exactitude and precision in, even though quite abstracts and not intuitive, mathematical terms. Our contemporary society recognises that between opinion and science there is a colossal difference; additionally, it is argued that the West (and western societies) has achieved much of its knowledge and progress due to the preponderance of science over the other areas (Chafetz, 2005; Zuberi, 2001). Historically, the assimilation of science in the fields of society, culture and, most importantly, politics and policy making became increasingly common in Europe after Voltaire's 1738 publication "Elements de la philosophie de Newton" – or Elements of the

Philosophy of Newton – in which he rationalises, and even tries to popularise, Newton's theories and line of thought in France. As a matter of fact, it provoked immense interest and reach in the field of philosophy – especially in Kant's work – compelling every academic henceforth to justify mathematically the possibility of nature's rational knowledge that can be seen in our every day.

An illustration of that regards the fact that, among philosophers, especially Plato, Aristotle, Kant and Descartes, there is an understanding that mathematics and quantitative data holds a productivity discourse that constitutes a form of representation of the modern (western) man, of validation and legitimation, and of modes of regulation. Subsequent to this notion that the world and society must be understood mathematically, Plato also argues that all knowledge rests in the mathematical idea. That means that, according to him, the mathematical language holds the true essence of things, values, concepts, etc. Under these circumstances, and following Descartes line of thought, David and Hersh (1986) believe that there is an overwhelming amount of digits in our current society. To them, society is drowning in the multitude of numbers and it does not concern the subjection or subjugation of one single computer, but rather to the computerisation and mechanisation of all communication mediums (p. 16). The communication of information and media in general is only one 'environment' in which mathematics affects the way it is perceived and understood. Even the formations of modern states are in the present day affected by this flow of quantified information. As a matter of fact, statistics can be seen today to have developed as science of the nation (Desrosieres, 1998). This movement of digitalisation of the processes of current social interaction, which has statistics as key element and core basis, also reaches a number of other different social environments. From science and scientific knowledge to health and nature, the quantification of data is now a prominent feature.

Indeed, this mathematisation of society "has become more and more hidden from view, forming an invisible universe that supports much of our lives" (Devlin, 1998, p. 12) where society relies on quantification and mathematics nor merely because its apparent objectivity validity but because it is a key element to comprehend how we conduct most aspects of our quotidian – from the enforcement of law to the exchange of goods and media communication (Porter, 1997, p. 9). Ultimately, this objectivation or 'rationalisation movement' affects most institutions, to which gives rise to a range of other information that sediments the practices of these individuals that belong to the general public and social spaces. One example of this movement is the mathematical discourse that has become, over the years, not only a logical discourse but also an objective one. Its 'truths', as named by Descartes, derives from 'safe hypothesis' and, therefore, are considered to be real, fair and objective. In fact, "numbers can make sense of a world otherwise too vast and intricate to get into proportion" (Blastland & Dilnot, 2008, p. 1). This existing interest derives from the importance of science in the world arena. Indeed, the Cartesian paradigm of the primary of reason, which implicates the methodological doubt and the rationalistic primacy, asserts that science is essentially rationalistic and cognitivist. Its model has been remodelled since its proposal in the 20th Century, but its premise is still valid: science aspires to objectivity as a means to try overcoming subjective conditions.

Historically, it has been suggested that there is a sturdy relationship between objectivity, mathematical data and science (Battersby, 2010; Desrosieres, 1998; Kuhn T., 1962; Stigler, 1986). Similarly to statistics, science is perceived as objective knowledge; that because, differently from a subjective reality, scientific reality "is that which has evolved to the point where it is the currently accepted basis of application and of further research and speculation" (Davis & Hersh, 1986, p. 273). Indeed, scientific claims differently from casual claims creates a believable fallacy due to the processes in which it had been to – peer review, numerous experiments, replication, etc. This process of mathematisation or naturalisation of scientific knowledge as true knowledge – meaning that reason infers humanity, civilization and society – has become ingrained in modern society and therefore has attributed and qualified scientific statistics as the means towards a "correct" way of thinking. Most importantly, science is also an area in which one can clearly notices its uses as a tool of achieving the 'journalistic truth' (Battersby, 2010). Science is considered to be the pursuit of knowledge and, therefore, it (all scientific knowledge and study) must be founded upon the belief that there is an universal, unbiased, objective reality that are precisely the ones which are going to be analysed and represented. In fact, in accordance to Stigler (1986) "[e]xternal assessments of accuracy have always been important to science. They can provide the only access to the measurement of systematic errors or biases" (p. 6).

Similarly, White (2013) argues: "mathematics is the science of definiteness, the necessary vocabulary of those who know"; it "is the language of definiteness, the necessary vocabulary of those who know, hence the intimate connection between mathematics and science". Ultimately, it is understood that the emergence of the modern scientific method initiated the process, which lead to the culmination of this new term "mathematisation of nature" and subsequently the mathematisation of society. Arguably, the structure of our society would be unthinkable without reference to mathematics (Desrosieres, 1998). Underlying this notion that everything is mathematisable is the idea that, as the world becomes gradually more mathematised, society tends to exclude these things that cannot be mathematised.

That being said, following a similar line of thought, Foucault believes in the idea of discontinuity in which discourses emerge and are socially constructed at the same time it disrupt the 'order of knowledge' and, therefore, statistical data guides the analysis of all other possibilities of expression, and its variations, as a means of attempting to assimilate the struggles in the search of this imposition of meaning (Fisher, 1996). Therefore, Foucault's notion of discontinuity facilitates the revealing of this impartiality myth, the key element of both current scientific knowledge and mathematics.

Journalism also has the power of constructing reality. Subsequently to the transition from traditional or medieval to the modern society, with its rationalisation process, the theocentric thought was abandoned and the socialisation of individuals went then to accomplish itself through the learning process of theoretical, practical-moral and esthetical problems, experienced in a decentralisation way in accordance to its own internal 'legalities' of these spheres of values. To the consolidation of these two systems widely identified intrinsically with the new society, the society and the market, one cannot ignore the role of journalism and this generalised system of exchange of (valuable) information that it played in this process. "This is the ability to intervene in the course of events, to influence actions of others and indeed to create events, by means of the production and transmission of symbolic forms" (Berger & Luckmann, 1966).

Social construction is arguably formed by inter subjectivity and one's own experiences. Tuchman (1978) makes a case that – bearing in mind the sociological conception of social actors – society helps, on the one side, to develop conscience and, on the other, through an intentional apprehension of the phenomena of shared social world, men and women are building and social phenomena collectively. She also believes that the notion of news as the mirror of reality defends "objectivity" as key element of the journalistic activity. As suggested by Graham Meikle (2009), these actions are also an indicator of a broader cultural phenomenon that is spreading globally modes of civil society organization through communication networks".

Berger and Luckmann (1966) further argue that the process of legitimation seen in social construction are composed by four levels:

1. The first level is pre-theorical and regards a "simple traditional affirmation" (p. 112). That is, it is the basis of all other evidences and subsequent premises as it represents self-evident knowledge
2. The second level "contains theoretical positions in rudimentary form" (p. 112). These premises are "highly pragmatic, directly related to concrete actions" and mostly concern moral maxims and proverbs.
3. "The third level of legitimation contains explicit theories by which an institutional sector is legitimated in terms of a differentiated body of knowledge" (p. 112). At this stage the process of legitimation starts to "provide fairly comprehensive frames of reference for the respective sector of institutionalized conduct" (p. 112).
4. The fourth and final level is where symbolic universes are imposed. "These are bodies of theoretical tradition that integrate different provinces of meaning and encompasses the institutional order in a symbolic totality" (p. 113).

Berger and Luckmann (1966) believe that this four-step process of legitimation justifies the institutional order by attributing cognitive validity (and legitimacy) to its 'objectivated meanings'. To them, "legitimation as a process is best described as a 'second-order' objectivation of meaning" (p. 110). "The function of legitimation is to make objectively available and subjectively plausible the 'first-order' objectivations that have been institutionalized" (Berger & Luckmann, 1966, p. 110).

Journalism is one of the most significant means of influence and a highly useful tool; thus, "marketing 'scientists' go to a lot of trouble learning what is most likely to have upon the viewer" (Chafetz, 2005, p. 20). Chafetz (2005) continues to reason that, much like statistics, science is not a reliable – or as reliable as portrayed – source of information either. According to him,

scientists themselves are corruptible. It is possible to find a scientist who will say, for money; just about anything you wish to have said, as the transcripts of trials show. Another is that scientific findings are limited by the assumptions that go into the design of experiments. Yet another, which applies most especially to experiments involving humans beings, is that it is impossible to control all the variables – to do that, you would have to produce a "lab rat" population of humans whose every detail would have to be monitored for conception, and even then you would fall short because of genetic differences among us and the effects of having lived in a certain environment. Still another is the fact that science is not the omniscient thing that in the optimistic 1950's and 60's we believed it was. Many of the modern scientific discoveries from the research and development labs came about by accident, when the problem that was solved was not the one for which a solution was sought (pp. 20-21).

Similarly Goldacre (2009) believes that because commercial interests plays, better yet, it is allowed to play such crucial role in the dissemination of science news and information, scientific data and evidence, statistical analysis and the practice of its publication itself are being greatly manipulated. The lack of pressure on the media to provide accurate data, and use research methods, as a means to enable to confront findings, indicates inadequate evidence, and so forth (Goldacre, 2009). To him, the nature of scientific methods under the current neoliberal society has turned science and scientific data into untrustworthy piece of information (Goldacre, 2009). Furthermore, capitalism and the need to produce profit have turned science into "bad science" (Goldacre, 2009). Goldacre (2009), Fjæstad (2007) thus believes that the media do not appreciate the importance of science and scientific histories, as, in accordance to him, journalists tend to obstruct rather than facilitate the communication with the public at large as journalism "distorts science in its own idiosyncratic way" (Goldacre, 2009, p. 225), "they play on the public's view of science as irrelevant, peripheral boffinry" (p. 226).

Still in accordance to Goldacre (2009), one of the reasons why this shift happened is due to the fact that many scientific fields or disciplines are now highly dependent on funding – regardless of where it comes from. "It is all about the money and power for lawyers. (…) Ah, but surely the media, also mentioned in the First Amendment, serve as a check on the unbridled power of the legal cartel" (Chafetz, 2005, p. 260). Nonetheless, this is not simply a one-way street in which science and scientists manipulate the media; but rather a two-way symbiotic relationship as medical practices is also influenced by the media "and so are academics" (Goldacre, 2009, p. 324). He then goes to argue that: "people read newspapers. Despite everything we think we know, their concepts seep in, we believe them to be true, and we act upon them, which makes it all the more tragic that their contents are so routinely flawed" (Goldacre, 2009, p. 324). The objectivity becomes thus the maker, the conceding of science.

PROBLEM

This research proposes to achieve is to produce an innovative body of knowledge that generates a completely new and unique comprehensive account of how statistics are used to articulate narratives and shape discourses of science in the news media and daily life. To do so, the project will look at key concepts such as objectivity, credibility and legitimation, the education of the mathematical language, as well as the mathematisation of society and nature. By understanding that "it has become almost a condition of scientific theory that it be expressible in mathematical language" (Davis & Hersh, 1986, p. 10) but that "averages ad relationships and trends and graphs are no always what they seem" (Huff, 1954, p. 10), it seeks to answer the following problems:

1.   How statistics are used to articulate narratives and shape discourses of science in the newsroom?
2.   How the general public decodes scientific statistics and discourses of science in the news?

This mathematical language is so appealing in our current number-driven culture that it is often employed to not only to legitimate stories but also to sensationalize, oversimplify and massify information. Due to its unique features, they are used in a vast array of news items – from sports and business to science and economics. However, without journalists who speak this language and readers who understand it, scientific statistics loose its meaning. The ways in which statistics are articulated and how the public decodes them is core to developing a better communication of statistics both in the news as well as on our daily life.

METHODS

Having established the theoretical basis of this research, which is relevant to the way in which the findings will be looked, it is now important to understand how the data will be gathered, organised and scrutinised. This section deals with the epistemological and methodological assumptions of the researchers and research whilst also examining in detail the data gathering technique throughout the project. Thus, this methodology section will rationalise the research practicalities and foundation while accounting for the data gathering and methodological approach to be used in this project. The primary purpose of this research is to scrutinise the uses and representations of statistics across media outlets when reporting science news by asking (1) how statistics are used to articulate narratives and shape discourses of science in the newsroom and (2) how the general public decodes scientific statistics and discourses of science in the news. Additionally, it seeks to produce exploratory research on how journalists manage quantitative data when gathering and disseminating news stories, most specifically how statistics are used by science journalists to articulate, validate and legitimate their stories. And how the general public understands this items as a means of validation and communication.

The methodological approach of this study is based on the triangulation of quantitative and qualitative research methodologies. These include the content analysis of printed news by science journalists, while driving a critical multimodal discourse analysis of a set of news articles, systematically selected from a theoretic-methodological basis construction, printed and published in the news media, both in Brazil and the United Kingdom in 2013. In sum, the research will use content analysis and critical discourse analyses, the former being the primary basis to this research. Additionally the scrutiny of ways in which statistics are used in newsroom as a means of legitimation will be examined through interviews. And that way, it goes then to systematise the selection newspapers and journalists to be interviewed. Lastly, this chapter provides the provisional research plan for the research.

The collected data analyses in response to the questioned problem and hope to elucidate the ways in which quantitative data is used to articulate and shape discourses of science in the newsroom and how the public decodes it. It aims to identify, explain and explore the relationship between statistics, and the articulation of narrative and discourses of science in the newsroom. Data were collected from a total of 564 (n=564) articles that focused on science news statistics, which allowed the compiling of a longitudinal analysis. The methodological approach for this study has guided the data collection as illustrated in this chapter. Content analysis was used to analyse the way in which science journalists have reported statistical data. Coding was used to group different elements contained in scientific news articles and turned this into quantitative data as to show the most relevant characteristics in relation to the uses of statistics in science news practice. A group of 18 unique codes were mostly used to highlight frequencies of: (1) year of publication; (2) newspaper; (3) byline; (4) type of news; (5) total number of sources quotes; (6) number of primary sources quoted; (7) number of secondary sources quoted; (8) nature of main source; (9) type of study; (10) singles study; (11) sample size; (12) main emphasis in headline; (13) who presents the statistics; (14) nature of statistics; (15) number of statistics; (16) nature of data; (17) visual data; (18) use of statistics. Discourse analysis was used to investigate how science journalists discursively construct the discourses of science news when using statistics. From the total universe of 564 articles, a close reading was conducted in 24 (twenty four) articles – 12 (twelve) in each newspaper – in order to perform an attentive reading to scrutinise this link between linguistic categories to ideological functions. The combination of these research tools yielded the possibility to rich in-depth interviews. This technique compelled of semi-structure interviews as to achieve an in-depth understanding of practices and methodologies used in the newsroom to deal with data.

Academic studies into science communication and the construction of science in the media have widely been placed within the boundaries of two models of scientific researches: relativism and constructivism. One of the most common misconceptions of paradigms is the understanding that this notion of paradigm shifts as well as the evolution and nature of science itself are an example of relativism. Kuhn (1962) denies this interpretation. He claims that science does not progress in a linear and continuous way. Conversely he argues that the understanding of scientific truth cannot be founded uniquely by objective criteria. Instead, it is defined by a consensus created by the scientific community – or rather a social construction.

When one considers reality to be socially constructed, to have an ability to intervene and influence actions through the means of symbolic forms, it is difficult to neglect the importance of context. The greatest and most pervasive fallacy of (philosophical) thinking is to ignore context (Dewey, 1927). Social sciences "are best understood by viewing people within their social, cultural, economic, geographic, and historical context" (SCRA, 2004). In brief, a multiple correspondence analysis is a technique of exploratory data analysis suitable to analyse two or more data entries. Content analysis is a scientific tool that makes replicable and valid inferences, adds new insights, greater understanding and practical actions from texts or data to their concepts. Thus, modelling the variance at multiple data correspondences rather than as one data allows variables to explain variance at theoretical levels, as well as observe the amount of variance explained in the outcome of each level. For this study two newspapers with high circulation and range of readership profiles will be examined. Within the UK scenery, The Guardian will be studied as they represent the country's "quality press" (Conboy, 2001). In Brazil, Folha de S. Paulo was chosen due to this broadsheet newspaper having the biggest circulation, geographic reach and presence among the largest Brazilian newspapers in the country.

Following the content analysis, it presents a close reading of a systematically selected sample of tweets from the total universe in order to perform a mindful and disciplines reading to understand the deeper meaning of the object of study (Brummett, 2010, p. 28). This research method completes with semi-structured interviews conducted with a small group of journalists from different media outlets in Britain and Brazil, who cover science news. The interviews are designed to argument the analyses of news articles. In doing so, this study provides knowledge on the practices and related methodologies used in the newsroom when gathering and disseminating data. Furthermore, it allows researchers to extract large amounts of data and information, which enables a richer work and outcome. Most scientific researches comprises of three phases. The first phase consists of an extended literature review. In the second, data is observed, collected and analysed. At its third phase, the researcher's objective is to gather information that is otherwise not available through the literature review or the data collection and analyses. The interview is the most widely used technique by researchers as to collect data in this last stage.

This approach can be seen in the work of Sayer (2000) and Bryman (2001). It has also been the subject of scrutiny of Herrera and Braumoeller (2004), as well as Hardy et al. (2000; 2005). A slightly different take on the issue of the uses of quantitative and qualitative methods in triangulation, comes from Neuendorf (2002), who argues for the use of qualitative and quantitative methods together, however, not necessarily for a hybrid use of critical discourse analysis and content analysis, as she suggests that these can be complementary but not necessary interlinked.

The intent is thus, to further understand the uses of scientific statistical information in news and in everyday life.

RESULTS

This section focuses on analysis the data collected. The focus of this chapter is to present and discuss the results of the three empirical methodological phases. Over 66 per cent of news containing science statistics in my sample is presented to the audiences in the form of hard news. When added to the number of feature articles, that number raises to well over 76 per cent of news articles. The dominance of hard news substantiates Stigler (1986), Desrosieres (1998), Battersby (2010) and Kuhn's (1962) inkling that there is a strong relationship between objectivity and science. Science is understood as an objective knowledge and therefore a tool of achieving the "journalistic truth" (Battersby, 2010). As the data suggests, statistical information is mostly used in hard news stories of science because of this unique quality of being, almost unquestionably, statically significant. These statistical statements are considered clear, succinct and to the point, and thus are a major source of reliable information. Conversely, these need to be taken in small and prudent doses. Science stories are, thus, a potentially powerful type of news. What gives it such importance is that science statistics is perceived as an objective truth - the ultimate journalistic goal. Indeed, as suggested by the statistics, the main provider of statistical data is Universities or rather academic journals. This confirms something that has been thoroughly agreed between all interviewed journalists. Tom Whipple, for one, believes that "I mean statistics are the reason why modern society works and exists. I don't have anything on to say and I mean the developments of [statistics] are the sole reason we don't burn witches. Yes, I think that statistics are very important" (Whipple, 2015). Table 1 shows the frequencies in the type of news presented to the public when communicating science statistics.

As seen the numbers dramatically fall when quantifying editorials (3.9 per cent), opinion column (8.5 per cent), promotional (2.3 per cent) and reportage (8.7 per cent).

Another interesting data provided by this study shows that just over 73 per cent of statistical studies quoted in scientific news articles are unknown. Similarly 69.2 per cent of articles do not state whether it was a single study or not. Nor its sample sizes – 81.2 per cent. This data confirms information that has been observed by scholars in other studies (Belair-Gagnon, 2015; Franklin & Carlson, 2011) that journalists tend not to share background or contextualise stories. For instance, Franklin and Carlson (2011) recent study on the uses of public relations material in quality newspapers in the United Kingdom showed that scientific stories based on factual claims corroborates "that on 70% of occasions these claims were entirely uncorroborated and in only 12% of cases they were corroborated completely" (2011, p. 102). As a response Whipple (2015) says that giving the reader context is "always relevant but sometimes and I'm rushing the time of the article. I'm sure there's occasions when I have not put it in, but I think it should always be there and…it is actually quite good test for me as an editor. If I'm reading an article over and, at some point, it did show result for, you know, a survey of 12 people, then it is quite embarrassing to have that in the paper. So it is quite useful to have that as a check up to myself. To say, would

Table 1. Types of news

		Frequency	Percent	Valid Percent	Cumulative Percent
Valid	Hard News	374	66.2	66.4	66.4
	Feature	57	10.1	10.1	76.6
	Editorial	22	3.9	3.9	80.5
	Opinion Column	48	8.5	8.5	89.0
	Promotional	13	2.3	2.3	91.3
	Reportage	49	8.7	8.7	100.0
	Total	563	99.6	100.0	
Missing	System	2	.4		
Total		565	100.0		

people find it odd if they read the sample size and if they would, then it really should not be publishing it or at least saying the sample size? You know, if it is really interesting, so the sample size of one [for example] a surgeon made a man with a [shattered] spine walk. Now, that sample size of one is such an extraordinary results and such a binary result that we have to go with it".

Additionally, still in accordance to my research, 26.2 per cent of scientific statistical information in news is based in single studies. Science journalists seldom go out of their way to look for further academic research – as a second study – to corroborate the information portrayed. Only 4.2 per cent of science news material comes from multiple studies. Table 2, Table 3, and Table 4 correspond to type of study, singularity of study and sample sizes respectively.

Table 2. Type of study

		Frequency	Percent	Valid Percent	Cumulative Percent
Valid	Observational	77	13.6	13.7	13.7
	Experimental	34	6.0	6.0	19.7
	Survey	39	6.9	6.9	26.6
	Unknown	413	73.1	73.4	100.0
	Total	563	99.6	100.0	
Missing	System	2	.4		
Total		565	100.0		

Table 3. Single study

		Frequency	Percent	Valid Percent	Cumulative Percent
Valid	Yes	148	26.2	26.3	26.3
	No	24	4.2	4.3	30.6
	Unknown	391	69.2	69.4	100.0
	Total	563	99.6	100.0	
Missing	System	2	.4		
Total		565	100.0		

Table 4. Sample size

		Frequency	Percent	Valid Percent	Cumulative Percent
Valid	Small	54	9.6	9.6	9.6
	Large	49	8.7	8.7	18.3
	Unknown	459	81.2	81.7	100.0
	Total	562	99.5	100.0	
Missing	System	3	.5		
Total		565	100.0		

When it comes to the uses of statistics per se 74.3 per cent of statistics were of descriptive nature. This number lowers to 56.6 per cent when analysing the data numerical data – compared to categorical data or both. Most importantly, 37.5 per cent made use of one statistics, following by 27.8 per cent who used four or more statistics. The author calls this pattern the "swim or sink" affect, meaning that journalists are so badly instructed or has such limited understanding of statistics that either they use one major statistics – using it as a objectifying source – or several as to show great knowledge – but which confuses or rather drowns the reader in numbers. For example, The Guardian's article "Nature: From Hills to Sea, UK wildlife is struggling: One in three species have halved over the last 50 year. Report finds limited number of bright spots" by Damian Carrington on May 22, 2013 presents the reader with, in total, 50 (fifty) numerical data (including, number of conservation groups, sample sizes, year, etc.) of which 24 (twenty four) are statistical data. Indeed, Grandelle (2015), editor of the "Society" section at O Globo (specialized in the area of environment and climate change) and science writer since 2009 agrees, "the reader feels attracted to numbers. And I feel attracted to it as well. Numbers are what people will talk about. That is only one example of how important numbers are, how indispensable statistics are. It is very hard to convince an editor to publish a piece if you don't convince him/her, and to do so you need a number." Thus, due to this attraction to numbers, science news journalists have often the tendency to overemphasise – and at times misrepresent – statistical information. Table 5 shows the nature of statistics used in the communication of science in the analysed news media.

Lastly, most statistical information in science news is used as a background to the story (29.7 per cent) as it legitimises stories. "Normally use it as a background in the story. I mean, normally, in certain journal articles, the statistics are not normally stand out extraordinary that give a point to why you are doing it" said Whipple (2015). This idea has been shared thoroughly among the journalists. Grandelle, for example, believes that "it is always important to recuperate numbers as well. A certain research will give you a new number, and you can recuperate with [a background] number. (…) This number is very interesting because it shows the amplitude of the problem" (2015). Lastly, Table 6 presents how statistical were used in the collected articles on science news.

With attention to shaped discourse and ways in which the public at large decodes it, this analysis focused in two articles. The "Nature: From Hills to Sea, UK wildlife is struggling: One in three species have halved over the last 50 year. Report finds limited number of bright spots" was shared 94 (ninety four) times in Twitter. Out of those, only two used its statistics as a means to legitimate the concern shared by the headline. None seemed to query the fact that in the fourth paragraph of the article, the author states that 3,148 species were analysed for the report. However, on the 21st paragraph is goes to say, "Just 5% of the estimated 59,000" species were analysed. Meaning that 95% of the data is unknown.

Table 5. Nature of statistics

		Frequency	Percent	Valid Percent	Cumulative Percent
Valid	Descriptive	420	74.3	74.6	74.6
	Inferential	72	12.7	12.8	87.4
	Both	71	12.6	12.6	100.0
	Total	563	99.6	100.0	
Missing	System	2	.4		
Total		565	100.0		

Table 6. Use of statistics

		Frequency	Percent	Valid Percent	Cumulative Percent
Valid	Produce News Story	91	16.1	16.2	16.2
	Substantiate Claims	86	15.2	15.3	31.4
	Contextualise Story	137	24.2	24.3	55.8
	Background of the Story	168	29.7	29.8	85.6
	Other	81	14.3	14.4	100.0
	Total	563	99.6	100.0	
Missing	System	2	.4		
Total		565	100.0		

That creates an inconsistency with the title – and general appeal – of the article, which states that the entire UK wildlife is struggling. A simple mathematical equation taken from the information provided in the article would indicate that concretely only 3,2 per cent of species and thus the UK wildlife are in decline. Conversely, Folha de S. Paulo's "Parcela de fumantes cai 20% em seis anos: Número vem de estudo da Unifesp com mais de 4.600 pessoas em 149 municípios" ("Smokers' share falls 20% in six years: Number comes from an Unifesp study with more than 4,600 people in 149 municipalities", translation by author) from December 12th, 2013 was shared 31(thirty one) times with 21 (twenty one) tweets presenting one or more statistical information. Out of those 125 tweets only one used statistics that were not presented in the article. This goes to show that in spite of the readers being attracted to numbers (Grandelle, 2015), they do not necessarily (1) understand the given data. Nor (2) reflect on and/or give enough consideration to the veiled meaning of numbers.

DISCUSSION

The framing of scientific statistical information in the mass media, and ways in which the public decodes it, has an influential impact in the social construction of reality and construction of science. Precious research has suggested there is an ongoing miscommunication between the scientific community, the media and the public due to the misrepresentation, miscommunication, inaccuracy and distortion of statistical information (Sumner, et al., 2014). The findings from this study suggests that news coverage of research on scientific issues has been highly misrepresented its statistical information by (1) under or overusing numbers, (2) not informing readers on the researches data methodologies, but most importantly (3) selection of data. In various aspects, this study has illustrated more general features of the way in which mass media reports social statistics (Best, 2001; 2004) and contribute to the social scientific construction of social problems (Osborne & Rose, 1999). Additionally, it has also proven the lack of statistical knowledge and time constrains of journalists (Lugo-Ocando & Brandão, 2015). As well as how statistical information needs to be contextualised (Franklin & Carlson, 2011) as well as correctly used (Huff, 1954). Numbers derived from academic journals have been widely used (and misused) without context, perpetuating thus the miss-education of the mathematical language. When science journalists choose not to provide context, they limit the information presented to the audiences. Moreover, it takes away the full picture. Scientific news is not worth without contextualization. And that is what makes or should make scientific statistical information and news important for our quotidian. The study thus reminds that the mass media is produced by people that are pressured into producing news quickly who, by doing so, avoid one of the core principles of journalism: context. The effect is to produce a constrained version of facts, a particular version of reality.

By the same token it opens space and presents a solution to the problem. The (mis)communication of science in the mass media has two main roots: (1) the lack of fluency in scientific and mathematical language of journalists and (2) the shortage of time for verification of accessed data. This inarticulacy in understanding this language is also driving cause for the public's misconstruction of science and mathematical information, hence the need for a better education of both the science journalist as well as the public at large. As a matter of fact, this Chinese Whisper scenario needs to be improved throughout. Scientists could better elucidate, in layman terms, scientific claims to journalists; those, ideally with more time, should be able to better understand this mathematical language; and the public better decode its discourse and meaning.

In several European countries, the scientific community has been meeting with the public as to create a scientific public sphere and to generate a more scientific sound population. It seeks not only the dissemination of scientific information but also the wider contextualization of academic research to the daily reality. Another less formal example of this need and creation of an open space for the discussion of science is the festival 'Pint of Science' which of next year will happen in 9 countries (UK, Ireland, France, Italy, US, Australia, Spain, Germany and Brazil), 50 cities and 3 nights around the globe. The festival aims to deliver science talks in an open, engaging and fun way by bringing them to our everyday pub. In 2012 two research scientists from Imperial College London put together an event called 'Meet the Researchers' that brought people affected by a multitude of diseases into their own lab as to demonstrate to them the kind of research they did. The event was hugely acclaimed and successful. Since then, the interest and need for scientific engagement with the community has grown and thus the 'Pint of Science' was born.

Indeed, the longitudinal mixed method outcome of this case study points to an existential need to the expansion of the scientific community to the general public. This study suggests that more than the need to further educate the public in mathematical and scientific language; it needs to have an embracing gathering/amalgamation of both the scientific and regular community. According to the Brazilian secretary of Basic Education of the Ministry of Education, Manuel Palacios da Cunha Melo, one of the biggest difficulties in this dialogue is the scepticism of many researchers who still believe that the layman will not understand they data. Still, he urges that the academia should try engaging more extensively to the community.

On the side of the journalistic community, this study makes it clear the need of it better understanding the data presented as well as critical thinking and more diversification of data sources. "Contrary to the assumptions of objectivity and factuality that journalists bear on crime statistics, these numbers are instead subject to the same type of agency and power games which are pretty much present in other beats and sources of information" (Lugo-Ocando & Brandão, 2015). This subjectivity should not be seen in scientific statistical information and thus, similarly to in the case of crime statistics, a wider range of studies and sources should be seek. Furthermore, it needs to be understood that data per se does not produce information by itself it needs to be contextualized.

The selective sources of media of science that have been refer to in this study raises issues regarding the influence of governmental sources in the communication of science. This influence can be something exceptionally worrying once statistical data is considered as an objective reference source. Taking into account that "a lot of statistical data comes from scientific articles; when it comes to corroborative data, the main sources are articles, the paper that is being published" (Grandelle, 2015); it sounds unfounded that most articles use government data sources in news of science. Grandelle (2015), however, explains that "governmental data are used because they are the main source; they are the authority figures that have more facility to collect data. For example, if you gather the meteorological data, here [in Brazil] comes from the Instituto Nacional de Meteorologia (INMET) – or National Institute of Meteorology – which is a governmental agency. There are private institutions, for example here in Brazil there is CLIMA TEMPO, but in the end CLIMA TEMPO tends to use data that comes from two governmental agencies: INMET and the Instituto Nacional de Pesquisas Espaciais (INPE) – or National Institute for Space Research. So the government has this significance. It is the government who gives/produces the raw data".

In journalism, it is quite common to use statistical information as a final product instead of a starting point. Throughout this process, from the starting point statistics to the final product statistics, some statistics lose its possible objective feature. That happens because journalists, even if science journalists, "work under very different conditions from scientists" (Seale, 2010, p. 862). The lack of time, pressure from editor and, most importantly in the case of science news, blind trust in academicals journals, often distorts these scientific statistics; losing thus its objective importance. Moreover, due to the lack of mathematical knowledge from the general public – case in point the UK where Dr. Emily Grossman (2015), during her presentation "Statistics in the Media" given on May 27th, 2015 at the University of Sheffield, stated that "in a 2012 study, when experts looked at the mathematical ability of 10 year olds, I'm sure a lot of you are familiar with the study, where it came out in the UK turn out in 26 out of 65 nations. In terms of mathematical abilities at GSCE levels, 16 and in fact there are 16 years old War three years behind the counterparts in the Far East. (…) As a matter of fact, it is estimated that half of the UK population have the maths ability in the same way to that of a primary school child. We are talking about eight million adults in working space age that have the function mathematical skills equivalent, really, of a nine-year-old child" (Grossman, 2015) – this now subjective statistics goes unnoticed. And this inability to detect subtle misrepresentations or misconceptions of statistical information – for example, correlation does not necessarily means causation – creates a vicious cycle where academics present a raw statistics which journalists seldom second check and the public accepts as fact.

As a final point, the relevance of this study lies in understanding the inter-dynamics of such news processes. Most importantly, by using three distinctive data set – that is, the content analysis, the discourse analysis and the interviews, this project produced a more encompassing idea of audiences and the mediation of scientific information to the latter, as well as a better understanding how such group decodes science news. Elucidating, thus, not only on the way they consume it but also how they can be better mediated to them. Ultimately, this unique data set can help journalists better explain science facts to lay readers and thus open communication with this set. All in all, it is hoped that the case study presented here will be of some assistance to future researchers and press offices designing approaches to releasing results of controversial studies to a wider public.

CONCLUSION

In conclusion, it would seem legitimate to understand statistics in science news as an unfamiliar legitimizing tool that most journalist use but few are familiar with the mathematical language. This has been the purpose of this chapter. This does not mean, however, that there is no space for statistical information in the news and daily life. To the opposite effect, there is a colossal need for statistical knowledge. Mathematical knowledge is intrinsic to the development of society and social development. Life could not be imagined without it. What need to be further developed are the study, training and contextualisation of such language. As seen by the findings, it needs an all-encompassing improvement in the understanding and usage of statistics. From the ways in which journalists select statistical data, to the way they present it to the audiences, all the way to the education of statistics and ways in which the public understands statistical information.

When the understanding of how scientific statistics are used to articulate and legitimate stories and how they are used to articulate narratives and shape discourses of science, it can be seen the importance of the understanding statistical information. Understanding the mathematical language is imperative. Once one understands mathematical terms, its potential assuring power becomes important. Most importantly, only when understands these terms one can securely pass such information forward. Thus, there is a vital need for general education of its knowledge.

However, whilst there is this need for general education of statistics, further understanding on how this could be better presented is needed. In this way, this chapter presents a necessity – a clear dependence on statistical data – but also a clear gap in the knowledge of scientifically statistical data; nonetheless, it does not present any response to how it could be better used and articulated.

It is recommended, thus, that such area be further developed. Expectation outcomes of such study would suggest a more encompassing partake of the public in the conception (and communication) of scientific studies. Case in point is the production of scientific information in European countries where the public is plays a role in the development of studies (where channels for communication are open).

This movement of digitalisation of the processes of current social interaction, which has statistics as key element and core basis, also reaches a number of other different social environments. From science and scientific knowledge to health and nature, the quantification of data is now a prominent figure. Nonetheless, the consequences to this over-mathematisation – and somewhat statistisation and digitalisation – it is still not known.

REFERENCES

Battersby, M. (2010). *Is that a Fact?* Ontario: Broadview Press.

Belair-Gagnon, V. (2015). *Social Media at BBC News: The Re-Making of Crisis Reporting.* Oxon, UK: Routledge.

Berger, P., & Luckmann, T. (1966). *The Social Construction of Reality: A Treatise in the Sociology of Knowledge.* London: Penguin Books.

Best, J. (2001). *Damned Lies and Statistics: Untangling numbers from the media, politicians, and activists.* Berkeley, CA: University of California Press.

Best, J. (2004). *More Damned Lies and Statistics: How numbers confuse public issues.* Berkeley, CA: University of California Press.

Blastland, M., & Dilnot, A. (2008). *The Tiger That Isn't - Seeing Through a World of Numbers.* London: Profile Books.

Boyle, D. (2000). *The Tyranny of Numbers: Why Counting Can't Make Us Happy.* London: Harper Collins.

Brummett, B. (2010). *Techniques of Close Reading.* London: Sage.

Bryman, A. (2001). *Social Research Methods.* Oxford, UK: Oxford University Press.

Butler, M. N. (1895). What Knowledge is of Most Worth? *Educational Review*, 105–120.

Chafetz, M. E. (2005). *Big Fat Liars: How Politicians, Corporation, and the Media Use Science and Statistics to Manipulate the Public.* Nashville, TN: Nelson Current.

Conboy, M. (2001). *The Press and Popular Culture.* London: Sage.

Dahlgren, P., & Sparks, C. (1991). *Communication and Citizenship: Journalism and the Public Sphere in the New Media Age.* London: Routledge.

Dahlgren, P., & Sparks, C. (1992). *Journalism and Popular Culture.* London: SAGE.

Davis, P. J., & Hersh, R. (1986). *Descartes' Dream: The World According to Mathematics.* London: Penguin Books.

Desrosieres, A. (1998). *The Politics of Large Numbers: A History of Statistical Reasoning.* London: Harvard University Press.

Devlin, K. (1998). *The Language of Mathematics: Making the Invisible Visible.* New York: W. H. Freeman and Company.

Dewey, J. (1927). *The Public Problems.* Swallow Press.

Eberstadt, N. (1995). *The Tyranny of Numbers - Mismeasurement and Misrule.* Washington, DC: The AEI Press.

Fisher, N. (1996). *Statistical Analysis of Circular Data.* Cambridge, UK: Cambridge University Press.

Fjæstad, B. (2007). Why Journalists Report Science as They Do. In M. W. Bauer, M. Bucchi, M. W. Bauer, & M. Bucchi (Eds.), *Journalism, Science and Society: Science Communication Between News and Public Relations.* London: Routledge.

Franklin, B., & Carlson, M. (2011). *Journalists, Sources, and Credibility: New Perspectives.* Oxon, UK: Routledge.

Goldacre, B. (2009). *Bad Science.* London: Fourth State.

Grossman, D. E. (2015, May 27). *Statistics in the Media.* Academic Press.

Hacking, I. (1965). *Logic of Statistical Inference.* London: Cambridge University Press. doi:10.1017/CBO9781316534960

Hardy, C., Lawrance, T. B., & Grant, D. (2005). Discourse and Collaboration: The Role of Conversations and Collective Identity. *Academy of Management Review*, *30*(1), 58–77. doi:10.5465/AMR.2005.15281426

Hardy, C., Palmer, I., & Philips, N. (2000). Discourse as a strategic resource. *Human Relations*, *53*(9), 1227–1248. doi:10.1177/0018726700539006

Herrera, Y., & Braumoeller, B. (2004). Symposium: Discourse and Content Analysis. *Qualitatite Methods*.

Huff, D. (1954). *How To Lie With Statistics*. London: Penguin Books.

Koch, T. (1990). *The News as a Myth: Fact and Context in Journalism*. Westport, CT: Greenwood Press.

Kovach, B., & Rosenstiel, T. (2001). *The Elements of Journalism*. London: Guardian Books.

Kuhn, T. S. (1962). *The Structure of Scientific Revolutions*. Chicago: University of Chicago Press.

Livingston, C., & Voakes, P. S. (2005). *Working with Numbers and Statistics: A Handbook for Journalists*. London: Lawrence Erlbaum.

Lugo-Ocando, J., & Brandão, R. F. (2015). *Stabbing News: Articulating Crime Statistics in the Newsroom*. Journalism Practice.

Meikle, G. (2009). *Interpreting News*. London: Palgrave Macmillan.

Mindich, D. T. (1998). *Just the Facts: How Objectivity Came to Define American Journalism*. New York: University Press.

Moore, D. (1997). The Basic Practice of Statistiscs. *The Freeman*.

Neuendorf, K. A. (2002). *The Content Analysis Guidebook*. Thousand Oaks, CA: Sage.

Nikolakaki, M. (2009). *Investigating Critical Routes: The Politics of Mathematics Education and Citizenship in Capitalism*. Retrieved from http://www.academia.edu/760799/investigating_critical_routes_the_politics_of_mathematics_education_and_citizenship_in_capitalism

Osborne, T., & Rose, N. (1999). Do the Social Sciences Create Phenomena? The Example of Public Opinion Research. *The British Journal of Sociology*, *50*(3), 367–396. doi:10.1111/j.1468-4446.1999.00367.x PMID:15259192

Porter, T. (1997). The triumph of numbers: civic implications of quantitative literacy. In L. Steen (Ed.), *Why Numbers Count: Quantitative Literacy for Tomorrow's America*. New York: College Board.

Sayer, R. A. (2000). *Realism and Social Science*. London: Sage. doi:10.4135/9781446218730

SCRA. (2004). Retrieved 2014 from http://www.scra27.org/about.html

Seale, C. (2010). How the Mass Media Report Social Statistics: A Case Study Concerning Research on End-of-Life decisions. *Social Science & Medicine*, *71*(5), 861–868. doi:10.1016/j.socscimed.2010.05.048 PMID:20609508

Signorielli, N. (1993). *Mass Media Images and Impact in Health*. Westport, CT: Greenwood Press.

Stigler, S. M. (1986). *The History of Statistics - The Measurement of Uncertainty before 1990*. Cambridge, MA: The Belknap Press of Harvard University Press.

Sumner, P., Vivian-Griffiths, S., Boivin, J., Williams, A., Venetis, C., & Davies, A. (2014). 12 9). The Association Between Exaggeration in Health Related Science News And Academic Press Releases: Retrospective Observational Study. *BMJ (Clinical Research Ed.)*, 1–8. PMID:25498121

Tuchman, G. (1978). *Making News: A Study in the Construction of Reality*. New York: Free Press.

White, W. F. (2013). *A Scrap-Book of Elementary Mathematics*. Retrieved from http://www.barnesandnoble.com

Zuberi, T. (2001). *Thicker than Blood: How Racial Statistics Lie*. Minneapolis, MN: Minnesota Press.

KEY TERMS AND DEFINITIONS

Chinese Whispers: Traditional children's play where a circle of people whispers given information to one, then this one to the next, and so forth.

Cumulative Percentage: Sum of the percentage of each region/category from the top to the bottom, designed to sum to 100 per cent.

Mathematical Language: System used to express, communicate and share mathematical information.

Percentage: Figure that provides the percentage of total cases that falls into the given region/category.

Quality Press: Category of (often British) newspaper distinguished by its seriousness.

Sink or Swim: Derived from a popular expression in the Portuguese language, it is often used to define something of extremes.

Valid Percentage: A percentage that excludes all missing cases.

This research was previously published in Handbook of Research on Driving STEM Learning With Educational Technologies edited by María-Soledad Ramírez-Montoya; pages 506-523, copyright year 2017 by Information Science Reference (an imprint of IGI Global).

354

Chapter 20
Naming Crime Suspects in the News:
"Seek Truth and Report It" vs. "Minimizing Harm"

Robin Blom
Ball State University, USA

ABSTRACT

Whereas some news outlets fully identify crime suspects with name, age, address, and other personal details, other news outlets refuse to fully identify any crime suspect—or even people who have been convicted for a crime. News media from a variety of countries have accused and fully identified people of being responsible for crimes, although those persons turned out to be innocent. Yet, when someone types the names of those people in online search engines, for many, stories containing the accusations will turn up at the top of the search results. This chapter examines the positive and negative aspects from those practices by examining journalistic routines in a variety of countries, such as the United States, Nigeria, and The Netherlands. This analysis demonstrates that important ethical imperatives—often represented in ethics codes of professional journalism organizations—can be contradictory in these decision-making processes. Journalists need to weigh whether they would like to "seek truth and report it" or "minimize harm" when describing crime suspects.

INTRODUCTION

It is not a question whether someone got caught with meth or another controlled substance, but rather who it is this time. Readers of many local newspapers in the Midwest of the United States are used to receiving reports about drug busts in their communities. At times it almost seems to be a daily occurrence:

Three people were arrested on a variety of felony charges after a methamphetamine lab was discovered in their South Side home.

DOI: 10.4018/978-1-5225-9869-5.ch020

As common with these types of stories, thereporters dutifully add the names of the arrestees. The report would look like something like this if it would make the next day's newspaper:

John Johnson, 36, and Pete Peterson, 32, were arrested at their home, at 747 E. Sixth Ave., after city police went there about 12:30 a.m. Thursday. Also found at the house were Jane Jones, 33, 4100 N. Keller St., and three children, ranging in age from 3 to 12.

And, as a bonus, the readers usually get to see the mug shots of the suspects that were taken at the police station or county jail after the arrest. Or, if someone from the newspaper staff rushed in soon enough, some pictures snapped at the scene could be part of the publication as well. It is common practice for thousands of media outlets around the world (and not just in the United States) to release such types of information in local crime stories—from rural weeklies to daily newspapers in large metro areas, as well as broadcast stations, blogs, and other types of citizen journalism outlets of all sizes.

Regardless of whether the three suspects from the example above are eventually convicted or not, a simple Google or Bing query—even many years later—for John, Pete, and Jane will most likely pull up their arrest story at, or near, the top of the search results. That could lead to big problems for all three down the road. Potential employers or graduate school admission officers would, perhaps, be less inclined to invite them for an interview. Banks may not provide them mortgages or loans to start a business. And their children could become isolated when other parents in the neighborhood don't want their offspring to play at a house where there are potentially illegal substances lying around—even when charges are dropped soon after the arrest.

In this case, it would have been better if they were Johan, Peter, and Sjaan—while living in The Netherlands—when they were arrested. Or Jon, Pétr, and Janna in Sweden. Because then their identities and pictures would likely not have appeared in a local daily right away after their arrest. Johan or Jon would have been "a 32-year-old resident" or the "32-year-old J." The identity would likely not be fully revealed at all, or only after conviction.

These reporting routines have been developed over a long time by journalists within their industries and could lead to the adoption of a "gold standard" of journalistic practices in individual media companies. In many cases (regardless of country), the "rules" on naming suspects is taught in journalism schools and in newsrooms as "the way we do things in our profession" without much thought about whether it is the best practice in *all* situations. As Fullerton and Patterson (2013) pointed out, "the most profound differences in press practices with respect to crime coverage result from ritualised, largely unexamined habits and from voluntary ethics policies – not from laws and formal regulation" (p. 124). Importantly, the authors also found that reporters have little knowledge about practices of colleagues and ethical codes in other countries. This probably applies to many journalists all over the planet.

It is certainly warranted to have larger discussions within media industries around the world as the digitalization of news could have large repercussions for many people who have digital footprints that they would like to—but can't—erase. Scientists warned about the influence of computers on people's daily life decades before the Internet became a household utility (see: Westin & Baker, 1972). Nowadays, social media messages float around the Twitterverse and other online repositories even when they are removed within minutes by their creators. Automatic Web crawlers or human Internet users have already captured and stored those virtual blips for eternity.

That becomes problematic when someone wants to forget some events from the past. "Since the beginning of time, for us humans, forgetting has been the norm and remembering the exception. Because of digital technology and global networks, however, this balance has shifted" (Mayer-Schönberger, 2011, p. 2). Social forgetfulness, the opportunity for a fresh start because no one can remember someone's particular history, is disappearing—as frustrating it may be for some (Blanchette& Johnson, 2002; Bannon, 2006). A criminal past or the accusation of being responsible for a crime may be a simple Internet search away to be known by others: "[o]ur pasts are becoming etched like a tattoo into our digital skins" (Lasica, 1998).

This chapter will discuss approaches to naming suspects during several stages of the judicial process in a variety of countries to establish a large range of practices and rationales for each of those routines, including Norway and the United Kingdom, among others. How are those practices around the world taking into account the threats to the presumption of innocence? What about the public right to know? Should there be a right to forget? And how are the potential negative experiences of victims taken into account? The answers of those questions provide an overview of how reporters and editors struggle with the classic battle between *seek truth and report it* and *minimizing harm*, as depicted in the Society of Professional Journalists' Code of Ethics, and with similar wording in many other ethics codes around the world. Moreover, the choices may also be influenced by local laws and regulations that lead to double standards within the coverage of some news organizations.

The goal is to provide the readers an overview of journalistic practices on naming suspects and the potential consequences of adopting one over the other in particular circumstances. In a period of time that people's history can easily be traced online, it is important that those re-evaluations take place to make sure that journalists inform the public about crime in their communication and also minimize harm for those involved, especially people not responsible for a crime. This analysis starts with an overview of the influence of organizational socializations journalistic routines and practices, in particular on news source selection and ethical decision-making. This will lead to a recommendation that there is a need for a more pragmatic approach in which journalists take into account the context of each case and all of its stakeholders (see: Husselbee, 1994).

Routines in the Newsroom

News production is a construction of themes and details to build stories that are gathered through routine practices that journalists have adopted on an ongoing basis (Strentz, 1989). This includes a high degree of consensus on storytelling and the way how to report news (Bennett, Gressett, & Halton, 1985). Routines are patterned, repeated practices or methods that people, such as news media workers, use to do their jobs. They are necessary to produce news efficiently. Without routines, journalists could not decide efficiently what to put into the news report and what issues and events must be left out (Brown, Bybee, Wearden, & Straughan, 1987).

Routines provide "regularity and manageability in a job that is inherently unmanageable" (Shoemaker, 1991, p.50). If reporters would not be able to cope with unexpected events, "news organizations, as rational enterprises, would flounder and fail" (Tuchman, 1973, p.111). Repeated practices save time in finishing a news piece and makes it easier to cope with deadlines set by news media organizations to get their message out on a set time on a daily basis or throughout a day(Niven, 2005). This also makes the news process cheaper (Sigal, 1986).

Routinization does not happen automatically when a person enrolls in an undergraduate journalism program or joins a news media organization. This happens over time by learning norms and values of an industry or work field. The journalistic routines are reinforced in the newsroom on a daily basis;

they are often unwritten rules followed by the majority of, if not all, members of a news outlet (Sigal, 1973). This process is called organizational socialization. Some studies, such as Breed's (1955) analysis of social control in the newsroom, show how reporters and editors are socialized to ascertain policies within organizations and work fields (also see: Bennett, Gressett, & Halton, 1985).

Taking into account societal forces on the norms, values, and beliefs of journalists, it still appears that individuals have much room to decide what ends up in the newspaper and what does not. Many journalism and mass communication professionals and scholars – and also the public – think that the personal views and beliefs influence the news selection process (Gaziano, 1987; Domke, Watts, Shah, & Pan, 1999; Lichtenberg, 2000; Lee, 2005).

Yet on the other hand, Reese (1991) argued that individuals are also "constrained in their power by structures beyond their immediate control" (p. 310). As a result of hundreds of years of organizational socialization within the field of journalism, newsmakers share criteria for news selection (Fishman, 1980).

Grossman and Kumar (1981) provided anecdotal evidence for organizational socialization in their book about reporting practices of White House correspondents. "[A]lthough newly arrived White House officials and reporters alike in the post-Watergate era may think of themselves as free agents, they variably follow the routines dictated by the needs of the organizations they work for" (p. 14). Each journalist tries to fulfill the organization's expectations bounded by the constraints placed by the outlet. Consequently, newly assigned reporters attempt to "follow the same routines as the reporters who preceded them to the White House" (p.14).

Especially the logistical and organizational limits affect what individuals within news media can do in providing news accounts to the public (Reese, 1991). Shoemaker (1991), therefore, proposed to examine "the extent to which the individual is merely carrying out a set of routine procedures" (p.49).

Cassidy (2006) compared the results of a content analysis of news articles by several news outlets and a survey of the reporters at those organizations, he found that factors on the routine level (peers on staff, supervisors, journalistic training, news sources, priorities of prestige publications, local competing news media, and wire service budgets) seemed to have more influence on what makes the news than individual demographics (e.g. age, educational history, racial/ethnic make-up, and political ideology).

Manning (2001) indicated that by looking at the journalistic routines used within one news organization, the news outcome could be predicted because of their adopted routines, but also warned that this view is too simplistic as a description of the effects of daily routines at news outlets on the news outcome. She maintained that it underemphasizes the extent to which individual characteristics, values, beliefs, and opinion make a significant difference.

There are indications that individual-level influence still is at work at news media organizations. This is not surprising considering the many individuals involved in the newsmaking process; within news media organizations, several kinds of conflicts influence the news outcome: conflicts between business and professional norms, between partisan and ideological factions, and between neutral and participant news values (Ettema, Whitney, &Wackman, 1987).Of course, the extent to which individuals can shape the news output is likely to differ by news organization and even by individual reporter or editor.

News Sources

Journalists need to make important decisions for each story about which sources to include. This selection procedure is also heavily routinized to turn events and issues into story as efficiently as possible. Journalists are often not able to witness events for themselves – they rely on stories of others (Berkowitz

& Beach, 1993). "Even when the journalist is in the position to observe an event directly, he remains reluctant to offer interpretations of his own, preferring instead to rely on his news sources. For the reporter, in short, most news is not what has happened, but what someone says has happened or will happen" (Sigal, 1973). Or as Gans (1980) put it, journalists "don't deal in facts, but in attributed opinions" (p.130). Even in cases when these attributed opinions are lies, "journalists can suggest that they have done so but only if they find other sources who allow themselves to be quoted to that effect" (Gans, 2003, p.47).

Journalists cannot take forever to complete stories; news holes need to be filled with their copy, and therefore, reports often need to be finalized before the next deadline (Bennett, 2005). As Sigal (1986) suggested, "Reporters need sources who can provide information on a regular and timely basis; they are not free to roam or probe at will" (p.16). To get a certain number of articles in the next day's newspaper, journalists need to receive lots of information in a short period of time in order to make the deadline (Hallin, Manoff, & Weddle, 1993). A steady flow of news is necessary. Journalists must make the "spontaneous predictable" and anticipate where newsworthy events develop (Bennett, 2005, p.166).

The choice of sources is an important force shaping the news. It is a decision of what information, like defining decision-making options, is included and which are excluded (Brown, Bybee, Wearden, & Straughan, 1987). In such way, sources are "primary definers" (McLeod, Kosicki, & McLeod, 2002, p. 244) of what happened, and thereby determine how that story is told (Kasoma & Maier, 2005). Sources try to influence what information gets out in the symbolic arena by managing what facts and opinions are discussed in public (Gans, 1980). Reporters, therefore, turn to people who provide information that can be used for news output on a regular basis. For instance, government agencies provide a "high volume of professionally produced, ready-to-report news matters" (Bennett, Gressett, & Halton, 1985, p. 50).

In many occasions, those who report on public affairs turn to bureaucrats, politicians, and other authorities. Journalists do this to hold (elected) officials accountable (the news media's watchdog function in society), but they are also easily accessible to provide information (Gandy, 1982; Hallin, Manoff, & Weddle, 1993).

Entman and Gross (2008) pointed out that this is often the case for news about criminal cases. Consequently, it is often slanted in favor of the prosecution, because there is often no credible source that voices a competing frame. "[U]nlike in coverage of policy debates over, say, social security, abortion, or the environment, there is no institutionalized political-party system to provide a more-or-less automatic two-sided debate among credible elites that journalists can reflect in their coverage" (p. 95).

Attorneys could provide a counterargument to accusations by the prosecutor, but public comments may not always be in the best interest for a defendant. Furthermore, the authors argued, pretrial reporting "tends generally to treat the presumption of innocence as a formality, largely limited to using the word allege" (p. 95).

Verifying Facts

Journalists always deal with the issue that some facts are verifiable in theory but not verifiable in practice (Tuchman, 1978). When a prosecutor "alleges" that a person has committed a crime, there is often not enough time to check out claims by sources to publish an article on the same day. Or worse, on many occasions, verifiable facts are just not readily available at all. This leads reporters to an alternative approach: reporting the truth-claims of sources. And because journalists often lack time to verify statements, this could deny them the opportunity to include multiple sides of stories and to find out if those claims are true *before* the next deadline, or when they are coping with real-time coverage (see:

Deuze, 2004; García-Avilés, 2014). As a result, reporters can indicate only that something happened (or is happening); journalists most likely will focus on what has happened rather than addressing questions on why something happened, or to provide a broader context (Perloff, 1998).

Journalists have little time to reflect on whether they have gotten at the truth when they turn in an assignment. And after all, in many instances they have been clearly wrong. For example, Sen. Joseph McCarthy was able to get his accusations in the news columns and broadcasts of U.S. news media during the anti-Communism era, even while many of them were found to be false. Furthermore, some reporters themselves thought McCarthy claims were false, but put the allegations in their news reports anyhow because they kept holding onto some newsroom routine practices, providing face-value coverage of important political figures (Bayley, 1981; Oshinsky, 1983; Hacket, 1984). Kovach and Rosenstiel (2001) illustrated this idea with a speech of Defense Secretary Robert McNamara on the war in Vietnam. His assertions were eventually found out not to be true, and the press "did not get at the truth of what he knew" (p. 37).

This contradicts the recommendations of the Hutchins Commission (1947), which warned—almost seven decades ago—about dangers of publishing accounts that are "factually correct but substantially untrue" (p. 219) By just reporting the facts - in this case: what a speaker claims - the distribution of lies cannot automatically be avoided. According to Rupar (2006), this shows that journalism is not just a matter of portraying "facts as they are," but also a "matter of assembling truth beneath and around 'facts as they are told'" (p. 128). Even when the claims are truthful, it still could be doubtful the picture drawn by the politician is a complete picture of the whole story.

Ethical Decision-Making

Journalists have important roles in society. As gatekeepers and story framers, there is a tremendous opportunity to inform fellow citizens about vital issues and events about success and failure in creating just societies. This task comes with immense responsibilities. Journalists can hurt people's feelings in news coverage and they need to make sound moral judgements in choosing the story elements and descriptions to be informative without unnecessarily offending or defaming certain individuals or groups.

Moral judgment is defined as "the process of choosing between right and wrong based upon what one finds important and is used to define the quality of reasons used by people making ethical choices" (Meader, Knight, Coleman, & Wilkins, 2015, p. 235). Those decisions between right and wrong (or good and bad) are made based on the values that a person or a group (united by a code of ethics) applies in such ethical choices. Values are "conceptions of the desirable that guide the way (people) select actions, evaluate people and events, and explain their actions and evaluations" (Schwartz, 1999, p. 24).

Ethical decisions can be difficult to take because they usually involve balancing positive and negative consequences for many stakeholders (Bugeja, 2008). This is particularly true "whenever two or more duties would lead to different decisions" (Christians, 2007, p. 122).

Although the foundation of many ethics philosophies do not change, the applications of the philosophies may take different meanings and lead to a new set of consequences within rapid changing social environments that are spurred by new communication forms and other technological innovations. Those developments lead to new questions about human rights in this Digital Age (Mathiesen, 2014) and the role of journalism in shaping those protections. As Christians and colleague (1991) pointed out, "Open news remains our national glory in a complicated world, and expectations of journalistic performance are higher than ever before" (p. 29).

Journalists likely have been exposed to at least some ethics training through their education and professional careers. Many journalism undergraduate programs have included media ethics education in their (core) curricula, either as a stand-alone course or in combination with media law. This exposes aspiring journalists to philosophies in ethical reasoning and case studies to explore the consequences of ethical decision-making in real life. And many (student) news outlets have adopted ethics codes from professional organizations, such as the Society of Professional Journalists (SPJ), which has adopted four sub-headers to explain the duties in covering news: (1) Seek truth and report it; (2) Minimize harm; (3) Act independently; and (4) Be accountable and transparent.

Codes of ethics provide journalists with some helpful guidance, yet they do not provide templates for adequate responses for each ethical dilemma. It is still up to the journalists to balance the interest of all stakeholders. "Journalistic codes of ethics seldom offer precise, bright-line rules that define problematic situations…. The flexible language of these codes leads to varied interpretations and a resultant lack of consensus on their meaning and application" (Morant, 2005, pp. 613-614). For instance, the code of ethics of the Nigerian Press Council (2016) proposes that publishing information about an individual is justified if a crime is being exposed, yet in many cases it is not sure that a suspect has committed an alleged crime. And the Press Council (2016) of South Africa points out that the right of privacy may only be overridden by the public interest and that the facts need to be true or substantially true. But, again, that may be hard to establish early in a crime investigation when suspects are interviewed and arrested.

Thus, codes of ethics do not provide guidance for a one size-fits-all solution when it comes to naming crime suspects in news coverage. In fact, using the SPJ codes as an example, the imperative of "seeking truth and report it" seems to challenge the imperative of "minimizing harm," according to Steele, Black, and Barney (1998).Thus, journalists need to balance on a case-by-case basis whether invading someone's privacy, or the extent to which someone's privacy is being invaded, is "necessary in order to permit others access to information needed to make equally important choices in their lives" (Etzioni, 1999, p. 23) or prevents harm to others. However, there is a variety of cases in which harm was done to the people's whose privacy was invaded by presenting them—mistakenly—as crime perpetrators. Despite many good intentions by journalists to adhere to journalists codes of ethics as much as they can, this does not prevent them from identifying the wrong people in crime cases. Consequently, such news coverage has haunted these false positives for many years after publications identified them as suspects of horrific crimes.

The False Positives

One of the most famous cases, because of the widespread—global—coverage, involves the person who was accused of planting a backpack with three pipe bombs at a park in Atlanta during the 1996 Summer Olympics that killed one person and injured 111 others. He was initially considered a hero for alerting the police when he discovered the explosives, which led to a large-scale evacuation that saved many lives. Yet, soon after, he was considered the prime suspect in the case. This led to large scrutiny by law enforcement, as well as the world media that followed him and his family around—even though he was just a "person of interest." Jewell has never been charged or indicted of any crime.

The news media played a vital role in continuous dissemination of information that made the person suspect, yet without any valid evidence (and, in hindsight, there was none). Alicia C. Shephard (1994), a senior writer for the *American Journalism Review*, wrote that "some restraint [by the news media] would have helped" in this particular case, because the finger pointing started before anyone was arrested, charged or indicted. In an unusual act, the U.S. attorney's office wrote a letter to the man's lawyers exonerating him: "This is to advise you that based on the evidence developed to date, your client [...] is not considered a target of the federal criminal investigation into the bombing on July 27, 1996, at Centennial Olympic Park in Atlanta. Barring any newly discovered evidence, this status will not change. I am hopeful that [...] will provide further cooperation as a witness in the investigation."

Another famous case, a decade later, involved several athletes from the Duke University lacrosse team. They were falsely accused of raping a student from another local university. Because the alleged victim was African-American and the students Caucasian, the case was framed as a potential hate-crime as well. Entman and Gross (2008) concluded that the press coverage of this case was not always one-sided and unfavorable to the students, yet the "early phase was also less balanced andexhibited a slant toward the prosecution" (p. 124).

Those early stories—filled with accusations against the players—are still easy to retrieve online. Peltz (2008) did a Google search and nine of first ten links were to stories in which it was not mentioned that the players were innocent. This could have large implications later on in life of these men, the author argued:

Imagine you are a harried hiring coordinator working for Big X Corporation. Before you sits a stack of 600 resumes, and your job today is to winnow the field by eliminating persons of dubious character. Your tool is Google ...[they] will probably not get the benefit of careful reading and follow-up searches concerning their charges. (p. 718)

The players were exonerated more than a year after they were accused. Their innocence was declared in a letter from the Attorney's Office of North Carolina, similar to Jewell. It is very rare the suspects receive a written account of their innocence in a case. Usually, charges are dropped or during a court case it is determined that there is not enough evidence to pronounce someone guilty. That is not the same as a declaration of innocence. Therefore, in many cases where there is no DNA evidence available to prove someone's innocence or other aspects of a case—in the public's eye—there is still the possibility that the suspects did commit the crime.

That is exactly what happened to another person who was accused of a crime he didn't commit:

[T]he libel actions have by no means addressed all the damage done to my personal and professional reputation, which I spent over 30 years building. ... I doubt the damage done can ever be repaired. Had I not been retired, I think the effect on my career would have been catastrophic. (see: Cathcart, 2011)

In another example, a man accused of raping a teenager, the struggle was worse. He spent ten years fighting to clear his name after he was not indicated by a grand jury and even won a defamation suit against his accusers. According to Reza (2005), "he had first taken a leave of absence and then left his job as a state prosecutor, undergone therapy, suffered daily threats and taunts from members of the public (to him and to his school-aged daughter), and endured constant attention from the media" (p. 771).

These cases are not overly rare, because a large percentage of state felony cases are dismissed after arrest in major urban centers, from 10 percent for driving-related offenses to 40 percent for assault cases. Similar numbers are found in federal cases, where prosecutors do not prosecute about one-third of the suspects for violent crimes. This pertains to many ten-thousands of people who were arrested but not prosecuted (Reza, 2005).

The Case for Naming Crime Suspects

The "assumptions about the value of names remain widely accepted, if not unchallenged, in U.S. practice" (Vultee, 2010). This is the case in other countries as well, such as the United Kingdom. This assumption is fueled by the desire for the press to be part of the broader marketplace of ideas, in which competing claims are assessed for their value. When it comes to information, it is assumed that "truth naturally overcomes falsehood when they are allowed to compete—[which] was used continually during the eighteenth century as a justification for freedom of expression" (Smith, 1988, p. 31).

In other words, according to Meyers (1993), the journalist's job is to gather and report all the details and "let the readers or viewers decide." The author also pointed out that such an interpretation of reporting practices "also divorces the journalist from her role as a moral agent, accountable to others" (p. 142). That is a deliberate approach from many news organizations in the United States and United Kingdom that value informing the public more than any other stakeholders, including the people accused of crime (Fullerton & Patterson, 2013).

This is noticeable for news outlets that run so-called mug shot websites, where all profile photos released by police in their distribution area, automatically, are placed online with all personal information of the arrestees and a description of the crime they are accused of by the police. For instance, mugshots and other personal information are directly published on the Tampa Bay Times website as soon as the police releases the information in the newspaper's four prime distribution counties (Hillsborough, Pasco, Pinellas, and Manatee). The images and the other information (name, photograph, booking ID, height, weight, age, gender, eye color, birth date, booking date and booking charge) remain searchable on the website for 60 days from the booking date. Several other newspapers have similar additions to their news sections, such as the *Chattanooga Times Free* Press. The pages are visited by thousands each day, which allow the outlets to sell lucrative advertising space to accompany the mugshots.

The *Tampa Bay Tribune* mugshot website has a disclaimer on its front page in which it states that the information mirrors open county sheriff's Web sites in the Tampa Bay area. Additionally, it acknowledges that the people appearing on the Website have not been convicted and are presumed innocent. "Do not rely on this site to determine any person's actual criminal record." The mugshots are removed from the Website after 60 days, yet that does not happen with all crime-related news coverage. However, the newspaper cannot prevent others from copying the crime reports and those stories may still float around the World Wide Web after being removed from the newspaper website.

Such openness about all the facts, including the names of suspects, may help victims of crime to step forward, if they have not done out of fear of repercussions by the perpetrator, concern of being stigmatized as a victim, or fearing to not be believed. In fact, a newspaper with all the details of a case could lead to criminals ending behind bars. A simple explanation that someone is investigated for sexual misconduct could lead to a breakthrough in multiple cases.

- **Arizona (Little Rock):** A Catholic priest was placed on administrative leave while police investigate allegations of sexual misconduct with a minor. The Rev. [John Doe], 53, wasn't charged with any crime.

This Associated Press local wire story about this man (his name was mentioned in full in the original report printed in the San Francisco Chronicle in the Fall of 2002), even emphasizing that he is not charged or arrested. It is only mentioned that the Douglas Police Department investigates him for misconduct of a minor. Further there is a short history about his work as a priest, but there is not any evidence attributed in the story that supports the allegations.

Yet, in similar cases, victims filed police reports after discovering that they were not alone. In the case of actor Bill Crosby (who at this point has not been convicted), dozens of women accused him of sexual assault after a few others had spoken out in public and made news headlines nationally and internationally. Lawyers of victims of British publicity agent Max Clifford praised the value of naming suspects of sexual crimes. After two women came forward, dozens of others did as well (Saunderson, 2014).

The Case against Naming Crime Suspects

In several West and North European countries the majority of daily newspapers do not publish full names of most suspects, such as in Norway, although the names would likely be published when an armed criminal is on the run. Names are usually published by almost all newspapers after people are formally charged and their cases go to trial (Bowers, 2013).

In Sweden, the full name may appear in crime coverage, but only after a person has been convicted by the courts. That would not even be the case in The Netherlands, except for a rare occasion. For instance, some media organizations provided the full name of the murderer of Pim Fortuyn, a popular politician who was killed a few days before the 2002 parliament elections; other outlets still used the killer's first name and initials for years, instead.

In an extraordinary case, one Dutch daily newspaper published not only the name of a convicted pedophile, but also his address (something that was unheard of in the Dutch press). This led to a mob scene outside of the apartment of the man with people demanding the pedophile to move out of town. This case was a source for heavy debate within the Dutch journalism industry and the newspaper's chief editor has publicly apologized for publishing the address. The newspaper also paid him 750 euro as compensation.

Whether you are a suspect or convict, in The Netherlands, the face is also rarely recognizable on a picture that accompanies a crime story. In a small amount of court stories, an artist impression of the scene may include a drawing of the suspect. But those impressions are more in the style of a caricature rather than a Rembrandt with all the fine details of facial expressions. The ability to recognize a specific person is small; and there is anecdotal evidence that suspects, judges, and prosecutors do not even recognize themselves in some of those drawings. Instead of drawings, some news outlets would publish a picture of a suspect or convict, yet would place a black box over the eyes of the suspect, which makes it much harder to recognize the person—even if you would pass the person in the street the next day. (Interestingly, this practice has been considered sensational in some of the ethics policies of daily newspapers, although that did not stop their reporters and editors from using pictures with some facial parts covered by the black box.)

There are many media outlets around the world that question the benefit for their audiences to know all personal details about a suspect, and whether they should do more to minimize harm to people that may later turn out to be innocent. For instance, more than 250 people have been exonerated in the United States while they were on death row, because DNA evidence dismissed them from involvement of the crime they were convicted for. When those people were named in newspaper reports before, during, and after the trial means they were falsely accused of brutal crimes.

Whether it's an old-fashioned news report or a modern online database, the main question remains the same: Are the people mentioned guilty of committing the crimes they are accused of? The main imperative of journalism is to tell the truth, but right after an arrest that is almost always impossible to say with limited access to evidence. Not all "facts" are checked and double-checked by the Justice Department at that point. Furthermore, not all "facts" are checked and double-checked by the journalists. That goes against the "most commonly repeated adage in U.S. criminal justice is the presumption of innocence: defendants are deemed innocent until proven guilty" (Baradaran, 2011, p. 723) and "Likewise in England, comments in the media about a person's guilt were criticized when the individual had not yet been found guilty (p. 735).

Reporters never know for sure what turns and twists a specific crime story will take during the course of a long judicial process. As James Carey (2002) explained, "premature scoops" could be "nothing more than gossip and sensationalism" (p. 80). That is the reason for why a growing number of U.S. college newspapers (e.g., University of Connecticut and Miami University) have decided to omit names from their daily police blotter if there is no need to identify a person to avoid additional harm to the community. The editors decide in individual cases whether identification is necessary.

Reza (2005) also questioned the necessity of naming suspects in many instances, because the majority of people who read the story will never will have any contact with that person. According to Solove (2007), "facts of the story may be of legitimate concern to the public, but the identification of the people involved might not further the story's purpose" (p. 133). Some journalists argue that publicity is not part of a court sentence and as Tor Mørseth, managing editor of *Bergens Tidende* (BT), told Bowers (2013), "identification of a person in media is an added burden, and we have taken a stand that we will not identify for this reason" (p. 80).

Rehabilitation: The Right to Be Forgotten

Related to that argument, an important reason for not naming convicted criminals (and thus as well in the stage when they were suspects) is the ability to rehabilitate after fulfilling their sentence. Full disclosure of all private facts could limit opportunities to make a living and support a family. That is less likely when a person is fully identified in news coverage. Other people may be less inclined to interact with someone they know has a criminal past (Fullerton & Patterson, 2013).

It has been advocated numerous times that courts should recognize a right to be forgotten. In that sense, citizens should have the right to have information deleted after a certain time, the right to have a "clean slate," and the right to be connected only to present information (Koops, 2011; McNealy, 2012).

The highest European court decided in 2014 that people have a right to have links removed from search websites, such as Google and Yahoo!, when the links connect Internet users to information that is deemed irrelevant or outdated. Hundreds of thousands of links and ten thousands of web pages have been removed since, although sometimes only for searches conducted in EU territory and not necessarily from other areas on the planet. However, media companies do not have to automatically honor all requests when it is assessed that there is a public interest in providing access to contended pages. Lower European courts have supported media companies in several of such cases.

It was not a surprise that the European Union would establish a right that would allow people to keep some sort of control of private information when there would not be an outweighing public interest in the information. Spanish courts have been supportive of the right to be forgotten argument and also French courts have long acknowledged the concept of *oubli*, or oblivion, that gives individuals the control of their past and future (Rosen, 2012; Ambrose &Ausloos, 2013).

The European approach is in direct conflict with protections found in the First Amendment of the United States, but that does not mean that that private information is automatically public (see: Warren

& Brandeis, 1890). The right of privacy is protected in many instances and limits news media somewhat in how and what to report in certain cases, although courts have refrained from clearly defining newsworthiness and its relation to privacy laws. And there is no overhauling legal framework that helps convicted criminals in their rehabilitation efforts by shielding them from press coverage.

Ironically, providing someone a second chance is regarded as a noble act in countries where the press predominantly is providing all details about crime suspects. Comeback stories are considered heroic and have often been glorified in many countries. Yet, for criminals such opportunity is made much harder with non-stop press coverage to take advantage of a new chance, whereas many criminals and innocent suspects would want nothing more. As Bannon (2006) explained, "Who has not experienced the liberating feeling of throwing off the baggage of the past and beginning afresh to confront the world? In a sense acts of pardon, amnesty, Catholic absolution in confession, are all mechanisms by which people can bury the past and begin anew" (p. 10).

Such pleas only count for juvenile crime suspects and convicts in many countries. This is even the case in the United States, although there is no consensus among journalists on such practice either. Reporters are more hesitant to fully identify juvenile suspects, in particular when they are not tried as an adult. Once rehabilitated, the child-turned-adult can petition the judge to destroy his record in certain cases for "its rationale - protecting juvenile offenders from attention that would stigmatize them and hinder their integration into society" (Reza, 2005, p. 785). Yet, as Howard Snyder, of the National Center for Juvenile Justice in Pittsburgh, explained in Hancock's (1998) article, "you can't expunge a newspaper article. Not now. Not ten years down the road." (p. 18-19).

But others disagree that juvenile criminals should be unnamed in news coverage: "No, naming a juvenile offender is not a breach of ethics. Not naming one would be, because it leave a hole in the story and could put the public at risk" (Kolb, 2011, p. 74). Many other journalists agree with this assessment and lean toward publishing all names of suspects, regardless of age. Many news managers at Ohio newspapers and television stations were often revealing the identity of juvenile suspects. (About 15 percent revealed the names in almost all instances.) The managers based their decision on the severity of the crime, age of the suspect, the distance of the crime to the distribution area of their news stories, and whether other news outlets had revealed the identity. The way the competition was covering the story also played a role (Hanson, 2004).

Imperfect Solutions

Whereas the European court decisions in favor of the right to be forgotten withholds media companies from disseminating certain news items after it has been published when it is deemed irrelevant or outdated, others have argued that is not enough. In the United Kingdom there have been repeated calls to make it a crime to publicly name a suspect in any police inquiry (Peachey, 2015). Some go even as far as arguing that U.S. courts should allow prior restraint on a narrowly tailored range of pre-trial information to avoid unfair trials, which also would mean that information about the suspect would not be discussed publicly until the first verdict of guilt or innocence by the courts (See: Phillipson, 2008).

Those calls for limiting press freedom are usually placed in context in which the media industry is capitalizing "on the public's insatiable hunger for sensations" to increase its profits (Mitrou, 2012, p. 4). In similar vein, Beale (2006) argued that "media content is shaped by economic and marketing considerations that frequently override traditional journalistic criteria for newsworthiness" (p. 398). Fullerton and Patterson (2013) pointed out that the 'tell-all-and-then-some' style of crime coverage is adopted by British media to "routinely probe an accused person's private life in search of villainous elements to explain alleged wickedness—but also to entertain" (p. 116).

Some of those criticisms may be correct in certain cases, but many journalists are in the business to inform audiences about the problems and successes in their communities—not the profit status of their employers. What may be lacking is a dialogue with those audiences about *how* the news is covered. Some news outlets have addressed this by appointing an ombudsperson to explain decisions made in the newsroom and answer questions from readers, listeners, or viewers in regards to such choices. But also other members of newsrooms have addressed concerns or comments to establish a better understanding of the public.

For instance, Scott Sherman (2010), a crime and court editor of the *Salt Lake Tribune*, explained in an article how the newspaper tended to deal with the question whether to name individual crime suspects:

The Tribune's decision to name or not name a person accused of a crime is never about protecting them from public scrutiny. We aim to inform our readers about events in their communities, but we also recognize the enormous responsibility we bear to be fair to those whose guilt or innocence will be decided by judge or jury.

Sherman went on to explain that covering news is "more than simply retelling the events –it requires thoughtful evaluation about what we cover and how we cover it." Furthermore, Sherman assumed that not many readers "will care to read follow-up stories on hearings, motions and ultimately a sentence for such a crime." Thus, the newspaper wanted to select only those stories that most important for public scrutiny to allow identification for the accused. Reporters would follow the case throughout the court system when it has been decided to use the name in early coverage.

This is to avoid that people are not only named when they are accused of committing a crime, but also when it turns out that those accusations were not correct. This would be especially damaging for a person when all Web searches would provide articles when he or she was suspect, but not when innocence have been proven or, otherwise, there was not enough evidence for a conviction. For instance, Shephard (1994) reported a case of a 15-year-old girl who allegedly had suffocated her half-sister. A local daily newspaper printed her name when she was convicted by the trial court, but did not name her when the conviction was overturned. Consequently, her name could come up in a Web search for being convicted of murder, while none of the stories that clear her from any liability could show up in during the same search using her name.

Several scholars have pointed out that these false positive findings—the identification of innocent people as suspects—must be debated in journalism more thorough to get a more pragmatic approach in naming suspects. For instance, Hodges (1994) maintained that "[i]n reporting on criminal behavior we should report all aspects of the criminal's private life that might help to understand the criminal and his or her acts," but not for sake of being complete. (p. 208).

Fullerton and Patterson (2013) pointed to a framework developed by Lennart Weibull, a senior researcher at the SOM Institute and professor in the Department of Journalism, Media and Communication at Gothenburg University. When a suspect is a private person without public function and the crime involves a private event, then journalists should refrain from publishing the name. On the flip side, when a crime case involves a public person at a public event, it is warranted to publish the name.

Yet, it becomes a more difficult decision when it involves a private citizen in a public event, or vice versa. Furthermore, the framework does not take into account the type of event or the impact for the public (e.g., news audiences may want more information about a serial killer targeting random people in a community than when there was a targeted, stand-alone murder, as disturbing that may be). The framework does also not take into account any concerns about rehabilitation either—even for public officials. For instance, Hodges (1994) argued that information about public officials only should be published "if their private activity might reasonable have a significant effect on their official performance" (p. 205).

Husselbee (1994) argued that "the journalist must be able to distinguish between a right to knowledge and a curious interest in knowing" (p. 145). The author advocated for a case-by-case evaluation that forces journalists to (1) evaluate what elements of a story the public need to know; (2) examine whether the story could effectively inform the public without personal information, or what would be the least amount of personal information that would be required to achieve the goal of informing the public; (3) determine the research procedure to verify the accuracy of information related to a case; (4) develop strategies to minimize harm to stakeholders; and (5) determine whether, and if so how, the decisions related to revealing private information will be communicated to the audience along with the news report(s).

In other words, there must be an important public purpose to know, meaning that news outlets should not automatically publish the names of all suspects, nor refuse to publish any. As journalistic routines and practices have been shaped through decades of organizational socialization it may take a while until newsrooms are willing to adopt a case-by-case approach. But internal newsroom discussions and broader debates within media industries can only be effective when discussants are aware of the wide range of policies, with all their pros and cons, to determine the fine lines on what details to report in crime news. Only then could media professionals find solutions to minimize or eliminate the number of false positives: stories about innocent people being linked to horrific crimes.

REFERENCES

Ambrose, M. L., & Ausloos, J. (2013). The right to be forgotten across the pond. *Journal of Information Policy*, *3*, 1–23. doi:10.5325/jinfopoli.3.2013.0001

Bannon, L. J. (2006). Forgetting as a feature, not a bug: The duality of memory and implications for ubiquitous computing. *CoDesign*, *2*(1), 3–15. doi:10.1080/15710880600608230

Baughman, S. B. (2011). Restoring the presumption of innocence. *Ohio State Law Journal*, *72*, 724–776.

Bayley, E. (1981). *Joe McCarthy and the Press*. Madison, WI: University of Wisconsin Press.

Beale, S. S. (2006). The news media's influence on criminal justice policy: How market-driven news promotes punitiveness. *William and Mary Law Review*, *48*, 397–481.

Bennett, S. C. (2012). The "right to be forgotten": Reconciling EU and US perspectives. *Berkeley Journal of International Law*, *30*, 161–195.

Bennett, W. (2005). *News: The politics of illusion* (5th ed.). New York: Pearson Longman.

Bennett, W., Gressett, L., & Halton, W. (1985). Repairing the news: A case study of the news paradigm. *Journal of Communication*, *35*(2), 50–68. doi:10.1111/j.1460-2466.1985.tb02233.x

Berkowitz, D., & Beach, D. (1993). News sources and news context: The effect of routine news, conflict and proximity. *The Journalism Quarterly*, *70*(1), 4–12. doi:10.1177/107769909307000102

Blanchette, J.-F., & Johnson, D. G. (2002). Data retention and the panoptic society: The social benefits of forgetfulness. *The Information Society: An International Journal, 18*(1), 33–45. doi:10.1080/01972240252818216

Bowers, J. O. (2013). *American and Norwegian press' approaches to identification of criminal suspects or arrestees: The public's right to know versus the private citizen's right to privacy, reputation, and presumption of innocence* (Unpublished master's thesis). University of Oregon.

Breed, W. (1955). Social control in the newsroom: A functional analysis. *Social Forces, 33*(4), 326–335. doi:10.2307/2573002

Brown, J., Bybee, C., Wearden, S., & Murdock Straughan, D. (1987). Invisible power: Newspaper news sources and the limits of diversity. *The Journalism Quarterly, 64*(1), 45–54. doi:10.1177/107769908706400106

Bugeja, M. (2008). *Living ethics: Across media platforms*. New York, NY: Oxford University Press.

Carey, J. (2002, Spring). What does "good work" in journalism look like? *Nieman Reports*, 79-81.

Cassidy, W. (2006). Gatekeeping similar for online, print journalists. *Newspaper Research Journal, 27*, 6–23.

Cathcart, B. (2011, October 8). The ordeal of Christopher Jefferies. *Financial Times Magazine*. Retrieved from http://www.ft.com/cms/s/2/22eac290-eee2-11e0-959a-00144feab49a.html

Christians, C. G. (2007). Utilitarianism in media ethics and its discontents. *Journal of Mass Media Ethics, 22*(2-3), 113–131. doi:10.1080/08900520701315640

Christians, C. G., Rotzoll, K. B., & Fackler, M. (1991). *Media ethics: Cases & moral reasoning* (3rd ed.). New York, NY: Longman.

Deuze, M. (2004). What is multimedia journalism? *Journalism Studies, 5*(2), 139–152. doi:10.1080/1461670042000211131

Domke, D., Watts, M., Shah, D., & Pan, D. (1999). The politics of Conservative Elites and the Liberal Media argument. *Journal of Communication, 49*(4), 35–58. doi:10.1111/j.1460-2466.1999.tb02816.x

Entman, R. M., & Gross, K. A. (2008). Race to judgment: Stereotyping media and criminal defendants. *Law and Contemporary Problems, 71*, 93–133.

Ettema, J., Whitney, D., & Wackman, D. (1987, 1997). Professional mass communicators. In D. Berkowitz (Ed.), Social meanings of news. Thousand Oaks, CA: SAGE Publications.

Etzioni, A. (1999). *The limits of privacy*. New York: Basic Books.

Fishman, M. (1980). *Manufacturing the news*. Austin, TX: University of Texas Press.

Fullerton, R. S., & Patterson, M. J. (2013). Crime news and privacy: Comparing crime reporting in Sweden, the Netherlands, and the United Kingdom. In J. Petley (Ed.), *Media and public shaming: Drawing the boundaries of disclosure*. New York: I. B. Tauris & Co.

Gandy, O. (1982). *Beyond agenda setting: information subsidies and public policy*. Norwood, NJ: Ablex Publishing.

Gans, H. (1980). *Deciding what's news: A study of CBS Evening News, NBC Nightly News, Newsweek, and Time*. New York: Random House.

Gans, H. (2003). *Democracy and the news*. New York: Oxford University Press.

García-Avilés, J. A. (2014). Online newsrooms as communities of practice: Exploring digital journalists applied ethics. *Journal of Mass Media Ethics, 29*(4), 258–272. doi:10.1080/08900523.2014.946600

Gaziano, C. (1987). News people's ideology and the credibility debate. *Newspaper Research Journal, 9*, 1–18.

Grossman, M., & Joynt Kumar, M. (1981). *Portraying the President: The White House and the News Media*. Baltimore, MD: John Hopkins University Press.

Hackett, R. (1984). Decline of a paradigm? Bias and objectivity in news media studies. *Critical Studies in Mass Communication, 1*(3), 329–359. doi:10.1080/15295038409360036

Hallin, D., Manoff, R., & Weddle, J. (1993). Sourcing patterns of national security reporters. *The Journalism Quarterly, 70*(4), 753–766. doi:10.1177/107769909307000402

Hancock, L. (1998, July/August). Naming kid criminals. *Columbia Journalism Review*, 18–19.

Hanson, G. (2004). Identifying juvenile crime suspects: A survey of Ohio TV stations, newspapers. *Newspaper Research Journal, 25*, 121–125.

Hodges, L. (1994). The journalist and privacy. *Journal of Mass Media Ethics, 9*(4), 197–212. doi:10.120715327728jmme0904_1

Husselbee, L. P. (1994). Respecting privacy in an information society: A journalists dilemma. *Journal of Mass Media Ethics, 9*(3), 145–156. doi:10.120715327728jmme0903_3

Hutchins Commission. (1947, 2004). "The Requirements," from Afree and responsible press. In J. Durham Peters & P. Simonson (Eds.), *Mass Communication and American Social Thought: Key texts, 1919-1968*. Lanham, MD: Rowman & Littlefield Publishers.

Kasoma, T., & Maier, S. (2005). *Information as good as its source: Source diversity and accuracy at nine daily U.S. newspapers*. Paper presented at the meeting of the International Communication Association, New York, NY.

Kolb, J. J. (2011, June). Coming of age: Naming juvenile criminal suspects shouldn't pose an ethical quandary. *Editor & Publisher*, 30.

Koops, B.-J. (2011). Forgetting footprints, shunning shadows. A critical analysis of the "right to be forgotten" in big data practice. *Scripted, 8*, 229–256.

Kovach, B., & Rosenstiel, T. (2001). *The elements of journalism: What newspeople should know and the public should expect*. New York: Three Rivers Press.

Lasica, J. D. (1998). The Net never forgets. *Salon*. Retrieved from http://www.salon.com/1998/11/25/feature_253/

Lee, T. (2005). The liberal media myth revisited: An examination of factors influencing perceptions of media bias. *Journal of Broadcasting & Electronic Media, 49*(1), 43–64. doi:10.120715506878jobem4901_4

Lichtenberg, J. (2000). In defence of objectivity revisited. In J. Curran & M. Gurevitch (Eds.), *Mass Media & Society* (3rd ed.; pp. 225–242). London: Arnold.

Manning, P. (2001). *News and news sources: A critical introduction.* Thousand Oaks, CA: SAGE Publication.

Mathiesen, K. (2014). Human rights for the digital age. *Journal of Mass Media Ethics, 29*(1), 2–18. doi:10.1080/08900523.2014.863124

Mayer-Schönberger, V. (2011). *Delete: The virtue of forgetting in the digital age.* Princeton, NJ: Princeton University Press.

McLeod, D., Kosicki, G., & McLeod, J. (2002). Resurveying the boundaries of political communication effects. In J. Bryant & D. Zillman (Eds.), *Media effects: Advances in theory and research.* Mahwah, NJ: Lawrence Erlbaum.

McNealy, J. E. (2012). The emerging conflict between newsworthiness and the right to be forgotten. *Northern Kentucky Law Review, 39*, 119–135.

Meader, A., Knight, L., Coleman, R., & Wilkins, L. (2015). Ethics in the digital age: A comparison of the effects of moving images and photographs on moral judgment. *Journal of Mass Media Ethics, 30*(4), 234–251. doi:10.1080/23736992.2015.1083403

Meyers, C. (1993). Justifying journalistic harms: Right to know vs. interest in knowing. *Journal of Mass Media Ethics, 8*(3), 133–146. doi:10.120715327728jmme0803_1

Mitrou, L., & Karyda, M. (2012). EU's data protection reform and the right to be forgotten: A legal response to a technological challenge? *5th International Conference of Information Law and Ethics.*

Morant, B. D. (2005). The endemic reality of media ethics and self-restraint. *Notre Dame Journal of Law, Ethics & Public Policy, 19*, 595–636.

Nigerian Press Council. (2016). *Code of ethics.* Retrieved from www.prescouncil.gov.ng/?page_id=281

Niven, D. (2005). An economic theory on political journalism. *Journalism & Mass Communication Quarterly, 52*(2), 247–263. doi:10.1177/107769900508200202

Oshinsky, D. (1983). *A conspiracy so immense: The world of Joe McCarthy.* New York: The Free Press.

Peachey, P. (2015, October 17). Hogan-Howe backs law against naming suspects in sex inquiries. *The Independent*, 20.

Peltz-Steele, R. J. (2008). Fifteen minutes of infamy: Privileged reporting and the problem of perpetual harm. *Ohio Northern University Law Review, 34*, 717–754.

Perloff, R. (1998). *Politics, Press, and Public in America.* Mahwah, NJ: Lawrence Erlbaum.

Phillipson, G. (2008). Trial by media: The betrayal of the First Amendment's purpose. *Law and Contemporary Problems, 71*, 15–29.

Press Council. (2016). *Code of ethics and conduct for South African print and online media.* Retrieved fromwww.presscouncil.org.za/ContentPage?code=PRESSCODE

Rachels, J. (1984). Why privacy is important. In F. Schoeman (Ed.), *Philosophical dimensions of privacy* (pp. 290–299). Cambridge, UK: Cambridge University Press. doi:10.1017/CBO9780511625138.013

Reza, S. (2005). Privacy and the criminal arrestee or suspect: In search of a right, in need of a rule. *Maryland Law Review (Baltimore, Md.), 64*, 755–874.

Rosen, J. (2012). The right to be forgotten. *Stanford Law Review, 64*, 88–92.

Rupar, V. (2006). How did you find that out? Transparency of the newsgathering process and the meaning of news. *Journalism Studies, 7*(1), 127–143. doi:10.1080/14616700500450426

Saunderson, D. (2014, April 30). Clifford case 'shows value of naming suspects'. *The Times,* 17.

Schwartz, S. (1992). *Universals in the content and structure of values: Theory and empirical tests in 20 countries.* New York, NY: Academic Press.

Shephard, A. C. (1994). Identifying juvenile suspects. *American Journalism Review,* 14.

Sherman, S. (2010, August 20). Reporters follow clear policy in naming suspects, victims in crime stories. *The Salt Lake Tribune.*

Shoemaker, P. (1991). *Gatekeeping.* Newbury Park, CA: Sage Publications.

Shoemaker, P., & Reese, S. (1996). *Mediating the message: Theories of influences on mass media content.* New York: Longman.

Sigal, L. (1973). *Reporters and officials: The organization and politics of newsmaking.* Lexington: D.C. Heath.

Sigal, L. (1986). Sources make the news. In R. Manoff & M. Schudson (Eds.), *Reading the news: A pantheon guide to popular culture* (pp. 9–37). New York: Pantheon Books.

Smith, J. A. (1988). *Printers and press freedom: The ideology of early American journalism.* New York: Oxford University Press.

Solove, D. J. (2007). *The future of reputation: Gossip, rumor, and privacy on the Internet.* New Haven, CT: Yale University Press.

Steele, B., Black, J., & Barney, R. D. (1998). *Doing ethics in journalism: A handbook with case studies* (3rd ed.). Boston, MA: Allyn & Bacon.

Strentz, H. (1989). *News reporters and news sources: Accomplices in shaping and misshaping the news* (2nd ed.). Ames, IA: Iowa State University Press.

Tuchman, G. (1973). Making news by doing work: Routinizing the unexpected. *American Journal of Sociology, 79*(1), 110–131. doi:10.1086/225510

Tuchman, G. (1978). Introduction: The symbolic annihilation of women by the mass media. In G. Tuchman, A. Kaplan Daniels, & J. Benét (Eds.), *Heart and home: Images of women in the mass media*. New York: Oxford University Press.

Vultee, F. (2010). Credibility as a strategic ritual: The Times, the interrogator, and the duty of naming. *Journal of Mass Media Ethics*, *25*(1), 3–18. doi:10.1080/08900521003621975

Warren, S., & Brandeis, L. (1890). The right to privacy. *Harvard Law Review*, *14*(5), 193–220. doi:10.2307/1321160

Westin, A. F., & Baker, M. A. (1972). *Databanks in a free society: Computers, record-keeping, and privacy*. New York: Quadrangle Books.

This research was previously published in Media Law, Ethics, and Policy in the Digital Age edited by Tendai Chari and Nhamo A. Mhiripiri; pages 207-225, copyright year 2017 by Information Science Reference (an imprint of IGI Global).

Chapter 21
Mediatized Witnessing and the Ethical Imperative of Capture

Sasha A Q Scott
Queen Mary University of London, UK

ABSTRACT

What does it mean to witness in an age saturated with media technology? This paper argues the need to rescue witnessing as a concept from its conflation with the watching and passive consumption of events. As an inherently political practice, the mediatization of witnessing is bound within questions of ethics and morality and has the potential to realign power and control in society. This article explores these issues through the witnessing of public death events: those shocking, exceptional and morally significant deaths that become 'public' through their mediation, observing that the continuous and contiguous production and consumption of media content has given rise to new performative rituals of local witnessing for (potentially) global audiences. I argue that the mediatization of witnessing serves to increase our moral awareness of seeing, rendering an ethical imperative of capture on those that witness, and thereby closing the veracity gap between events and their meaning.

INTRODUCTION

Witnessing is an enduring and essential form of communication. Present in the earliest religious and legal texts, witnessing constitutes an inherently political practice that involves questions of ethics, agency, truth and experience. The term has broad rhetorical appeal, containing a linguistic weight that encodes both the event and the actor with status and significance. In distinction from the viewer, the witness exists within events and is responsible to them; they are active, embedded and empowered. We are all potential witnesses, whom digital media has invested with the power to capture, share and narrate the minutia of our everyday lives - from the banal to the exceptional – through the processes of mediatization. This article starts from the observation that this continuous and contiguous production and consumption of media content has given rise to new performative rituals of local witnessing for (potentially) global audiences. Yet there is an increasing tendency to conflate the status of bearing witness with the mediated

DOI: 10.4018/978-1-5225-9869-5.ch021

watching and passive consumption of events. This serves to both undermine the power of witnessing as a concept and reduce witnessing to little more than technological mediation, and is something that should be resisted. This article explores these issues through the witnessing of public death events: those shocking, exceptional and morally significant deaths that become 'public' through their mediation and the subsequent media event they become (Sumiala, 2014).

The article argues that examining the mediatization of witnessing is important for our understanding of the ethical implications of ubiquitous media. I use the term mediatization as reference to the ways in which media and technology have shaped the contemporary condition of witnessing as a cultural and social form. As Zelizer (1998, p.10) explains, witnessing is implicated in transforming events by either materially altering their course or subsequently impacting our understanding. This is why the death event is particularly useful for exploring these ideas: moments of moral concern that might otherwise have been lost being captured and communicated to the world. Drawing from a range of recent examples, I argue that the audio-visual evidence recorded on a smartphone constitutes a witnessing testimony, forming a public record that bridges traditional boundaries between the public and private, the phatic and factual, and the body and machine. This article explores how these performative witnessing rituals contain the potential for contesting power and control in a global society.

I begin by discussing the relationship between media, witnessing and the death event and introducing the selection of case studies to highlight exactly what I mean by performative rituals of witnessing. There follows a review of recent approaches to witnessing and media that underscores the essential moral status the witness holds in society (Allan, 2014; Reading, 2009, 2011; Tait, 2011). I explore this 'mediatization of witnessing' through interrogating the role of the visual and the conditions of capture. This shows digital capture to be much more than a simple question of recording and representation, but rather as action, as imperative, and as a process of differentiation. Analysis draws upon Winfied Schulz's (2004) typology of the four dimensions of mediatization (extension, substitution, amalgamation and accommodation) but moves beyond thinking narrowly in terms of media 'logics'. The ensuing discussion illustrates how the witness, the image, and digital connectivity are all inalienably entwined with both the death event and the conditions of death.

This article shows witnessing to be an act of human agency, one by which we become a part of the dialectic between the powerful and the powerless. As Cook (2007) explains, because the witness is defined by circumstance (over choice) witnessing is a moral act. The purposive nature of witnessing assigns it with a selfless credibility, defined by an engagement beyond simple spectatorship because it is an ethical mode of watching. As such, I argue that we can observe an ethical imperative of capture that falls upon the mediatized witness.

WITNESSING AND THE DEATH EVENT

The ethical imperative to bear witness has been described by Allan (2014) as an 'epistemic conviction' for journalists, and indeed the role of professional media actors in witnessing global events has a rich body literature of behind it (Chouliaraki, 2015; Couldry 2004; Cottle, 2006; Dayan & Katz, 1992; Ellis, 2000;). Broadcast media have turned the ordinary citizen into witnesses of events such as the moon landings, the assassination of JFK, the fall of the Berlin wall and the terrorist attacks of 9/11 that have come to define moments in history by creating a shared communal (yet mediated) memory. These events live on through a system of collective representations that are near universal mnemonics, connecting individuals through space and time to a unitary symbolic narrative. In Ellis's terminology, modern citizens have become 'mundane witnesses' (2009, p.73), a status that is common and routine when once it signified the opposite. Mundane witnessing folds the horrors of war into the TV game show that shares its scheduling; a refugee crisis taking parity alongside a sporting triumph. The problem with this conjunction of witnessing and watching is that the grotesque and the mundane occupy the very same space, and most often it is the mundane that comes to dominate. As Tait (2011) quite rightly states, in an age of ubiquitous media it is more important than ever to distinguish between witnessing and watching. These two practices are not equal; there is nothing prosaic in bearing witness.

In order to rescue the term, we must clarify these distinctions. I focus on the phenomenon of public death events because they articulate an explicit distinction between the momentous and the mundane. Death causes rupture to the collective fabric; it brings questions of our own and our community's mortality and ultimately threatens continuity and identity. Death can also, conversely, come to clarify meaning and give purpose to the lived world as death causes a distillation of the very essence of what we hold worth living for. In this sense, death becomes the continuum for our normative values and beliefs. For a death to become transformed from an individual loss into a public one depends on certain sociopolitical circumstances and the cultural work of reporting, speeches, commentary, ritual, marches, meetings and more. Here, a 'public' is an audience, (as both spectators and witnesses), but it is also a community, a socialised body, and as such carries with it the inference of some kind of shared civic interest (Habermas, 1991). Thus, if witnessing concerns standards of morality and that which is deemed socially significant, then the public death event is a rich prism through which to explore them.

Our point of departure is not with the distant TV audiences of Frosh and Pinchevski's media witnessing (2009), but the individuals who are physically present at the scene, cameraphone in hand. Most often, our banal rituals of capture and gaze will be elevated to that of witnessing by chance. In these moments, local injustices and struggles can become elevated onto the global stage by performative rituals of local witnessing. I use the 'performative' here in the sense that these acts are doing something to the event, and in doing so change their meaning (i.e. performing some kind of social action). Additionally, these are ritual acts in the sense that they are strategies of differentiation that distinguish and privilege certain objects and actions from others (Bell, 1992, p.74). These performative rituals are not reducible to the sensory experience of events because witnessing, as Peters tells us, is also a discursive act that recalls that experience for the absent audience: 'witnessing thus has two faces: the passive one of seeing and the active one of saying' (2001, p. 709). It is here that the witness can take on an extraordinary power.

It is this dyadic relationship that I now explore through comparative analysis of two collections of events. First, I turn to death events that took place during popular uprisings in Iran, Tunisia and Egypt from 2009, and the incredible stories of Neda Soltan, Mohammed Bouazizi, and Khaled Said. The identities of the individuals who captured these deaths has largely been lost or forgotten and instead it is the digital testimony that remains. These three examples show how the visual testimony of a local injustice can at once challenge entrenched and violent political structures in the local frame whilst also coming to represent a pollution of shared human values in the global frame. The second series of events involve the deaths of African Americans by police officers or whilst in police custody in the United States. The digital recordings of the deaths of Eric Garner, Walter Scott and Freddie Gray challenge a different form of authority and control: a recurrent and institutionalised racism that casts the black life as both threatening and disposable (Yancy & Butler, 2015). In these more recent events the identities of the camera-welding activists is known and their experiences a matter of public record. The original footage is supplemented with interviews and media coverage that opens up a dynamic new discursive space for testimony to reside and consequently enriches our understanding of its role. Before we can fully engage with these issues it is necessary to locate events within wider conversations about the intersection of witnessing and mediatization.

MEDIATION AND MEDIATIZATION: WITNESSING AND MOBILE TECHNOLOGY

Due largely to its mix of relative stability and high plasticity as a form of cultural communication our conceptual understanding of witnessing has endured almost unaltered from the earliest religious texts in which it appears (Thomas, 2009, p.91). The eighth commandment states 'thou shalt not bear false witness against thy neighbour', and whilst precise interpretations compete throughout the books of Deuteronomy and Leviticus, is clear across them all that witnessing is not a symbolic practice, but rather an ethical one of social necessity. Just as Proverbs 14(25) tells us 'a true witness delivereth souls', so the Qur'an states 'every soul will come, and with it a driver and a witness' (Qaf, 50(21)), embedding witnessing in existential concerns. In a natural continuation, the moralism of witnessing is inextricably linked to conceptions of martyrdom, Peters provocatively suggesting 'within every witness, perhaps, stands a martyr' (2001, p.713). The ultimate price the witness pays for their moral conviction is with their life. In Greek, the etymology is the same: Martus means witness. The point here is that both witness and martyr are imbued with a moral truth claim, cast as the voice of the afflicted and prepared to make the ultimate sacrifice to protect the credibility and veracity of their testimony. In doing so they create a boundary between two opposing belief systems and imbue their side of that division with both moral and ethical capital. Cook explains that martyrdom is not a singular act; it involves first the martyr (the witness transformed through death), an audience, and crucially the communicative agent, allowing the transmission of the narrative to that audience (2007, p.3). Additionally, if we understand law to be a society's demarcation of the ethical boundaries of behaviour, it is entirely logical that the witness should occupy a privileged place in almost every legal system known.

As a theoretical construct witnessing endures precisely because it plays this moral role in society. Boltanski (1999) emphasises this point when he argues that once witnessing becomes separated from any sense of morality or responsibility for those involved it ceases to be witnessing and is instead reduced to mere spectatorship. Thus, we do not need to entirely reconceptualise witnessing in response to processes of mediatization, but it is important to ask how, as a cultural form, it has adapted to the reconfigured symbolic environment. The impetus being on changing contexts, rather than alterations in stable forms. Media alter patterns, but pre-existing conditions shape those alterations (Jansson, 2013, p.282), and it is for this reason that mediatization becomes such a useful concept. Following Krotz (2007), mediatization is taken to be a meta-process similar to globalization, individualization and commercialization, and at its most simple is a theoretical construct with which to understand particular societal changes due to the role of media and technology. This is the transmedia landscape, wherein moments of significance are enabled and enacted not simply 'via' or 'because' of any single medium, but rather through, across and even beyond media (Hepp, 2013). This is media as context, content and technology, and reducible to none alone. Whereas mediation refers (narrowly) to information passing through or being dependent on an intermediary agent, mediatization concerns social and cultural factors that become entangled with and inseparable from technological processes of mediation.

Central to questioning the mediatization of witnessing is the digital capture of the event in both context and condition. Our postmodern subjectivity is bound to the visual, with the relentless production and consumption of images reconfiguring private/public boundaries (Ibrahim, 2012). Thus, an account of the mediatized witness concerns the networked individual who instinctively and ritualistically raises their recording device when faced with a shocking, traumatic and significant event for one purpose only: to capture (and by inference disseminate) their testimony. Here the purposive act is only complete once the corresponding file is uploaded, signifying a self-reflexivity that links the immediate spatial present to the wider discursive frame. This constitutes a remarkable contributory factor in the 'visual economy' wherein visceral images are observed to create spectacular events as much as they record them (Anden-Papadopoulis, 2013; Ibrahim, 2010; Poole, 1997) The conception of a visual economy (rather than culture) is important in expressing the idea that the visual involves dynamics of power and inequality just as much as it concerns representation and narrative.

Kato et al. (2005) discuss how the conventional camera was itself the signifier of an 'event' worthy of capture, its deployment symbolically demarcating a space or time as distinct from the mundane. In contrast, the embedded multimodality of the cameraphone constantly bridges between the material present and immaterial 'other'. The politics of watching is not contained within the device: it is inseparable from the networked potential that ubiquitous connectivity brings. The web to which our devices connect cannot be understood simply as technology we 'go to'; rather it is a sociotechnical system made up of physical objects, human actors, algorithmic protocol, regulations, norms and social structures (Benski & Fisher, 2014, p.4). As Shanks and Svabo (2013) tell us, the camera phone has become a something of a sensory prosthetic, a virtual sense organ if you will. We live in a world where to see is to believe, and experience must be recorded, shared and vitally viewed by others if it is to be felt as authentic. At any public event, we are now surrounded by camera phones held aloft for the recording, sharing, narration and authentication of experience: this banal imaging being integrated into the wider visual economy (Ibrahim, 2015). These rituals have become normalized as cultural processes of embodied meaning making. They are also inherently performative, with actors employing their mobile devices to situate themselves - spatially and temporally - in a symbolic demarcation of identity (Koster, 2003).

Andén-Papadopoulis presents the notion of the 'citizen camera-witness' in reference to the cameraphone-wielding activist that tells the story of protest and oppression to the world via their mobile device. She observes:

Those who are not only on-the-scene of breaking news events, but also translate this actuality in affective yet strongly exhibitive camera-phone imagery, perhaps carry the most significant form of capital to be considered a witness in the current global visual economy. (Andén-Papadopoulis, 2013, p.7)

Andén-Papadopoulis describes how the simple act of recording can be elevated into a distinct cultural form. This capturing of moments of moral significance means we cannot settle for an account of photography as purely representational. Kember and Zylinska make the argument for understanding the ontology of the photograph as predominantly that of becoming, of being different to what once was (2012, p.71-77). Photography is so very important because of its incredible proximity to life itself: the speed, quality, virility, and accessibility of the tools of capture and sharing increase the power of the liminal in opposing and redefining existing power structures. The photograph is no longer documenting times past but synchronously constituting the present and potential futures.

DIGITAL MARTYRS

In Tehran on June 20th 2009 the 26-year-old music student Neda Soltan (1983-2009) was walking with her father as part of a peaceful protest contesting the recent election results when she was shot through the heart. The moments after the shot, as her life passed from her, were captured on a mobile phone in a 47 second video (NEDAyeeIRAN, 2009). The amateur camera work and crude audio encode the imagery with an authenticity that is unavoidable, communicating an embodied, affective experience from 'within' the event more faithfully than any professionally shot footage ever could. We see the camera turn from recording the protests toward Neda as the shot is heard. In that moment, a domestic act became a moral practice, normatively linked to pain and death, right and wrong, justice and freedom. From a story being told, suddenly an event was witnessed; a private sensory experience transformed instantly into a mediated public testimony. In this way, conventional binaries between the self and other, body and machine, private and public, local and global, and citizen and journalist, were made obsolete. The original video (two others appeared later) has been viewed millions of times, and immediately became a viral sensation, again an example of the incredible extension of the natural limits of human communication. Neda was declared the first 'Digital Martyr' (Rajabi, 2012), and has been described as the most widely witnessed death in human history (Mahr, 2009). The power of Neda's story as an exemplar for mediatized witnessing comes from the moral clarity of events: she was actively facing her persecutors, walking the streets in a declarative display of her beliefs. The bystander would not have been imbued with such moral authority. But how should we define this amalgamation of elements when Neda the Martyr is the central witness (to the brutality of the regime), the camera-wielding bystanders were witness (to Neda's death), the video-as-object is witness (as testimony), and we as global audience are also witness to events? In highlighting the three applications of witnessing as '(1) the agent who bears witness, (2) the utterance or text itself, and (3) the audience who witnesses, Peters (2001, p.709) displays the true complexity of witnessing as a noun.

So the mediatization of witnessing concerns much more than an event or individual, and is reducible to neither. Anna Reading describes this 'mobile witnessing' as a 'fluid and travelling involvement in data capture, data sharing and receipt, through global networks mobilized through multiple mobilities' (2009, p61). The implication being that by accommodating and extending the free movement of data, mediatization opens new opportunities to expose the wrongs that witnessing infers. Take the case of Mohammed Bouazizi (1984-2011), the young Tunisian man humiliated by a local official concerning an apparent violation of a trivial trading law, who went to protest his innocence. His dissent was ignored, and through frustration, anger and shame performed self-immolation. Bouazizi's death was filmed on camera phone and distributed online, seen by many as a catalyst for the uprising, and becoming entrenched in the wider narrative of the Tunisian revolution. Bouazizi's was also not the only self- immolation of this kind in Tunisia. Abdeelem Trimech commited suicide in this way in Monastir in 2010 for similar reasons, but without the extension afforded by media Trimech's death was not captured and his narrative was tragically lost. Similarly, in Egypt 28-year-old Khaled Said (1982-2010) was taken from an internet café by two police officers and publically beaten to death. Whilst his death was publically witnessed it was not digitally captured at the time. It was not until his body was surreptitiously photographed in the morgue that processes of mediatization took hold. His family posted the images online, quickly substituting any legal process. Said's story became amalgamated into the wider narrative of revolution, martyrdom and social life in Egypt. The digital image once again extended the natural limit of communication - completely replacing the futile previous attempts to highlight his cause through traditional channels - and accommodated in wider media and cultural practices. Said's death was witnessed in the street, but in the first instance a cameraphone and later social media platforms illustrate the mediatization of events, transforming their socio-political significance. Said's story highlights how mediatized witnessing is an inherently political act, performing as counter-gaze against powerful elites and hierarchies. The speed and reach of exposure giving new voice to the witness, amplifying their testimony beyond imagination.

HOLDING POWER TO ACCOUNT

When Ramsey Orta realised the altercation between his friend, Eric Garner, and several New York police officers was becoming more than ordinary it was natural, instinctive and virtually instant to switch between being a viewer and a witness: "I was already on my phone," Orta explained, "I always seen them cops doing something to somebody else, so I figured I'd just record it." (quoted in Sanburn, 2014). The video of Garner's death that Orta captured reverberated through the mediascape and continues to have political impact today. It dominated world news bulletins, trended on Twitter and Facebook, and has been viewed millions of times via various YouTube iterations. Garner's repeated cry of 'I can't breath' has become an enduring symbol and slogan of the wider Black Lives Matter political rights movement. We see Orta-the-witness perform a purposive act with the explicit intention of creating or communicating testimony of events recognised to be of moral or ethical significance. Technology did not create the witness here, but rather collapsed traditional distinctions of time and space associated with witnessing, testimony and the legal-moral process. As Orta explains "It just gives me more power to not be afraid to pull out my camera anytime" (ibid, 2014). This illustrates Peters' striking observation that the witness can be understood as the paradigmatic case of the medium: the means or agent for communicating information and experience to those not party to the original (2001 p.709). And as we know, mediation is anything but neutral: 'mediation involves the movement of meaning' (emphasis added, Silverstone, 1999, p.13) across texts, discourses, or events.

In April 2015 Feidin Santana was returning home in North Charleston, South Carolina, when he saw a struggle between a local man and a police officer. Instinctively, he started filming on his mobile phone. The resulting video captured the police officer Michael Slager shoot dead Walter Scott as he ran away. Despite confronting the officers on the scene at the time, Santana did not share the video with friends or the authorities through fear: 'I felt that my life, with this information, might be in danger' he later said (Helsel, 2015). As time passed it became clear the police were falsifying their record of events. According to police reports and city officials, officer Slager claimed he had feared for his life and that Scott had taken his Taser gun. Watching events unfold, Santana became increasingly aware of the true importance of his video; he reports feeling an obligation and a 'duty to act' 'I saw the cop of top of Mr Scott...I was hearing the Taser, I was just trying to record...so, he...he can be aware that there is some person you know, witnessing...and recording' (quoted in Eversley, 2015). This is the ethical imperative laid bare. Santana was conscious he had not simply seen, but witnessed, and as Ibrahim argues, to witness 'is to partake' (2010, p.126). So, Santana reached out, via Facebook. He sent an anonymous screenshot to the group Black Lives Matter, and from there the video made its way to Walter Scott's family and then into the public domain.

Santana witnessed these events with his own eyes. Circumstance thrust an ordinary man into an extraordinary situation: with or without a cameraphone, he was the only witness to a moral wrongdoing. The dynamics of mediatization fundamentally impacted events: media extended the natural limits of communication in two striking ways. First, Santana was no longer bound by the fallibility of his own memory, recall, standing or trustworthiness. Without the video as testimony the legal case would have been reduced to the word of a young Hispanic man from an economically deprived area against that of an officer of the law. Second, when Santana was vulnerable and isolated he was able to connect via digital networks and reach directly to those who could help, and not be exposed to the dangers of what was by then a visibly corrupted legal system; the network directly undermining the hierarchy. Furthermore, media processes came to substitute incumbent social processes. As soon as the video was public the legal case was essentially over and any police investigation ultimately irrelevant. This is closely connected to the amalgamation of established social processes with those of media as the trial - in the legal sense of the term - was inseparable from the media event surrounding it. The legal system was simply there to confirm what was incontrovertible in the public mind (at the time of writing Slager remains in prison charged with murder). Finally, this was all seamlessly accommodated across all sectors of society. To illustrate how completely this took place it is perhaps most effective to imagine its opposite, as Scott's attorney asked: 'What if there was no video? What if there was no witness?' (Helsel, 2015). In his actions, Santana was inserted directly into events in what Halverson et al. (2013) term 'vertical integration' whereby an individual's personal narrative is woven into the wider pre-existing narrative framework, which before would have been spatially, temporally and conceptually out of reach.

THE ETHICAL IMPERATIVE OF CAPTURE

Alan Badiou in, *Ethics, An Essay on the Understanding of Evil* (2001), states:

[Ethics] should be referred back to particular situations, it should become the enduring maxim of singular processes, it should concern the destiny of truths, in the plural...There is no ethics in general. There are only - eventually - ethics of processes by which we treat the possibilities of a situation.

Whilst the bystander is transformed into the witness by chance, that transformation has moral and political force: the context of a given situation - i.e. the occurrence of wrongdoing - defines witnessing as an 'ethical' form. So it would seem that in the age of digital technologies and the visual economy, the ethics of situations that Badiou describes assigns the contemporary witness with an ethical imperative to capture. In his witnessing of murder, Feidin Santana's self-awareness was striking. First of the morality of his role when he says he started recording 'so he [Scott] could feel that there was someone there', and secondly of the power of his evidence. And as the quote shows, the witness is not reducible to the technology: in his own words Santana tells he was witnessing and recording. Santana was speaking on his phone as he saw events unfold and his description shows a natural and instinctive transition into witnessing. Conscious or otherwise, Santana's words and actions explicitly reflect an ethical imperative that witnessing so often involves.

The ethical imperative itself is a central concept that can be found right back to the parable of the Good Samaritan, unable to pass by suffering that he has seen with his own eyes. One cannot 'un-see' as it were, and once seen a moral responsibility to our fellow man ensues. This is a central tenet of all faiths and indeed some legal systems hold up the ethical imperative (French law in particular carries a penalty for failing to come to someone's assistance). The ethical imperative of capture is a natural extension of this principle. It might not be consciously acknowledged by those involved, but the evidence shows it to be an inescapable and defining aspect of contemporary witnessing. Whilst Sue Tait (2011) talks of the moral responsibility a witness bears, this is in the context of the journalist that has consciously taken the role of witness as a profession. In contrast, the ethical imperative I define here draws its cultural weight from the power of chance and circumstance. It is exactly because the witness is outside any formal professional or political role that they carry their distinct claim to truth.

The ethical imperative concerns the potential of technology as an act of connectivity: to immediate political events, to a moral/legal audience, and even to more abstracted ideas of a 'common humanity'. In Luc Boltanski's (1999) discussion of media and the moralities of watching through technology, he explains how moral responsibility can come from contractual, natural (familial), or circumstantial commitments. Any obligation to involve oneself directly in events is one of 'nearness' or 'distance'. Mediation, he argues, serves to increasingly distance the observer from direct responsibility. My argument here confirms the obligation of the witness through their 'nearness' (proximity is defined a priori in this context), but it questions mediation as always 'distancing' the ethical. Here, the act of digital capture serves to bridge between the witness and the victim (or event), increasing the ethical/moral binding. The power of distancing is no longer about morality and instead concerns protection: the camera phone substitutes physical bodily insertion into dangerous scenes. The performative ritual of capture alters the balance and location of power. It protects the witness with distance through instant sharing and uploading, substituting sole responsibility for testimony and negating the rarefied witness status as the sole conduit of truth. The witness is no longer the primary threat to the wrongdoer: digital testimony takes on this role.

The proliferation of digitally networked mobile technology has awoken an awareness of the moral implications of seeing. The mediatization of witnessing reflects a constant potential for the wired body to become a central actor in global narratives, a latent energy waiting to be triggered. I have discussed a series of events that are particularly striking and have a shared set of characteristics, but they are not stand-alone. The murder of Lee Rigby in London in 2013 shows the same markers; the deaths Philandro Castile, Sandra Bland, Alton Sterling and Freddie Gray all carry elements of the subversive capture of an unjust death that questions power. Although reflecting a different moral framework, even the deaths of Muammar Gadaffi and Saddam Hussein can be understood as incidents of mediatized witnessing.

The instinctive and ritualistic reach for the cameraphone in moments of rupture reflects an awareness of the role of testimony to the very epistemic meaning of events. We are all therefore endowed with a moral imperative. Perhaps we can update Peters' suggestion that in every witness stands a martyr, that now in every voyeur stands a potential witness. This can only be a good thing for the wider social whole. It represents not only an empathetic awareness of the self in relation to the socialised body, but it is also another small step in empowering the disenfranchised in society. It is empowering the powerless, even just by implication. We see this most explicitly in the US context, where real change is happening first because of what has been witnessed, but increasingly because of what may be witnessed in the future. Altering the institutionalised racism of an organisation like the US police force is a generational process; curtailing deviant behaviour because of fear it will be witnessed on cameraphone and broadcast across the globe is immediate.

DIGITAL TESTIMONY AND THE VERACITY GAP

In every act of witnessing lays an audience that needs convincing of the truth of testimony, be it in a courtroom or global public opinion (Cook, 2007, p.15). The etymology of testimony is telling: The Latin *superstes* refers to those who experience events and live to tell others of it, whereas *terstis* refers to those who position, themselves as a third between two others (Pakman, 2004, p.268). So, it would seem the witness is destined to provide testimony to a public, a process that involves 'distancing and reflecting on the original event, which is...by definition, contested in the process of testimony' (ibid p.289). In order to do so, witness experience must bridge what Peters terms 'the veracity gap': the discrepancy between those with first-hand knowledge and those without. Mediatization serves to close that gap, not just through the material production of verifiable testimony but by extending the affective power of that testimony and the passages it takes through our social spaces. Our mobile technologies are literally embedded with our bodies, held tight in our pockets. Events are brought close through haptic motors or auditory signals we have tailored to our bodily response mechanisms. Our social media timelines, email alerts and newsfeeds are personalised through self and algorithmic selection, conditioning an increased trust in what we see and read. As a result, the veracity gap closes.

Forces of Mediatization have resulted in performative rituals of witnessing beyond the immediate event. Following Neda's death we saw thousands of YouTube commemorative videos proclaiming her martyrdom with the host pages becoming virtual reliquaries for mourners. As a communion of grief they are cathartic, ritualistic and performative. In a similar process, Twitter hashtags such a #BlackLivesMatter and #IAmMichaelBrown become performative mantras that signify both acts of witnessing and an endorsement of testimony that frame and locate events. They are declarative acts of identity, solidarity and inclusion. They not only give a spatial focus to congregation, but also incubate a form of allegiance and integration between participants removed from events across space and time. In much the same way as pilgrims write comments in visiting books, slip notes in the Western Wall, or leave a burning candle in places of worship, the comments sections below a YouTube video or on a Facebook memorial page allow for the distant witness to perform a redemptive ritual that helps reaffirm community and inclusion. The sharing of links and posting of images circumvents the passivity of a mass media audience that can now actively participate in the redistribution and reformation of original witness testimony, creating social imaginaries and a collective memory. The social media practice of posting a 'selfie' photograph accompanied by a declarative mantra of solidarity such as 'I am Khaled Said' or 'I am Michael Brown' has now become such a formalised response pattern to be easily recognised as a postmodern ritual. These highly symbolic acts are not completely new, but are instead contemporary manifestations of enduring rituals that are rife in all the major religions. The taking of bread and wine in Catholic communion is the symbolic re-enactment of the witnessing recorded in the First Epistle of Corinthians; to recite the Haggadah is to bear witness to the Jewish liberation from slavery; the Shia practices of Muharram serve as witness to the martyrdom of Imam Hussein ibn Ali: all symbolic acts of witnessing which correlate with the practices described herein. Their ritualisation is the fundamental human practice of making these experiences common and shared.

It is easy to read the Mediatization of witnessing as extending the limit of human communication, to use Shulz's terminology. In the closed political spaces of Tehran, Cairo, Charleston and Ferguson, media practices have substituted traditional activities and yet they have not remained exclusively online. The response to Neda's murder culminated in an international 'Neda day'. Thousands of people gathered in protests across the globe wearing Neda masks designed by an Iranian exile in Paris and downloadable as a .JPG from http//.wearealloneneda.wordpress, (replete with an instruction card and the strict condition that no other images or banners be used). Standing as unified symbolic witnesses to Neda's death, the mask actions made for striking imagery that resonated back once again to the digital space. Similarly, the images of Khaled Said and Mohammed Bouazizi were everywhere in Tahrir Square and the streets of Tunisia respectively. In the United States the names of Michael Brown, Eric Garner and Walter Scott are repeated still: when marchers chant 'Black Lives Matter' they are bearing witness, weighting and encoding events as morally and ethically wrong. The placards they carry show images captured on camera phones and bear hashtags - an addressivity marker that serves a mechanical function in search, retrieval and the inclusion in digital conversations - on their hand painted signs: the online and offline feeding each other in perpetuity.

CONCLUSION

A topic as complex as witnessing has interest for a range of academic disciplines. In focusing on the witnessing of death events I have been purposively selective; the examples cited all share a (relatively) unambiguous moral interpretation that opens a space to explore the relationship between the witness, the spectator, and processes of mediatisation. As such the issues raised have resonance with notions of citizen journalism, law, visual culture, audience studies and wider social and cultural theory (particularly ritual). Mediatized witnessing has many forms, linked through material, affective and networked connections and may be confined to all yet none at once. The notion of mediatized witnessing as I present it here captures the convergence of a traumatic event with an agential witness in the first instance, and the event with a witnessing 'audience' (perhaps we can go as far as calling them a jury?) via a witnessing 'text' in the secondary instance. These are liminal moments of rupture and transgression that represent opportunity for redefining assumed or imposed hierarchies. The more formalised or entrenched an act of witnessing becomes (entering into some kind of judicial process either officially or more usually in the court of public opinion) the more recognisable the ritual process around it takes shape and prescribed categories, conventions and structures are increasingly able to be overturned, negated and reinvented.

Witnessing is at once the sensory experience of an event and the communication of that experience to those removed from it. Whilst mobile technology has increased spectatorship, voyeurism and gaze, it also opens new opportunities for ethical interventions and socialised responses. We can think of these 'witnessed' moments as representing both transgression and opportunity. They are moments that Turner (1969) would recognise as anti-structure, when power (in whatever form) is undermined by the witness. Whilst it is perfectly possible to capture moments of interest free from ethical involvement, the embedded instantaneity of our digital devices nonetheless empowers those who find themselves in these moments of significance to capture, exploit and extend the liminal opportunities opened through ruptures of time and space. The mediatization of witnessing therefore defines an active process, with the witness imbued with moral capital and a responsibility to events. Chance and circumstance render an ethical imperative of capture on those that find themselves in these moments of significance. This paper has illustrated how the long-term evolution of media's role in contemporary society has impacted on witnessing as a cultural form, giving rise to new performative rituals of local witnessing. In physics, latent energy is understood as the potential capacity to affect change; mediatization both increases that potential energy and can serve as the initiate in its release. Witnessing holds a liminal power to reassign and redefine meaning and as such the capacity for the witness to hold entrenched stakeholders to account appears to have been increased. Perhaps most significantly, the mediatization of witnessing serves to close the veracity gap between events and their ultimate meaning.

ACKNOWLEDGMENT

This work is supported by the EPSRC through the Media and Arts Technology CDT [EP/G03723X/1].

REFERENCES

Allan, S. (2014). Witnessing in crisis: Photo-reportage of terror attacks in Boston and London. *Media, War and Conflict.*, *7*(2), 133–151. doi:10.1177/1750635214531110

Andén-Papadopoulos, K. (2013). Citizen Camera-Witnessing: Embodied political dissent in the age of 'mediated mass self-communication'. *New Media & Society*, *16*(5), 1–17.

Badiou, A. (2002). *Ethics: An essay on the understanding of evil.* London: Verso Books.

Bell, C. (1992). *Ritual Theory, Ritual Practice.* Oxford, UK: Oxford University Press.

Benski, T., & Fisher, E. (2014). Introduction: Investigating Emotions and the Internet. In T. Benski & E. Fisher (Eds.), *Internet and Emotions* (pp. 1–14). London, New York: Routledge.

Boltanski, L. (1999). *Distant suffering: Morality, media and politics.* Cambridge, UK: Cambridge University Press. doi:10.1017/CBO9780511489402

Chouliaraki, L. (2015). Digital witnessing in conflict zones: The politics of remediation. *Information Communication and Society*, *18*(11), 1362–1377. doi:10.1080/1369118X.2015.1070890

Cook, D. (2007). Martyrdom. In *Islam.* Cambridge, UK: Cambridge University Press.

Cottle, S. (2006). Mediatized Rituals: Beyond Manufacturing Consent. *Media Culture & Society*, *28*(3), 411–432. doi:10.1177/0163443706062910

Couldry, N. (2004). *Media Rituals: A Critical Approach.* London, New York: Routledge.

Dayan, D., & Katz, E. (1992). *Media Events: The Live Broadcasting of History.* Cambridge, MA: Harvard University Press.

Ellis, J. (2009). Mundane witness. In P. Frosh & A. Pinchevski (Eds.), *Media Witnessing: Testimony in the Age of Mass Communication* (pp. 73–88). Hampshire: Palgrave Macmillan UK. doi:10.1057/9780230235762_4

Eversley, M. (2015). Man who shot S.C. cell phone video speaks out. *USA Today*. Retrieved from: http://www.usatoday.com/story/news/2015/04/08/walter-scott-feidin-santana-cell-phone-video/25497593/

Frosh, P., & Pinchevski, A. (Eds.). (2009). *Media Witnessing: Testimony in the Age of Mass Communication.* Hampshire: Palgrave Macmillan UK. doi:10.1057/9780230235762

Habermas, J. (1991). *The Structural Transformation of the Public Sphere: An inquiry into a category of bourgeois society.* Cambridge, MA: MIT press.

Halverson, J. R., Ruston, S. W., & Trethewey, A. (2013). Mediated Martyrs of the Arab Spring: New Media, Civil Religion, and Narrative in Tunisia and Egypt. *Journal of Communication*, *63*(2), 312–332. doi:10.1111/jcom.12017

Helsel, P. (2015). Walter Scott Death: Bystander Who Recorded Cop Shooting Speaks Out. *NBC News*. Retrieved from http://www.nbcnews.com/storyline/walter-scott-shooting/man-who-recorded-walter-scott-being-shot-speaks-out-n338126

Hepp, A. (2013). *Cultures of Mediatization*. Cambridge, UK: Polity Press.

Ibrahim, Y. (2010). Distant Suffering and Postmodern Subjectivity: The Communal Politics of Pity. *Nebula*, 7(1-2), 122-135.

Ibrahim, Y. (2012). The Politics Of Watching: Visuality and the New Media Economy. *International Journal of E-Politics*, *3*(2), 1–11. doi:10.4018/jep.2012010101

Ibrahim, Y. (2015). Instagramming life: Banal imaging and the poetics of the everyday. *Journal of Media Practice*, *16*(1), 42–54. doi:10.1080/14682753.2015.1015800

Jansson, A. (2013). Mediatization and Social Space: Reconstructing Mediatization for the Transmedia Age. *Communication Theory*, *23*(3), 279–296. doi:10.1111/comt.12015

Kato, F., Okabe, D., Ito, M., & Uemoto, R. (2005). Uses and Possibilities of the Keitai Camera. In *Personal, Portable and Pedestrian. Mobile Phones in Japanese Life* (pp. 300–310). Cambridge, MA: MIT Press.

Kember, S., & Zylinska, J. (2012). *Life After New Media: Mediation as a vital process*. Cambridge, MA: MIT Press.

Koster, J. (2003). Ritual performance and the politics of identity: On the functions and uses of ritual. *Journal of Historical Pragmatics*, *4*(2), 211–248. doi:10.1075/jhp.4.2.05kos

Krotz, F. (2007). The meta-process of mediatization as a conceptual frame. *Global Media and Communication*, *3*(3), 256–260. doi:10.1177/17427665070030030103

Mahr, K. (2009). 'Neda Agha-Soltan'. *Time Magazine* (online). Retrieved from http://content.time.com/time/specials/packages/article/0,28804,1945379_1944701_1944705,00.html. 10.6.14

NEDAyeeIRAN. (2009, June 23). *Neda Iran* [video file]. Retrieved from https://www.youtube.com/watch?v=d90bwM4No_M

Pakman, M. (2004). The epistemology of witnessing: Memory, testimony, and ethics in family therapy. *Family Process*, *43*(2), 265–271. doi:10.1111/j.1545-5300.2004.04302010.x PMID:15603508

Peters, J. (2001). Witnessing. *Media Culture & Society*, *23*(6), 707–723. doi:10.1177/016344301023006002

Poole, D. (1997). *Vision, Race and Modernity: A Visual Economy of the Andean Image World*. Princeton, NJ: Princeton University Press.

Rajabi, S., & Hejazi, A. (2012). Neda: Manifestations of a Digital Martyr. In *Finding Religion in the Media: Work in Progress on the 'third spaces of digital religion* (pp. 51–62). Colorado: The Centre for Media, Religion and Culture, University of Colorado.

Reading, A. (2009). Mobile Witnessing: Ethics and the Camera Phone in the War on Terror. *Globalizations*, *6*(1), 61–76. doi:10.1080/14747730802692435

Reading, A. (2011). Memory and digital media: Six dynamics of the globital memory field. In M. Nieger, O. Meyers, & E. Zandberg (Eds.), *On Media Memory* (pp. 241–252). London: Palgrave Macmillan UK. doi:10.1057/9780230307070_18

Sanburn, J. (2014). The Witness: One year after filming Eric Garner's fatal confrontation with police, Ramsey Orta's life has been upended. *Time Magazine*. Retrieved from http://time.com/ramsey-orta-eric-garner-video/

Schulz, W. (2004). Reconstructing mediatization as an analytical concept. *European Journal of Communication, 19*(1), 87–101. doi:10.1177/0267323104040696

Shanks, M., & Svabo, C. (2013) Mobile Media Photography: New Modes of Engagement. In J. Larson & M. Sandbye (Eds.), Digital Snaps: The New Face of Photography (pp. 227-246). London: I.B. Tauris & Co Ltd.

Silverstone, R. (1999). *Why Study Media?* London: Sage.

Sumiala, J. (2014). Mediatization of Public Death. In K. Lundby (Ed.), *Mediatization of Communication* (Vol. 21, pp. 681–701). Berlin, Boston: Walter de Gruyter GmbH & Co KG.

Tait, S. (2011). Bearing witness, journalism and moral responsibility. *Media Culture & Society, 33*(8), 1220–1235. doi:10.1177/0163443711422460

Thomas, G. (2009). Witness as a cultural form of communication: Historical roots, structural dynamics and current appearances. In P. Frosh & A. Pinchevski (Eds.), *Media Witnessing: Testimony in the Age of Mass Communication* (pp. 88–111). Houndmills: Palgrave Macmillan. doi:10.1057/9780230235762_5

Turner, V. (1969). *The Ritual Process: Structure and Anti-Structure*. Cornell Ithaca, New York: University Press.

Yancy, G., & Butler, J. (2015) What's Wrong With 'All Lives Matter'? *New York Times Opinion Pages*. Retrieved from http://opinionator.blogs.nytimes.com/2015/01/12/whats-wrong-with-all-lives-matter/?_r=0

Zelizer, B. (1998). *Remembering to Forget: Holocaust Memory Through the Camera's Eye*. Chicago: University of Chicago Press.

This research was previously published in International Journal of E-Politics (IJEP), 8(1); edited by Sofia Idris; pages 1-13, copyright year 2017 by IGI Publishing (an imprint of IGI Global).

Chapter 22
Online Free Expression and Its Gatekeepers

Joanna Kulesza
University of Lodz, Poland

ABSTRACT

This chapter covers the pressing issues of online free expression at the time of global telecommunication services and social media. What once was the domain of the state has become the prerogative of private global companies – it is their terms of service and sense of social responsibility that have replaced local perceptions of morality and set limits to individual personal rights. Whether protecting privacy or defending against defamation, it is the Internet Service Provider who can offer tools far more effective and prompt than any national court and law enforcement agency. And even though the right to free expression is firmly rotted in the global standard of article 19 UDHR, nowhere than online are the differences in its interpretation, originated by history, morality and religion, more palpable. The paper aims to discuss each of the three composite rights of free expression (the right to hold, impart and receive information and ideas) and identify the actual limitations originated by national laws. The author emphasizes states' positive obligation to take active measures aimed at protecting free expression, ensuring that all human rights are "protected, respected and remedied". This obligation makes the interrelationship between national lawmakers and international telecommunication service providers complex as the latter serve as the actual gate keepers of free expression in the information society. The paper covers a discussion on how different countries deal with this challenge through various approaches to ISP liability, including the notice-and-take down procedure as well as content filtering (preventive censorship). The author goes on to criticize those mechanisms as enabling ISPs too much freedom in deciding upon the shape and scope of individuals' right to impart and receive information.

INTRODUCTION

The paper discusses the contemporary perspective of the right to free expression when exercised online with particular regard to the rights and obligations of Internet Service Providers (ISPs). The author briefly recapitulates the origin, definition and interpretation of the three composite rights enshrined in article 19 UDHR: the right to hold, impart and receive information and ideas. She puts emphasis on their

DOI: 10.4018/978-1-5225-9869-5.ch022

limitations legitimately enforced by states. States' duty to protect free expression is than identified as their negative obligation to refrain from infringement as well as a positive one, to guarantee that human rights are "protected, respected and remedied" within national legal systems. Than the role of Internet Service Providers is introduced as the gate keepers of free expression in the information society. Different schemes for national ISP liability mechanisms are presented: the notice-and-take down procedure as well as Internet content filtering (preventive censorship). Kulesza goes on to criticize both mechanisms as enabling ISPs too much freedom in deciding upon the shape and scope of individuals' right to impart and receive information.

FREEDOM OF EXPRESSION: DEFINITION, MEANING, AND ENFORCEMENT

Freedom of expression is deeply rooted in the human rights system – it's one of the fundamental freedoms enshrined in the Universal Declaration of Human Rights (UDHR), adopted as a statement of international consensus on the need to protect certain rights and liberties of individuals against unjustified infringement by state authorities and third parties (United Nations 1948 and 2011, Schauer 1982 and 2004). The wording of its Article 19, phrasing the right to free expression, has been repeated in numerous international treaties and served as a standard of free speech for national courts and international tribunals. Article 19 of the UDHR grants every human the right "freedom of opinion and expression". The very language of the article specifies the three inclusive freedoms that come with the freedom of expression. The "right to freedom of opinion and expression" includes "freedom to hold opinions", as well as the liberty to receive information and (last but not least) to impart it, "regardless of frontiers" (United Nations 1948). Confines for exercising these complementary rights are defined in Article 29 para. 2, which subjects their implementation "to such limitations as are determined by law" and introduced "for the purpose of securing due recognition and respect for the rights and freedoms of others". Restrictions may be set up also in order to meet the "just requirements of morality, public order and the general welfare in a democratic society". The ambiguous wording of the limitative clause results from the "aggressive" compromise of 1948 (Morsnik 1999) and brings numerous interpretative challenges up till today.

The 1948 compromise was possible primarily due to two factors. First, because of the recent horrid remembrances of World War II, driving the world leaders, debating the scope and shape of the Declaration, to emphasize their disaccord with mass human rights violations. The other crucial factor was the non-binding character of the Declaration. When a binding assertion was required, the international community needed almost twenty more years for a suitable form of its stipulations to be successfully introduced into a treaty. The contents of the corresponding Article 19 of the International Covenant on Civil and Political Rights (ICCPR) derive richly from the UDHR original (United Nations 1966). In para. 1 the Article includes a confirmation of the universality of "the right to hold opinions without interference", while putting the human right guarantee into more detail in para. 2. It grants each human the right to "freedom of expression" which – again – includes three complementary liberties: to "seek, receive and impart information and ideas", regardless of frontiers. In the neighboring para. 3 the limitative clauses are repeated, giving state authorities the possibility to set legal boundaries on the exercise of human rights for reasons of national security or public order, to protect public health or morals as well to guarantee the rights of others. Should states decide to introduce such "necessary" limitations, they may do so only through an act of law.

Details of the interpretation of the right have been set by numerous UN bodies. One directly mandated by the UN to enforce Article 19 ICCPR is the Human Rights Council (the successor of the United Nations Commission on Human Rights) (United Nations 2005). This is a inter-governmental body vested with the task of identifying and investigating grave violations of human rights by UN members states. It primarily works through annual reports ("Universal Periodic Review)" of state parties on their implementation of the ICCPR as well as through non-binding guidelines on the interpretation of individual rights. It also issues recommendations directed at states found to be in violation of human rights, following the individual complaint procedure and pursued by a "follow-up procedure" aimed at verifying the implementation of the particular recommendations (United Nations 1966). Its mandate includes the power to submit to the Security Council a request to introduce sanctions against states in grave violations of human rights.

These procedures are subject to criticism, falling along two complimentary lines. The guidelines are regarded as too general for country specific implementation, which complements the lack of state parties' political will to implement them. What is more, the Council often supports countries weak in the implementation of human rights standards, using their national human rights organizations as a cover up for their own violations (Mertus 2009).

In its research and policy shaping activities the Council is supported by the Advisory Committee. The Committee is a group of independent experts providing the Council with "expertise and advice on thematic human rights issues". In 2011 the Committee presented the Council with guidelines on the interpretation of Article 19 ICCPR, as a laying ground for Council guidelines on the particular interpretation of the right of free expression (United Nations 2011). The agreement was reached after two years of intense discussions and consultations with states and civil society. The Committee emphasizes that any limitations to the exercise of the right to free speech may only be introduced through acts of law, where a rule of law is to be understood as "formulated with sufficient precision to enable an individual to regulate his or her conduct accordingly" and "made accessible to the public". Traditional, religious or other such customary law sources are not considered "law" for the purpose of the regulation. A clear guideline for the governments to actively protect the right to impart and receive information by ones within their jurisdiction is enshrined in para. 25, which states that "a law may not confer unfettered discretion for the restriction of freedom of expression on those charged with its execution" (United Nations 2011). This stipulation supports the contents of para. 15, which requires "states to take all necessary steps to foster independence" of new media and ensure individual access thereto. New media are referred to in para. 43 as "operation of websites, blogs or other internet-based, or other information dissemination systems, including (…) internet service providers or search engines". When explaining in what form the limitations foreseen in para. 3 of Article 19 ICCPR may be introduced, the Committee emphasizes, that "the restrictions must be provided by law", may only be introduced on one of the grounds set out in Article 19 and must conform to the strict tests of necessity and proportionality. What is more, when restrictions are applied, that must be done only for the "purposes for which they were prescribed and must be directly related to the specific need on which they are predicated".

The work of the Committee visualizes the right to free expression as a negative obligation of states to refrain from infringing the individual right to have and share information. The Committee does not directly address the issues of limitations put onto the individual right to free expression by private parties nor does it introduce any positive obligations of states to actively protect individuals from such infringements in this very document. It has been doing so however successively since 2004, starting with the Sub-Commission on the Promotion and Protection of Human Rights of the (then) UN Commission on

Human Rights in the form of "Draft Norms on the Responsibilities of Transnational Corporations and Other Business Enterprises with Regard to Human Rights" (United Nations 2003). Referred to as the UN "Protect, Respect and Remedy" Framework for Business and Human Rights the document includes a set of human rights guidelines applicable to non-state parties and was adopted by the Human Rights Council unanimously in 2008 (nicknamed "the Ruggie Report" after the name of the UN Special Representative, tasked with preparing the report serving as the blueprint for the guidelines) (Ruggie, 2006, 2008 and 2011). The "Protect, Respect and Remedy" Framework includes three groups of obligations. The first group covers duties resting upon states, compelling them to protect individuals against human rights abuses by third parties (the obligation to "protect"). This goal ought to be obtained through appropriate policies, law, and adjudication. Crucial to effective protection of human rights is the obligation to show due diligence in assessing human rights risks arising out of corporate responsibility to respect human rights. Through external analysis of human rights threats states are to present their will to effectively respect human rights of individuals within their jurisdiction (meeting the obligation to "respect"). Eventually, states are obliged to provide for effective legal remedies against human rights violations by non-state parties (the obligation to "remedy").

The contents of the right to free expression may therefore be identified in much detail based on the work of the HRC. The crucial problem is its enforcement. For the reasons of cultural differences in interpretation of the guidelines' general language and lack of a suitable, efficient enforcement mechanism there is little chance of an effective enforcement procedure in the near future. As a result no enforceable universal standard for freedom of expression is currently in place. All the work of the UN bodies on the scope and shape of right to free expression may serve as interpretative guidelines. There is however one regional framework that prides itself on effectiveness – the European Convention on Human Rights treaty system. It's functioning envisages the principles defined within the HRC work. Below a closer look at this regional regime, as a practical example of a enforceable consensus, is briefly discussed.

FREEDOM OF EXPRESSION: THE EUROPEAN CONSENSUS

ICCPR derived from Article 19 of the UDHR, however the consensus reached in 1966 was also fueled by negotiations around the first European treaty aimed at protecting human rights, inspired by the success of the UDHR (Bates 2010). Next to the developing trade and industry system of the European Coal and Steel Community, a pan-European legal regime of human rights' protection was being developed. Following successful negotiations, in November 1950 the European Convention for the Protection of Human Rights and Fundamental Freedoms (known as the European Convention on Human Rights; ECHR) was signed, laying the foundations for the work of the Council of Europe (CoE) and the European Court of Human Rights (ECtHR). Deriving from numerous articles of the UDHR, also its stipulations on the freedom of expression resembled those of Article 19 UDHR.

Article 10 ECHR puts the general clauses from Article19 UDHR into more detail. Its wording grants everyone "the right to freedom of expression", including "freedom to hold opinions and to receive and impart information and ideas". Emphasis should be put on the three-element construction of the right, resembling the original Article 19 UDHR scheme, including the right to have, share and access any and all forms of expression. None of those integral freedoms should be infringed through an "interference by public authority". They all ought to be granted to everyone with no discrimination and "regardless of frontiers". A limitative clause in Article 10 para. 2 allows for constraints placed upon the exercise of those freedoms solely when particular conditions are met. Exercise of the freedom of expression may be limited through the introduction of "formalities, conditions, restrictions or penalties" prescribed by law and "necessary in a democratic society" (Arai-Takahashi 2002). The particular reasons, for which the right may be limited are named directly in the text of the convention and have been thoroughly explained in the ECtHR jurisprudence. They include: "the interests of national security, territorial integrity or public safety, for the prevention of disorder or crime, for the protection of health or morals, for the protection of the reputation or rights of others, for preventing the disclosure of information received in confidence, or for maintaining the authority and impartiality of the judiciary".

ECtHR noted on numerous occasions that Article 10 refers to states, and introduces their negative obligation to refrain from interference with the exercise of individual right to free expression, unless particular circumstances, described in Article 10 para. 2 are met. In particular states are obliged to refrain from interfering with the delivery of information or ideas individuals wish to share with others under their jurisdiction. Despite requests, the Court denied the Article 10 clause as a guarantee to access information as such, in particular public information and administrative documents. As the ECtHR noted in Leander v. Sweden: "the right to freedom to receive information basically prohibits a Government from restricting a person from receiving information that others wish or may be willing to impart to him." but at the same time "cannot be construed as imposing on a State, (…) positive obligations to (…) disseminate information of its own motion". The right to receive information may rarely be understood to impose an obligation upon a state to disclose personal information on the individual making a claim for access thereto. Enforcement of such right should be assured primarily through the introduction of "effective and accessible procedure" enabling the applicants to have access to "all relevant and appropriate information" (Council of Europe 2011).

An interesting, recent turn in this line of adjudication seems to be introduced by the 2009 decision in the Társaság a Szabadságjogokért (TASZ) v. Hungary case. The case is of particular interest for these deliberations, as it refers to a "public watchdog" organization, operating primarily on-line. Numerous administrative obstacles introduced by Hungarian authorities were considered in this landmark decision as an infringement of the right to access information, guaranteed by Article 10. Referring to its earlier jurisprudence, the Court observed that "preliminary obstacles created by the authorities in the way of press functions call for the most careful scrutiny". It regards state's duty "not to impede the flow of information sought by the applicant" as an imminent part of its obligations under Article 10 (Council of Europe, 2011).

In its jurisprudence the Court also presented an interpretation of another element constitutive of the freedom of expression as defined in Article 10 – of its universality. In Cox v. Turkey the Court observed that the term "regardless of frontiers" which describes the territorial scope of the right "implies that the Contracting States may only restrict information received from abroad within the confines of the justifications set out in Article 10 § 2" (Council of Europe 2011). They may not therefore exercise outside their territorial jurisdiction any more stringent limitations than those effective within their borders.

ECtHR imposes upon state parties one more obligation under Article 10 freedom of expression guaranties. Until recently positive obligations of states were introduced primarily with regard to privacy protection (Article 8 ECHR) or the right to assembly (Akandji-Kombe 2007). With regard to Article 10 initially states were only under a (negative) obligation to refrain from infringing the right to freedom of expression, while no positive obligation of the states to protect that right from infringement by non-state, private actors was implied. That was the case until 2008, when ECtHR confirmed states' positive obligation to safeguard individuals' possibility to exercise their right to receive and impart information within the limits set in the Convention. In Khurshid Mustafa And Tarzibachi v. Sweden the Court claimed "it cannot remain passive where a national court's interpretation of a legal act, (...) appears unreasonable, arbitrary, discriminatory or, more broadly, inconsistent with the principles underlying the Convention" (European Court of Human Rights 2008). It therefore claimed state parties' obligation to oversee private disputes among individuals within their jurisdictions, in order to safeguard the human rights' guarantees set by the Convention.

Summarizing the European approach the right to freedom of expression may be regarded as states' obligation to guarantee each individual within their jurisdiction the right to hold, receive and impart information regardless of frontiers, unless limitations are introduced within acts of national law when considered necessary in a democratic society. Such limitations may only be exercised by state authorities or entities acting on their behalf. State parties are also under a positive obligation to protect the right from unauthorized infringement by private parties. Safeguarding the execution of those obligations it is the ECtHR that has the authority to hold states responsible for individual breaches of their obligations designated within the convention. The personal complaint procedure proves to be a relatively successful tool in implementing the detailed, European standard of free speech (Bowcott 2012, Greer 2000).

Naturally the European consensus, even though recognized and enforced by numerous states, is not a worldwide paradigm. It thoroughly varies from the U.S. interpretation of the contents of the right to free speech, as based upon the First Amendment and may be set against a comprehensively different cultural background than that of e.g. Asian or African communities. Therefore it may only serve as an example of a possible interpretation of the Article 19 bottom-line universal standard. It is primarily national laws that create the legitimate legal background for the actions of individuals imparting information to various jurisdictions or legal entities, such as communication companies, attempting to render services. In the era of the World Wide Web the challenge of identifying the appropriate application of national legal standards is of particular importance. Below is described the role which telecommunication companies and other Internet Service Providers (ISPs) are obliged to play according to different national laws and regional regulations, as their day-to-day operations leave a lasting mark on the practical significance of Article 19 UDHR and ICCPR.

INTERNET SERVICE PROVIDER: AN ATTEMPTED DEFINITION

"Internet Service Provider" is a term used to describe entities rendering a wide range of services. According to the EU e-commerce directive – a document fundamental to the issue of ISP liability, the term "service provider" is used to describe "any natural or legal person providing an information society service", where the latter are defined in Article 1(2) of Directive 98/34/EC (European Commission 2000). According thereto an "Information Society service" is "any service normally provided for remuneration, at a distance, by electronic means and at the individual request of a recipient of services" (European Commission 2000). This definition was aimed to cover any and all telecommunication companies, offering Internet services, such as providing Internet connectivity to individual users (access providers) or enabling web-hosting services (host providers). The term includes also services consisting of designing and/or hosting websites (to some extent the term covers therefore content providers) (Hoeren 2009). Some authors refer to a fourth category of ISPs, who offer their services through on-line based applications: application-providers (EUROIspa 2008). The phrase covers therefore numerous and diversified groups of entities sharing one joint feature: they provide commercial services enabling Internet access through

IP-assigned devices (be it computers, tablets, "smart-phones" or other "smart" devices, collectively referred to as "the Internet of Things"; IoT) (Weber, Weber 2010). The U.S. Copyright Act offers somewhat similar definition, according to which the term "means a provider of online services or network access, or the operator of facilities therefore" and includes entities "offering the transmission, routing, or providing of connections for digital online communications, between or among points specified by a user, of material of the user's choosing, without modification to the content of the material as sent or received." At the same time numerous national regimes, like acts of e.g. Chinese law contain no legal definition of an ISP or a particular scheme for their liability. Nevertheless – unlike in Europe – those enabling Internet access or hosting digitized data may be held liable for that data (hosted or enabled) based on numerous provisions of statutory law, like regulations on copyright, state secrets or internal security. Guidelines on their liability may be found in "The Interpretation of the Supreme People's Court on Certain Issues Concerning the Application of Laws in the Hearing of Cases Involving Computer Network Copyright Disputes" dated 21 Dec. 2000 (CCH Asia Pte. Ltd. (2005) .The term therefore covers entities such as telecommunications companies, on-line service providers and even every day users (should they be administering or moderating a website enabling others to create content). Their technical capability to disable access to certain data alleged illegal is their only joint feature. Therefore an Internet Service Provider is any entity technically capable of hosting electronic content and disabling access thereto as provided by national laws.

The first challenge ISPs need to face is therefore setting their scope of services against the national definition or understanding of an on-line or telecommunications service provider. Should they meet the criteria set therein, they ought to obey by particular state's limitations on free speech, introduced through acts of national law. Should they act against those regulations they will face civil liability or criminal responsibility within the state where they operate. Should they however go against human rights guarantees, states within which they operate may be held internationally liable. According to the "Protect, Respect and Remedy" Framework any limitations on free speech introduced by non-governmental entities (such as ISPs) or exercised without judicial authorization are against states' international responsibilities. At the same time the national telecommunications regulations usually vest services providers with the power to shape the scope and limits of individual right to receive and impart information, be it through Internet monitoring and filtering mechanisms (preventive censorship of all electronic content originating from acts of law or local ethical standards, primarily business ethics) or notice-and-take down procedures. Thisgives ISPs much power in the information society. The popularity of the global network and its architecture give them the capability to decide what kinds of content may be accessed on-line by the users they render their services to.

ISP LIABILITY: A REGIONAL DICHOTOMY

Regulatory approach to ISP liability falls along two lines. While in Europe and the U.S. state authorities generally do not impose a general obligation onto service providers to monitor the information they provide access to, which they transmit or store, such an obligation is being introduced (explicitly or derived from stipulations of various acts of law) in most Asian and African national regimes (EUROIspa 2008).

Article 15 of the e-commerce Directive provides a good example of a the European general scheme, resembling the U.S. 1996 Digital Millennium Copyright Act (DMCA) notice-and-takedown procedure. The notice-and-takedown procedures generally hold the ISPs free from liability as long as they are unaware of the illegality of the materials they enable access to. Once informed of the illegal character of the data, they are obliged to disable access thereto under the pain of own subsidiary liability. The e-commerce Directive introduces a number of situations, where ISPs might be held liable for on-line content (Articles 12-15). They include providing access to communication networks, transmitting data and hosting information. ISPs are obliged to discontinue enabling access to certain content upon receiving a notification of its illegal character, under the pain of own responsibility. Should an ISP be made aware of a potentially infringing character of the content it enables or hosts and decide not to disable access thereto, they will be the ones facing legal consequences brought about by such content, regardless of the direct responsibility of the individual who had uploaded or created it. ISP liability may therefore result from failing to take down content about the illegal character of which a notice to the ISP was issued. Details of the procedures of issuing such notice and the time periods given to ISP to analyze and execute a decision made upon their contents are left to national legislations, which vary thoroughly (Asbo Baistrocchi 2003, Wood et al 2002). The lack of a detailed notice-and-takedown procedure guidelines within the Directive has been criticized as a threat to human rights, in particular the right to free speech (Asbo Baistrocchi, 2003). Lack of a uniform pan-European procedure allows for much flexibility in the implementation of the Directive, especially since national regulations often include interpretative clauses, which as a result lay upon the ISPs the obligation to decide on their own upon the legality of hosted material. Should an ISP not block access to illegal content of which they are informed, they will be facing liability for the damage that this content might cause. The ISP's decisions on the character of the hosted data and the following decision on (dis)continuing enabling access thereto are of detrimental consequences to the providers, since should they be wrong, they will be facing legal responsibility. This situation brings an undesired chilling effect: ISPs are limiting their own risk of potential lawsuits by blocking the access to any reported content, as potentially exposing them to liability. This makes the ISPs censors of on-line content, deciding upon which content will be imparted to the larger public. The right to free expression of users (in particular their constituent right to impart information) is being restrained based on the decision of a single private law entity, based on a interpretative clause of an act of law. Such practice is clearly contrary to the comments provided by HRC in its 2011 document, where in pt. 25 it states that a limitative clause must be foreseen by law, where "a norm, to be characterized as a "law", must be formulated with sufficient precision to enable an individual to regulate his or her conduct accordingly (…)" (United Nations 2011).What is more, "a law may not confer unfettered discretion for the restriction of freedom of expression on those charged with its execution" (United Nations 2011). A phrase that seems to provide detailed guidelines for ISP liability schemes follows: "Laws must provide sufficient guidance to those charged with their execution to enable them to ascertain what sorts of expression are properly restricted and what sorts are not" (United Nations 2011). Neither the EU notice and takedown procedure, nor the interpretative documents provided for in numerous Asian states meet those guidelines. The current practice may therefore be considered contrary to the interpretations of the contents of the right to free expression provided by both: ECtHR and the HRC, presented above.

The U.S. version of the notice-and-takedown procedure, as enshrined in the DMCA provides clearer guidelines. Although relating to only one category of illegal content (copyright infringing data), the DMCA puts in much detail both: the form of the notice and the mechanism following its issuance (Moore Clayton 2009). The DMCA introduces rigid periods of time for particular phases of the take-down procedure. Regardless its legislative meticulousness it is considered a threat to free expression on-line, primarily due to the national interpretation of international free speech standards (Tian 2009, European Audiovisual Observatory 2004).

Another important matter relating to content liability is the ISP criminal responsibility. This issue is raised with most significance when it comes to copyright infringement, but the criminalization of libel still existent in national legal systems also ought to raise concerns as a possible footpath for ISP subsidiary liability. Numerous national court judgments confirm criminal ISP responsibility for hosted content. They often found ISPs responsible for "contributory copyright infringement" rather than a direct offence, however such a construct may raise questions as instituting a subsidiary criminal liability. Whether the ISP may be regarded as a warrant (entrusted with a particular legal obligation) and therefore criminally liable for its omission seems doubtful in the light of the two issues raised above (the unclear scope of subjects the obligation is addressed to and the contents of the required action designated in an insufficiently detailed manor to bring criminal liability).

Regardless their shortcomings, neither the Directive nor the DMCA oblige the ISP to actively seek information potentially deemed illegal. That is not the case with the majority of national legislative acts and their legally binding interpretations made face ISP rights and duties in Asia and Africa. ISPs' strict criminal responsibility next to direct civil liability for hosting illegal content are a legal standard in numerous countries, mainlyin Asia and the Near East. Open Network Initiative names China, Iran, Uzbekistan, Burma, Vietnam and Turkmenistan as world's top "filtering" countries when it comes to censoring political content (it regards the filtering of political content in those states "extensive") (Deibert 2008). Their national policies include extensive Internet "filtering", obliging ISPs to monitor the content they enable and disable access to all information that might be regarded dangerous to widely defined state interest (Deibert 2008).

Internet filtering is also gaining some popularity in Europe. The recent EU Directive on child pornography provides states with an option to block access to on-line images of adolescent nudity (European Commission 2010). In Europe state-imposed filtering is usually introduced through a court order, obliging a particular national ISP to block access to a certain website the content of which is found contrary to national law (as exercised by Danish, German and numerous other European national courts in their orders against ISPs providing access to e.g. the controversial The Pirate Bay website). This mechanism is questionable with regard to human rights, since it infringes the right to impart and receive information, as confirmed by the recent Organization for Security and Co-operation in Europe (OSCE) report (OSCE 2010). OSCE clearly states, that "Internet access policies, defined by governments, should be in line with the requirements of (...) Article 10 of the European Convention on Human Rights" and defines the very Internet access as a human right (OSCE 2010).

CONCLUSION

The analysis presented above aims to prove that ISP filtering of on-line content, whether following the notice-and-takedown procedure or exercised following a legal or an ethical obligation, is a serious threat to the freedom of expression, as granted by international human rights guarantees. Blocking or disabling access to certain on-line content infringes the individual right to communication, derived from Article 19 ICCPR. Every time when access to information uploaded by a service recipient is disabled, the individual right of that user to impart information is infringed. Article 19 para. 3 ICCPR provides for particular, exceptional circumstances, in which the individual right to free speech may be limited. International jurisprudence and doctrine, including the Committee on Human Rights report recognizes the possibility to introduce limitations onto free speech in those exceptional circumstances through an act of law, exercised by state authorities, in particular the judicature. As expressed explicitly in both: the UN "Protect, Respect and Remedy" Framework for Business and Human Rights and the ECtHR jurisprudence the states are not only under a negative obligation to refrain from limiting free speech, but also under a positive obligation to protect the individual right to free expression from invasions by third parties. Under no circumstances may those invasions be executed by private entities, unless when executing a court order. Therefore, the current scope of ISP rights and obligations must be deemed to wide. Nationals laws authorize them to decide upon the scope of electronic content available on-line. Their individual decisions of disabling access to certain content uploaded by an individual Internet user sets the limits of that user's individual right to free expression. Such practice constitutes a serious threat to the human right expressed in Article 19 UDHR and ought to be replaced with more detailed guidelines for ISPs when they ought to hold liability for content they enable.

REFERENCES

Akandji-Kombe, J.-F. (2007). *Positive obligations under the European Convention on Human Rights; A guide to the implementation of the European Convention on Human Rights; Human rights handbooks, No. 7*. Council of Europe.

Arai-Takahashi, Y. (2002). *The Margin of Appreciation Doctrine and the Principle of Proportionality in the Jurisprudence of the ECHR*. New York: Intersentia.

Asbo Baistrocchi, P. (2003). Liability Of Intermediary Service Providers In The EU Directive On Electronic Commerce. *Computer & High Technology Law Journal, 19*, 111–130.

Bates, E. (2010). *The Evolution of the European Convention on Human Rights: From Its Inception to the Creation of a Permanent Court of Human Rights*. Oxford University Press.

Council of Europe Research Division. (2011). *Internet: case-law of the European Court of Human Rights*. Available at. http://www.echr.coe.int/ECHR/EN/Header/Case-Law/Case-law+analysis/Research+reports/

Deibert, R. (2008). *Access Denied: The Practice and Policy of Global Internet Filtering*. MIT Press.

European Commission. (2000). *Directive 2000/31/EC of the European Parliament and of the Council of 8 June 2000 on certain legal aspects of information society services, in particular electronic commerce, in the Internal Market (further herein: e-commerce directive)*. Author.

European Commission. (2010). *Proposal for a Directive of the European Parliament and of the Council on combating the sexual abuse, sexual exploitation of children and child pornography, repealing Framework Decision 2004/68/JHA*. Author.

European Court of Human Rights (2008) Khurshid Mustafa et Tarzibachi v. Sweden, (23883/06)

Hoeren, T. (2009). Liability for Online Services in Germany. *German Law Journal, 10,* 561-584.

Mertus, J. (2009). *The United Nations and Human Rights: A Guide for a New Era*. Oxon, UK: Taylor & Francis.

Moore, T., & Clayton, R. (2009). The Impact of Incentives on Notice and Take-down. In E. M. Johnson (Ed.), *Managing Information Risk and the Economics of Security* (pp. 199–223). New York: Springer. doi:10.1007/978-0-387-09762-6_10

Morsink, J. (1999). *The Universal Declaration of Human Rights: Origins, Drafting, and Intent.* University of Pennsylvania Press. doi:10.9783/9780812200416

OSCE. (2010). *Freedom of Expression on the Internet Study of legal provisions and practices related to freedom of expression, the free flow of information and media pluralism on the Internet in OSCE participating states.* Available at: http://www.osce.org/fom/80723

Ruggie, J. (2006). *Interim report of the Special Representative of the Secretary-General on the issue of human rights and transnational corporations and other business enterprises.* UN Doc. E/CN.4/2006/97.

Ruggie, J. (2008). *Protect, Respect and Remedy: a Framework for the Business and Human Rights: Report of the Special Representative of the Secretary-General on the issue of human rights and transnational corporations and other business enterprises, John Ruggie.* UN Doc. E/HRC/8/5.

Ruggie, J. (2011). *Report of the Special Representative of the Secretary-General on the issue of human rights and transnational corporations and other business enterprises, John Ruggie, Guiding Principles on Business and Human Rights: Implementing the United Nations "Protect, Respect and Remedy" Framework.* A/HRC/17/31.

Schauer, F. (1982). *Free Speech: A Philosophical Enquity.* Cambridge, UK: Cambridge University Press.

Schauer, F. (2004). Media Law, Media Content, and American Exceptionalism. In European Audiovisual Observatory, Political Debate and the Role of the Media: The Fragility of Free Speech. European Audiovisual Observatory.

Tian, Y. (2009). *Re-Thinking Intellectual Property: The Political Economy of Copyright Protection in the Digital Era.* Oxon, UK: Taylor & Francis.

United Nations. (1948). *Universal Declaration of Human Rights.* G.A. Res. 217A (III), U.N. Doc. A/810.

United Nations. (1966). International Covenant on Civil and Political Rights (ICCPR), G.A. res. 2200A (XXI), 21 U.N. GAOR Supp. (No. 16) at 52. *U.N. Doc. A, 6316,* 999.

United Nations. (2003). *Social and Economic Council, Sub-Commission on the Promotion and Protection of Human Rights.* E/CN.4/Sub.2/2003/12/Rev.2.

United Nations. (2005). *2005 World Summit Outcome.* GA Res 60/1, 9, UN Doc. A/ RES/60/1.

United Nations. (2011). *Human Rights Committee.* General comment No. 34, Article 19: Freedoms of opinion and expression CCPR/C/GC/34.

Watt, N., & Bowcott, O. (2012). David Cameron calls for reform of European court of human rights. *The Guardian.* Retrieved from http://www.guardian.co.uk/law/2012/jan/25/david-cameron-reform-human-rights

Weber, R. H., & Weber, R. (2010). *Internet of things: legal perspectives*. Berlin: Springer. doi:10.1007/978-3-642-11710-7

Wood, C., Drayson, C., Dye, J., Thomasin, J., McDonell, P., Dillon, M., ... Sykes, K. (2002). Great Britain. In G. Spindler & F. Börner (Eds.), *E-commerce law in Europe and the USA* (pp. 246–253). Berlin: Springer. doi:10.1007/978-3-540-24726-5_5

Index

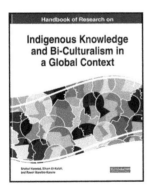

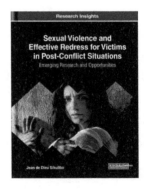

Ensure Quality Research is Introduced to the Academic Community

Become an IGI Global Reviewer for Authored Book Projects

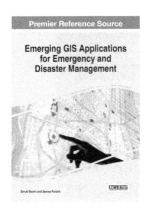
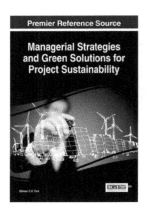

The overall success of an authored book project is dependent on quality and timely reviews.

In this competitive age of scholarly publishing, constructive and timely feedback significantly expedites the turnaround time of manuscripts from submission to acceptance, allowing the publication and discovery of forward-thinking research at a much more expeditious rate. Several IGI Global authored book projects are currently seeking highly-qualified experts in the field to fill vacancies on their respective editorial review boards:

Applications and Inquiries may be sent to:
development@igi-global.com

Applicants must have a doctorate (or an equivalent degree) as well as publishing and reviewing experience. Reviewers are asked to complete the open-ended evaluation questions with as much detail as possible in a timely, collegial, and constructive manner. All reviewers' tenures run for one-year terms on the editorial review boards and are expected to complete at least three reviews per term. Upon successful completion of this term, reviewers can be considered for an additional term.

If you have a colleague that may be interested in this opportunity,
we encourage you to share this information with them.

IGI Global's Transformative Open Access (OA) Model:
How to Turn Your University Library's Database Acquisitions Into a Source of OA Funding

In response to the OA movement and well in advance of Plan S, IGI Global, early last year, unveiled their OA Fee Waiver (Offset Model) Initiative.

Under this initiative, librarians who invest in IGI Global's InfoSci-Books (5,300+ reference books) and/or InfoSci-Journals (185+ scholarly journals) databases will be able to subsidize their patron's OA article processing charges (APC) when their work is submitted and accepted (after the peer review process) into an IGI Global journal.*

How Does it Work?

1. When a library subscribes or perpetually purchases IGI Global's InfoSci-Databases including InfoSci-Books (5,300+ e-books), InfoSci-Journals (185+ e-journals), and/or their discipline/subject-focused subsets, IGI Global will match the library's investment with a fund of equal value to go toward subsidizing the OA article processing charges (APCs) for their patrons.

   Researchers: Be sure to recommend the InfoSci-Books and InfoSci-Journals to take advantage of this initiative.

2. When a student, faculty, or staff member submits a paper and it is accepted (following the peer review) into one of IGI Global's 185+ scholarly journals, the author will have the option to have their paper published under a traditional publishing model or as OA.

3. When the author chooses to have their paper published under OA, IGI Global will notify them of the OA Fee Waiver (Offset Model) Initiative. If the author decides they would like to take advantage of this initiative, IGI Global will deduct the US$ 1,500 APC from the created fund.

4. This fund will be offered on an annual basis and will renew as the subscription is renewed for each year thereafter. IGI Global will manage the fund and award the APC waivers unless the librarian has a preference as to how the funds should be managed.

Hear From the Experts on This Initiative:

"I'm very happy to have been able to make one of my recent research contributions, 'Visualizing the Social Media Conversations of a National Information Technology Professional Association' featured in the *International Journal of Human Capital and Information Technology Professionals*, freely available along with having access to the valuable resources found within IGI Global's InfoSci-Journals database."

– **Prof. Stuart Palmer**,
Deakin University, Australia

For More Information, Visit: www.igi-global.com/publish/contributor-resources/open-access or contact IGI Global's Database Team at eresources@igi-global.com.

Milton Keynes UK
Ingram Content Group UK Ltd.
UKHW032157231123
433158UK00001B/23